INVESTMENT LAW WITHIN
INTERNATIONAL LAW

Developments within various subfields of international law influence international investment law, but changes in investment law also have an impact on the evolution of other fields within international law. With contributions from leading scholars and practitioners, they examine specific links between investment law and other subfields of international law, such as the law on armed conflict, human rights, sustainable development, trade, development and EU law. In particular, this book scrutinises how concepts, principles and rules developed in the context of such subfields could inform the content of investment law. Solutions aimed at resolving problems in other settings may provide instructive examples for addressing current problems in the field of investment law, and vice versa. The underlying question is whether key subfields of public international law, notably international investment law, are open to cross-fertilisation or whether they are evolving further into self-contained regimes.

FREYA BAETENS is Assistant Professor of Public International Law at Leiden University and Visiting Professor at the World Trade Institute in Berne. Concurrent with her academic activities, she is an associate lawyer with VVGB Advocaten/Advocats, Brussels, advising clients on public international law and EU law matters. She has published on a wide range of topics, including treaty interpretation, state responsibility, equality, sustainable development, interaction between legal regimes, discrimination in international migration law and EU external relations.

INVESTMENT LAW WITHIN INTERNATIONAL LAW

Integrationist perspectives

Edited by

FREYA BAETENS

CAMBRIDGE
UNIVERSITY PRESS

CAMBRIDGE
UNIVERSITY PRESS

University Printing House, Cambridge CB2 8BS, United Kingdom

Published in the United States of America by Cambridge University Press, New York

Cambridge University Press is part of the University of Cambridge.

It furthers the University's mission by disseminating knowledge in the pursuit of education, learning and research at the highest international levels of excellence.

www.cambridge.org
Information on this title: www.cambridge.org/9781107038882

© Cambridge University Press 2013

First published 2013

Printed by CPI Group (UK) Ltd, Croydon CRO 4YY

A catalogue record for this publication is available from the British Library

Library of Congress Cataloging in Publication data
Investment law within international law : integrationist perspectives / edited by Freya Baetens.
pages   cm
Includes bibliographical references.
ISBN 978-1-107-03888-2 (Hardback)
1. Investments, Foreign (International law)   I. Baetens, Freya, editor of compilation.
K3830.I475 2013
346′.092–dc23   2012051782

ISBN 978-1-107-03888-2 Hardback

Additional resources for this publication at www.cambridge.org/baetens

CONTENTS

v

CONTRIBUTORS

WOLFGANG ALSCHNER is a PhD candidate in international law at the Graduate Institute of International and Development Studies (IHEID) in Geneva, Switzerland. Before that, he studied international law, international relations and economics in Dresden, Beirut and Geneva. In addition, he has been working as a consultant in the Section on International Investment Agreements (IIA) of UNCTAD.

PHILIPP AMBACH is Special Assistant to the President of the International Criminal Court. He previously obtained his 1st and 2nd State Examination in law at Humboldt Universität, Berlin, and Oberlandesgericht Düsseldorf, in 2004 and 2007, respectively, and in 2009 wrote a PhD in international criminal law at the Freie Universität, Berlin. In 2007, he worked as a prosecutor in the Office of the Public Prosecutor of Cologne, Germany; from 2008 to 2009 as Associate Legal Officer in the Appeals Chamber of the International Criminal Tribunal for the former Yugoslavia; and from 2009 to 2010 as Associate Legal Officer in the Appeals Chamber of the International Criminal Tribunal for Rwanda.

FREYA BAETENS, Cand.Jur. and Lic.Jur. (Ghent); LLM (Columbia); PhD (Cambridge), is Assistant Professor of Public International Law at Leiden University and Visiting Professor at the World Trade Institute, Berne. She has been a Research Fellow of the Max Planck Institute for Comparative Public Law and International Law, Heidelberg, and editor of the *Max Planck Encyclopedia of Public International Law*. She is a member of the Executive Board of the Society of International Economic Law (SIEL) and a Fellow with the Centre for International Sustainable Development Law (CISDL), McGill University, Montreal. She is on the editorial board of the *Leiden Journal of International Law* and the academic review board of the *Cambridge Journal of International and Comparative Law*. Concurrent with her academic activities, she is an associate lawyer with VVGB Advocaten/Advocats, Brussels, advising clients on international law and EU law matters.

N. JANSEN CALAMITA is the Director of the Investment Treaty Forum and Senior Research Fellow at the British Institute of International and Comparative Law, London. He also holds the post of lecturer in Public International Law at the University of Birmingham. Prior to these posts, he was a member of the Faculty of Law at the University of Oxford, and a visiting fellow of Mansfield College, Oxford. Before becoming a full-time academic, he served in the Office of the Legal Advisor in the US Department of State, representing the United States before the Iran–US Claims Tribunal and in bilateral investment matters, and also in the Office of Legal Affairs at the United Nations as a member of the UNCITRAL Secretariat. He has also been in private practice in New York. He is a graduate of Boston University Law School (J.D. summa cum laude) and the University of Oxford (BCL).

DIANE A. DESIERTO specialises in international economic law, dispute resolution and ASEAN law, holding degrees from Yale Law School (JSD 2011, LLM 2009) and the University of the Philippines (LLB/JD equiv. cum laude 2004, BSc Economics summa cum laude 2000). At Yale, she was Howard M. Holtzmann Fellow in International Arbitration and Dispute Resolution; Lillian Goldman Perpetual Scholar; Editor of the *Yale Journal of International Law*; 2010–2011 Yale Fellow of HE Judge Bruno Simma and HE Judge Bernardo Sepulveda-Amor at the International Court of Justice, The Hague, the Netherlands; and was awarded the Ambrose Gherini Prize in International Law for her JSD dissertation (*Necessity and National Emergency Clauses: Sovereignty in Modern Treaty Interpretation*, International Litigation in Practice Series, vol. 3, 2012). She has taught international law at several Philippine law faculties, before taking up her current position as Assistant Professor at Peking University School of Transnational Law, while also continuing as a partner at Desierto Ammuyutan Purisima and Desierto Law.

MARY E. FOOTER is Professor of International Economic Law and Head of the Business, Trade and Human Rights Unit at the Human Rights Law Centre, University of Nottingham School of Law. She holds a Master's degree in Dutch civil law from the University of the Netherlands Antilles, an LLM in Public International Law from University College London and a PhD (cum laude) from the Erasmus University, Rotterdam. She has served as Senior Programme Legal Counsel at the International Development Law Organization and as expert consultant to the WTO and the EU. She is series editor of the *Edward Elgar Series on International Economic Law*, a member of the Editorial Board of the *Manchester Journal of International Economic*

Law, the *European Journal of Risk Regulation,* and a member of the Advisory Board of *Legal Issues in International Integration* and of the e-journal *Law, Social Justice and Global Development.* She is a member of the Executive Board of the European Society of International Law, the Executive Council of the British Branch of the International Law Association, the ILA International Trade Law Committee and the Society of International Economic Law.

MARKUS W. GEHRING is a university lecturer in Sustainable Development Law at the Law Faculty, Deputy Director of the Centre for European Legal Studies (CELS) and Fellow in Law at Robinson College, Cambridge University. He holds an *ad personam* Jean Monnet Chair in Sustainable Development Law at the University of Ottawa, Canada, and serves as affiliated lecturer in European and International Law at the Department of Politics and International Studies. He holds an LLM from Yale and a Dr. jur. from Hamburg. He practised European and international trade law with Cleary Gottlieb in their Brussels office. Prior to joining Robinson College, he was a tutor in Public International Law at University College, Oxford. He serves as Lead Counsel for Sustainable International Trade, Investment and Competition Law with the Centre of International Sustainable Development Law (CISDL), McGill University, Montreal and was a member representative of the Concerted Action on Trade and Environment (CATE) research initiative, funded by the European Commission.

ANASTASIOS GOURGOURINIS practises law in Greece as a member of the Athens Bar specialising in international economic law. He is an elected lecturer in International Law at the National and Kapodistrian University of Athens, Faculty of Law, and is a Special Legal Adviser to the Hellenic Ministry of State and Strategic Investments. He completed his doctoral thesis at University College London in 2010, focusing on the fragmentation of international law, and, more specifically, the normative role of equity and equitable principles in the WTO. Among his current and recent publications are: 'Equity in International Law Revisited (with Special Reference to the Fragmentation of International Law)', *American Society of International Law Proceedings,* 103 (2009): 79–82; 'Delineating the Normativity of Equity in International Law', *International Community Law Review,* 11 (2009): 327–47; 'The Distinction between Interpretation and Application of Norms in International Adjudication', *Journal of International Dispute Settlement,* 2 (2011): 31–57; and '*Lex Specialis* in WTO and Investment Protection Law', *German Yearbook of International Law,* 53 (2010): 579–621.

MARIA GRITSENKO is an associate in the International Arbitration and Litigation Group of Skadden, Arps, Slate, Meagher & Flom (UK) LLP. Her expertise includes investment treaty and investment contract disputes, as well as international commercial arbitration proceedings under a variety of different rules. Originally from Ukraine, she trained as a lawyer in France and the United States. She holds a Master's degree in public international law from the Pantheon-Assas University, Paris II, and an LLM from the University of Michigan Law School, Ann Arbor.

NICOLAS HACHEZ, LLM (NYU), LLB (Louvain), is Project Manager and Research Fellow at the Institute for International Law and at the Leuven Centre for Global Governance Studies, University of Leuven. His research interests mainly include global governance studies, international legal theory, international human rights law and international investment law. He has published on various issues connected to those disciplines, such as corporate social responsibility, the role of non-state actors and of private regulation in global governance, or the relations between international investment law and other branches of international law. Formerly, he worked as an attorney in the Brussels office of an international law firm, where he focused his practice on international investment law and European Community law.

THOMAS HENQUET studied at the University of Amsterdam (LLM) and Yale University (LLM). He practised law in the Amsterdam office of Clifford Chance, specialising in litigation/arbitration and international law. In his current position as legal counsel in the International Law Division of the Netherlands Ministry of Foreign Affairs, his practice includes investment protection.

GLEIDER I. HERNÁNDEZ is Lecturer in Law at Durham Law School, Durham University. Previously, he served as Associate Legal Officer at the International Court of Justice (2007–2010), acting as law clerk to Vice-President Peter Tomka and Judge Bruno Simma from 2008 to 2010. He holds a DPhil from the University of Oxford, where he researched the concept of the international judicial function from the perspective of the International Court of Justice. Previously, he read for an LLM (Hons) at Leiden University, the Netherlands, and for BCL and LLB degrees at McGill University, Montreal, Canada.

MOSHE HIRSCH holds the Maria von Hofmannsthal Chair in International Law, and has been the Director of the Forum of International Law and the chairperson of the Committee on Advanced Studies of the Faculty of Law and Department of International Relations, Hebrew University of Jerusalem since 2005. He is also a Member of the list of the Panel of Conciliators and Arbitrators maintained by the International Centre for the Settlement of Investment Disputes (ICSID) (since November 2008). He was a Visiting Lecturer at the Academy of International Trade Law, Macao; the Jay Altmayer Distinguished Visiting Professor of Law, Tulane University School of Law, New Orleans; and Visiting Professorial Fellow at the Institute of International Economic Law, Georgetown University, Washington. He served as a member of the committee established by the Israeli Ministry of Justice to prepare a new statute on sovereign immunity and as a member of the Israeli–Palestinian Research Group on the Jerusalem Area, established under the auspices of the Olof Palme International Center, Stockholm, Sweden. He has been a researcher and member of the think tank on the Future Status of Jerusalem, at the Jerusalem Institute for Israel Studies since 1989, and a member of the Israel Bar Association since 1988.

AVIDAN KENT is a PhD candidate at the University of Cambridge, focusing on international trade and investment and climate change law, with degrees from the University of Haifa (LLB) and McGill University (LLM). He is an Associate Fellow at the Centre of International Sustainable Development Law and a member of the Israeli Bar.

URSULA KRIEBAUM is Associate Professor for Public International Law at the Department of European, International and Comparative Law, University of Vienna. Her academic research focuses on international investment protection law and arbitration, and international and European human rights law. She has worked in the office of the legal adviser of the Austrian Ministry of Foreign Affairs, and is the author of several publications in the fields of international investment law and arbitration. She also acts as consultant for law firms in investment arbitration and human rights cases.

JUDITH LEVINE is Senior Legal Counsel at the Permanent Court of Arbitration, The Hague. From 2003 to 2008, she was an attorney in the arbitration group at White & Case LLP, New York, where she represented corporations and sovereign states in ICSID, ICC, AAA and UNCITRAL arbitrations. Her prior roles include law clerk at the International Court of Justice, adviser to the Australian Attorney-General, associate at the High Court of Australia, lecturer at the University of New South Wales (UNSW) and for the Chartered Institute of Arbitrators, and member of the Australian delegation to UNCITRAL Working Group II. She holds a BA/LLB (University Medal) (UNSW) and LLM (NYU).

RALPH ALEXANDER LORZ has held the Chair of German and Foreign Public Law, European Law and Public International Law at Heinrich Heine University of Düsseldorf since 2000. From 2007 to 2009 and again from 2012 to the present, he was on a sabbatical leave serving as Vice-Minister for Higher Education, Research and the Arts in the state government of Hesse. He has studied at the universities of Mainz, Marburg and Mannheim, earned an LLM degree at Harvard Law School in 1994 and is admitted to practise law in Germany and New York. His research work focuses on the European Common Market and international economic law.

VID PRISLAN is a Research Fellow and PhD candidate at the Grotius Centre for International Legal Studies, Leiden Law School. He holds a Diploma in International Relations from the University of Ljubljana and an LLM in International Law from Leiden University. He is an experienced researcher in the field of public international law, has assisted counsel in contentious cases before the PCA and the ICJ, and has regularly provided expert advice to governments and private parties in territorial and maritime delimitation disputes, and in the context of various investment arbitration proceedings. He is book review editor of the *Leiden Journal of International Law*.

PIERRE-OLIVIER SAVOIE is counsel in the Trade Law Bureau, Department of Foreign Affairs and International Trade, Ottawa, Canada. He has acted as counsel to the government of Canada in several NAFTA Chapter Eleven arbitrations, as well as in several FIPA negotiations. Prior to joining the Trade Law Bureau in 2009, he worked in the international arbitration and commercial litigation groups at White & Case LLP, New York, clerked for Justice Marie Deschamps at the Supreme Court of Canada and for judges Peter Tomka and Mohammed Bennouna at the International Court of Justice.

CHRISTOPH SCHREUER is a graduate of the universities of Vienna, Cambridge and Yale. Over an academic career spanning more than forty years, he has published numerous articles and several books in the field of international law. Since 1992, he has concentrated on international investment law; the main product of which is a 1,500-page commentary on the Convention on the Settlement of Investment Disputes between States and Nationals of Other States under the title *The ICSID Convention: A Commentary*. He has written expert opinions in many investment cases and has served as an arbitrator in ICSID and UNCITRAL cases. He has spent most of his academic career at the Department of International Law of the University of Salzburg, Austria. From 1992 to 2000, he was the Edward B. Burling Professor of International Law and Organization, Paul H. Nitze School of Advanced International Studies (SAIS), Johns Hopkins University, Washington, DC. From 2000 to 2009, he was Professor of International Law at the University of Vienna, Austria. Since 2008, he has been Of Counsel with the law office Wolf Theiss.

NICO SCHRIJVER is Professor of International Law and Academic Director of the Grotius Centre for International Legal Studies, Leiden University and is a member of the Senate of the Dutch Parliament. He serves as the President of the International Law Association, is vice-chair of the UN Committee on Economic, Social and Cultural Rights, and is a member of the Royal Netherlands Academy of Arts and Sciences, the Permanent Court of Arbitration and the Institut de droit international. He is the author of *Sovereignty over Natural Resources. Balancing Rights and Duties* (Cambridge University Press, 1997), *The Evolution of Sustainable Development in International Law* (2008) and *Development without Destruction. The UN and Global Resource Management* (2010).

SILKE STEINER, MA (Bruges), Dr.iur. (Graz), is working as an assistant professor at the Department of European, International and Comparative Law, University of Vienna. Before joining the University of Vienna, she studied law in Graz and EU external relations at the College of Europe, Bruges, and worked at the Austrian Ministry of Foreign Affairs. Her special areas of research include European institutional law, the EU's external relations, fundamental principles and judicial protection on the EU level, as well as international economic law.

LEONIE TIMMERS obtained her LLB in Law with International Relations from the University of Sussex, Brighton. She went on to complete her LLM in Public International Law at Leiden University, where she graduated cum laude. Her chapter in this book is based on her LLM thesis for which she obtained the Leiden Journal of International Law Thesis Prize. She started working as an associate in the Caracas office of Norton Rose, where she has been involved in several arbitrations against the Bolivarian Republic of Venezuela, before moving to her current post at the Norton Rose London office. Her main areas of interest are public international law and investment arbitration.

ELISABETH TUERK is a legal expert in the United Nations Conference on Trade and Development (UNCTAD), Section on International Investment Agreements in UNCTAD's Division on Investment and Enterprise. She manages the Section's research work and contributes to its technical assistance and capacity-building work, and to the management and organisation of UNCTAD's intergovernmental meetings and events. In her previous UNCTAD assignment, she worked as an Economic Affairs Officer at the Trade Negotiations and Commercial Diplomacy Branch, Division on International Trade in Goods and Services and Commodities of the UNCTAD. Prior to joining UNCTAD, she worked as staff attorney for the Trade and Investment Program of the Center for International Environmental Law (CIEL), Geneva. She holds a Magistra Degree in Law and a Magistra Degree in International Management from the Karl-Franzens University, Graz, Austria, as well as a Master's degree from the World Trade Institute in Berne, Switzerland.

FRIEDL WEISS is a professor in the Department of European, International and Comparative Law at the University of Vienna, as well as Visiting Professor at the universities of Bratislava and Bocconi, Milan. Previously he was Lecturer in Law at the London School of Economics and Political Science, held the Chair of International Economic Law and International Organisations at the University of Amsterdam, as well as various visiting professorships, including at the universities of Louvain-la-Neuve, Panthéon-Assas Paris II, HEI Geneva, Minnesota, Tulane and Wuhan. His research focus includes European and international (economic) law, international organisations, including those of international economic governance and European Community law. He holds a doctorate in law, a Licence spéciale en droit Européen from the European Institute of the Free University of Brussels, as well as an MA in Public International Law and European Law from the University of Cambridge. He has been legal adviser in the EFTA Secretariat, a legal consultant in GATT, and is a member and a former rapporteur of the ILA Committee on International Trade Law, as well as a former member of the ILA committees on International Law on Sustainable Development on Foreign Investment.

JAN WOUTERS is Professor of International Law and International Organizations, Jean Monnet Chair Ad Personam EU and Global Governance, and Director of the Leuven Centre for Global Governance Studies and Institute for International Law at the Katholoeke Universiteit Leuven (KU Leuven). He is Visiting Professor at the College of Europe (Bruges), in the Master of

Laws in International Economic Law and Policy (University of Barcelona), in the European Master's Degree in Human Rights and Democratisation (Venice), and in the Executive Master of European and International Business Law (University of Sankt-Gallen). He is President of the Flemish Foreign Affairs Council, which advises the Flemish Government, and practises law as Of Counsel at Linklaters, Brussels. He is the Editor of the *International Encyclopedia of Intergovernmental Organizations* and the Vice-Director of *Revue belge de droit international*. He studied law and philosophy in Antwerp and Yale universities, was a Visiting Researcher at Harvard Law School and obtained his PhD at KU Leuven.

RUMIANA YOTOVA is currently pursuing a PhD in international law at Cambridge University under the supervision of Professor James Crawford. Previously, she obtained a LLM Adv. degree in Public International Law (cum laude) at Leiden University, a Master of Law degree (with excellence) at Sofia University, and a Diploma in English and EU Law at Cambridge University. In 2009, she also obtained a Diploma in Public International Law (cum laude) at The Hague Academy of International Law. She acquired practical experience in her work as a research associate of Professor James Crawford, and as a legal trainee at the Permanent Court of Arbitration and the European Commission, Directorate General Maritime Affairs and Fisheries.

TABLE OF CASES

PREFACE

The last two decades have witnessed an exponential increase in investor–state arbitrations. Investment tribunals now regularly render binding decisions as to whether states have violated protection standards guaranteed under various investment treaties. The pace by which these tribunals deliver their awards has turned investment law into one of the most dynamic fields of public international law. Developments in other subfields of international law influence the development of international investment law, but also vice versa, changes in investment law have an impact on the evolution of other fields of international law.

As the majority of publications focus on the application and interpretation of investment protection standards, the interaction of international investment law with other subfields of international law has not yet been so extensively explored. To fill this gap, academics and practitioners contributing to this collection examine specific links between investment law and such other rules of international law. In particular, this book scrutinises how concepts, principles and rules developed in the context of other subfields of international law could, or should, inform the content of investment law. Solutions conceived for resolving problems in other settings may provide instructive examples for addressing current problems in the field of investment law, and vice versa. This serves as an aid for several contributors to determine whether various subfields of public international law, particularly international investment law, are open to cross-fertilisation or whether they are evolving ever further into self-contained regimes.

This book contains a peer-reviewed selection of the most innovative and outstanding papers resulting from presentations at the international conference on 'The Interaction of International Investment Law with Other Fields of Public International Law', which took place on 8 and 9 April 2011 at Leiden University. This conference brought together experts from the field of international investment law with renowned scholars and practitioners from other subfields of international law.

Every part of this volume addresses one particular interrelationship: the authors of each part have had the opportunity to examine each other's ideas so as to guarantee a coherent approach to the matter, thereby avoiding a fragmented discussion.

One important comment received in the course of preparing this volume was that a book such as this one could pursue two goals: (1) an overall, single volume, assessment of the literature 'with some extra edge'; or (2) a selection of the most relevant issues. So, in which category does this work belong? The answer would be that this book pursues mainly the first goal, but without any claim to exhaustiveness, while each individual part focuses more on the second goal. Fully achieving the first goal would be impossible without publishing a series of volumes on the topic, while merely focusing on the second goal might result in a rather incoherent collection. For that purpose, this book has been divided into broad themes, whereby the contributions to each part are of a more specific nature: aiming to add to existing scholarship by analysing new angles. This inevitably entails choices in terms of topics that are addressed, so, for example, in Part II, aside from two contributions with a general approach from a novel angle (sociological and constitutional) by Hirsch and Calamita, two more specific topics are analysed which bear high current relevance (indigenous peoples and the right to property) by Levine and Timmers.

Following the brief historical introduction by Nico Schrijver, who uses the early foreign investment policy of the Netherlands as a case study, some chapters build on previous research, such as those examining the relationship between investment and sustainable development, human rights or trade. Other topics are highly novel and controversial, for example, as elaborated upon in the contributions on investment and armed conflict in Part I. Attention is also paid to the relationship of investment with regional developments, such as those occurring in the EU and in developing countries. The main aim of this book is to assess these interactive relationships so as to inspire future debate and scholarship.

Part I: international investment and armed conflict

This volume commences with the, perhaps, most unusual interrelationship of all: the link between international investment and armed conflict. Rarely were two legal fields seemingly so distinct; yet cannot virtually every conflict be found to be rooted in economic ground? This part shows that two of the most specialised subfields of international law interact and will probably do so increasingly in the future. Although historically many investor claims have arisen out of armed conflict and have been examined under customary international law, in contemporary scholarship it is uncommon to analyse current investment treaty rules in the light of the law on armed conflict, and vice versa.

The starting shot is fired by a universally acknowledged *éminence grise* of international investment law, Christoph Schreuer, who delivers an in-depth examination of the protection of foreign investment in times of armed conflict. He concedes that there is no obvious or express link between international investment law, on the one hand, and the law that applies in situations of armed conflict or hostilities, on the other. However, rules on protection of foreign investors are not automatically suspended as soon as an armed conflict looms; on the contrary, bilateral investment treaties (BITs) often contain clauses that address precisely such situations: 'full protection and security' clauses. This chapter examines how such clauses have been applied and interpreted by arbitral tribunals in cases such as *Amco Asia v. Republic of Indonesia*, including the question as to why such claims have been brought rather rarely. Another point of interest pertains to how the interpretation of these clauses has been extended beyond physical security in certain more recent cases. Moreover, during armed conflict, it is explored how foreign investors could be protected under other investment treaty obligations, for example, expropriation or national treatment clauses. Finally, this chapter assesses potential expansion of investment protection during armed conflict.

The baton is then passed to a public international law scholar, Gleider I. Hernández, who continues on the theme of full protection and security clauses. He sees international investment law as containing a tension between its existence as a primarily treaty-based *lex specialis* and its claim to being a projection of principles of general international law. It is, indeed, consistent with the inner logic of international investment law that only those rules of investment protection which *must* yield to the law of armed conflict *should be expected* to yield. Yet in an international legal order where even fundamental human rights may become subject to derogation in situations of armed conflict, certain questions concerning the scope and applicability of international investment law must be answered. As investment law transcends its origins as a primarily self-contained regime, there are areas in which it borrows extensively by analogy from international humanitarian law, such as the protection of aliens. However, claims of the continued application of investment law in situations where humanitarian law supersedes general international law are scrutinised with a certain dose of scepticism in this chapter.

The final chapter in Part I is perhaps the most extraordinary one: it does not address the role of foreign investors during armed conflict from the perspective of the protection that is owed to them, but rather the opposite: what are the *duties* of such investors? As Special Assistant to the President of the International Criminal Court, Philipp Ambach is well placed to assess the international criminal responsibility of transnational corporate actors doing business in zones of armed conflict. He maintains that investor protection during armed conflict highlights only one group of interests worthy of protection. Civil communities also need protection, not only from the immediate effects of the armed conflict, but from the persons or entities 'pulling the strings' as well. Business corporations that maintain trade relations with partner groups or entities that are at the same time engaged in armed conflicts may become indirectly involved in the commission of serious crimes. Through the provision of financial resources to regional armed groups, for the exploitation of natural resources in conflict zones, for example, international business actors may even incur criminal liability if they know that their resources are also used to provide these armed groups with weapons that are subsequently used against civilians. The crimes committed may amount to international crimes, such as war crimes, crimes against humanity or even genocide. In such cases, corporate actors may even come under scrutiny by the International Criminal Court for their participatory role in such crimes, if the individual criminal liability of the person(s) in control of such financial transactions on behalf of a corporate actor can be established.

Part II: international investment and human rights

From international humanitarian law to human rights law, the need to balance corporate and community interests continues in time of peace. The interrelationship between international investment and human rights is often examined in scholarly writings, but this part zooms in on less-often explored aspects of that relationship.

Starting with a sociological perspective to investment and human rights treaties, Moshe Hirsch, a legal scholar as well as international relations specialist at the Hebrew University of Jerusalem, explains how analysis of the decisions of investment tribunals relating to human rights instruments reveals that, while investment tribunals very often rely on international rules regarding state responsibility or treaty law, they are generally reluctant to accord significant weight to human rights treaties in the context of international investment. The generally negative approach of investment tribunals towards the application of human rights treaties may be explained by various factors, whereby this chapter focuses on sociocultural factors relating to the social settings in which rules of international law are formed, interpreted and implemented. It is argued that the legal interactions between various branches of international law (either integration or fragmentation) can be analysed as social interactions between the relevant communities. These legal interactions are affected by the particular features of relevant social settings, as well as the mutual relationships between the relevant social groups. More specifically, the sociocultural distance between the particular international legal settings affects the inclination of relevant decision-makers to incorporate or reject parallel legal rules developed in other branches of international law. Consequently, greater sociocultural 'distance' between the involved social settings and groups is likely to decrease the prospects for mutual incorporation of legal rules developed in the other legal sphere. In the light of the deep-rooted tensions between the relevant communities, it is not surprising that investment tribunals are generally reluctant to accord significant weight to human rights treaties during the resolution process of international investment disputes. Thus, the considerable sociocultural distance between these settings parallels the normative distance between these branches of international law.

This theoretical approach is subsequently tested in practice by Judith Levine, Senior Legal Counsel at the Permanent Court of Arbitration, with regard to the interaction of international investment law and the rights of indigenous peoples. The crossover of these subfields may arise in the context of international investment arbitration in cases where: (a) indigenous people are the investor–claimants in an arbitration against a state (e.g., *Grand River*); (b) an investor complains about action taken by a state relating to the regulation or protection of the rights of indigenous peoples; (c) an investor complains about a state's failure to protect the investor against actions taken by indigenous groups (e.g., *Burlington*); (d) a group of indigenous people, who are non-parties but have an interest in the investment arbitration, intervenes as *amicus curiae* (e.g., *Glamis Gold*). Based on a study of recent cases before international investment and human rights adjudicatory bodies, the author argues that tribunals faced with arguments about the relevance of indigenous rights have so far either managed to avoid confronting the issues directly or acknowledged the developing body of international indigenous law, but stopped short of applying it due to the circumstances of the particular case and the treaty language in question. The final part of the chapter looks at some rare instances where, at the stage of drafting investment agreements, the interaction of investment law and indigenous rights has been addressed in the treaty text itself, such as the China–New Zealand Free Trade Agreement.

One region where the interaction of international investment law and human rights law is often felt as a conflict of norms, rather than a peaceful coexistence, let alone fruitful cross-fertilisation, is Latin America. Leonie Timmers, associate lawyer at Norton Rose, zooms in on a highly topical question: is the protection against expropriations in Venezuela merely a right to property *in theory*? The starting point is that it is essential for the effectiveness of the legal order that state compliance with obligations towards individuals, particularly the right to property, can be legally enforced. Within this context, this contribution examines the enforcement mechanisms in Venezuela where, since the socialist revolution, several expropriations have taken place. The author analyses the position of three groups of individuals: land owners, local investors and foreign investors. The objective is to investigate whether the legal protection of these three groups is effective and efficient, leading to equal protection under the law for all. It is argued that discrimination does take place, in the sense that foreign investors are better protected through their access to international dispute settlement fora, which enables them to obtain a more effective remedy. Several solutions are proposed, such as the strengthening of the inter-American human rights system through the development of individual access to international dispute settlement, and through reforms allowing the court to examine more cases of an economic nature. As long as this is not the case, the right to equal treatment of private property will, at least for Venezuelans, remain a right in theory, not in practice.

The final contribution to this part takes a step back, seeking to unveil the broader picture that emerges through the practical applications. N. Jansen Calamita, Director of the Investment Treaty Forum at the British Institute of International and Comparative Law and lecturer at the University of Birmingham, explores the constitutional considerations behind international human rights and the interpretation of international investment treaties. While the interaction of legal communities has been explored in some depth by other scholars, it is rather doubtful whether this dynamic, even if accepted as valid in principle, can explain the reception of human rights-oriented arguments before investment treaty tribunals. In the first place, and contrary to the position taken by Hirsch, this author submits that it is not at all clear that human rights arguments have received a cold reception. For example, the principle of proportionality, a cornerstone of the European human rights system, has been increasingly embraced, through inference and analogy, by investor–state tribunals in the application of a variety of substantive protections, for example, fair and equitable treatment, and indirect expropriation. Moreover, investor–state tribunals have looked specifically to the case law of the European Court of Human Rights in giving application to substantive investment treaty standards. Directly engaging with Chapter 4, the author posits that a sociological interpretation of the interaction between investment treaties and human rights treaties, while intellectually stimulating, lacks the capacity for validation. More useful would be an analysis of the tribunals' reasoning where this matter has been raised, as well as of the jurisdictional clauses under which these tribunals function. These data-points, together with the positive rules of treaty interpretation, suggest a more fruitful path both to understanding the behaviour of investment tribunals and considering future drafting options in order to provide a more textual authority for the treatment of human rights issues in investment arbitration.

Part III: international investment and sustainable development

Part III addresses the sustainable development–investment interaction, including, in addition to the 'classic' environment-related topics, also social, cultural and other forms of development. Such an approach allows for authors to examine various forms of development in an innovative manner.

How can international investment agreements (IIAs) be improved so as to support sustainable development objectives? That is the central question in Chapter 8, embarked upon by Markus W. Gehring and Avidan Kent, from the universities of Cambridge and Ottawa. In the face of the current turmoil in the business, finance and management world, this chapter aims to explain in basic terms what an investment really is and how it contributes to global sustainable development. Domestic corporate lawyers, government officials and NGO representatives lack a detailed knowledge about investments and the laws governing them. A more solid understanding could contribute to the de-mystification of investments by examining how they interact with other important priorities such as sustainable development. Despite the seeming lack of inclusion of sustainable development within the current regulatory framework of investments at the international level, some steps have been taken in the right direction. Certain international organisations, such as the International Institute for Sustainable Development (IISD), have started developing Model BITs that include sustainable development objectives for all parties involved in these treaties. While some may see these Model BITs as not feasible in the present political climate, a few countries have nevertheless begun to include more sustainable development concepts in their own Model BITs. Other states have looked more closely at the possibility of using exception clauses in their Model BITs to achieve the same goals. Another way of introducing sustainable development concepts into IIAs has been to draft the dispute settlement provisions in alignment with current sustainable development practices. However, while development goals are increasingly addressed in IIAs, this has been done, according to the authors, in an indirect manner and in a primarily defensive mode. Moreover, allowing for exceptions, reservations and the like may seem to seek to shield contracting parties permanently or temporarily from assuming the full scope of obligations under the IIA.

The same question is also examined from an institutional angle by Wolfgang Alschner and Elisabeth Tuerk, consultant and legal expert at the United Nations Conference on Trade and Development (UNCTAD), respectively, who present a range of policy options for sustainable development in the specific context of IIAs. Today many states have adopted a more proactive attitude to aligning IIAs with sustainable policy considerations. As pointed out in the 2010 World Investment Report, states are renegotiating, amending and denouncing their BITs in larger efforts to re-balance the international investment regime. Two sets of policy options are available to states. On the one hand, they can improve the language and reassess the scope of their treaties, resulting in new IIAs that include interesting 'best practices' in this context. Beyond adding flexibilities and specifying treaty language to avoid undesired impacts on regulatory prerogatives for pursuing sustainable development impacts, recent IIAs also include provisions that supplement 'hard' investment obligations with 'softer' sustainability standards and that refer to investment-related sustainability issues, such as environmental labour or corporate social responsibility (CSR). On the other hand, states can use alternative, informal means to re-balance their IIAs, such as fostering a sustainability-oriented interpretation in the case of investor–state dispute settlement. While leaving the task of interpreting IIA obligations in an investor–state dispute to arbitral tribunals, proactive state involvement may help to make IIAs more predictable and development-friendly.

International organisations cannot, of course, provide all the answers as, particularly in the field of international law-making, the primary role is reserved for states. Some states are more active in this regard than others: and Canada is a prime example of this, as explained by Pierre-Olivier Savoie, counsel in Canada's Trade Law Bureau. He elaborates on reservations, CSR and other mechanisms in support of sustainable development in Canada's Model Foreign Investment Promotion and Protection Agreement (FIPA). First, the FIPA provides mechanisms allowing a party to conduct sustainable development even though it does not impose obligations on investors like the IISD Model BIT does. Such mechanisms include reservations and general exceptions, while other substantive provisions require the FIPA parties to take certain measures to ensure the transparency of regulatory measures. The Model FIPA also recognises that it is inappropriate to relax domestic health, safety or environmental standards to encourage investment. Second, reservations allow for regulatory flexibility and do not shield contracting parties from assuming their obligations under FIPAs. Reservations are negotiated between FIPA parties and constitute an integral part of the treaty. Such reservations can be made for both existing and future non-conforming measures with respect to some substantive obligations, such as national treatment, most-favoured-nation (MFN) treatment, performance requirements and provisions relating to the senior management and board of directors. Third, BITs that are similar to the IISD Model likely require extensive negotiations, as confirmed by Canada's experience with its FIPA. This is probably why countries with Model BITs similar to the FIPA (e.g., United States) have fewer of these treaties than countries with models that do not allow for carving out non-conforming existing and future measures (e.g., France and Germany).

The final word in this part goes to a scholar, Diane A. Desierto, Peking University School of Transnational Law, who looks at the sustainable development criterion in investment as a decisive element in determining the applicability of IIAs. Of all constitutive elements of 'an investment' identified in *Joy Mining* v. *Egypt* and *Salini* v. *Morocco*, subsequent arbitral tribunals have given least attention to the theoretical development of 'a significant contribution to a host State's development'. Is such a 'contribution' to be assessed in singularly microeconomic terms

(e.g., tax revenues and project returns) or, as seen from innovations in
the IISD Model BIT, could investment tribunals adopt a more integrative
perspective in the assessment of such 'contributions', taking into account
key aspects of sustainable development such as the host state's environmental and cultural obligations? The paradox of circumscribing 'investment' into unduly restrictive microeconomic and commercial definitions
in IIAs is that it may also cause the IIA to be inapplicable in cases with
investor–claimants who themselves are protected subjects of a host state's
international obligations with respect to sustainable development. The
2011 NAFTA arbitral award in *Grand River* v. *United States* provides an
interesting example of how the claimants – all members of indigenous
peoples (Six Nations of the Iroquois Confederacy, or the Haudenosaunee) – ultimately failed to meet evidentiary grounds to show that their
traditional commercial activities constituted 'an investment' object of
NAFTA protection. To this end, this chapter discusses whether the
threshold issue of IIA applicability should be resolved by way of more
nuanced 'investment' definitions in the newer generation of IIAs, thus
purposely building in sustainable development through treaty design.
Alternatively, in the light of recent annulments in *Sempra* v. *Argentina*
and *Enron* v. *Argentina*, it is assessed whether it is tenable to leave the
issue to the divergent positions of arbitral tribunals on IIA applicability
in their interpretations of the broad exceptions clauses ('essential security
interests' or 'necessity' clauses) that remain extant from the older generation of IIAs.

Part IV: international investment, trade and developing countries

The role of development, as already touched upon Chapter 11, is further
scrutinised in the following four chapters. As development is all too often
narrowed down to its economic aspects, some contributions in this part
specifically focus on trade, while others consider different sides of development, such as social, political or cultural development.

The interaction between investment and trade as main pillars of
economic development is, in the words of Mary E. Footer, University
of Nottingham, a 'relationship that never went away'. Drawing on the
evolution of these two areas of economic activity over the course of six
decades, this relationship is examined from a historical and contemporary perspective. States have often sought to regulate international investment within the context of a broader trade or commercial treaty regime,
for which they have used fora like the UN General Assembly, the OECD

or UNCTAD, or have turned to 'soft' law instruments. The contemporary relationship between the two multilateral systems has evolved both substantively and procedurally. From a substantive perspective, this chapter engages in an analysis of: (1) the principle of non-discrimination, as exemplified by MFN and national treatment standards; and (2) the principles of equity and justice, as evidenced by the doctrine of legitimate expectations and the concept of denial of justice. The chapter then shows that both the WTO dispute settlement system and the system of investor–state dispute resolution have taken a procedural turn in the last five years, the effects of which hinder the proper exercise of public power by states, whether WTO members or host states in the field of foreign investment. The foregoing analysis questions the future of the relationship between international investment law and trade, and, in particular, the ongoing exercise of public power in a situation of global economic governance.

The next contributor, Anastasios Gourgourinis, is a lawyer, lecturer and adviser for the Hellenic Ministry of State and Strategic Investments. He reviews the international minimum standard of treatment of aliens as 'one standard to rule them all?' This chapter discusses how trade and investment provisions concerning the administration of domestic regulation, and more specifically the treatment afforded to foreign traders/ investors, have been influenced by the international customary minimum standard. In other words, the international minimum standard of treatment of aliens is viewed as a 'floor' for the protection of foreign traders and investors vis-à-vis, on the one hand, due process standards regarding the administration of domestic regulation under WTO law, and, on the other, fair and equitable treatment standards prescribed by various IIAs. Emphasising the triangular normative relationship regarding the administration of domestic regulation between the customary rule as *lex generalis* and the provisions of the trade and investment regimes as *leges speciales*, the author argues that, on the basis of the same or similar facts, norms derived from the two regimes may lead to the same or similar juridical consequences, so that investors can assume that they will prevail on a fair and equitable treatment claim if their home state has earlier prevailed, for example, on an Article X:3 GATT claim at the WTO, and vice versa. The chapter concludes by identifying potential problematic issues, such as forum shopping and double redress, as potential consequences of this normative overlap.

The chapter by Ursula Kriebaum, University of Vienna, adopts a developing-country approach towards investment treaty standards. Most arbitral tribunals have not systematically considered a country's level of development when assessing the threshold for the violation of BIT standards. Nevertheless, some arbitral tribunals were prepared to consider the social, economic and political situation prevailing in the country when applying the investment protection standards in particular cases. All of these cases concerned a lowering of the standards in situations of political or economic difficulty and instability. The tribunals often used the concept of 'legitimate expectations' when considering such factors, finding that the reasonableness of investors' expectations had to be measured against the background of the situation prevailing in the host state. Some tribunals seem to have acted on the assumption that a certain minimum standard exists which provides a specific 'bottom line of treatment'. If the state crosses this bottom line, it would inevitably lead to a violation of the investment protection standard – an approach which is questioned by the author.

The last word in this part is offered to a practitioner, Maria Gritsenko, associate lawyer at Skadden, Arps, Slate, Meagher & Flom, who explores the possibility of applying a 'variable' standard of protection for developing countries. International investment protection standards have sometimes been interpreted less stringently based on the host country's state of development, as analysed in Chapter 14. Gritsenko disagrees with Kriebaum's conclusion, submitting that such an approach would suggest that the international standard of treatment of investors can somehow be lower in developing countries, which would run at cross-purposes with the idea of international investment law being a specific response to the demand for protection of foreign investors in developing countries. This chapter reviews the instances in which a country's state of development was brought to the attention of the arbitrators and discusses whether there is a 'variable' standard of protection. If this is not the case, the question arises as to whether, and at what stage of deciding an investment dispute (liability or quantum), the tribunals should consider that the defendant state is a developing country.

Part V: international investment and the European Union

So far, several chapters have paid attention to the actions of various international organisations, as well as individual developed and developing states. However, the most dynamic 'elephant in the room' is perhaps the European Union, where several developments are ongoing, initiated after the entry into force of the Lisbon Treaty in 2009, which may eventually influence the development of international investment law in its entirety. This specific part on the European Union was included to address the highly topical issue of the recent expansion of competences on the European level, which may significantly change the current mostly bilateral nature of the investment treaty landscape. Other regional blocks do not have a clear homogeneous investment policy, nor is any similar centralisation taking place to the same extent in any such blocks.

Friedl Weiss and Silke Steiner, University of Vienna, embark on an analysis of the investment regime under Article 207 of the Treaty on the Functioning of the European Union (TFEU), to find it a legal conundrum that raises many questions with regard to the scope of 'foreign direct investment' (FDI) and the future of intra-EU BITs. The Lisbon Treaty extended the EU's exclusive competence for its common commercial policy to include FDI only, leaving 'indirect investment' arguably within the competence of EU member states. The European Commission has encountered criticism concerning its intention to replace existing BITs of EU member states. The proposed new policy focuses, *inter alia*, on balancing investor protection, on the one hand, and 'the right to protect the public capacity to regulate and meet the EU's obligation to exercise policy coherence for development', on the other. However, under the proposed approach, arbitral tribunals are not only authorised, but indeed required to perform a balancing act between potentially conflicting public policy goals (investor protection versus competing or conflicting public policy goals). This effectively implies a delegation of public policy-making to international arbitral tribunals. As the Commission's proposal for a regulation on transitional arrangement for BITs between member states and third countries travels through the EU legislative process, criticism has been voiced with regard to some of the proposed policy changes. This chapter seeks to contrast and evaluate the positions taken by the Commission, the Council of Ministers and the European Parliament on various policy changes.

The gauntlet thrown by the authors of Chapter 16 is subsequently picked up by Thomas Henquet, legal counsel at the Netherlands Ministry of Foreign Affairs, who presents some inspiring ideas on the uneasy relationship between international investment and the European Union, as he experiences it on a daily basis. As elaborated upon in Chapter 16, the stated aim of the European Commission, largely endorsed by the Council, is to gradually replace BITs between EU member states and third states with agreements between the EU and such states. To that end, EU policy will be developed on the basis of 'best available practices' of member states. For the Netherlands, as for many member states, it is important that the new policy does not detract from its strong position as an investment country, both as an investment host state and an investor home state. This strong position of the Netherlands is at least partly due to its BITs. In addition to having entered into BITs with a large number of states, Dutch BITs offer favourable provisions to investors, including broad definitions of the terms 'investment' and 'national'. The aim of the contribution is to identify some of the 'best available practices' of Dutch BITs with a view to inspiring and guiding future EU policy.

Next to challenges, the new EU competence regarding FDI also provides law-makers with a number of opportunities, as submitted by Rumiana Yotova, Cambridge University. Article 207 of the TFEU constitutes the first express inclusion of 'foreign direct investment' into the scope of EU common commercial policy and thus exclusive competence. Although this is a step towards clarifying the rights and obligations of EU member states *inter se* with respect to FDI, it also raises potential controversies that remain to be resolved by the future implementing regulations. While the obvious advantage of a new consolidated intra-EU BIT is providing a level playing field for all EU investors operating within the EU, there are challenges too, which are already identifiable in the Commission's Communication on a Comprehensive European International Investment Policy. Illustrative thereof is the provisional definition of FDI, which is exclusively EU law-centred without any reference to the extensive investment arbitration case law setting out the relevant criteria as to what constitutes an investment, raising uncertainties concerning unprotected 'portfolio' investments. Another example is the disregard for case law precedents on the scope of investors' legitimate expectations. Finally, this contribution discusses the Commission's intention to regulate and modify the right of investors to refer their dispute to investor–state arbitration so as to enhance transparency and consistency through quasi-permanent arbitrators and appeal procedures.

Part VI: outlook: international investment in the twenty-first century

For the epilogue, four scholars were given a free hand to predict, speculate or even philosophise about the future of international investment law in the twenty-first century. The core question put to them was: if one were to organise a conference on the interaction of international investment law with other fields of public international law in twenty or fifty years' time, what would the controversial topics be?

Nicolas Hachez and Jan Wouters, University of Leuven, foresee that international arbitration, as the preferred dispute settlement system in international investment disputes, will increasingly come under fire in the next decades as the current format does not provide sufficient room for the preservation of the public interest. Although reforms have been adopted or are underway to open up arbitral proceedings and provide opportunities for the participation of public interest groups, the authors assert that these changes are unlikely to soothe the current worries. Several ambitious proposals have already been put forward, notably the idea of setting up a permanent institution that could hear cases at first instance or serve as an appeals mechanism. They conclude, however, that 'despite a pressing need for (r)evolution, conservatism firmly holds the international investment legal regime, especially on the part of capital-exporting countries, as their corporations value highly the possibility of resorting to arbitration'. One can only hope that, 'in the absence of a sea change, small tides of reform will, in the course of the twenty-first century, progressively shape a fairer and more open dispute settlement system that is more concerned with the general interest'.

Vid Prislan, Leiden University, draws all the threads from the previous chapters together, to demonstrate that there is more than one avenue for investment tribunals to consider non-investment obligations in deciding investor–state disputes. The general latitude that investment tribunals enjoy with regard to the scope of legal rules that they are entitled to apply, as well as the rules on treaty interpretation that enable them to take account of the broader normative environment in the interpretative process, provide them with a sufficient degree of flexibility to properly consider obligations arising under instruments other than the investment treaty, without necessarily exceeding their jurisdictional limits. He argues that the regulation of the interaction between investment law and other subfields of international law requires primarily a policy response. Investment arbitral tribunals should not be entrusted with deciding which societal concerns have priority; their task is primarily in finding the precise balance between the acts that may reasonably be found to constitute interference with investors' rights, and acts that fall within the state's legitimate right to regulate.

Ralph Alexander Lorz, Heinrich Heine University of Düsseldorf, opts for a different approach: rather than looking at dispute resolution, he takes a step back and assesses the fragmentation, consolidation and the future relationship between international investment law and general international law as such. In his eyes, the challenge to overcome the problems of fragmentation and to strike a balance between the competing demands is a twofold one. First, in terms of the persons involved, this calls for the reunification of various legal communities that are currently still largely separate. Second, in legal terms, this requires the identification of overlapping roles and, insofar possible, revisiting and reviewing such roles so as to eliminate potential incompatibilities. Notwithstanding these challenges, however, perhaps the best news to be taken from the contributions to this book is that reconciliation seems generally possible. To some extent, the author already sees this happening in personal terms: academics as well as practitioners are active in multiple branches of the law. With regard to the subject matter, it is clear that no matter how specialised the subfields of public international law already are, and will increasingly become in the future, they maintain common roots and traits. Once this path of mutual exchange is taken, many positive cross-fertilisation effects can be expected in the future. Such effects may come about via either through judicial or legislative means, whereby the role of new players in the international field, such as the WTO, the EU and several developing countries, should not be underestimated.

International law-makers and adjudicatory bodies can no longer ignore the various interactions between international investment law and other fields of public international law – this is the quintessential idea put forward by all contributions to this volume. Matters cannot simply be left to run their course, although some adjudicatory bodies have already shown impressive ingenuity in finding pragmatic solutions to imminent problems. However, a more systematic approach towards creating a new generation of international agreements is required; which implies a challenging responsibility for academics and practitioners alike who are involved in negotiating, applying and interpreting the international treaties of the twenty-first century.

Freya Baetens

I Introduction

The ever-increasing internationalisation of the global economy that has taken place since the end of the Second World War has led to an enormous growth in foreign investment. This became particularly pronounced during the 1990s, when foreign investment quadrupled.[1] Yet the phenomenon of foreign investment has long been known to the Dutch. The construction in 1619 of a train-oil factory on Smeerenburg in the Spitsbergen islands by the Noordsche Compagnie, and the acquisition in 1626 of Manhattan Island by the Dutch West Indies Company are proudly referred to as the earliest cases of foreign direct investment (FDI) in Dutch history.[2] Throughout the seventeenth century, the Dutch East India Company and the Dutch West Indies Company also began to create trading settlements around the globe. Their trading activities generated enormous wealth, making the Netherlands one of the most prosperous countries of that time. Even after the end of the colonial era, the Netherlands remained a significant player in the world economy. Ranking today as the fifteenth largest economy in the world measured by its gross domestic product, it continues to be among the largest sources, as well as recipients, of investment in the world, in both absolute and relative terms. In terms of FDI stocks, in 2010 the Netherlands ranked as the eighth largest recipient of investments (US$589.8 billion) and seventh largest source of investments (US$890.2 billion).[3] In 2009, it had a reported inflow of approximately US$34.5 billion and an outflow of US $26.9 billion. And while FDI inflows showed a negative figure in 2010, FDI outflows in the same year rose even further, to US$31.9 billion. It is not

---

[1] UNCTAD, *World Investment Report 2005* (Geneva: UNCTAD, 2005), p. 2.
[2] See F. de Goey, 'Dutch Overseas Investments in the Very Long Run (*c.* 1600–1990)', in R. van Hoesel and R. Narula (eds), *Multinational Enterprises from the Netherlands* (London: Routledge, 1999), pp. 32–60 at p. 35.
[3] UNCTAD, *World Investment Report 2011* (Geneva: UNCTAD, 2011).

surprising, therefore, that the Netherlands has long had a special interest in both the promotion and protection of foreign investment.

II   Dutch foreign investment policy and investment treaty landscape

While the large inflow of foreign direct investment is largely attributable to the strategic location of the Netherlands and its generally very favourable investment climate, foreign investment outflow is owed foremost to the presence of major multinational corporations operating from within the Netherlands. In fact, until the 1970s, Dutch foreign investment outflows could not be considered in isolation from the international activities of four industrial enterprises – Shell, Philips, Unilever and AKZO – which all began operating on an international scale at an early stage.[4] Because of the many international activities of Dutch companies, the Netherlands also traditionally attaches great importance to establishing and maintaining an adequate international legal system for the protection of foreign investment – bilaterally as well as multilaterally. Therefore, the Netherlands actively supported the creation of the International Centre for the Settlement of Investment Disputes (ICSID) in the context of the World Bank, and was among the first to ratify the ICSID Convention in 1966.[5] It also supported the efforts to adopt a Convention on the Protection of Foreign Property under the auspices of the Organisation for Economic Co-operation and Development (OECD) in the 1960s. The adoption of such a convention was considered particularly desirable by the Dutch Government, since no substantive rules on investment protection were included in the ICSID Convention.[6] At around the same time, the Netherlands also took the first steps to ensure the security and protection of investments of its nationals abroad on a bilateral level. The first agreement to be solely devoted to the encouragement and protection of investment

---

[4] See, generally, R. van Hoesel and R. Narula (eds), *Multinational Enterprises from the Netherlands* (London: Routledge, 1999).

[5] Convention on the Settlement of Investment Disputes between States and Nationals of Other States, Establishing the International Centre for the Settlement of Investment Disputes (ICSID Convention), Washington, 18 March 1965, entered into force on 14 October 1966: 575 *UNTS* 159, 4 *ILM* 532 (1965). The Netherlands' instrument of ratification was deposited on 14 September 1966, while the Convention entered into force on 14 October 1966.

[6] See Explanatory Memorandum accompanying the ratification of the ICSID Convention in the Dutch Parliament, Parliamentary Year 1965–1966, 8610, No. 3, p. 3.

was the Convention on Capital Investment and the Protection of Property which was signed with Tunisia in 1963.[7] In subsequent decades, the number of bilateral investment treaties (BITs) concluded by the Netherlands grew rapidly, and today it boasts with the seventh largest network of bilateral agreements for the promotion and protection of investments in the world, having concluded BITs with as many as ninety-eight states,[8] ninety-four of which are currently in force.[9] Nonetheless, BITs are still regarded as the second best option and the Dutch Government has always given priority to multilateral instruments for the protection of investments.[10] The government has been a strong supporter of the Multilateral Agreement on Investment (MAI), as this was expected to bring about an important stimulus for Dutch investments abroad and foreign investments in the Netherlands.[11] After the failure of the MAI, the Netherlands continued to support negotiations on a multilateral investment agreement in the context of the World Trade Organization (WTO).[12]

[7] Convention Between the Government of the Kingdom of the Netherlands and the Government of the Tunisian Republic concerning the Encouragement of Capital Investment and the Protection of Property, signed on 23 May 1963, entered into force on 19 December 1964, 1965 *UNTS* 238.

[8] This figure includes 8 older agreements on economic (and technical) cooperation which are still in force. The figure separately treats BITs which were subject to State succession, such as the BIT with the Czech and Slovak Republic which was succeeded by the Czech Republic and Slovakia respectively and the BIT with the Federal Republic of Yugoslavia which was succeeded by Serbia and Montenegro, respectively. On the other hand, the figure does not take into account BITs which were subsequently re-negotiated, namely those with Korea (1974), Egypt (1976), Romania (1983), China (1985), Oman (1987), and Bulgaria (1988), or ceased to apply because of the dissolution of a treaty partner as in the case of the BIT with Yugoslavia (1976).

[9] The BITs with Brazil, Chile, Eritrea and Zambia have not yet entered into force. Brazil and Chile have notified the Netherlands that they do not intend to ratify their respective agreements. The BITs with Venezuela and Bolivia are still included in this figure, even though the respective countries have recently terminated their BITs with the Netherlands. However, the provisions of these treaties continue to be effective for a further period of fifteen years from the date of termination.

[10] See *Beleidsdoorlichting Handelspolitiek: Eindrapport*, Policy Review Commercial Policy, Final Report, Ministry of Economic Affairs, November 2007, available at: www.rijksbegroting.nl/binaries/pdfs/beleidsdoorlichtingen/ez-handelspolitiek.pdf, at p. 30, accessed 11 January 2013.

[11] The government's position was explained in Letter of the State Secretary for Economic Affairs, 13 March 1998, Tweede Kamer der Staten-Generaal, Parliamentary Year 1997–1998, 25 941, No. 1, p. 2. See also 'Protectionisme dreigt nu MAI is mislukt', *Economische Zaken*, vol. 19, 13 November 1998.

[12] See Report of the Parliamentary Commission on Economic Affairs, 12 May 1998, Tweede Kamer der Staten-Generaal, Parliamentary Year 1997–1998, 25 941, No. 4, p. 5; and Letter of

At the same time, the Netherlands has traditionally remained very liberal towards inward foreign investment, with freedom of capital movement and national treatment of foreign investors being the norm. Foreign firms are able to invest in virtually any sector of the Dutch economy, with the exception of a few public monopolies such as the media sector. In general, the Netherlands inward investment policy belongs among the most open in the world and, instead of conducting a protectionist policy, the Dutch Government prefers to play an active role in attracting foreign investment to the Netherlands with its proactive policy of acquisition.[13] The Netherlands has also been adamant in guaranteeing a strong degree of protection to the property of foreigners, and the state has generally refrained from large-scale expropriations. The Dutch legal system provides a strong degree of protection to the property of foreigners, not only because of the firm constitutional guarantees on the protection of private property,[14] but also as a result of international human rights standards,[15] which find direct application in the Dutch domestic legal order in view of the monist relationship between international law and domestic law provided for in the Dutch Constitution.[16]

---

the State Secretary for Economic Affairs, 23 November 1998, Tweede Kamer der Staten-Generaal, Parliamentary Year 1998–1999, 25 941, No. 5, p. 8.

[13] The contours of the current acquisition policy are described in the policy memorandum *In actie voor acquisitie. Hoe Nederland profiteert van buitenlandse investeringen* (*In Action for Acquisition. How Foreign Investments Benefit the Netherlands*), The Hague, August 2006, p. 4, attached to Letter of State Secretary for Economic Affairs, 28 August 2006, Tweede Kamer der Staten Generaal, Parliamentary Year 2006–2007, 30 300 XIII, No. 98.

[14] Article 14(1) of the Dutch Constitution, although not referring to the right to property as such, provides that: 'Expropriation may take place only in the public interest and on prior assurance of full compensation, in accordance with regulations laid down by or pursuant to Act of Parliament.' This and other translations of constitutional provisions used in this contribution are taken from 'The Constitution of the Kingdom of the Netherlands', *Netherlands International Law Review* 30 (1983): 387.

[15] Property rights are protected by Article 1 of Protocol No. 1 to the European Convention on Human Rights (20 March 1952, entered into force 18 May 1954, 213 *UNTS* 262) and Article 17 of the Charter of Fundamental Rights of the European Union (OJ C364/9, 18 December 2000). See also P. C. E. van Wijmen and J. P. Loof, 'The Influence of Article 1 Protocol No. 1 on the Dutch Legislation concerning Expropriation', in J. P. Loof, H. Ploeger and A. van der Steur (eds), *The Right to Property: The Influence of Article 1 Protocol No. 1 ECHR on Several Fields of Domestic Law* (Maastricht: Shaker Publishing, 2000), pp. 111–26.

[16] Article 93 of the Dutch Constitution provides that: 'Provisions of treaties and of resolutions by international institutions, which may be binding on all persons by virtue of their contents, shall become binding after they have been published.' Furthermore, Article 94 provides: 'Statutory regulations in force within the Kingdom shall not be applicable if

The liberal and open policy of the Netherlands with regard to both inward and outward foreign investment manifests itself in the extensive investment protection guarantees provided for in Dutch BITs. These traditionally provide coverage for various types of investments and a broad range of investors, including, for example, legal entities incorporated in third states, with few limitations. The protection afforded by these treaties is capacious, and includes not only the assurance of fair and equitable treatment, full protection and security, national and most-favoured-nation (MFN) treatment, and a prohibition on expropriation without compensation, but also broad umbrella clauses, as well as clauses on transfer of funds, subrogation and taxation.[17] With their extensive protection guarantees, Dutch BITs have made an important contribution to the creation of a transparent, predictable and stable environment for Dutch companies operating internationally. These companies are now offered the security that their investments made on the territory of the other country during the term of the treaty will be protected by a set of basic rules that, unlike domestic legislation, cannot be unilaterally changed by the host state. Importantly, any breach of these rules can be invoked directly by investors through recourse to investor-state arbitration.[18]

Like the agreements of other capital-exporting countries, however, Dutch BITs have also begun increasingly to be perceived as restraining the regulatory space of host states and favouring the protection of foreign investment over other societal interests.[19] Moreover, in view of their broad scope of application, they have been criticised for allowing investors of third states to make use of their extensive benefits through the

---

such application is in conflict with provisions of treaties that are binding on all persons or of resolutions by international institutions.' Hence, not only may these provisions be invoked in domestic judicial proceedings, but they also prevail, in case of discrepancy, over both the constitution and Acts of Parliament. On the effects of international law in the Dutch domestic legal system, see E. A. Alkema, 'Foreign Relations in the Netherlands Constitution of 1983', *Netherlands International Law Review* 31 (1984): 307.

[17] On these provisions, see N. J. Schrijver and V. Prislan, 'The Netherlands', in C. Brown and D. Krishan (eds), *Commentaries on Selected Model Investment Treaties* (Oxford University Press, 2013), pp. 535–91.

[18] As a rule, Dutch BITs contain broad arbitration clauses, which provide investors with the possibility of commencing ICSID or other types of arbitration in case of a dispute with the host state concerning an investment protected under the treaty.

[19] See generally on this critique, S. A. Spears, 'The Quest for Policy Space in a New Generation of International Investment Agreements', *Journal of International Economic Law* 13 (2010): 1037.

practice of treaty-shopping.[20] The effects of these criticisms have already become visible as a few states that were respondents in arbitrations on the basis of Dutch BITs recently decided to terminate their agreements with the Netherlands.[21] But while not necessarily leading to a rupture in the investment treaty system, these developments nonetheless point out the need to further study the interaction between foreign investment and other fields of international law. The contributions to this book deliver a thought-provoking and timely step towards charting such interplay.

III   New generation of Dutch BITs: beyond investment protection?

The focus of Dutch BITs, like the BITs of other capital-exporting coun-tries, has long been solely on the promotion and protection of foreign investment, while issues such as the protection of environment or the improvement of labour standards in the state recipient of the investment were not directly mentioned. This is not surprising given that for more than five decades foreign investment has been considered as a key determinant in the pursuit of economic growth and development, from which positive spill-over effects were assumed to follow automatically. The large majority of Dutch BITs record in their preambles the desire of the contracting parties 'to strengthen their traditional ties of friendship and to extend and intensify the economic relations between them, particularly with respect to investments by the nationals of one Con-tracting Party in the territory of the other Contracting Party', and recognize 'that agreement upon the treatment to be accorded to such investments will stimulate the flow of capital and technology and the economic development of the Contracting Parties and that fair and equitable treatment of investments is desirable'. The emphasis is thus on the quid pro quo that has traditionally informed the system of investment treaty protection: in exchange for contributing to the flow

---

[20] See, e.g., *Aguas del Tunari SA* v. *Republic of Bolivia*, ICSID Case No. ARB/02/3, Decision on Respondent's Objections to Jurisdiction, 21 October 2005, para. 330 and *Saluka Investments BV (The Netherlands)* v. *The Czech Republic*, UNCITRAL, Partial Award, 17 March 2006, paras 240–1. See R. van Os and R. Knottnerus, *Dutch Bilateral Investment Treaties: A Gateway to 'Treaty Shopping' for Investment Protection by Multinational Companies* (Amsterdam: SOMO, 2011); M. Skinner, C. A. Miles and S. Luttrell, 'Access and Advantage in Investor–State Arbitration: The Law and Practice of Treaty Shopping', *Journal of World Energy Law and Business* 3 (2010): 260, at pp. 275–6.

[21] This has recently happened in the case of the BITs with Venezuela and Bolivia.

of capital and technology into the economy of the host state, the investors of the other contracting party are promised fair and equitable treatment which is in accordance with other standards contained in the investment treaty. But the exclusive focus on foreign investment promotion and protection, coupled with the extensive investment protection guarantees provided for in these treaties, has given rise to criticism that BITs serve as tools for elevating investors' interests above other societal concerns in the host state.[22]

Some capital-exporting countries, in particular the United States and Canada, have consequently begun to amend their BITs by introducing detailed provisions defining what constitutes non-compensable regulatory expropriation. They have also chosen to insert other language that narrows the scope of key obligations or incorporates general exceptions clauses exempting the host state from potential liability resulting from regulation based on public health, environmental protection, labour matters or other aspects concerning the public good.[23] The Netherlands, for its part, has not yet undertaken an official review of its BITs to determine whether they strike an appropriate balance between principles of investment protection and the need of the host state for regulatory discretion. This is not surprising, since it has not yet been a respondent in an investment arbitration and, therefore, has had little incentive so far to dilute the protections contained in its BITs. However, in line with the policy that it previously pursued in the MAI negotiations,[24] it has nonetheless started to include in the preamble of its newer BITs additional recitals that stipulate that the promotion and protection of investments must not be pursued at the expense of other important societal values.

---

[22] On the need to strengthen the social dimension of investment treaties alongside their economic one, see F. Ortino, 'The Social Dimension of International Investment Agreements: Drafting a New BIT/MIT Model?' *International Law FORUM du droit international* 7 (2005): 243.

[23] On this, see, e.g., Spears, 'The Quest for Policy Space', and J. Beechey and A. Crockett, 'New Generation of Bilateral Investment Treaties: Consensus or Divergence?' in *Contemporary Issues in International Arbitration and Mediation: The Fordham Papers 2008* (Leiden: Nijhoff, 2009), pp. 5–25.

[24] The position of the Netherlands in the context of MAI negotiations was that the latter should not undermine international obligations on sustainable development, respect for internationally recognised social rights, and guarantees for cultural identity and cultural diversity. Commission on Economic Affairs, 12 May 1998, Tweede Kamer der Staten-Generaal, Parliamentary Year 1997–1998, 25 941, No. 4, p. 6; and Letter of the State Secretary for Economic Affairs, 23 November 1998, Tweede Kamer der Staten-Generaal, Parliamentary Year 1998–1999, 25 941, No. 5, p. 2.

Thus, the preambles of a number of Dutch treaties concluded in the last decade, as well as the Dutch Model BIT which has been used since 2004, expressly recognise 'that the development of economic and business ties will promote internationally accepted labour standards', and affirm that the treaty objective of encouragement and reciprocal protection of investments 'can be achieved without compromising health, safety and environmental measures of general application'.[25] The placing of non-investment policy objectives on the same normative plane as investment policy objectives is an important improvement when one considers that preambles are integral parts of treaty texts and often serve as important guides to the interpretation of treaty provisions.[26] The reference to non-investment policy objectives, it is apparently hoped, shall ensure that such objectives are taken into account in the interpretation of substantive protection standards. In practice, however, not all Dutch BITs that were concluded in the past decade actually contain these statements.[27] Moreover, the additional preambular paragraphs are included in only a fraction of Dutch BITs that are currently in force.[28]

Yet, undoubtedly, Dutch BITs were never concluded with the intention that the protection of foreign investment should take place at the expense of other societal concerns. Thus, the addition of non-investment policy objectives in the new generation of Dutch BITs is perhaps a useful clarification, but it certainly must not be interpreted as implying that older Dutch BITs shall be applied without due regarding being paid to the needs of the host states. In interpreting one of these older BITs, the Tribunal in *Saluka*, after noting that the preamble contained 'a more

---

[25] See the treaties with Mozambique (2001), Namibia (2002), Suriname (2005), Dominican Republic (2006) and Oman (2009), whereas the treaty with Burundi (2007) contains only the recital on health, safety and environment.

[26] Article 31(1) VCLT requires a treaty to be interpreted 'in good faith in accordance with the ordinary meaning to be given to the terms of the treaty in their context and in the light of its object and purpose', the context comprising, among others, the treaty's preamble. Several arbitral tribunals established on the basis of Dutch BITs have had recourse to the treaty's preamble to shed light on the content of specific substantive provisions. See, e.g., *Aguas del Tunari SA* v. *Republic of Bolivia*, ICSID Case No. ARB/02/3, Decision on Respondent's Objections to Jurisdiction, 21 October 2005, para. 241, and *Saluka Investments BV (The Netherlands)* v. *The Czech Republic*, UNCITRAL, Partial Award, 17 March 2006, para. 300.

[27] The treaties with Armenia (2005), Bahrain (2007), Algeria (2007) and Macao (2008) are silent on these issues.

[28] Six of the ninety-four BITs currently in force contain such clauses. They are listed in n. 2, above.

subtle and balanced statement of the Treaty's aims than is sometimes appreciated', properly concluded that:

> the protection of foreign investments is not the sole aim of the Treaty, but rather a necessary element alongside the overall aim of encouraging foreign investment and extending and intensifying the parties' economic relations. That in turn calls for a balanced approach to the interpretation of the Treaty's substantive provisions for the protection of investments.[29]

IV   The need to embed legal investment obligations in the broader fabric of international law

The need for a balanced approach in interpreting investment protection standards in Dutch BITs becomes more pronounced when one considers the totality of foreign policy goals of the Netherlands. Surely, the strengthening of the international economic legal order that takes place by means of bilateral and multilateral investment treaties undoubtedly belongs to the officially proclaimed foreign economic policy goals of the Dutch Government.[30] But there are also other foreign policy objectives. One of them is, importantly, the promotion and protection of human rights, which has even been elevated since 1978 to the status of 'cornerstone' or 'main pillar' of Dutch foreign policy.[31] Another is an active international development cooperation policy, pursued by the Netherlands since the mid-1960s. The Netherlands is one of the few OECD countries that has achieved the 0.7 per cent GDP target as official development assistance (ODA). In general, Dutch foreign policy is geared towards promoting the rule of law in international relations, which is part of the mission of the Dutch Government enshrined in Article 90 of the Dutch Constitution.[32]

Acknowledging the breadth of foreign policy goals is an important step in understanding that the system of foreign investment protection was never intended to function independently and in isolation from other

---

[29] *Saluka Investments BV (The Netherlands)* v. *The Czech Republic*, UNCITRAL, Partial Award, 17 March 2006, para. 300.

[30] See *Beleidsdoorlichting Handelspolitiek: Eindrapport*, Ministry of Economic Affairs, November 2007, available at: www.rijksbegroting.nl/binaries/pdfs/beleidsdoorlichtingen/ez-handelspolitiek.pdf, at pp. 8, 16, 29–30.

[31] See N. J. Schrijver, 'A Missionary Burden or Enlightened Self-Interest?: International Law in Dutch Foreign Policy', *Netherlands International Law Review* 57 (2010): 209.

[32] This reads: 'The Government shall promote the development of the international rule of law.'

international norms and concerns.[33] It is, however, beyond doubt that conceptualising the interplay of non-investment norms and concerns with the legal regime of foreign investment requires further study. The present book with contributions collected by Dr Freya Baetens is a laudable and an important step in this direction.

Nico Schrijver

---

[33] In the WTO context the Dutch Government commissioned a study on the implementation of non-trade objectives, such as compliance with labour standards and human rights, and protection of the environment and animal welfare, with special emphasis on the impact on the trading position of developing countries. See P. van den Bossche, N. Schrijver and G. Faber, *Unilateral Measures Addressing Non-trade Concerns: A Study on WTO Consistency, Relevance of Other International Agreements, Economic Effectiveness and Impact on Developing Countries of Measures concerning Non-product-related Processes and Production Methods* (The Hague: Ministry of Foreign Affairs, 2007).

PART I

International investment and armed conflict

1

The protection of investments in armed conflicts

CHRISTOPH SCHREUER

Recent events in Libya have turned the spotlight on an aspect of international investment law that has, so far, attracted little attention. Investments, almost by definition, require stability and cannot thrive in situations of violence and political volatility. Libya is host to a number of important foreign investments, notably in the energy sector. The current armed struggle has seriously affected these investments and is likely to lead to a series of disputes with foreign investors. At the same time Libya is party to bilateral investment treaties (BITs) with several countries, including Austria, Belarus, Belgium–Luxembourg, Croatia, France, Italy, Malta, Portugal and Switzerland.[1]

Similar situations have arisen, and are likely to arise in the future, in other parts of the world. Therefore, a discussion about the protection of foreign investments in times of armed conflict is by no means relevant only to the current situation in Libya.

A   Treaties in times of armed conflict

Investment law is in large measure governed by treaties. Therefore, the preliminary question that arises is if, and to what extent, the outbreak of armed conflict affects the continued application of treaties relating to the protection of foreign investments. The International Law Commission of the United Nations (ILC) has for some time pursued the project of codifying the rules governing the effects of armed conflict on treaties. Starting in 2004, its Special Rapporteur was Sir Ian Brownlie; in 2009, the ILC appointed Lucius Caflisch as Special Rapporteur. An advanced set of Draft Articles on the topic, published in 2010,[2] may be taken as reflecting the current state of international law.

---

[1] Libya is not a party to the Energy Charter Treaty, signed 17 December 1994, entered into force 16 April 1998, OJ L380/24.
[2] UN ILC Draft Articles on the Effects of Armed Conflict on Treaties, A/65/10.

The Draft Articles define 'armed conflict' as armed force between states or protracted armed force between government authorities and organised armed groups.[3] Therefore, international as well as non-international armed conflicts are covered. As far as non-international armed conflicts are concerned, these would have to be more than merely sporadic.

The Draft Articles contain a presumption of continuity of treaties: the outbreak of an armed conflict does not *ipso facto* terminate or suspend the operation of treaties.[4] In addition, the Draft Articles offer a list of treaties the subject matter of which implies continued operation during armed conflicts. This list includes 'treaties of friendship, commerce and navigation and analogous agreements concerning private rights'; it also includes 'treaties relating to commercial arbitration'.[5] Where a treaty contains express provisions on its operation in situations of armed conflict these provisions shall apply.[6] As will be shown below, some bilateral investment treaties contain specific provisions that address the consequences of armed conflict.

Termination or suspension of a treaty in times of armed conflict would be subject to certain formalities. An intention by a state party to terminate or suspend requires notification; a state party thus affected may object. This procedure would lead to the obligation to resort to dispute settlement. The rights and obligations of states with regard to dispute settlement, as far as they have remained applicable, despite the existence of the armed conflict, under other provision of the Draft Articles, remain unaffected

---

[3] Draft Article 2(b): '"Armed conflict" means a situation in which there has been a resort to armed force between States or protracted resort to armed force between governmental authorities and organized armed groups.'

[4] Draft Article 3: 'Absence of *ipso facto* termination or suspension. The outbreak of an armed conflict does not *ipso facto* terminate or suspend the operation of treaties as: (a) between States parties to the treaty that are also parties to the conflict; (b) between a State party to the treaty that is also a party to the conflict and a State that is a third State in relation to the conflict.'

[5] Draft Article 5: 'The operation of treaties on the basis of implication from their subject matter: (1) In the case of treaties the subject matter of which involves the implication that they continue in operation, in whole or in part, during armed conflict, the incidence of an armed conflict will not as such affect their operation ... Annex: Indicative list of categories of treaties referred to in draft article 5 ... (d) Treaties of friendship, commerce and navigation and analogous agreements concerning private rights; ... (l) Treaties relating to commercial arbitration ...'

[6] Draft Article 7: 'Express provisions on the operation of treaties: where a treaty itself contains [express] provisions on its operation in situations of armed conflict, these provisions shall apply.'

by a notification of termination or suspension.[7] Even where suspension or termination takes place the treaty may contain clauses that are separable.[8] Obligations existing under international law independently of a treaty are unaffected by a termination or suspension as a consequence of an armed conflict.[9] Therefore, as a rule, treaties dealing with the protection of foreign investments, such as BITs, continue to apply after the outbreak of armed hostilities. This is particularly so where these treaties address the consequences of armed conflicts.

Some BITs contain general security clauses. These clauses reserve the right of states to take measures to safeguard their essential interests in emergency situations. Security clauses of this kind are discussed below in section D.

BITs may contain several types of clauses dealing with violent situations, including armed conflict. These treaty provisions safeguard the interests of investors even in situations of armed conflict. Some of these treaty clauses have been interpreted and applied by investment tribunals. The most common provision of this kind that may be found in most BITs is a clause guaranteeing full protection and security (section B, below). In addition, some BITs contain clauses that specifically address wars and other armed conflicts. One type of these 'war clauses' merely promises non-discrimination in the treatment of losses incurred through armed conflict and similar situations (section C.1, below). The other type goes further and

---

[7] Draft Article 8: 'Notification of intention to terminate, withdraw from or suspend the operation of a treaty: 1. A State engaged in armed conflict intending to terminate or withdraw from a treaty to which it is a party, or to suspend the operation of that treaty, shall notify the other State party or States parties to the treaty, or its depositary, of that intention ... 3. Nothing in the preceding paragraphs shall affect the right of a party to object, in accordance with the terms of the treaty or applicable rules of international law, to termination, withdrawal from or suspension of the operation of the treaty ... 4. If an objection has been raised within the prescribed time limit, the States parties concerned shall seek a solution through the means indicated in Article 33 of the Charter of the United Nations. 5. Nothing in the preceding paragraphs shall affect the rights or obligations of States with regard to the settlement of disputes insofar as they have remained applicable, pursuant to draft articles 4 to 7, despite the incidence of an armed conflict.'

[8] Draft Article 10: 'Separability of treaty provisions: Termination, withdrawal from or suspension of the operation of the treaty as a consequence of an armed conflict shall, unless the treaty otherwise provides or the parties otherwise agree, take effect with respect to the whole treaty except where: (a) The treaty contains clauses that are separable from the remainder of the treaty with regard to their application ...'

[9] Draft Article 9: 'Obligations imposed by international law independently of a treaty: The termination of or the withdrawal from a treaty, or the suspension of its operation, as a consequence of an armed conflict, shall not impair in any way the duty of any State to fulfil any obligation embodied in the treaty to which it would be subject under international law independently of that treaty.'

actually promises compensation for losses incurred under these circumstances provided certain conditions are met (section C.2, below).

B Full protection and security

Most investment treaties contain provisions granting protection and security for investments.[10] Many of these treaties, including the NAFTA,[11] refer to 'full protection and security'.[12] Others, such as the Energy Charter Treaty,[13] refer to 'most constant protection and security'. Some put 'security' before 'protection'. These variations in language do not appear to carry any substantive significance.

There is no doubt that this provision is designed to protect investors and investments against violent action. In fact, in a number of cases tribunals seem to have assumed that this standard applies exclusively to physical security and to the host state's duty to protect the investor against violence directed at persons and property stemming from state organs or private parties.[14] More recently, authority has emerged to the effect that this standard extends to legal protection.[15]

1 Violence by state organs

Clauses guaranteeing protection and security have been applied in a number of cases. In some of these cases the violent action came from

---

[10] Provisions on full protection and security are contained in Libya's BITs with Austria, Belgium–Luxembourg (subject to a public order exception), Italy, Portugal and Switzerland.

[11] Article 1105(1) North American Free Trade Agreement, adopted 17 December 1992, entered into force 1 January 1994, 32 *ILM* 289 (1993).

[12] For the historical origin of the concept, see A. Newcombe and L. Paradell, *Law and Practice of Investment Treaties: Standards of Treatment* (Alphen aan den Rijn: Kluwer Law, 2009), pp. 307–8; J. D. Salacuse, *The Law of Investment Treaties* (Oxford University Press, 2010), pp. 208–10.

[13] Energy Charter Treaty, Article 10(1).

[14] *PSEG* v. *Turkey*, Award, 19 January 2007, at paras 257–9; *Enron* v. *Argentina*, Award, 22 May 2007, paras 284–7; *BG Group* v. *Argentina*, Award, 24 December 2007, paras 323–8; *Sempra* v. *Argentina*, Award, 28 September 2007, paras 321–4; *Plama* v. *Bulgaria*, Award, 27 August 2008, para. 180; *Rumeli* v. *Kazakhstan*, Award, 29 July 2008, para. 668; *Saluka Investments BV (The Netherlands)* v. *The Czech Republic*, Partial Award, 17 March 2006, paras 483, 484; *Eastern Sugar* v. *The Czech Republic*, Partial Award, 27 March 2007, para. 203; *Parkerings* v. *Lithuania* , Award, 11 September 2007, para. 355.

[15] For detailed discussion see C. Schreuer, 'Full Protection and Security', *Journal of International Dispute Settlement* 1(1) (2010): 6–10.

state organs. It is clear that the state is responsible for actions perpetrated by its organs.[16] The applicability of a treaty provision on protection and security to direct attacks on the investor's person and property by organs of the host state is beyond doubt. In *Biwater Gauff* v. *Tanzania* the Tribunal said:

> The Arbitral Tribunal also does not consider that the *'full security'* standard is limited to a State's failure to prevent actions by third parties, but also extends to actions by organs and representatives of the State itself.[17]

In *AMT* v. *Zaire*,[18] the investment had been subject to looting by elements of Zaire's armed forces. The applicable treaty provided that 'protection and security of investment shall be in accordance with applicable national laws, and may not be less than that recognized by international law'. The Tribunal found that the treaty provision imposed upon Zaire a duty of vigilance to take all necessary measures of precaution. Zaire had breached this obligation by taking no measure that would ensure the protection and security of the investment. It followed that Zaire was in breach of its treaty obligation.[19] The Tribunal said:

> Zaire has breached its obligation by taking no measure whatever that would serve to ensure the protection and security of the investment in question … Zaire is responsible for its inability to prevent the disastrous consequences of these events adversely affecting the investments of AMT which Zaire had the obligation to protect.[20]
>
> Zaire has manifestly failed to respect the minimum standard required of it by international law.[21]
>
> The responsibility of the State of Zaire is incontestably engaged by the very fact of an omission by Zaire to take every measure necessary to protect and ensure the security of the investment made by AMT in its territory.[22]

---

[16] See the International Law Commission's Articles on State Responsibility, Article 4: 'Conduct of organs of a State: 1. The conduct of any State organ shall be considered an act of that State under international law, whether the organ exercises legislative, executive, judicial or any other functions, whatever position it holds in the organization of the State, and whatever its character as an organ of the central government or of a territorial unit of the State. 2. An organ includes any person or entity which has that status in accordance with the internal law of the State.'

[17] *Biwater Gauff* v. *Tanzania*, Award, 24 July 2008, para. 730 (original emphasis).

[18] *AMT* v. *Zaire*, Award, 21 February 1997, 5 *ICSID Reports* 11.   [19] At paras 6.02–6.11.

[20] At para. 6.08.   [21] At para. 6.10.   [22] At para. 6.11.

Interestingly, the Tribunal did not base responsibility on the attribution of the acts of the soldiers to the state, but on the state's failure to protect the investment.

Toto v. *Lebanon*[23] concerns the construction of a highway. The investor had complained about the failure of the Lebanese Government to remove Syrian troops from the construction site. In its Decision on Jurisdiction, the Tribunal made the tentative finding that the alleged inaction of Lebanon, if proven, would constitute a failure to protect under the BIT between Italy and Lebanon.[24]

2   Private violence

Another important application of the protection and security standard concerns the state's duty to protect the investor against violence stemming from non-state actors. These may be rebels or insurgents engaged in a struggle against the government or private groups engaged in violent action against the investment.

In *Asian Agricultural Products Ltd (AAPL)* v. *Sri Lanka*,[25] the investment had been destroyed in the course of a counter-insurgency operation by the Sri Lankan security forces. The applicable treaty provided that foreign investments 'shall enjoy full protection and security'. The Tribunal found no conclusive evidence as to whether the destruction had been caused by the state's security forces or by the rebels.[26] The Tribunal stated that while a state is not, in principle, responsible for the actions of insurgents, it had a duty of protection that applied regardless of whether the damaging acts originated from the insurgents or government forces. The Tribunal said:

> It is a generally accepted rule of International Law, clearly stated in international arbitral awards and in the writings of the doctrinal authorities, that:
>
> (i) A State on whose territory an insurrection occurs is not responsible for loss or damage sustained by foreign investors unless it can be shown that the Government of that state failed to provide the standard of protection required, either by treaty, or under general customary law, as the case may be; and

---

[23] *Toto Costruzioni* v. *Lebanon*, Decision on Jurisdiction, 11 September 2009. In its Award of 17 June 2012, the Tribunal decided that Lebanon had not failed to comply with the full protection and security standard.
[24] At paras 110–18.   [25] *AAPL* v. *Sri Lanka*, Award, 21 June 1990, 4 *ICSID Reports* 246.
[26] At para. 85(D).

(ii) Failure to provide the standard or protection required entails the state's international responsibility for losses suffered, regardless of whether the damages occurred during an insurgents' offensive act or resulting from governmental counter-insurgency activities.[27]

On that basis the Tribunal found Sri Lanka responsible.[28] After a detailed analysis of the course of events the Tribunal concluded:

> the Tribunal considers that the Respondent through said inaction and omission violated its due diligence obligation which requires undertaking all possible measures that could be reasonably expected to prevent the occurrence of killings and property destructions.[29]

The guarantee of full protection and security extends to a duty to protect against violent action stemming from private persons falling short of the ILC's definition of armed conflict as set out above.[30] This may be demonstrated with the help of two cases involving hotels.

Wena Hotels v. *Egypt*,[31] involved the forcible seizure of two hotels by employees of a state entity (Egyptian Hotels Company (EHC)) with whom the investor had contractual relations. The weapons used consisted of sticks and cudgels. The treaty applicable in that case provided that investments 'shall enjoy full protection and security'. Government officials did not participate in the forcible seizure, but the police and other authorities took no effective measures to prevent or redress the seizure. The Tribunal had no doubt that Egypt violated its obligation to accord full protection and security.[32] This result was based on the finding that Egypt was aware of EHC's intentions to seize the hotels and took no action to prevent it from doing so. Nor did the police and the competent ministry take any immediate action to restore the hotels to the investor. Also, no substantial sanctions had ever been imposed on the perpetrators. The Tribunal said:

---

[27] At para. 72.

[28] At paras 78–86. The Tribunal interpreted the requirement of due diligence as a reference to the minimum standard under customary international law. At paras 67–9.

[29] At para. 85(B).

[30] See also *Elettronica Sicula SpA (ELSI) (United States of America* v. *Italy)*, ICJ Reports 1989, p. 15, paras 105–8; *Técnicas Medioambientales Tecmed SA* v. *The United Mexican States*, Award, 29 May 2003, 43 ILM 133 (2004), at paras 175–7; *Noble Ventures Inc.* v. *Romania*, Award, 12 October 2005, paras 164–6; *Pantechniki* v. *Albania*, Award, 30 July 2009, paras 71–84.

[31] *Wena Hotels Ltd* v. *Arab Republic of Egypt*, Award, 8 December 2000, 41 ILM 896 (2002).

[32] At para. 84.

84. The Tribunal agrees with Wena that Egypt violated its obligation under Article 2(2) of the IPPA to accord Wena's investment 'fair and equitable treatment' and 'full protection and security'. Although it is not clear that Egyptian officials other than officials of EHC directly participated in the April 1, 1991 seizures, there is substantial evidence that Egypt was aware of EHC's intentions to seize the hotels and took no actions to prevent EHC from doing so. Moreover, once the seizures occurred, both the police and the Ministry of Tourism took no immediate action to restore the hotels promptly to Wena's control. Finally, Egypt never imposed substantial sanctions on EHC or its senior officials, suggesting Egypt's approval of EHC's actions.

Amco v. *Indonesia*[33] was not decided on the basis of a BIT, but in the framework of customary international law. In that case, the investment consisted of a lease and management contract for a hotel. The local partner in the contract took over the hotel by force with the assistance of members of the Indonesian armed forces. The Tribunal held that the forcible takeover was not attributable to the government of Indonesia. But it found that Indonesia was in breach of international law, since it had failed to protect the investor against the takeover of the hotel by its citizens. The Tribunal said:

It is a generally accepted rule of international law, clearly stated in international awards and judgments and generally accepted in the literature, that a State has a duty to protect aliens and their investment against unlawful acts committed by some of its citizens ... If such acts are committed with the active assistance of state-organs a breach of international law occurs.[34]

3   Standard of liability

It is generally accepted that the obligation to provide protection and security does not create absolute liability. Rather, the standard is one of 'due diligence', that is, a reasonable degree of vigilance.[35] In *AAPL* v. *Sri*

---

[33] *Amco Asia Corporation and Others* v. *The Republic of Indonesia*, Award, 20 November 1984, 1 *ICSID Reports* 413.

[34] At para. 172.

[35] *Elettronica Sicula SpA (ELSI) (United States of America v. Italy)*, *ICJ Reports* 1989, p. 15, para. 108. See also *Técnicas Medioambientales Tecmed SA* v. *The United Mexican States*, Award, 29 May 2003, 43 *ILM* 133 (2004), at para. 177; *Noble Ventures Inc.* v. *Romania*, Award, 12 October 2005, para. 164; *Wena Hotels Ltd* v. *Arab Republic of Egypt*, Award, 8 December 2000, 6 *ICSID Reports* 68, para. 84; *Saluka Investments BV (The Netherlands)* v. *The Czech Republic*, Partial Award, 17 March 2006, para. 484; *MCI* v. *Ecuador*, Award, 31

Lanka,[36] the Tribunal rejected claimant's argument that the provision granting 'full protection and security' had created a strict or absolute liability, stating:

> the Tribunal declares unfounded the Claimant's main plea aiming to consider the Government of Sri Lanka assuming strict liability under Article 2(2) of the Bilateral Investment Treaty, without any need to prove that the damages suffered were attributable to the State or its agents, and to establish the State's responsibility for not acting with 'due diligence'.[37]

In the same sense, the Tribunal in *Wena* v. *Egypt* said about the interpretation of the full protection and security clause in the BIT between Egypt and the United Kingdom that:

> In interpreting a similar provision from the bilateral investment treaty between Zaïre and the United States, another ICSID panel has recently held that 'the obligation incumbent on [the host state] is an obligation of vigilance, in the sense that [the host state] shall take all measures necessary to ensure the full enjoyment of protection and security of its [sic] investments and should not be permitted to invoke its own legislation to detract from any such obligation'.[38] Of course, as still another ICSID panel has observed, a host state's promise to accord foreign investment such protection is not an 'absolute obligation which guarantees that no damages will be suffered, in the sense that any violation thereof creates automatically a "strict liability" on behalf of the host State'.[39] A host state 'is not an insurer or guarantor ... it does not, and could hardly be asked to, accept an absolute responsibility for all injuries to foreigners[40].[41]

It follows from the above practice that the standard of full protection and security involves the obligation of the host state to exercise restraint in the use of armed force where a protected investor is involved. It also involves the obligation to protect the investment against rebel forces and other forms of private violence. This obligation does not create strict liability, but rather an obligation of due diligence, that is, it exists to the extent of the reasonable use of the host state's capabilities.

July 2007, paras 245–6; *Plama* v. *Bulgaria*, Award, 27 August 2008, para. 181; *Biwater Gauff* v. *Tanzania*, Award, 24 July 2008, paras 725, 726; *Rumeli* v. *Kazakhstan*, Award, 29 July 2008, para. 668; *Siag* v. *Egypt*, Award, 1 June 2009, para. 447.

[36] *AAPL* v. *Sri Lanka*, Award, 21 June 1990, 4 *ICSID Reports* 246, paras 45–53.

[37] At para. 53.   [38] Referring to *AMT* v. *Zaïre*, Award, 21 February 1997, para. 6.05.

[39] Referring to *AAPL* v. *Sri Lanka*, Award, 21 June 1990, para. 48.

[40] Referring to *AAPL* v. *Sri Lanka*, Award, 21 June 1990, para. 49.

[41] *Wena Ltd* v. *Arab Republic of Egypt*, Award, 8 December 2000, para. 84.

C   War clauses in investment treaties

1   Non-discrimination clauses

Many BITs contain clauses referring to war or to other forms of armed conflict, states of emergency, revolution, insurrection, civil disturbance or similar events. In their simple form these clauses provide for national treatment and most-favoured-nation (MFN) treatment in relation to any measures, such as restitution or compensation that the states may take.

Article 7 of the Libya–Portugal BIT contains such a clause:

> Article 7: Compensation for damages or losses
>
> Each Party shall provide to investors of the other Party, whose investments suffer losses in the territory of the first Party owing to war or armed conflict, revolution, a state of national emergency, disobedience or disturbances or any other event considered as such, treatment that restitutes the conditions of these investments that existed before the damage had occurred, or compensation, or any other settlement that is no less favourable than that Party accords to the investments of its own investors, or of any third State, whichever is more favourable. Any payment made under this article shall be, without delay, freely transferable in convertible currency.

Provisions of this type are not uncommon in BITs.[42] NAFTA, Article 1105(2) also contains the obligation to non-discriminatory treatment with respect to measures adopted relating to losses suffered owing to armed conflict or civil strife.

Clauses of this type do not create substantive rights to restitution or compensation beyond non-discrimination vis-à-vis host state nationals or nationals of third countries. In other words, their effect depends on measures taken by the host state in relation to these investors.[43]

In *CMS* v. *Argentina*, the Tribunal said with respect to a similar provision in Article IV(3) of the Argentina–US BIT:

> The plain meaning of the Article is to provide a floor treatment for the investor in the context of the measures adopted in respect of the losses suffered in the emergency, not different from that applied to nationals or other foreign investors. The Article does not derogate from the Treaty

---

[42] Libya's BITs with Belgium–Luxembourg, France and Italy contain similar clauses.

[43] See also *AAPL* v. *Sri Lanka*, Award, 21 June 1990, paras 65–7; *LG&E* v. *Argentina*, Decision on Liability, 3 October 2006, paras 243, 244; *Enron* v. *Argentina*, Award, 22 May 2007, para. 320.

rights but rather ensures that any measures directed at offsetting or minimizing losses will be applied in a non-discriminatory manner.[44]

2 Extended war clauses

Some treaties contain extended war clauses. These extended war clauses relate to war or to other armed conflict, state of emergency, revolution, insurrection, civil disturbance or similar events. They typically include the non-discrimination clause just described. But they go further in that they also contain absolute standards. Under these clauses losses suffered by investors at the hands of the host state's forces or authorities through requisitioning or destruction not required by the necessities of the situation are treated in analogy to expropriation. In other words, such acts require compensation that is prompt, adequate and effective. Article 12 of the Energy Charter Treaty is an example for such an extended war clause.[45]

Article 15 of the BIT between Austria and Libya contains such an extended war clause.[46] Its first paragraph reflects the standard of non-discrimination previously discussed. Its second paragraph goes beyond non-discrimination and provides for an absolute standard of restitution or compensation:

> Article 5: Compensation for Losses
>
> (1) An investor of a Contracting Party who has suffered a loss relating to its investment in the territory of the other Contracting Party due to war or to other armed conflict, state of emergency, revolution, insurrection,

---

[44] *CMS* v. *Argentina*, Award, 12 May 2005, para. 375

[45] Article 12 of the ECT provides: 'Compensation for losses: (1) Except where Article 13 applies, an Investor of any Contracting Party which suffers a loss with respect to any Investment in the Area of another Contracting Party owing to war or other armed conflict, state of national emergency, civil disturbance, or other similar event in that Area, shall be accorded by the latter Contracting Party, as regards restitution, indemnification, compensation or other settlement, treatment which is the most favourable of that which that Contracting Party accords to any other Investor, whether its own Investor, the Investor of any other Contracting Party, or the Investor of any third state. (2) Without prejudice to paragraph (1), an Investor of a Contracting Party which, in any of the situations referred to in that paragraph, suffers a loss in the Area of another Contracting Party resulting from: (a) requisitioning of its Investment or part thereof by the latter's forces or authorities; or (b) destruction of its Investment or part thereof by the latter's forces or authorities, which was not required by the necessity of the situation, shall be accorded restitution or compensation which in either case shall be prompt, adequate and effective.'

[46] Libya's BIT with Croatia contains a similar clause.

civil disturbance or any other similar event, or acts of God or *force
majeure*, in the territory of the latter Contracting Party, shall be accorded
by the latter Contracting Party, as regards restitution, indemnification,
compensation or any other settlement, treatment no less favourable than
that which it accords to its own investors or to investors of any third state,
whichever is most favourable to the investor.

(2) An investor of a Contracting Party who in any of the events referred to
in paragraph (1) suffers loss resulting from:

(a) requisitioning of its investment or part thereof by the forces or
authorities of the other Contracting Party, or

(b) destruction of its investment or part thereof by the forces or authorities of the other Contracting Party, which was not required by the
necessity of the situation,

shall in any case be accorded by the latter Contracting Party restitution or
compensation which in either case shall be prompt, adequate and effective
and, with respect to compensation, shall be in accordance with Article 4 (2)
and (3).

It will be noted that under paragraph (2) compensation is due only if the
adverse act was caused by government forces or authorities and not by
rebel forces. The duty to make restitution or pay compensation in the
case of requisitioning of the investment or part thereof is independent of
military necessity: even if the requisitioning was mandated by military
necessity, restitution or compensation is still due. By contrast, restitution
or compensation for destruction is due only if the forces acted in excess
of military necessity. In other words, collateral damage arising from
military action that is lawful under the *ius in bello* is not covered. This
corresponds to the situation under customary international law.

Two cases demonstrate that the requirements contained in extended war
clauses are not easy to meet. In *AAPL v. Sri Lanka*,[47] Article 4 of the applicable
BIT between Sri Lanka and the United Kingdom contained an extended war
clause. Its first paragraph provided for non-discrimination as regards restitution, indemnification, compensation or other settlement in cases of losses
suffered owing to war or other armed conflict, revolution, a state of national
emergency, revolt, insurrection or riot. The second paragraph provided:

(2) Without prejudice to paragraph (1) of this Article, nationals and
companies of one Contracting Party who in any of the situations referred
to in that paragraph suffer losses in the territory of the other Contracting
Party resulting from

---

[47] *AAPL* v. *Sri Lanka*, Award, 21 June 1990, 4 *ICSID Reports* 246.

(a) requisitioning of their property by its forces or authorities, or

(b) destruction of their property by its forces or authorities which was not caused in combat action or was not required by the necessity of the situation,

shall be accorded restitution or adequate compensation. Resulting payments shall be freely transferable.

The Tribunal refused to grant a remedy under this provision because there was no conclusive proof that the losses were incurred as a consequence of acts committed by government forces. The Tribunal said:

it has to be noted that the foreign investor who invokes the applicability of said Article 4(2) assumed a heavy burden of proof, since he has ... to establish:

(i)   that the governmental forces and not the rebels caused the destruction;

(ii)   that this destruction occurred out[side] of 'combat';

(iii) that there was no 'necessity' in the sense that the destruction could have been reasonably avoided due to its unnecessary character under the prevailing circumstances.

... there is no convincing evidence produced which sufficiently sustains the Claimant's allegation that the firing which caused the property destruction came from the governmental troops, and no reliable evidence was adduced to prove that the shrimps were lost due to acts committed by the security forces; ...

Therefore the Arbitral Tribunal finds that the first condition required under Article 4(2) cannot be considered fulfilled in the present case, due to the lack of convincing evidence proving that the losses were incurred due to acts committed by the governmental forces.[48]

The Tribunal found that the second and third conditions were also not met: the destruction was caused by 'combat action' in the sense of Article 4(2)(b).[49] In addition, the Tribunal was unable to conclusively determine the issue of military necessity.[50]

In *AMT* v. *Zaire*,[51] the looting and destruction had taken place at the hands of elements of the armed forces in uniform involving the use of army weapons. In interpreting an extended war clause of the type discussed here, the Tribunal reached the conclusion that the soldiers in uniform did not, in fact, represent the country's armed forces, since they had acted individually and not in any organised manner.

---

[48] At paras 58–60.   [49] At paras 61–2.   [50] At paras 63–4.
[51] *AMT* v. *Zaire*, Award, 21 February 1997.

Therefore, the destruction was caused by separate individuals and not the 'forces'. The Tribunal said:

> In the present case, it is true from the information received that they were the military, at least persons in military attire who manifestly acted individually without any one being able to show either that they were organized or that they were under order, nor indeed that they were concerted.
>
> The nature of the looting and the destruction of property which were looted show clearly that it was not 'the army' or 'the armed forces' that acted as such in the circumstance. And this in no way resembles expropriation or requisition by the State.[52]

These cases show that extended war clauses subject the investor's right to restitution or compensation to a number of stringent requirements. The practice on these clauses indicates that these conditions are not easy to meet. Any requisitioning or destruction must have occurred at the hands of the government's forces and not as a consequence of action by rebel forces or individuals. In a war situation it is often difficult to prove the source of the destruction. Requisitioning is easier to trace to government forces and will usually go hand in hand with some formality.

Military necessity is relevant only in case of destruction, but not of requisitioning. The existence of military necessity for the destruction of the investment or part thereof will be difficult to ascertain. Much will depend on who has to bear the burden of proof. In *AAPL v. Sri Lanka*, the Tribunal put the burden of proof for the existence of military necessity upon the claimant. This would appear to be an unreasonably onerous requirement. It should be incumbent upon the state exercising military force to justify it in terms of military necessity.

D   Security clauses in investment treaties

Some treaties, especially US BITs, contain general security exceptions.[53] The NAFTA in Article 2102 also contains a provision of this kind. Article XI of the BIT between Argentina and the United States is an example:

> Article XI
>
> This Treaty shall not preclude the application by either Party of measures necessary for the maintenance of public order, the fulfillment of its

---

[52] At paras 7.08–7.9.
[53] For more detailed treatment, see Newcombe and Paradell, *Law and Practice of Investment Treaties Standards of Treatment*, pp. 488–500.

obligations with respect to the maintenance or restoration of international peace or security, or the protection of its own essential security interests.[54]

A more recent version based on the 2004 US Model BIT is self-judging in that it contains the words 'that it considers necessary'.[55]

This provision has received much attention, especially as it relates to the customary international law requirements for a state of necessity as reflected in Article 25 of the ILC's Articles on State Responsibility. This discussion and the relevant cases do not concern an armed conflict, but an alleged economic emergency.[56]

The application of a security exception of this kind has radical and far-reaching consequences. In the words of the CMS *Ad Hoc* Committee:

> Article XI is a threshold requirement: if it applies, the substantive obligations under the Treaty do not apply.[57]

> Article XI, if and for so long as it applied, excluded the operation of the substantive provisions of the BIT.[58]

Therefore, if the security exception applies, the investor is deprived of the BIT's protection. This would also exclude reliance on the treaty's full protection and security standard. Of course, the protection afforded by customary international law remains unaffected.

The conditions for the application of such a security exception are relatively easily met in a situation involving armed force. The Article speaks of public order and of essential security interests. This would cover not only international or civil wars, but also terrorism and armed rebellion. The reference to 'the maintenance or restoration of international peace or security' echoes Article 39 of the UN Charter. Therefore, action in pursuance of Security Council resolutions under chapter

---

[54] For a detailed analysis of this clause, see R. Dolzer, 'Emergency Clauses in Investment Treaties: Four Versions', in M. H. Arsanjani, J. Katz Cogan, R. D. Sloane and S. Wiessner (eds), *Looking to the Future: Essays on International Law in Honor of W. Michael Reisman* (Leiden: Martinus Nijhoff, 2011), pp. 705–18.

[55] On the issue of the self-judging nature of security exceptions, see Newcombe and Paradell, *Law and Practice of Investment Treaties Standards of Treatment*, pp. 492–5.

[56] See especially *LG&E* v. *Argentina*, Award, 3 October 2006, paras 226–61; *CMS* v. *Argentina*, Award, 12 May 2005, paras 332–78; *CMS* v. *Argentina*, Decision on Annulment, 25 September 2007, paras 101–50; *Sempra* v. *Argentina*, Award, 28 September 2007, paras 364–91; *Sempra* v. *Argentina*, Decision on Annulment, 29 June 2010, paras 173–219; *Enron* v. *Argentina*, Award, 22 May 2007, paras 322–42; *Enron* v. *Argentina*, Decision on Annulment, 30 July 2010, paras 347–408.

[57] At para. 129.   [58] At para. 146.

VII of the Charter may also be covered by this exception. It is evident that the potential danger to the rights of investors posed by security exceptions of this kind in investment treaties is considerable.

The Energy Charter Treaty contains a more elaborate security clause that explicitly refers to armed conflict. Article 24(3) of the ECT provides:

> (3) The provisions of this Treaty other than those referred to in paragraph (1) shall not be construed to prevent any Contracting Party from taking any measure which it considers necessary:
>
> (a) for the protection of its essential security interests including those
>
> (i) relating to the supply of Energy Materials and Products to a military establishment; or
>
> (ii) taken in time of war, armed conflict or other emergency in international relations;
>
> (b) relating to the implementation of national policies respecting the non-proliferation of nuclear weapons or other nuclear explosive devices or needed to fulfil its obligations under the Treaty on the Non-Proliferation of Nuclear Weapons, the Nuclear Suppliers Guidelines, and other international nuclear non-proliferation obligations or understandings; or
>
> (c) for the maintenance of public order.

The savings clause at the beginning of Article 24(3) refers to Article 24(1), which in turn refers to Article 12. Article 12 contains an extended war clause as discussed above. Therefore, the right to restitution or compensation in case of requisitioning or destruction as provided by Article 12 remains unaffected by the security clause of Article 24(3).

The reference in Article 24(3) to essential security measures taken in time of war, armed conflict or other emergency in international relations leaves no doubt that an international armed conflict is covered by this security exception. But the limiting words 'in international relations' leave open the question of whether non-international armed conflicts are covered. The answer to this question will depend on whether the limitation to 'international relations' is read as referring only to the immediately preceding 'other emergency' or to the entire subsection (3)(a)(ii).

E   Armed conflict and *force majeure*

In some cases the existence of violent situations has played an incidental role in investment cases. In a number of cases, parties to investment disputes invoked armed conflicts and other situations of violence as an excuse for the non-performance of their obligations. This is not a peculiarity of investment arbitration. For the sake of completeness, a few examples for the invocation of *force majeure* in investment cases are summarised here.

In *Autopista* v. *Venezuela*,[59] the investor was entitled to a road toll increase under the terms of a concession agreement. These toll increases had been prevented by civil unrest and rioting. Venezuela pleaded *force majeure*. The Tribunal found that a successful invocation of *force majeure* required that three conditions be met. These were impossibility of performance, unforeseeability of the intervening event and non-attributability of the intervening event to the defaulting party.[60] On the facts of the case, the Tribunal found that the situation had been foreseeable and hence rejected Venezuela's reliance on *force majeure*.[61]

In *Toto* v. *Lebanon*,[62] the claimant had complained about a long delay in court proceedings.[63] The Tribunal noted that in the intervening period there had been terrorist bombings, assassinations, a war with Israel and two instances of severe internal fighting. This, together with the claimant's own inaction, led the Tribunal to conclude that under the *prima facie* test it did not have jurisdiction over this complaint.[64]

In *RSM* v. *République Centrafricaine*,[65] the investor excused its failure to perform certain aspects of a contract by relying on *force majeure*. The argument was based on political and civic troubles, which had led to a coup d'état, and on the general security situation in the country. The contract defined *force majeure* as 'tout événement imprévisible, irrésistible et indépendant de la volonté de la Partie l'invoquant, tels que tremblement de terre, grève, émeute, insurrection, troubles civils, sabotage, faits de guerre ou conditions imputables à la guerre'.[66] The Tribunal examined the attributes of unforeseeability, irresistibility and non-attributability to the party invoking it.[67] On that basis it found that the security situation in the Central African Republic amounted to a situation of *force majeure*.[68]

---

[59] *Autopista* v. *Venezuela*, Award, 23 September 2003.   [60] At para. 108.

[61] At paras 106–19.

[62] *Toto Costruzioni* v. *Lebanon*, Decision on Jurisdiction, 11 September 2009.

[63] At paras 139–68.   [64] At paras 165–8.

[65] *RSM* v. *République Centrafricaine*, Décision sur la compétence et la responsabilité, 7 December 2010.

[66] At para. 147, 'any unforeseeable and unpreventable event, independent of the wish of the Party which invokes it, be they earthquakes, strikes, rebellion, insurrections, civil unrest, sabotage, acts of war or conditions due to war' (translation by the editor).

[67] At paras 148–184.   [68] At para. 185.

F   Conclusion

So far, the known effects of armed conflict on investment protection have been few and sporadic. But, as we have seen, the legal potential is considerable and it is quite likely that we will see more cases in the future.

Treaties for the protection of investments do not generally become inapplicable in times of armed conflict. In fact, some of the provisions in these treaties are designed to afford protection in situations of violent struggle. However, some of these treaties contain broad security clauses that exempt host states from compliance with the treaties' substantive standards in violent emergency situations.

Most treaties guarantee full protection and security. This standard involves an obligation by the host state to spare the investment from violent actions. It also requires a measure of protection against violent interference by private parties and by rebel forces.

Some treaties contain clauses that specifically refer to armed conflicts. In their simple and more frequent form these war clauses merely promise non-discrimination when it comes to measures designed to remedy the consequences of armed conflicts. Some treaties go further and contain a positive obligation of restitution or compensation in cases of requisitioning or destruction of investments. However, this obligation is subject to a number of restrictive requirements.

Therefore, investor protection in times of armed conflict will in large measure depend on the availability of favourable treaties upon which the investor can rely. The current situation is far from uniform and offers a patchwork of treaty provisions that favour some investors in some countries, but leave other investors without treaty protection. The example of Libya shows vividly that only investors from certain nations enjoy treaty protection. Even for investors who can rely on treaties, their position is by no means uniform. To some extent this may be remedied by the availability of MFN clauses. A satisfactory solution would require a much denser network of bilateral treaties or a widely ratified multilateral treaty.

2

The interaction between investment law and the law of armed conflict in the interpretation of full protection and security clauses

GLEIDER I. HERNÁNDEZ*

A Introduction

From the perspective of the generalist international lawyer, international investment law certainly gives the air of a legal order which, if not already distinct, is fragmenting away from public international law. The unfamiliar case names, the profusion of bilateral investment treaties (BITs) and the specialised terminology used in the investment law sphere all contribute to this aura. Yet, whatever this first impression, investment law continues to draw heavily from public international law in a variety of fields, due to a variety of factors, from the treaty basis for investment law to the continued prominence of public international lawyers practising investment law. That international investment practice remains firmly rooted within the general work of international lawyers is not a matter for serious question.

As this edited collection demonstrates, there is nascent doctrinal interest in the interaction of international investment law with other specialised regimes of international law. The present study will focus on the interaction of international investment law with the law governing armed conflict; a phenomenon of increasing importance, given the emergence of situations of violence in states that have, in recent years, actively entered into BITs. Many of these BITs contain so-called 'full protection and security' clauses, which impose a positive obligation on contracting states to take measures to provide a certain measure of protection; and, as

* A draft of this chapter was presented at the 'Interaction of International Investment Law with Other Fields of Public International Law' conference, held in Leiden on 8–9 April 2011, whence this edited collection originates. The author is grateful to Dr Freya Baetens, Dr Diane Desierto and Mr Thomas Lieflānder for their invaluable comments on drafts of this work.

will be developed in this chapter, the question remains whether this obligation can be said to remain unaffected by the emergence of a situation of armed conflict.

In situations of rioting or other isolated disturbances, there is theoretically no reason to excuse a state from its treaty obligations. In fact, under customary international law, claims relating to possible or inevitable damage to aliens during periods of serious disorder, and the possible scope of protection by a host state, has long been the concern of arbitral tribunals.[1] Applying the concept of *force majeure*, a series of arbitral awards decided before 1930 and concerning Latin American states developed the principle of non-responsibility of a host state for extraordinary events of social strife and disorder.[2] That principle is qualified by the obligation of the host state to exercise *due diligence*; that is, to use the police and the military forces to protect the interests of foreigners to the extent feasible and practicable under the circumstances, both before the event and while it unfolds.[3] The claimant has the burden of demonstrating the failure of the host state to act with due diligence in meeting its obligations,[4] usually to an internationally recognised standard; and certainly no claim will be accepted if the host state can demonstrate that foreigners have received the same treatment as nationals of the host state.[5]

---

[1] See, e.g., *Sambiaggio* (1903) X *RIAA* 499, in which Art. 4 of the Italy–Venezuela Treaty of 1861 provided for 'the fullest measure of protection and security of person and property'; *British Claims in the Spanish Zone of Morocco* (1925) II *RIAA* 615, 642 *et seq.* (statement of Arbitrator Huber); and A. V. Freeman, 'Responsibility of States for Unlawful Acts of their Armed Forces', *Recueil des Cours* 88 (1955-II): 263.

[2] *Spanish Zone of Morocco Claim* (1924), (1925) 2 *RIAA* 615, 642; *Pinson* v. *United Mexican States* (1928), (1952) 5 *RIAA* 327, 419. For more examples, see R. Dolzer and C. Schreuer, *Principles of International Investment Law* (Oxford University Press, 2008), p. 166; and I. Brownlie, *Principles of Public International Law*, 7th edn (Oxford University Press, 2008), p. 455.

[3] Dolzer and Schreuer, *Principles of International Investment Law*, p. 166, citing *Melilla* v. *Ziat, Ben Kiran* (1924), (1949) 2 *RIAA* 730; *Pinson* v. *United Mexican States* (1928), (1952) 5 *RIAA* 327; and *United States Consular and Diplomatic Staff in Tehran* (*United States* v. *Iran*), Judgment, *ICJ Reports* 1980, 3, p. 29.

[4] Brownlie, *Principles of Public International Law*, p. 455, referring to L. B. Sohn's and R. R. Baxter's comments on the Harvard Research Draft.

[5] A. McNair, *International Law Opinions* (Cambridge University Press, 1956), vol. II, p. 245. See also *AAPL* v. *Sri Lanka*, Award, 21 June 1990, 4 *ICSID Reports* 246, 30 *ILM* 577 (1991), para. 85, where it was found that the governmental authorities should have undertaken precautionary measures in order to resolve the situation peacefully before launching an armed attack against the investor's facilities. *AAPL* v. *Sri Lanka* will be discussed below, at Section C.2(a), in relation to the obligation to provide physical security when in a state of armed conflict.

Certainly, the protection of assets from the arbitrary actions of state organs makes sense. However, the question arises as to whether it is realistic to insist on applying this rule blindly in all situations. Are states bound to provide full protection and security in lands held by rebel forces? What if human rights issues are at stake? Wartime is a particular factual situation, where decisions must often be taken precipitously, with little deliberation. The question of what legal obligations continue to apply in the event of armed conflict thus remains salient.

The present chapter is an attempt to consider the workings of investment law during situations of armed conflict through the prism of public international law. The first substantive section will consider the impact of armed conflict in public international law generally, and make the claim that international humanitarian law, or the law of armed conflict, constitutes a form of *lex specialis*, which can come to modify, in case of conflict between them, treaty obligations such as those contained in BITs. The second substantive section will examine practice in the investment law sphere in relation to 'full protection and security' clauses, in order to assess whether investment law has adopted an approach consistent with international law. It is true that many BITs also contain 'security exceptions' that could be invoked in situations of armed conflict. For reasons of clarity, these will not be addressed here, as the case law on such provisions has generally been applied in situations of 'financial necessity'; moreover, the relationship of security exceptions to the customary law concept of necessity raises numerous conceptual questions too broad to be addressed in this study. [6]

---

[6] A concept resulting from the Argentine financial crisis of 1999–2002, considered by the tribunals in *CMS Gas Transmission Company* v. *Argentina*, Award, 12 May 2005, 44 *ILM* 1205 (2005); *CMS Gas Transmission Company* v. *Argentina*, Decision of the *Ad Hoc* Committee on the Application for Annulment, 25 September 2007, 46 *ILM* 1136 (2007); *Sempra Energy International* v. *Argentina*, ICSID Case No. ARB/02/16, Award, 28 September 2007; *Sempra Energy International* v. *Argentina*, ICSID Case No. ARB/02/15, Decision on Annulment, 29 June 2010; *Enron Corporation and Ponderosa Assets, LP* v. *Argentina*, ICSID Case No. AR/01/3, Award, 22 May 2007; *LG&E Energy Corp., LG&E Capital Corp. and LG&E International, Inc.* v. *Argentina*, Decision on Liability, 3 October 2006; and *Continental Casualty Company* v. *Argentina*, ICSID Case No. ARB/03/9, Decision on Jurisdiction, 22 February 2006. For analysis of this case law, see T. Christakis, 'Nécessité n'a pas de loi? La nécessité en droit international', *Colloque de Grenoble: La nécessité en droit international* (2007): 11; J. Kurtz, 'Adjudging the Exceptional at International Investment Law: Security, Public Order and Financial Crisis', *International and Comparative Law Quarterly* 59 (2010): 325; M. Waibel, 'Two Worlds of Necessity in ICSID Arbitration: *CMS* and *LG&E*', *Leiden Journal of International Law* 20 (2007): 637; A. Bjorklund, 'Emergency Exceptions: State of Necessity and *Force*

It appears that the inner logic of investment law has, with a few exceptions, adhered relatively strongly to the basic tenets of public international law, although there exist divergences that could yet suggest possible future fragmentation. As such, the 'disintegrative inclination' of international investment law might yet be counter-balanced through a presumption of compliance with international law.

B   Definitions

1   Definitions of armed conflict

The discussion in this chapter will proceed on the assumption that the existence of an armed conflict is not in issue. However, it bears recalling that situations of armed conflict are well defined in international humanitarian law, as that legal regime becomes applicable only when an armed conflict actually occurs. Common Article 2 of the four Geneva Conventions becomes applicable in 'all cases of declared war or of any other armed conflict which may arise between two or more of the High Contracting Parties, even if the state of war is not recognized by one of them'.[7] That definition concerns situations of international armed conflict, being one between states. With regard to non-international armed conflicts, Article 1, paragraph 1, of the Second Additional Protocol to the Geneva Conventions applies in the case of

> armed conflicts ... which take place in the territory of a High Contracting Party between its armed forces and dissident armed forces or other organized armed groups which, under responsible command, exercise such control over a part of its territory as to enable them to carry

---

Majeure', in P. Muchlinksi, F. Ortino and C. Schreuer (eds), *Oxford Handbook of International Investment Law* (Oxford University Press, 2008), p. 459; A. Reinisch, 'Necessity in International Investment Arbitration: An Unnecessary Split of Opinions in Recent ICSID Cases? Comments on *CMS* v. *Argentina* and *LG&E* v. *Argentina*', *Transnational Dispute Management* 3(5) (2006): 1.

[7] Geneva Convention (I) for the Amelioration of the Condition of Wounded and Sick in Armed Forces in the Field, Geneva, signed 12 August 1949, entered into force 21 October 1950, 75 *UNTS* 31, Art. 2; Geneva Convention (II) for the Amelioration of the Condition of Wounded, Sick and Shipwrecked Members of Armed Forces at Sea, signed 12 August 1949, entered into force 21 October 1950, 75 *UNTS* 85, Art. 2; Geneva Convention (III) Relative to the Treatment of Prisoners of War, signed 12 August 1949, entered into force 21 October 1950, 75 *UNTS* 135, Art. 2; Geneva Convention (IV) Relative to the Protection of Civilian Persons in Time of War, signed 12 August 1949, entered into force 21 October 1950, 75 *UNTS* 287, Art. 2.

out sustained and concerted military operations and to implement [Additional Protocol II].[8]

These definitions are regularly applied without question as to their authoritativeness,[9] but investment lawyers could also look elsewhere. In his proposed Draft Article 2 on the Effects of Armed Conflict on Treaties, which was drafted to maintain broad conformity between the fields of international humanitarian law and treaty law in a definition of armed conflict,[10] Special Rapporteur Caflisch instead used the more 'modern' definition deployed in 1995 by the Appeals Chamber of the International Tribunal for the Former Yugoslavia in the *Tadić* case: 'An armed conflict exists whenever there is a resort to armed force between States or protracted armed violence between governmental authorities and organized armed groups or between such groups within a State.'[11] Whatever definition might come to prevail in the case law of investment tribunals, these *points de repère* should provide substantial continuity between international investment law and the law of armed conflict in respect of these basic terms of reference.

2 Armed conflict in public international law

a International humanitarian law as *lex specialis*

The question has naturally arisen as to the effect of a situation of armed conflict on the application of rules of international law, especially those

---

[8] Second Protocol Additional to the Geneva Conventions of 12 August 1949, and relating to the Protection of Victims of Non-International Armed Conflicts (Protocol II), signed 8 June 1977, entered into force 7 December 1978, 1125 *UNTS* 609, Art. 1, para. 1.

[9] See, e.g., ICJ, *Armed Activities in the Territory of the Congo (DR Congo v. Uganda)*, Judgment, *ICJ Reports* 2005, p. 168, p. 244, para. 218; ICTY, *Prosecutor v. Duško Tadić*, Decision on the Defence Motion for Interlocutory Appeal on Jurisdiction, Case No. IT-94-1-A, Decision, 2 October 1995, para. 70. The Tribunal's subsequent case law has consistently recalled the definition of a non-international armed conflict arrived at in *Tadić*.

[10] L. Caflisch, 'First Report on the Effects of Armed Conflicts on Treaties', Report of the International Law Commission on the Work of its Sixty-Second Session, GAOR 65th Sess., Supp. No. 10 (A/65/10); UN Doc. A/CN.4/627, 22 March 2010, p. 4, para. 30. At paras 31–40, it is suggested that inspiration for the wording derives directly from Art. 2 of the Institut de droit international's resolution titled 'The Effects of Armed Conflicts on Treaties' of the Institute of International Law, adopted at its Helsinki session on 28 August 1985.

[11] *Prosecutor v. Tadić*, Decision on the Defence Motion for Interlocutory Appeal on Jurisdiction, para. 70. Although simplified, the ICTY's definition drew heavily from Common Article 2 of the four Geneva Conventions and Art. 1, para. 1, of the Second Additional Protocol to the Geneva Conventions: see Caflisch, 'First Report on the Effects of Armed Conflicts on Treaties', para. 30.

of a conventional nature, as the Vienna Convention on the Law of Treaties expressly excludes the possible effects of armed conflicts from its scope.[12] One possible method is to view the law of armed conflict as *lex specialis*. The *lex specialis derogate legi generali* principle, which allows states to 'contract out' of general international law, is well understood, codified as it is under Article 55 of the Articles on the Responsibility of States.[13] For the principle to apply, however, the competing norms and provisions have to cover the same subject matter, and there must exist an actual inconsistency, or direct conflict, between them.[14] The *lex specialis* principle does not apply when the more specific treaty is silent on a matter, as general international law, or the more general treaty provision, then continues to apply. In effect, states must 'contract out' of the *jus dispositivum*,[15] although this may take a number of forms: 'special law

[12] Vienna Convention on the Law of Treaties (1969), Vienna, signed 23 May 1969, entered into force 27 January 1980, 1155 *UNTS* 331 (Vienna Convention or VCLT), Art. 74, para. 1, provides that the provisions of the Convention 'shall not prejudge any question that may arise in regard to a treaty between one or more States and one or more international organizations ... from the outbreak of hostilities between States'.

[13] ILC, Articles on the Responsibility of States for Internationally Wrongful Acts, in Report of the International Law Commission on the Work of its Fifty-Third Session, GAOR 56th Session, Supp. No. 10; UN Doc. A/56/10, ch. V (2001), at Art. 55, which indicates that the Articles do not apply 'where and to the extent that the conditions for the existence of an internationally wrongful act or the content or implementation of the international responsibility of a State are governed by special rules of international law'. See also *North Sea Continental Shelf* (*FR Germany* v. *Denmark*; *FR Germany* v. *Netherlands*), *ICJ Reports* 1969, p. 3, p. 43, para. 72; and the Report of a study group of the United Nations International Law Commission, 'Fragmentation of International Law: Difficulties Arising from the Diversification and Expansion of International Law', UN Doc. A/CN.4/L.682, 13 April 2006, p. 34, para. 56: 'The principle that special law derogates from general law is a widely accepted maxim of legal interpretation and technique for the resolution of normative conflicts.'

[14] ILC, Articles on the Responsibility of States, Commentary to Art. 55, p. 358, para. 4. But cf. Sir Gerald Fitzmaurice's suggestion that the *lex specialis* principle 'can only apply where the specific and general provision concerned deal with the same substantive matter': G. G. Fitzmaurice, 'The Law and Procedure of the International Court of Justice 1951–1954: Treaty Interpretation and Other Treaty Points', *British Year Book of International Law* XXXIII (33) (1957): 203, at p. 237.

[15] C. Binder, 'Changed Circumstances in Investment Law: Interfaces between the Law of Treaties and the Law of State Responsibility with a Special Focus on the Argentine Crisis', in C. Binder, U. Kriebaum, A. Reinisch and S. Wittich (eds), *International Investment Law for the 21st Century: Essays in Honour of Christoph Schreuer* (Oxford University Press, 2009), pp. 608–30, at pp. 622–3. See also Iran–US Claims Tribunal, *Amoco Int. Finance Corp.* v. *Iran*, Award, 14 July 1987, 15 *Iran–US CTR* 189, p. 222, para. 112: 'As a *lex specialis* in the relations between the two countries, the Treaty supersedes the *lex generalis*, namely customary international law. This does not mean, however, that the

may be used to apply, clarify, update, or modify as well as set aside general law'.[16] Even so, what states do not expressly contract out of remains applicable, albeit in a residual form:

> the point of the *lex specialis* rule is to indicate which rule should be applied ... the special, as it were, steps to become applicable instead of the general. Such replacement remains, however, always only partial. The more general rule remains in the background providing interpretative direction to the special one.[17]

In the *Nuclear Weapons* Advisory Opinion, the International Court of Justice qualified precisely thus the impact of international humanitarian law on another specialised regime within public international law: specifically, the international law protecting human rights. Describing international humanitarian law as *lex specialis* to resolve an apparent conflict between the two regimes, it concluded that while international humanitarian law should not displace or supersede international human rights law completely, in cases of conflict, the former regime could come to modify the interpretation of the latter regime. In the words of the Court:

> the protection of the International Covenant of Civil and Political Rights does not cease in times of war, except by operation of Article 4 of the Covenant whereby certain provisions may be derogated from in a time of national emergency. Respect for the right to life is not, however, such a provision. In principle, the right not arbitrarily to be deprived of one's life applies also in hostilities. The test of what is an arbitrary deprivation of

---

latter is irrelevant in the instant Case. On the contrary, the rules of customary international law may be useful in order to fill in possible *lacunae* of the law of the Treaty, to ascertain the meaning of undefined terms in its text, or more generally, to aid interpretation and implementation of its provisions.' See also *Military and Paramilitary Activities in and against Nicaragua (United States v. Nicaragua)*, Jurisdiction and Admissibility, Judgment, *ICJ Reports* 1984, p. 392, p. 424, para. 73.

[16] ILC, 'Report on the Fragmentation of International Law', p. 409, para. 8.

[17] ILC, 'Report on the Fragmentation of International Law', para. 102. This approach was endorsed in ICJ, *Case concerning Oil Platforms (Iran v. United States)*, Merits, Judgment, *ICJ Reports* 2003, p. 161, paras 32, 41, 73; and by an ICSID Tribunal in *Archer Daniels Midland Company and Tate & Lyle Ingredients Americas, Inc. v. The United Mexican States*, ICSID Case No. ARB(AF)/04/05, 21 November 2007, paras 113–23. Kurtz, 'Adjudging the Exceptional', p. 354, argues that the reasoning used in *Oil Platforms* would allow the customary test of necessity to continue to apply, in residual fashion, to interpret treaty provisions of the sort under study here. But cf. *United Parcel Service of America Inc. v. Canada*, UNCITRAL Arbitration, Award on the Merits, 24 May 2007, 46 *ILM* 922, paras 59–62, where a NAFTA tribunal held that specific provisions of the NAFTA constituted *lex specialis* and thus applied to the exclusion of the customary rules on attribution codified in Arts 4 and 5 of the ILC Articles on the Responsibility of States.

life, however, then falls to be determined by the applicable *lex specialis*,
namely, the law applicable in armed conflict which is designed to regulate
the conduct of hostilities. Thus whether a particular loss of life, through
the use of a certain weapon in warfare, is to be considered an arbitrary
deprivation of life contrary to Article 6 of the Covenant, can only be
decided by reference to the law applicable in armed conflict and not
deduced from the terms of the Covenant itself.[18]

The same approach could be used to reconcile the law governing the
interpretation of BITs and investment protection more generally with the
law of armed conflict. If one takes as a given the essentially treaty-based
nature of investment law, it seems logical that that regime should also
yield to the law of armed conflict in the same manner as does general
international law.

b   Two *leges speciales* in conflict: international humanitarian law and international investment law

However, this also raises a second question: it stands to reason that
bilateral investment treaties also form collectively a self-contained *lex
specialis* which stands apart from general international law, entitling the
foreign investor to the enhanced protection under the standards contained in the treaty itself, yet with the said treaty being interpreted against
the background of general international law. In the case of collision
between two specialised regimes, in which each legal regime might
'suggest different ways of dealing with a problem',[19] ascertaining which
rules are to apply becomes difficult.

One can reasonably infer from the ICJ's Opinion in *Nuclear Weapons*
that it would treat international investment law, applicable under normal
circumstances, similarly to international human rights law: the state of
armed conflict triggers the application of international humanitarian law,
thus displacing the standard regime. Moreover, in *Israeli Wall* the Court
reiterated its previous finding in *Nuclear Weapons* that many norms of
international humanitarian law are 'intransgressible':

> With regard to international humanitarian law, the Court recalls that in
> its Advisory Opinion on the Legality of the Threat or Use of Nuclear
> Weapons it stated that 'a great many rules of humanitarian law applicable
> in armed conflict are so fundamental to the respect of the human person

---

[18] *Legality of the Threat or Use of Nuclear Weapons*, Advisory Opinion, *ICJ Reports* 1996,
p. 225, para. 25.
[19] ILC, Report on the Fragmentation of International Law, para. 2.

and "elementary considerations of humanity" …', that they are 'to be observed by all States whether or not they have ratified the conventions that contain them, because they constitute intransgressible principles of international customary law'… In the Court's view, these rules incorporate obligations which are essentially of an *erga omnes* character.[20]

Whatever mysterious legal effect may eventually come to attach to the qualification of 'intransgressible' by the Court is immaterial; but there is no evidence or practice whatsoever to justify the position that international investment agreements such as BITs, the preambles to which state that their goal is limited to promoting investment or fostering economic ties, can implicitly displace general international law.[21] Simma and Kill have elsewhere argued, in relation to international human rights norms embodied in multilateral treaties, that without express derogation from that generally applicable regime, it is impossible to interpret clauses providing for full security and protection or security exceptions in BITs as derogating from the states' otherwise applicable legal obligations.[22] Transposing the essence of this argument to the law of armed conflict, in the absence of express derogation, it would be untenable to stretch the interpretation of a full protection and security clause, or a necessity clause, beyond the general regime and into the regime of last resort embodied by international humanitarian law, a *lex specialis* designed to provide a floor for human rights protection in times of armed conflict.[23]

c The effect of armed conflict on treaty obligations at the International Law Commission (ILC)

Another source of interpretative guidance for assessing the effect of a state of armed conflict on the application or interpretation of BITs might

---

[20] ICJ, *Legal Consequences of the Construction of a Wall in the Occupied Palestinian Territory*, Advisory Opinion, *ICJ Reports* 2004, p. 136, para. 157, citing *Nuclear Weapons*, p. 257, para. 79.

[21] B. Simma and T. Kill, 'Harmonizing Investment Protection and International Human Rights: First Steps towards a Methodology', in C. Binder, U. Kriebaum, A. Reinisch and S. Wittich (eds), *International Investment Law for the 21st Century: Essays in Honour of Christoph Schreuer* (Oxford University Press, 2009), pp. 678–707, at p. 705, suggest that this precludes the provisions of BITs from displacing human rights obligations.

[22] Simma and Kill, 'Harmonizing Investment Protection and International Human Rights, p. 705.

[23] This interpretation is consistent with Caflisch, 'First Report on the Effects of Armed Conflicts on Treaties', Draft Article 7, para. 81 (commentary at paras 77–80), which provides that: 'where the treaty expressly provides, it shall continue to be operative in situations of armed conflict'.

be ILC Special Rapporteur Lucius Caflisch's 'First Report on the Effects of Armed Conflicts on Treaties'.[24] The 'First Report' was drafted bearing in mind the exhortation that it be made clear that the Draft Articles are without prejudice to international humanitarian law, which constitutes the *lex specialis* governing armed conflict.[25] Accordingly, Caflisch embodies a presumption favouring the continuity of international humanitarian law in his Draft Article 3, which should apply equally to bilateral investment treaties. This would be so even if one could conclude that the rules of international humanitarian law could be departed from by way of a plea of necessity under customary international law, as it bears recalling that necessity, a circumstance precluding wrongfulness, is intended as a *defence* against the attribution of responsibility for a wrongful act to a state. It is not an exception allowing for derogation from the applicable law.

Draft Article 4 specifies further rules to assist in ascertaining whether a treaty is to be terminated or suspended in the event of an armed conflict. It should be recalled that a state of armed conflict does not automatically permit termination or suspension of treaty obligations, of course: the treaty provisions might well be unaffected by that change in circumstances. Accordingly, one must interpret the relevant provisions in line with the rules set out in Articles 31 and 32 of the Vienna Convention, taking account of the 'nature and extent of the armed conflict and its effect on the treaty, the subject matter of the treaty and the number of parties to the treaty'.[26] Draft Article 4 also aims to provide criteria against which a notification of termination or suspension (for which there is a procedure under Draft Article 8; see below) can be measured; and it should, of course, be noted that, according to Draft Article 10, termination or suspension of a treaty takes effect with respect to the treaty as a whole unless the treaty contains clauses that are separable from the remainder of the treaty.[27]

---

[24] Although Sir Ian Brownlie prepared four reports prior to his untimely passing, for reasons of space, this study will make reference primarily to Caflisch's 'First Report', which proposes amendments to the relevant Draft Articles and builds on Sir Ian's work.

[25] This was the position of the United Kingdom and the United States: Caflisch, 'First Report on the Effects of Armed Conflicts on Treaties', para. 24.

[26] Draft Article 4, in Caflisch, 'First Report on the Effects of Armed Conflicts on Treaties', para. 51.

[27] Draft Article 10, *ibid.*, para. 98. The inclusion of that Article aims to harmonise the rules for termination or suspension of the treaty with the general regime laid out in Art. 44, para. 3, *lit.* (c) of the Vienna Convention: *ibid.*, paras 99–101.

The existence of armed conflict alone is insufficient to modify treaty relations between states: Draft Article 5 stipulates that the incidence of an armed conflict will not 'as such' affect the operation of the treaty.[28] In enumerating treaties falling under this category, the Special Rapporteur includes 'treaties of friendship, commerce and navigation and analogous agreements concerning private rights' as the sort of treaty whose continued applicability has, through state practice, proved 'so necessary that [states] have continued to apply them ... despite having experienced the catastrophic consequences of the incidence of an armed conflict'.[29] These types of treaties are, moreover, to be distinguished from treaties concluded with the specific purpose of remaining applicable in times of armed conflict, as evidenced in Draft Article 5, paragraph 2:

> Treaties relating to the law of armed conflict and to international humanitarian law, treaties for the protection of human rights, treaties relating to international criminal justice and treaties declaring, creating or regulating a permanent regime or status or related permanent rights, including treaties establishing or modifying land boundaries or maritime boundaries and limits, remain in or enter into operation in the event of armed conflict.[30]

Draft Article 5 is clarified by the addition of Draft Article 7, which requires express provision in a treaty that it will continue to operate during armed conflict, and Draft Article 8, which provides a clear procedure for the notification of termination, withdrawal or suspension.[31] Taken together, it is clear that formal, express action is required from a state that seeks to rely on the outbreak of armed conflict so as not to comply fully with its treaty obligations.[32] Finally, Draft Article 9 provides that, irrespective of what a state has covenanted, it remains

---

[28] Draft Article 5, *ibid.*, para. 70 (commentary at paras 52–69).

[29] Draft Article 5, *ibid.*, para. 52.

[30] Draft Article 5, para. 2, *ibid.*, para. 70 (commentary at paras 55, 62–3).

[31] Draft Article 8, *ibid.*, para. 96, which implements a system whereby notification takes effect only upon receipt of formal notification from a state party to a treaty to another state party that it intends to terminate or withdraw from a treaty or to suspend the operation of that treaty. Moreover, the notification mechanism in Draft Article 8 is such that it is meant to complement, not replace, the rules already extant in the Vienna Convention, and any dispute-settlement mechanisms already in place (i.e., Art. 33 of the UN Charter, or any compromissory clauses referring to arbitral or judicial tribunals).

[32] Similarly, see the proposed Draft Article 12, *ibid.*, para. 110, which would provide, as a general rule, that 'subsequent to an armed conflict, the States parties may regulate, on the basis of a new agreement, the revival of treaties terminated or suspended as a result of the armed conflict'.

bound to whatever obligation embodied in the treaty to which it would be subject under international law independently of that treaty.[33] Together, these Articles would serve to confirm the position taken herein, that investment treaties would not, unless express provisions were included to that effect, serve to displace international humanitarian law.[34]

The next section will, therefore, delve into two particular categories of provisions contained in investment treaties that impose obligations that might come to be affected by the emergence of armed conflict. Accordingly, this chapter will now examine full protection and security clauses, under which states undertake to provide certain safeguards so as to protect investments against the outbreak of physical violence. So-called 'security exceptions' or 'necessity' clauses will not be examined here: although these may also be relevant, they raise the complex plea of necessity,[35] a concept that has received separate scholarly treatment elsewhere.[36] Because full protection and security clauses *impose* specific obligations, while security exceptions allow for the *derogation from* specific obligations, the analytical framework structuring these respective provisions is sufficiently distinct to justify this distinction.

---

[33] Draft Article 9, *ibid.*, para. 97.

[34] The question, nevertheless, remains open as to what legal effect attaches to the qualification of 'intransgressible' to a norm, as the ICJ did not elaborate further in its Advisory Opinion in *Nuclear Weapons*: see, above, n. 20.

[35] Although it has very rarely been upheld on the facts, the principle of necessity has been recognised in cases ranging from the *Russian Indemnity* arbitration (*Russia/Turkey*), 11 November 1912, 12 *RIAA* 44, to the case law of the ICJ in *Gabčíkovo-Nagymaros Project* (*Hungary* v. *Slovakia*), *ICJ Reports* 1997, p. 7, and *Legal Consequences of the Construction of a Wall in the Occupied Palestinian Territory*, Advisory Opinion, *ICJ Reports* 2004, p. 136, to the case law of ITLOS (e.g., *MV Saiga (No. 2)* (*Saint Vincent and the Grenadines* v. *Guinea*), 38 *ILM* 1323). There have also been recent, rapid developments in arbitral awards: see *CMS Gas Transmission Company* v. *Argentine Republic*, ICSID Case No. ARB/01/8, Award, 12 May 2005, 14 *ICSID Reports* 152, criticised on its interpretation of necessity in *CMS Gas Transmission Company* v. *Argentine Republic* (ICSID Case No ARB/01/08), Decision on application for annulment, 25 September 2007, 14 *ICSID Reports* 251); *LG&E Energy Corp., LG&E Capital Corp. and LG&E International, Inc.* v. *Argentina*, Decision on Liability, 3 October 2006; *Continental Casualty Company* v. *Argentina*, ICSID Case No. ARB/03/9, Decision on Jurisdiction, 22 February 2006; and *Sempra Energy* v. *Argentine Republic*, ICSID Case No. ARB/02/16, Award, 28 September 2007; subsequently annulled in *Sempra Energy International* v. *Argentine Republic*, ICSID Case No. ARB/02/15, Decision on Annulment, 29 June 2010.

[36] For further reading on the topic of necessity in investment arbitration, see, above, n. 6.

C Full protection and security clauses before investment tribunals

1 Protection under full protection and security clauses

The subject of recent scholarly attention,[37] full protection and security clauses found early expression in bilateral treaties of friendship, commerce and navigation (FCN treaties), and had an extensive life in the customary international law rules relating to the protection of the property of aliens through claims of state responsibility and the invocation of diplomatic protection.[38] Such clauses are drafted with many variations (including, *inter alia*, 'full protection and security',[39] 'the most constant protection and security',[40] the looser standards of 'protection' or 'full protection',[41] 'protection and security'[42] and, finally, the variant 'full legal protection and security'[43]). It also bears noting that some BITs include

---

[37] See, e.g., C. Schreuer, 'Full Protection and Security', *Journal of International Dispute Settlement* 1(2) (2010): 353; and G. Cordero Moss, 'Full Protection and Security', in A. Reinisch (ed.), *Standards of Investment Protection* (Oxford University Press, 2008), p. 133.

[38] C. McLachlan, L. Shore and M. Weiniger, *International Investment Arbitration: Substantive Principles* (Oxford University Press, 2007), p. 247. The modern, treaty-based formula derives from the draft for a multilateral convention to protect private foreign investment prepared by Hermann Abs and Lord Shawcross, 'Draft Convention on Investments Abroad', *Journal of Public Law* 9 (1960): 115, 116, Art. 1. See also *United States Diplomatic and Consular Staff in Tehran* (*United States* v. *Iran*), Judgment, *ICJ Reports* 1980, p. 3, pp. 31-2, paras 63-8, where the Court found that Iran's failure to take any steps to protect the US Embassy in Tehran against non-state militants was a violation of international law.

[39] This takes a number of forms: 'full protection and security' (United States–Uruguay BIT (2005), Art. 5(1); Sri Lanka–United Kingdom BIT (1980), Art. 2(2) and Egypt–United Kingdom BIT (1975), Art. 2(2)); 'full physical security and protection' (Eritrea–Netherlands BIT (2003), Art. 3(1); Hungary–Netherlands BIT (1987), Art. 3(2)); 'adequate protection and security' (Indonesia–Syria BIT (1997), Art. 2(2); 'full and constant protection and security' (China–Djibouti BIT (2003), Art. 2(2); Japan–Korea BIT (2002), Art. 10(1); 'complete and adequate protection and security' (Jordan–Yemen BIT (1996), Art. 2(2)).

[40] 'The most constant protection and security' (Thailand–Vietnam BIT (1991), Art. 3(2); Bangladesh–Japan BIT (1998), Art. 5(1); Hungary–Thailand BIT (1991), Art. 3(2)).

[41] 'Protection' (Lithuania–Norway BIT (1992), Art. III; Bulgaria–Croatia BIT (1996), Art. 2 (1); Spain–Cuba BIT (1994), Art. 3(1); Jordan–Poland BIT (1997), Art. 3(1)); 'full protection' (Marshall Islands–Taiwan BIT (1999), Art. 3(1)).

[42] US–Zaire BIT (1984), Art. II(4).

[43] The obligation to provide 'full legal protection and security' may be found in the Germany–Argentina BIT, Art. 4(1), applied in *Siemens AG* v. *The Argentine Republic*, ICSID Case No. ARB/02/8, Award, 6 February 2007.

no such protection clauses whatsoever.[44] Whatever these various formulations, arbitral practice has generally tended to interpret these in a
similar manner,[45] thus allowing for a certain generalisation as to their
scope of application, for example, as regards the relationship of full
protection and security to the cognate concept of fair and equitable
treatment[46] or an international minimum standard.[47] From these we
can make some deductions as to the effect of such clauses in situations
of armed conflict, to which they heretofore have not been applied. It
seems that, in relation to physical security at least, international courts
and investment tribunals consider full protection and security clauses not
as independent treaty standards sufficiently distinct from customary

---

[44] For example, Estonia–Sweden BIT (1992), Egypt–Kazakhstan BIT (1993), India–
Kazakhstan BIT (1996), Argentina–New Zealand BIT (1999) and Iran–Kazakhstan BIT
(1996).

[45] A. Newcombe and L. Paradell, *Law and Practice of Investment Treaties: Standards of
Treatment* (Alphen aan den Rijn: Kluwer Law, 2009), p. 308; Cordero Moss, 'Full
Protection and Security', p. 134.

[46] Several BITs provide that investments shall be accorded fair and equitable treatment *and*
shall enjoy full protection and security, including the Czech–Slovak BIT, Art. 2(2)(i),
applied in *Československá Obchodní Banka, AS* v. *Slovak Republic*, ICSID Case No. ARB/
97/4, Award, 29 December 2004; United Kingdom–Egypt BIT, Art. 2(2), applied in *Wena
Hotels Ltd* v. *Arab Republic of Egypt*; United Kingdom–Sri Lanka BIT, Art. II (2)(a),
applied in *AAPL* v. *Sri Lanka*. Other BITs provide that full protection and security will be
provided *under* the obligation to provide fair and equitable treatment: see, e.g.,
Netherlands–Czech and Slovak Republic BITs, applied in *CME Czech Republic BV (the
Netherlands)* v. *Czech Republic*, Partial Award, 13 September 2001, and *Saluka* v. *Czech
Republic*, Partial Award, 17 March 2006; and Netherlands–Poland BIT, Art. 3.2, applied
in *Eureko* v. *Poland*, Partial Award, 19 August 2005. Full protection and security has been
interpreted *in accordance with* the principle of fair and equitable treatment in France–
Argentina BIT, Art. 5.1, applied in *Compañía de Aguas del Aconquija SA and Vivendi
International* v. *Argentine Republic (II)*, ICSID Case No. ARB/97/3, Award, 20 August
2007.

[47] The full protection and security standard has been linked to treatment not less than that
required by international law in the United States–Czech Republic BIT, Art. II 2(a),
applied in *Lauder* v. *Czech Republic*, Award, 3 September 2001; United States–Argentina
BIT, Art. II.2(a), applied in *Azurix Corp* v. *The Argentine Republic*, ICSID Case No. ARB/
01/12, Award, 14 July 2006; United States–Ecuador BIT, Art. II (3)(a), applied in
Occidental Exploration and Production Company v. *The Republic of Ecuador*, LCIA Case
No. UN 3467, Award, 1 July 2004; United States–Romania BIT, Art. II (2)(a), applied in
Noble Ventures v. *Romania*; United States–Turkey BIT, Art. II (3), applied in *PSEG
Global Inc. and Konya Elektrik Üretim ve Ticaret Limited Sirketi* v. *Republic of Turkey*,
ICSID Case No. ARB/02/5, Award, 19 January 2007; United States–Zaire BIT, Art. II (4),
applied in *American Manufacturing & Trading, Inc. (AMT)* v. *Republic of Zaire*, ICSID
Case No. ARB/93/1, Award, 21 February 1997; United States–Mexico BIT, applied in
Técnicas Medioambientales Tecmed SA v. *The United Mexican States*, Award, 29 May
2003, 43 *ILM* 133 (2004); United States–Uruguay BIT (2005), Art. 5(1).

international law standards, but, rather, primarily as a reference to international minimum standards under customary international law.[48] The possibility that a state might be held responsible for the acts of non-state actors will be addressed next. Finally, the question as to whether non-physical security, and especially 'legal security', is part of the obligation of protection will be considered.

2 Physical security

a Violence committed by state organs

The obligation to provide full protection and security clearly finds a scope of application in the context of the physical safety of persons and

---

[48] This question has come to the fore, most prominently, when examining Art. 1105(1) of the North American Free Trade Agreement (NAFTA), signed 17 December 1992, entered into force 1 January 1994, 1993 *ILM* 289, according to which each party undertakes to 'accord to investments of investors of another Party treatment in accordance with international law, including fair and equitable treatment and full protection and security'. Article 1105 is drafted unlike any BIT, expressly referring to 'Minimum Standard of Treatment' in its heading; as Schreuer, 'Full Protection and Security', p. 363, notes, this suggests express evident reference to general international law which is wholly absent from most bilateral investment treaties. The NAFTA Free Trade Commission's 'official interpretation' clearly considers that the obligations imposed under the NAFTA should go no further than the customary international law minimum standard of treatment of aliens: '1. Article 1105(1) prescribes the customary international law minimum standard of treatment of aliens as the minimum standard of treatment to be afforded to investments of investors of another Party. 2. The concepts of "fair and equitable treatment" and "full protection and security" do not require treatment in addition to or beyond that which is required by the customary international law minimum standard of treatment of aliens' (FTC Note of Interpretation, 31 July 2001, available at: www.international.gc.ca/trade-agreements-accords-commerciaux/disp-diff/NAFTA-Interpr.aspx?lang=en, accessed 25 September 2011). This official interpretation has been endorsed by NAFTA tribunals in *Pope & Talbot* v. *Canada*, Award in Respect of Damages, 31 May 2002, 41 *ILM* 1347 (2002), paras 17–69; *Mondev Intl Ltd* v. *United States of America*, Award, 11 October 2002, 6 *ICSID Reports* 192, paras 100 ff.; *United Parcel Service of America Inc.* v. *Canada*, Award, 22 November 2002, 7 *ICSID Reports* 288, para. 97; *ADF Group Inc.* v. *United States of America*, Award, 9 January 2003, 6 *ICSID Reports* 470, paras 175–8; *Loewen Group, Inc. and Raymond L. Loewen* v. *United States of America*, Award, 26 June 2003, 7 *ICSID Reports* 442, paras 124–8; *Waste Management, Inc.* v. *The United Mexican States*, Award, 30 April 2004, 43 *ILM* 967 (2004), paras 90–1; *Methanex* v. *United States*, Award, 3 August 2005, Pt IV, ch. C, paras 17–24; *Thunderbird* v. *Mexico*, Award, 26 January 2006, paras 192, 193. See also *United Mexican States* v. *Metalclad Corp.*, Judgment, Supreme Court of British Columbia, 2 May 2001, 5 *ICSID Reports* 236, paras 61–5. The official BIT practice of both the United States and Canada has also followed this interpretation: see, e.g., the Chile–United States FTA (2003), Art. 10.4; United States–Uruguay BIT (2004), Art. 5; US Model BIT (2004), Art. 5; and Canada Model BIT, Art. 5.

installations connected with protected investments.[49] Several tribunals have concluded that the standard in fact applies exclusively or preponderantly to physical security and to the host state's duty to protect the investor against violence directed at persons and property stemming from state organs or private parties.[50] In *Saluka* v. *Czech Republic*, the Tribunal stated expressly that the scope of the 'full security and protection' clause was not to cover just any kind of impairment of an investor's investment, but more specifically to protect the physical integrity of an investment against interference by use of force caused by civil strife and/ or physical violence.[51] As such, it is clear as to why interpretation of this clause is at the heart of reconciling the rules of armed conflict with the rules of investment protection.

The leading case in this regard is *Asian Agricultural Products Ltd (AAPL)* v. *Sri Lanka*,[52] the first dispute in which an international tribunal had an opportunity to deal with the provisions of a bilateral investment treaty on compensation for damages caused during wars and national emergencies. Indeed, the central theme in the award was the interplay between the interpretation of the treaty obligations to provide full protection and security, and the customary international law governing the principles on destruction by government agents.[53] In *AAPL* v. *Sri Lanka*, the claimant's submission that the BIT created a higher standard of investment protection than customary international law was rejected by the Tribunal, which concluded that the inclusion of terms such as 'full protection' in that BIT did not refer to any standards higher than the minimum standard of due diligence traditionally required by general international law.[54] The Tribunal's ultimate finding was that, in times

---

[49] A good definition to this effect was given in *PSEG* v. *Turkey*, Award, 19 January 2007, para. 258.

[50] See, e.g., *PSEG* v. *Turkey*, paras 257–9; *Enron* v. *Argentina*, Award, 22 May 2007, paras 284–7; *BG Group* v. *Argentina*, Award, 24 December 2007, paras 323–8; *Sempra* v. *Argentina*, Award, 27 September 2007, paras 321–4; *Plama* v. *Bulgaria*, Award, 27 August 2008, para. 180; *Rumeli* v. *Kazakhstan*, Award, 29 July 2008, para. 668; *Parkerings* v. *Lithuania*, Award, 11 September 2007, para. 354. Broadly speaking, the interpretation in these awards is consonant with the principle contained in Article 4 of the Articles on the Responsibility of States that a state is responsible for actions perpetrated by its organs.

[51] *Saluka* v. *Czech Republic*, para. 483; Schreuer, 'Full Protection and Security', p. 354.

[52] *AAPL* v. *Sri Lanka*, Award, 21 June 1990, 4 *ICSID Reports* 246, 30 *ILM* 577 (1991).

[53] M. Sornarajah, *The International Law on Foreign Investment*, 3rd edn (Cambridge University Press, 2010), p. 213.

[54] See also P. Rambaud, 'Des obligations de l'État vis à vis de l'investisseur étranger: la sentence CIRDI du 27 juin 1990, *société Asian Agricultural Products Ltd (AAPL) c. Sri Lanka*', *Annuaire français de droit international*, 38 (1992): 501, 504, who observes how

of civil disturbance a host state was under a duty to confer adequate protection on foreign investors. In circumstances where governmental forces had committed acts of destruction during combat action, there would be liability if the claimant could establish that the action went beyond what was objectively necessary and caused wanton and unnecessary destruction.[55]

What was most interesting about *AAPL* v. *Sri Lanka* was that the obligation of full protection and security was applied by the Tribunal both as a matter of customary law and of treaty obligation, a point which has been criticised in the literature as an undue expansion of jurisdiction under BITs.[56] It also raises questions as to the extent to which obligations existing outside the BIT can be adjudicated by such tribunals: for example, had Sri Lanka been involved in a non-international armed conflict with the Tamil rebels, could the Tribunal have applied the relevant provisions of the Hague and Geneva conventions on the protection of property in armed conflict, or would this have fallen outside its jurisdiction?

The interpretation of full protection and security clauses in other arbitral panels is in broad conformity with the *AAPL* v. *Sri Lanka* award. In *AMT* v. *Zaire*,[57] where the relevant BIT provided that 'protection and security of investment ... may not be less than that recognized by international law', the respondent's armed forces had looted the claimant's investment. The Tribunal held that the treaty provision imposed upon Zaire a duty of vigilance that would not be inferior to the minimum standard of international law, which had been breached by the failure of the state to take any measures to ensure the protection and security of the investment.[58] The Tribunal stated:

the Tribunal unanimously rejected AAPL's 'strict liability' argument as contrary to every possible canon of interpretation embodied in Article 31 of the Vienna Convention: the ordinary meaning of the text; an interpretation of the text in the light of the treaty's object and purpose; an interpretation of the treaty in the light of other relevant rules of international law; or even the principle of effectiveness.

[55] *AAPL* v. *Sri Lanka*, paras 57–8.

[56] Sornarajah, *The International Law on Foreign Investment*, p. 214, has argued that it is open to question whether the Tribunal could assume jurisdiction on the basis of the treaty and apply rules not stated expressly therein, and that arguably the Tribunal had arrogated for itself 'virtually limitless' jurisdiction by addressing the issue through customary international law.

[57] *AMT* v. *Zaire*, Award, 21 February 1997, 5 *ICSID Reports* 11.

[58] *AMT*, paras 6.02–6.11.

Zaire has breached its obligation by taking no measure whatever that would serve to ensure the protection and security of the investment in question ... Zaire is responsible for its inability to prevent the disastrous consequences of these events adversely affecting the investments of AMT which Zaire had the obligation to protect.

Zaire has manifestly failed to respect the minimum standard required of it by international law.

The responsibility of the State of Zaire is incontestably engaged by the very fact of an omission by Zaire to take every measure necessary to protect and ensure the security of the investment made by AMT in its territory.[59]

More recently, in *Eureko* v. *Poland*,[60] the claimant alleged harassment of its senior officials by Polish governmental authorities, and invoked a treaty provision providing for 'full security and protection' by the host state. The Tribunal in that case did not find the treaty obligation to require more than the customary international law standard of protection. It thus found that there was no conclusive evidence that Poland was the author or instigator of the actions in question, and that it was not convinced in any event that the harassment breached the standard of full security and protection.[61]

Taken as a whole, these cases would suggest that as worded, full protection and security clauses do not seem to impose more than an international minimum standard of protection under customary international law. It is perhaps true that they could impose additional obligations, were they to be more specific than customary international law;[62] but the practice of arbitral tribunals on this point seems inconclusive.

b   Protection against non-state actors

The duty on the part of the state to provide protection to the foreigner and his property is twofold: it requires states to protect investors both against violence stemming from third parties,[63] as well as against violence

---

[59] *AMT*, para. 6.11.   [60] *Eureko BV* v. *Poland*, Partial Award, 19 August 2005.

[61] *Eureko BV*, paras 236–7. The Tribunal did concede that certain of the acts were disturbing and came close to the threshold of breaching the treaty, and added that if such actions were to be repeated and sustained, the responsibility of Poland could be incurred.

[62] See, below, Section C.3, for further discussion of the 'full legal protection and security' clause found in *Siemens* v. *Argentina*.

[63] *Eastern Sugar* v. *Czech Republic*, Partial Award, 27 March 2007, para. 203: 'the criterion in [the Czech–Netherlands BIT] concerns the obligation of the host state to protect the investor from *third* parties, in the cases cited by the Parties, mobs, insurgents, rented thugs and others engaged in physical violence against the investor in violation of the state

caused by the host state and its organs.[64] The recent *Biwater Gauff* v. *Tanzania* award confirms this: the Tribunal did not 'consider that the *"full security"* standard is limited to a State's failure to prevent actions by third parties, but also extends to actions by organs and representatives of the State itself'.[65] It is clear that the wording of full protection and security clauses suggests that host states are under an obligation to take active measures to protect investments from adverse effects, and that the adverse effects need not be limited to actions of the host state (and its armed forces), but may also stem from private parties such as rebel groups or demonstrators. However, the standard of liability in case of violations of full protection and security remains that of due diligence, and not of absolute liability.

A state has an obligation to act if it has knowledge of an imminent danger of such destruction of property by insurrectionists or by a riotous mob.[66] The distinction lies primarily in the standard of diligence required in order to meet the obligation of protection. As shown above, when a state or its organs instigate damage to the investment, there is a presumption that responsibility is attributed to the state unless it can invoke circumstances precluding wrongfulness;[67] this presumption could also apply in the case of an armed conflict, whether international or non-international. When non-state actors are involved, and especially in conditions of civil disorder, the causal link between the state's behaviour and the harmful events that befell the investment need not be established definitively. The obligation to provide full protection and security does not oblige a state to refrain from causing

---

monopoly of physical force. Thus where a host state fails to grant full protection and security, it fails to act to *prevent* actions by third parties that it is required to prevent.' See generally H. E. Zeitler, 'The Guarantee of "Full Protection and Security" in Investment Treaties Regarding Harm Caused by Private Actors', *Stockholm International Arbitration Review* 3 (2005): 1.

[64] *Parkerings* v. *Lithuania*, Award, 11 September 2007, para. 354.

[65] *Biwater Gauff* v. *Tanzania*, Award, 24 July 2008, para. 730.

[66] An old rule: see *Sambiaggio Case*, 10 *RIAA* 499, p. 534; *Home Missionary Society Case* (1920) 6 *RIAA* 42; C. F. Amerasinghe, *State Responsibility for Injuries to Aliens* (Oxford: Clarendon Press, 1967), pp. 281–2; I. Brownlie, *The System of the Law of Nations: State Responsibility* (Oxford University Press, 1983), p. 162.

[67] The same standard could apply if the relationship of the non-state actors to the state was such, or was transformed through a series of acts into a situation where the non-state actors were effectively *agents* of the state, or effectively exercising elements of government authority: see *Hostages in Tehran*, p. 35, para. 74, and Iran–United States Claims Tribunal, *Kenneth P. Yeager* v. *The Islamic Republic of Iran*, *IUSCT Reports*, vol. 17, p. 92, p. 104, para. 43.

damage, but rather to exercise due diligence, or take the necessary measures of vigilance, in order to prevent damage.[68]

Various cases concerning situations of civil strife or disorder demonstrate that the full protection and security provision is not interpreted as imputing absolute liability on the respondent State, but rather, that the obligation of a State is that of due diligence in protecting investors from forcible interference.[69] For our purposes, it stands to reason that in a situation of non-international armed conflict where non-state actors are causing damage to investments, the same obligations would apply.

The case of *Amco* v. *Indonesia* is interesting as it was decided under customary international law at a time before investment disputes began to be brought under BITs. In that dispute, the investor's local partner (PT Wisma) in a lease and management contract forcibly took over the hotel that was the subject of the investment, with the assistance of members of the Indonesian armed forces. The Tribunal held that the forcible takeover was not attributable to the government of Indonesia. However, it found that Indonesia was in breach of international law, since it had failed to protect the investor against the takeover of the hotel by its citizens. The Tribunal concluded that:

> it is a generally accepted rule of international law, clearly stated in international awards and judgments and generally accepted in the literature, that a State has a duty to protect aliens and their investment against unlawful acts committed by some of its citizens ... If such acts are committed with the active assistance of state-organs a breach of international law occurs.[70]

In the *ELSI* case, a chamber of the International Court of Justice was to apply a provision of a BIT between the United States and Italy, through which the two states granted each other 'the most constant protection and security for their persons and property'.[71] In assessing the conduct of the Italian authorities in failing to prevent workers from occupying the factory owned by the investors, the Court's chamber adjudged Italy's conduct to be adequate: 'the reference ... to the provision of "constant protection and security" cannot be construed as the giving of a warranty

---

[68] Cordero Ross, 'Full Protection and Security', p. 138.

[69] Schreuer, 'Full Protection and Security', p. 357.

[70] *Amco Asia Corporation, Pan American Development Limited, PT Amco Indonesia v. Republic of Indonesia*, Award, 20 November 1984, 1 *ICSID Reports* 413, para. 172.

[71] Article V, para. 1, United States–Italy FCN treaty, in ICJ, *Elettronica Sicula SpA (ELSI) (United States of America v. Italy)*, *ICJ Reports* 1989, p. 15, p. 63, para. 103.

that property shall never in any circumstances be occupied or disturbed'.[72] The ICJ's decision in *ELSI* established that while a host state is under an obligation to take measures to provide protection,[73] that obligation is not of an absolute character. Tellingly, this was so even given that the FCN treaty itself supplemented the 'most constant protection and security' standard by adding 'and shall enjoy in this respect the full protection and security required by international law'.[74] The Chamber interpreted this to mean that while 'protection and security' was to conform with the minimum international standard, this provision set standards which could go further in their protection than required by general international law.[75] In so doing, the Chamber interpreted the reference to international law not as a limitation of the standard to the international minimum, but instead considered the international minimum standard to constitute a residual 'floor' below which the treaty standard could not fall.[76]

The threshold for engaging the standard is rather high. For example, in *Tecmed* v. *Mexico*, the claimant alleged that the Mexican authorities had failed to take effective action against social demonstrations and disturbances at the site of the landfill at issue in that case. The Tribunal, applying a provision calling for 'full protection and security to the investments … in accordance with International Law', found that there was insufficient evidence to prove that the Mexican authorities had 'encouraged, fostered or contributed' to the actions in question.[77] The Tribunal also held that there was no evidence that the authorities had not acted 'reasonably, in accordance with the parameters inherent in a democratic State', to the 'direct action' movements that disturbed operations.[78] This reasoning also obtained in *Noble Ventures* v. *Romania*,[79] another dispute concerning the interpretation of a full protection and security clause in the light

---

[72] *ELSI*, p. 65, para. 108.   [73] Schreuer, 'Full Protection and Security', p. 355.

[74] Article V, para. 3, United States–Italy FCN treaty, in *ELSI*, para. 103.

[75] *ELSI*, para. 111.

[76] See also *AMT* v. *Zaire*, paras 6.06–6.07; and *Azurix Corp* v. *The Argentine Republic*, ICSID Case No. ARB/01/12, Award, 14 July 2006, para. 361, which affirmed that the international law standard was to be understood as a floor for the treaty-based protection. The Tribunal in *Azurix* affirmed that the content of the treaty-based and customary law obligations was substantially similar, whether interpreted according to the ordinary meaning of the treaty's wording or according to the standard under international law.

[77] *Tecmed* v. *Mexico*, para. 176.

[78] *Tecmed*, paras 175–7. The Tribunal specifically mentioned that its finding also applied to the judicial system.

[79] *Noble Ventures Inc.* v. *Romania*, Award, 12 October 2005.

of demonstrations and protests, in this case by employees of the claimant. In rejecting the claim, the Tribunal referred to Italy's conduct in the *ELSI* case, finding that Romania's conduct was 'no more harmful' than Italy's had been in the earlier case, and that it was difficult to identify any specific failure on the part of the respondent to exercise due diligence in protecting the claimant.[80]

The investment decisions cited above, if taken as a coherent body of case law, thus suggest uniformly that the standard of diligence exercised by a state is not absolute, and that the situation of civil disorder is to be taken into account when assessing the level of diligence required. In fact, the standard of diligence itself is variable according to the intensity of the strife, the resources that can be diverted for the purpose of protection and other similar factors: 'the rule must be applied with a great deal of sensitivity'.[81] Take, for example, *Pantechniki* v. *Albania*,[82] a claim concerning riots and looting that caused damage to the investment. In response to the claimant's allegation that Albania was under a duty not only to protect actively the claimant's investment against riots and looting, but also to take precautionary measures to prevent such events from occurring, the Tribunal held that the extent of a state's duty under a full protection and security provision depended to some extent on the resources available to that state.[83] Concluding that the Albanian authorities were powerless in the face of the magnitude of the events that caused damage to the claimant's investments, the Tribunal did not find the

---

[80] *Noble Ventures*, paras 164–6.

[81] Sornarajah, *The International Law on Foreign Investment*, p. 135.

[82] *Pantechniki* v. *Albania*, Award, 30 July 2009, paras 71–84.

[83] *Pantechniki*, para. 77. This has echoes of Arbitrator Huber's holding in *Spanish Zone of Morocco*, p. 644, in which, when discussing the diligence required of a state when protecting aliens, he noted that a state is 'obliged to exercise only that degree of vigilance which corresponds to the means at its disposal … the vigilance which from the point of view of international law a state is required to exercise, may be characterised as *diligentia quam in suis*'. See also Brownlie, *Principles of Public International Law*, p. 526, who argues that the *diligentia quam in suis* principle (from Roman law: a level of care that one applies in one's own affairs) calls for an objective national treatment standard that measures conduct based on what could be reasonably expected of the state in question in the light of its resources. This would be a 'modified objective standard' according to Newcombe and Paradell, *Law and Practice of Investment Treaties*, p. 310: 'the host State must exercise the level of due diligence of a host state in its particular circumstances'. See also N. Gallus, 'The Influence of the Host State's Level of Development on International Investment Treaty Standards of Protection', *Journal of World and International Trade* 6 (2005): 711, and Freeman, 'Responsibility of States for Unlawful Acts of their Armed Forces', pp. 277–8.

respondent to have failed to comply with its duty to extend full protection and security. A state of armed conflict would logically require a similar approach.

The same contextual, case-by-case approach seemed also to be followed in *Wena Hotels Ltd* v. *Arab Republic of Egypt*,[84] even though the Tribunal there found that the respondent state was liable under a full protection and security clause for damage caused by private actors. *Wena Hotels* v. *Egypt*, a case concerning the forcible seizure of two hotels owned by the claimant by employees of an Egyptian state entity (Egyptian Hotels Company (EHC)), involved the interpretation of an applicable treaty provision that investments 'shall enjoy full protection and security'. Although government officials did not participate in the seizure, the police and other authorities took no effective measures to prevent or redress the seizure. The Tribunal concluded that Egypt had violated its obligation to accord full protection and security, as the state had been aware of the intentions to seize the hotels by EHC, yet took no action to prevent this. Moreover, the police and the competent ministry took no immediate actions to restore the hotels to Wena's control; nor did Egypt impose any substantial sanctions on EHC or its senior officials, 'suggesting Egypt's approval of EHC's actions'.[85] In essence, therefore, Egypt's conduct (and its legal connection to the perpetrators) was such that it was distinguishable on the facts from the conduct of Indonesia, Italy, Mexico, Romania and Albania in the cases above. All the arbitral tribunals cited above (as well as the ICJ) have consistently applied the same standard of due diligence in protecting investors from forcible interference. Measures taken to meet this obligation are not assessed on whether the desired protection was achieved, but, rather, on the basis that the host state has acted diligently; it is thus an obligation of means or of conduct.[86] The same should be expected to apply, *mutatis mutandis*, in the case of non-state actors engaged in a non-international armed conflict, although host states engaged in investment arbitration might in such circumstances invoke the provisions on security exceptions embodied in many BITs.

3   Beyond physical security: 'legal' security

There has been some discussion as to whether full protection and security obligations extend beyond physical safety. This protection does

---

[84] *Wena Hotels Ltd* v. *Arab Republic of Egypt*, Award, 8 December 2000, 41 *ILM* 896 (2000).
[85] *Wena Hotels*, para. 84.   [86] Cordero Ross, 'Full Protection and Security', p. 139.

not seem to require investor states to safeguard against all non-physical threats, such as in *PSEG* v. *Turkey*, where the Tribunal rejected claims to the effect that the obligation of protection required the maintenance of a stable and predictable business environment,[87] or in *Eureko* v. *Poland*, where the Tribunal concluded that a stable investment climate is part of the obligation of fair and equitable treatment, but not of full protection and security.[88]

The same does not appear to be true, however, regarding the availability of legal safeguards, as there seems to exist case law guaranteeing *legal* security as part of the obligation to provide full protection and security. Although no breach was declared, the ICJ Chamber in *ELSI* considered the availability of the legal mechanism as an element of full security and protection to be enjoyed by the investor, finding that the legal mechanism was present and that the obligation was not breached.[89] In *CME*, the Tribunal concluded that the Czech Republic was obliged to ensure that, neither by amendments of its laws nor by actions of its administrative bodies, is the agreed and approved security and protection of the investment withdrawn or devalued.[90] Although they diverged on the ultimate finding, in *Lauder* the Tribunal affirmed the Czech Republic's duty to keep the judicial system available and to examine investors' claims properly.[91] In *Tecmed*, even though the Tribunal found no violation by Mexico, the availability of the legal system was deemed to be an element of the full protection and security to be enjoyed by the investor.[92] In *Saluka*, the Tribunal also affirmed the obligation of the Czech Republic to make available appeal mechanisms against police searches and administrative decisions affecting the investment.[93] Although the terms of the award are less express in relation to *legal* security, one could also consider the award in *CSOB*, where the Tribunal concluded that Slovakia's conduct in the interpretation of the terms of the contract deprived the investor of any meaningful protection for its loan, and thus breached the commitment to grant full protection and security.[94]

An unusual award is that in *Siemens*,[95] where Article 4(1) of the Germany–Argentina BIT provided for the obligation to provide 'full legal

---

[87] *PSEG* v. *Turkey*, para. 259.   [88] *Eureko* v. *Poland*, paras 240, 248, 250–1, 253.

[89] *ELSI*, para. 111.   [90] *CME* v. *Czech Republic*, para. 613.

[91] *Lauder* v. *Czech Republic*, para. 314. For further discussion, see Cordero Moss, 'Full Protection and Security', p. 145.   [92] *Tecmed* v. *Mexico*, para. 171.

[93] *Saluka* v. *Czech Republic*, paras 493, 496.

[94] *CSOB* v. *Slovak Republic*, para. 170.   [95] *Siemens* v. *Argentina*, para. 303.

protection and security';[96] it was concluded there that Argentina's obligation to provide legal security for the investment was, substantially, to guarantee the *certainty* of the legal system.[97] In this respect, provisions guaranteeing *legal* security would enable the investor to pursue its rights effectively.[98] But, as with the cases described in the preceding paragraph, the BIT need not refer *verbatim* to the term 'legal': in *Vivendi II*, the Tribunal concluded that the standard of 'full protection and security' embodied in the France–Argentina BIT applied to any act or measure that deprives an investor's investment of protection and full security, and could threaten either physical possession or the legally protected terms of operation of the investment, as either could be subject to harassment without being physically harmed or seized.[99]

Finally, although there is little case law on this point, it would seem that the obligation to provide legal security would continue to apply irrespective of the existence of a state of armed conflict, or at the very least, once that conflict had come to an end. In *Wena Hotels*, the Tribunal found that one of the violations of the obligations connected with full protection and security was the fact that Egypt did not impose sanctions against the perpetrators of the seizure.[100]

D Conclusion

The basic premise of international investment law is that it creates a treaty relationship between two states in which they undertake to waive their sovereign immunity in case of suit, and agree to provide investors of the nationality of the other contracting state with a certain standard of treatment. Such treaties are not normative in the sense that they seek to dispense entirely with international law; they simply seek to streamline the process by which business is conducted.

It is true that, by giving individual investors *ius standi* to take their disputes before investment tribunals directly, investment law is given immense force as it no longer relies on the diplomatic protection afforded by their national states. But one should not confuse the individual–state relation established here with some grand normative

---

[96] The exact wording of Art. 4(1) of the Germany–Argentina BIT: see, above, n. 43.
[97] *CME v. Czech Republic*, para. 613.
[98] Schreuer, 'Full Protection and Security', p. 352.
[99] *Vivendi v. Argentina II*, para. 7.4.17.
[100] *Wena Hotels Ltd v. Arab Republic of Egypt*, paras 82, 84, 94–5.

redefinition of a new legal order. Investment law draws from the same underlying principles that govern public international law: the interpretation of treaty obligations; the rules of state responsibility and attribution; diplomatic protection; and questions of remedies. The underlying logic behind BITs is no more, and no less, than to create *treaty rights* between states under international law. The rights and obligations created in BITs for private entities are the implementation of the mutual consent of parties, under Article 25 of the ICSID Convention, to permit private entities to submit their disputes to international arbitration.[101] Viewed in this light, therefore, investment law remains very much rooted within the international legal order. A specialised regime it may be, but investment law is not a fragment that has spun away from the orbit of general public international law.

Moreover, the examination of practice with regard to full protection and security clauses has demonstrated that, at least with regard to a state of armed conflict, investment law draws in general from the same basic principles that govern public international law. Despite the occasional divergence or conflict, there is no systemic distinction emerging in the sphere of investment protection, giving rise to different rules of interpretation or the application of different sources of law than those used for public international law as a whole. Treaty obligations such as 'full protection and security' are not interpreted in a totalising manner, displacing international humanitarian law or the law of armed conflict more generally. As such, it is perhaps safe to assert that international investment law will remain wedded to the governing principles of international law for the foreseeable future.

Yet it is apposite to address Simma's and Kill's claim that there is a 'disintegrative inclination' prevailing in the area of international investment law,[102] whereby international investment law is being considered in

---

[101] A. Tzanakopoulos, 'Denunciation of the ICSID Convention under the General International Law of Treaties', in R. Hoffman and C. Tams (eds), *International Investment Law and General International Law: From Clinical Isolation to Systemic Integration?* (Baden-Baden: Nomos Verlaggesellschaft, 2011), p. 75, esp. pp. 89–90. In fact, first Bolivia's and now Ecuador's denunciations of the ICSID Convention suggest that even the rights acquired by investors under BITs are not seen as desirable for states as they once were, and this indirect right has been revoked. Bolivia submitted its notice of withdrawal under Article 72 of the ICSID Convention on 2 May 2007, taking effect on 2 November 2007; Ecuador submitted its notice of withdrawal on 6 July 2009, taking effect on 6 January 2010.

[102] Simma and Kill, 'Harmonizing Investment Protection', p. 679, citing M. Hirsch, 'Conflicting Obligations in International Investment Law: Investment Tribunals' Perspective',

'splendid isolation' in relation to other rules of public international law, and especially those of international human rights law.[103] It is true that the jurisdiction of most arbitration tribunals is limited to the interpretation or application of the BIT under which they are convened.[104] Such limited jurisdiction would conceivably encourage investment tribunals to confine their analysis purely to the treaty provisions governing the matter, to the detriment of general international law. Yet two observations stemming from the analysis herein should serve to dispel this notion, at least as far as full protection and security provisions relate to the law of armed conflict.

First, investment treaties are, like any other treaties, subject to the same principles of treaty interpretation, which confirms the relevance of the rules of interpretation contained in Articles 31 and 32 of the Vienna Convention on the Law of Treaties.[105] Even if states fail to make explicit provision for armed conflict in BITs, there nevertheless remains a legal basis for considering the impact of armed conflict on treaty-based obligations of protection for investors. As argued in section 2, above, in case of normative conflict between the rules of international humanitarian law and the provisions of a BIT, the laws governing armed conflict constitute a *lex specialis* that would modify or displace the interpretation of a BIT provision when a state of armed conflict could be said to exist. The 'intransgressible' nature of the laws of armed conflict only serves to buttress this conclusion.

Even if one were to reject this qualification, the laws of armed conflict could, just as Simma and Kill argue in relation to international human

---

in T. Broude and Y. Shany (eds), *The Shifting Allocation of Authority in International Law. Considering Sovereignty, Supremacy and Subsidiarity: Essays in Honour of Professor Ruth Lapidoth* (Oxford: Hart, 2008), p. 323, at p. 324.

[103] B. Simma, 'Foreign Investment Arbitration: A Place for Human Rights?' *International and Comparative Law Quarterly* 60 (2011): 572, at p. 576.

[104] Like the jurisdiction of any international court or tribunal, the jurisdiction of international arbitral tribunals 'is based on the consent of the parties and is confined to the extent accepted by them': ICJ, *Armed Activities on the Territory of the Congo (New Application: 2002) (Democratic Republic of the Congo v. Rwanda)*, Jurisdiction and Admissibility, *ICJ Reports* 2006, p. 3, para. 88. See also C. McLachlan, 'The Principle of Systemic Integration and Article 31(3)(c) of the Vienna Convention', *International and Comparative Law Quarterly* 54 (2005): 279, at p. 288.

[105] *AAPL v. Sri Lanka*, p. 594, para. 39; *Duke Energy Electroquil Partners & Electroquil SA v. Republic of Ecuador*, ICSID Case No. ARB/4/19, Award, 18 August 2008, para. 173; *Continental Casualty Company v. Argentine Republic*, ICSID Case No. ARB/03/9, Award, 5 September 2008, para. 164. See also McLachlan, Shore and Weiniger, *International Investment Arbitration*, p. 66.

rights law, constitute 'relevant rules' of treaty interpretation in accordance with Article 31(3)(c) of the Vienna Convention. The International Court of Justice, in *Mutual Assistance in Criminal Matters*[106] and also in *Oil Platforms*,[107] confirmed the relevance of Article 31(3)(c) of the Vienna Convention in acting as a 'harmonising'[108] bridge between the provisions of a bilateral treaty and the parallel general international law on the matter; or what Campbell McLachlan terms 'systemic integration'.[109] This also coheres with the conclusions of the ILC in its 'Final Report on the Fragmentation of International Law', where it concludes that general law can inform, even 'crucially', the interpretation of a special treaty rule:[110] as the ILC concludes, it is a 'key point ... that the normative environment cannot be ignored and that when interpreting the treaties, the principle of integration should be borne in mind'.[111]

Investment treaties, and the legal framework that they help to structure, fundamentally remain 'creatures of international law', and thus predicate their existence and operation on being part of the international legal order.[112] Given the inherent nature of treaties as *leges speciales*, one can therefore employ a rebuttable presumption that the parties to a treaty did not intend to upset some other rule of international law.[113] This 'presumption of compliance' was already employed in the days of the Permanent Court of International Justice, in effect creating a presumption that treaties are intended to produce

---

[106] *Certain Questions of Mutual Assistance in Criminal Matters* (*Djibouti* v. *France*), Judgment, *ICJ Reports* 2008, p. 177, p. 219, paras 112–13.

[107] *Oil Platforms* (2003), esp. para. 41.

[108] ILC, 'Report on the Fragmentation of International Law', p. 408, para. 4. Tzanakopoulos, 'Denunciation of the ICSID Convention', p. 86, argues that this general principle of harmonisation is broadly similar to the principle of interpreting domestic law in harmony with international law. See further, generally, A. Tzanakopoulos, 'Domestic Courts as the "Natural Judge" of International Law', in J. Crawford and S. Nouwen (eds), *Select Proceedings of the European Society of International Law, vol. 3: 2010* (Oxford: Hart, 2012), p. 155.

[109] McLachlan, 'The Principle of Systemic Integration', p. 280.

[110] ILC, 'Report on the Fragmentation of International Law', para. 414.

[111] *Ibid.*, para. 419.

[112] McLachlan, 'The Principle of Systemic Integration', p. 280, citing A. McNair, *The Law of Treaties* (Oxford University Press, 1961), p. 466. He further argues that the principle of systemic integration flows so inevitably from the nature of a treaty as an agreement governed by international law (see VCLT, Art. 2(1)(a)) that it 'has the status of a constitutional norm within the international legal system'.

[113] Simma and Kill, 'Harmonizing Investment Protection', p. 694. They argue that this interpretative method can effectively transmit the normative content of external rules in a way that promotes coherence among legal regimes.

effects in accordance with existing rules of law;[114] and as Simma and Kill have demonstrated, it has frequently been used in various contexts by the present International Court.[115]

Of course, when states clearly wish to derogate from existing international law they may do so, to an extent.[116] A period may yet emerge when BITs expressly envisage derogating from the law of armed conflict, and it is in fact commonplace for treaties to be concluded to alter or

---

[114] See *Territorial Jurisdiction of the International Commission of the River Oder*, Judgment, 10 September 1929, PCIJ Ser. A., No. 23 (1929), p. 20, on ambiguity in some of the language in the Treaty of Versailles: 'it would hardly be justifiable to deduce from a somewhat ill-chosen expression an intention to derogate from a rule of international law so important as that relating to the ratification of conventions'. In *Right of Passage over Indian Territory (Portugal v. India)*, Preliminary Objections, Judgment, *ICJ Reports* 1957, p. 125, p. 142, the ICJ held that: 'it is a rule of interpretation that a text emanating from a Government must, in principle, be interpreted as producing and intending to produce effects in accordance with existing law and not in violation of it'.

[115] In *ELSI*, p. 42, para. 50, the Italy–United States FCN treaty was silent on whether the requirement of local remedies would apply to claims by either party. The Chamber concluded that it found itself 'unable to accept that an important principle of customary international law should be held to have been tacitly dispensed with, in the absence of any words making clear an intention to do so'. In *Oil Platforms* (2003), para. 41, the Court applied the same principle to find that the 1955 bilateral treaty was not intended 'to operate wholly independently of the relevant rules of international law on the use of force ... The application of the relevant rules of international law relating to this question thus forms an integral part of the task of interpretation entrusted to the Court.' Simma and Kill, 'Harmonizing Investment Protection', p. 689, suggest that in *Oil Platforms*, 'the Court employed a presumption that the 1955 Treaty was not intended to produce results that diverged with international law on the use of force'. See also *Mutual Assistance in Criminal Matters*, p. 219, paras 113–14, where the Court suggested that the provisions of a bilateral treaty of friendship and cooperation between the parties were relevant rules under Art. 31(3)(c) of the Vienna Convention, and thus had 'a certain bearing' on the Court's interpretation of the bilateral Convention at issue in that case.

[116] Certainly, the principle that particular treaty provisions may validly derogate from previously existing rules of international law has been recognised by the PCIJ in *Acquisition of Polish Nationality*, Advisory Opinion, 15 September 1923, PCIJ Ser. B, No. 7 (1923), pp. 15–16, and by the ICJ in *North Sea Continental Shelf*, paras 25 and 42, para. 72. However, see *Oil Platforms*, Separate Opinion of Judge Simma, p. 330, para. 9: states do not have a completely free hand in the legal ordering of their relations, especially in relation to *jus cogens* norms, which impose a 'legally insurmountable limit to permissible treaty interpretation'. Judge Simma's point takes on particular relevance when one considers how the Court has characterised the rules of international humanitarian law as 'intransgressible', and in the light of Art. 26 of the Articles on the Responsibility of States, which prevents the preclusion of wrongfulness of 'any act of a State which is not in conformity with an obligation arising under a peremptory norm of general international law'. See also R. Gardiner, *Treaty Interpretation* (Oxford University Press, 2008), pp. 264–5.

depart from existing rules of international law.[117] However, the fundamental proposition remains that where parties to treaties do not appear to have expressly intended to alter existing rules of customary law, an interpreter is justified in adopting an interpretation that coheres with those rules already in force.[118] Applying this principle coherently, and in a systematic manner, one can ensure the continued interrelation between investment law and other fields of public international law.

[117] In fact, Hugh Thirlway has remarked that states will often conclude treaties for the precise purpose of producing effects that are not in accordance with the law that was previously binding upon them: H. Thirlway, 'The Law and Procedure of the International Court of Justice, Part Three' *British Year Book of International Law* LXII (62) (1991): 1, at pp. 60–1.

[118] Simma and Kill, 'Harmonizing Investment Protection and International Human Rights', p. 690. At *ibid.*, pp. 690–1, and in relation to international human rights law, they argue that even when parties to a treaty expressly declare an intention to supersede pre-existing rules of law in their treaty relations, the interpretive impact of those external rules whose exclusion is contemplated will be minimised. The argument could be applied, *mutatis mutandis*, as regards the interpretation of an investment tribunal interpreting a hypothetical BIT which would expressly derogate from the law of armed conflict. However, it bears recalling that there has been no BIT to date that has expressly excluded the application of the laws of armed conflict in treaty relations between parties. The reason for this is difficult to discern, but may in part be related to the 'intransgressible' qualification that attaches to a great many of such norms and rules.

3

International criminal responsibility of transnational corporate actors doing business in zones of armed conflict

PHILIPP AMBACH[*]

A Introduction

It is indisputable that international business representatives and corporations engaging in economic activities in zones of armed conflict have a reasonable interest in ensuring that their goods and transactions are adequately protected from any loss or harm. This protection may go well beyond the physical security of goods and agents, and be expressed through 'protection and security' clauses that are often part of the legal provisions in international bilateral or multilateral investment agreements.[1] However, investor protection during armed conflict highlights only one set of interests that are worth protecting. At least equally important is the protection of the interests of the civil communities affected by armed conflict. These communities need protection not only from the immediate effects of armed conflict, but also from the persons or entities orchestrating and/or fuelling these conflicts. The vast majority of armed conflicts of our times are, if not based on, at least closely tied in with the economic interests of the belligerent parties or stakeholders behind the scenes. Business corporations that maintain trade relations with partner groups or entities that are, at the same time, engaged in an internal or international armed conflict may become directly or indirectly involved in the commission of serious crimes. Many international

---

[*] This chapter is based on a contribution to the conference 'The Interaction of International Investment Law with Other Fields of Public International Law', at Leiden Law School, 8 and 9 April 2011. The views expressed are those of the author alone and cannot be attributed to the International Criminal Court.

[1] See Christoph H. Schreuer, 'Full Protection and Security', *Journal of International Dispute Settlement* 1(2) (2010): 353–69; *Amco Asia Corporation and Others* v. *The Republic of Indonesia*, Award, 1 *ICSID Reports* 413, 20 November 1984; *Suez and Others* v. *Argentina*, Decision on Liability, ICSID Case No. ARB/03/19; IIC 442 (2010), 30 July 2010.

corporate actors provide financial resources to regional armed groups through the trade of goods that are the product of exploitation of natural resources in conflict zones, such as gold, diamonds, oil, uranium and other precious or strategic resources. These business actors may incur criminal liability if they are aware that their goods or funds serve to provide these armed groups with weapons or other means of warfare subsequently used against civilians. The crimes committed may amount to international crimes, such as war crimes, crimes against humanity or genocide. In such cases, corporate actors may even come under scrutiny by the International Criminal Court (ICC) for their participatory role in such crimes, if the individual criminal liability of the person(s) in control of such financial transactions on behalf of a corporate actor can be established.

B Frequent trade scenarios between the armed group and the corporate actor

International humanitarian law does not contain any explicit provisions governing situations where international business corporations are engaged in economic transactions in areas of armed conflict that, directly or indirectly, impact on that conflict. However, the conduct of corporate actors may directly collide with one of the most fundamental principles of international humanitarian law: the protection of civilians in armed conflict. Financial or trading activities of international corporate actors in areas embroiled in armed conflict may in fact destabilise the region and even pour oil on the fire of a looming conflict, if the economic transactions serve to strengthen one or more of the – possibly multiple – warring parties.

The exploitation of natural resources has recently become the primary means of financing and protracting armed violence in a number of conflict zones. A plethora of reports exists from UN-mandated investigative commissions and non-governmental human rights organisations documenting the link between the exploitation of natural resources, on the one hand, and armed conflict, on the other.[2] Prominent examples are Sierra Leone, Liberia, Democratic Republic of Congo (DRC) and East

---

[2] See UN GA Resolution A/RES/55/56, 29 January 2001; Panel of Experts on the Illegal Exploitation of Natural Resources and Other Forms of Wealth of the Democratic Republic of the Congo, UN Docs S/2002/1146, 16 October 2002; S/2003/1027, 28 October 2003; and S/2008/773, 12 December 2008; James G. Stewart, *Corporate War Crimes: Prosecuting Pillage of Natural Resources*, Open Society Justice Initiative, October 2010, available at: www.opensocietyfoundations.org/sites.default/files/pillage-manual-2nd-edition-2011.pdf.

Timor. These 'resource wars' are sustained by commercial actors purchasing resources from the different parties involved in armed conflict.
The ongoing conflict in the Great Lakes Region of the DRC represents
one of the most current and sad examples. In a resolution of December
2008, the UN Security Council called upon all states 'to take appropriate
steps to end the illicit trade in natural resources, including if necessary
through judicial means', to cease illegal exploitation of natural resources
in the region.[3] In mentioning 'judicial means' to tackle the situation the
Security Council resolution made it clear that the criminal prosecution of
those who engage in trade with armed groups may be a key component in
effectively combating the protracted commission of crimes by armed
groups in the region. The Security Council went beyond a mere condemnation of the crimes committed and expressed, albeit implicitly, its conviction that the conduct of international corporate actors may amount to
criminal behaviour, triggering individual criminal responsibility.

Possible scenarios for such 'resource wars' are fairly straightforward
and, unfortunately, recurrent. Armed groups bring areas rich in natural
resources under their control, and build their own economy centred on
the exploitation and trade of these resources. In order to maintain such
territorial and economic control, coercion and force are being used
against the affected population. These measures frequently amount to
serious human rights violations and crimes of an international dimension. The nature of such 'armed groups' is not necessarily limited to
guerrilla forces operating against state authorities. It encompasses any
larger group with an inner command structure, a degree of stability and
organisation, the ability to carry out sustained military operations and,
arguably, some territorial control.[4] These groups may be organised in a

---

[3] UN SC Resolution 1856 (2008), 22 December 2008, p. 8, para. 21.

[4] The requirements could be defined in direct reference to the International Criminal
Tribunal for the former Yugoslavia's (ICTY) decision of the Appeals Chamber in the
Tadić case (ICTY, *Prosecutor* v. *Duško Tadić*, Case No. IT-94-1-AR72, Decision on the
Defence Motion for Interlocutory Appeal on Jurisdiction, 2 October 1995), defining
the necessary amount of internal organisation and stability of an armed group to be a
party in a non-international armed conflict (see *ibid.*, para. 70). See also ICTY, *Prosecutor*
v. *Duško Tadić*, Case No. IT-94-1-T, Judgment, 7 May 1997, para. 562; ICC, *Prosecutor* v.
Thomas Lubanga Dyilo, Case No. ICC-01/04-01/06, Judgment, 14 March 2012 (*Lubanga*
Judgment), paras 534–7. It is noteworthy, however, that the exercise of territorial control
would not appear to be a constitutive element of the definition of an armed conflict not of
an international character pursuant to Art. 8(2) of the ICC Statute, see *ibid.*, para. 536;
Otto Triffterer (ed.), *Commentary on the Rome Statute of the International Criminal
Court: Observer's Notes*, 2nd edn (Munich/Oxford: C. H. Beck/Hart, 2008), Art. 8,

bipolar fashion, consisting of a civil-political-economic branch, as well as an armed wing that is responsible for the commission of crimes. Even state actors exploiting their own country by violent means affecting the civilian population may be the business partner in question. The scenario described is a frequent occurrence in war-torn or failed states rich in natural resources where a plurality of armed groups struggle for power and, therefore, seek access to these resources by all necessary means.[5] In engaging in economic transactions with these armed groups, or even by providing them with warfare technology, know-how or manpower,[6] international corporate actors support, protract and possibly even intensify the armed conflict and thus the suffering of the affected civilian population. They may even incur criminal liability, under certain circumstances, for the crimes committed by the armed groups, if these crimes stand in a close enough relation to the economic transaction.

International criminal liability of corporate representatives for business transactions facilitating grave crimes is not a novelty in international criminal law. However, international courts and tribunals have devoted little to no attention to the issue since the post-Second World War criminal proceedings held against German businessmen involved in the war through their respective businesses.[7] This may be explained in part by the general state of paralysis of initiatives in the area of international criminal justice during the Cold War. For the post-Cold War era, the focus of the newly established mechanisms of international criminal

---

marginal n. 351 (p. 502); William A. Schabas, *The International Criminal Court: A Commentary on the Rome Statute* (Oxford University Press, 2010), pp. 204–5.

[5] Two examples of currently ongoing criminal proceedings before international courts illustrate the growing prominence of 'resource wars' based on the illicit exploitation of national resources and use of force against civilians, as well as the growing importance of this field of law: the case against Charles Taylor before the Special Court for Sierra Leone (SCSL) (Case No. SCSL-03-1-A) and the case against Jean Pierre Bemba before the International Criminal Court (ICC) (Case No. ICC-01/05 -01/08). See also Stewart, *Corporate War Crimes*, p. 9.

[6] Private military companies are increasingly hired and employed as security personnel or even as combatants by parties engaged in armed conflicts. See Hannah Tonkin, *State Control over Private Military and Security Companies in Armed Conflict*, Cambridge Studies in International and Comparative Law, No. 84 (Cambridge University Press, 2011).

[7] A number of post-Second World War cases established the criminal liability of corporate actors for international crimes, see *US* v. *Friedrich Flick et al.*, US Military Tribunal IV, 22 December 1947; *US* v. *Carl Krauch et al.*, US Military Tribunal VI, 29–30 July 1949. For a comprehensive overview, see Volker Nerlich, 'Core Crimes and Transnational Business Corporations', *Journal of International Criminal Justice* 8 (2010): 898–901.

justice lay in post-conflict transitional justice. The UN *Ad hoc* International Criminal Tribunals for the former Yugoslavia and for Rwanda, as well as a number of hybrid internationalised *ad hoc* courts, have been set up predominantly as a measure to bring justice to post-conflict communities for past crimes.[8] It is only through the establishment of the ICC in July 2002 that the international community created a permanent criminal justice mechanism with a mandate to put an end to impunity for the perpetrators of the worst international crimes and to pre-empt the commission of such crimes in the future. Setting the focus on international corporate actors who fuel armed conflicts is a necessary development away from a merely reactive justice system that has been geared towards post-conflict settings; it leads towards a more dynamic system of international criminal justice that actively intervenes in ongoing armed conflict and cuts its resources.[9]

C A possible criminal dimension of international business transactions

Many forms of illegal support of armed groups by international corporate actors are sanctioned by either applicable national laws, international treaties applicable through relevant implementing legislation or UN embargoes adopted pursuant to chapter VII of the Charter of the United Nations and enforced through national legislations.[10] However, national criminal proceedings against international corporate actors have remained few.[11] A reason for this may be that the crimes are often

---

[8] It bears noting that the UN *Ad hoc* International Criminal Tribunal for the former Yugoslavia (ICTY) had already been established in 1993 through UN SC Resolutions 808 (1993) and 827 (1993), although the Dayton Accords officially ending the war in Bosnia-Herzegovina were only concluded in November 1995.

[9] James G. Stewart speaks of the role of international criminal justice 'as an element of global governance rather than transitional justice', see James G. Stewart, 'Atrocity, Commerce and Accountability: The International Criminal Liability of Corporate Actors', *Journal of International Criminal Justice* 8 (2010): 316, 326.

[10] For an overview, see Reinhold Gallmetzer, 'Prosecuting Persons Doing Business with Armed Groups in Conflict Areas', *Journal of International Criminal Justice* 8 (2010): 948–9.

[11] See Gallmetzer, 'Prosecuting Persons Doing Business with Armed Groups in Conflict Areas'. However, for a recent example of a domestic prosecution of an international business actor assisting in massive state crimes against civilians, see the Court of Appeal in The Hague, the Netherlands, *Gerechtshof Den Haag, In the Case of Frans van Anraat*, Judgment, Cause list No. 22-000509-06 (LJN: BA4676), 9 May 2007, available at: www.haguejusticeportal.net/eCache/DEF/7/548.html.

committed far away from those states where the corporate actors are incorporated and exercise their principal business activities; the geographic distance may shift these crimes out of the focus of national investigators. Further, effective criminal prosecution by the state hosting the foreign economic transaction may not be forthcoming as these 'host' states often have a fragile and corrupt justice system and lack resources to carry out the complex criminal investigations – if they are not themselves the trade partner.

However, the investigation and prosecution of international corporate actors is not limited to the national level. Corporate actors may also incur criminal responsibility for international core crimes before an *international* justice mechanism.[12] Leaving aside for a moment the question of whether, and to what extent, such criminal responsibility is necessarily aimed at individuals directing the corporate activities of their businesses or whether it can also be attributed to the corporate actors in a collective manner,[13] there are a number of scenarios in which the crimes linked to the economic transactions of corporate actors may amount to international crimes. If, and when, the link between the crime and the economic transaction is strong enough, international corporate actors may come into the focus of criminal investigators of international criminal courts and tribunals.

D Relevant conduct resulting in criminal responsibility for international crimes

I Scenarios connecting the corporate transactions with crimes on the ground

A common scenario in which international corporate actors are involved in armed conflict is the trade of arms between these actors and armed groups or regional associations with an armed wing. If the weapon recipient proceeds to use these arms in order to commit grave acts of

---

[12] Crimes under international law differ from domestic crimes in that they are *directly* punishable under international law. See Gerhard Werle, *Principles of International Criminal Law*, 2nd edn 2009 (The Hague: T. M. C. Asser Press, 2009), paras 114–18. The so-called 'core' crimes are such crimes that can be found in the Statutes of both *Ad Hoc* Tribunals of the UN as well as the ICC: crimes against humanity, war crimes, genocide and the crime of aggression (the latter being solely codified in Art. 8*bis* of the Rome Statute). See K. Ambos, *Internationales Strafrecht*, 3rd edn (Munich: C. H. Beck, 2011), § 7, paras 122 *et seq.*

[13] See below, section E.I.

violence amounting to international crimes, and the involved corporate actor is aware of the intended use of the sold goods, a (participatory) liability for the committed crimes may be the consequence.[14] In another scenario, the international corporate actor purchases natural resources or raw materials, such as cobalt, gold, diamonds, crude oil, etc., from a regional business partner with an armed wing. The traded resources have been previously obtained by that partner through pillage or any other violent form of exploitation of the civilian population, such as forced labour in mines. In the first scenario, the crimes committed on the ground with the received weaponry may amount to killings, torture and forcible displacement of civilians or any other person protected under international law.[15] In the latter scenario, crimes like pillage, torture and enslavement may be some of the typical crimes committed on the ground in order to produce, obtain and subsequently trade these resources.

II International crimes that could be committed with the involvement of the corporate actor

1 Crimes against humanity

Crimes committed in the above scenarios may give rise to an international dimension if certain framework conditions are met. Crimes against humanity require as a minimum corollary element that the relevant acts be committed as part of a widespread or systematic attack against the civilian population.[16] The crime can be committed both during war and in times of peace. Further, the attack may be launched

---

[14] See below, sections E and F.

[15] See the four Geneva Conventions of 12 August 1949 and their two Additional Protocols of 1977, as well as various international and regional human rights treaties, such as the International Covenant on Civil and Political Rights and UN General Assembly Resolution 2200A (XXI), 16 December 1966.

[16] See Art. 5 of the ICTY Statute; Art. 3 of the Statute of the International Criminal Tribunal for Rwanda (ICTR); and Art. 7(1) of the Rome Statute of the ICC. Article 5 of the ICTY Statute requires in addition as a jurisdictional requirement that the crime be committed in armed conflict (see ICTY, *Prosecutor* v. *Dragoljub Kunarac et al.*, Case Nos IT-96-23 & 23/1-A, Appeals Chamber, para. 83). Article 3 of the ICTR Statute stipulates that the crimes be committed 'on national, political, ethnic, racial or religious grounds'. The enumerated discriminatory grounds are likewise jurisdictional in nature. See ICTR, *Prosecutor* v. *Joseph Nzabirinda*, Case No. ICTR-01-77-T, 23 February 2007, Trial Chamber, para. 23.

by non-state actors, that is, regional armed groups.[17] However, for such groups a certain level of organisation, structure and regional (military) authority may be required.[18] Individual acts encompass, among other things, acts of murder, enslavement, deportation and torture. Thus, as long as these acts of violence against civilians are being carried out as part of a widespread or systematic attack against the civilian population, the underlying crimes may amount to crimes against humanity, as sanctioned in the statutes of the *Ad hoc* Tribunals of the UN as well as the ICC.[19]

2   War crimes

Trading by international corporate actors with armed groups in a zone of armed conflict may also result in the business representative's involvement in the commission of war crimes. Such crimes are best described as violations of a rule of international humanitarian law that create direct criminal responsibility under international law.[20] As a general precondition, the crime has to be committed during, and in connection with, an armed conflict, that is, a resort to armed force between states, or protracted armed violence between government authorities and organised armed groups or between such groups within a state.[21] In other words, war crimes can also be committed in purely *internal* armed conflicts.[22]

---

[17] *Argumentum ex* Art. 7(2)(a) of the Rome Statute (State *or* organizational policy, emphasis added). See also ICC, Elements of Crimes, ICC-ASP/1/3(Part II-B), 9 September 2002, Art. 7, Introduction, para. 3; Werle, *Principles of International Criminal Law*, paras 813–17; ICTR, *Prosecutor* v. *Clément Kayishema and Obed Ruzindana*, Case No. ICTR-95-1-T, Trial Chamber, 21 May 1999, paras 125–6.

[18] See ICC Decision Pursuant to Art. 15 of the Rome Statute on the *Authorization of an Investigation into the Situation in the Republic of Kenya*, Case No. ICC-01/09-19, Pre-Trial Chamber II, 31 March 2010, para. 90; however, see also ICC, *Prosecutor* v. *William Samoei Ruto, Henry Kiprono Kosgey and Joshua Arap Sang*, Dissenting Opinion by Judge Hans-Peter Kaul to Pre-Trial Chamber II's *Decision on the Prosecutor's Application for Summons to Appear for William Samoei Ruto, Henry Kiprono Kosgey and Joshua Arap Sang*, Case No. ICC-01/09-01/11, Pre-Trial Chamber, 15 March 2011, paras 8 *et seq.*; K. Ambos, *Internationales Strafrecht*, para. 186.

[19] Article 5(a), (c), (d) and (f) of the ICTY Statute; Art. 3(a), (c), (d) and (f) of the ICTR Statute; Art. 7(a), (c), (d) and (f) of the Rome Statute.

[20] Werle, *Principles of International Criminal Law*, para. 773.

[21] ICTY, *Prosecutor* v. *Duško Tadić*, Case No. IT-94-1-AR72, Decision on the Defence Motion for Interlocutory Appeal on Jurisdiction, Appeals Chamber, 2 October 1995, para. 70; ICTR, *Prosecutor* v. *Théoneste Bagosora et al.*, Case No. ICTR-98-41-T, Trial Chamber, 18 December 2008, para. 2229.

[22] Werle, *Principles of International Criminal Law*, paras 825 *et seq.*; ICTR, *Prosecutor* v. *Jean-Paul Akayesu*, Case No. ICTR-96-4-T, Trial Chamber, 2 September 1998, paras

Lastly, the crime(s) committed must stand in a functional relationship to the armed conflict creating a 'nexus' between the crime(s) and the conflict.[23] Different sets of specific crimes can be focused upon in the above scenario, namely: acts of killing or other violence[24] against protected persons not taking an active part in the hostilities;[25] acts geared towards the utilisation of protected persons by way of slavery and forced labour;[26] or acts directed against property, such as plunder, confiscation or pillaging.[27] Any of these acts could constitute relevant conduct in the above scenarios of resource wars involving international corporate trading partners.

a **The war crime of pillage in focus** The pillage or plunder of natural resources[28] merits specific attention in the context of the involvement of corporate actors in conflict zones. The crime of pillage can be defined as all forms of intentional and unlawful appropriation of property in an armed conflict of a sufficiently serious nature for which individual criminal responsibility attaches under international criminal law,[29] or, in more simple terms, theft during war.[30] It is explicitly enumerated in Article 8(2)(b)(xvi) of the Rome Statute for an international armed

604–16; ICTY, *Tadić*, Decision on the Defence Motion for Interlocutory Appeal on Jurisdiction, paras 116, 134.

[23] ICTY, *Tadić*, Decision on the Defence Motion for Interlocutory Appeal on Jurisdiction, para. 70; Werle, *Principles of International Criminal Law*, para. 846; ICTR, *Bagosora*, Trial Judgment, para. 2231.

[24] See, e.g., Art. 2(a), (b), (c) of the ICTY Statute; Art. 4(a) and (e) of the ICTR Statute; and Art. 8(2) in various subparagraphs.

[25] *Prosecutor v. Zejnil Delalić et al.* (*Čelebići Camp*), Case No. IT-96-21-A, Appeals Chamber, 20 February 2001, para. 420.

[26] See *Prosecutor v. Mladen Naletilić et al.* (*Tuta/Štela*), Case No. IT-89-34-T, Trial Chamber, 31 March 2003, paras 250, 251, 302. This crime, however, has so far been accepted only as existing in international armed conflict; see *ibid.*, para. 251.

[27] Based on the *grave breaches* provisions of the Geneva Conventions, war crimes against property criminalise not only the expropriation, but also the destruction of property (see Art. 2(d) of the ICTY Statute; Art. 8(2)(a)(iv), 8(2)(b)(xiii), 8(2)(e)(xiii) of the Rome Statute); however, for the topic under discussion, the focus shall remain on the unlawful appropriation (for economic purposes).

[28] The terms 'pillage' and 'plunder' can be used synonymously, see ICTY, *Prosecutor v. Blagoje Simić et al.*, IT-95-5-T, Trial Chamber, 17 October 2003, para. 98; *Shorter Oxford English Dictionary*, 5th edn, vol. II, pp. 2206, 2252; see also Stewart, *Corporate War Crimes*, para. 11.

[29] ICTY, *Prosecutor v. Dario Kordić and Mario Čerkez*, Case No. IT-95-14/2-A, Appeals Chamber, 17 December 2004, paras 79–84.

[30] Stewart, *Corporate War Crimes*, p. 10 (Introduction).

conflict and in Article 8(2)(e)(v) for an internal armed conflict.[31] The ICTY Statute defines the crime of 'plunder of public or private property' as a violation of the laws or customs of war, also applicable in internal armed conflict, under Article 3(e).[32] The ICTY has furthermore found in the case of *Prosecutor* v. *Tihomir Blaškić* that 'pillage is explicitly prohibited in Article 33 of the Geneva Convention IV, and Article 4, paragraph 2(g) of Additional Protocol II. In addition, Articles 28 and 47 of the Hague Regulations of 1907 expressly forbid pillage. The prohibition against pillage may therefore be considered to be part of customary international law'[33] in both international and non-international armed conflict.[34]

The crime of pillage describes one of the principal illicit means by which armed groups gain possession of goods in order to sell them to international corporate actors in an effort to finance their (para-)military operations. It is only recently that this 'systematic' pillaging (as opposed to appropriation by individual combatants for their private gain) has again come into focus in an international criminal investigation after having been briefly the subject of judicial attention in post-Second World War trials against German business representatives for the pillaging of natural resources.[35]

---

[31] Article 8(2)(b)(xvi) and (e)(v) of the Rome Statute reads: 'Pillaging a town or place, even when taken by assault'. In addition, Art. 8(2)(a)(iv) of the Rome Statute, based, *inter alia*, on the *grave breaches* provision in Art. 147 of the Geneva Convention IV, stipulates the 'extensive destruction and appropriation of property, not justified by military necessity and carried out unlawfully and wantonly'. However, the objects of conduct can only be protected property as defined in the Geneva Conventions I, II and IV, such as hospitals and the vehicles and material required for medical care (see Geneva Convention I, Arts 19, 20, 33–6; Geneva Convention II, Arts 22–8, 38, 39; Geneva Convention IV, Arts 18, 21, 22), but also real or personal property in occupied territory (see Art. 53 of the Geneva Convention IV).

[32] The provision on 'extensive … appropriation of property' in Art. 2(d) of the ICTY Statute is likewise based on the *grave breaches* provisions of the Geneva Conventions (see above). See ICTY, *Prosecutor* v. *Radoslav Brđanin*, Case No. IT-99-36-T, Trial Chamber, 1 September 2004, paras 584–6. See also Art. 4(f) of the ICTR Statute.

[33] ICTY, *Prosecutor* v. *Tihomir Blaškić*, Case No. IT-95-14-A, Appeals Chamber, 29 July 2004, paras 147, 148.

[34] See ICTR, *Akayesu*, Trial Judgment, paras 604–16; Jean-Marie Henckaerts and Louise Doswald-Beck, *Customary International Humanitarian Law Study*, vol. I (Cambridge University Press, 2005), pp. 182–5.

[35] See Art. 6(b) of the Nuremberg Charter of the International Military Tribunal; see also *US* v. *Krauch et al.* (IG Farben), 8 *Trials of War Criminals before the Nuremberg Military Tribunal under Control Council Law No. 10*, 1081 (1952): 1129 *et seq.*

b Does pillage have to be committed for private or personal use?

The jurisprudence of the UN *Ad hoc* Tribunals is clear that 'the prohibition on the wanton appropriation of enemy public or private property extends to both isolated acts of plunder for private interest and to the "organized seizure of property undertaken within the framework of a systematic economic exploitation of occupied territory"'[36]; however, it is not clear whether the ICC Statute likewise provides that the crime of pillage can be committed as part of a framework of systematic economic exploitation of occupied territory in order to finance military action. The Elements of Crimes of the Rome Statute[37] represent a list of guidelines to assist the ICC in the interpretation and application of the crimes under the statute.[38] Regarding the crime of pillage as enumerated in Article 8(2)(b)(xvi) and 8(2)(e)(v) of the Rome Statute, the Elements of Crimes require that 'the perpetrator intended to deprive the owner of the property and to appropriate it *for private or personal use*'.[39] The crime of pillage as described in the ICC Elements of Crimes would thus appear to differ from the definition of the crime by the UN *Ad hoc* Tribunals by virtue of the additional qualitative requirement of private or personal use. Cases of systematic pillaging of natural resources by armed groups in order to sustain their own existence and to finance their own resources and participation in an armed conflict would evidently not qualify as 'private or personal use'. Even if the armed group in question is not an official state actor, one would overstretch the term 'private use' if it were to be applied to the economic activities of regional armed groups claiming a certain territorial control. In other words, a restrictive interpretation of the crime of pillage as suggested by the ICC Elements of Crimes would fail to cover those cases of pillaging that are carried out in

---

[36] ICTY, *Prosecutor* v. *Tihomir Blaškić*, Case No. IT-95-14-T, Trial Chamber, 3 March 2000, para. 184, quoting ICTY, *Prosecutor* v. *Mucić et al.*, Case No. IT-96-21, '*Čelebići Camp*', 9 October 2001, Trial Chamber, paras 590–1; ICTY, *Dario Kordić and Mario Čerkez*, Case No. IT-95-14/2-T, Trial Chamber, 26 February 2001, para. 352.

[37] As adopted at the 2010 Review Conference (RC/11), see at: www.icc-cpi.int.

[38] See Art. 9(1) of the Rome Statute.

[39] ICC, Elements of Crimes, Art. 8(2)(b)(xvi) and 8(2)(e)(v), Element No. 2 (emphasis added). The Elements of Crimes stipulate in a footnote that 'appropriations justified by military necessity cannot constitute the crime of pillaging'; however, pillage is *per se* prohibited pursuant to Art. 33 of the Geneva Convention IV, as well as Art. 47 of the 1907 Hague Convention Respecting the Laws and Customs of War on Land and its Annex: Regulations concerning the Laws and Customs of War on Land, The Hague, 18 October 1907 (Hague Regulations 1907). See also Werle, *Principles of International Criminal Law*, paras 997–9.

a systematic and industrial fashion by military or paramilitary units for military or commercial purposes – in brief, the gravest cases of pillage.

However, the wording of Article 8(2)(b)(xvi) and 8(2)(e)(v) of the Rome Statute reflects the terminology established in international customary law, which does *not* contain the provision of 'private or personal use'.[40] The latter provision can be found only in the Elements of Crimes, which, by their nature, merely assist in the interpretation of Articles 6–8 of the statute, but are not *binding*.[41] The requirement of 'private or personal use' is therefore unnecessarily restrictive and does not reflect the current standards of protection provided by customary international law to private or public property[42] in either international or non-international[43] armed conflict. Judges in future international trials applying Article 8(2)(b)(xvi) and 8(2)(e)(v) of the Rome Statute are thus well advised to consider the liability of corporate actors for the pillaging of natural resources in conflict zones in the light of contemporary international jurisprudence[44] rather than the ICC's Elements of Crimes. Otherwise, an important impunity gap could evolve in modern resource-fuelled armed conflicts.

3 Genocide

Lastly, international corporate actors could be held liable for participation in the crime of genocide through their commercial activities in relevant conflict zones. The crime of genocide, as defined in the Genocide Convention of 1948,[45] can be committed through a number of alternative

---

[40] Hague Regulations 1907, Arts 28, 47; Art. 33 of the Geneva Convention IV. See also SCSL, *Prosecutor* v. *Brima et al.*, Case No. SCSL-04-16-T, Trial Judgment, 20 June 2007, para. 751; SCSL *Prosecutor* v. *Fofana et al.*, Case No. SCSL-04-14-T, Trial Judgment, 2 August 2007, para. 160; Stewart, *Corporate War Crimes*, paras 3–9, 16–18.

[41] Article 9(1) provides that 'Elements of Crimes *shall assist* the Court in the interpretation and application' (emphasis added), which underlines their non-binding nature. See Triffterer, *Commentary on the Rome Statute of the International Criminal Court*, Art. 9, paras 30, 39.

[42] ICTY, *Prosecutor* v. *Enver Hadžihasanovi and Amir Kubura*, Case No. IT-01-47-T, Trial Chamber, 15 March 2006, para. 52: 'ces règles ne permettent pas des pillages arbitraires et injustifiés pour les besoins de l'armée ou pour les besoins de ses membres'; SCSL, *Fofana et al.*, Trial Judgment, para. 160.

[43] See Art. 4(2)(g) of the Additional Protocol II of 1977 to the Geneva Conventions.

[44] See above, nn. 40 and 42.

[45] See Art. II of the Convention on the Prevention and Punishment of the Crime of Genocide, adopted by Resolution 260 (III) A of the UN General Assembly, 9 December 1948 (Genocide Convention).

or cumulative acts with the intent to destroy, in whole or in part, a national, ethnical, racial or religious group.[46] The relevant acts are not limited to killing or causing serious physical harm to members of the group, but also encompass other, less direct conduct such as, *inter alia*, the prevention of births within a group (as a form of biological genocide) or forcibly transferring children of the group to another group (as a form of cultural genocide).[47] Characteristic of this crime is the specific intent or (primary) goal of the perpetrator to destroy a defined group in whole or in part.[48]

Corporate actors are usually driven by predominantly economic objectives, therefore, any specified destructive intent will be hard to prove. However, a number of participatory forms of the crime of genocide do not require the participant to have the genocidal intent him- or herself.[49] Scenarios are conceivable where corporate actors may cross the line towards criminal liability even for the crime of genocide, as will be discussed in detail in section E, below.

4 Crime of aggression

As the first statute since the London Agreement establishing the International Military Tribunal to try crimes committed by nationals of European Axis powers during the Second World War, the Rome Statute contains the provision of the crime of aggression (Article 5(d) of the statute). Article 8*bis* of the Rome Statute describes the crime of aggression as the 'planning, preparation, initiation or execution, by a person in a position effectively to exercise control over or to direct the political or military action of a State, of an act of aggression which, by its character, gravity and scale, constitutes a manifest violation of the Charter of the United Nations'.[50] It is conceivable that international corporate actors who assist state authorities in delivering weapons or other warfare

---

[46] See Art. 6 of the Rome Statute; Art. 2(2) of the ICTR Statute; Art. 4(2) of the ICTY Statute. See also ICTR, *Prosecutor v. Ferdinand Nahimana et al.*, Case No. ICTR-96-11-A, Appeals Judgement, 28 November 2007, para. 492.

[47] See *Prosecutor v. Ferdinand Nahimana et al.*, Case No. ICTR-96-11-A. See also Werle, *Principles of International Criminal Law*, para. 724. See also ICTR, *Prosecutor v. Tharcisse Muvunyi*, Case No. ICTR-2000–55A-T, Trial Chamber, 12 September 2006, para. 482; ICTR, *Akayesu*, Trial Judgment, para. 731.

[48] ICTR, *Prosecutor v. Athanase Seromba*, Case No. ICTR-2001-66-A, Appeals Chamber, 12 March 2008, para. 175; ICTR, *Akayesu*, Trial Judgment, paras 498, 520.

[49] Article 2(3) of the ICTR Statute and Art. 4(3) of the ICTY Statute stipulate a list of punishable acts in a verbatim repetition of Article III of the Genocide Convention.

[50] Article 8*bis* of the Rome Statute, inserted by Resolution RC/Res.6 of 11 June 2010.

logistics incur participatory liability in the preparation and/or execution of an act of aggression. However, the activation of the ICC's jurisdiction for the crime of aggression is subject to a decision of the Assembly of States Parties after 1 January 2017 (Article 15*bis* of the Rome Statute). The practical importance of the crime of aggression for international corporate actors is therefore at present limited compared with the afore-mentioned crimes.

E   Criminal responsibility

International corporate actors can be involved in activities in zones of armed conflict in a variety of manners and with differing intensity. Their involvement can range from direct assistance in hostilities as providers of security personnel[51] through arms supply, to economic ties in the trade of natural resources that are either the product of serious human rights violations or the trade of which engenders the subsequent submission of grave crimes or both. Translated into legal terms, the involvement of international corporate actors in international crimes may range from direct and active participation alongside local actors, to auxiliary activities to the crimes of others by provision of material, logistic or financial support. In assessing the relevant criminal conduct and possible mode of participation of international corporate actors, two main questions require adequate attention: first, who exactly can be subject to proceedings before international criminal courts and tribunals; and, second, through which modes of criminal liability can criminal conduct be attributed to the actors that were previously identified? These questions shall be examined in turn.

I   Criminal responsibility of a corporate actor versus an individual?

Many national legal systems around the world are founded on the principle of individual guilt for criminal conduct (*nulla poena sine culpa*).[52] The perpetrator has to carry out the criminal act with the

---

[51] See *United States of America* v. *Slough et al.* (Blackwater5), as well as links to other cases involving private contractors, available at: www.asser.nl, subsection 'Cases'.

[52] This is true in particular for the majority of continental European legal traditions and systems. See ICRC, 'Customary IHL, Practice (2), Practice Relating to Rule 102. Individual Criminal Responsibility (III–VI), available at: www.icrc.org/customary-ihl/eng/docs/v2_rul_rule102.

knowledge that what he or she is doing is criminal and that he or she incurs criminal responsibility for his or her conduct. The perpetrator's guilt has to encompass all (subjective and objective) elements of the criminal conduct; the conduct has to be ethically and morally reproachable to an individual person.[53] These legal systems do not allow for an inference of guilt from a single individual within a corporation to the corporation as a whole or vice versa. Some legal systems, however, encompass the concept of criminal liability of corporations.[54] Corporations are legally best described as 'legal persons' (as opposed to natural persons). Legal justifications for such corporate criminal liability differ, and penal consequences are often limited to pecuniary sanctions against the corporation as a whole. If one were to take a doctrinal approach, it could be argued that the criminal accountability in such a case is lodged with a group of responsible persons legally or factually leading and representing the corporate actor. By way of a functional analogy to the principle of individual criminal responsibility, a collective 'corporate' responsibility could be established based on the systemic practices within the corporate entity as well as the board's joint control over its operations, as a substitute of the guilt of an individual.[55] The collective knowledge of the corporate leadership regarding the criminal consequences of a particular transaction, or a specific project involving a plurality of transfers of goods or other relevant transactions, would have to be proven in order to establish subjective elements (*mens rea*) necessary to establish criminal liability. However, the issue of corporate criminal responsibility has not (yet) taken proper shape in the sphere of international criminal law.[56] Neither the UN *Ad hoc* Tribunals nor the ICC exercise jurisdiction over legal persons. Article 25(1) of the Rome Statute stipulates that 'the Court shall have jurisdiction over natural persons pursuant to this Statute'. A proposal submitted by France during the preparatory stage of the

---

[53] See, for Germany, Art. 46(1), s. (1) of the German Penal Code (Strafgesetzbuch, StGB). See also German Constitutional Court (Bundesverfassungsgericht) BVerfGE 20, 323, para. 31.

[54] Common law legal systems, such as Ireland and England, the Netherlands, France, Norway, Belgium, Finland and Denmark. See Adolf Schönke and Horst Schröder, *Strafgesetzbuch Kommentar*, 27th edn (Munich: C. H. Beck, 2006), preliminary annotations to §§ 25 *et seq.*, para. 122.

[55] Schönke and Schröder, *Strafgesetzbuch Kommentar*, para. 129.

[56] Furthermore, the suggested doctrinal approach tries to tie the criminal responsibility to 'individualisable' common characteristics, such as the individuals' knowledge of certain corporate transactions together with their leading role in the corporate entity (Board), and as such is ultimately rooted in the doctrine of individual responsibility.

adoption of the Rome Statute to include legal persons as possible addressees of statutory crimes did not find approval by the majority of the states founding the Rome Statute.[57] The statutes of the international tribunals contain similar provisions to the Rome Statute.[58] Likewise, other international or internationalised criminal tribunals do not provide for corporate criminal liability in their constitutive texts.[59] It follows that *de lege lata* there is no instrument currently available for international courts and tribunals to hold international corporate actors responsible through their corporate identity. It should be noted, however, that an international debate is gaining momentum on ways to address involvement of international corporate actors in criminal activity internationally.[60] The question has been raised whether there is a rule in international customary law which provides for the accountability and punishment of legal persons for international core crimes.[61] Further, there seems to be at least a prohibition addressed at international corporate actors regarding the commission of core crimes, even if criminal consequences for a breach of a particular prohibition are not yet part of the corpus of international customary law.[62]

However, the absence of a clear position in international customary law stipulating the criminal liability of international corporations for international crimes does not mean that *individual* corporate officials are likewise exempt from international criminal jurisdiction. Usually,

---

[57] See Proposal submitted by France, Art. 23, Individual Criminal Responsibility, Legal Persons, Doc. A/Conf.183/C.1/L.3, 16 June 1998, *Official Records of the United Nations Diplomatic Conference of Plenipotentiaries on the Establishment of an International Criminal Court (Reports and other documents)*, vol. III, p. 258. See also *ibid.*, vol. II, *Summary of the Meetings of the Committee of the Whole*, Doc. A/CONF.183/C.1/SR.1, paras 32 *et seq.*, p. 133.

[58] See Art. 5 of the ICTR Statute and Art. 6 of the ICTY Statute, limiting jurisdiction to natural persons.

[59] While the SCSL Statute does not explicitly limit its jurisdiction to *natural* persons, a plain reading of, in particular, Art. 1(1) makes clear that the SCSL limits its jurisdiction to natural persons. See also Law on the Establishment of the Extraordinary Chambers in the Courts of Cambodia (ECCC), with inclusion of amendments as promulgated on 27 October 2004, NS/RKM/1004/006, Art. 1 and chapter II (Competence).

[60] See Desislava Stoitchkova, 'Towards Corporate Liability in International Criminal Law', University of Utrecht, Intersentia 2010; Norman Farrell, 'Attributing Criminal Liability to Corporate Actors: Some Lessons from the International Tribunals', *Journal of International Criminal Justice* 8 (2010): 875.

[61] Nerlich, 'Core Crimes', p. 898.

[62] For an insightful discussion of the issue, see Nerlich, 'Core Crimes and Transnational Business Corporations', pp. 898 *et seq.*

even in larger corporations, decisions on specific transactions are taken by a rather small panel of chief executive officers (CEOs) or stakeholders who head the corporation and who represent its 'directing minds'.[63] If it can be established, based on the evidence of a particular case, that pursuant to the decision of an individual member of the corporation or a small panel of identifiable CEOs a certain economic transaction – be it a transfer of goods such as weapons or a financial transfer – has been carried out which then serves to facilitate the commission of international crimes, a sufficiently close link between the corporate officials and the crime may be established, if a number of additional preconditions are met. These shall be briefly discussed in the following.

The main problem in ascribing any individual criminal responsibility to individual corporate officials is their factual and physical remoteness from the crimes, committed often thousands of kilometres away, as well as the fact that often these individuals have never even set foot in the country or region where the crimes are being committed. Other than in most domestic criminal cases, the involvement of international corporate actors in international crimes remains remote from the physical perpetration of crimes as well as the direct perpetrators. The only link exists through an economic tie or, more broadly, an organisational structure at the end of which stands the commission of international crimes. These situations, however, bear a striking resemblance to the modern leadership crime cases before international courts and tribunals. In these cases, the accused stand in the dock accused of having committed crimes through organisational structures, be this through political or military chains of command. The UN *Ad hoc* Tribunals continue to adjudicate such cases regarding both the genocide in Rwanda 1994 and the Yugoslav war which erupted at the beginning of 1992. Both tribunals have tried a number of political and military leaders whose involvement in the atrocities on the ground was indirect and through organisational structures, rather than through any direct and visible involvement in the crimes.[64] It is therefore instructive, as a first step, to assess in the following the tribunals' jurisprudence in this particular regard in order to distil guiding principles on how to define criminal responsibility of individual corporate officials when dealing with their specific remoteness from the crimes.

---

[63] Farrell, 'Attributing Criminal Liability to Corporate Actors', p. 875.
[64] See, e.g., ICTY, *Prosecutor* v. *Momčilo Krajišnik*, Case No. IT-39-00-A, Appeals Chamber, 17 March 2009; ICTR, *Prosecutor* v. *Théoneste Bagosora et al.* (*Military I*), Case No. ICTR-96-7, Trial Chamber, 18 December 2008.

As a subsequent step, it is important to examine how the tribunals' jurisprudence can be brought in harmony with the ICC Statute. While the ICC has not yet produced any significant jurisprudence on the involvement of economic actors in international crimes, the statute already provides some guidance on how such cases could be dealt with in the future. Further, the Office of the Prosecutor (OTP) of the ICC has acknowledged in connection with the situation in the Democratic Republic of Congo that 'there is general concern that the atrocities allegedly committed in the country may be fuelled by the exploitation of natural resources there and the arms trade, which are enabled through the international banking system', and 'that investigation of the financial aspects of the alleged atrocities will be crucial to prevent future crimes and for the prosecution of crimes already committed'.[65] The OTP is actively monitoring individuals who are suspected of financing alleged atrocities, as expressed publicly by the ICC prosecutor on various occasions.[66]

II   Modes of criminal responsibility pursuant to the international statutes

Individual criminal liability does not attach solely to individuals who physically commit a crime; it may extend to those who participate in and contribute to the commission of a crime in a number of ways, as long as a sufficient connection to the crime can be established.[67] Individual criminal liability of representatives of corporations for international crimes can be ascribed broadly in two forms: either the company official acts in close cooperation with his or her business partners as a co-author of crimes; or the individual corporate actor's

---

[65] ICC Press Release on communications received by the Office of the Prosecutor of the ICC, No. pids.009.2003-EN, 16 July 2003, pp. 3–4.

[66] See Statements of the ICC Prosecutor, available at: www.icc-cpi.int; see also Gallmetzer, 'Prosecuting Persons Doing Business with Armed Groups in Conflict Areas', pp. 950–1. Gallmetzer further refers to the OTP's network of law enforcement agencies (LEN) as a useful tool to achieve *national* prosecution of corporate actors doing business with armed groups in conflict zones; *ibid.*, pp. 952 *et seq.* For further information on the LEN, see ICC Prosecutorial Strategy 2009–2012, 1 February 2010, paras 17, 32, available at: www.icc-cpi.int.

[67] ICTY, *Prosecutor* v. *Blagoje Simić et al.*, Case No. IT-95-5-T, Trial Chamber, 17 October 2003, para. 135. For a general overview, see Robert Cryer, Håkan Friman, Darryl Robinson and Elizabeth Wilmshurst, *An Introduction to International Criminal Law and Procedure*, 2nd edn (Cambridge University Press, 2010), s. 15, pp. 361 *et seq.*

contribution to the crime is of an auxiliary nature, while the design and control of the crime is left to the business partner.

1 Accountability of corporate representatives as a (co-)perpetrator of a crime

a Joint criminal enterprise versus co-perpetration In the case of the international corporate representative co-authoring a crime with a local business partner, both the corporate actor and the local group engage in collective criminal conduct for which both sides are held accountable as principal perpetrators of the crime. Such joint commission of crimes as principals has been described by the ICTY as 'joint criminal enterprise' (JCE).[68] The ICTR, the Special Court for Sierra Leone (SCSL), as well as the Extraordinary Chambers in the Courts of Cambodia have adopted this doctrine.[69] The notion of joint or co-perpetratorship does not appear explicitly in *any* of the statutes of the aforementioned institutions. The doctrine of JCE as a form of systemic attribution of criminal responsibility to its members[70] has been developed from post-war jurisprudence in one of the first and most important judgments of the ICTY, *Prosecutor v. Duško Tadić*,[71] and served as a means to fill the *lacuna* of joint criminal liability in the statutes of the *ad hoc* courts and tribunals.[72] Pursuant to this doctrine, a group of individuals can be held commonly criminally responsible as principals of the crime if, pursuant to their common plan, design or purpose, one or more crimes against international law are committed.[73] No physical or otherwise direct involvement in the crime

---

[68] ICTY, *Tadić*, Appeal Judgment, paras 227 *et seq*. For the determination of JCE as a form of 'commission' of a crime pursuant to Art. 7(1) of the ICTY Statute, see ICTY, *Prosecutor* v. *Miroslav Kvočka et al.*, Case No. IT-98-30/1-A, Appeals Chamber, 28 February 2005, para. 80.

[69] ICTR, *Prosecutor* v. *Aloys Simba*, Case No. ICTR-01-76-T, Trial Chamber, 13 December 2005, paras 385 *et seq.*; SCSL, *Prosecutor* v. *Alex Tamba Brima et al.*, Case No. SCSL-2004-16-A, Appeals Chamber, 22 February 2008; see also Werle, *Principles of International Criminal Law*, para. 456; ECCC Case 002 *Ieng Thirith et al.*, Criminal Case File No. 002/19-09-2007-ECCC/OCIJ (PTC38), Decision on the Appeals against the Co-Investigating Judges Order on Joint Criminal Enterprise (JCE), Pre-Trial Chamber, 20 May 2010.

[70] Ambos, *Internationales Strafrecht*, § 7 para. 23.

[71] See, in particular, ICTY, *Tadić*, Appeal Judgment, paras 194 *et seq*.

[72] Regarding the differing provision of the Rome Statute in Art. 25(3)(a), see below. See also Cryer *et al.*, *An Introduction to International Criminal Law and Procedure*, s. 15.3, pp. 367 *et seq*.

[73] ICTY, *Tadić*, Appeal Judgment, para. 188; ICTY, *Prosecutor* v. *Kupreškić*, Case No. IT-95-16-T, Trial Chamber, 14 January 2000, para. 772.

is required; the contribution need not be indispensable (i.e., causal) or even substantial.[74] Further, the participation of an accused in the JCE need not involve the commission of a crime, and can thus be an act that is not illicit in and of itself as long as it furthers the execution of the common criminal purpose.[75] Imagine a corporate representative acting in collusion with an armed group in providing weapons or armed security personnel in order to take control of territories or facilities with a view to ensuing economic exploitation of said territories; while the provision of resources by the corporate actor is on its face not illegal,[76] it can nevertheless constitute participatory conduct in a JCE if the seizure of the area encompassed the commission of international crimes as part of the common plan. Moreover, ICTY jurisprudence stipulates that a defendant who participates in a common plan to commit an international crime can be held responsible even for the commission of unplanned crimes, if these crimes were only foreseeable and the defendant willingly took the risk of their occurrence.[77] By virtue of this 'extended' form of JCE,[78] the (corporate) actor who merely accepted the forcible transfer of civilians as a consequence of his or her contributions to the general purpose may be held accountable for ensuing excess

---

[74] ICTY, *Kvočka et al.*, Appeal Judgment, paras 97–8. However, the ICTY Appeals Chamber found in its *Brđanin* Appeal Judgment that the contribution by each participant 'should at least be a significant contribution to the crimes for which the accused [are] to be found responsible'. *Prosecutor v. Brđanin*, Case No. IT-99-36-A, Appeals Chamber, 3 April 2007, para. 430.

[75] ICTY, *Prosecutor v. Momčilo Krajišnik*, Case No. IT-00-39-A, Appeals Chamber, 17 March 2009, para. 218, referring to, *inter alia*, *Kvočka et al.*, Appeal Judgment, para. 99; ICTR, *Prosecutor v. E. & G. Ntakirutimana*, Case No. ICTR-96-17-A, Appeals Chamber, 13 December 2004, para. 466.

[76] Provided the weapon delivery is not in contravention of any international treaty prohibiting the proliferation of specific weapons or any UN embargo on the delivery of weapons to the area/actors in question.

[77] ICTY, *Tadić*, Appeal Judgment, para. 228; ICTY, *Kvočka et al.*, Appeal Judgment, para. 83. See also Cryer *et al.*, *An Introduction to International Criminal Law and Procedure*, s. 15.3.2, p. 371.

[78] The ICTY has established three distinct forms of JCE; all three forms share an identical *actus reus* as outlined above, but differ as to the *mens rea* requirements. The first form of JCE requires intent directed at the crimes committed; the second form of JCE (applicable in so-called 'concentration camp cases') requires knowledge of the system of ill-treatment within the confines of a concentration or other prison camp, as well as the intent to further the common concerted system of ill-treatment. See ICTY, *Tadić*, Appeal Judgment, para. 228. The third form is the 'extended' form of JCE as explained above. For the exact distinction of all three forms, see ICTY, *Prosecutor v. Mitar Vasiljević*, Case No. IT-98–32-A, Appeals Chamber, 25 February 2004, paras 97 *et seq.*

crimes beyond the original framework of the common plan, such as rapes, torture and killings, if these crimes were a natural and foreseeable consequence of the execution of the common plan and the participant could only foresee these crimes and 'willingly took the risk' that they be committed[79] (often described as (advertent) recklessness or, in civil law terms, *dolus eventualis*).[80] However, it bears noting that this form of commission as established by the ICTY is subject to controversy,[81] and finds no direct equivalent in the Rome Statute of the ICC.[82]

b Co-perpetration under the Rome Statute The Rome Statute takes a more rigid approach on the definition of the joint commission of a crime. Article 25(3)(a) of the Rome Statute explicitly regulates the individual as well as the joint commission of a crime. It stipulates that a person can be held criminally responsible if he or she commits a statutory crime as an individual or 'jointly with another'. In the jurisprudence of the Pre-Trial and Trial Chamber in the case against *Thomas Lubanga Dyilo*, the distinction between principals of a crime (i.e., those who commit the crime as a perpetrator) and accessories (i.e., those who merely assist the principals in the commission of a crime) is to be made by the criterion of 'control over the crime'.[83] Although none of the co-perpetrators has overall control over the offence because all participants depend on one another for its commission, all participants share control over the crime because each of them could frustrate its commission by not carrying out his or her task.[84] Each co-perpetrator's contribution to the common

---

[79] ICTY, *Tadić*, Appeal Judgment, para. 228.

[80] Cryer et al., *An Introduction to International Criminal Law and Procedure*, s. 15.3.2, p. 371.

[81] See ECCC, Decision on Joint Criminal Enterprise, paras 74 *et seq*.; Werle, *Principles of International Criminal Law*, para. 464.

[82] Cryer et al., *An Introduction to International Criminal Law and Procedure*, s. 15.3.3, pp. 372 *et seq*.

[83] ICC, *Lubanga*, Judgment, paras 994–1006; ICC, *Prosecutor v. Thomas Lubanga Dyilo*, Decision on the Confirmation of Charges (public redacted version), Case No. 01/04-01/ 06-803-tEN, 29 January 2007 (*Lubanga* Confirmation Decision), para. 410. When making a legal determination, judges of the ICC are to analyse its consistency with the Statute, which is pursuant to Art. 21(1)(a) of the Rome Statute the first source of applicable law (together with the Elements of Crimes and the Rules of Procedure and Evidence). The consideration of the jurisprudence of the UN *Ad hoc* Tribunals is only a secondary source of law and only as far as it reflects international customary law (Art. 21 (1)(b)).

[84] ICC, *Lubanga*, Judgment, paras 989, 999–1006; ICC, *Lubanga*, Confirmation Decision, paras 340 *et seq*.; ICC, *Prosecutor v. Germain Katanga and Mathieu Ngudjolo Chui*,

crime has to be in and of itself essential to the commission of the crime.[85] In other words, each co-perpetrator's contribution has to be causal (*condition sine qua non*) for the commission of the crime, non-action would prevent the joint crime in its intended form.[86] In contrast, JCE merely requires a 'significant' contribution, which neither has to be essential (i.e., causal) nor substantial for the commission of the joint crime.[87] In the context of corporate transactions it will in many cases prove difficult to establish that a corporate actor's contribution amounted to control over the crime, as the connection to the direct perpetrators on the ground will be too remote to frustrate or otherwise influence the commission of a crime at any given point.[88] In these cases, as the ICC jurisprudence currently stands,[89] the Rome Statute has stricter requirements than the jurisprudence of the UN *Ad hoc* Tribunals that apply the JCE doctrine, thus putting a heavy evidentiary burden on the prosecutor.

c **Subjective requirements of criminal liability (*mens rea*)** In addition to the specific requirements on the objective side of the commission of a crime, the requirements regarding the mental element represent another challenge to hold corporate actors accountable as co-perpetrators for international crimes. As a JCE member, the individual perpetrator has to share the group's intent with regard to the underlying crime(s).[90] In other words, pursuant to the jurisprudence of the UN *Ad hoc* Tribunals, the perpetrator has to be aware of the substantial likelihood

---

Decision on the Confirmation of Charges, Case No. 01/04-01/07, 30 September 2008, paras 482 *et seq.*; ICC, *Prosecutor v. Omar Hassan Ahmad Al Bashir*, Decision on the Confirmation of Charges, Case No. ICC-02/05-01/09, 4 March 2009, paras 210 *et seq.*

[85] ICC, *Lubanga*, Judgment, paras 999–1006; ICC, *Lubanga*, Confirmation Decision, paras 346–4.

[86] Note, however, the Separate Opinion of Judge Adrian Fulford to the ICC *Lubanga* Judgment, Doc. No. ICC-01/04-01/06-2842, paras 6 *et seq.*

[87] ICTY, *Brdanin*, Appeal Judgment, para. 430. For a definition of the notion 'substantial', see also ICC, *Lubanga*, Judgment, paras 991, 997 and ample further jurisprudence of international tribunals in fn. 2704, *ibid.*

[88] While the provision of logistics or weapons by a corporate actor may often prove to be a *condition sine qua non* for the armed group in the conflict zone to carry out the crimes as encompassed in the common purpose, the corporate actor may lose control over the 'whether' and the 'how' of the commission of the crime the moment that the delivery of the material is effected. See ICC, *Lubanga Dyilo*, Confirmation Decision, para. 330.

[89] The ICC *Lubanga* Pre-Trial and Trial Chambers' notion of 'control over the crime' has not yet been either validated or dismissed by the ICC Appeals Chamber.

[90] ICTY, *Tadić*, Appeal Judgment, para. 220.

that a crime will be committed in the execution of his (volitional) acts; he or she has to accept the crime.[91] In the case of the ICC, Article 30(1) of the Rome Statute defines the necessary mental element for the commission of a crime as 'intent and knowledge'. Article 30(2) stipulates that a person has intent where he or she 'means to engage in the [criminal] conduct' and 'in relation to a consequence, that person means to cause that consequence or is aware that it will occur in the ordinary course of events'. Pursuant to the ICC Pre-Trial Chamber's jurisprudence, Article 30 of the Rome Statute encompasses criminal intent with a strong volitional element (*dolus directus* of the first degree) and, as a lesser form of *mens rea* encompassed by Article 30, the intent requirement as acknowledged by the jurisprudence of the UN *Ad hoc* Tribunals.[92]

The predominant aim of corporate actors (i.e., the representatives directing the corporate entity) is generally economic gain. In order to achieve this monetary aim, the corporate actor may accept the unpleasant reality that with the help and provision of the corporation's funds or equipment crimes are being committed. Such acceptance of the expected commission of crimes does not mean that the corporate actor genuinely means to engage in the criminal conduct and therefore intends the result as manifested in the commission of crimes. However, as demonstrated above, such acceptance of the crimes as a consequence of the corporate actor's involvement generally suffices to establish the necessary *mens rea* in order to be held liable before the ICC – provided that the corporate

---

[91] ICTY, *Blaškić*, Appeal Judgment, paras 41–2; ICTY, *Prosecutor v. Pavle Strugar*, Case No. IT-01-42-T, Trial Chamber, 31 January 2005, paras 235–6; ICTR, *Nahimana et al.*, Appeal Judgment, para. 481. See also Werle, *Principles of International Criminal Law*, para. 393.

[92] ICC, *Lubanga*, Judgment, paras 1011–13; ICC, *Lubanga*, Confirmation Decision, paras 350 *et seq.*; ICC, *Katanga and Ngudjolo Chui*, Confirmation Decision, paras 529–30; ICC, *Prosecutor v. Jean Pierre Bemba Gombo*, Decision Pursuant to Article 61(7)(a) and (b) of the Rome Statute on the Charges of the Prosecutor Against Jean-Pierre Bemba Gombo, Case No. ICC-01/05-01/08, 15 June 2009, paras 352–69. Pre-Trial Chamber I in the *Lubanga* case found in addition that Art. 30 of the Rome Statute encompasses *dolus eventualis*, whereby the perpetrator merely envisages the likelihood of the commission of a crime as the consequence of his or her acts (advertent recklessness) (see ICC *Lubanga*, Confirmation Decision, paras 352–5). However, the Pre-Trial Chamber in the *Bemba* case explicitly disagreed with this notion, arguing instead as a result of an in-depth analysis of the matter that Art. 30 excludes *dolus eventualis* (ICC, *Bemba*, Confirmation Decision, paras 358–69). Supportive of the latter interpretation, see ICC, *Lubanga*, Judgment, para. 1011; Ambos, *Internationales Strafrecht*, s. 7, paras 67–9; R. Cryer *et al.*, *An Introduction to International Criminal Law and Procedure*, s. 15.2, p. 367; Werle, *Principles of International Criminal Law*, paras 408–13.

actor's material contribution is essential for the realisation of the crime and the corporate actor is aware of this.

d   Reality check: evidentiary obstacles   At the same time, it has to be noted that, in practice, significant evidentiary obstacles remain for the establishment of a corporate actor's intent for the commission of crimes on the ground. Goods such as weapons or other auxiliary means for the commission of international crimes often pass through a number of intermediaries prior to arriving at their final addressee, making it difficult to trace back what the intent and knowledge of the corporate actor encompassed when sending the goods in the first place. In these situations, it may prove extremely difficult to find the necessary (mostly circumstantial) evidence to meet the high standards for a conviction in a criminal court.[93] Thus, apart from those cases where a collusive common purpose of local war lords and corporate actors to 'clean' a certain territory or facilities with the aim of illicit exploitation can be demonstrated, it may at times prove difficult for the ICC – or any other (international) criminal court – to establish sufficient evidence that an individual corporate actor intended (*ergo*: at a minimum accepted) to commit international crimes as a co-perpetrator jointly with an armed group.[94]

2   Corporate representative's participation in a crime as an accessory

a   The concept of aiding and abetting   Customary international law recognises that accessory liability to crimes perpetrated by the principals

---

[93] See also Farrell, 'Attributing Criminal Liability to Corporate Actors', pp. 879–80. Pursuant to the jurisprudence of the ICTY, for a finding of guilt in an alleged crime, a reasonable trier of fact must have reached the conclusion that all the facts that are material to the elements of that crime have been proven beyond reasonable doubt by the prosecution. See ICTY, *Prosecutor* v. *Dragomir Milošević*, Case No. IT-98-29/1-A, Appeals Chamber, 12 June 2009, para. 20, citing ICTY, *Prosecutor* v. *Milan Martić*, Case No. IT-95-11-A, Appeals Chamber, 8 October 2008, para. 55; ICTY, *Prosecutor* v. *Sefer Halilović*, Case No. IT-01-48-A, Appeals Chamber, 16 October 2007, para. 109.

[94] The evidentiary burden would be substantially alleviated if one accepted the ICC Pre-Trial Chamber's interpretation in the *Lubanga* case that Art. 30 of the Rome Statute encompasses *dolus eventualis* – a notion which has been contradicted by the *Lubanga* Trial Chamber in its Judgment, paras 1009–11. As with the ICTY's notion of JCE type III (see above), the corporate actor could even be held accountable as a perpetrator if he only foresaw and accepted the risk that crimes *may* (not *will*) be committed as a result of his or her acts. Cf. ICC, *Lubanga*, Judgment, para. 1012.

(main perpetrators) may also encompass crimes geographically and structurally remote from the accessory to the crime (here: the international corporate actor).[95] The Rome Statute stipulates in Article 25(3)(c) that anyone who, 'aids, abets or otherwise assists in its commission' shall be criminally responsible. The UN *Ad hoc* Tribunals contain similar provisions.[96] In the jurisprudence of the ICTY, the *actus reus* of aiding and abetting consists of practical assistance, encouragement or moral support which has a substantial effect on the perpetration of the crime.[97] No cause and effect relationship between the conduct of the aider and abettor and the commission of the crime, or proof that such conduct served as a condition precedent to the commission of the crime, is required.[98] Further, the assistance need not be rendered at the location or time when the crime is committed.[99] These requirements are noteworthy in the corporate context as any economic transaction between the corporate actor and the armed group that serves to facilitate the commission of crimes in any way may suffice as necessary conduct on the objective side of a crime's commission. A corporate actor that regularly buys natural resources off a local war lord and thereby financially sustains the war lord's illegal regime of producing these goods through forced labour and mistreatment of civilians, would, objectively, fulfil the *actus reus* of the crime of aiding and abetting. This could also be said of a corporate actor that provides an armed group with weapons or logistics which are used to carry out crimes.

[95] ICTY, Prosecutor v. Mile Mrkšić and Veselin Šljivančanin, Case No. IT-95-13/1-A, Appeals Chamber, 5 May 2009, para. 81; Kai Ambos, 'Individual Criminal Responsibility', in Otto Triffterer (ed.), *Commentary on the Rome Statute of the International Criminal Court*, 2nd edn (Munich/Oxford: C. H. Beck/Hart, 2008), Art. 25, para. 17.

[96] Article 7(1) of the ICTY Statute; Art. 6(1) of the ICTR Statute.

[97] ICTY, *Blaškić*, Appeal Judgment, para. 46; ICTR, *Prosecutor v. Tharcisse Muvunyi*, Case No. ICTR-00-55-A, Appeals Chamber, 29 August 2008, para. 79; ICTR, *Prosecutor v. Athanase Seromba*, Case No. ICTR-2001-66-A, Appeals Chamber, 12 March 2008, paras 44, 139.

[98] ICTY, *Prosecutor v. Mile Mrkšić and Veselin Šljivančanin*, Case No. IT-95-13/1-A, Appeals Chamber, 5 May 2009, para. 81; ICTY, *Blaškić*, Appeal Judgment, para. 48; ICTR, *Prosecutor v. Dominique Ntawukulilyayo*, Case No. ICTR-05-82-A, Appeals Chamber, 14 December 2011, para. 214.

[99] ICTY, *Blaškić*, Appeal Judgment, para. 49. In a recent Appeal judgment, the ICTY held that if the aider and abettor is remote from relevant crimes, his or her acts have to be 'specifically directed' towards the facilitation of the crimes. *ICTY, Prosecutor v. Momčilo Perišić*, Case No. IT-04-81-A, Appeals Chamber, 28 February 2013, paras 33–44. It remains to be seen whether the Appeals Chamber will uphold this jurisprudence, which would appear to stand in some contrast to its previous jurisprudence, in future decisions.

According to the jurisprudence of the UN *Ad hoc* Tribunals, the state of mind, or *mens rea*, required of the aider and abettor is the knowledge that his or her acts assist the commission of the principal's offence.[100] It is not necessary that the aider and abettor *intended* to provide assistance to a particular crime.[101] In the *Kvočka et al.* case, the Trial Chamber of the ICTY defined the difference between co-perpetration and aiding and abetting as being of a subjective nature: if 'the participant shares the *intent* of the criminal enterprise', he is a co-perpetrator; if he 'only' possesses *knowledge*, he is an aider and abettor.[102] Following this jurisprudence, it would thus be sufficient if the corporate actor only knew that his or her financial transactions or provision of goods would serve in the commission of crimes. This requirement would obviously be fulfilled in cases of weapon deliveries to an armed group that is publicly reputed to systematically commit crimes against civilians, and the corporate actor knows that the weapons provided would most likely facilitate the commission of further crimes. But also trade of natural resources with a local armed group in the knowledge that this group obtains the resources through pillaging, forced labour, enslavement or other international crimes would fulfil the mode of responsibility of aiding and abetting, even if the corporate actor disapproves of the crimes committed.[103]

b   The additional subjective requirement of Article 25(3)(c) of the Rome Statute   However, the provision of the ICC Statute describing the auxiliary[104] mode of liability of aiding and abetting differs slightly from the provision of the UN *Ad hoc* Tribunals in its subjective requirements: Article 25(3)(c) of the Rome Statute requires *in addition* to the

---

[100]   ICTR, *Ntawukulilyayo*, Appeal Judgment, para. 222.

[101]   ICTY, *Blaškić*, Appeal Judgment, para. 49; ICTY, *Prosecutor* v. *Mitar Vasiljević*, Case No. IT-98-32-A, Appeals Chamber, 25 February 2004, para. 102; ICTR, *Nahimana et al.*, Appeal Judgment, para. 482.

[102]   ICTY, *Prosecutor* v. *Miroslav Kvočka et al.*, Case No. IT-98-30/1-T, Trial Chamber, 2 November 2001, paras 265 *et seq.*, at paras 319–20.

[103]   Such interpretation of the *mens rea* standard necessary for aiding and abetting was shared by the Dutch Court of Appeal in The Hague in the case of *Frans van Anraat*, a Dutch businessman who in 1987 and 1988 had supplied the Iraqi regime of Saddam Hussein with large amounts of Thiodiglycol (TDG) in full knowledge that it was a precursor chemical for mustard gas and that the gas would be applied against Kurdish civilians. See *Gerechtshof Den Haag, In the Case of Frans van Anraat* (above), paras 11.16–11.18, 12.1.1.

[104]   See, affirming this view, the Majority Opinion in ICC, *Lubanga*, Judgment, paras 996–8.

auxiliary's knowledge of the crime of the principal that the assistance be rendered 'for the purpose of facilitating the commission of such a crime'. While it is not necessary that the aider and abettor share the perpetrator's specific intent required for a specific crime, the Rome Statute seemingly requires the aider's and abettor's intent to be directed towards the assistance of a crime, and therefore goes beyond the ordinary *mens rea* requirement of Article 30 of the Statute.[105] As the term 'purpose' generally implies a specific subjective requirement that is 'stricter than mere knowledge', the subjective requirement of Article 25(3)(c) goes beyond the standards as stipulated by the jurisprudence of the UN *Ad hoc* Tribunals.[106] This additional requirement has repercussions on the adjudication before the ICC of international crimes committed in the corporate context. As stated above, the primary interest of the corporate actor typically lies in economic profit. The commission of crimes as an effect of the business transaction, be this a delivery of services, or goods or any other auxiliary business activity, will often be an unpleasant consequence deplored by the corporate actor while, at the same time, he or she accepts the crimes as 'collateral damage'. In this case, he or she could not be held liable as an aider or abettor pursuant to Article 25(3)(c) of the Rome Statute as he or she would be missing the necessary volitional element; while pursuant to the jurisprudence of the UN *Ad hoc* Tribunals he or she could be held liable as an auxiliary. If one considers, together with the UN *Ad hoc* Tribunals, that the knowledge standard for aiding and abetting properly reflects customary international law, the question arises as to why the drafters of the Rome Statute raised the *mens rea* requirement without any apparent need to do so.[107]

---

[105] Ambos, 'Individual Criminal Responsibility', Art. 25, para. 23; Werle, *Principles of International Criminal Law*, para. 492. See also Farrell, 'Attributing Criminal Liability to Corporate Actors', p. 882.

[106] Ambos, 'Individual Criminal Responsibility', Art. 25, para. 23. See, however, Perišić Appeal judgment, paras 34–44, on the 'specific direction' requirement. Interestingly, the majority of the judges considered specific direction to be an objective element of criminal responsibility (*actus reus*). See Joint Separate Opinion of judges Theodor Meron and Carmel Agius, Case No. IT-04-81-A, 28 February 2013. See, in contrast to this – doubtful – new jurisprudence ICTY, *Mrkšić and Šljivančanin* Appeal judgment, para. 159.

[107] It bears noting that the ICC is under no obligation to reflect the state of customary law as it is a treaty-bound organisation. See ICC, *Katanga and Ngudjolo Chui*, Confirmation Decision, para. 508. For a detailed and comprehensive discussion of the issue, see also Farrell, 'Attributing Criminal Liability to Corporate Actors', pp. 882–93.

c   Assisting the commission of a group crime, Article 25(3)(d) of the
Rome Statute   However, possible future proceedings before the ICC
against international economic actors may turn the problem with Article
25(3)(c)'s *mens rea* requirement to a mere academic exercise: Article
25(3)(d) of the Rome Statute provides that a person who contributes in
any way to the commission of a crime by a group of persons acting with a
common purpose can be held criminally responsible if he or she inten-
tionally contributed to the crime in the mere knowledge of the group's
intention to commit the crime.[108] As for the objective requirements, this
mode of liability serves as a catch-all rule encompassing any form of
assistance, regardless of whether it is significant or substantial, let alone
essential for the commission of the group crime.[109] In most cases, in the
focus of international criminal courts, the local or national business
partner of the international corporate actor will be a corporate, political
or other entity comprising a plurality of persons pursuing a common
and, at least in part, criminal purpose that the business transaction is
destined to assist or facilitate. Hence, the vast majority of cases that the
UN *Ad hoc* Tribunals' legal framework would deal with as cases of aiding
and abetting international crimes would fall with regard to the *actus reus*
of the crime under Article 25(3)(d) of the Rome Statute.

---

[108] Subparagraph (d) is an almost literal copy of Art. 2, para. (3)(c) of the International
Convention for the Suppression of Terrorist Bombings, UN Doc. A/RES/52/164 (1998);
ILM 249 (1998); 2149 *UNTS* 284. The subparagraph differs from traditional conspiracy
provisions in that it requires a direct participatory act and at least a contribution to the
collective attempt of a crime. See Ambos, 'Individual Criminal Responsibility', Art. 25,
para. 24.

[109] In the case of the *Prosecutor* v. *Callixte Mbarushimana* before the ICC, the Pre-Trial
Chamber opined that by way of a *de minimis* gravity threshold, 'in order to be criminally
responsible under article 25(3)(d) of the Statute, a person must make a significant
contribution to the crimes committed or attempted'. See ICC, *Prosecutor* v. *Callixte
Mbarushimana*, Decision on the Confirmation of Charges, Case No. ICC-01/04-01/10-
465-Red, 16 December 2011, para. 285. At the same time, the Pre-Trial Chamber
rejected the idea that the contribution should be more than significant, that is, substantial or even essential (*ibid.*, paras 278–82). The Appeals Chamber refrained from a
discussion of the Pre-Trial Chamber's definition as it was not relevant to the outcome
of the appeal (ICC, *Prosecutor* v. *Callixte Mbarushimana*, Case No. ICC-01/04-01/10 OA
4, Judgment on the Appeal of the Prosecutor against the Decision of Pre-Trial Chamber
I, 16 December 2011, entitled 'Decision on the Confirmation of Charges', 30 May 2012,
paras 65–6). For a forceful argument against the Pre-Trial Chamber's postulate of a
gravity threshold in Art. 25(3)(d) of the Rome Statute, see *ibid.*, Separate Opinion of
Judge Silvia Fernandez de Gurmendi, paras 7 *et seq.* For a general overview, see Werle,
Principles of International Criminal Law, para. 494.

Further, under this mode of responsibility, the contributor's mental element is in the first place directed towards the own contributive act ('such contribution shall be intentional'[110]), while mere knowledge suffices regarding the crime intended by the principal perpetrators ('be made in the knowledge of the intention of the group to commit the crime').[111] On its face, the term 'intentional' could be understood as reminiscent of a specific intention provision (*dolus specialis*), which can be found, for instance, in the 'intent to destroy' mental requirement of Article 6 of the Rome Statute on the crime of genocide. However, the existence of additional specific subjective requirements contained in subparagraphs (i) and (ii) of Article 25(3)(d) directed at the principals' crimes rather suggests that the term 'intentional' merely qualifies the contributor's own contribution,[112] and reflects, in a declaratory manner, the general *dolus* provision 'knowledge and intent' of Article 30 of the Rome Statute.[113] It remains unclear, however, whether this knowledge and intent of the contributor in Article 25(3)(d), second sentence, is directed at the contributive act *as such* (i.e., the purchase of goods, the selling of weapons) or at the fact that the act *contributes to a crime*. Again, the subjective qualifications of subparagraphs (i) and (ii) of Article 25(3)(d) regarding the contributor's mental disposition towards the principals' crime(s) suggest that the contributor's intent regarding his or her own conduct is indeed limited to the knowledge of the act *as such*.[114]

Finally, it is not entirely clear whether Article 25(3)(d) of the Rome Statute requires that the contributor to the group crime be aware of the *specific* crime(s) intended by the group. While the wording of Article 25(3)(d) allows for such a narrow interpretation ('made in the knowledge of the intention ... to commit *the crime*'[115]), a systemic analysis of Article 25(3)

---

[110] Rome Statute, Art. 25(3)(d), second sentence.

[111] Rome Statute, Art. 25(3)(d)(ii). See also Farrell, 'Attributing Criminal Liability to Corporate Actors', pp. 880–1.

[112] Rome Statute, Art. 25(3)(d), second sentence.

[113] Ambos, 'Individual Criminal Responsibility', Art. 25, para. 28; concurring, Werle, *Principles of International Criminal Law*, para. 495 and n. 268.

[114] Conversely, even if one demanded that the intent has to be directed towards the knowledge that the auxiliary's act contributes to the (attempted) commission of a group crime, this would merely create the same subjective requirement as in the case of aiding and abetting pursuant to the jurisprudence of the UN *Ad hoc* Tribunals (intent as regards the own participatory act), and would therefore not threaten to 'overburden' Art. 25(3)(d) of the Rome Statute as regards its *mens rea* requirements vis-à-vis other modes of liability.

[115] Rome Statute, Art.25(3)(d)(ii) (emphasis added).

may suggest otherwise. When subparagraphs (c) and (d) of Article 25(3) refer to the 'commission of such a crime', they in fact refer to the chapeau of Article 25(3), stipulating a person's liability for 'a crime within the jurisdiction of the Court'. It follows the inner logic of the provision of Article 25(3) that the term 'the crime' in subparagraph (d)(ii) likewise refers to the chapeau of Article 25(3) and not the *specific* crime envisaged by the group. Furthermore, the jurisprudence of the UN *Ad hoc* Tribunals has firmly established that it is not necessary that the aider and abettor knows either the precise crime that was intended or the one that was, in the event, committed.[116] The auxiliary must merely be aware of the 'essential elements' of the crime committed by the principal offender.[117] This jurisprudence can be considered as an expression of international customary law.[118]

There are good reasons to apply this jurisprudence to the ICC's provision for aiding and abetting, since overburdening the mental element of the aider and abettor would threaten to obfuscate the *mens rea* distinction between the principal perpetrator pursuant to Article 25(3)(a) and the auxiliary in Article 25(3)(c) and (d) of the Rome Statute.[119] In the light of the identical *telos* of the UN *Ad hoc* Tribunals' and the ICC's provisions on criminal liability of an auxiliary to the crime, it is reasonable to assume that the contributor in Article 25(3)(d) merely needs to be aware of the essential elements of the crime that was ultimately committed by the principals. Translated into the context of the corporate actor trading with armed groups, it could suffice in the circumstances of the case that the corporate actor was aware that armed attacks against civilians are being carried out with the traded weapons. Knowledge of specific killings, executions or other serious bodily harm resulting from

---

[116] ICTY, *Blaškić*, Appeal Judgment, para. 50: 'If [the auxiliary] is aware that one of a number of crimes will probably be committed, and one of those crimes is in fact committed, he has intended to facilitate the commission of that crime, and is guilty as an aider and abettor', quoting, as an example, the 'Risikoerhöhungstheorie' ('theory of added peril') in German law, BGHSt. 42, 135–9. See also ICTY, *Mrkšić and Šljivančanin*, Appeal Judgment, paras 49, 159; ICTR, *Nahimana et al.*, Appeal Judgment, para. 482.

[117] The auxiliary must merely be aware of the 'essential elements' of the crime committed by the principal offender; see ICTY, *Vasiljević*, Appeal Judgment, para. 102; ICTY, *Prosecutor* v. *Vidoje Blagojević and Dragan Jokić*, Case No. IT-02-60-A, Appeals Chamber, 9 May 2007, para. 221.

[118] See Ambos, *Internationales Strafrecht*, § 7, para. 41; Werle, *Principles of International Criminal Law*, para. 492.

[119] Werle, *Principles of International Criminal Law*, para. 492.

such attacks would arguably not be necessary. Likewise, the corporate actor's knowledge would suffice that in the mine from which the purchased diamonds originate, civilians are being subjected to illicit exploitation and forced labour – knowledge of specific killings, torture, detention and slavery would not have to be proven in court.[120]

F Conclusion

International criminal responsibility for international corporate actors still remains largely uncharted territory. While some domestic legal systems acknowledge corporate criminal liability of legal persons, it is not, however, established whether customary international law provides for this. In recent years, the possible involvement of international corporate actors in grave crimes has increasingly caught international attention, as illustrated in resolutions of the UN General Assembly and the Security Council, as well as statements of the Office of the Prosecutor of the ICC. Recent examples of resource wars, in particular on the African continent, demonstrate that international corporate actors involved in business within zones of ongoing armed conflict often fuel and exacerbate these conflicts. It is now time to adjust the system of international criminal justice to the modern landscape of perpetrators of the worst crimes in armed conflict – including corporate actors. The statutes of the UN *Ad hoc* Tribunals and the Rome Statute contain provisions that allow the criminal prosecution of individual corporate representatives. While it may be difficult to obtain the evidence necessary to hold those actors criminally accountable before an international criminal court due to their remoteness from the crimes, the first case has yet to be made. For the victims of these conflicts there is much to lose – and much to gain for peace and international justice.

---

[120] As a caveat to these examples, it has to be underlined that the exact factual circumstances that have to be embraced by the contributor's *mens rea* are subject to the specific circumstances of each case, and can therefore not be generalised too far. The above examples are thus rather of an illustrative nature.

PART II

International investment and human rights

4

Investment tribunals and human rights treaties: a sociological perspective

MOSHE HIRSCH*

I Introduction

Sociology of law involves the study of how social factors influence the development and enforcement of law.[1] As elaborated below, sociological analysis casts a new light on a significant dimension of the relationships between different branches of international law and enriches our understanding of the social factors involved in the inclination by legal decision-makers to incorporate or reject legal rules developed in other branches of international law. This chapter aims to analyse the particular set of interactions between two branches of international law – human rights and investment treaties – from a sociocultural perspective. The basic argument of this chapter is that legal interactions between various branches of international law may also be analysed as *social interactions between the relevant communities*.

Sociological analysis of international law[2] begins from the premise that individuals' behaviour and normative choices are significantly affected by

* I am grateful to Ohad Abrahami for excellent research assistance. This chapter draws upon M. Hirsch, 'The Interaction between International Investment Law and Human Rights Treaties: A Sociological Perspective', in Y. Shany *et al.* (eds), *Multi-Sourced Equivalent Norms* (Oxford: Hart, 2011), p. 211; M. Hirsch, 'Human Rights and Investment Tribunals' Jurisprudence Along the Private/Public Divide', in T. Weiler and F. Baetens (eds), *New Directions in International Economic Law: In Memorial of Thomas Walde* (New York: Brill, 2011), p. 5.
[1] 'Sociology of Law', in N. Abercrombie, S. Hill and B. S. Turner (eds), *The Penguin Dictionary of Sociology*, 4th edn (London: Penguin, 2000), p. 338.
[2] See, e.g., M. Hirsch, 'The Sociology of International Law', *University of Toronto Law Journal* 55 (2005): 891; A. T. Lang, 'Some Sociological Perspectives on International Institutions and the Trading System', in C. B. Picker, I. D. Bunn and D. Arner (eds), *International Economic Law: The State and Future of the Discipline* (Portland: Hart, 2008), p. 73; R. Goodman and D. Jinks, 'How to Influence States: Socialization and International Human Rights Law', *Duke Law Journal* 54 (2004): 621; R. Goodman and D. Jinks,

their social context and sociocultural factors.[3] The sociological core
assumptions regarding the influential role of social factors on individual
behaviour are extended to the economic realm by *economic sociology*.[4]
Existing literature demonstrates that sociocultural factors (such as values
and norms) influence international economic relations among states and
individuals.[5]

Different legal rules regulating international economic activities reflect
different sociocultural values and affect social processes, such as socialisation, conformity and social exclusion. The link between international
economic law and sociocultural factors is evident in the special rules
for trade in cultural goods and services (e.g., films and television pro-
grammes), 'seen as vehicles for transmitting intangibles that are the
essence of a society: ideas, values, identity and a sense of shared experience and community'.[6] This relationship between international trade
and culture is also discernable with regard to trade in other products
and services. Similarly, the impact of sociological factors on the formation, content and implementation of regional trade agreements (RTAs) is
well documented in economic and legal literature. From a sociological

'Incomplete Internationalization and Compliance with Human Rights Law', *European
Journal of International Law* 19 (2008): 725.

[3] On this presumption in sociology, see, e.g., A. Giddens, *Sociology*, 5th edn (Cambridge,
Polity Press, 2006), pp. 7–8; M. Hollis, *The Philosophy of Social Science* (Cambridge
University Press, 1994), pp. 112–13; S. H. Heap, M. Hollis, B. Lyons, R. Sugden and
A. Weale, *The Theory of Choice: A Critical Guide* (Blackwell, Oxford, 1992), pp. 63–4;
J Scott, *Sociological Theory* (Aldershot: Elgar, 1995), p. 1.

[4] M. Granovetter, 'Economic Action and Social Structure: The Problem of Embeddedness',
in R. Swedberg (ed.), *Economic Sociology* (Cheltenham: Elgar, 1996), pp. 239, 245. See also
F. Dobbin, 'The Sociological View of the Economy', in F. Dobbin (ed.), *The New Economic
Sociology: A Reader* (Princeton University Press, 2004), p. 5.

[5] For empirical studies on impact of social factors on trade and investment, see, e.g.,
M. Noland, 'Affinity and International Trade', Institute for International Economics
Working Paper No. WP 05-3 3, June 2005, p. 8 and references therein. See also
A. Cheptea, 'Trade and Cultural Affinity', paper presented at the 2007 RES Conference,
23 February 2007, available at: editorialexpress.com/cgi-bin/conference/download.cgi?
db_name=res2007&paper_id=643; J. Frankel, *Regional Trading Blocs in the World Eco-
nomic System* (Washington, DC: Institute for International Economics, 1997), pp. 45–6;
J. I. Siegel, A. N. Licht and S. H. Schwartz, *Egalitarianism, Cultural Distance, and FDI:
A New Approach*, 2 January 2008, available at SSRN: ssrn.com/abstract=957306. See also
M. Grinblatt and M. Keloharju, *Distance, Language, and Culture Bias: The Role of Investor
Sophistication*, Yale ICF Working Paper No. 00-04, Yale SOM Working Paper No. ICF
00-04, February 2000, available at SSRN: ssrn.com/abstract=222169.

[6] A. McCaskill, 'Culture and the International Trade Rules: Issues and Outlook', available at:
www.cdc-ccd.org/First_Conference_en/McCaskill_en.doc.

perspective, it is clear that these agreements are embedded in sociocultural relations among state societies. Thus, the formation of RTAs is influenced by sociocultural factors, and the provisions of RTAs often reflect different sociocultural values prevailing in the involved societies and the particular region.[7]

Analysis of sociological factors involved in various international economic activities is likely to affect legal policy regarding the interpretation of various legal rules, including the relationships between different branches of international law, particularly norms deriving from international investment law and human rights treaties.

II Investment tribunals' approach to international human rights law

The relationship between various norms established through different international instruments has recently attracted considerable attention from international law scholars.[8] Questions relating to the interactions between investment law and other spheres of international law have scarcely been discussed in international legal literature.[9] The ongoing proliferation of international investment agreements, the increasing number of treaties in other branches of international law, and the considerable growth of investor–state arbitration are likely to enhance the prospects for overlaps between obligations included in investment and non-investment instruments. Thus, arguments regarding the relationship between norms arising from investment and non-investment instruments (either consistent or inconsistent rules) are brought by

[7] For a sociological analysis of regional trade agreements, see M. Hirsch, 'The Sociology of International Economic Law: Sociological Analysis of the Regulation of Regional Agreements in the World Trading System', *European Journal of International Law* 19 (2008): 277.

[8] See ILC, 'Report on the Work of its 58th Session: Conclusion 2, Conclusions of the work of the Study Group on the Fragmentation of International Law: Difficulties Arising from the Diversification and Expansion of International Law', 2006, UN Doc. A/61/10, para. 251. See also 'Diversity or Cacophony?: New Sources of Norms in International Law Symposium', *Michigan Journal of International Law*, 25 (Special Issue) (2004).

[9] See M. Hirsch, 'Interactions between Investment and Non-Investment Obligations in International Investment Law', in P. Muchlinski, F. Ortino and C. Schreuer (eds), *The Oxford Handbook of International Law on Foreign Investment* (Oxford University Press, 2008), p. 262; however, A. van Aaken, 'Fragmentation of International Law: The Case of International Investment Protection', *Finnish Yearbook of International Law* (2008), University of St Gallen Law and Economics Working Paper No. 2008-1, available at: ssrn.com/abstract=1097529.

different parties (host states, foreign investors and NGOs) arising at different stages of international litigation, that is, during discussions on liability (*Suez* v. *Argentina*)[10] and remedies (e.g., *Santa Elena* v. *Costa Rica*).[11]

In certain cases, investment tribunals were ready to interpret investment treaty provisions according to legal rules developed in other branches of international law and apply them to investment disputes. In fact, investment tribunals very often resorted to international rules regarding state responsibility[12] or treaty law.[13] Similarly, investment tribunals were ready to apply 'general principles of law' with regard to investments involving corruptive or fraudulent practices.[14]

When encountering *inconsistent* rules derived from international investment and human rights laws, investment tribunals may draw upon secondary rules developed in the sphere of public international law for the purpose of ordering the hierarchy between rules; rules such as Article 53 of the Vienna Convention on the Law of Treaties (regarding *jus cogens*) and Article 30 of the same convention (regarding the *lex posteriori* rules).[15] While investment tribunals frequently resort to the interpretative provisions of the Vienna Convention, they have not so far significantly invoked the above regulatory rules included in Article 30 or 53 of this convention.

---

[10] *Suez, Sociedad General de Aguas de Barcelona SA and Vivendi Universal SA* v. *Argentine Republic*, ICSID, Case No. ARB/03/19 (France–Argentina and Spain–Argentina BITs), Decision on Liability, 30 July 2010, para. 256, available at:www.italaw.com/documents/SuezVivendiAWGDecisiononLiability.pdf.

[11] *Santa Elena* v. *Costa Rica*, ICSID Review: Foreign Investment Law Journal 15 (2000): 169, para. 71 (regarding the relationship between international environmental treaty and investment obligations).

[12] On the application of rules of state responsibility by investment tribunals, see, e.g., K. Hober, 'State Responsibility and Attribution', in P. Muchlinski, F. Ortino and C. Schreuer (eds), *The Oxford Handbook of International Law on Foreign Investment* (Oxford University Press, 2008), p. 549.

[13] On the application of the 1969 Vienna Convention on the Law of Treaties by investment tribunals, see C. Schreuer, 'Diversity and Harmonization of Treaty Interpretation in Investment Arbitration', *Transnational Dispute Management* 3 (April 2006), available at: www.transnational-dispute-management.com.

[14] *World Duty Free* v. *Kenya*, ICSID Case No. ARB/00/7, Award, 4 October 2006, paras 136–57, available at: www.italaw.com/documents/WDFv.KenyaAward.pdf; *Inceysa Vallisoletana SL* v. *Republic of El Salvador*, ICSID Case No. ARB/03/26, Award, 2 August 2006, para. 242, available at: www.italaw.com/documents/Inceysa_Vallisoletana_en_001.pdf.

[15] On these rules of general international law, see, e.g., M. Hirsch, 'Sources of International Investment Law', ILA Study Group on the Role of Soft Law Instruments in International Investment Law, 21 July 2011, pp. 23–6, available at: http://papers.ssrn.com/sol3/papers.cfm?abstract_id=1892564.

Analysis of investment tribunals' decisions relating to human rights instruments reveals that while these tribunals often incorporate rules of general international law (particularly on state responsibility and treaty law), they adopt a quite consistent approach *opposing* the incorporation of international human rights law in investment disputes.[16] With the exception of the 2002 *Mondev* award,[17] investment tribunals have declined to thoroughly examine the specific provisions of international human rights instruments invoked by the parties, notwithstanding the various arguments raised during different stages of litigation by the various parties.

Investment tribunals have offered various reasons for their reserved approach with regard to the application of human rights instruments in investment relations. These include lack of sufficiently elaborated arguments by the parties (e.g., the *Azurix*[18] and *Siemens*[19] cases); lack of jurisdiction (e.g., the *Biloune*,[20] *Euro-Tunnel*[21] and *Aguas del Tunari*[22] cases); and the difference between the two branches of international law (e.g., the *Azurix* Annulment award[23]

---

[16] See, e.g., M. Hirsch, 'Investment Tribunals and Human Rights: Divergent Paths', in P. M. Dupuy, E. U. Petersmann and F. F. Francioni (eds), *Human Rights in International Investment Law and Arbitration* (Oxford University Press, 2009), p. 97.

[17] *Mondev International Ltd* v. *United States of America*, ICSID Case No. ARB(AF)/99/2, Award, 1 October 2002, para. 1, available at: www.italaw.com/documents/Mondev-Final.pdf.

[18] *Azurix* v. *Argentina*, ICSID Case No. ARB/01/12, Award, 14 July 2006, para. 3, available at: www.italaw.com/documents/AzurixAwardJuly2006.pdf.

[19] *Siemens* v. *Argentina*, ICSID Case No. ARB/02/8, Award, 6 February 2007, para. 79, available at:www.italaw.com/documents/Siemens-Argentina-Award.pdf.

[20] *Biloune* v. *Ghana*, UNCITRAL, 1993, 95 *ILR* 183, 2002–203.

[21] *Channel Tunnel Group* v. *Governments of the United Kingdom and France*, Partial Award, 30 January 2007, paras 151, 153, available at: www.pca-cpa.org/upload/files/ET_PAen.pdf.

[22] *Aguas del Tunari SA* v. *Bolivia*, ICSID Case No. ARB/02/3, Petition of La Coordinadora para la Defensa del Agua y Vida, and others to the Arbitral Tribunal, 29 August 2002, paras 47 and 48, available at: www.italaw.com/documents/Aguaaboliviapetition.pdf. Letter from the President of the Tribunal in the Matter of *Aguas del Tunari* v. *The Republic of Bolivia*, 29 January 2003, available at: www.law.berkeley.edu/faculty/ddcaron/Documents/ICSID%20Arbitrations/ARB-02-3_NGO_Petition_ICSID_Response_2003.pdf.

[23] The Azurix Annulment Committee stated as follows: '128. Argentina also has referred by analogy to the European Convention on Human Rights and NAFTA. As the extent of the protections afforded by an investment protection treaty depends in each case on the specific terms of the treaty in question, the Committee regards comparisons with differently-worded treaties as of limited utility, especially treaties outside the field of investment protection. It is noted that the European Court of Human Rights has held that (subject to possible exceptions) a shareholder in a company does not have standing to bring a claim for a violation of the company's rights under Article 1 of Protocol No. 1 of the European Convention on Human Rights, and that the mere fact that there has been a

and the *Siemens* case[24]). In some cases the tribunals did not elaborate the reasons for this approach.[25]

In several cases, investment tribunals were ready to examine the impact of the European human rights law on investment disputes (the *Mondev*, *Tecmed*[26] and *Azurix* awards). Thus, for instance, the *Tecmed* and *Azurix* tribunals cited the case law of the European Court of Human Rights (ECtHR) (the *James* case)[27] in order to underline the vulnerability of investors in foreign countries. A later attempt by Argentina to apply the same ECtHR judgment was dismissed by the *Siemens* tribunal, which emphasised the inconsistency between the European Convention's rules regarding the 'margin of appreciation' and international investment law.[28] In the *Saipem* case, the tribunal cited the ECtHR jurisprudence to conclude that rights under judicial decisions are protected property capable of being the object of an expropriation, and that court decisions can amount to an

---

violation of the company's rights under Article 1 of Protocol No. 1, does not of itself mean that there has been a violation of the shareholder's rights under that provision. However, such an approach does not inform the situation where a law or treaty might confer certain rights directly on a shareholder which would be violated by an injury to the company, or answer the question whether the shareholder could have standing to bring a claim in that event.' *Azurix Corp.* v. *The Argentine Republic*, Decision on the Application for Annulment of the Argentine Republic, para. 128, available at:http://icsid.worldbank. org/ICSID/FrontServlet?requestType=CasesRH&actionVal=viewCase&reqFrom=Home& caseId=C5.

[24] *Siemens* v. *Argentina*, above n. 19, para. 354.

[25] See, e.g., *Sempra* v. *Argentina*, ICSID Case No. ARB/02/16, Award, 28 September 2007, paras 4, 93, 225, available at: www.italaw.com/documents/SempraAward.pdf. Similarly, certain activities mentioned in the Decision on Annulment in the *Mitchell* v. *DRC* (mainly seizure of property and incarceration) raise human rights issues, but there is no indication that the tribunal addressed these issues. *Patrick Mitchell* v. *Democratic Republic of Congo*, ICSID Case No. ARB/99/7, Decision on the Application for Annulment of the Award, 1 November 2006, para. 1, citing para. 23 of the Award of 9 February 2004 (not publicly available). Cited in C. Reiner and C. Schreuer, 'Human Rights and International Investment Arbitration', below. n. 54, at 88.

[26] *Tecmed* v. *Mexico*, ICSID Case No. ARB(AF)/00/2, Award, 29 May 2003, para. 122, available at: www.italaw.com/documents/Tecnicas_001.pdf; *Azurix* v. *Argentina*, above, n. 18, para. 261.

[27] *James and Others* v. *The United Kingdom* [1986] ECHR 2 (21 February 1986), para. 50. See *Tecmed* v. *Mexico*, above, n. 26, para. 122; *Azurix* v. *Argentina*, above, n. 18, para. 261.

[28] *Siemens* v. *Argentina*, above, n. 19, para. 354. On this part of the award, see L. Liberti, 'The Relevance of Non-investment Treaty Obligations in the Assessment of Compensation', *Transnational Dispute Management* 4(6) (2007).

expropriation.[29] In the *CMS* case, the tribunal concluded, after analysing the relevant circumstances, that the issues disputed by the parties did not raise the 'question of affecting fundamental human rights'.[30]

In all of the above cases dealing with the interaction between investment and human rights instruments, not one investment tribunal has absolved a party from its investment obligations or reduced the amount of compensation as a result of the consideration of human rights instruments.

III Sociocultural distance and interactions between branches of international law

As discussed above, while investment tribunals very often resort to international rules regarding state responsibility or treaty law, they are generally reluctant to accord significant weight to human rights treaties in international investment law. The generally negative approach displayed by investment tribunals towards the application of human rights treaties may be explained by various factors. This chapter focuses on sociocultural factors relating to the social settings in which these rules of international law are formed, interpreted and implemented.

Sociologists of law have long emphasised that law is 'always rooted in communities'; and laws are considered by these scholars as expressive types of these communities.[31] The basic argument of this chapter is that legal interactions among branches of international law may also be analysed as *social interactions* between the relevant communities. These

---

[29] *Saipem SpA* v. *Bangladesh*, ICSID Case No. ARB/05/07, Decision on Jurisdiction and Recommendation on Provisional Measures, 21 March 2007, paras 130 and 132.

[30] *CMS Gas Transmission* v. *Argentina*, ICSID Case No. ARB/01/08, Final Award, 12 May 2005, para. 121. For Argentina's argument in this regard, see para. 114, available at: www.italaw.com/documents/CMS_FinalAward_000.pdf.

[31] R. Cotterrell, *Law, Culture and Society: Legal Ideas in the Mirror of Social Theory* (Aldershot: Ashgate, 2006), pp. 117, 161. The link between societal processes and normative behaviour has long been recognised in sociological literature, and the founders of sociology appreciated the central role of law (together with economy, politics and cultural institutions) in the modern world. R. Banakar and M. Travers, 'Classical Sociology and Law', in R. Banakar and M. Travers (eds), *An Introduction to Law and Social Theory* (Oxford: Hart, 2002), pp. 9, 10; W. M. Evan, 'Law and Society', in E. F. Borgatta and M. L. Borgatta (eds), *Encyclopedia of Sociology*, vol. 3 (New York: Macmillan, 1992), p. 1075.

legal interactions are affected by the particular features of relevant social settings, as well as by the mutual relationships between the relevant social groups. More specifically, the *sociocultural distance*[32] between the particular international legal settings affects the inclination of relevant decision-makers to incorporate or reject legal rules developed in other branches of international law. Generally, greater sociocultural 'distance' between the involved social settings and groups decreases the prospects for mutual incorporation of legal rules developed in the other legal sphere. Thus, the inclination or disinclination of investment tribunals to accord a significant role to human rights treaties is influenced by the cultural distance between these two branches of international law. This chapter does not aim to develop a sophisticated scale for measuring sociocultural distance between various branches of international law, but rather to assess the distance between international investment and human rights laws and discuss its implications.

IV   The sociocultural distance between investment and human rights laws

The social settings in which international investment[33] and human rights laws emerge and are interpreted are very different. The members of the two communities pursue extremely different career paths. While most

---

[32] The element of cultural distance in predicting *trade* between countries is often included in the famous 'gravity model'. Generally, national cultural distance can be defined as the degree to which the shared norms and values in one country differ from those in another. Various studies suggest that an increasing cultural distance (manifested, e.g., by language, religious beliefs, colonial past) reduces the amount of trade between countries. S. Beugelsdijk, H. de Groot, G. J. Linders and A. Slangen, 'Cultural Distance, Institutional Distance and International Trade', ERSA Conference Papers, ersa04p265, 2004, pp. 3–5, available at: www-sre.wu-wien.ac.at/ersa/ersaconfs/ersa04/PDF/265.pdf; A. Cheptea, 'Trade and Cultural Affinity', paper presented at the 2007 RES Conference, 23 February 2007, available at: editorialexpress.com/cgi-bin/conference/download.cgi?db_name=res2007&paper_id=643; G. Hofstede, *Culture's Consequences: Comparing Values, Behaviors, Institutions, and Organizations across Nations* (London: Sage, 2001); B. Tadesse and R. White, 'Does Cultural Distance Hinder Trade in Goods? A Comparative Study of Nine OECD Member Nations', *Journal of Open Economies Review* 21 (2010): 237; B. Tadesse and R. White, 'Cultural Distance as a Determinant of Bilateral Trade Flows: Do Immigrants Counter the Effect of Cultural Distance?' *Applied Economics Letters*, forthcoming, available at: papers.ssrn.com/sol3/papers.cfm?abstract_id=1078045.

[33] On other cultural aspects of some investment agreements and decisions, see A. Froehlich, 'Cultural Matters in Investment Agreements and Decisions', in A. Reinisch and C. Knahr (eds), *International Investment law in Context* (Utrecht: Eleven International, 2008), p. 141.

human rights lawyers work in legal divisions of NGOs or academia, foreign investment lawyers (and arbitrators) are predominantly senior lawyers/practitioners, legal scholars or former judges affiliated with major international law firms.[34]

While human rights lawyers are often linked to a certain social movement and are determined to take sides in political or moral struggles,[35] most investment lawyers are anxious to maintain a professional and neutral position.[36] These divergent career paths mean that the members of the two communities undergo starkly different socialisation processes.[37] Thus, for instance, while investment lawyers are inclined to emphasise the importance of the unimpeded flow of capital, legal predictability and stability, as well as a market economy ideology; human rights lawyers are more concerned with universal values and underline the primacy of human rights over other international legal rules (including international economic treaties).

Each community has a distinct heritage and narratives. For example, while 'the great petroleum arbitrations' during the 1960s and 1970s 'occupy a quasi-mythical position' in international investment law;[38] the adoption of the Universal Declaration of Human Rights and the Tiananmen Square massacre constitute central collective narratives for human rights lawyers. The members of the two communities employ different terminologies. Thus, for example, while human rights lawyers

---

[34] On 'mixing of roles' of arbitrators and lawyers, see Y. Dezalay and B. Garth, *Dealing in Virtue: International Commercial Arbitration and the Construction of a Transnational Legal Order* (University of Chicago Press, 1996), pp. 49–51. See also C. A. Rogers, 'Regulating International Arbitrators: A Functional Approach to Developing Standards of Conduct', *Stanford Journal of International Law* 41 (2005): 53, 56–7. On the important role of large law firms in international arbitration, see Dezalay and Garth, *Dealing in Virtue*, pp. 8, 37–8, 48, 53.

[35] On 'cause' (or 'public interest') lawyers and their determination to take sides in political and moral struggles, see C. S. Shdaimah, 'What's in a Name?: Cause Lawyers as Conceptual Category', Bepress Legal Series Paper No. 903, 2006, available at: law.bepress.com/cgi/viewcontent.cgi?article=4436&context=expresso.

[36] On the importance of neutrality as an element of the 'virtue' of arbitrators, see Dezalay and Garth, *Dealing in Virtue*, pp. 8, 83. On the significance of being distant from politics, see *ibid.*, pp. 45, 98.

[37] 'Socialisation' refers to life-long social experience by which individuals develop their human potential and learn patterns of their culture. Socialisation is an ongoing process by which societies transmit norms and values to new members of the social group. The principal 'agents of socialisation' are the family, school, peer group and the mass media. M. Renzetti and D. J. Curran, *Living Sociology*, 2nd edn (Upper Saddle River, NJ: Pearson, 2000), pp. 106–9; R. J. Brym and J. Lie, *Sociology* (Belont, CA: Wadsworth, 2003), pp. 92–105.

[38] See, e.g., Dezalay and Garth, *Dealing in Virtue*, p. 74.

frequently refer to 'the Covenants' or the CERD, many of them hardly understand terms like MFN, NIEO or 'umbrella clauses'. These different vocabularies point to the fundamental conceptual differences between these spheres of international law.[39] This difference between human rights and investment languages and concepts became clear, for instance, when the *Siemens* tribunal flatly rejected the doctrine of 'margin of appreciation'[40] afforded to states by the ECtHR.[41]

International investment and human rights laws have dissimilar 'legal cultures',[42] and the members of each community hold different views regarding the role of law[43] and the role of tribunals.[44] These two settings diverge along the private–public divide. International

---

[39] On the significance of the language of law, shared tradition and 'kind of brotherhood' of lawyers, Lawrence Friedman noted: 'Any occupational group will make use of verbal shorthand: indeed, any group with shared experiences will do so. Lawyers share a common training, in law schools and universities, This gives them a common culture ... Words, phrases, and memories, drilled into lawyers' heads during training, unite the profession, link it to a shared tradition, mark it as a kind of brotherhood, separated from the layman's world.' L. M. Friedman, *Law and Society: An Introduction* (Upper Saddle River, NJ: Prentice-Hall, 1977), p. 89.

[40] On the margin of appreciation doctrine under international law and the European Convention on Human Rights, see A. Mowbray, *European Convention on Human Rights* (Oxford University Press, 2007), pp. 629–33; Y. Shany, 'Toward a General Margin of Appreciation Doctrine in International Law?' *European Journal of International Law* 16 (2006): 907; E. Benvenisti, 'Margin of Appreciation, Consensus, and Universal Standards', *New York University Journal of International Law and Politics* 31 (1999): 843.

[41] *Siemens v. Argentina*, above, n. 19, para. 354.

[42] As Nelken explains, legal culture is one way of describing relatively stable patterns of legally oriented social behaviour and attitudes. The identifying elements of legal culture range from facts about institutions, such as the number and role of lawyers and controlled, to various forms of behaviour, such as litigation and aspects of ideas, values, aspirations and mentalities. Though numerous studies identify legal culture with the nation-state, patterns of legal culture can, and must, also be sought both at the subnational as well as at the transnational level. D. Nelken, 'Using the Concept of Legal Culture', *Australian Journal of Legal Philosophy* 29 (2004): 1, 3. On the concept of legal culture, see also R. Cotterrell, *Law, Culture and Society* (Aldershot: Ashgate, 2006), pp. 81–96. On the elements of legal culture, see D. Nelken, 'Towards a Sociology of Legal Adaptation', in D. Nelken and J. Feest (eds), *Adapting Legal Cultures* (Oxford: Hart, 2001), pp. 3, 25–6.

[43] On legal cultures and international law, see T. M. Franck, 'The Legal Culture and Culture Culture', *Proceedings of the Annual Meeting: American Society of International Law* (January 1999), available at www.asil.org/files/legalculture.pdf; E. Jouannet, 'French and American Perspectives on International Law: Legal Cultures and International Law', *Maine Law Review* 58 (2006): 292, available at: http://cerdin.univ-paris1.fr/IMG/pdf/French_and_American_Perspectives-version_CERDIN.pdf.

[44] On the economic role in creating the culture of international commercial arbitration, see T. Ginsburg, 'The Culture of Arbitration', *Vanderbilt Journal of Transnational Law* 36

investment and human rights laws deal with asymmetric legal relations between states and individuals, including corporations. States are in a superior position vis-à-vis individuals and foreign investors. Sovereign states may, for example, change the domestic law applicable to individuals, and are in a better position to influence changes in international law.[45] Consequently, legal rules developed in those spheres aim to compensate individuals and corporations found in an inferior position under the domestic law. This goal is predominantly attained by enhancing the latter's legal protection at the international level. While international investment and human rights laws strive to cope with similar structural challenge, they have evolved along different conceptual lines.

International human rights law has largely developed within the public law sphere, and it primarily applies to the relationship between individuals (including legal persons) and the state.[46] Consequently, different freedoms, rights, authorities and obligations have been assigned to individuals and states. In light of the original inferior position of individuals, human rights law has established a long list of individual rights and freedoms to protect weaker individuals in their relationships with government authorities.

(2003): 1335. On legal traditions in international commercial arbitration, see L. Trakman, 'Legal Traditions and International Commercial Arbitration', *American Review of International Arbitration*, (Spring 2007), UNSW Law Research Paper No. 2007-29, available at: papers.ssrn.com/sol3/papers.cfm?abstract_id=986507. See also P. Martinez-Fraga, 'The Convergence of Legal Cultures in Arbitration and Amendments to the New York Convention: If it is Not Broken, Why Fix it, but if it is Good, Make it Better', Jean Monnet/Robert Schuman Paper Series, October 2006, vol. 6, No. 20, available at: www6.miami.edu/eucenter/EU_Long%20Paper20_fall06_MartinezFraga.pdf.

[45] See, e.g., C. N. Brower and S. W. Schill, 'Is Arbitration a Threat or a Boon to the Legitimacy of International Investment Law?' *Chicago Journal of International Law* 9 (2008/9): 471, 478; M. Hirsch, *The Arbitration Mechanism of the International Center for the Settlement of Investment Disputes* (Dordrecht: Kluwer, 1993), pp. 133–4; T. Wälde, 'The Present State of Research Carried Out by the English-speaking Section of the Centre for Studies and Research', *Hague Academy Report on International Investment Law* (2007), pp. 76–9.

[46] The distinction between *jus privatum* (private law) and *jus publicum* (public law) is attributed to the Roman jurist Ulpian, who drew a distinction between laws that govern relations between citizens and the government, and the principles that govern the relations of citizens with one another. T. Rowland, 'Private Law', in *The Philosophy of Law: An Encyclopedia*, vol. II (New York: Garland Publishing, 1999), p. 687. For an insightful analysis of the history of the public–private divide, see M. J. Horwitz, 'The History of the Public/Private Distinction', *University of Pennsylvania Law Review* 130 (1982): 1423–8.

Aiming to cope with a parallel structural pattern, international investment law took a different route; focusing on the private law aspects of the relations between host governments and foreign investors. Consequently, investment tribunals are inclined to attach considerable weight to reciprocal promise-based obligations (arising, for instance, from the investment contract) and reliance-based obligations (arising, for instance, from the host state's pledges), primarily formed during the negotiations and the 'entry stage'.[47] International investment law (both investment treaties and tribunals' jurisprudence) largely aims to protect various private law undertakings made between the host state and the foreign investor.

The public–private divergence between international human rights law and investment law[48] also arises from the different scope of application, as well as from the cogent and non-reciprocal nature of the rules applicable in these spheres. While investment obligations primarily bind the host state and the foreign investor *inter se*, international human rights obligations reflect fundamental values of the international community[49] and have *erga omnes* application.[50]

The public nature of international human rights law clearly arises from the mandatory character of these rights. In contrast to private *jus dispositivum* obligations, some fundamental human rights are considered as *jus cogens*.[51] Furthermore, unlike the emphasis on reciprocal obligations

[47] During the negotiations towards a contract and the 'entry stage', the gap between the parties' legal capacities is relatively small. Following this stage, the superior position of the host state regarding its influence upon the content of both domestic and international law is glaring. In light of these asymmetric relations, investment tribunals are inclined to level the normative field and emphasise the obligations included in the investment agreement and presentations made during the 'entry stage', as well as various circumstances prevailing at this critical stage, such as the information available to both parties in this phase.

[48] On the public–private divide and investment disputes, see G. van Harten, 'The Public–Private Distinction in the International Arbitration of Individual Claims Against the State', 24 August 2009, available at SSRN: http://ssrn.com/abstract=1461125; W. W. Burke-White and A. von Staden, 'Private Litigation in a Public Law Sphere: The Standard of Review in Investor–State Arbitrations', University of Pennsylvania Law School, Public Law Research Paper No. 09–23, 28 August 2009, available at SSRN: http://ssrn.com/abstract=1465899.

[49] See, e.g., Preamble, Institute of International Law, Resolution on Obligations *Erga Omnes* in International Law, available at: www.idi-iil.org/idiE/resolutionsE/2005_kra_01_en.pdf.

[50] See, e.g., Institute of International Law, Resolution on Obligation *Erga Omnes*.

[51] On the peremptory nature of fundamental human rights, see, e.g., T. Koji, 'Emerging Hierarchy in International Human Rights and Beyond', *European Journal of International Law* 12 (2001): 917, 927; T. Meron, 'On a Hierarchy of International Human Rights', *American Journal of International Law* 80 (1986): 1.

in investment law, the compelling nature of human rights obligations results in the prohibition on the use of countermeasures infringing fundamental human rights.[52]

An examination of the *institutional* features of human rights and investment law also reveals the public–private split between these two spheres. Investors' rights are primarily protected by arbitral tribunals that are for the most part established by bilateral or trilateral investment treaties. Investment arbitral tribunals are regularly established on an *ad hoc* basis, premised on the parties' autonomy[53] and consent,[54] so they tend to adopt the private *inter partes* model that characterises international commercial arbitration.[55]

Thus, for instance, in the *Aguas del Tunari* v. *Bolivia* case, a request by an NGO to, *inter alia*, submit *amicus curiae* briefs (based also on the

---

[52] See Art. 50(1)b) of the International Law Commission's Rules on Responsibility of States for Internationally Wrongful Acts (2001), available at: http://untreaty.un.org/ilc/texts/instruments/english/draft%20articles/9_6_2001.pdf. See also Art. 60(5) of the 1969 Vienna Convention on the Law of Treaties, (1969) 8 *ILM* 679, 701; 1979 *ILC Yearbook*, vol. II, Pt 2, 116; 1992 *ILC Yearbook*, vol. II, Pt 2, 32–3. M. Craven, 'Legal Differentiation and the Concept of the Human Rights Treaty in International Law', *European Journal of International Law* 11 (2000): 489.

[53] On the major role of parties' autonomy and private aspects of international economic arbitration, Bagheri notes: 'In essence, arbitration is an institution by which individuals adjudicate disputes privately insofar as the law allows. The distinguishing factor of this form of private justice is its consensual and voluntary nature.' M. Bagheri, 'Party Autonomy in its Jurisdictional Capacity: The Place of International Commercial Arbitration', in M. Bagheri (ed.), *International Contracts and National Economic Regulation* (London: Kluwer, 2000), pp. 95, 106. This author also states: 'The supremacy of private initiative in international trade and investment is recognized once it is translated into the legal notion of party autonomy in international economic transactions' (p. 113).

[54] See, e.g., the following statement regarding the jurisdiction of ICSID tribunals: 'Consent of the parties is the cornerstone of the jurisdiction of the Centre', Report of the Executive Directors on the Convention on the Settlement of Investment Disputes Between States and Nationals of other States, 1965, available at: www.worldbank.org/icsid/basicdoc/partB-section05.htm. On the major role of the parties' consent in arbitral investment proceedings and the ensuing limited competence to address human rights issues, see C. Reiner and C. Schreuer, 'Human Rights and International Investment Arbitration', in P. M. Dupuy, E. U. Petersmann and F. Francioni (eds), *Human Rights in International Investment Law and Arbitration* (Oxford University Press, 2009), p. 82.

[55] See, e.g., Wälde, 'The Present State of Research', pp 75–6; G. van Harten, *Investment Treaty Arbitration and Public Law* (Oxford University Press, 2007), pp. 5–6, 58; G. van Harten and M. Loughlin, 'Investment Treaty Arbitration as a Species of Global Administrative Law', *European Journal of International Law* 17 (2006): 121, 126–45. On the dominant private features of international arbitration, see also C. Rogers, 'The Vocation of International Arbitrators', *American University International Law Review* 20 (2005): 944, 957, 993–4.

1966 International Covenant of Civil and Political Rights)[56] was turned down by the tribunal, explaining that:

> it is the Tribunal's unanimous opinion that your core requests are beyond the power or the authority of the Tribunal to grant. *The interplay of the two treaties involved* [the ICSID Convention and the BIT] *and the consensual nature of arbitration places the control of the issues you raise with the parties, not the Tribunal.*[57]

One of the significant factors influencing the character of investment tribunals as *inter partes* or public dispute settlement mechanisms relates to the exposure of their proceedings to the public, as well as the participation of public interest groups in the legal proceedings. Generally, investment arbitration proceedings are not open to the public, tribunals do not disclose copies of written pleadings and other documents submitted to them, and oral hearings are also closed to the public.[58] The prevailing atmosphere of confidentiality in most investment arbitral proceedings tends to intensify the adjudicators' perception that their principal role is settling a private dispute between the specific parties, while diminishing the weight given to broader public interest often related to human rights.

In contrast to *ad hoc* investment arbitration, human rights tribunals (like the European and Inter-American courts of human rights) present plain public features: they are permanent courts and their proceedings are regularly open to the public. Unlike the enforcement of investment obligations, exposure of human rights violations to the public is a major instrument for inducing states to respect their international obligations ('the politics of shame').[59]

---

[56] *Aguas del Tunari SA* v. *Republic of Bolivia*, ICSID Case No. ARB/02/3 (Netherlands–Bolivia BIT), NGO Petition to Participate as *Amici Curiae*, 29 August 2002, available at: http://ita.law.uvic.ca/documents/Aguaaboliviapetition.pdf.

[57] Letter from President of Tribunal Responding to Petition, 29 January 2003, available at www.ita.law.uvic.ca/documents/Aguas-BoliviaResponse.pdf (emphasis added).

[58] As noted by Knahr and Reinisch, the most restrictive rules are included in UNCITRAL Arbitration Rules, ICSID tribunals handle confidentiality issues rather restrictively, and access to documents is easier in the context of NAFTA chapter 11 proceedings. For a detailed analysis of the arbitration rules of UNCITRAL, ICSID and NAFTA, see C. Knahr and A. Reinisch, 'Transparency versus Confidentiality in International Investment Arbitration: The Biwater Gauff Compromise', *International Courts and Tribunals* 6 (2007): 97, 98–103; J. Delaney and D. B. Magraw, 'Procedural Transparency', in P. Muchlinski, F. Ortino and C. Schreuer (eds), *The Oxford Handbook of International Law on Foreign Investment* (Oxford University Press, 2008), p. 721.

[59] See, e.g., J. H. Lebovic and E. Voeten, 'The Politics of Shame: The Condemnation of Country Human Rights Practices in the UNCHR', *International Studies Quarterly* 50 (2006): 861.

Tribunals regularly fulfil two principal functions: settling disputes between the particular rival parties and developing standards for future behaviour. Different tribunals emphasise different roles, and the perception of adjudicators often influences the content of their decisions. Generally, tribunals emphasising their law-making role are more likely to take into account wider public policy considerations (including those relating to human rights), seeking a due balance between the competing principles. On the other hand, tribunals that perceive their role as 'merely' settling the specific dispute between the particular parties (the *'inter partes* model') are less likely to grant significant weight to the broader policy issues reflected in non-investment treaties. Most investment tribunals incline to adopt the *'inter partes* model' (which is prevalent in commercial arbitration) and grant precedence to their role as settlers of disputes between the particular litigants.[60]

The predominantly private character of investment tribunals, and their emphasis on the private–commercial aspects of investment disputes, may well explain the ingrained inclination of those tribunals not to focus on public policy issues (such as human rights obligations) involved in investment disputes. Most of those investment tribunals that did refer to human rights jurisprudence often cited the case law of the European Court of Human Rights in order to protect investors' rights.[61]

The relationship between the human rights and investment communities is often characterised by mistrust and antagonism. These hostile relationships were prominent during attempts to establish the comprehensive Multilateral Agreement on Investment (MAI) that failed in 1998,[62] as well as during the failed negotiations to formulate an additional WTO agreement on investment (1996–2004). Indeed, one of the

---

[60] See, e.g., *Glamis Gold* v. *United States of America*, Award, 8 June 2009, paras 3 and 7, available at: www.naftalaw.org/Disputes/USA/Glamis/Glamis-USA-Award.pdf; Wälde, 'The Present State of Research', pp. 75–6; van Harten, *Investment Treaty Arbitration and Public Law*, pp. 5–6, 58.

[61] See, e.g., on *Tecmed*, *Azurix* and *Saipem* awards in section II, above.

[62] On the MAI, see M. J. Trebilcock and R. Howse, *The Regulation of International Trade*, 2nd edn (New York: Routledge, 2005), pp. 459–60; M. Matsushita, T. J. Schoenbaum and P. C. Mavroidis, *The World Trade Organization: Law, Practice and Policy*, 2nd edn (Oxford University Press, 2006), pp. 833–5; A. B. Zampetti and P. Sauve, 'International Investment', in A. T. Guzman and A. O. Sykes (eds), *Research Handbook in International Economic Law* (Northampton, MA: Elgar, 2007), pp. 211, 249–51.

significant factors leading to these negotiation failures relates to the opposition of human rights and environmental NGOs.[63]

To sum up, in light of the considerable sociocultural distance between investment and human rights law, and the deep-rooted tensions between the relevant communities, it is not surprising that investment tribunals are generally reluctant to accord significant weight to human rights treaties in international investment law. Thus, the substantial sociocultural distance between these sociocultural settings parallels the normative distance between these branches of international law.

When a *non*-investment tribunal encountered legal issues involving investment and human rights rules, it did not hesitate to grant significant weight to human rights treaties. When the Southern African Development Community Tribunal discussed international legal rules applicable to expropriations undertaken by the government of Zimbabwe, it did not hesitate to apply human rights treaties.[64] In contrast to investment tribunals, however, this is a permanent tribunal (established in 1992), and its members are appointed for a five-year term and may be re-appointed for an additional five-year term.[65]

---

[63] See, e.g., UNCTAD, 'Lessons from the MAI', 1999, pp. 24–25 available at: www.unctad.org/en/docs/psiteiitm22.en.pdf; Trebilcock and Howse, *The Regulation of International Trade*, pp. 457–61; Matsushita *et al.*, *The World Trade Organization*, pp. 836–8; Zampetti and Sauve, 'International Investment', pp. 249–51; 'WTO: Members Decide on Way Forward in Doha Round', *Bridges Weekly Trade News Digest*, vol. 7, No. 43, 17 December 2003. See also R. Geiger, 'Multilateral Approaches to Investment: The Way Forward', in J. E. Alvarez and K. P. Sauvant, *The Evolving International Investment Regime* (Oxford University Press, 2011), pp. 153, 159.

[64] *Campbell* v. *Zimbabwe* Southern African Development Community Tribunal, (2008), pp. 19–21, 47–51, available at: www.zwnews.com/Ruling281108.pdf.

[65] The tribunal was established in 1992 as part of the SADC Treaty (South African Development Community), Art. 9(g); and became operational in 2005, see website at: www.sadc.int/tribunal. Its jurisprudence is based on the SADC Treaty, along with other treaties, general rules of public international law and principles of the Law of States (Art. 21 of the Tribunal's Protocol). The tribunal comprises five regular members, along with a pool of five replacement members selected by the president in case a regular member is ill or unavailable (Art. 3(2) of the Protocol). Sessions are administered by a panel of three members unless the tribunal decides on a full bench of five (Art. 3(3) of the Protocol). The sessions are held in public unless the tribunal or one of the parties requests otherwise (Rule 45 of the Tribunal's Rules of Procedure). Members are appointed for a period of five years with the option of being appointed for another five (Art. 6(1) of the Protocol). On the SADC Tribunal, see also, e.g., the tribunal website at: www.sadc.int/tribunal; O. C. Ruppel and F. X. Bangamwabo, 'Chapter 8 – The SADC Tribunal: A Legal Analysis of its Mandate and Role in Regional integration', *Monitoring Regional Integration in Africa Yearbook*, 1 (2008); J. Pauwelyn, 'Going Global, Regional or Both? Dispute Settlement in the Southern African Development Community (SADC) and Overlaps with the WTO and Other Jurisdictions', *Minnesota Journal of International Law* 13 (2004): 231, 239–40.

V   Buds of change?

Social factors and processes change over time, and social patterns affecting the sociocultural distance between investment and human rights law are also likely to be modified. The inclination of investment arbitrators to incorporate or reject rules derived from human rights instruments may be altered, for example, following changes in the 'demographic composition' of investment arbitrators (including their social background), changes in the mutual interactions between the two communities (e.g., increasing direct interpersonal interactions between the members of the two communities) or modifications in the external environment in which investment tribunals operate.

Recent developments highlight certain buds of change and they may signify more willingness on the part of investment arbitrators to increase the weight of human rights treaties in investment disputes. Several recent developments are likely to exert further pressure on investment arbitrators to accord a greater weight to broader public interests (including human rights): the trend to enhance the transparency of investment tribunal proceedings to the public;[66] the growing criticism of certain private features underlying the contemporary investment arbitration system;[67] the resolution of the EU Parliament (April 2011) calling, *inter alia*, for the inclusion of human rights provisions in future investment treaties with developing countries;[68]

---

[66] On this trend, see, e.g., *Biwater Gauff* v. *United Republic of Tanzania*, ICSID Case No. ARB/05/22, Procedural Order, 29 September 2006, para. 114, available at: icsid.worldbank.org/ICSID/FrontServlet?requestType=CasesRH&actionVal=showDoc&docId=DC531_En&caseId=C67; Knahr and Reinisch, 'Transparency versus Confidentiality in International Investment Arbitration', p. 97; W. W. Park, *Arbitration of International Business Disputes* (Oxford University Press, 2006), pp. 42–3; J. E. Vinuales, '*Amicus* Intervention in Investor–State Arbitration', *Dispute Settlement Journal* 61 (2007): 72.

[67] See, e.g., van Harten, *Investment Treaty Arbitration and Public Law*, pp. 5–6, 58–9; W. W. Burke-White and A. von Staden, 'Private Litigation in a Public Law Sphere: The Standard of Review in Investor–State Arbitrations', *Yale Journal of International Law* 35 (2010): 283, at pp, 288, 297–8. See also the European Parliament Resolution, 6 April 2011, below, n. 68, Articles 24 and G.

[68] Article 37 of the European Parliament Resolution on the future European international investment policy, 6 April 2011 provides: '37. Notes that investment risk is generally higher in developing and least developed countries and that strong, effective investor protection in the form of investment treaties are key to protecting European investors and can improve governance, thereby bringing about the stable environment needed to increase FDI into these countries; notes that, for investment agreements to further benefit these countries, they should also be based on investor obligations in terms of compliance

and the Australian Government's statement expressing opposition to investor–state dispute settlement.[69]

The increasing awareness of investment tribunals to the public interest is reflected in a series of decisions on the impact of corruptive practices on investment proceedings. The *World Duty Free* tribunal emphasised the impact of bribery on the public:

> The answer, as regards public policy, is that *the law protects not the litigating parties but the public*; or in this case, the mass of tax-payers and other citizens making up one of the poorest countries in the world.[70]

Similarly, the tribunal in the *El Salvador* case found that the claimant's investment had been fraudulently made (involving forged documents). The tribunal stated that international public policy bars the parties from benefiting from their own fraud, and ruled that the dispute was not arbitrable under the El Salvador–Spain treaty.[71]

More importantly, two recent investment awards explicitly state that investor rights do not trump international human rights. Facing arguments that the right to water trumps Argentina's obligations under bilateral investment treaty,[72] the *Suez* tribunal rejected any contradiction between these legal rules and hinted that human rights and investment treaty obligations have an equal legal status:

---

with human rights and anti-corruption standards as part of a broader partnership between the EU and developing countries for the purpose of reducing poverty; calls on the Commission to assess viable future partners, drawing on Member State best practices with BITs', available at: www.europarl.europa.eu/sides/getDoc.do?type=TA&reference=P7-TA-2011-0141&format=XML&language=EN.

[69] See J. Kurtz, 'The Australian Trade Policy Statement on Investor–State Dispute', *ASIL Insights* 15(22) (2011), available at: www.asil.org/insights110802.cfm.

[70] *World Duty Free* v. *Kenya*, above, n. 14, para. 181 (emphasis added).

[71] *Inceysa Vallisoletana SL* v. *Republic of El Salvador*, above, n. 14. Similarly, the arbitrator (Lagergren) stated in the famous case No. 1110 (1963) of the International Chamber of Commerce that bribery constituted a 'gross violation of good morals and international public policy', and he ruled that jurisdiction must be declined in this case (cited in *Duty Free World* v. *Kenya*, para. 148).

[72] The tribunal summarised the argument as follows: 'Argentina and the *amicus curiae* submissions received by the Tribunal suggest that Argentina's human rights obligations to assure its population the right to water somehow trumps its obligations under the BITs and that the existence of the human right to water also implicitly gives Argentina the authority to take actions in disregard of its BIT obligations.' *Suez and Vivendi* v. *Argentina*, ICSID Case No. ARB/03/19, Decision on Liability, 30 July 2010, para. 262, available at: www.italaw.com/documents/SuezVivendiAWGDecisiononLiability.pdf.

> Argentina is subject to both international obligations, i.e. human rights and treaty obligation, *and must respect both of them equally*. Under the circumstances of these cases, Argentina's human rights obligations and its investment treaty obligations are not inconsistent, contradictory or mutually exclusive. Thus, as discussed above, Argentina could have respected both types of obligations.[73]

It seems that the *Phoenix* tribunal went one step further, implicitly recognising the primacy of certain fundamental human rights over investors' rights. While discussing the close links between investment treaties and general international law,[74] the tribunal provided the following example:

> To take an extreme example, nobody would suggest that ICSID protection should be granted to investments made in violation of the most fundamental rules of protection of human rights, like investments made in pursuance of torture or genocide or in support of slavery or trafficking of human organs.[75]

To sum up, though investment tribunals have generally been reluctant to accord significant weight to human rights treaties and, until now, declined to absolve parties (it is significant to write 'parties' and not 'states') from their investment obligations or to reduce the amount of compensation, the above new developments may signify some change regarding the increasing awareness of investment tribunals to the public interest, including enhancing the role of human rights instruments in international investment law.

VI Concluding remarks

The small number of publications addressing the sociology of international law is conspicuous in light of the noticeable contribution of sociological theories to the disciplines of law[76] and international relations

---

[73] *Suez and Vivendi* v. *Argentina*, para. 262 (emphasis added).
[74] *Phoenix Action Ltd* v. *Czech Republic*, ICSID Case No. ARB/06/5, Award, 15 April 2009, para. 77, available at: www.italaw.com/documents/PhoenixAward.pdf.
[75] *Phoenix* v. *Czech Republic*, para. 78.
[76] On the sociology of law, see, e.g., Cotterrell, *Law, Culture and Society*; D. Milovanovic, *An Introduction to the Sociology of Law*, 3rd edn (Monsey, NY: Criminal Justice Press, 2003); R. Cotterrell, *The Sociology of Law*, 2nd edn (Oxford: Butterworths, 1992); G. Gurvitch, *Sociology of Law*, Law and Society Series (Piscataway, NJ: Transaction Publishers, 2001); W. M. Evan, *The Sociology of Law* (New York: Free Press, 1980), p. 1; R. Banakar and M. Travers (eds), *An Introduction to Law and Social Theory* (Oxford: Hart, 2002).

theory.[77] The preceding sections seek to analyse the approach of investment tribunals vis-à-vis human rights treaties from a sociocultural perspective. As discussed above, investment tribunals are generally reluctant
to accord significant weight to human rights treaties in international
investment law.

This chapter has argued that the relationships between these two
branches of international law may be analysed as social interactions
between the relevant communities. These legal interactions are affected
by the particular features of relevant social settings, as well as the mutual
relationships between the relevant social groups. More specifically, it is
argued that the sociocultural distance between the particular international legal settings affects the inclination of relevant decision-makers
to incorporate or reject parallel legal rules developed in other branches
of international law. An analysis of the relationships between the social
settings involved in international human rights and investment laws
reveals a considerable sociocultural distance between these branches of
international law. In light of this distance, and the deep-rooted tensions
between the relevant communities, it is not surprising that investment
tribunals are generally reluctant to accord significant weight to human
rights treaties in international investment law.

The existing social and normative distance between investment and
human rights laws is likely to change in the future as past experience
shows that the relationship between various branches of international law
is often dynamic. Future sociocultural changes within each community – or
changes in the social interactions between the relevant communities –
may narrow the normative distance between international human rights
and investment law. Though investment tribunals have generally been

---

[77] On the constructivist approach in international relations theory, see, e.g., M. Barnett,
'Social Constructivism', in J. Baylis and S. Smith (eds), *The Globalization of World
Politics*, 3rd edn (Oxford University Press, 2005), p. 251; A. Wendt, *Social Theory of
International Politics* (Cambridge University Press, 1999); E. Adler, 'Cognitive Evolution:
A Dynamic Approach for the Study of International Relations and their Progress', in
E. Adler and B. Crawford (eds), *Progress in Postwar International Relations* (New York:
Columbia University Press, 1991), p. 43; J. G. Ruggie, *Constructing the World Polity*
(London: Routledge, 1998), pp. 11–14; M. Finnemore, 'Construction of Norms of Humani-
tarian Intervention', in P. J. Katzenstein (ed.), *The Culture of National Security: Norms and
Identity in World Politics* (New York: Columbia University Press, 1996), p. 153; E. Adler,
'Seizing the Middle Ground: Constructivism in World Politics', *European Journal of
International Relations* 3 (1997): 319; E. Adler, 'Constructivism and International Rela-
tions', in W. Carlsnaes, T. Risse and B. A. Simmons (eds), *Handbook of International
Relations* (London: Sage, 2001), p. 95.

reluctant to accord significant weight to human rights treaties and, until now, have declined to absolve parties from their investment obligations or to reduce the amount of compensation, recent developments may signify some change regarding the increasing awareness of investment tribunals to the public interest, including the role of human rights instruments in international investment law.

The interaction of international investment arbitration and the rights of indigenous peoples

JUDITH LEVINE[*]

1 Introduction

This chapter explores the interaction of international investment law with the rights of indigenous peoples. The crossover of these growing subfields of public international law may arise in a variety of ways in the context of investor–state arbitration, as described in section 2 of this chapter. First, indigenous people might be the investor claimants in an arbitration against a state and invoke the specific protections owed to indigenous peoples in support of their claim. Second, a foreign investor might complain about measures taken by a host state that were put in place for purposes of regulating or protecting the rights of indigenous peoples. Third, a foreign investor might complain if a host state has failed to protect against actions taken by indigenous groups that adversely affect the investment. Fourth, a group of indigenous people, who are not parties to an arbitration but nevertheless have an interest in the case, might intervene in the proceedings to make submissions about the potential relevance of the rights of indigenous peoples.

Section 3 examines how some arbitral tribunals have recently dealt with (or chosen not to deal with) arguments that the rights of indigenous peoples should be taken into account when interpreting and applying the provisions of investment treaties. Arbitral tribunals constituted pursuant to investment treaties are not the only bodies to have confronted the crossover of investment and indigenous rights. As described in section 4, human rights bodies have also had occasion to consider conflicting rights of indigenous people with the rights of foreign investors under investment

---

[*] This chapter was presented as part of the human rights panel at the April 2011 Leiden conference on the 'Interaction of International Investment Law with Other Fields of Public International Law'. Any views expressed in this chapter are personal to the author and are not attributable to the permanent Court of Arbitration.

treaties. The most direct, and least controversial, way in which an investment tribunal might take into account the rights of indigenous peoples would be if the investment treaty itself provided a textual basis for doing so. Section 5 highlights how a few states have expressly acknowledged the possible interaction of international investment law and indigenous rights in the actual text of their investment treaties.

Such express references in investment treaties to indigenous rights specifically, or even to human rights more generally, remain quite rare. As discussed in section 6, absent express provision in a treaty, some commentators have argued that adjudicative bodies, when faced with two possible treaty interpretations, should opt for the one that is most consistent with other norms of international law, under a presumption that states would have intended to comply with all their obligations under international law. Todd Weiler, for example, noted that indeed 'harmonious construction is mandatory'.[1] Moshe Hirsch observed that the individuals who typically constitute the arbitral tribunals in investment treaty disputes have different professional outlooks to those who specialise in human rights, and that this divide has given risen to a *de facto* barrier to harmonising international investment and human rights norms.[2] As will be seen, the recent cases dealing with the overlap of indigenous rights with investment law present an interesting counterpoint to this observation, both as to the constitution of the tribunals and as to the approach they have taken towards 'reconvergence' or 'harmonisation' of the two fields of international law.

Before proceeding with the above topics, two preliminary matters are set out in this introduction. First, the author sheds some light on the recent experience of the Permanent Court of Arbitration (PCA) with respect to international investment arbitration and human rights generally. Second, the potential sources of law concerning the rights of indigenous peoples are briefly canvassed.

1.1   The PCA's experience with investment arbitration and human rights

Established in 1899, the PCA is the oldest intergovernmental organisation dedicated to the resolution of international disputes.[3] The PCA

---

[1] T. Weiler, Human rights panel discussion, April 2011 Conference, Leiden University.

[2] M. Hirsch, 'Investment Tribunals and Human Rights Treaties: A Sociological Perspective', Chapter 4, this volume.

[3] International Convention for the Pacific Settlement of International Disputes, adopted 29 July 1899, entered into force 4 September 1900 (1898–99), 187 CTS 410. Available at: www.pca-cpa.org/showpage.asp?pag_id=1187.

today is a vibrant institution situated at the juncture between public and private international law, and dedicated to meeting the rapidly evolving dispute resolution needs of the international community.[4] In addition to its continuing prominence as registry for large-scale inter-state and intra-state arbitrations,[5] the PCA administers disputes between private parties and states, and has a unique role as designating or appointing authority under the UNCITRAL Rules of Arbitration.[6] During the last ten years the PCA has seen more case activity than it did cumulatively during the previous hundred years.[7]

One large factor in this renaissance has been the surge in investor–state arbitrations under bilateral and multilateral investment treaties.[8] The PCA has administered more than eighty-eight investor–state arbitrations since 2001, when *Saluka Investments BV* v. *Czech Republic* was instituted.[9] As at March 2013, there were over forty-eight investor–state arbitrations on the PCA's docket, including under bilateral investment treaties, the Energy Charter Treaty and the North American Free Trade Agreement (NAFTA). In a handful of these cases, the parties raised human rights issues. The PCA operates under a duty of confidentiality. Therefore, absent an express waiver by the parties, it is not possible to describe these cases in any detail. However, the following broad brush strokes are offered to illustrate the type of scenarios in which human rights issues have emerged in investor–state arbitrations administered by the PCA.[10]

---

[4] See generally, P.-J. le Cannu and D. Drabkin, 'Assessing the Role of the Permanent Court of Arbitration in the Peaceful Settlement of International Disputes', *L'Observateur des Nations Unies* 27 (2010): 181; M. L. Kuscher, 'The Role of the Permanent Court of Arbitration: Ensuring Efficiency, Transparency, and Neutrality', paper presented at Conference of the World Jurist Association, Mauritius, April 2011 (publication forthcoming).

[5] For example, in the *Abyei* arbitration between the government of Sudan and the Sudan People's Liberation Movement/Army, available at: www.pca-cpa.org/showpage.asp?pag_id=1306. See B. Daly, 'The Abyei Arbitration: Procedural Aspects of an Intra-State Border Arbitration', *Leiden Journal of International Law* 23 (2010): 801.

[6] The UNCITRAL Arbitration Rules were adopted by the UN General Assembly in 1976 and a revised version was adopted in 2010, available at: www.uncitral.org/uncitral/en/uncitral_texts/arbitration/2010Arbitration_rules.html. See generally S. Grimmer, 'The Permanent Court of Arbitration and the UNCITRAL Arbitration Rules', *CEU Ediciones, Serie Arbitraje y Resolución Alternativa de Controversias*, No. 5, 2009.

[7] See, e.g., PCA Annual Report 2011, available at: www.pca-cpa.org/showpage.asp?pag_id=1069.

[8] J. Levine, 'Navigating the Parallel Universe of Investor–State Arbitrations under the UNCITRAL Rules', in C. Brown, K. Miles and L. Nottage (eds), *Evolution and Revolution in Investment Arbitration* (Cambridge University Press, 2011), 369.

[9] Available at: www.pca-cpa.org/showpage.asp?pag_id=1149.

[10] In no PCA-administered investment arbitration as at the time of the Leiden Conference in April 2011, had a party made arguments specifically about the intersection of

In at least four cases, the investor claimants (or individuals associated with the claimants) have commenced separate complaint proceedings with regional or international human rights bodies based on their treatment by the host state. Some of the facts giving rise to the human rights complaints are the same as those underpinning the alleged violations of investment treaty protections that form the subject of the parallel arbitrations. In at least three cases, investor claimants have referenced the findings of regional or international human rights bodies, as well as reports of NGOs, to provide factual context and to support their complaints about the host state's conduct.

In at least three cases, regional human rights treaties or the jurisprudence from human rights courts have been invoked by claimants in support of their legal arguments. For example, human rights case law has been offered to reinforce arguments about non-retroactivity of treaties, to support arguments of excessive delay in national courts in connection with denial of justice claims, to prove the lack of independence in the judiciary to show that exhaustion of local remedies would be futile, or to flesh out the obligations under a minimum standard of treatment. In at least one case, the respondent state argued that overlap and incompatibilities between the BIT in question and a regional human rights regime deprived the tribunal of jurisdiction.[11]

In the PCA's experience therefore, it is neither exclusively investors nor exclusively states that have been the parties raising human rights issues. Similarly, as described in section 2, indigenous rights issues have been invoked in investment arbitrations sometimes by investors, sometimes by states, and sometimes even by non-parties.

---

investment law and *indigenous* rights. Thus, indigenous rights presented a relatively safe topic for the author to explore without divulging sensitive details of pending PCA cases. The author does not purport to be an expert on indigenous rights, although she has encountered indigenous rights issues in private practice on commercial arbitrations involving Latin America; during editorial work for the *Indigenous Law Bulletin* (UNSW, Australia); working at the High Court of Australia on various cases relating to aboriginal rights and native title; and as an adviser to the Australian Attorney-General.

[11] The parties to this case have consented to publication of the jurisdictional award. See *Eureko BV v. Slovak Republic*, PCA Case No. 2008-13, Award on Jurisdiction, Arbitrability and Suspension, 26 October 2010, available at: www.pca-cpa.org/showpage.asp?pag_id=1414, paras 58, 69, 111, 131.

1.2   Sources of law protecting the rights of indigenous peoples

A complex web of legal protections might apply to indigenous peoples.[12] On a domestic level, indigenous rights may be dealt with via a multi-layered system of constitutional protections – federal, state and local legislation and regulations – as well as case law. There are several international instruments specific to indigenous peoples, the most notable being the UN Declaration on the Rights of Indigenous Peoples of 2007 (UNDRIP).[13] UNDRIP was adopted by the General Assembly with 143 states in favour, eleven abstentions and four against (Australia, Canada, New Zealand and the United States). All four have since expressed support for UNDRIP.[14] Another key international instrument specific to the rights of indigenous peoples is the International Labour Organization Convention concerning Indigenous and Tribal Peoples in Independent Countries (ILO Convention 169).[15]

More general international instruments on human rights, such as the International Covenant on Civil and Political Rights of 1966 (ICCPR)[16] and the International Convention on the Elimination of All Forms of Racial Discrimination (CERD)[17] are also of potential relevance to protecting the rights of indigenous peoples. Likewise, regional human rights instruments and decisions of regional human rights bodies may provide sources of protection to indigenous people, for example, the American Convention on Human Rights (American Convention)[18] and the African Charter on Human and Peoples' Rights (African Charter).[19]

---

[12] For a detailed description, see, e.g., International Law Association Committee on the Rights of Indigenous People, Interim Report (2010), available at: www.ila-hq.org/en/committees/draft-committee-reports-the-hague-2010.cfm; A. Xanthaki, 'Indigenous Rights in International Law over the Last 10 Years and Future Developments', *Melbourne Journal of International Law* 10 (2009): 27; S. J. Anaya, *Indigenous Peoples in International Law*, 2nd edn (New York: Oxford University Press, 2004).

[13] GA Resolution 61/295, UN GAOR, 61st sess., 107th plen mtg, UN Doc. A/RES/61/295, 13 September 2007, text available at: www.un.org/esa/socdev/unpfii/en/drip.html.

[14] See, e.g., Canada's announcement, available at: www.ainc-inac.gc.ca/ap/ia/dcl/stmt-eng.asp; Australia's announcement was on 3 April 2009; New Zealand's announcement was on 20 April 2010. The US position is currently under review, and Colombia and Samoa have since removed their abstentions.

[15] 1989 International Labour Organization Convention Concerning Indigenous and Tribal Peoples in Independent Countries, 28 *ILM* 1382 (1989), text available at: www.ilo.org/dyn/normlex/en/f?p=1000:12100:0::NO::P12100_ILO_CODE:C169.

[16] 1966 International Covenant on Civil and Political Rights, 999 *UNTS* 171.

[17] 1965 International Convention on the Elimination of All Forms of Racial Discrimination, 660 *UNTS* 195.

[18] 1969 American Convention on Human Rights, 1144 *UNTS* 123.

[19] 1981 African Charter on Human and Peoples' Rights, 1520 *UNTS* 217.

The above sources seek to protect the rights of indigenous peoples, *inter alia*, to: (i) self-determination;[20] (ii) traditional and cultural activities and natural resources;[21] (iii) be consulted and participate in matters that affect them;[22] (iv) development and management of indigenous lands;[23] (v) be free from discrimination;[24] (vi) access sacred sites;[25] (vii) maintain and develop contacts across borders;[26] and (viii) redress for violations of these rights.[27] The extent to which some of these sources are binding, for example, as having 'crystallised into customary law and/or reflect[ing] existing treaty obligations' is the subject of some uncertainty.[28] As will be seen, the relevance of these sources within the context of an investment arbitration has also been the subject of debate and will depend on the legal and factual circumstances in any case.

2 Scenarios in which the rights of indigenous peoples have arisen in investor–state arbitrations

Although there are not many reported cases of investor–state arbitrations where indigenous rights issues have arisen, the few examples that do exist demonstrate that the issues can arise via different players and means.

First, indigenous people may be the *investor claimants* in an arbitration against a state. Such claimants might invoke indigenous rights as a 'sword' to strengthen their claims of violation of the investment treaty. This occurred in the case of *Grand River Enterprises. v. United States*

[20] UNDRIP, Art. 3; ICCPR, Art. 1(1); African Charter, Art. 20(1).
[21] UNDRIP, Arts 5, 8, 11–12, 14–15, 20, 25–9, 31–2, 36; ILO Convention, Arts 13–15, 23, 32; ICCPR, Arts 1(2), 27; CERD, Art. 5(d)(vi); American Convention, Art. 16; African Charter, Arts 17(2), 21(1).
[22] UNDRIP, Arts 5, 18, 27; ILO Convention, Arts 6–7; ICCPR, Art. 25; CERD, Art. 5(c); American Convention, Art. 23; African Charter, Art. 13.
[23] UNDRIP, Arts 8, 10, 25–9, 32; ILO Convention, Arts 13–19.
[24] UNDRIP, Arts 2, 9, 14(2), 16, 21(1), 22(2), 24(1), 29(1); ILO Convention, Arts 3(1), 4(3), 20(2), 24; ICCPR, Art. 26; American Convention, Arts 1, 24; African Charter, Arts 18(3), 28; see generally CERD.
[25] UNDRIP, Arts 11–12.   [26] UNDRIP, Art. 36; ILO Convention, Art. 32.
[27] UNDRIP, Arts 8, 11, 20, 28, 32; ILO Convention, Art. 12; American Convention, Art. 44.
[28] International Law Association Committee on the Rights of Indigenous Peoples, First Report (2008), p. 3, available at: www.ila-hq.org/en/committees/index.cfm/cid/1024. See also, International Law Association Committee on the Rights of Indigenous People, Interim Report (2010), pp. 6, 13, 15–16, 23, 35, 43–52, available at: www.ila-hq.org/en/committees/draft-committee-reports-the-hague-2010.cfm; Xanthaki, 'Indigenous Rights in International Law' pp. 34–7.

('*Grand River*'), [29] in which the individual claimants were members
of indigenous peoples, or First Nations, belonging to the Six Nations of
the Iroquois Confederacy, also known as the Haudenosaunee. The claimants were involved in tobacco production and distribution, and were
considered Canadian citizens for the purposes of NAFTA. In December
2004, they commenced an arbitration against the United States, contend-
ing that certain actions taken by some US states to implement the 1998
Master Settlement Agreement (the deal which was brokered between
certain states and major tobacco manufacturers to settle a mass
tobacco-related lawsuit) violated their rights as Canadian investors under
NAFTA Chapter Eleven. The claimants argued, *inter alia*, that as indigenous people, they were entitled to a 'heightened level of vigilance and
care', which required more proactive consultations.[30] They contended
that the United States had treated them 'contrary to the basic human
rights norms that condition how the customary international law standard of fair and equitable treatment should be interpreted particularly
when the interests of First Nations members and communities are at
stake'.[31] According to the claimants:

> As an evolving norm of customary international law, the duty of States to
> respect and protect the rights and interests of First Nations across
> borders, in good faith, must be considered in the interpretation of treaty
> rights when interests of First Nations individuals are directly involved.[32]

The way in which the *Grand River* tribunal dealt with such arguments is
discussed in more detail in section 2.2 below.

A second way in which the rights of indigenous people might arise in
investor–state arbitrations is in the context of *state actions* motivated
(partially or totally) by policies to regulate or protect indigenous people.
Thus, rather than the claimants invoking indigenous rights, it would be
the states whose actions were either directly or indirectly justified on the
basis of indigenous rights. In this way, indigenous rights might be

---

[29] *Grand River Enterprises Six Nations Ltd et al.* v. *United States of America*, NAFTA,
documents relating to the case are available at: www.state.gov/s/l/c11935.htm.
[30] *Grand River*, Claimants' Memorial on the Merits, 10 July 2008, paras 2, 171, 189–91,
available at: www.state.gov/documents/organization/107684.pdf.
[31] *Grand River*, para. 3.
[32] *Grand River*, para. 150. See also the *Amicus Curiae* Submission of the Office of the
National Chief of the Assembly of Nations, filed on 19 January 2009 in support of the
claimants' arguments, p. 2, available at: www.state.gov/documents/organization/117812.
pdf.

invoked more as a 'shield' than as a 'sword'.[33] In the case of *Glamis Gold Ltd* v. *United States of America* ('*Glamis Gold*'),[34] the investor was a Canadian gold-mining enterprise that complained that the United States had expropriated its investment in violation of obligations under NAFTA, due to actions taken by the United States for purposes of, *inter alia*, regulating or protecting rights of indigenous people. The investor's project had been opposed by members of the Quechan Indian Nation, who believed that it would destroy important cultural and sacred sites, including the 'Trail of Dreams'. The *Glamis Gold* case is discussed in further detail below.[35]

A third scenario in which indigenous rights may arise in an investment arbitration is that in which a foreign investor complains about a *failure by a state* to protect the foreign investor against actions taken by groups of indigenous peoples. For example, in *Burlington Resources Inc.* v. *Ecuador* ('*Burlington*'),[36] the claimant, a US oil company, sued Ecuador for violations of the US–Ecuador BIT. One alleged violation was that Ecuador failed to fulfil its obligation to provide the investment with full protection and security.[37] Burlington argued that Ecuador had failed to take sufficient steps to overcome local indigenous opposition to the

---

[33] See references to the 'black economic empowerment' cases in South Africa and the 'Indigenization Laws' in Zimbabwe below at n. 35.

[34] *Glamis Gold Ltd* v. *United States of America*, NAFTA, documents relating to the case are available at: www.state.gov/s/l/c10986.htm.

[35] Another interesting set of cases relating to the protection of indigenous peoples involve the South African 'black economic empowerment' laws and their impact on foreign investors, such as *Pietro Foresti et al.* v. *Republic of South Africa*, ICSID Case No. ARB (AF)/07/01, Award, 4 August 2010, available at: http://icsid.worldbank.org/ICSID/Front-Servlet?requestType=CasesRH&actionVal=showDoc&docId=DC1651_En&caseId=C90, and claims by European investors against Zimbabwe stemming from its 'indigenization' land laws. See discussion in U. Kriebaum, 'Human Rights of the Population of the Host State in International Investment Arbitration', *Journal of World Investment and Trade* 10 (2009): 653, at p. 666; L. E. Peterson, 'Human Rights and Bilateral Investment Treaties: Mapping the Role of Human Rights Law within Investor–State Arbitration', *Rights and Democracy*, 2009, available at: www.dd-rd.ca/site/_PDF/publications/globalization/HIRA-volume3-ENG.pdf.

[36] *Burlington Resources Inc.* v. *Republic of Ecuador*, ICSID Case No. ARB/08/05, Decision on Jurisdiction, 2 June 2010, available at: http://ita.law.uvic.ca/documents/BurlingtonRe-sourcesInc_v_Ecuador_Jurisdiction_Eng.pdf.

[37] Under the Treaty between the United States and Ecuador concerning the Encouragement and Reciprocal Protection of Investments, 11 May 1997, Art. II(3)(a). For another example of an investment arbitration brought under that Treaty, see *Chevron Corporation and Texaco Petroleum Co.* v. *The Republic of Ecuador*, PCA Case No. 2007-2, 2011, see at: www.pca-cpa.org/showpage.asp?pag_id=1432.

project, which had involved protests, death threats, violent attacks and property damage.[38] With regard to this alleged failure, the tribunal found that the BIT's requirement of a six-month waiting period before arbitral proceedings could commence was not satisfied because Burlington had not notified the respondent of the existence of this particular dispute before instituting proceedings.[39] This outcome highlights a dilemma that investors might face in situations of opposition from indigenous groups. On the one hand, the investor may wish to take a diplomatic stance to encourage the government to assist the investor in dealing with the situation sensitively. On the other hand, the investor needs to assert to the government in clear terms that if the government fails to take action, there is a dispute for the purpose of establishing jurisdiction under the treaty.

Finally, there may be cases where a non-party to the investment arbitration, who nevertheless has an interest in its outcome, seeks to intervene in the proceedings in some capacity in order to bring the rights of indigenous peoples (or lack thereof) to the attention of the tribunal. In the *Glamis Gold* case, for example, the tribunal granted leave to accept a non-party submission by the Quechan Indian Nation.[40] The Quechan submission described 'the established and emerging customary international law principles that impose extensive obligations on States to respect and protect indigenous peoples' sacred sites; their rights to access and use these sites; and their cultural, spiritual, and religious practices'.[41] The Quechan Nation submitted that:

> the Tribunal is required to be mindful of how it construes [Articles 1105 and 1110 of NAFTA] so that they do not require or authorize State conduct of the kind that would conflict with international norms protecting indigenous people ... Such an approach is the only way to ensure consistency in wider public international law.

The tribunal's reaction to the Quechan submission is described further in the next section.

The *Grand River* case saw interventions both from Canada (arguing *against* the invocation of indigenous rights as customary international law) and from the Assembly of First Nations (arguing *in favour* of the invocation of indigenous rights as customary law). Canada, as a

---

[38] *Burlington*, paras 26–37.   [39] *Burlington*, paras 316–18.
[40] *Glamis Gold*, Decision on Application of and Submission by Quechan Indian Nation, 16 September 2005, available at: www.state.gov/documents/organization/53592.pdf.
[41] *Glamis Gold*, Non-party Submission of Quechan Indian Nation, 19 August 2005 (Quechan submission), available at: www.state.gov/documents/organization/52531.pdf.

contracting party to NAFTA, made a submission pursuant to NAFTA, Article 1128, regarding the interpretation of NAFTA, Article 1105. Canada's submission stated, *inter alia*, that ILO Convention 169 and the UNDRIP do not constitute customary international law, and so do not fall within the ambit of Article 1105(1).[42]

The National Chief of the Assembly of First Nations (AFN) wrote a letter to the tribunal to express support for the claimants and to provide the tribunal 'with an informed view about some of the arguments made by the parties concerning the rights of Indigenous peoples under international law'.[43] The letter was submitted after the deadline for non-party submissions, but was nevertheless included as a supporting exhibit to the claimants' reply, and in that context was read and considered by the tribunal.[44] In the letter, the AFN pointed to the obligation of good faith under international law which obligated the government to act in a manner consistent with promises made to, or for the benefit of, indigenous peoples. It was submitted that the promise of 'fair and equitable treatment' in Article 1105 of NAFTA meant that the claimants were entitled to base their legitimate expectations upon their rights as indigenous peoples honoured by NAFTA government officials. Further, the letter pointed to the good faith duty in the ILO Convention 169 to consult indigenous peoples when government action threatens their rights to territory or their economic livelihood, and urged that the failure by the United States to sign the UNDRIP 'cannot mean that their officials should be free to ignore the basic principles of international law reflected in it'.[45] How the tribunal dealt with the arguments of Canada and the AFN is discussed in more detail below.

3   How investment tribunals have dealt with arguments about the rights of indigenous peoples: two examples

This section briefly sets out the different ways in which the *Glamis Gold* and the *Grand River* tribunals dealt with arguments about the interaction of international investment law with international indigenous peoples' rights.

---

[42] *Glamis Gold*, Art. 1128 Submission of Canada, 19 January 2009, available at: www.state. gov/documents/organization/115489.pdf.

[43] *Grand River*, Letter from the National Chief of the Assembly of First Nations to the Tribunal, 19 January 2009, available at: www.state.gov/documents/organization/117812. pdf.

[44] *Grand River*, Award, 12 January 2011, para. 60, available at: www.state.gov/documents/ organization/156820.pdf.

[45] *Grand River*, Award.

3.1   Glamis Gold Ltd *v.* United States

Glamis Gold Ltd, a Canadian mining company, brought a NAFTA claim against the United States for alleged injuries relating to a proposed gold mine in southeastern California. Glamis claimed that certain federal government actions and California state measures with respect to open-pit mining operations resulted in the expropriation of its investments in violation of NAFTA, Article 1110, and denied its investments the minimum standard of treatment under international law in violation of NAFTA, Article 1105. The California measures included regulations requiring back-filling and grading for mining operations in the vicinity of Native American sacred sites. Glamis claimed damages of more than US $50 million. As noted above, the mining project had been opposed by the Quechan people, who believed it would destroy important cultural and sacred sites including the 'Trail of Dreams'.

In *Glamis Gold*, it was the Quechan people themselves, rather than either of the parties, that urged the tribunal to take into account international norms protecting indigenous people. The Quechan people claimed that 'neither party's brief sufficiently outlined the international and domestic legal and policy frameworks that support indigenous cultural resource protection'.[46] According to the Quechan people, the tribunal should consider that the 'preservation and protection of indigenous rights in ancestral land is an obligation of customary international law which must be observed, by both the NAFTA Parties and any treaty interpreter, in accordance with the principle of good faith'.[47] They advocated that:

> In any dispute that directly involves the rights and/or interests of indigenous peoples, it is patent that international law norms establishing or otherwise concerning indigenous peoples should be considered as being included in the 'rules of international law that are applicable' with respect to that dispute. This is true regardless of whether the indigenous peoples [are parties to the case or not].
>
> In other words, under NAFTA Article 1131(1), the Tribunal is required to be mindful of how it construes [Articles 1105 and 1110 of NAFTA] so that they do not require or authorize State conduct of the kind that would conflict with international norms protecting indigenous people ... Such an approach is the only way to ensure consistency in wider public

---

[46] Quechan submission, p. 1.
[47] Quechan submission, p. 1, drawing attention in particular to Art. 12 of the UNDRIP, Art. 5 of the ILO Convention 169 and Art. XIX of the American Convention.

international law and is also mandated in the customary international law
rules on treaty interpretation.[48]

The Quechan people also argued that an investor seeking compensation
for 'an alleged taking of property cannot rely upon a claim to acquired
rights in which no legitimate expectation to enjoy such rights existed'.[49]
They urged the tribunal to consider that 'Glamis knew, or should have
known, that any right granted to it to exploit ancestral Quechan lands,
could only be enjoyed upon satisfaction of the concomitant domestic and
international obligations owed by the Respondent to the Quechan
people, to take whatever positive steps were necessary to protect and
promote their interests in such land'.[50]

The tribunal agreed to accept the Quechan submission, having considered the views of the parties and having formed the view that the
submission satisfied the NAFTA Free Trade Commission's Statement on
non-disputing party participation.[51] In doing so, the tribunal expressly
recalled that its acceptance did 'not signify agreement or disagreement
with the substance of the submission', and that 'the granting of leave did
not require the tribunal to address the submission at any point in the
Arbitration'.[52]

Indeed, when it came time to issuing the award in June 2009, the
tribunal noted that it was:

> aware that the decision in this proceeding has been awaited by private
> and public entities concerned with environmental regulation, the inter-
> ests of indigenous peoples, and the tension sometimes seen between
> private rights in property and the need of the State to regulate the use
> of property. These issues were extensively argued in this case and
> considered by the Tribunal. However, given the Tribunal's holdings,
> the Tribunal is not required to decide many of the most controversial
> issues raised in this proceeding ... It believes that its case specific
> mandate and the respect demanded for the difficult task faced squarely
> by some future tribunal instead argues for it to confine its decision to the
> issues presented.[53]

---

[48] Quechan submission, p. 89, citing the 1969 Vienna Convention on the Law of Treaties
and jurisprudence of the World Trade Organization Appellate Body.

[49] Quechan submission, p. 19.   [50] *Ibid.*

[51] *Glamis Gold*, Decision on Application of and Submission by Quechan Indian Nation, 16
September 2005, available at: www.state.gov/documents/organization/53592.pdf.

[52] *Glamis Gold*, para. 15. See also *Glamis Gold*, Award of 8 June 2009, para. 274, available at:
www.state.gov/documents/organization/125798.pdf.

[53] *Glamis Gold*, para. 8.

The tribunal extensively recounted the expert evidence and parties' arguments as to the cultural significance of sites to the Quechan people, but made no mention of any of the arguments made or sources cited in the Quechan Indian Nation's submission. The tribunal ultimately denied the claimant's expropriation claim on the ground that the measures complained of did not cause a sufficient economic impact to effect an expropriation.[54] The tribunal found that Glamis had failed to establish that any of the cited actions violated the obligation of the United States to provide fair and equitable treatment, which it held to a very stringent test (the *Neer* test).[55] In formulating this test, the tribunal did not cite to any arguments in any of the non-party submissions.

Thus, despite the attempts of the Quechan people to bring the interaction of investment treaty protections and indigenous peoples' rights to the attention of the tribunal, the tribunal declined to rule on such issues in circumstances in which it could dispose of the case on other grounds.

3.2   Grand River Enterprises et al. v. United States

A different approach was taken by the tribunal in the *Grand River* case the following year. Grand River Enterprises Six Nations Ltd (a Canadian corporation), Jerry Montour, Kenneth Hill and Arthur Montour were the claimants. They were technically Canadian citizens for purposes of NAFTA, but first and foremost considered themselves members of the Iroquois (or Haudenosaunee) nation. The claimants were engaged in the manufacture, production and distribution of tobacco, particularly under the 'Seneca' brand of cigarettes. They sought more than US$600 million in damages allegedly resulting from a 1998 settlement agreement between various state attorneys-general and the major tobacco companies, and certain state legislation that partially implements the settlement. They alleged violations of NAFTA, Articles 1102 (national treatment), 1103 (most-favoured-nation (MFN) treatment), 1104 (better of national or MFN treatment), 1105 (minimum standard of treatment under international law) and 1110 (expropriation).

---

[54] *Glamis Gold*, pp. 238 ff.

[55] *Glamis Gold*, pp. 353 ff. The *Neer* test derives from the case of *Neer* v. *Mexico*, 4 *Reports of International Arbitration Awards* 60 (15 October 1926), in which it was held at para. 4 that: 'the treatment of an alien, in order to constitute an international delinquency, should amount to an outrage, to bad faith, to wilful neglect of duty, or to an insufficiency of governmental action so far short of international standards that every reasonable and impartial man would readily recognize its insufficiency'.

The claimants argued, *inter alia*, that as indigenous people, they were entitled to a 'heightened level of vigilance and care' in being proactively consulted by the states. They argued that the United States had treated them 'contrary to the basic human rights norms that condition how the customary international law standard of fair and equitable treatment should be interpreted particularly when the interests of First Nations members and communities are at stake'. They submitted that:

> As an evolving norm of customary international law, the duty of States to respect and protect the rights and interests of First Nations across borders, in good faith, must be considered in the interpretation of treaty rights when [the] interests of First Nations individuals are directly involved.[56]

As noted above, the claimants appended to their Memorial a letter of support from the National Chief of the Assembly of First Nations urging the tribunal to take a similar approach to their task. The tribunal, in its award of January 2011, declined jurisdiction over three of the claimants, on the basis that they had not made an investment in the United States, as there was no established 'enterprise' within the meaning of NAFTA, Article 1139.[57] In this respect, the tribunal held that 'assertions of undocumented understandings "customary among indigenous peoples"' were too vague and lacking in evidentiary support.[58]

With respect to the remaining claimant, Mr Arthur Montour Jr, the tribunal denied the claim on the merits; however, the tribunal did engage to some extent with the arguments relating to the role of indigenous peoples' rights in this investment arbitration. The tribunal agreed that the states of the United States 'do not appear to have been at all sensitive to the particular rights and interests of the Claimants or the indigenous nations of which they are citizens' and stated that:

> The Tribunal cannot avoid noting the strong international policy and standards articulated in numerous written instruments and interpretive decisions that favour state action to promote such rights and interests of indigenous peoples.[59]

---

[56] *Grand River*, Claimants' Memorial on the Merits, 10 July 2008, paras 2, 171, 189–91, available at: www.state.gov/documents/organization/107684.pdf.

[57] *Grand River*, Award, 12 January 2011, paras 103–6, available at: www.state.gov/documents/organization/156820.pdf.

[58] *Grand River, ibid.*   [59] *Grand River*, para. 186.

However, the tribunal ultimately found that 'whatever unfair treatment was rendered [to Mr Arthur Montour Jr] ... it did not rise to the level of an infraction of the fair and equitable treatment standard of 1105, which is limited to the customary international law standard of treatment of aliens'.[60] With respect to duties of consultation, the tribunal stated:

> It may well be, as the Claimants urged, that there does exist a principle of customary international law requiring governmental authorities to consult indigenous peoples on governmental policies or actions significantly affecting them ... in any event, any obligations requiring consultation run between the state and indigenous peoples as such, that is, as collectivities [not as individuals].[61]

Even if consultations with individuals were required, the tribunal stated that 'it would be difficult to construe such a rule as part of the customary minimum standard of protection that must be accorded to every foreign investment pursuant to Article 1105'. The tribunal explained that the standard sets a floor, and was not meant to vary from investor to investor:

> The notion of specialized procedural rights protecting some investors, but not others, cannot readily be reconciled with the idea of a minimum customary standard of treatment due to all investments.[62]

Thus, on Article 1105, the tribunal held that:

> Article 1105 ... does not incorporate other legal protections that may be provided [to] investors or classes of investors under other sources of law. To hold otherwise would make Article 1105 a vehicle for generally litigating claims based on alleged infractions of domestic and international law and thereby unduly circumvent the limited reach of Article 1105 as determined by the Free Trade Commission in its binding directives.[63]

There was some consolation to the claimants in the tribunal's costs order. The tribunal acknowledged their status as indigenous peoples and the less than ideal treatment they had received at the hands of the respondent and therefore declined to order costs against them:

> In departing from the 'in-principle' rule of Article 40 [of the UNCITRAL Rules], the Tribunal has considered factors going beyond the narrow question of which party was 'unsuccessful'. It has taken into account, in particular, the Claimants' atypical situation as First Nations ... entrepreneurs

---

[60] *Grand River*, para. 187.   [61] *Grand River*, para. 210.   [62] *Grand River*, para. 213.
[63] *Grand River*, para. 219.

carrying on cross-border trade in the tradition of their ancestors. It is mindful of the economic difficulties faced by ... many indigenous communities, as the result of historical factors, and of the role of Claimants' business ventures ... as an important source of employment and income. The Tribunal believes that it would have been appropriate for [US authorities] to give greater recognition to, through appropriate consultations, the interests and concerns of Native American communities and entrepreneurs potentially affected by the MSA and related measures. Even if there be no right of redress established under NAFTA, the Tribunal believes that 'an appreciation of these matters can fairly be taken into account in exercising the Tribunal's discretion in terms of costs and expenses'.[64]

4 How other bodies have dealt with the interaction of international investment law with the rights of indigenous peoples

Investment–treaty arbitration is not the most common forum for the airing of complaints on behalf of indigenous peoples about their treatment under standards of international law. Such arguments are more likely to be seen at the level of national litigation or claims before regional or international human rights bodies. The intersection of the rights of indigenous peoples with the rights of foreign investors under a BIT actually has arisen in the context of a case before the Inter-American Court of Human Rights (IACHR). For example, in the case of *Sawhoyamaxa Indigenous Community* v. *Paraguay*,[65] it was alleged by the Inter-American Commission for Human Rights that Paraguay had violated the community's right to property under Article 21 of the American Convention. The Commission argued that:

> Paraguay has not guaranteed the right to property over their ancestral lands of the members of the Sawhoyamaxa Community, consequently depriving said Indigenous Community not only of the material possession of their lands but also from the fundamental basis to develop their culture, their spiritual lives, their integrity and their economic survival.[66]

---

[64] *Grand River*, para. 247, quoting *Mondev International Ltd* v. *United States*, ICSID Case No. ARB(AF)/99/2, Award, 11 October 2002, para. 159.

[65] IACHR, *Case of the Sawhoyamaxa Indigenous Community* v. *Paraguay*, Judgment, Merits, Reparations and Costs, 29 March 2006, available at: www.corteidh.or.cr/docs/casos/articulos/seriec_146_ing.pdf.

[66] *Sawhoyamaxa Indigenous Community*, para. 113. Reportedly, in a more recent case in 2012 an indigenous group from a different South American country petitioned the

In response, one of Paraguay's arguments (though not one of its principal arguments), pointed to the potential rights of a German foreign investor under the Paraguay–Germany BIT:

> the refusal by the land owner to sell the lands to the *INDI* so that said area might, in turn, be transferred to the Sawhoyamaxa Community has proven to be a stumbling block. Moreover, the owner is protected under a treaty between Paraguay and Germany on the promotion and reciprocal protection of capital investments from both countries.[67]

In relation to this argument, the Court held:

> with regard to the third argument put forth by the State, the Court has not been furnished with the aforementioned treaty between Germany and Paraguay, but, according to the State, said convention allows for capital investments made by a contracting party to be condemned or national-ized for a 'public purpose or interest', which could justify land restitution to indigenous people. Moreover, the Court considers that *the enforcement of bilateral commercial treaties negates vindication of non-compliance with state obligations under the American Convention; on the contrary, their enforcement should always be compatible with the American Convention, which is a multilateral treaty on human rights* that stands in a class of its own and that generates rights for individual human beings and does not depend entirely on reciprocity among States.[68]

The Court found the state's arguments to be 'insufficient to justify non-enforcement of the right to property of the Sawhoyamaxa Community'.[69]

5 How (a few) states have dealt with the rights of indigenous peoples in the text of investment treaties

The above examples from NAFTA tribunals and the IACHR show that international courts and tribunals have, to varying degrees, attempted to find some balance or compatibility in the standards of protection for investors, on the one hand, with protection of indigenous rights, on the other. The task might have been simpler had the treaties in question specifically addressed issues of overlap. A few states have incorporated language into their investment and free trade treaties that addresses some aspects of potential overlap between indigenous rights and investment protection.

Commission for protective measures related to an investment arbitration, but the request was subsequently withdrawn.

[67] *Sawhoyamaxa Indigenous Community*, para. 115.
[68] *Sawhoyamaxa Indigenous Community*, para. 140 (emphasis added).
[69] *Sawhoyamaxa Indigenous Community*, para. 141.

5.1 New Zealand FTAs and protection of Maori rights

New Zealand has inserted an exception in several of its recent investment treaties agreements, leaving it scope to take measures that might otherwise be in breach of investment protections, if such measures were taken in order to protect the indigenous Maoris pursuant to the Waitangi Treaty.[70] Such exceptions can be found in New Zealand's free trade agreements with China, Hong Kong, Thailand, Singapore and Malaysia.[71] The following language appears in chapter 15, 'General Provisions and Exceptions' of the ASEAN–Australia–New Zealand Free Trade Agreement of 2010:

> Article 5: Treaty of Waitangi
>
> 1. Provided that such measures are not used as a means of arbitrary or unjustified discrimination against persons of the other Parties or as a disguised restriction on trade in goods and services, nothing in this Agreement shall preclude the adoption by New Zealand of measures it deems necessary to accord more favourable treatment to Maori in respect of matters covered by this Agreement including in fulfillment of its obligations under the Treaty of Waitangi.[72]

5.2 South Africa's BITs and 'disadvantaged' groups

There are also examples from South Africa's bilateral investment treaties (BITs), which include language qualifying the obligations to accord foreign investors national or MFN treatment.[73] For instance, the South Africa–Mauritius BIT provides in Article 3:

> 4. The provisions of paragraphs (2) [national treatment] and (3) [MFN] shall not be construed so as to oblige one Contracting Party to extend to the investors of the other Contracting Party the benefit of any treatment, preference or privilege resulting from …

---

[70] See discussion in Peterson, 'Human Rights and Bilateral Investment Treaties', p. 42.
[71] New Zealand–China Free Trade Agreement, available at: www.chinafta.govt.nz/1-The-agreement/2-Text-of-the-agreement/18-Chapt-17-Exceptions/index.php; Thailand–New Zealand Closer Economic Partnership Agreement, Art. 15.8, available at: www.mfat.govt.nz/downloads/trade-agreement/thailand/thainzcep-december2004.pdf.
[72] Available at: www.asean.fta.govt.nz/chapter-15-general-provisions-and-exceptions.
[73] See discussion in Kriebaum, 'Human Rights of the Population of the Host State', p. 663.

(c) Any law or measure in pursuance of any law, the purpose of which
is to promote the achievement of equality in its territory, or designed to
protect or advance persons, or categories of persons, disadvantaged by
unfair discrimination in its territory.[74]

6   Reconciling the two fields of law in the absence of express treaty provision

Such treaty provisions as those extracted in the above section are rare
among the 3,000 plus investment treaties entered into between states.
Most tribunals presented with arguments concerning the interaction of
international investment law and the laws concerning indigenous protection obligations will not have the benefit of express treaty language as
guidance. In the absence of express treaty language, parties, tribunals and
commentators have invoked a number of techniques to take into account
different branches of international law in the application of an international investment treaty.

It has been pointed out that the provisions of the BIT may provide
some scope for a tribunal to take human rights considerations into
account. For example, the narrowness or breadth of the jurisdiction
clause in a BIT might guide how far a particular human rights issue
can be looked at by an investment tribunal.[75] The applicable law clause of
a BIT might also open the possibility of taking into account human rights
law either as part of the national law of the host state or as part of the
'rules of international law'.[76] The application of an 'in accordance with
host State law' clause might also lead a tribunal to find that investments
in violation of host state human rights norms would not enjoy the
protection of a BIT.[77]

Tribunals might also consider human rights norms as a matter of
treaty interpretation. Article 31(3) of the Vienna Convention on the

---

[74] Available at: www.unctad.org/sections/dite/iia/docs/bits/mauritius_southafrica.pdf. See
also discussion of the so-called 'black economic empowerment' cases in Peterson,
'Human Rights and Bilateral Investment Treaties'.
[75] See Kriebaum, 'Human Rights of the Population of the Host State', p. 660–1, e.g., whether
the jurisdiction clause provides for arbitration of 'any disputes made by an investor
against a Contracting Party' or be confined to 'any disputes about whether the Contracting Party has breached provisions of the Treaty'.
[76] Kriebaum, 'Human Rights of the Population of the Host State', pp. 661–2.
[77] Kriebaum, 'Human Rights of the Population of the Host State', pp. 664–7.

Law of Treaties requires that in the interpretation of a treaty 'there shall be taken into account, together with the context ... any relevant rules of international law applicable in the relations between the parties'.[78] Some commentators have noted that, as a general interpretive approach, a 'presumption of compliance' can assist tribunals.[79] This assumes that, unless expressly provided, treaty parties would not have intended that their agreement offends existing rules of international law. The presumption favours the interpretation of different obligations of international law in coherence with each other. Thus, if a tribunal is faced with two different possible interpretations of a BIT, one that is consistent with concurrent human rights obligations and one that is not, then the tribunal should favour the interpretation that is consistent with human rights obligations. The examples given in this chapter from cases touching on both investment protection and the rights of indigenous peoples illustrate how a number of the above techniques have been propounded by parties and non-parties and, in some cases, have been embraced by the decision-makers themselves.

Moshe Hirsch noted that 'increasing public transparency and participation of NGOs in investment proceedings is likely to exert further pressure on investment arbitrators to accord a greater weight to broader public interests ... including those reflected in non-investment international treaties'.[80] The trend of participation by non-parties is certainly reflected in the examples considered in this chapter from the field of

---

[78] 1969 Vienna Convention on the Law of Treaties, Art. 31(3)(c). See discussion in Kriebaum, 'Human Rights of the Population of the Host State', pp. 667–71; B. Simma and T. Kill, 'Harmonizing Investment Protection and International Human Rights: First Steps Towards a Methodology', in C. Binder, U. Kriebaum, A. Reinisch and S. Wittich (eds), *International Investment Law for the 21st Century: Essays in Honour of Christoph Schreuer* (Oxford University Press, 2009), pp. 678–707; M. Jacob, 'International Investment Agreements and Human Rights', in *Research Paper Series on Human Rights, Corporate Responsibility and Sustainable Development* (Duisberg, Germany: INEF, 2010), para. 3.2.3, available at: www.humanrights-business.org/files/international_investment_agreements_and_human_rights.pdf.

[79] G. I. Hernández, 'The Interaction Between Investment Law and the Law of Armed Conflict in the Interpretation of Full Protection and Security Clauses', see Chapter 2, this volume, Jacob, 'International Investment Agreements and Human Rights', para. 3.2.3; Simma and Kill, 'Harmonizing Investment Protection and International Human Rights'; Kriebaum, 'Human Rights of the Population of the Host State'.

[80] M. Hirsch, 'Conflicting Obligations in International Investment Law: Investment Tribunals' Perspective', in Y. Shany and T. Broude (eds), *The Shifting Allocation of Authority in International Law: Considering Sovereignty, Supremacy and Subsidiarity* (Oxford: Hart, 2008), p. 343.

indigenous peoples' rights. He further considered that investment tribunals have so far generally been reluctant to accord significant weight to human rights treaties in international investment law, an observation shared by others.[81] The *Glamis Gold* case is perhaps one example consistent with this observation, but the *Grand River* case suggests that some tribunals may be more open to considering the potential relevance of international norms concerning indigenous peoples, even if the case did not result in a victory for the claimants. Hirsch also argued that this 'generally negative approach of investment tribunals towards the application of human rights treaties may be explained by various factors [including] sociocultural factors relating to the social settings in which these rules of international law are formed, interpreted and implemented'.[82] Todd Weiler noted that it is incumbent upon international tribunals to construe treaty provisions in a manner consistent with a state's other international obligations, but considered that a primary obstacle to such development lies with the practitioners in the two fields. He regarded 'the divergence in professional outlook and approach, exhibited by practitioners of these related fields of public international law as something akin to a *de facto* barrier to doctrinal entry', suggesting that if the barriers can be reduced, 're-convergence may be possible as between the two fields'.[83]

One observation made in different contributions to this volume is that the decision-makers in investment arbitration systems tend to be lawyers in private practice with backgrounds in commercial disputes, whereas human rights adjudicators tend to come from more academic or public law backgrounds.[84] In the context of the cases discussed in this chapter, however, that is not strictly accurate. For example, in the *Glamis Gold* case, the presiding arbitrator was a law professor who was the president of a university and who had chaired a commission on international

---

[81] M. Hirsch, synopsis for conference programme, available at: http://media.leidenuniv.nl/legacy/iil-conference–call-for-discussant-proposals.pdf. See also Simma and Kill, 'Harmonizing Investment Protection and International Human Rights', pp. 678–9. But see J. D. Fry, 'International Human Rights Law in Investment Arbitration: Evidence of International Law's Unity', *Duke Journal of Comparative and International Law* 18 (2007): 77.

[82] M. Hirsch, synopsis for conference programme, available at: http://media.leidenuniv.nl/legacy/iil-conference–call-for-discussant-proposals.pdf.

[83] T. Weiler, synopsis for conference programme, available at: http://media.leidenuniv.nl/legacy/iil-conference–call-for-discussant-proposals.pdf.

[84] M. Hirsch, 'Investment Tribunals and Human Rights Treaties: A Sociological Perspective', see Chapter 4, this volume.

religious freedoms. Only one of the co-arbitrators was a lawyer from private practice, and the other was a law professor who had served as president of the American Society for International Law.[85] In *Grand River*, the presiding arbitrator was a practitioner, but he had also served as president of the Bar Association of India and co-chaired the Human Rights Institute of the IBA. One of the co-arbitrators (who incidentally survived an arbitrator challenge by the United States)[86] was a human rights professor and the UN special rapporteur on the situation of human rights and fundamental freedoms of indigenous peoples. He had participated in the drafting of UNDRIP, published extensively on indigenous rights and had even acted for indigenous parties in matters before the IACHR. The other co-arbitrator was also a law professor and had served as a commissioner on the Eritrea–Ethiopia Claims Commission. All three arbitrators in the *Burlington* case were professors as well as lawyers whose practices were not limited to commercial matters, but also included appearances before the ICJ.[87] The breadth of experience of the arbitrators in the cases described in this chapter might be coincidental, or it might be indicative that it is no longer possible to slot international arbitrators into certain professional categories. In the PCA's experience, there are now many outstanding candidates for arbitrators with experience across a broad spectrum of private and public, national and international legal practice areas.

7 Conclusion

The interaction of international investment law with the rights of indigenous peoples has not been the subject of great attention to date. However, indigenous rights have been raised in a number of different contexts in investment arbitration, at the instigation of claimants, states or nonparties. Tribunals faced with arguments about the relevance of indigenous rights have so far either managed to avoid confronting the issues directly or acknowledged the developing body of international indigenous law, but

---

[85] The *Glamis Gold* arbitrators were Professor M. K. Young, Professor D. D. Caron and Mr K. D. Hubbard.

[86] The *Grand River* arbitrators were Mr F. S. Nariman, Mr J. R. Crook and Professor J. Anaya. As to the challenge to Professor J. Anaya, see Letter from ICSID to Prof. Anaya, 28 November 2007, available at: www.naftaclaims.com/Disputes/USA/GrandRiver/GRE-USA-Anaya_Challenge-28–11–07.pdf.

[87] The *Burlington* arbitrators were Professor G. Kaufmann-Kohler, Professor B. Stern and Professor F. Orrego Vicuña.

stopped short of applying it due to the circumstances of the particular case and the treaty language in question. Exceptionally, a few states have expressly provided for such rights in their investment treaties, adopting a solution that allows for more direct, and less controversial, application of indigenous rights than the alternative techniques of interpretation. Greater awareness of indigenous rights in the context of investment treaty arbitration has, at least in the cases described in this chapter, perhaps been facilitated by the appointment of arbitrators with diverse legal experience, and allowing submissions from the viewpoints of representatives of the indigenous peoples themselves.

6

The protection against expropriations in Venezuela: a right to property in theory?

LEONIE TIMMERS

Introduction

'We don't know what we can do. We're trying to defend our rights. But it seems that here there are no rights. We have no rights' said Rafael Garrido after the Venezuelan president, Hugo Chávez, had expropriated his jewellery store and certain other buildings in the centre of Caracas because, according to Chávez, 'it's not possible for these buildings, with so much history ... to be occupied by businessmen'.[1] President Chávez is not afraid to express that in order for his 'socialist revolution' to be successful, all private property which does not subordinate to the socialist project, will rapidly be expropriated.[2]

Chávez' career started in 1992 when he committed a failed coup d'état against former President Carlos Andrés Perez. When he was arrested he appeared on national television, where he famously recognised the failure of the coup, although merely '*por ahora* ...' ('for now').[3] He did indeed return to the national stage, and this time he was elected democratically on the platform of a reformation of the entire economic and political system. This promise was to be taken quite literally: he had the constitution rewritten, changed the name of the country to the Bolivarian Republic of Venezuela,[4] and adapted the national flag by adding an extra

---

[1] A. Fernandez, 'Business Owners Move Out of Building "Expropriated" by Venezuela's Chavez', *Latin American Herald Times*, 10 February 2010, available at: www.laht.com/article.asp?ArticleId=352004&CategoryId=10717.

[2] Observatorio de Derechos de la Propriedad, at: http://paisdepropietarios.org.

[3] For more information, see R. Gott, *Hugo Chávez and the Bolivarian Revolution* (London: Verso, 2005), p. 23.

[4] This change of name was a symbol of the 'secular cult' surrounding Simón Bolívar, the man who liberated Venezuela (and other Latin American countries) from Spanish rule. Gott, *Hugo Chávez*, p. 91.

star and changing the direction of the horse in the national coat of arms to the left to represent the direction in which the revolution should be heading. While this shows that Chávez was radical from the beginning, it actually took him some years to openly admit that he aimed to achieve the 'Socialism of the 21st Century',[5] but it immediately became clear that his socialism was to be 'based on expropriations'.[6]

The wave of expropriations[7] started in the Orinoco Belt, an area that harbours many foreign oil companies. Chávez mandated the existing foreign companies to renegotiate their oil contracts and transform from purely private corporations into mixed companies, with a majority share in the hands of the state, while corporations that did not accept the new terms were (un)kindly asked to leave. Subsequently, the government targeted the services, construction, banking and food sectors,[8] whereas the latest round of expropriation seems to include farms and private homes. The Venezuelan president has determined that properties that can be categorised as 'inactive spaces' may be expropriated in order to resolve the housing crisis prevalent in the country.[9] The definition of 'inactive' has been rather broad: it encompasses operating farms, empty garages, parking lots and second homes. Chávez has defended these rigorous measures by arguing that the bourgeoisie itself used to 'expropriate the people',[10] and that public companies are much more efficient than private companies. It may well be that these statements are more based on aspirations than on reality; there is not

---

[5] J. Forero, 'Chávez Restyles Venezuela With "21st-Century Socialism"', New York Times, 30 October 2005, available at: www.nytimes.com/2005/10/30/international/americas/30venezuela.html.

[6] A. Contreras, 'Venezuela Socialism is Based on Expropriations', El Universal, 22 January 2010, available at: www.eluniversal.com/2010/01/22/en_ing_esp_venezuelan-socialism_22A3319291.shtml.

[7] Please note that different terms are used for the taking of property. These include 'confiscation', 'nationalisation' or, in very critical literature, even 'appropriation'. This chapter will use the term 'expropriation' as this is an overarching term that can incorporate both nationalisation and confiscation (the latter being automatically in breach of international law). For an explanation of the characteristics of each term, see M. Sornarajah, The International Law on Foreign Investment, 3rd edn (Cambridge University Press, 2010), pp. 364–7.

[8] Sornarajah, The International Law on Foreign Investment.

[9] I. Vincentelli, 'The Uncertain Future of ICSID in Latin America', Law and Business Review of the Americas 16 (2009): 438–40.

[10] 'Chávez dice que los ricos le han quitado la propiedad privada al pueblo', El Universal, 18 June 2009, available at: www.eluniversal.com/2009/06/18/pol_ava_chavez-dice-que-los_18A2400923.shtml.

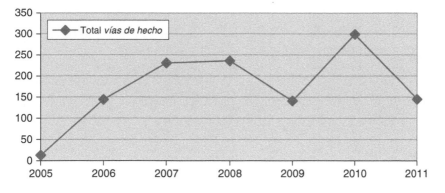

Figure 6.1 Total *vías de hecho* 2005–2011

'a single expropriated property in Venezuela that produces what it produced when it was privately owned'.[11]

The right to expropriate is an inherent feature of sovereignty, and more specifically a state's permanent sovereignty over its natural resources, thus it does not in and of itself constitute an unlawful act.[12] However, Chávez' actions give the impression that this right is unlimited and can be used as a sanction or threat. This position is not supported in either national or international law; an expropriation is lawful only under strict conditions, namely, when it: (1) serves a public purpose; (2) is not arbitrary and discriminatory; (3) follows principles of due process; and (4) is accompanied by prompt, adequate and effective compensation.[13] These conditions demonstrate that state sovereignty needs to be balanced against the right to property of the expropriated object.

Expropriations that do not conform to these conditions, and are therefore unlawful limitations of the right to property, are called '*vías de hecho*' under Venezuelan law. The NGO *Observatorio de Derechos de Propiedad* has made a classification of the total number of *vías de hecho* between 2005 and August 2010 in Venezuela. Figures 6.1 and 6.2 show

---

[11] Editorial, 'Hugo Chávez's Expropriation Binge', *Investor's Business Daily*, 17 May 2010, available at: www.investors.com/NewsAndAnalysis/Article/534341/ 201005172027/ Hugo-Chavezs-Expropriation-Binge.aspx. See also 'Venezuelan Economy: Towards State Socialism', *The Economist*, 18 November 2010, available at: www.economist.com/node/ 17527250.

[12] N. Schrijver, *Sovereignty over Natural Resources: Balancing Rights and Duties* (Cambridge University Press, 1997), p. 289; *Texaco* v. *Libya*, 17 *ILM* 1 (1977), para. 59.

[13] R. Dolzer and C. Schreuer, *Principles of International Investment Law* (Oxford University Press, 2008), p. 91.

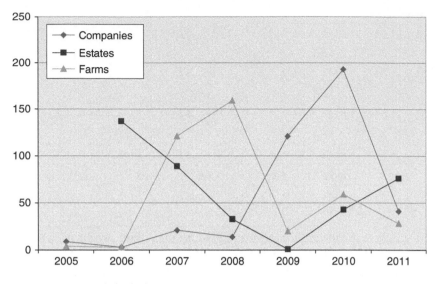

Figure 6.2   *Vías de hecho* by type, 2005–August 2011

that whereas in 2005 there were thirteen cases of unlawful expropriations, this increased to 299 cases in 2009. It is also shown that these
expropriations affect three areas: companies, estates and farms, and this
sheds some light on the main victims of these expropriations. They are,
first, Venezuelan land and farm owners (hereinafter landowners);
second, Venezuelan nationals who own companies (hereinafter national
investors); and, finally, foreigners who own companies in Venezuela
(hereinafter foreign investors).

The exact nature of the right to property and the extent to which it can
be limited has caused much discussion.[14] However, one issue that is
generally accepted is that the right to property is a human right for *all*,
in that everyone, irrespective of their background, is entitled to enjoy
this right. Thus, at the crux of the right to property is the issue of
non-discrimination and equal treatment: protection of this right should
not depend on whether one is rich or poor, government or citizen,
foreigner or national. This is reflected in the Venezuelan Constitution,
which provides in Article 115 that '*every* person has the right to the use,
enjoyment, usufruct and disposal of his or her goods'.[15] It is also

---

[14] See T. van Banning, *The Human Right to Property* (Antwerp: Intersentia, 2002).
[15] Constitution of the Bolivarian Republic of Venezuela, Gaceta Oficial No. 36.860.30, 30
December 1999, Art. 115 (emphasis added).

provided in the Universal Declaration on Human Rights[16] and the American Declaration of Human Rights.[17]

'Rights', or more specifically 'human rights', are codified because they are widely recognised as essential for the well-being of individuals, but are nevertheless often not respected. This, then, sheds light on the purpose of granting a 'right' to property; it is codified in law so that, where a violation of this right occurs, people have a tool to challenge such violation, based on the idea that a right without a remedy would be merely a right *in theory*, and thus no right at all.

It is interesting that, in spite of the fact that the right to property is clearly stipulated in national and international law, the owner of the jewellery store in Caracas exclaimed, referring to the right to protect his property from expropriation, that 'it seems that here there are no rights'. Was this merely ignorance about the existence of a right to property or does this concern the lack of a remedy when this right is violated? Does the right to property, or the mechanisms protecting this right, fulfil its purpose and grant a right for *all*, or is there discrimination as to who *can* and who *cannot* enforce such right and obtain a remedy? In other words, is the right to property a right in practice or merely one in theory?

This chapter intends to answer these questions by looking at the protection available under domestic and international law for those persons affected by the *vías de hecho*, or *unlawful* expropriations. As a consequence, the objects of these expropriations are seen as 'victims' for the purpose of this work, which entails the risk that the chapter might be accused of being biased in favour of the 'victims' of expropriation and neglecting the position of the state. However, such apparent 'bias' can be explained by the particular focus of this work; that is, in relation to the issue of expropriation, one can elaborate on any of the following four stages: (1) rights, (2) obligations, (3) responsibility and reparations and (4) remedies. A focus on obligations, for example, would mean examining instances of alleged expropriation and identifying what the obligations of the state were in the specific instance, as well as the extent to

---

[16] '*Everyone* has the right to own property', Universal Declaration on Human Rights, 10 December 1948, GA Resolution 217A (III), UN Doc. A/810 at 71 (1948), Art. 17 (emphasis added).

[17] '*Everyone* has the right to the use and enjoyment of his property', American Declaration of Human Rights, 22 November 1969, OAS Treaty Series No. 36; 1144 *UNTS* 123, Art. 21 (emphasis added).

which the state adhered to these obligations in the cases at hand.[18] In contrast, the present analysis focuses on stage (4): the remedies that the victims of an expropriation have at their disposal when a state has breached their right to property. In other words, this concerns the stage in which a state has already breached its obligations and is responsible for paying reparations. This focus does not in any way intend to suggest that the right to property is unlimited or that it should always prevail over the right to expropriate.

The structure of this chapter is as follows: first, the 'traditional' safeguards granted by domestic remedies and diplomatic protection will be examined. Second, the possibilities for redress under investment law will be analysed and, third, the final section will address the protection under the Inter-American Convention on Human Rights. It will be argued throughout this chapter that the right to property is, in practice, not a right for *all*, because it mainly protects one of the affected groups: foreign investors. For national landowners or national investors who fall victim to an expropriation, the right to property appears to be a right solely in theory.

Section 1: domestic courts and diplomatic protection

1.1   Domestic courts

1.1.1   Background and access

An expropriation, defined as the 'compulsory taking of private property by the state',[19] concerns essentially a dispute between the state and the victim who owns property in that state. Therefore, the most self-evident point of redress is a domestic court. Applying to such court demonstrates respect for national sovereignty, because it gives the host state an opportunity to assess the matter within its own legal system and to provide a remedy for the behaviour of its state organs.[20] The domestic legal system

---

[18] See, e.g., literature on what constitutes an expropriation; Sornarajah, *The International Law on Foreign Investment*; I. Iruretagoiena Agirrezabalaga, *El arbitraje en los litigios de expropiacion de inversiones extranjeras* (Barcelona: Bosch, 2010).

[19] D. Harris, *Cases and Materials on International Law*, 7th edn (London: Sweet & Maxwell, 2010), p. 474.

[20] U. Kriebaum, 'Local Remedies and the Standards for the Protection of Foreign Investment', in C. Binder, U. Kriebaum, A. Reinisch and S. Wittich (eds), *International Investment Law for the 21st Century: Essays in Honour of Christoph Schreuer* (Oxford University Press, 2009), p. 421.

is open to both nationals and foreigners and thus provides, in principle, a remedy for all victims of illegal expropriations on an equal basis.

1.1.2 Protection

In order to bring a case before a Venezuelan domestic court, domestic rules governing the procedure for lawful expropriations must be in place. While this section will not examine the applicable domestic laws in much detail, it will nevertheless give a short outline of such laws in order to look at the legislative basis for a legal action. The Venezuelan Constitution – which was rewritten in 1999 when the current administration started its term – establishes that an expropriation is a legitimate restriction of the right to property provided that it serves the public interest and is accompanied by payment of fair compensation.[21] These conditions are further clarified in Articles 14 and 36 of the *Ley de Expropiación*, which sets out a list of activities that fall within the aforementioned public or general interest, as well as a set of guidelines for the determination of fair compensation, respectively. Article 7 of the *Ley de Expropiación* determines the correct procedure for an expropriation, which entails: (i) a formal provision that declares the public utility; (ii) a statement that its implementation indispensably requires total or partial transfer of the property or right; (iii) a fair price for the goods to be expropriated; and (iv) timely payment in cash of fair compensation. These rules would seem to indicate that the right to property is well-protected in Venezuela.

However, a new law was approved in 2007[22] and renewed in 2010,[23] which allowed President Chávez to legislate via decrees with status of law[24] in areas including transport, economics, state institutions and property. *Leyes Habilitantes* are provided for by the constitution[25] in order 'to concede powers to the Executive for a determined period of time to approve decrees that permit the implementation of important transformative policies which would otherwise take too long to enact due to bureaucratic obstacles'.[26] The 'important transformative policy' that gave rise to the need for this law in 2007 was the 'emergency caused by

---

[21] Venezuelan Constitution, Arts 115 and 116 and *Ley de Expropiación por Causa de Utilidad Pública o Social*, Gaceta Oficial No. 37.475, 1 July 2002, Art. 2.

[22] *Ley Habilitante*, Gaceta Oficial No. 38.617, 1 February 2007.

[23] *Ley Habilitante*, Gaceta Oficial Extraordinaria No. 6.009, 17 December 2010.

[24] So-called *Decretos con Rango, Valor y Fuerza de Ley*.

[25] Venezuelan Constitution, Arts 203 and 236.8.

[26] 'Venezuela's Enabling Law: 5 Questions & 5 Answers', *Correo del Orinoco International*, 30 December 2010, available at: venezuelanalysis.com/analysis/5906.

torrential rains in the country'.[27] As a result, many laws have been enacted in order to provide a place for the *indemnificados* to live.[28]

One example is the 2011 *Ley de Emergencia de Viviendas*, which allows the taking of 'otiose and underutilised' land for the benefit of the *indemnificados*.[29] Also, in relation to the agrarian sector, the expropriation of farms and agrarian land is facilitated by the 2010 reforms to the *Ley de Tierras y Desarollo Agrário*, which prohibit *Latifundium* (ownership of large amounts of land) and empowers the government to 'assume direct responsibility for the production and distribution of food'. It is based on the idea that 'the land belongs to the tiller', thus to the people that work on it.[30]

While this idea might engender some sympathy, the fact that before 2009 some 2,500 hectares of agrarian land had already been 'rescued' and only a small portion of which is actually producing food, whereas none of this land has been transferred to the persons that work on it, provides a worrying precedent.[31] The reality is that the farmers never become owners of the land, but instead of being employed by a landlord, they are employed by the state (read: dependent on the state).[32] Thus, while the constitution offers protection against expropriation, subsequent laws seem to allow for a broad interpretation of 'public interest'.

1.1.3 Benefits and risks

It can be concluded that one definite benefit of domestic remedies is their broad access in that all victims of expropriations may apply to a national court. Furthermore, national law gives a clear outline of the requirements for an expropriation to be lawful. However, the decrees adopted under the *Ley Habilitante* might be used by the government as a means to justify more *vías de hecho*.

However, domestic courts do not always provide reliable fora for the effective protection of the interests of expropriation victims, as judges may

---

[27] 'Venezuela's Enabling Law: 5 Questions & 5 Answers'.
[28] A popular term used for those who have lost their homes as a result of the heavy rainfall.
[29] *Ley de Emergencia de Viviendas y Terrenos Urbanos*, Gaceta Oficial Extraordinaria No. 6.018, 29 January 2011.
[30] *Ley de Tierras y Desarollo Agrário*, Gaceta Oficial Extraordinaria No. 5.991, 29 July 2010.
[31] 'Temen más invasiones con reforma a Ley de Tierras', *El Universal*, 11 June 2010, available at: www.cedice.org.ve/detalle.asp?ID=3856.
[32] Y. Valery, 'Venezuela: aprobada reforma a Ley de Tierras', *BBC News*, 16 June 2010, available at: www.bbc.co.uk/mundo/economia/2010/06/100615_0357_venezuela_ley_-de_tierras_ao.shtml.

be (pressured to be) biased in favour of the state, and procedures can be cumbersome and time consuming.[33] This is particularly the case in Venezuela. While the Venezuelan Constitution sets out that the 'judicial power is independent and the Supreme Tribunal of Justice will enjoy autonomy in its function, finance and administration',[34] and has established a transparent process for selection and removal of judges,[35] reality portrays a wholly different picture. Since 1999, numerous laws have been enacted that allow for a circumvention of the safeguards provided for by the constitution.

One of those laws is particularly worrying. The National Constituent Assembly, which was in charge of redrafting the 1999 Constitution, set up the 'Emergency Judicial Commission' in 2002, charged with the creation of a 'transparent, impartial, autonomous, swift and uncomplicated judiciary'[36] by removing judges involved in corruption and for inexcusable procedural delays.[37] *Prima facie*, this commission seems to assist in the implementation of the constitution; however, as the decree establishing it does not set out specific guidelines for the suspension or removal of judges, the commission has dismissed numerous judges without following a clear procedure, thus violating the principles endorsed in the constitution. This issue was addressed by the Inter-American Court of Human Rights (IACtHR) in 2008 in a case concerning the dismissal of three judges for 'inexcusable miscarriage of justice'.[38] The IACtHR decided that the judges had not been granted a fair trial before an impartial court and ordered that they be reinstated in the judiciary. In spite of this judgment, the judges have not been reinstated in the judiciary. Also, the commission maintains its functions – which are supposed to be only temporary – and has done such a rigorous job that none of the judges presently on the bench entered before 1999.[39] It is therefore a valid concern that certain judges have been dismissed for political reasons rather than because of misconduct.[40]

---

[33] C. Schreuer, *The ICSID Convention: A Commentary* (Cambridge University Press, 2001), p. 347.

[34] Venezuelan Constitution, Art. 254.   [35] Venezuelan Constitution, Arts 255–7.

[36] *Reorganización del Poder Judicial*, Gaceta Oficial No. 36.805, 11 October 1999, para. 2.

[37] *Reorganización del Poder Judicial*, Arts 6–7.

[38] *Case of Apitz Barbera et al. (First Court of Administrative Disputes)* v. *Venezuela*, IACtHR, Judgment, 5 August 2008, Series C No. 182.

[39] Inter-American Commission on Human Rights, *Democracy and Human Rights in Venezuela*, 30 December 2009, OEA/Ser.L/V/II, Doc. 54, para. 251.

[40] L. Castaldi, 'Judicial Independence Threatened in Venezuela: The Removal of Venezuelan Judges and the Complications of Rule of Law Reform', *Georgetown Journal of International Law*, 37 (2005/6): 477–506.

However, dismissal is only one way in which judges who rule against the wishes of the government are penalised. The most notorious example is that of Judge Afiuni, who ordered the conditional release of a banker who had been detained for more than two years without a conviction,[41] and whose detention had been described by the UN Working Group on Arbitrary Detention as arbitrary.[42] This caused President Chávez to call her a 'bandit' and suggest she be sent to prison for thirty years.[43] She was eventually sentenced to thirty-five years' imprisonment for corruption, aiding in the evasion of justice and conspiracy. The IACHR and the Working Group on Arbitrary Detention have since heavily criticised her detention.[44]

In the light of the above, judges who exercise judicial review of an executive decision bear a great risk of dismissal, and might even suffer more severe consequences. It therefore may not come as a surprise that between October 2010 and September 2011, 82 per cent of the cases brought against acts of government organs were rejected.[45] Therefore, bringing a case in a Venezuelan court against an expropriation is unlikely to give any investor or landowner a fair trial, let alone an effective chance to retain its property or obtain compensation.

1.2   Diplomatic protection

1.2.1   Background and access

Diplomatic protection was developed at a time when states were still regarded as the only subjects of public international law. This meant that corporations or individuals did not have any form of legal standing to bring a claim against a state for the violation of international rules. It seemed iniquitous that a foreign national was left without a remedy

---

[41] 'Criminals or Dissidents', *The Economist*, 17 February 2011, available at: www.economist. com/node/18184396.

[42] Human Rights Council, 'Report of the Working Group on Arbitrary Detention', 18 January 2010, Doc. A/HRC/13/30, p. 6.

[43] 'Tribunal fijó fecha de juicio contra Afiuni para el 9 de julio', *El Universal*, 20 June 2012, available at: www.eluniversal.com/nacional-y-politica/120620/tribunal-fijo-fecha-de-jui-cio-contra-afiuni-para-el-9-de-julio.

[44] IACtHR Report, 2009, para. 297; UN News Centre, *Venezuelan Leader Violates Independence of Judiciary: UN Rights Experts*, available at: www.un.org/apps/news/story.asp? NewsID=33273&Cr=judges&Cr1.

[45] Provea, 'Balance de la situación de derechos humanos: Octubre 2010 a Septiembre 2011', available at: www.derechos.org.ve/pw/wp-content/uploads/03Balance.pdf, p. 39.

when his action was unsuccessful or impossible in a national court. Therefore, it became common practice to allow the state of nationality to act on behalf of its nationals, either by negotiating with the injuring state or by pursuing legal action.[46] The ratio for this right was explained by the Permanent Court of Justice (PCIJ) in the *Panevezys-Saldutiskis* case: 'a state is in reality asserting its own right, the right to ensure in the person of its nationals respect for the rules of international law'.[47]

While a state may exercise diplomatic protection for any internationally wrongful act affecting its nationals, this section will limit itself to a discussion of diplomatic protection of foreign investors, the exercise of which is subject to two conditions. First, there needs to be a nationality link between the investor and the state bringing the diplomatic protection claim. As the foreign investor is often a corporation with shareholders from different nationalities, it is important to determine who is a national for the purposes of diplomatic protection. Since the *Barcelona Traction* case it is clear that only 'the state under the laws of which [the company] is incorporated and in whose territory it has its registered office'[48] may exercise diplomatic protection. The International Court of Justice (ICJ) thus dismissed the claim by Belgium, brought on behalf of Belgian shareholders who owned 88 per cent of a company incorporated in Canada. It was held that granting a right of diplomatic protection for shareholders would open the floodgates and 'create an atmosphere of insecurity and confusion in international economic relations'.[49] However, the Court did establish three exceptions to this general rule in the *Barcelona Traction* case, which were further developed in the *Diallo* case.[50] It was established that shareholders are entitled to diplomatic protection only when (i) their direct interests have been violated,[51] (ii) the corporation has ceased to exist or (iii) the corporation has the nationality of the injuring state and incorporation in that state was a precondition to setting

---

[46] P. Muchlinski, 'The Diplomatic Protection of Foreign Investors: A Tale of Judicial Caution', in C. Binder, U. Kriebaum, A. Reinisch, S. Wittich (eds), *International Investment Law for the 21st Century. Essays in Honour of Christoph Schreuer* (Oxford University Press, 2009), p. 342.

[47] *Panevezys-Saldutiskis Railway* (*Estonia* v. *Lithuania*), (1939) PCIJ Ser. A/B No. 76, p. 16.

[48] *Barcelona Traction, Light and Power Company Ltd* (*Belgium* v. *Spain*), Judgment, *ICJ Reports* 1970, p. 3, para. 70.

[49] *Barcelona Traction*, para. 96.

[50] *Ahmadou Sadio Diallo* (*Republic of Guinea* v. *Democratic Republic of the Congo*), Preliminary Objections, Judgment, *ICJ Reports* 2007, p. 582.

[51] *Barcelona Traction*, para. 47.

up a business.[52] It needs to be stressed that these exceptions are still highly controversial. The second condition is the need to exhaust local remedies, which can be a time-consuming and costly matter.[53]

Most Venezuelans have a bitter memory of the early exercises of 'diplomatic protection', which was often paired with the use of force. The history books still cover *El Bloqueo de 1902–1903*, when the German fleet bombed Venezuelan ports and sank Venezuelan vessels as a response to the confiscation of German, British and Italian properties and unpaid debts.[54] This so-called 'gunboat diplomacy' was not rare in Latin America and led to the formation of two important doctrines. First, the Drago Doctrine, which provided that no force could be used in the collection of outstanding debts in another country.[55] This doctrine evolved into hard law with the adoption of the Drago–Porter Convention by the Second International Hague Peace Conference in October 1907, where states committed themselves to not resorting to force in the collection of foreign debts unless the other state refuses to submit to arbitration.[56] Second, the Calvo Doctrine, also known as the 'national standard', was critical of treatment which ensured better protection for foreign investors than for nationals, and therefore argued that disputes with foreign investors were to be governed by national laws and settled in domestic courts.[57] The idea behind this doctrine – treating nationals and foreigners equally – is also supported in this chapter. However, this author would decline to agree with Calvo's premise that in order to achieve equal treatment, all disputes should be resolved in national courts. This suggestion might have made sense when the doctrine was formulated (1896), since there was no neutral international forum for the settlement of disputes, but nowadays there is more reason to aim for the opposite: a better protection of the interests of *nationals* in an *international* forum. To use it nowadays as an argument to reject invest-ment arbitration is merely an endorsement of a so-called 'race to the bottom', as domestic courts in many states do not offer the same

---

[52] *Diallo*, paras 91–3. See also International Law Commission, Draft Articles on Diplomatic Protection, UN GAOR, 61st Sess., Supp. No. 10, UN Doc. A/61/10 (2006), Art. 11.

[53] Muchlinski, 'The Diplomatic Protection of Foreign Investors', pp. 343–5.

[54] J. Anzola, 'From Gunboats to Arbitration', *Transnational Dispute Management*, 5 (2008): 2.

[55] A. Hershey, 'The Calvo and Drago Doctrines', *American Journal of International Law* 1 (1907): 31.

[56] A. Newcombe and L. Paradell, *Law and Practice of Investment Treaties: Standards of Treatment* (Alphen aan den Rijn: Kluwer Law, 2009), p. 10.

[57] Schrijver, *Sovereignty over Natural Resources*, p. 178.

protection as international arbitration.[58] Such endorsement goes against the spirit of the progressive realisation of human rights, as it would actually decrease the rights of foreigners, instead of increase the rights of nationals.

Today, the role of diplomatic protection has significantly diminished and the use of force is no longer allowed. In the wave of expropriations in Venezuela, there has been only one instance in which diplomatic protection was exercised by Spain for a group of Spanish landowners whose properties had been expropriated. This did, in fact, convince the Venezuelan Government to enter into negotiations and to pay reparations.[59]

1.2.2 Benefits and risks

A benefit of relying on the protection of the home state instead of initiating a personal claim is that the home state – depending on its size – can usually exercise more pressure on the host state to comply with its international obligations. The host state might not want to ruin its relations with the home state over a simple incident, and may therefore be inclined to comply with the request without too many difficulties.

However, the fact that a state of nationality may bring a claim also gives rise to considerable risks, because the decision whether to exercise diplomatic protection lies entirely in the hands of that state.[60] This usually means that a state will espouse such a claim only when the protection of the investment is important for the national interest.

The other risk of relying on diplomatic protection, particularly in relation to Venezuela, is that Venezuela has not accepted the ICJ's compulsory jurisdiction.[61] Therefore, unless it specifically accepts jurisdiction for the particular case, or unless jurisdiction is already accepted through a specific treaty, the Court would not have jurisdiction over a diplomatic protection claim brought on behalf of victims of expropriation in Venezuela.

---

[58] W. Verweij and N. Schrijver, 'The Taking of Foreign Property under International Law: A New Legal Perspective', *Netherlands Yearbook of International Law* 15 (1984): 26.

[59] A. Alcoceba Gallego, A. Manero Salvador and F. Quispe Remón, *La Protección de la Inversión Española en los Estados Miembros del ALBA. Marco Jurídico de las Inversiones Españoles en Bolivia, Ecuador y Venezuela* (Madrid: Ed. Civitas, 2010), p. 76; see also L. Vinogradoff, 'Primeros Españoles indemnizados por la expropiación de tierras en Venezuela', *ABC*, 3 May 2006, available at: www.abc.es/hemeroteca/historico-03-05-2006/abc/Nacional/primeros-espa%C3%B1oles-indemnizados-por-la-expropiacion-de-tierras-en-venezuela_1421384297092.html.

[60] Dolzer and Schreuer, *Principles of International Investment Law*, p. 211.

[61] ICJ, 'Declarations Recognizing the Jurisdiction of the Court as Compulsory', available at: www.icj-cij.org/jurisdiction/index.php?p1=5&p2=1&p3=3.

1.3   Conclusion on domestic courts and diplomatic protection

In conclusion, resorting to a domestic court or, as a foreign investor, relying on diplomatic protection of the home state does not seem to offer encouraging prospects for a successful claim. Domestic courts in Venezuela are, in principle, available for all victims of expropriation, but the newly adopted laws and the existence of a judiciary that has repeatedly been found biased by international human rights bodies, give reason to believe that domestic courts do not provide an effective remedy. Diplomatic protection is available only for foreign investors, and while the pressure exercised by another state may be very powerful, the state of nationality will not easily commit itself to such action, unless the investment is important enough for a state to risk the deterioration of diplomatic relations – which will rarely be the case.

Section 2: investor–state arbitration

2.1   Background

Venezuela was, just like other Latin American countries, initially hesitant to allow investors to settle investment disputes in an international forum, and instead preferred to adjust or 'internationalise' its investment contracts.[62] In the Venezuelan perception, signing up to the International Centre for the Settlement of Investment Disputes (ICSID) would have been incompatible with the Calvo doctrine and the related principle of sovereignty over natural resources, because it provides for an international mechanism for the settlement of investment disputes.[63] However, the tide turned in the 1990s, when the Venezuelan Government under President Caldera initiated the *Apertura Petrolera* programme – which was meant to attract foreign oil companies to the country[64] – and ratified[65] the ICSID Convention, which entered into force for Venezuela on 1 June 1995.[66] A total of

---

[62] I. Vincentelli, 'The Uncertain Future of ICSID in Latin America', *Law and Business Review of the Americas* 16 (2009): 410.

[63] Schrijver, *Sovereignty over Natural Resources*, p. 187.

[64] Anzola, 'From Gunboats to Arbitration', p. 9.

[65] The Convention was signed on 18 August 1993 and ratified on 2 May 1995.

[66] ICSID, List of Contracting States and other Signatories of the Convention, available at: icsid.worldbank.org/ICSID/FrontServlet?requestType=ICSIDDocRH&actionVal=ContractingStates&ReqFrom=Main.

twenty-nine cases have been brought against the state since then, of which six have been concluded.[67]

However, this trend has reversed again during the Chávez administration; during the fifth summit of the *Alianza Bolivariana para los Pueblos de Nuestra América* (ALBA) movement,[68] presidents Morales and Chávez announced that all ALBA countries that were also ICSID members would withdraw from the Convention and denounce all the BITs in force.[69] Bolivia and Ecuador were the first countries to live up to their promise by withdrawing from ICSID,[70] and Venezuela did so on 24 January 2012. In accordance with Article 71 of the ICSID Convention, this denunciation became effective on 25 July 2012.

What consequences these actions have for investors will be discussed in the final part of this section. However, it seems important to stress at the outset that: (i) the denunciation of the ICSID Convention does not affect pending cases against Venezuela; (ii) in the opinion of this author, investors (who have accepted Venezuela's offer to arbitrate) may continue to file cases against Venezuela before the ICSID even after the date that the denunciation becomes effective due to Article 72 of the ICSID Convention; and (iii) even if an ICSID Tribunal decides that Article 72 has a distinct meaning from the one advocated in this chapter, investors have the opportunity to resort to *Ad hoc* Tribunals to resolve investment disputes with Venezuela or to bring a claim against one of the state-controlled corporations before, for example, the International Chamber of Commerce or the Stockholm Chamber of Commerce.

This section will first consider questions in relation to access to the ICSID system, and will further analyse the benefits and dangers of investor–state arbitration as a method of dispute settlement for expropriation claims in Venezuela.

2.2   Access

It is well known that in order to access the ICSID system, one must first comply with the requirements laid down in Article 25(1) of the ICSID

---

[67] ICSID, available at: icsid.worldbank.org/ICSID/FrontServlet.

[68] Its principal members are Bolivia, Ecuador, Venezuela, Cuba and Nicaragua.

[69] Vincentelli, 'The Uncertain Future of ICSID in Latin America', p. 423.

[70] Bolivia was the first country to withdraw from ICSID on 2 May 2007, and Ecuador on 6 July 2009. T. Nelson, '"History Ain't Changed": Why Investor–State Arbitration Will Survive the "New Revolution"', in M. Waibel, A. Kaushal, K. Chung and C. Balchin (eds), *The Backlash Against Investment Arbitration* (The Hague: Kluwer Law, 2010), pp. 573–4.

Convention. For the purpose of this chapter, it is interesting to further examine two such requirements, namely, the required consent to submit a dispute to the ICSID and the nationality requirement of the investor.

2.2.1   Consent to arbitration

Venezuela has concluded BITs with twenty-seven different countries,[71] of which twenty-four are in force.[72] All these BITs contain a 'consent to arbitration' clause. The large majority of BITs provide that friendly consultations should take place between the parties before resorting to arbitration, and that a claim may be submitted to arbitration only if such consultations have not resolved the dispute within three or six months. Some BITs give the investor a choice between resort to the domestic court system or to arbitration. Seven of the BITs contain a fork-in-the-road clause, stipulating that once an investor has chosen to resort to a domestic court or an investment tribunal, this choice shall be final. This clause incorporates the roman maxim *electa una via, non datur recursus ad alteram*[73] and is intended to avoid procedural 'multiplicity or duplicity'.[74] Where the investor chooses arbitration, it may resort to several forums. All BITs, apart from the one concluded with the Russian Federation, provide for the ICSID as a forum for the settlement of disputes. Furthermore, sixteen BITs establish that resort may be had to the ICSID Additional Facility. and practically all BITs in force (except for the Venezuela–France BIT) provide for *ad hoc* arbitration under the UNCITRAL rules, in case the ICSID is not available. The BIT with the Russian Federation also puts forward the Stockholm Chamber of Commerce as a possible forum, and the BIT with Iran allows dispute resolution through the International Chamber of Commerce. Thus, for those investors that can rely on a BIT there are a range of options, but protection is still largely dependent on the 'luck' of having the right nationality. The United States,

---

[71] It is interesting to note that the latest BITs have been concluded with anti-Western countries such as Iran, Belarus and the Russian Federation.

[72] The BITs with Brazil, Italy and the Russian Federation are not yet in force, whereas Venezuela terminated the BIT with the Netherlands.

[73] 'Once a course of action has been chosen, there is no recourse to another'. V. Tejera Pérez, 'Do Municipal Investment Laws Always Constitute a Unilateral Offer to Arbitrate? *The Venezuelan Investment Law: A Case Study*', in I. Laird and T. Weiler (eds), *Investment Treaty Arbitration and International Law*, 2 vols (New York: Jurisnet LLC, 2008), vol. II, p. 7.

[74] For an analysis of the fork-in-the-road provisions in Venezuelan BITS, see Tejera Pérez, 'Do Municipal Investment Laws Always Constitute a Unilateral Offer to Arbitrate?'.

for example, which is Venezuela's largest commercial partner,[75] has not concluded a BIT with the country. Investors from countries with which Venezuela has not concluded BITs could alternatively rely on an investment agreement with the state.

2.2.2 Nationality of the investor

The introduction to this chapter outlined that the main victims of expropriation in Venezuela are foreign investors, national investors and national landowners. The ICSID criteria for nationality make clear that only one group of 'victims' has access to investor–state arbitration at ICSID, namely, foreign investors. For national investors, there is one option that would allow them – if carefully planned – to obtain access to the ICSID, and that is 'nationality planning'.

While ICSID jurisdiction is limited to disputes between a contracting party and a 'national' of another contracting party, there is one exception to this principle, contained in Article 25(2) of the Convention, namely: that, 'because of foreign control' a juridical person of the host state is considered a national of the other contracting party. Thus, for example, where a company in Venezuela is fully controlled by a Dutch company, instead of the company being treated as Venezuelan, it is treated as Dutch and could thus rely on the Netherlands–Venezuela BIT against Venezuela. Nationality planning, also referred to as 'treaty shopping', refers to the practice of restructuring national companies in order to insert a foreign investor into the corporate chain so as to gain protection under the BIT and access to investor–state arbitration.[76] This structure is not only set up by national investors, who would not otherwise have access to any international forum, but also by foreign investors from states that do not have a BIT in place with Venezuela.

Aguas del Tunari v. *Bolivia* concerned the restructuring of a Bolivian company that was put under the control of a Dutch holding company so as to be able to rely on the Netherlands–Bolivia BIT. The arbitral tribunal in that case held that this practice is valid and legitimate, because 'the language of the definition of national in many BITs evidences that such

---

[75] E. Hernández-Bretón, 'Protección de Inversiones en Venezuela', in A. Dreyzin de Klor and D. Fernández Arroyo (eds), *Inversiones Extranjeras. Derecho del Comercio Internacional y Actualidades* (Caracas: DeCITA, 2005), p. 221.

[76] C. Schreuer, 'The Future of Investment Arbitration', in M. Arsanjani, J. Cogan, R. Sloane and S. Wiessner (eds), *Looking at the Future, Essays on International Law in Honor of W. Michael Reisman* (The Hague: Martinus Nijhoff, 2011), p. 795.

national routing of investments is entirely in keeping with the purpose of the instruments and the motivations of the state parties'.[77] In a dispute that arose out of the previously mentioned nationalisation measures in the Orinoco Oil Belt, the *Mobil Corporation* v. *Venezuela* case, the arbitral tribunal held that restructuring investments to protect them against mistreatment by Venezuela 'by gaining access to ICSID arbitration through the BIT ... was a perfectly legitimate goal',[78] as long as it relates to the protection for *future* disputes, rather than a dispute that is already ongoing.[79]

Such restructuring requires careful planning, taking into account the exact wording of the BIT, as illustrated by two cases involving national investors who restructured their company in order to insert a foreign investor into the corporate chain. First, the *Tokios Tokelés* v. *Ukraine* case, where the claimant, a Lithuanian company that was fully owned by Ukrainian nationals, filed a claim with the ICSID, relying on the Lithuania–Ukraine BIT, for unjustified actions by the Ukrainian Government against its Ukrainian subsidiary, Taki Spray.[80] The arbitral tribunal did not accept Ukraine's argument that Tokios Tokelés was not a 'genuine entity' of Lithuania;[81] it held that the 'foreign control' required under Article 25(2)(b) of the ICSID Convention was established by the fact that Tokios Tokelés was incorporated in Lithuania and was thus a 'national' of 'another contracting party'.[82] It did not 'lift the corporate veil' by looking behind the incorporation and establishing who controlled the company (i.e., Ukrainian nationals).

The second case in which the arbitral tribunal took a wholly different approach to establishing foreign control is *TSA Spectrum* v. *Argentina*.[83] This case concerned an Argentinean company (TSA) that was wholly owned by a Dutch company (TSI), which, in turn, was controlled by an

---

[77] *Aguas del Tunari* v. *Bolivia*, ICSID Case No. ARB/03/2, Jurisdiction, 21 October 2005, para. 332.

[78] *Mobil Corporation and others* v. *Bolivarian Republic of Venezuela*, ICSID Case No. ARB/ 07/27, Jurisdiction, 10 June 2010, para. 204.

[79] *Mobil Corporation*, para. 205.

[80] A. Martin, 'International Investment Disputes, Nationality and Corporate Veil: Some Insights from *Tokios Tokelés* and *TSA Spectrum de Argentina*', *Transnational Dispute Management* 8 (2011): 3.

[81] *Tokios Tokelés* v. *Ukraine*, ICSID Case No. ARB/02/18, Jurisdiction, 29 April 2004, para. 21.

[82] *Tokios Tokelés*, para. 42.

[83] *TSA Spectrum de Argentina SA* v. *Argentina*, ICSID Case No. ARB/05/5, Admissibility, 19 December 2008.

Argentinean national (Mr Jorge Justo Neuss), a majority shareholder. TSA relied on the Netherlands–Argentina BIT for its claim against Argentina for termination of a concession contract.[84] The approach of the arbitral tribunal in *Tokios Tokelés* had been to establish 'foreign control' by looking at the place of incorporation to determine nationality, which in *TSA* would have been the Netherlands. However, the tribunal in *TSA* went further and relied on the 'controlling nationality' test, thus 'lifting the corporate veil' to see who was ultimately in control of the corporation;[85] which led to Mr Jorge Justo Neuss, so TSA's claim was dismissed.

It is interesting to note that in February 2012, a claim was brought before the ICSID by Gambrinus, a Barbados-based company led by executives of Venezuela's largest private company, *Empresas Polar*.[86] This claim is a clear example of nationality planning by a Venezuelan national in order to obtain access to international arbitration: it concerns the state's expropriation of the fertiliser company Fertinitro, in which Gambrinus held a 10 per cent stake. Should the tribunal take the 'place of incorporation' approach in respect of Fertinitro (owned by a Barbadian company), the claim would succeed. However, should the 'controlling nationality' approach be taken as to Fertinitro (ultimately controlled by Venezuelans), the claim would fail. It seems worthwhile to keep track of the *Gambrinus* case since, first, the outcome is likely to determine which course of action will be taken by Venezuelan investors seeking to resolve their disputes through international arbitration, and, second, despite the lack of binding precedent in investment arbitration it may establish a pattern as to the acceptability of nationality planning.

In conclusion, it might be beneficial for national investors to restructure their investment to insert a foreign investor in the corporate chain so as to obtain access to protection by the ICSID; however, in the light of the different approaches taken by tribunals in different cases, this requires proper planning, considering the specific wording of the BIT.[87]

---

[84] C. Verrill, 'Introductory Note to ICSID: *TSA Spectrum de Argentina SA* v. *Argentine Republic*', *ASIL in Focus* (2008), available at: www.asil.org/infocus090520.cfm.

[85] *TSA Spectrum*, para. 147.

[86] *Gambrinus Corp.* v. *Bolivarian Republic of Venezuela*, ICSID Case No. ARB/11/31; see also B. Ellsworth and R. Sandiford, 'Exclusive: Top Venezuela Firm filed Arbitration against Chavez', Reuters, 16 February 2012, available at: www.reuters.com/article/2012/02/16/us-venezuela-arbitration-idUSTRE81F0SO20120216.

[87] See for a critique, Sornarajah, *The International Law on Foreign Investment*, pp. 327–9.

2.3   Benefits and risks

For those investors who have the 'privilege' of being able to bring a claim before an investment arbitration tribunal the advantages are many. First and foremost, is the fact that investors do not need to wait for their home state to take action against the host state, but can initiate a claim themselves.

However, the risk that investors in Venezuela are facing is the fact, which was outlined above, that Venezuela has withdrawn from ICSID. It was outlined above that the possibility of withdrawing from ICSID is provided for in Article 71 of the Convention, which stipulates that a state can withdraw from ICSID by written notice and that such withdrawal shall take effect six months from the date of the written notice.[88] However, the effects of this clause are significantly limited by Article 72, which provides that the withdrawal will not 'affect the rights or obligations ... of that state ... arising out of consent to the jurisdiction of the Centre ... before such notice'.[89] This provision is an expression of the general rule, also contained in Article 25(1), that no party can withdraw its consent unilaterally.

To clarify the exact meaning of Article 72, it is helpful to consider the *travaux préparatoires* of the ICSID Convention. Even though several delegates proposed limitations to Article 72 to ensure that a state would not be compelled 'to remain forever in an organisation to which it did not want to belong', no such limitations were included since it was considered that 'a general statement would not be binding on the state which had made it until it had been accepted by an investor'.[90] Thus, it seems that one needs to look at the wording of the arbitration clause contained in the document providing consent to ICSID arbitration to determine whether it contains unconditional consent or an agreement to consent.[91] The Venezuela–Barbados BIT, for example, provides that disputes '*shall*, at the request of the national concerned, *be submitted* to the International Centre for Settlement of Investment Disputes'.[92]

---

[88] See above.

[89] Convention on the Settlement of Investment Disputes Between States and Nationals of Other States, 18 March 1965, 575 *UNTS* 159, Art. 72.

[90] *Documents concerning the Origin and the Formulation of the Convention, Memorandum of the Meeting of the Whole, 25 February 1965*, vol. II, Pt 2 (Washington, DC: ICSID Publications, 1968), pp. 1010–11.

[91] E. Gaillard, 'The Denunciation of the ICSID Convention', *New York Law Journal* 237 (2007): 3.

[92] Article 8.1 (emphasis added).

This is a clear example of consent to ICSID jurisdiction which would fall within Article 72 of the Convention. On the other hand, the Venezuela–Argentina BIT provides that 'in case of recourse to international arbitration, the investor and the host state *may agree to submit* to [ICSID or *ad hoc* arbitration under UNCITRAL]'.[93] Here the situation is different, since further agreement is needed before an ICSID arbitration can commence. It is likely that such provision does not bind a denouncing state under Article 72.

However, it remains to be seen whether the same position is taken by ICSID tribunals. It is interesting to note that requests for arbitration have been filed against Bolivia and Ecuador, on the basis of Article 72, after their denunciations of the ICSID, and even after such denunciations became effective. However, no tribunal has pronounced on the existence of ICSID jurisdiction in such cases: in the *Quiport SA* case, the parties reached a settlement,[94] while in the *Pan American Energy* case, no decision has been made yet.[95]

Furthermore, just as consent to the ICSID Convention does not imply consent to submit cases to arbitration, withdrawal from the ICSID Convention does not imply the withdrawal of consent to arbitration.[96] Even if Venezuela executes its second threat, and withdraws from all BITs, this would have to be done in conformity with the treaty provisions on termination, which means that investments established before the termination of the BIT would still have an additional period of protection of between ten and fifteen years, because of the so-called 'survival clause' contained in each BIT.[97] Therefore, BITs and the consent to arbitration clauses in investment agreements are still in force and cases may continue to be brought before the mechanisms for dispute settlement stipulated therein. Sixteen of the Venezuelan BITs in force allow for claims under the ICSID Additional Facility Rules,[98] and additionally for the option of *ad hoc* arbitration under the

---

[93] Article 11.3 (emphasis added).
[94] *Quiport SA* v. *Republic of Ecuador*, ICSID Case No. ARB/09/23.
[95] *Pan American Energy LLC* v. *Plurinational State of Bolivia*, ICSID Case No. ARB/10/8.
[96] A. Mezgravis, 'The Standard of Interpretation Applicable to Consent and its Revocation in Investment Arbitration', *Transnational Dispute Management* 8 (2011): 31.
[97] E. Gaillard, 'Anti-Arbitration Trends in Latin America', *New York Law Journal* 239 (2008): 3.
[98] These rules allow for the administration of disputes where one of the parties is not a party to the ICSID Convention. ICSID, Additional Facility Rules, ICSID/11/Rev. 1, January 2003, Art. 2.

UNCITRAL rules.[99] The problematic aspect of a UNCITRAL award is that the judiciary of the host state may, under Article 5(2) of the New York Convention, deny the execution of the arbitral award when it considers that such execution would be against public order.[100] The Venezuelan Supreme Tribunal has indeed already relied on the argument of maintaining public order to annul an arbitral award in a commercial case rendered by an ICC tribunal,[101] and might well be willing to do so again. However, this problem is easily solved by the fact that an investor may enforce a UNCITRAL award in any of the 146 state parties to the New York Convention in which the Venezuelan state has assets.[102]

Therefore, the 'risk' of withdrawal is not really a risk, because parties will still be able to resort to the ICSID under the Additional Facility Rules or resolve their dispute via UNCITRAL.

2.4   Conclusion on investor–state arbitration

Investor–state arbitration grants wide protection to those who can benefit from accessing the system, which is dependent on having the 'right' nationality, namely, from a country that has concluded a BIT with Venezuela. Alternatively, Venezuelan investment law may be relied upon, but this does not guarantee access to ICSID. National investors may obtain access by restructuring their company so as to insert a foreign investor of the 'right' nationality in their corporate chain, as long as it is

---

[99] Venezuela signed the New York Convention in 1995; it entered into force on 9 May 1995.

[100] A. Mezgravis, 'El Orden Público Sustantivo, el Orden Público Procesal y la Arbitrabilidad como Causales de Denegación del Laudo: Especial Referencia a Venezuela y Otros Países de América Latina', in C. Soto Coaguila (ed.), *Arbitraje Comercial y Arbitraje de Inversiones. Convención de Nueva York de 1958 Reconocimiento y Ejecución de Sentencias Arbitrales Extrajeras* (Lima: Instituto Peruano de Arbitraje, 2009), p. 804.

[101] *VTV* v. *Elettronica Industriale SPA*, Political-Administrative Chamber of the Supreme Tribunal of Justice, Case No. 00-2759, Decision No. 00855, 5 April 2006, available at: www.tsj.gob.ve. See also Mezgravis, 'El Orden Público Sustantivo', p. 806.

[102] United Nations Convention on the Recognition and Enforcement of Foreign Arbitral Awards, 10 June 1958, 330 *UNTS* 38, Arts 1–5. Note that this possibility is threatened by the recent decision of the Venezuelan Government to return all gold that was stored abroad to the country, which severely limits the assets of Venezuela abroad and therefore the chances of foreign investors of obtaining full compensation from a foreign court. G. Gupta, 'With much Fanfare, Venezuela's First Batch of Repatriated Gold comes Home', *Christian Science Monitor*, 29 November 2011, available at: www.csmonitor. com/World/Americas/Latin-America-Monitor/2011/1129/With-much-fanfare-Venezuela-s-first-batch-of-repatriated-gold-comes-home.

planned carefully. Finally, the effects of Venezuela's withdrawal from the ICSID remain limited due to the extended time of protection ensured by Article 72 of the ICSID Convention and the survival clause in BITs.

Section 3: human rights law

3.1 Background

Venezuela is a party to the American Convention on Human Rights (ACHR) and is therefore obliged to 'respect and ensure the rights in the Convention',[103] including the right to property enshrined in Article 21 of the ACHR which provides that:

> 1. Everyone has the right to the use and enjoyment of his property. The law may subordinate such use and enjoyment to the interest of society. 2. No one shall be deprived of his property except upon payment of just compensation, for reasons of public utility or social interest, and in cases and according to the forms established by law.[104]

Thus, 'victims' of expropriations in Venezuela are entitled to initiate a claim under the Inter-American system should their right to property be violated.

The ACHR has two supervisory organs: the Inter-American Commission on Human Rights (IACHR) and the Inter-American Court of Human Rights (IACtHR).[105] Individuals, groups of individuals and legally recognised NGOs may file a petition to the Commission against any state party to the ACHR.[106] Although the Commission merely issues recommendations,[107] it has the power to decide on the admissibility of petitions and so 'filters' cases before they reach the IACtHR.[108] If the Commission concludes that the case is admissible, the Court may issue a judgment on the issue, which is binding and without appeal.[109]

---

[103] Organization of American States, American Convention on Human Rights, 'Pact of San Jose', Costa Rica, 22 November 1969, 1144 *UNTS* 143, Art. 1(1).

[104] ACHR, Art. 21.

[105] This mirrors the European human rights system that existed before the entry into force of the 11th Protocol in 1998. Jo. M. Pasqualucci, *The Practice and Procedure of the Inter-American Court of Human Rights* (Cambridge University Press, 2003), p. 4.

[106] ACHR, Art. 44. Thus, legal persons cannot file a claim, see below, section 3.2.3.

[107] ACHR, Arts 50–1.

[108] C. Tomuschat, 'The European Court of Human Rights and Investment Protection', in C. Binder, U. Kriebaum, A. Reinisch, S. Wittich (eds), *International Investment Law for the 21st Century. Essays in Honour of Christoph Schreuer* (Oxford University Press, 2009), p. 640.

[109] ACHR, Arts 67–8.

This section will first consider who can access the Inter-American system by looking at jurisdictional issues. It will then examine whether this system provides for valuable protection against illegal expropriations by looking at the benefits and risks of the system.

3.2   Access

3.2.1   Exhaustion of local remedies

Before a petition can be brought to the Commission, a preliminary issue needs to be complied with, namely, the exhaustion of local remedies.[110] However, as the reason for establishing a regional human rights court is precisely the lack of functioning national courts for certain sensitive issues, the exhaustion of local remedies is not a fixed requirement. According to Article 46(2), it may be waived when:

> (a) the domestic legislation of the state concerned does not afford due process of law for the protection of the right concerned, (b) the claimant has been denied access to local remedies or is prevented from exhausting them, (c) there is an unwarranted delay in rendering the final judgment on the remedies.[111]

These exceptions have been further clarified in the jurisprudence of the Court, where it is established that remedies need not be exhausted when they are inadequate or ineffective.[112] Moreover, the exhaustion of local remedies rule applies only when the respondent state brings a preliminary objection claiming that local remedies have not been exhausted.[113]

It has been observed in section 1 that while Venezuela has a solid constitutional basis for the protection of property leading to the assumption that domestic remedies are available and effective, recent judicial practice shows that the judiciary is partial and rarely decides against the government.[114] Several Venezuelan claimants before the IACtHR have argued that this implies that remedies are inadequate and ineffective, and therefore fall within the exceptions of Article 46(2).[115] The Commission

---

[110] ACHR, Art. 46(1)(a).   [111] ACHR, Art. 46(2).

[112] *Case of Velasquez-Rodriguez* v. *Honduras*, IACtHR, Judgment, 29 July 1988, Ser. C No. 4, paras 63–6.

[113] Case of the *Saramaka People* v. *Suriname*, IACtHR, Judgment, 28 November 2007, Ser. C, No. 172, paras 43–4.

[114] See above, pp. 136–8.

[115] See, e.g., *Jesús Mohamad Capote, Andrés Trujillo y Otros* v. *Venezuela*, IACHR Case No. 4348.02, Report No. 96/06, Admissibility, 23 October 2006, para. 69; *Allan R. Brewer*

has proven to be not unreceptive to this argument,[116] but nevertheless noted that in order to fall within one of the exceptions, claimants cannot simply rely on the general perception that the Venezuelan judiciary lacks independence. In other words, the Commission cannot make pronouncements as to whether all Venezuelan courts are partial all the time, but if the lack of judicial independence is demonstrated on the basis of the situation in the petitioned case, the Commission will certainly take it into account.[117]

3.2.2   Legal persons

It needs to be established who is a 'person' for the purposes of the ACHR. *Prima facie*, it would seem that the ACHR covers only natural persons, as Article 1(2) provides that 'for the purposes of this Convention, "person" means every human being'.[118] Thus, the Commission maintained for a long time that it did not have jurisdiction over claims by juridical persons.[119] Therefore, when a claim was filed to the Commission on behalf of 105 shareholders of the *Banco de Lima* against the Peruvian Government after it had presented its plan 'to expropriate all of the shares of the Peruvian Banks remaining in private hands',[120] the Commission held that:

> in the Inter-American system, the right to property is a personal right. The Commission is empowered to vindicate the rights of an individual whose property is confiscated, but is not empowered with jurisdiction over the rights of juridical beings, such as corporations or as in this case, banking institutions.[121]

However, the Commission and the Court have now somewhat softened their approach in relation to claims by juridical persons. The Commission has started granting rights that are ultimately for the benefit of legal persons, although the claims still have to be brought by natural persons. In the case concerning the Venezuelan television channel Globovisión,[122]

Carías v. *Venezuela*, IACHR Case No. 84-07, Report No. 97/09, Admissibility, 8 September 2009, para. 92.

[116] See *Jesús Mohamad Capote*, para. 69; *Allan Brewer Carías*, para. 92.
[117] *Jesús Mohamad Capote*, para. 69.   [118] ACHR, Art. 1(2).
[119] See, e.g., *Tomas Enrique Carvallo Quintana* v. *Argentina*, IACHR Case No. 11.859, Report No. 67/01, Admissibility, 14 June 2001, para. 55.
[120] *Banco de Lima Shareholders* v. *Peru*, IACHR Case No. 10.169, Report No. 10/91, Inadmissibility, 22 February 1991, para. 1.
[121] *Banco de Lima*, para. 3.
[122] *Case of Gabriela Perozo et al.* v. *Venezuela*, IACtHR, Judgment, 28 January 2009, Ser. C No. 194, paras 2–3. This channel is the only 'opposition channel' left, after Chávez

a group of employees and shareholders were systematically attacked and harassed by private citizens and state agents, so the victims petitioned the Commission for precautionary measures. The Commission, and later the Court, granted such measures in favour of the individuals who had brought the petition, but also more generally, by demanding that Venezuela adopt all measures 'to safeguard and protect the life, personal integrity, and freedom of expression of the reporters, executives, and workers of Globovisión and of other persons found at the facilities of that media company', and 'the measures necessary to provide perimeter protection for the headquarters of the Globovisión media company'.[123] Careful reading reveals that these measures are actually protecting the legal person Globovisión instead of merely natural persons.

Another case in which the Court dealt more directly with the interpretation of Article 1(2) in relation to legal persons is the *Cantos* v. *Argentina* case.[124] Mr Cantos was the owner of a business group in Argentina; the premises of several companies associated with his business group were searched by the Argentinean revenue department and numerous financial documents were 'seized without being inventoried'. These seizures led to financial losses of the companies.[125] The Commission admitted Mr Cantos' petition and transferred it to the Court. Argentina made preliminary objections relying on Article 1(2) of the ACHR to argue that Mr Cantos' business group was not protected by the Convention because it was a legal person. The Court rejected this argument, arguing that such interpretation would lead to an absurd result[126] and would remove 'an important group of human rights from protection by the Convention'.[127] The fact that Article 1(2) excludes juridical persons did not mean that 'an individual may not resort to the Inter-American system for the protection of human rights to enforce his fundamental rights, even when they are encompassed in a legal figure or fiction created by the same system of law'.[128] The Court

---

closed down all other radio and TV channels that were critical of him because these channels allegedly failed to comply with certain regulations. See 'Hugo Chavez Closes 34 Venezuelan Radio Stations', *The Telegraph*, 2 August 2002, available at: www.telegraph.co.uk/news/worldnews/southamerica/venezuela/5961183/Hugo-Chavez-closes-34-Venezuelan-radio-stations.html; 'Venezuela TV Channels Taken Off Air', BBC News, 24 January 2010, available at: news.bbc.co.uk/2/hi/americas/8477428.stm.

[123] *Asunto de la Emisora de Televisión 'Globovisión' respecto Venezuela*, Provisional Measures, Order of the IACtHR, 4 September 2004, Ser. E, p. 11.

[124] *Cantos* v. *Argentina*, IACtHR, Judgment, 7 September 2001, Ser. C No. 85.

[125] *Cantos*, para. 2.   [126] *Cantos*, para. 25.   [127] *Cantos*, para. 28.

[128] *Cantos*, para. 29.

clarified that this situation occurs, for example, in the case of shareholders and where an individual, such as Mr Cantos, files on behalf of himself and the company.[129]

These cases indicate that, while legal persons *as such* cannot petition the Commission, the rulings of the Commission and the Court may *benefit* legal persons as long as a natural person brings the claim. Thus, the restricting effect of Article 1(2) of the ACHR is nowadays less visible.

3.3   Protection

Once the jurisdictional requirements have been met, the actual width of Article 21 of the ACHR becomes important in order to determine the scope of what is protected under the Article. First, it is interesting to note that Article 21 protects the right to *property*,[130] rather than protecting *investments*. Thus, there is no need for a 'specific economic usage' of the property for it to be protected,[131] so it also protects Venezuelan land-owners whose farms or homes have been expropriated.

With the development of the Court's jurisprudence, it has become clear that the concept of property is to be interpreted broadly. In the *Ivcher Bronstein* case, a Peruvian–Israeli national who held a majority of shares in a television channel, was deprived of his nationality by the Fujimori Government.[132] This prevented him from being a majority shareholder in a television channel,[133] and therefore violated his right to property. The IACtHR held that the participation of Mr Baruch Ivcher Bronstein as a major shareholder 'constituted a property over which Mr. Ivcher had the right to use and enjoyment'.[134] In relation to the expropriation of property, it has been outlined above that Article 21

---

[129] *Cantos*, para. 30.

[130] On this issue, the ACHR has improved the clarity of the property provisions in comparison with the ECHR, which protects 'possessions'. L. Wildhaber and I. Wild-haber, 'Recent Case Law on the Protection of Property in the European Convention on Human Rights', in C. Binder, U. Kriebaum, A. Reinisch and S. Wittich (eds), *International Investment Law for the 21st Century: Essays in Honour of Christoph Schreuer* (Oxford University Press, 2009), pp. 657–9.

[131] U. Kriebaum, 'Local Remedies and the Standards for the Protection of Foreign Invest-ment', in C. Binder, U. Kriebaum, A. Reinisch and S. Wittich (eds), *International Investment Law for the 21st Century: Essays in Honour of Christoph Schreuer* (Oxford University Press, 2009), p. 232.

[132] *Case of Ivcher Bronstein v. Peru*, IACtHR, Judgment, 6 February 2001, Ser. C No. 74.

[133] Under Peruvian law, only nationals can own a business in telecommunications.

[134] *Ivcher Bronstein*, para. 123.

provides the conditions for a lawful expropriation.[135] While the Court has never dealt directly with the merits of a case solely concerning expropriation, several cases came close to an assessment of the expropriation conditions so the issue was discussed in some detail. It is interesting to briefly examine these cases, particularly to analyse the approach of the Court to compensation.

In the abovementioned case of *Ivcher Bronstein*, the Court held that concerning whether Mr Ivcher's right to property was violated, it 'should not restrict itself to evaluating whether a formal dispossession or expropriation took place, but should look beyond mere appearances and establish the real situation behind the situation that was denounced'.[136] This seems to indicate that creeping or indirect expropriations would also fall under the scope of protection.[137] After finding that Peru had violated both Article 21(1) and (2) by arbitrarily expropriating Mr Ivcher's shares, the Court went on to order restitution and compensation. However, the IACtHR did not prescribe the amount of compensation to be paid, but left this determination to the domestic authorities to be decided under the applicable rules of domestic legislation.[138] While an arbitral tribunal constituted under Peruvian domestic law awarded damages in the *Ivcher* case,[139] the deferral of the compensation issue to domestic courts could also, at least in Venezuela, possibly mean that damages will be low or will not be awarded at all. The IACtHR continued to follow this approach in other cases, such as the *Cesti Hurtado* v. *Peru* case, where it expressed hesitance to award compensation to a family corporation by holding that, because of the height of the claimed damages and the commercial nature of the claim, 'the Court considers that this determination corresponds to the ... national institutions rather than to an international human rights tribunal'.[140] The dangers of leaving the determination of compensation to domestic courts became evident in

---

[135] ACHR, Art. 21.   [136] *Ivcher Bronstein*, para. 124.

[137] P. Nikken, 'Balancing of Human Rights and Investment Law in the Inter-American System of Human Rights', in P-M. Dupuy, E-U. Petersmann and F. Francioni (eds), *Human Rights in International Investment Law and Arbitration* (Oxford University Press, 2009), p. 250.

[138] *Ivcher Bronstein*, para. 191(8).

[139] *Case of Ivcher Bronstein* v. *Peru, Monitoring Compliance with Judgment*, Order of the IACtHR, 21 September 2005, para. 14.

[140] *Case of Cesti Hurtado* v. *Peru, Reparations*, IACtHR, Judgment, 31 May 2001, Ser. C No.78, para. 46.

this case, where damages were initially awarded but were later annulled by the Peruvian Court of Appeal.[141]

The more recent *Case of Chaparro Álvarez and Lapo Íñiguez* v. *Ecuador* might indicate that the IACtHR has taken some measures to ensure that domestic courts grant a fair amount of damages. It outlined the complexity it encountered in determining the 'commercial value of the company'[142] in question, which had been arbitrarily seized by the authorities on the basis of allegations of drug trafficking. Furthermore, the Court listed some aspects that should be taken into account when determining such value and established that it did not have sufficient evidence on those issues. In spite of this complexity, the Court granted US$150,000 in compensation to the claimant, basing this amount on an expert opinion and on the principle of equity.[143] It then ordered the establishment of an independent arbitral tribunal under domestic law, which should determine the exact amount of compensation to be paid to the claimant. However, even if the tribunal concludes that compensation should be lower than US$150,000, the claimant may keep the money already granted. The Court further established a time limit within which the local arbitral tribunal must reach its decision.[144] In the meanwhile, while some efforts have been made to establish an arbitral tribunal, it has still not pronounced on the compensation to be paid.[145] This decision might indicate a change of approach, and certainly for the better. While, for reasons of evidence, it is understandable that the Court generally defers the question of compensation to national authorities, it should not lead to reduced protection of the victim.

3.4　Benefits and risks

The benefit of the Inter-American system is that, in principle, it protects all victims of expropriations in Venezuela, namely, Venezuelan land-owners and investors, as well as foreign investors (under the condition that cases on behalf of foreign investors are brought by a natural person). The fact that no cases have yet been brought by any of the expropriation

---

[141] *Case of Cesti Hurtado* v. *Peru, Monitoring Compliance with Judgment*, Order of the IACtHR, 17 November 2004 and 22 September 2006, para. 14.

[142] *Case of Chaparro Álvarez and Lapo Íñiguez* v. *Ecuador*, IACtHR, Judgment, 21 November 2007, Ser. C No. 170, para. 232.

[143] *Chaparro Álvarez*, paras 231–2 　　[144] *Chaparro Álvarez*, paras 232–3.

[145] *Case of Chaparro Álvarez and Lapo Íñiguez* v. *Ecuador*, IACtHR, Judgment, 22 February 2011, Monitoring Compliance with Judgment, paras 16–24.

victims in Venezuela might be due to the general perception among those victims that it is preferable to negotiate a settlement with the government, rather than taking the risk of being unsuccessful in court. However, the jurisprudence of the Court shows that it is increasingly worth pursuing a claim before the IACtHR. In this light, it is important for Venezuelan NGOs promoting the protection of human rights in general,[146] or property rights more specifically,[147] and for lawyers who pursue human rights claims, to bring this option to the attention of their clients or the general public.

The first risk, or perhaps disadvantage, is the fact that cases cannot be submitted directly to the IACtHR, but need to be sent there by the Commission if it finds them admissible, so only a small number of cases are sent to the Court 'on the basis of the best interests of human rights'.[148] This means that the majority of cases never reach the IACtHR. To give an example: the Commission received 1,658 petitions in 2011 of which forty originated from Venezuela.[149] Just twenty-three cases were submitted to the IACtHR in that year, only one of which involved Venezuela.[150] Thus, for the majority of cases, there is no prospect of ever obtaining a binding judgment, and it is questionable whether Venezuelan authorities will adhere to a non-binding document with recommendations from the Commission, since so far they have consistently been ignored.

The second risk is related to the first. As said before, the Court has never decided a case related solely to an expropriation, but by examining the cases which involved violations of the right to property more generally, it can be observed that these cases always dealt with the right to property in the context of a wider problem. For example, a number of cases against Nicaragua concerned violations of the right to property, but these claims were brought in the context of the Sandinista revolution and related to assets of a specific group of people, namely, those associated with the Somoza dictatorship.[151] Alternatively, cases touched upon the

---

[146] For example, Provea (www.derechos.org.ve) or Espacio Publico (www.espaciopublico.org).

[147] Observatorio de Derechos de Propiedad (http://paisdepropietarios.org).

[148] IACHR, 'What is the IACHR?', available at: www.cidh.oas.org/what.htm.

[149] None of these petitions concerned the right to property, Inter-American Commission on Human Rights, Annual Report of the Inter-American Commission on Human Rights 2011, 9 April 2012, OEA/Ser.L/V/II, p. 47.

[150] This case did not concern the right to property, IACHR, Annual Report 2011, pp. 62–3.

[151] See, e.g., *Martinez Riguero* v. *Nicaragua*, IACHR, Case No. 7788, Resolution No. 20/86, 10 April 1986 and *Martin* v. *Nicaragua*, IACHR, Case No. 10. 770, Report No. 12/94, Admissibility, 1 February 1994.

right to property in combination with other human rights. For example, in the abovementioned case of *Ivcher Bronstein*, the Court was concerned with violations of the right to a nationality, due process, judicial protection and freedom of speech.[152] Therefore, as the IACtHR decides so few cases, it is unlikely that the Commission will decide to submit a pure expropriation case to the Court.

Even if claims concerning expropriation were to eventually reach the IACtHR, it might be difficult to execute those judgments in Venezuela, in spite of the fact that judgments issued by the Inter-American Court are binding.[153] There are strong indications that the Venezuelan Government and the Supreme Tribunal of Justice (STJ) are 'unimpressed' by judgments of international mechanisms, especially those of the IACtHR, and do not feel obliged to comply with them. For example, when the claimant in the *Rafael Montserrat Prato* case asked the Court to present information about his case to the Commission and the IACtHR, the Court, in an almost rude passage, responded that: 'the Venezuelan judiciary is autonomous ... therefore, it does not recognize the judgments of any international organ or the idea that such organ is hierarchically superior'.[154]

This idea was further developed in 2003, when the STJ declared that all decisions of, *inter alia*, the IACtHR would always be subjected to a test of constitutionality, and that they would be executed only if they did not violate constitutional principles.[155] It came as no surprise that in 2008, the Supreme Tribunal relied on the alleged 'unconstitutionality' of the IACtHR decision in the *Case of Apitz Barbera* v. *Venezuela* (discussed in section 1) to decide that this judgment could not be executed.[156] The STJ held that execution of this judgment would go

---

[152] *Ivcher Bronstein* v. *Peru*, 2001.

[153] ACHR, Arts 67–8. The Court tests compliance by asking for periodic reports in which the state party must outline what it has done to comply with the judgment and by asking for the reaction of the victims on these reports (see Rules of Procedure of the Inter-American Court of Human Rights, reprinted in 'Basic Documents Pertaining to Human Rights in the Inter-American System', OAS/Ser.L/V/I.4 rev. 13, 2010, Art. 69).

[154] Translation by the author. *Rafael Enrique Montserrat Prato*, Constitutional Chamber of the Venezuelan Supreme Tribunal, Case No. 00-0190, Decision No. 776, 18 May 2001, available at: www.tsj.gob.ve.

[155] *Jesús Eduardo Cabrera Romero*, Constitutional Chamber of the Venezuelan Supreme Tribunal, Case No. 04-3301, Decision No. 1942, 15 July 2003, available at: www.tsj.gob.ve.

[156] See above, p. 137.

against essential constitutional principles and values of the Bolivarian Republic of Venezuela and would lead to an institutional chaos.[157]

As a consequence, Venezuela is not only violating its obligations as a state party to the ACHR and disregarding the well-known rule of international law that domestic law cannot be used to justify non-compliance with international obligations,[158] but it is also breaching the Venezuelan Constitution which provides in Article 23 that: 'the treaties, pacts and conventions relating to human rights which have been executed and ratified by Venezuela have a *constitutional rank* and *prevail over internal legislation* ... and shall be *immediately and directly applied by the court*'.[159] This attitude of indifference by the Venezuelan STJ is a risk for the execution of IACtHR judgments. While the IACtHR can, under Article 65 of the ACHR, inform the General Assembly of the United Nations of a member state's non-compliance with a judgment, this would merely bring the issue to the political sphere. In sum, it seems unlikely, in light of the fact that Venezuela is a very important supplier of petroleum, that the General Assembly would do anything more than condemning this attitude on paper.

3.5   Conclusion on the Inter-American human rights system

The Inter-American system is an accessible system as it provides a platform for all victims of expropriations in Venezuela. However, those benefits seem outweighed by the fact that very few cases can benefit from a binding decision by the IACtHR. Furthermore, the Venezuelan STJ has proved to be willing to risk committing an international wrongful act by subjecting decisions of the IACtHR to a 'constitutionality' test, which limits claimants' chances of a satisfactory outcome of this long process.

---

[157] *La interpretación acerca de la conformidad constitucional del fallo de la Corte Interamericana de Derechos Humanos de fecha 5 de agosto de 2008*, Constitutional Chamber of the Venezuelan Supreme Tribunal, Case No. 08-1572, Decision No. 1939, 18 December 2008, available at: www.tsj.gob.ve.

[158] Vienna Convention on the Law of Treaties, 22 May 1969, 1155 *UNTS* 331, Art. 27; ILC Articles on State Responsibility for Internationally Wrongful Acts, UNGA Resolution 56/83, UN GAOR 56th Sess., Annex, Agenda Item 162, UN Doc. A/RES/56/83, 2001, Art. 32; and see, in relation to the ACHR, *Case of Hilaire, Constantine and Benjamin et al.* v. *Trinidad and Tobago*, IACtHR, Judgment, 1 September 2001, Ser. C No. 81, para. 84.

[159] Venezuelan Constitution, Art. 23 (emphasis added).

Conclusion

This chapter started from the premise that human rights are codified in order to provide people with a tool to challenge violations of their rights. Against this background, it has been analysed whether the right to property, or the mechanisms protecting this right, fulfil their purpose and grant a right for *all* or if there is discrimination as to who can and who cannot enforce such right and obtain a remedy. This analysis was executed in the context of the recent wave of unlawful expropriations in Venezuela, by looking at the protection available for three identified groups of 'victims': landowners, national investors and foreign investors.

First, the remedies before domestic courts were examined. It was demonstrated that, although Venezuelan legislation provides for an independent and impartial judiciary, practice shows that the Venezuelan judiciary rarely decides against the government because of the high political risks that this would entail. Therefore, although all 'victims' can pursue a claim in domestic courts, this option does not mean much in practice. The chapter then analysed the option of diplomatic protection, once a popular means by which Western countries could ensure that their nationals were protected against recalcitrant host states in the South. The force with which Western states protected their nationals abroad led to firm opposition from Latin American states to the European-imposed rules that had developed 'in response to the requirements of the Western business civilization, and were, therefore, naturally biased in their favour'.[160] It was also demonstrated that investors usually benefit from diplomatic protection only if it is in the interests of their home state to pursue an action, so investors are never in control of the process. This explains why diplomatic protection has played only a limited role following the rise of investor–state arbitration.

The content and scope of investor–state arbitration was discussed in section 2, where it could be observed that for those who can access the system, extensive protection is offered. However, access requires the existence of an investment and the existence of a BIT between the home state and Venezuela, because reliance on Venezuelan foreign investment law promises little success. While national investors may try to belong to this group by restructuring their investment and inserting a foreign

---

[160] O. Lissitzyn, 'International Law in a Divided World', *International Conciliation* 542 (1963): 58, cited in Verweij and Schrijver, The Taking of Foreign Property under International Law, p. 22.

company in the corporate chain, it depends on the arbitral tribunal's willingness to recognise the effect of such restructuring. It was also demonstrated that the impact of Venezuela's withdrawal from the ICSID should not be overestimated, as the ICSID system provides sufficient protection through Article 72 of the Convention.

Finally, section 3 considered the protection of Venezuelan expropriation victims under human rights law. The right to property is protected under the ACHR; however, it has been evidenced that neither the Commission nor the Court have so far directly examined 'pure' expropriation claims and have dealt with the right to property only in combination with breaches of other rights. Furthermore, while there is no restriction on the nationality of claimants who are natural persons, claims by legal persons are still not allowed in the Inter-American system. Therefore, this option seems most relevant for Venezuelan landowners, but it is likely that only a limited number of claimants can benefit from a binding judgment by the IACtHR, because the majority of cases are declared inadmissible by the Commission.

This analysis indicates that not everyone has an equal chance of enforcing his or her right to property, at least not in practice. Foreign investors undoubtedly benefit from the best protection, because they have access to investor–state arbitration. The decision of the tribunal in the *Gambrinus* claim will demonstrate whether investor–state arbitration is also an option for Venezuelan investors. Alternatively, national investors may pursue a claim before the IACHR. Finally, for national landowners, who might well be most affected by the expropriations, the only possibility is to try to gain access to the Inter-American system. After examining these issues, it seems clear that there is some truth in the statement that for Venezuelan nationals whose property has been expropriated 'it seems that ... there are no rights'. While on paper all victims are protected against unlawful expropriation, the extent to which this right can be enforced differs significantly.

While times have changed considerably since the Argentinean lawyer Carlos Calvo formulated his famous doctrine in which he strived for equal treatment between nationals and foreigners through the settlement of all disputes in national courts, such equal treatment has still not been achieved. Is this the reason why a number of Latin American countries have recently showed signs of distrust towards the system of investment arbitration? The arguments used by the ALBA movement for their opposition to the ICSID are strikingly similar to the arguments of the Latin American countries at the time of the Drago and Calvo doctrines, and later during the discussions in the 1950s on the principle of permanent sovereignty over natural resources: foreigners should not enjoy better protection against expropriation and should therefore be subjected to the jurisdiction of the host state. Disputes on the merits and compensation should be settled in national courts rather than by an international 'imperialist' mechanism such as the ICSID.

However, there are several reasons why these arguments no longer have the same validity as they might have had before. First, such arguments do not sit well with the idea of the progressive realisation of human rights; where there is discrimination, one should strive to improve the position of those who are discriminated against (nationals) instead of decreasing the protection for the privileged (foreigners), and this will not be achieved through domestic settlement in national courts. Second, there is an increased consensus that sovereignty should be limited in many areas, which is visible, for example, in the development of humanitarian law rules for non-international armed conflicts. However, the idea underlying Calvo's doctrine remains valid: nationals and foreigners should be treated equally because, as outlined in the introduction of this chapter, the right to property does not discriminate between national and foreigner, so it is important to improve this situation. One possible solution would be to reform the Inter-American system by allowing direct petitions to the Court, and to increase the number of sessions of the IACtHR so that the Commission would not need to be so selective and the Court could hear more cases, including those of an economic nature. However, as long as equal treatment between nationals and foreigners does not exist, the right to property will remain, for many Venezuelans, a right *in theory*.

7

International human rights and the interpretation of international investment treaties: constitutional considerations

N. JANSEN CALAMITA

I Introduction

There is an irony about the way in which the international law of investment has developed. Throughout much of the twentieth century the international protection of foreign investors was the almost exclusive province of customary international law,[1] and during this period pitched ideological battles were fought to define the standards of protection due to foreign investors under customary international law.[2] At the same time, while states and academic commentators debated substantive standards of protection, investors, having no standing in international law, wary of subjecting themselves to adjudication by municipal institutions in host states, and cognizant of the vagaries involved in persuading their states of nationality to espouse claims of diplomatic protection on their behalf, devised creative strategies for resolving potential disputes with host states, involving the use of international arbitration and contractual clauses incorporating public

---

[1] The qualification here refers to the Friendship, Commerce and Navigation treaties, entered into by states prior to the advent of the modern international investment treaty. The United States was the chief proponent of this architecture for delineating standards of treatment of foreign nationals. See generally Kenneth J. Vandevelde, *United States Investment Treaties: Policy and Practice* (Boston, MA: Kluwer Law, 1992), pp. 7–43.

[2] For relatively concise overviews of the debate in customary international law, compare Andreas F. Lowenfeld, *International Economic Law* (Oxford University Press, 2002), chs 13–15 and M. Sornarajah, *The International Law on Foreign Investment*, 2nd edn (Cambridge University Press, 2005), ch. 10. See generally Thomas Wälde, 'A Requiem for the 'New Economic Order': The Rise and Fall of Paradigms in International Economic Law and a Post-Mortem with Timeless Significance', in Gerhard Hafner *et al.* (eds), *Liber Amicorum Professor Ignaz Seidl-Hohenveldern* (The Hague: Kluwer Law, 1998), p. 771.

international law as the law of the contract.[3] It was hardly an efficient system. Standards of protection were uncertain and mechanisms for dispute resolution were *ad hoc* and unpredictable in application and effectiveness. Geopolitically, the situation was destabilizing – another flashpoint for disagreement and tension among states, East–West, North–South, especially in those circumstances in which one state took the formal step of espousing a claim against another on behalf of its nationals operating abroad.

The conclusion of the ICSID Convention in 1965, and the accelerated adoption of bilateral and multilateral investment treaties beginning in the 1980s (and vastly accelerating in the 1990s) heralded a change.[4] Instead of contentious and uncertain norms of customary international law, states agreed to standards of treatment for foreign investors set out in investment treaties.[5] Instead of relying upon the espousal of claims on behalf of nationals by states, investors were empowered to raise their claims directly under the treaties entered into by their states.[6] Instead of *ad hoc* arbitral arrangements of variable effectiveness, investors could now in many cases avail themselves of the facilities of the ICSID to provide a framework for the resolution of investment disputes detached from the interference of national legal systems.[7] It was, it seemed, the dawning of a new era in which the protection of foreign investors would be guaranteed, states would benefit from liberated flows of foreign direct investment, and disputes with respect to specific investments would be resolved effectively and efficiently without each dispute becoming an inter-state dispute.

[3] See Robert B. von Mehren and P. Nicholas Kourides, 'International Arbitrations between States and Foreign Private Parties: The Libyan Nationalization Cases', *American Journal of International Law* 75 (1981): 476; Georges R. Delaume, 'State Contracts and Transnational Arbitration', *American Journal of International Law* 75 (1981): 893; Christopher Greenwood, 'State Contracts in International Law: The Libyan Oil Arbitrations', *British Yearbook of International Law* (1982): 27.

[4] See, e.g., Jesawald W. Salacuse, 'BIT by BIT: The Growth of Bilateral Investment Treaties and Their Impact on Foreign Investment in Developing Countries', *International Law* 24 (1990): 665.

[5] See, e.g., Francis A. Mann, 'British Treaties for the Promotion and Protection of Investments', *British Yearbook of International Law* (1981): 241, at p. 249; Pamela B. Gann, 'The US Bilateral Investment Treaty Program', *Stanford Journal of International Law* 21 (1985): 373.

[6] Mann, 'British Treaties for the Promotion and Protection of Investments'.

[7] On the conclusion of the ICSID Convention in particular, see Aaron Broches, 'The Convention on the Settlement of Disputes between States and Nationals of Other States', *Recueil des Cours* 136 (1972-II): 331; P. F. Sutherland, 'The World Bank Convention on the Settlement of Disputes', *International and Comparative Law Quarterly* 28 (1979): 367.

And yet this new era has only partly come to pass. For as the international law of investment has developed, through the treaty practice of states and the accumulation of published arbitral awards and decisions arising out of investor–state disputes, new issues, some likely not foreseen and some purposely deferred, have come to the fore.

On the one hand, the framework established by the ICSID Convention and other dispute settlement mechanisms created under investment treaties has proven to be remarkably effective at resolving disputes. While one cannot be statistically definitive owing to the continuing confidentiality of some investor–state proceedings, experience suggests that states have respected the agreements they have made to resolve disputes arising under investment treaties pursuant to various forms of arbitration. Moreover, it also appears that not only have states respected the dispute resolution processes they have established under these treaties through their participation in investor–state arbitrations, but they have also been willing thus far to respect the arbitral process at the critical and essential stage of performance of the arbitral award, even when otherwise disagreeing with the result.[8] There are, of course, exceptions to these general truths, and there have been some notable instances in which particular states have either refused to perform investment treaty awards voluntarily,[9] or in accordance with the ICSID Convention,[10] or where certain states have chosen to withdraw from either some or all of their investment treaties[11] or the ICSID Convention itself.[12] Such evidence does not, however, undermine the essential point: that the investor–state

---

[8] See generally Alan S. Alexandroff and Ian A. Laird, 'Compliance and Enforcement', in Peter Muchlinski, Federico Ortino and Christoph Schreuer (eds), *The Oxford Handbook of International Investment Law* (Oxford University Press, 2008), p. 1175.

[9] The Franz Sedelmayer saga is a notable example of protracted post-award litigation in the face of state recalcitrance. See Pål Wrange, '*Sedelmayer* v. *Russian Federation*, No. Ö 170-10. 2011 NYTT Juridiskt Arkiv 475. Supreme Court of Sweden, July 1, 2011', *American Journal of International Law* 106 (2012): 347.

[10] See, e.g., Matt Moffett, 'Besting Argentina in Court Doesn't Seem to Pay', *Wall Street Journal*, 21 April 2012, p. A11 (chronicling outstanding ICSID awards against Argentina).

[11] For example, in 2008 Ecuador terminated nine investment treaties – with Cuba, the Dominican Republic, El Salvador, Guatemala, Honduras, Nicaragua, Paraguay, Romania and Uruguay. See United Nations Conference on Trade and Development, 'Denunciation of the ICSID Convention and BITs: Impact on Investor–State Claims', IIA Issues Note, December 2010 (describing withdrawal of Bolivia and Ecuador from the ICSID and Ecuador's termination of a number of its investment treaties).

[12] See, e.g., ICSID News Release, 'Bolivia Submits a Notice under Article 71 of the ICSID Convention', 16 May 2007. See also Silvia Karina Fiezzoni, 'The Challenge of UNASUR Member Countries to Replace ICSID Arbitration', *Beijing Law Review* 2 (2011): 134.

mechanisms agreed to in investment treaties have proved to be remarkably good at doing what they were established to do: resolve disputes between investors and states in a binding and effective way.

Yet, while the arbitral mechanisms that states have chosen in order to resolve disputes arising under investment treaties have proven to be remarkably effective in providing for the binding resolution of disputes, dispute resolution is only part of the story. The truth is that as the number of investment treaties concluded among states approaches nearly 3,000, the content of the standards of protection afforded under those treaties remains almost as uncertain and as controversial as it ever was under customary international law. Even though the language used in these treaties has displayed a remarkable uniformity, the meaning of much of that language remains indeterminate. Thus, for example, that which constitutes 'measures tantamount to expropriation' under a bilateral investment treaty is no more certain than that which constitutes an indirect expropriation in customary international law. Determining what conduct constitutes a violation of the obligation to provide foreign investors with 'fair and equitable treatment' under an investment treaty remains as unpredictable as determining what conduct constitutes a violation of the 'minimum standard of treatment' as a matter of custom. And, indeed, this is not to mention the new ambiguities created by the inclusion of clauses in investment treaties without analogues in customary international law, such as the meaning of 'investment', guarantees of most-favoured-nation (MFN) treatment to investors and treatment promising that foreign investors will receive 'national treatment' with respect to their investments. Insofar as clarification of the standards of protection owed to foreign investors was a goal of the move by states from customary international law protections to investment treaty protections, it is a goal that has yet to be achieved.

On a theoretical level, the reason for this shortfall seems plain: in investment treaties, with some notable exceptions discussed below, states often have agreed to texts and adopted standards addressed to the state's capacity to regulate freely within the public sphere without at the same time (a) having reached an underlying political and economic settlement on the public values necessary to give those standards legal certainty; or (b) having delegated interpretive authority to constitutional–administrative dispute resolution structures, that is, courts, that might serve to develop such a settlement with some degree of coherence. This combination of imprecise, ambiguous standards and *ad hoc* arbitral resolution has lead to a lack of coherence in the development of a 'system' of international investment treaty-based law.

The absence of articulations of public goods (beyond investment protection) in most international investment treaties has led to calls for these treaties to be interpreted by reference to other areas of international law, such as international human rights law. Relying upon Article 31(3)(c) of the Vienna Convention on the Law of Treaties, it has been suggested that taking into account the international human rights obligations of parties to international investment treaties will serve the purpose of providing greater balance to the interpretation of investment treaties, and even greater clarity.[13] This chapter looks at this claim. Section II expands upon the political–legal character of investment treaties, explaining how these agreements have largely adopted standards-type norms instead of rules-type norms in articulating the protections owed by host states to foreign investors. Section III looks at the difficult issues created by such imprecise treaty drafting in the interpretation and application of the protection against indirect expropriation found in investment treaties. Section IV considers proposals to resolve this interpretive difficulty through the use of the principle of proportionality and reference to human rights instruments. Section V concludes with the suggestion that rather than relying upon unpredictable applications of rules of treaty interpretation, states would be better advised to clarify their investment treaties and explicate the scope of the guarantees of protection provided thereunder – as a number of states have begun to do.

II   The political–legal character of investment treaties: standards without norms

Like constitutional–administrative systems in many municipal orders, international investment treaties establish standards of protection owed by the state towards the individual, in this case the investor, and create mechanisms by which disputes as to the application of those standards may be resolved.[14] And as in many municipal systems, the protections so

---

[13] See Jasper Krommendijk and John Morijn, '"Proportional" by What Measure(s)? Balancing Investor Interests and Human Rights by Way of Applying the Proportionality Principle in Investor–State Arbitration', in Pierre- Marie Dupuy, Ernst-Ulrich Petersmann and Francesco Francioni (eds), *Human Rights in International Investment Law and Arbitration* (New York: Oxford University Press, 2009), p. 422.

[14] Whether the investment treaty regime is part of a larger process of constitutionalisation across international economic law generally has been the subject of much theorising, speculation and, occasionally, advocacy by academic commentators. See, e.g., David

provided are articulated in broad terms, that is, as 'standards' of protection, rather than express 'rules' that require interpretation in order to be given operational meaning.[15] The use of broadly framed standards, as opposed to more particularised rules, is not uncommon in domestic orders, whether in private law (e.g., 'unconscionability' or 'reasonable person') or public law (e.g., 'due process', 'natural justice' and *ordre public*). The use of standards, whether in legislation or treaties, involves the adoption of inherently flexible terms and reflects the difficulties with rules-based law-making.[16] As a functional matter, drafters simply cannot anticipate all the situations in which a rule might be applied and, consequently, cannot be expected (and often do not attempt) to explicate in legislation, or in legislative guidance materials, the precise application of the law in all circumstances.[17]

More than functionality, however, the use of standards is often a political choice that enables the responsible parties to adopt language of deliberate indeterminacy in order to secure agreement.[18] Terms may be chosen precisely because their generality and indeterminacy allows them to be acceptable to a range of actors involved in the legislative or treaty-making process.[19] Because each actor is able to ascribe its own subjective meaning to the standard at the time of adoption, further debate and disagreement, which might make more

Schneiderman, *Constitutionalizing Economic Globalization* (Cambridge University Press, 2007); Ernst-Ulrich Petersmann, *Constitutional Functions and Constitutional Problems of International Economic Law* (Fribourg: Fribourg University Press/Boulder Press, 1991); Deborah Z. Cass, *The Constitutionalization of the World Trade Organization* (Oxford University Press, 2005); Gus van Harten, *Investment Treaty Arbitration and Public Law* (Oxford University Press, 2007).

[15] See, e.g., Duncan Kennedy, 'Form and Substance in Private Law Adjudication', *Harvard Law Review* 89 (1976): 1754; Pierre Schlag, 'Rules and Standards', *UCLA Law Review* 33 (1985): 379, at pp. 382–3; Louis Kaplow, 'Rules Versus Standards; An Economic Analysis', *Duke Law Journal* 42 (1992): 557, at pp. 568–70.

[16] See generally, Michael Dorf, 'Legal Indeterminacy and Institutional Design', *New York University Law Review* 78 (2003): 875, at p. 877: 'Even if there can be agreement on high-order procedures – such as "count every vote" – or principles – such as "treat people equally" – the maddening complexity of the world and the fact of moral diversity often render agreement on specifics impossible.' See Kenneth W. Abbott and Duncan Snidal, 'Hard and Soft Law in International Governance', *International Organization* 54 (2000): 421, at p. 429.

[17] Cf. Abbott and Snidal, 'Hard and Soft Law in International Governance', p. 429 (addressing the issue in the context of treaties).

[18] See Kennedy, 'Form and Substance in Private Law Adjudication', pp. 1702–6, 1709–10.

[19] See Lon Fuller, 'The Forms and Limits of Adjudication', *Harvard Law Review* 92 (1978): 353, at pp. 393–405.

specific rules impossible to agree at the legislative stage, are deferred until a later point, specifically until the point at which the standard must be applied.

The use of standard-type norms brings its own set of difficulties. At its most extreme, the use of standards may lead to legal indeterminacy,[20] which may itself threaten the rule of law. While one might think that Michael Dorf overstates matters when he observes that 'if the application of a rule requires deliberation about its meaning, then the rule cannot be a guide to action in the way that a commitment to the rule of law appears to require',[21] there is a point to be taken. The rule of law requires that actors be able to ascertain the law and form a rational view about its likely application.[22] In municipal orders, at least, it may be possible to address problems of indeterminacy through the establishment of constitutional and administrative institutions entrusted and empowered to interpret and apply standards, and to do so by reference to the constitutional values that the administrative system or the system of judicial review is designed to vindicate. The reference to core normative values in the interpretation and application of standards is essential in order to give such standards a principled juridical meaning – almost by definition such standards cannot be given meaning solely by reference to text.[23] Municipal orders employing standards (and adhering to the rule of law) thus rely upon *both* the existence of transparent institutions with the constitutional legitimacy to make such interpretations and give such application *and* on the existence of a more or less identifiable body of social and political values, which may serve as the context within which the system of review operates.[24] In the absence

---

[20] Indefinite standards are, of course, but one possible cause of legal indeterminacy. Causes may also include conflicting rules, a lack of rules or standards, and the uncertain application of such rules or standards as exist. See Robert Alexy, *A Theory of Argumentation*, trans. Ruth Adler and Neil MacCormick (Oxford University Press, 1989), p. 1.

[21] Michael Dorf, 'Legal Indeterminacy and Institutional Design', *New York University Law Review* 78 (2003): 875, at p. 877. See Jules L. Coleman and Brian Leiter, 'Determinacy, Objectivity, and Authority', *University of Pennsylvania Law Review* 142 (1993): 549, at p. 582; Richard A. Epstein, 'Some Doubts on Constitutional Indeterminacy', *Harvard Journal of Law and Public Policy* 19 (1995): 363.

[22] Although the content of the rule of law is contested, knowledgeability and predictability are generally accepted characteristics. See, e.g., Robert Summers, 'The Principles of the Rule of Law', *Notre Dame Law Review* 74 (1999): 1692, at pp. 1693–5.

[23] See Ronald Dworkin, *Taking Rights Seriously* (Cambridge, MA: Harvard University Press, 1977), pp. 25–7.

[24] Kathleen M. Sullivan, 'The Justices of Rules and Standards', *Harvard Law Review* 106 (1992): 22, at pp. 58–61.

of such a normative underpinning, or such constitutional institutions, the interpretation and application of standards becomes unmoored from positive sources of legitimacy, and the process of interpretation and application almost surely becomes arbitrary, essentially subjective and illegitimate.[25]

Of course, even in the context of a legal system like a mature municipal order, in which constitutionally legitimised structures exist to give resolution to contested issues of interpretation and application of standard-type norms, resort to standards reduces legal certainty, since their application is always circumstance- or fact-dependent. While the reduction of legal certainty tends to erode legitimacy and undermine the rule of law,[26] the constitutional position of the decision-maker may nevertheless serve to preserve legitimacy even as the process produces decisions that are difficult to predict *ex ante*. Again, however, the construction of public values through the judiciary presupposes that the interpretation and application of the standards (a) takes place in a constitutional framework that allows for authoritative interpretation and application; (b) the process of interpretation and application is transparent and subject to public scrutiny; and (c) rests upon a clear articulation of the normative value set called upon to give juridical meaning to the standards. And it is here that the similarities between constitutional–administrative systems of domestic law and the regime of international investment law break down. As discussed further below, in international investment law not only is it difficult to find evidence of a politically legitimised normative value set upon which to base the interpretation and application of standard-type norms, but the structures in place for dispute resolution are ill-suited to provide constitutional guidance.

---

[25] In the municipal context, the suggestion is sometimes made that: 'where constitutional materials do not clearly specify the value to be preferred, there is no principled way to prefer any claimed human value to any other. The judge must stick close to the text and the history, and their fair implications, and not construct new rights.' Robert Bork, 'Neutral Principles and Some First Amendment Problems', *Indiana Law Journal* 47 (1971): 1, at p. 8. In principle, this view is unobjectionable, but much depends upon what one means by 'constitutional materials'. I do not here argue that reference beyond the 'four corners' of the text or even beyond the direct drafting history of the text necessarily leads one into the realm of the subjective and arbitrary.

[26] See Thomas Franck, 'Legitimacy in the International System', *American Journal of International Law* 82 (1988): 705, at p. 713.

III Indeterminacy in investment treaties: the example of indirect expropriations

To highlight the problem of standards and values in investment law, one might consider the protection against uncompensated expropriations (direct and indirect) found in virtually every investment treaty currently in force.[27] The conceptual problem in the context of indirect expropriations is to distinguish between those regulatory acts that, because of the extent of their consequences, should be treated as an 'indirect expropriation' requiring compensation and those that should not.[28] Many acts which a state may take through regulation and enforcement can serve to diminish the value of investments by limiting the ways in which assets may be used and enjoyed. The protection against uncompensated 'indirect expropriations', however, does not mean that the state must pay compensation for every attributable act of regulation or enforcement which diminishes the value of an investment. Plainly that is not what the expropriation provisions of investment treaties require. As one of the architects of the early bilateral investment treaty programme of the United States has put it: 'no State, of course, is prepared to surrender its power to regulate the use of property or is willing to commit to the payment of compensation each time it exercises that power'.[29] At the same time, however, clearly some regulatory action by the state will 'cross the line', and the provision providing for protection against both direct and indirect expropriations is obviously designed to prevent the state from doing indirectly through regulation that which it could not accomplish directly through seizure without compensation.

In fact, few investment treaties provide any suggested criteria for drawing this distinction,[30] that is, few investment treaties present the arbitrators of disputes arising under them with a firm foundation for resolving conflicts between investor rights, on the one hand, and public goods, on the other. Indeed, during the period of the greatest expansion of the numbers of investment treaties currently in force – roughly from

---

[27] See United Nations Conference on Trade and Development, Bilateral Investment Treaties 1995–2006: Trends in Investment Rulemaking, UNCTAD/ITE/IIT/2006/5 (2007); *ibid.*, Taking of Property, UNCTAD/ITE/IIT/15 (2000).

[28] Rosalyn Higgins, 'The Taking of Property by the State: Recent Developments in International Law', *Recueil des Cours* 176 (1982): 259, at p. 331.

[29] Kenneth J. Vandevelde, *Bilateral Investment Treaties: History, Policy, and Interpretation* (New York: Oxford University Press, 2010), p. 279.

[30] But see, below, section V.

the end of 1989 when there were 385 investment treaties to the end of 1999 when that number had reached 1,857 – almost no investment treaties expressed *any* specific criteria upon which to draw a distinction between non-compensable regulation, on the one hand, and measures tantamount to expropriation and requiring compensation, on the other.[31]

The absence of textual detail in investment treaties with respect to the protection against uncompensated expropriation is not, of course, because the customary international law on the meaning of expropriation is so clear. It is not.[32] Rather, if anything, it may be hypothesised that it is precisely because the concept of expropriation is contested in customary international law that states have resorted to vague, 'standards-type' drafting when addressing this core protection.[33] On this hypothesis, the reason for the 'omission' of precise language as to the scope of the expropriation protection in many treaties may be understood as a

---

[31] See United Nations Conference on Trade and Development, Taking of Property, UNCTAD/ITE/IIT/15, 2000. Indeed, even in a treaty as sophisticated and developed in its treatment of investment protection issues as the North American Free Trade Agreement (especially for its time – 1993/4), the meaning of expropriation is left notably vague. It was only through the experience of defending claims under that treaty that Canada and the United States developed treaty language in 2004 that gives greater clarity to the meaning of expropriation and the obligation to compensate. See Canada Model Foreign Investment Protection Agreement, Annex B.13(1), 2004, and US Model Bilateral Investment Treaty, Annex B, 2004. On the changes in treaty-making practice, especially since 2004, see, below, section V.

[32] Compare Alexander P. Fachiri, 'Expropriation and International Law', *British Yearbook of International Law* 5 (1925): 173 with John F. Williams, 'International Law and the Property of Aliens', *British Yearbook of International Law* 9 (1928): 1. The general literature on indirect expropriation in customary international law is vast. See generally George Christie, 'What Constitutes a Taking of Property Under International Law?', *British Yearbook of International Law* 38 (1962): 307; Rosalyn Higgins, 'The Taking of Property by the State', p. 259; Patrick M. Norton, 'A Law of the Future or a Law of the Past? Modern Tribunals and the International Law of Expropriation', *American Journal of International Law* 85 (1991): 474; George Aldrich, 'What Constitutes a Compensable Taking of Property? The Decisions of the Iran–United States Claims Tribunal', *American Journal of International Law* 88 (1994): 585; Vaughan Lowe, 'Regulation or Expropriation?' *Current Legal Problems* 55 (2002): 447; Stephen R. Ratner, 'Regulatory Takings in Institutional Context: Beyond the Fear of Fragmented International Law', *American Journal of International Law* 102 (2008): 475.

[33] By way of example, one might consider the negotiation of the 1980 Egypt–US BIT. See Kenneth J. Vandevelde, 'The Bilateral Investment Treaty Program of the United States', *Cornell International Law Journal* 21 (1988): 201, at pp. 232–3, n. 208 (providing background to the negotiations in which Vandevelde acted as counsel to the US negotiating team).

political choice of vague standards instead of specified rules in order to reach a textual agreement, but without resolving the parties' underlying normative issues.

IV   An interpretive role for proportionality and human rights?

In response to the imprecision of investment treaty texts, a number of investor–state arbitral awards have invoked the principle of proportionality as a tool with which to strike a balance between the rights of investors, as broadly guaranteed in investment treaties, and the rights of states to regulate for the public good, as left implicit in those same treaties.[34] This is an interesting development in no small part because none of the treaties involved in these cases has included language that expressly calls for the application of a principle of proportionality or requires a balancing as such. Academic commentators have also taken notice of the invocation of proportionality in investment treaty arbitration, and a number have presented proportionality as a remedy for the perceived ills of international investment law, usually by way of protecting states from the broadly phrased obligations they have undertaken in their investment treaties and the broad enforcement of these obligations by the arbitral tribunals they have established.[35]

While the acceptance of proportionality into international law, either as custom or as a general principle of law recognised by civilized nations, is open to more question and doubt than is sometimes acknowledged,[36] this is not the focus of this chapter. Rather, the chapter focuses on the use of proportionality as such and on the role that international

---

[34] See, e.g., *Técnicas Medioambientales Tecmed SA* v. *Mexico*, ARB(AF)/00/2, Award, 29 May 2003, para. 122.

[35] See, e.g., Alex Sweet Stone, 'Investor–State Arbitration: Proportionality's New Frontier', *Law and Ethics of Human Rights* 4 (2010): 47, at p. 49; Anne van Aaken, 'Defragmentation of Public International Law through Interpretation: A Methodological Proposal', *Indiana Journal of Global Legal Studies* 16 (2009): 483; Benedict Kingsbury and Stephan Schill, 'Investor–State Arbitration as Governance: Fair and Equitable Treatment, Proportionality and the Emerging Global Administrative Law', in Albert Jan van den Berg (ed.), *50 Years of the New York Convention*, ICCA Congress Series, No. 14 (Alphen aan den Rijn: Kluwer Law, 2009), p. 5.

[36] Chinese administrative law, for example, recognises no such principle, and the question thus becomes upon what doctrinal peg proportionality's invocation is to be hung if it is not itself a rule of customary international law or 'a general principle of law recognised by civilized nations'. See Han Xiuli, 'The Principle of Proportionality in *Tecmed v. Mexico*', *Chinese Journal of International Law* 6 (2007): 635, at p. 650. Contra Anne van Aaken, 'Defragmentation of Public International Law through Interpretation', p. 502.

human rights law might play in addressing two key issues implicated by the use of proportionality in any context: interest identification and weight.

At its most abstract level, the concept of proportionality posits that 'individuals affected by [state] decisions should not be required to bear a burden that is unnecessary or disproportionate to the ends being pursued'.[37] From this premise comes the well-known tripartite framework of questions, or at least issues, that a tribunal invoking proportionality ought to address: (1) *suitability*: are the means used by the state suitable (reasonably likely) to achieve the aim it pursues?; (2) *necessity*: are the means adopted necessary (indispensable) to achieve the aim pursued?; (3) *proportionality stricto sensu*: even if there are no less restrictive means, is the burden on the individual excessive relative to the benefits secured by the state objective?[38]

Proportionality by its terms therefore requires a balancing. But as a matter of practical reasoning, this balancing requires *ab initio* an identification and qualification of that which is to be balanced, that is, the rights and interests at stake. In a municipal constitutional or administrative system, at least, one might hope to find those rights and interests expressed in a constitutional document or, at least, find a constitutional structure designed to give definitive exposition to the rights of the polity.[39] In investment treaties, however, one is presented with quite a different situation. In investment treaties, as a matter of generality, one finds broad 'standards' of protection, relative silence with regard to the residual rights of the state, and an absence of institutions charged with rendering systemic interpretations of the treaty text.

To return to the protection against uncompensated expropriation, by way of example, the language adopted in most investment treaties remains at a remarkably general level.[40] Thus, with regard to the text – the starting point for any interpretive effort – the language with respect to expropriation is generally not helpful either in specifying the contours of the identified investor rights or saying much, if anything, about the

---

[37] Jeffrey Jowell and Anthony Lester, 'Proportionality: Neither Novel nor Dangerous', in Jeffrey Jowell and Dawn Oliver (eds), *New Directions in Judicial Review* (London: Stevens, 1988), pp. 51, 69.

[38] See, e.g., Case C-331/88, *Fedesa* [1990] ECR I-4023.   [39] See, above, section II.

[40] See, e.g., Austria–Egypt Agreement for the Promotion and Protection of Investments, 2001, Art. 4(1): 'Investments of investors of either Contracting Party shall not be expropriated in the territory of the other Contracting Party except for a public purpose by due process of law and against compensation.'

states' residual rights with respect to regulation. Reading expropriation provisions in investment treaties, one is left with the conclusion that while states have been willing to agree that expropriations need to be compensated, they have been unwilling (or unable) to articulate the circumstances in which an expropriation will be said to have occurred. What is especially interesting in this respect is that whereas investment treaties often have very specific rules with respect to the manner in which compensation should be calculated in the event an expropriation is found,[41] with respect to the circumstances that will constitute an expropriation in the first instance, there is usually nothing more to go on than the undefined term 'expropriation'.

To move beyond the text to extrinsic evidence gets one little further. In the main, the drafting histories of investment treaties are not available[42] and, indeed, when they have been made public, they have proved to be largely inconclusive in identifying the core values and objectives of the protections specified.[43] Similarly, with respect to textual expressions of the general object and purpose of the treaty, as expressed through perambulatory clauses, for example, in the great majority of investment treaties there is limited basis upon which to calibrate the broad protections guaranteed elsewhere in the treaty. The preambles of most investment treaties simply emphasise that the object and purpose of the agreement is to promote and protect

---

[41] See, e.g., Austria–Egypt Agreement for the Promotion and Protection of Investments, Art. 4(2): 'Such compensation shall be equivalent to the fair market-value of the investment, as determined in accordance with recognized principles of valuation taking into account such as, *inter alia*, the capital invested, replacement value, appreciation, current returns, goodwill and other relevant factors, immediately prior to or at the time when the decision for expropriation was announced or became publicly known, whichever is the earlier.'

[42] See, e.g., *Vannessa Ventures Ltd* v. *Venezuela* , ICSID Case No. ARB(AF)/04/6, Decision on Jurisdiction, 22 August 2008, para. 58; *Desert Line Projects LLC* v. *Yemen*, ICSID Case No. ARB05/17, Award, 6 February 2008, para. 109; *Wintershall Aktiengesellschaft* v. *Argentina*, ICSID Case No. ARB/04/14, Award, 8 November 2008, para. 108.

[43] See, e.g., *Fireman's Fund Insurance Co.* v. *Mexico* ICSID Case No. ARB(AF)/02/01, Decision on the Preliminary Question, 17 July 2003, para. 94; *Canadian Cattlemen for Fair Trade* v. *United States*, NAFTA Tribunal, Award on Jurisdiction, 28 January 2008, para. 158; *Aguas del Tunari SA* v. *Bolivia*, ICSID Case No. ARB/02/3, Decision on the Respondent's Objections to Jurisdiction, 21 October 2005, para. 274. See also Kaj Hobér, 'Misconduct by Proxy? Trying to Understand Article 22 of the ECT', in M. Á. Fernández-Ballesteros and David Arias (eds), *Liber Amicorum Bernardo Cremades* (Madrid: Wolters Kluwer, 2010), pp. 573, 580 (noting the limited usefulness of *travaux* in interpreting Art. 22 of the Energy Charter Treaty).

investments in the respective states.[44] In some instances, the pre-ambles may be more elaborate, as discussed in section V, but in the majority of cases, such as in the investment treaties entered into by European states,[45] there are seldom any statements in the preambles or text of the treaty to suggest other purposes. Thus, one finds few, if any, references to obligations of the investor with respect to its investment, or to the enduring power of the state to regulate in pursuit of public goods, or even to derogate from the protections granted in extreme circumstances, such as in the exercise of the state's essential security interests. This generalisation holds true in the great mass of treaties, whether between developed and developing states or between developing states themselves.

Investment treaties generally do not provide references to the residual regulatory rights of the state or the human rights of the host state population. In searching for a basis for the identification of rights and interests which might be included in a balancing of textually identified investor rights, therefore, in most cases one is left with a textual void. The text of the investment treaty, however, is not the only source for the interpretation of its provisions. Under the recognised rules of treaty interpretation there are other sources to which an arbitral tribunal may have reference when interpreting an investment treaty's guarantees. Through this interpretive process some have suggested that it may be possible to identify rights and interests beyond those expressed positively in the treaty text in order to provide balanced interpretations informed by the principle of proportionality.[46] In cer-tain cases, for example, the applicable law provision of an investment treaty and/or the jurisdictional clause may provide an express basis for an interpretive reference to sources of law external to the investment

---

[44] In this regard, the preamble in the 2003 investment treaty between the United Kingdom and Bosnia-Herzegovina is representative of a great many investment treaties: 'Desiring to create favourable conditions for greater investment by nationals and companies of one State in the territory of the other State: Recognising that the encouragement and recipro-cal protection under international agreement of such investments will be conducive to the stimulation of individual business initiative and will increase prosperity in both States; [The Parties] have agreed as follows'.

[45] See, e.g., Austria–Egypt Agreement for the Promotion and Protection of Investments (2001); German Model BIT (2008); France Model BIT (2006). See N. Jansen Calamita, 'The Making of Europe's International Investment Policy: Uncertain First Steps', *Legal Issues in European Integration* 38 (2012): 301–30.

[46] See Krommendijk and Morijn, '"Proportional" by What Measure(s)?', p. 422.

treaty, such as international law generally and human rights treaties in particular.[47] In addition, even without such an applicable law clause, Article 31(3)(c) of the Vienna Convention on the Law of Treaties operates to require that the interpretation of a treaty 'take into account other relevant rules of international law applicable in the relations between the parties'.[48] Under this provision, such 'relevant rules' may in principle include international human rights treaties to which the parties to an investment treaty are also parties.[49]

Because of its general applicability, Article 31(3)(c) provides a potential gateway for reference to human rights instruments in the interpretation of investment treaties.[50] Article 31(3)(c), however, is not a particularly straightforward provision; it leaves a good many questions open about how interpretation should proceed under its terms. Article 31(3)(c) thus raises interpretive questions as to the meaning of 'take into account', 'rules of international law' and 'applicable', as well as important operative questions about the criteria for the relevance of other rules[51] and whether all the parties to a multilateral agreement must also be parties to the other treaty relied upon – an issue particularly raised in the context of regional investment treaties.[52] For the purposes of this chapter, the meaning of 'take into account' is of particular interest as it raises a global question about what role the introduction of human rights treaties via the mechanism of Article 31(3)(c) might have in the interpretive process.

---

[47] See Ursula Kriebaum, 'Human Rights and the Population of the Host State in International Investment Arbitration', *Journal of World Investment and Trade* 10 (2009): 653, at pp. 660–1.

[48] See generally Campbell McLachlan, 'Investment Treaties and General International Law', *International and Comparative Law Quarterly* 57 (2008): 361.

[49] See Report of the Study Group of the International Law Commission, 'Fragmentation of International Law: Difficulties Arising from the Diversification and Expansion of International Law', 58th Sess., 1 May–7 June and 3 July–11 August 2006, UN Doc. A/CN.4/L.682, 13 April 2006, paras 471–2.

[50] Article 31(3)(c) applies simply by virtue of the treaty being a creation of international law and therefore subject to the rules of general international law, including the law of treaties. See N. Jansen Calamita, 'Countermeasures and Jurisdiction: Between Effectiveness and Fragmentation', *Georgetown Journal of International Law* 42 (2011): 233, at pp. 276–80.

[51] On the application of Art. 31(3)(c) generally, *see Oil Platforms* (*Iran v. US*), Merits, 2003 *ICJ Reports*, 2003, pp. 25, 161, paras 41–2.

[52] On this latter issue, see, e.g., Report of the Panel, 'European Communities: Measures Affecting the Approval and Marketing of Biotech Products', WT/DS291–3/R, 29 September 2006, p. 333, para. 7.68.

By way of brief example one might consider Article 11 of the International Covenant on Economic, Social and Cultural Rights (ICESCR).[53] The text of Article 11 indicates that 'the States Parties to the present Covenant recognize the right of everyone to an adequate standard of living for himself and his family, including adequate food, clothing and housing, and to the continuous improvement of living conditions'. Among many debates about the meaning of Article 11 has been whether or not Article 11 implies a 'right to water'. While a right to water is not mentioned in the terms of Article 11, a number of UN bodies, including the General Assembly, have interpreted its guarantee as including such a right.[54] On the basis of these interpretations, the 'right to water' has been asserted in a number of investor–state disputes both as general 'context' to be taken into account in the interpretation of the investment treaty's terms, and more directly as an affirmative defence to the state's performance of its investment treaty obligations.[55]

In principle there is a difference between reference to relevant rules of international law for the purposes of interpretation and the invocation of other rules of international law as creating a conflict precluding the execution of international obligations.[56] In the latter situation general principles of international law provide a number of tools that may be called upon to resolve such conflicts: the principle of *lex specialis*;[57] the principle of *lex posterior*;[58] and the principle that the latest expression of the states' intentions resolves any conflict.[59] In order to determine whether a conflict exists, however, the treaties must first be interpreted.

---

[53] International Covenant on Economic, Social and Cultural Rights, 16 December 1966, 999 *UNTS* 3, entered into force 3 January 1976.

[54] See General Assembly Resolution 64/292, A/RES/64/292, 3 August 2010; Committee on Economic, Social and Cultural Rights, General Comment No. 15: The Right to Water, UN Doc. E/C.12/2002/11, 20 January 2003. See also Michael J. Dennis and David P. Stewart, 'Justiciability of Economic, Social, and Cultural Rights: Should There be an International Complaints Mechanism to Adjudicate the Rights to Food, Water, Housing, and Health?' *American Journal of International Law* 98 (2004): 462. See generally Kerstin Mechlem, 'Treaty Bodies and the Interpretation of Human Rights', *Vanderbilt Journal of Transnational Law* 42 (2009): 905.

[55] See Jorge E. Vinuales, 'Access to Water in Foreign Investment Disputes', *Georgetown International Environmental Law Review* 21 (2009): 733.

[56] See Campbell McLachlan, 'The Principle of Systemic Integration and Article 31(3)(c) of the Vienna Convention', *International and Comparative Law Quarterly* 54 (2005): 279, at p. 286.

[57] See Martii Koskenniemi, 'Study on the Function and Scope of the *lex specialis* Rule and the Question of Self-contained Regimes', ILC (LVI)/SG/FIL/CRD.1 and Add. 1, para. 160.

[58] See Vienna Convention on the Law of Treaties, Art. 30(3).

[59] See Joost Pauwelyn, *Conflict of Norms in Public International Law* (Cambridge University Press, 2005), p. 328.

One view of Article 31(3)(c)'s instruction to 'take into account' is that it serves as an avenue for the introduction of the principle of proportionality into the interpretation of treaty obligations. Van Aaken, for example, has argued that Article 31(3)(c) allows for the reconciliation of 'intra-constitutional conflicts of public international law through interpretational means, such as balancing and the principle of proportionality, by using human rights law in the interpretation of nonhuman rights law'.[60] On this view, Article 31(3)(c), as applied in the context of the interpretation of an investment treaty, requires a balancing of the provisions of the investment treaty under interpretation with such rules of international law (e.g., international human rights law) as may be applicable and relevant.[61] Put into operational terms, van Aaken suggests that:

> the judge has to first consider whether human rights law informs the interpretation of the non-human rights treaty under Article 31(1) of the Vienna Convention. Second, the judge has to consider whether human rights law is applicable between the parties under Article 31(3)(c) ... [Third, t]he judge then has to balance the principle of the treaty to be interpreted, which is presumably in conflict with the human rights principle in question.[62]

Van Aaken's construction of Article 31(3)(c), and its reliance on the principle of proportionality, does not tell us much about what it means to 'take account of' human rights treaties (if we assume them to be 'applicable' between the parties and relevant). Rather, it returns us to the principle of proportionality. Some comments on proportionality have been offered above, and this is not the place for a detailed critique of the concept.[63] It may suffice to observe here, however, in the context of Article 31(3)(c), that proportionality is in the end nothing more than a technical framework by which one may organise an argument. Absent an infusion of normative content from external sources, proportionality simply functions as a scale without weights.[64] Thus, even if we assume

---

[60] van Aaken, 'Defragmentation of Public International Law through Interpretation', p. 501.

[61] van Aaken, 'Defragmentation of Public International Law through Interpretation', p. 506.

[62] van Aaken, 'Defragmentation of Public International Law through Interpretation', p. 506.

[63] For a general critique of the principle of proportionality, see Grégoire C. N. Webber, 'Proportionality, Balancing, and the Cult of Constitutional Rights Scholarship', *Canadian Journal of Law and Jurisprudence* 23 (2010): 179.

[64] Cf. Ole Spiermann, 'Twentieth Century Internationalism in Law', *European Journal of International Law* 18 (2007): 785, at p. 802: 'proportionality as such is a balance without weights'.

that a rational and principled process of balancing is possible,[65] and we are able to identify in general terms that which is to be balanced,[66] we do not (and cannot) know how the balance called for by the principle of proportionality will be struck until we know the identity of the interests we intend to recognise, what weight they are to be given, and to whom we intend to entrust that balancing. This, of course, brings us back to the point noted earlier about the importance of establishing a sociopolitical (or 'constitutional' if one prefers) value set that can provide a basis for the principled and legitimised recognition of the rights and interests to be put into the proportionality balance. Absent such criteria for determining what goes on the scales and what does not, we are beset with indeterminacy, subjectivity and an absence of consensual validation.[67] Proportionality simply provides no answers to these concerns and, indeed, may actually obfuscate the importance of the political process of contesting and establishing constitutional values.

In response to this concern, the suggestion has been made that in the investment treaty context the 'constitutional' values are already

---

[65] Conceptions of proportionality take a consequentialist view that protected rights are susceptible to balancing against the public interest. This premise, however, raises the issue of commensurability. Are the matters which the proportionality equation purports to balance commensurable so that it is possible to undertake such balancing in a principled way? Proportionality seems to assume a scale on which the value of protecting rights and the value of protecting the public interest can be measured, compared and balanced. See Denise Meyerson, 'Why Courts Should Not Balance Rights Against the Public Interest', *Melbourne Law Review* 31 (2007): 873, at p. 881. But it may be objected that in order for the inquiry to be in any way principled, it requires a common scale upon which the weights of principles and the weights of interferences can be measured. Without such a common scale, asking whether the public's interest in securing benefit x is more weighty than the individual's interest in exercising right y (or the cost of the individual's inability to exercise right y in a certain way) is subject to the criticism of being without constraint, and perhaps being irrational because the lack of commensurability is likely to lead to open-ended decision-making on the balance of all reasons and facts. See Jürgen Habermas, *Between Facts and Norms: Contributions to a Discourse Theory of Law and Democracy*, trans. William Rehg (Cambridge: Polity Press, 1996), p. 259.

[66] That is, the rights under an international investment treaty and other 'relevant rules of international law applicable in the relations between the parties'.

[67] See Thomas Schultz, 'The Concept of Law in Transnational Arbitral Legal Orders and some of its Consequences', *Journal of International Dispute Settlement* 2 (2011): 59, at p. 69: 'The issue is this: in the absence of ascertainable and agreed higher standards against which to judge the correct allocation of resources effected by a system of norms, any reference to "justice" in a discussion on the virtues and vices of a rule system necessarily would amount to a scientifically unsupportable expression of individual or collective preferences.'

established, if not in the investment treaty itself because if its imprecision, then in terms of human rights treaties because of their universality.[68] The idea, however, that reference to human rights treaties will serve to clarify systemic values in international investment law seems unlikely. Like the investment treaties they are meant to help interpret, international human rights treaties are themselves largely indeterminate and lack sufficiently clear normative content to serve as a principled interpretive guide to the rights and obligations in other treaties.[69] While the vagueness and ambiguity of expressed rights in international human rights treaties is most acute with respect to economic, social and cultural rights,[70] even civil and political rights, which are less contested, are often indeterminate as well.[71] Moreover, while most international human rights treaties provide for some delegation for the purposes of their general interpretation, these delegated bodies have heretofore lacked the power or legitimacy to give binding, systemic legal readings of their treaty texts.[72] As a consequence, in the event such treaties might be raised for interpretation and application in an arbitral setting, such as may arise in an investment treaty dispute, the imprecision of human rights treaty terms (and the absence of authoritative interpretation) raises further concerns about the indeterminacy of the parties' rights and obligations and the *ex ante* ability of affected parties to know the law.[73]

---

[68] See Krommendijk and Morijn, '"Proportional" by What Measure(s)?', p. 422.

[69] See, e.g., John Tobin, 'Seeking to Persuade: A Constructive Approach to Human Rights Treaty Interpretations', *Harvard Human Rights Journal* 23 (2010): 1; Ryan Goodman and Derek Jinks, 'How to Influence States: Socialization and International Human Rights Law, *Duke Law Journal* 54 (2004): 621, at p. 676; Louise Doswald-Beck and Sylvian Vité, 'International Humanitarian Law and Human Rights Law', *International Review of the Red Cross* 293 (1993): 94, at p. 106: 'The major difficulty of applying human rights law as enunciated in the treaties is the very general nature of the treaty language.'

[70] See generally, Henry J. Steiner, Philip Alston and Ryan Goodman, *International Human Rights in Context: Law, Politics, Morals*, 3rd edn (Oxford University Press, 2008), pp. 280–94.

[71] Tobin, 'Seeking to Persuade', p. 1 (citing the shifting scope of the prohibition against torture and the ambiguous parameters of the right to a fair trial). In understanding why human rights treaties contain such imprecise terms, and lack delegation mechanisms for binding, authoritative interpretation, one may note again the consent dynamic whereby the use of vague language and ambiguous terms is chosen to facilitate textual agreement. See Abbott and Snidal, 'Hard and Soft Law in International Governance', p. 429.

[72] See generally Mechlem, 'Treaty Bodies and the Interpretation of Human Rights', p. 905.

[73] See, above, section III.

V The present as the past: the new reality of investment treaties

The risk of total incoherence in the interpretation and application of the vast network of investment treaties is ameliorated somewhat by adjudicative dialogue whereby different arbitral tribunals and adjudicative bodies, aware of one another's activities, exchange ideas and views indirectly and imperfectly.[74] While this dialogic process of the development of the law grates against international law's foundational notion of consent-based norm creation, it is the dynamic that states have created through their treaty practice in a great many BITs. It is, however, neither the only nor the most important dynamic prevalent in investment treaty law. For just as scholars have begun to identify and theorise a *de facto* multilateralisation of investment treaty obligations through a dynamic dialogue of arbitral tribunals interpreting largely similar imprecise investment treaty texts, states have once again reminded us of their central, controlling role in the field.

In many ways, the kind of investment treaty that has been the focus of this chapter to now is a thing of the past. Beginning with the revision of the Canadian and US model investment treaties in 2004, state treaty-making practice has developed swiftly and substantially.[75] In a trend that can now be seen in North and South America, Asia and Oceania, states have become far more sophisticated in their investment-related treaty practices than they were even ten years ago. While there is not the space here for a full recitation of this development, a few salient points may be noted. First, states have moved away from entering into BITs and have moved towards entering into free trade agreements (FTA) with investment chapters. As a consequence, the context within which investment protections are found in a FTA is far more varied and broad looking than in a classic BIT. Second, states in the Americas, Asia and Oceania are no longer content to leave the object and purpose of their agreements unexpressed or with a singular focus on investment protection. States are now far clearer and far more comprehensive in their expressions of treaty purpose, for example, making express shared intentions to retain regulatory freedom both generally, but also in specially

---

[74] See Gabriel Kaufmann-Kohler, 'Arbitral Precedent: Dream, Necessity or Excuse?' *Arbitration International* 23 (2007): 357.

[75] See David A. Gantz, 'The Evolution of FTA Investment Provisions: From NAFTA to the US–Chile Free Trade Agreement', *American University International Law Review* 19 (2004): 679.

identified areas.[76] Third, states have given attention to the drafting of substantive protections, clarifying the meaning of these provisions so as to give textual express to the balance that states wish to see struck between investor protection and state regulatory freedom. Thus, for example, in a host of recent investment treaties, states have adopted explanatory annexes with respect to the meaning of the protection against uncompensated indirect expropriations.[77] These annexes serve to indicate the understanding of the parties as to the meaning of expropriation in a way that the undefined use of the term (and implicit reference to customary international law) simply cannot.

This move towards precision in investment treaty drafting is an interesting one, especially given the dynamics described above with respect to the treaty-making process.[78] What is evident from this practice is that states have become more cautious and more considered in the way in which they take on obligations towards foreign investors. This development has been driven both by shifting global investment flows and because – as the states that have spurred this development have discovered (i.e., Canada, Mexico and the United States) – imprecision in investment treaties can lead to unwelcome and unforeseen challenges to state regulatory action. Through this development, it is suggested, states are coming closer in at least some recent treaties to identifying a core shared value set which animates their agreements. In principle, this should make the application and interpretation of these agreements more predictable. It may even make reference to constitutional adjudicative techniques like 'proportionality' more legitimate.

---

[76] See, e.g., United States–Uruguay BIT (2005) (recognising the rights of the parties to regulate and specifically with respect to 'the protection of health, safety, and the environment, and the promotion of consumer protection and internationally recognized labour rights'); Japan–India Comprehensive Economic Partnership Agreement (2011) ('reaffirming their rights to pursue their economic and development goals and their rights to realise their national policy objectives'); ASEAN–Australia–New Zealand Free Trade Agreement (2010).

[77] See, e.g., Central America–Dominican Republic–United States Free Trade Agreement (2004), Annex 10-B; Korea–United States Free Trade Agreement (2010), Annex 11-B; Canada–Peru Free Trade Agreement (2009), Annex 812.1; ASEAN Comprehensive Investment Agreement (2009), Annex 2; Australia–Chile Free Trade Agreement (2009), Annex 10-B; Japan–India Comprehensive Economic Partnership Agreement (2011), Annex 10.

[78] See, above, section II.

PART III

International investment and sustainable development

8

International investment agreements and the emerging green economy: rising to the challenge

MARKUS W. GEHRING AND AVIDAN KENT[*]

I   Overview of the relationship between the green economy and foreign direct investment

In the 2012 Rio+20 Summit the world's nations committed themselves to the promotion of the green economy, in the context of sustainable development and poverty eradication.[1] The term 'green economy' was defined by the United Nations Environment Programme (UNEP) as 'one that results in improved human well-being and social equity, while significantly reducing environmental risks and ecological scarcities'.[2] Elsewhere the 'green economy' was described as an economy that 'should contribute to eradicating poverty as well as sustained economic growth, enhancing social inclusion, improving human welfare and creating opportunities for employment and decent work for all, while maintaining the healthy functioning of the Earth's ecosystems'.[3]

Foreign direct investment (FDI), as defined by the Organisation for Economic Co-operation and Development (OECD), 'reflects the object-ive of establishing a lasting interest by a resident enterprise in one economy (direct investor) in an enterprise (direct investment enterprise) that is resident in an economy other than that of the direct investor'.[4] It is usually assumed that such investments include several features, such as

---

[*] With special thanks to Erika Arban and Misha Benjamin for invaluable research assist-ance. This chapter shares thoughts with previous work of the authors.

[1] UNCSD, 'The Future We Want', 2012, available at: www.uncsd2012.org/content/documents/727The%20Future%20We%20Want%2019%20June%201230pm.pdf.

[2] UNEP, 'Towards a Green Economy: Pathways to Sustainable Development and Poverty Eradication', 2011, available at: www.unep.org/greeneconomy/greeneconomyreport/tabid/29846/default.aspx, p. 16.

[3] UNCSD, 'The Future We Want', para. 56.

[4] Secretary-General of the OECD, *OECD Benchmark Definition of Foreign Direct Investment*, 4th edn (Paris: OECD, 2008), available at: www.oecd.org/dataoecd/26/50/40193734.pdf, para. 117.

the transfer of funds, long-term activity, at least partial participation of the investor in the management of the project and business risk.[5] The promotion of FDI is regulated mainly by international investment agreements (IIAs). These treaties are designed to provide security and certainty for foreign investors in order to promote FDI, with the object of achieving the ultimate goal of development.

The relationship between FDI and the green economy can be described as 'dual-natured'.[6] On the one hand, the activity of transnational corporations (TNC) can, and often does, promote certain aspects of sustainable development. The outcome document of the Rio+20 Summit, 'The Future We Want', did, indeed, mention the importance of the private sector in promoting the green economy.[7] The private sector's investment, it is stated, is especially important with respect to climate change,[8] job creation,[9] biodiversity,[10] the development of environmentally sound technologies,[11] and sustainable agriculture and productivity.[12] On the other hand, it has been argued by many that the activity of TNCs can also frustrate sustainable development goals. For example, the UN Special Representative of the Secretary-General on the issues of human rights and transnational corporations revealed serious allegations of violations of a wide range of human rights by TNCs.[13] Similarly, some FDI also adversely affect the environment. The establishment of coal-fired power plants is one such example.[14]

---

[5] Rudolf Dolzer and Christoph Schreuer, *Principles of International Investment Law* (Oxford University Press, 2008), p. 60.

[6] This term was recently used to describe the more specific relationship between FDI and climate change, see in United Nations Conference on Trade and Development (UNCTAD), *World Investment Report 2010, Investing in a Low Carbon Economy* (New York: UNCTAD, 2010), p. 136 (UNCTAD Report 2010).

[7] UNCSD, 'The Future We Want', para. 46.

[8] UNCSD, 'The Future We Want', para. 127.

[9] UNCSD, 'The Future We Want', para. 154.

[10] UNCSD, 'The Future We Want', para. 201.

[11] UNCSD, 'The Future We Want', para. 271.

[12] UNCSD, 'The Future We Want', para. 110.

[13] Report of the Special Representative of the Secretary-General on the issue of human rights and transnational corporations and other business enterprises, John Ruggie, 'Promotion and Protection of all Human Rights, Civil, Political, Economic, Social and Cultural Rights, Including the Right to Development', UN Doc. A/HRC/8/5/Add.2, 2008, available at: http://daccess-dds-ny.un.org/doc/UNDOC/GEN/G08/136/61/PDF/G0813661. pdf?OpenElement.

[14] See, e.g., the factual background of the *Vattenfall* case, *Vattenfall AB, Vattenfall Europe AG, Vattenfall Europe Generation AG & Co. KG (Sweden and Europe)* v. *Federal Republic of Germany*, ICSID Case No. ARB/09/6, Award, 11 March 2011.

The relationship between FDI and sustainable development, it should be noted, is also two-sided. While FDI can support sustainable development, sustainable development can also support the interests of TNCs. The great economic potential embedded in the prospect of a 'green economy' is indeed noticeable.[15] For example, in the context of climate change, according to some estimates the demand for emission credits may reach US$100 billion by 2050.[16] An increase in the demand for low-carbon technologies is therefore expected, and consequently also great economic gains to the owners of these technologies. Moreover, ignoring sustainable development issues can be bad for businesses. For example, as identified by the Stern Review, the effects of climate change are expected to damage economic growth and disrupt the economy 'on a scale similar to those associated with the great wars and the economic depression of the first half of the 20th century'.[17]

It can be understood, therefore, that there is much to gain by the integration of the green economy, sustainable development and FDI policies. Such integration can take place in several fora. For example, it has been suggested that the protection offered by IIAs should be integrated within the Kyoto Protocol's flexible mechanisms, as means to promote low-carbon investments.[18] But as stated by Sussman, in light of the complex questions climate change negotiators must already face, adding negotiation over a multilateral investment agreement into this process seems impractical.[19] Moreover, the failure of past attempts to conclude investment treaties in multilateral frameworks (the OECD or the WTO, for example) raises even more doubts as to the viability of this idea.

Another, perhaps more practical possibility, would be to integrate the green economy's goals into IIAs. As explained in this chapter, the integration of these goals in IIAs can take place on several levels. First, the objectives of the green economy and sustainable development can be

---

[15] See, e.g., Céline Kauffmann and Cristina Tébar Less, *Transition to a Low-carbon Economy: Public Goals and Corporate Practices* (Paris: OECD, 2010), available at: www.oecd.org/dataoecd/40/52/45513642.pdf, paras 105–9.

[16] UNFCCC, 'Investment and Financial Flows to Address Climate Change', 2007, available at: http://unfccc.int/cooperation_and_support/financial_mechanism/items/4053.php, para. 637.

[17] Sir Nicholas Stern, 'The Stern Review on the Economics of Climate Change', 30 October 2006, available at: http://webarchive.nationalarchives.gov.uk/+/http://www.hm-treasury.gov.uk/stern_review_report.htm, p. ii.

[18] Edna Sussman, 'The Energy Charter Treaty's Investor Protection Provisions: Potential to Foster Solutions to Global Warming and Promote Sustainable Development', in Cordonier Segger *et al.* (eds), *Sustainable Development in World Investment Law*, p. 528.

[19] Sussman, 'The Energy Charter Treaty's Investor Protection Provisions', p. 529.

integrated before the conclusion of IIAs. For example, impact assessment mechanisms can assist decision-makers in understanding the impact, whether positive or negative, an investment treaty may have on sustainable development objectives. Second, sustainable development can be integrated within the procedural dimensions of the dispute settlement mechanisms of IIAs. For example, the principle of public participation, as phrased by the International Law Association's 'New Delhi Declaration of Principles of International Law Relating to Sustainable Development',[20] and reaffirmed as an objective of the green economy in the Rio+20 Summit,[21] can be integrated through the inclusion of the public's right to submit *amicus curiae* briefs in investment disputes, or by allowing free access to documents. Lastly, the objectives of the green economy can be integrated within the substantive provisions of IIAs. For example, the substantive rules of IIAs can be phrased in a manner that does not restrict states from enacting environmental or social laws. Moreover, IIAs can also be designed so as to actively promote the transition to a green economy. This can be achieved, *inter alia*, by creating a privileged business environment for 'green' investments.

According to the concepts of sustainable development and the green economy, when states are embarking on new IIA negotiations they should take three dimensions into account: economic development, social development and environmental protection. While there is a widespread consensus on the need for green, sustainable economic growth, most will also agree that FDI is a key component of any development agenda. However, although the concept of sustainable development has been enshrined as an explicit objective in several binding international treaties, it is at the core of the mandate of many international organisations, and it is also the subject of various soft law declarations and standards. Sustainable development remains challenging to include in new IIAs.

The following section explains how sustainable development and green economy objectives can be integrated into international investment law. It reviews both the procedural and substantive dimensions of IIAs, the tools available for states in order to integrate the goals of the green economy into their IIAs, and the challenges faced by policy-makers when making policy choices in this field.

---

[20] International Law Association (ILA), 'New Delhi Declaration of Principles of International Law Relating to Sustainable Development', *Netherlands International Law Review* 49(2) (2002): 299.

[21] UNCSD, 'The Future We Want', paras 58(c), 76.

II   The green economy in the drafting of IIAs

A   Procedural dimension

1   Impact assessment as a new dimension[22]

a   **Overview**   Foreign direct investment can bring social, economic and environmental benefits to countries. Indeed, FDIs have a positive impact on such issues as income growth, modernisation, employment and productivity.[23] Yet without careful crafting, investment agreements can frustrate sustainable development objectives and create potential conflicts between commercial, social and environmental goals.[24] Moreover, well-drafted agreements can achieve more than their inherent goals. For example, trade and investment agreements can, at least potentially, also support and promote climate change or poverty eradication objectives. One way to avoid potential conflicts, on the one hand, and promote possible synergies, on the other, is the use of impact assessment mechanisms.[25]

Impact assessments are comprehensive independent studies in which the future impact of negotiated agreements is assessed. In the past, the focus of these mechanisms was limited to the environmental effects of trade agreements. These assessments are known as environmental impact assessments (EIAs). Nowadays, however, the scope of impact assessments is increasingly expanding. For example, some impact assessments are specifically designed to review the impact of international trade or foreign investment on human rights.[26]

---

[22] This part draws on Markus Gehring, 'Impact Assessments of Investment Treaties', in Cordonier Segger et al. (eds), Sustainable Development in World Investment Law, p. 149.

[23] OECD, Committee on International Investment and Multinational Enterprises, Foreign Direct Investment for Development: Maximising Benefits, Minimising Costs (Paris: OECD, 2002), available at: www.oecd.org/dataoecd/47/51/1959815.pdf.

[24] For a review of the potential conflicts, see Marie-Claire Cordonier Segger, Markus W. Gehring and Andrew Paul Newcombe (eds), Sustainable Development in World Investment Law (Alphen aan den Rijn: Kluwer Law, 2011).

[25] For a more detailed review of this topic, see Gehring, 'Impact Assessments of Investment Treaties'.

[26] For a detailed review, see James Harrison and Alessa Goller, 'Trade and Human Rights: What does "Impact Assessment" Have to Offer?' Human Rights Law Review 8(4) (2008): 587. An example of impact assessment for foreign investment, see Rights & Democracy, Human Right Impact Assessments for Foreign Investment Projects: Learning from Community Experience in the Philippines, Tibet, the Democratic Republic of Congo, Argentina, and Peru (Montreal: Rights & Democracy, 2007), available at: www.dd-rd.ca/site/_PDF/publications/globalization/hria/full%20report_may_2007.pdf.

More widely, and in accordance with the 'holistic' concept of sustainable development,[27] some impact assessment mechanisms attempt to provide a fuller picture by assessing the economic, environmental and social implications of investment and trade agreements. For example, the EU Commission's 'Handbook for Sustainability Impact Assessment' proposes the examination of such issues as energy use, poverty, gender equality, external debt, public health, living conditions, access to education, labour standards, unemployment and more.[28] These wider assessments are known as sustainability impact assessments (SIAs). The importance of impact assessments for the green economy was emphasised recently in 'The Future We Want' declaration, in which the world's nations resolved to 'strengthen the institutional framework for sustainable development, which will, *inter alia*':[29]

> (g) promote the science–policy interface through inclusive, evidence-based and transparent scientific assessments, as well as access to reliable, relevant and timely data in areas related to the three dimensions of sustainable development, building on existing mechanisms, as appropriate; in this regard, strengthen participation of all countries in international sustainable development processes and capacity building especially for developing countries, including in conducting their own monitoring and assessments.

Impact assessment mechanisms can be found both at the domestic and international level: on the national level, domestic environmental and planning laws require an impact assessment for major projects; on the international level, some trade and investment negotiations include requirements for assessing the impact that negotiated agreements might have on sustainable development. For example, as part of the EU–Canada negotiations for a Comprehensive Economic and Trade Agreement (CETA), SIAs were prepared so as to assess the impact of both international trade and investment on economic, social and environmental issues.[30]

---

[27] The EU Commission's 'Impact Assessment Guidelines' mentions that one of the objectives of impact assessments is to ensure coherence and consistency with the EU's sustainable development strategies. See European Commission, 'Impact Assessment Guidelines', 15 January 2009, SEC(2009)92, available at: http://ec.europa.eu/governance/impact/commission_guidelines/docs/iag_2009_en.pdf, p. 6.

[28] European Commission, External Trade, 'Handbook for Sustainability Impact Assessment', 2006, available at: http://trade.ec.europa.eu/doclib/docs/2006/march/tradoc_127974.pdf, pp. 52–6.

[29] UNCSD, 'The Future We Want', para. 76(g).

[30] See the report commissioned by the European Commission, 'A Trade SIA Relating to the Negotiation of a Comprehensive Economic and Trade Agreement (CETA) Between the

Impact assessments of trade agreements often follow four steps.[31] (1) The 'screening and scoping' phase, in which the relevant issues are framed and the measures that are most likely to impact the environment (or broader issues in the case of SIAs) are identified. This step often includes expert meetings and public consultations. (2) The next stage is the initial review, in which the potential impact of the negotiated agreement (or more accurately, of the measures identified in the first step) on the environment (or on issues such as social well-being, in the case of SIAs) is identified. The scope of this examination varies from one mechanism to another. While in certain countries only local effects are examined (Canada, for example), in other jurisdictions transboundary and global effects are also assessed (the EU, for example). (3) Following the initial review, a preliminary assessment will often be published. The purpose of this review is to inform the negotiators about the projected impacts of trade liberalisation in the identified areas. (4) Lastly, an *ex post* final assessment is prepared following the conclusion of the negotiations and after the final text of the agreement has been approved. The final assessment outlines how some negotiating positions might have changed due to the content of the preliminary assessment, as well as the trade-offs and balances made between economic liberalisation and environmental protection.

Sustainability impact assessments can promote the goals for the green economy in several ways. As in the field of international trade, when applied to foreign investments SIAs allow negotiators to identify aspects of agreements that require mitigation or enhancement measures in order to achieve the fullest benefits of investment.[32] By assessing economic, environmental and social impacts of potential measures, decision-makers have a better idea of the advantages and disadvantages of each proposal. SIAs allow decision-makers to fully understand the synergies between the different fields, and how one policy can support another. Alternatively,

EU and Canada', Final Report, June 2011, available at: www.eucanada-sia.org/docs/EU-Canada_SIA_Final_Report.pdf. On investment, see at p. 337.

[31] The exact typology varies between one jurisdiction to another. However, in essence, these stages are mostly similar. For example, for the EU typology of these stages, see EU Commission, 'Handbook for Sustainability Impact Assessment', pp. 12, 17–19 or EU Commission, 'Impact Assessment Guidelines', p. 7. For a more detailed review of the typology proposed in this chapter, see Gehring, 'Impact Assessments of Investment Treaties', pp. 154–5.

[32] For a detailed review of SIAs, see Gehring, 'Impact Assessments of Investment Treaties', p. 145.

by addressing more than just environmental or economic aspects, SIAs equip decision-makers with better tools to perform the trade-offs which are necessary in places where the promotion of one policy inherently frustrates the goals of another. Lastly, where the public is effectively invited to take part in this process, SIAs also increase the democratic legitimacy and the quality of negotiated agreements.

The use of impact assessment mechanisms has increased in recent years. The following section provides a brief overview of the approaches to impact assessment mechanisms applied by Canada, the United States and the European Union in the field of international trade.[33] Some of these are also applicable to foreign investment arising in the specific context of FTAs.

b   Canada   Canada's first foray into impact assessment of investment came at the end of the WTO Uruguay Round in 1994, when it carried out an *ex post* environmental review of the Round's Agreements. In 1999, the Liberal Government introduced the internally binding 'Strategic Environmental Assessment of Plans and Policies' (SEA), a directive mandating that every government policy should be assessed for its environmental impact prior to implementation.[34] In February 2001, the cabinet adopted the Environmental Assessment (EA) of Trade Negotiations as the stand-alone assessment tool.[35] This assessment focuses almost entirely on environmental issues. However, despite its limited focus, the Canadian Government refers to this instrument as an indispensable decision-making tool for the promotion of sustainable development by engaging representatives from other levels of government, the public, the private sector and non-governmental organisations in the process.[36]

The process of EAs includes six phases:[37] (1) notice of intent, in which the purpose of the proposed negotiations is explained; (2) initial EA,

---

[33] For a more detailed review, see Gehring, 'Impact Assessments of Investment Treaties', pp. 156–68.

[34] See Foreign Affairs and International Trade Canada, 'Framework for Conducting Environmental Assessments of Trade Negotiations', February 2001, available at: www.international.gc.ca/trade-agreements-accords-commerciaux/ds/Environment.aspx?lang=en&view=d.

[35] Canada, 'Framework for Conducting Environmental Assessments of Trade Negotiations'.

[36] Foreign Affairs and International Trade Canada, *Handbook for Conducting Environmental Assessments of Trade Negotiations*, March 2008, available at: www.international.gc.ca/enviro/assets/pdfs/EnvironA/overview/handbook-e.pdf.

[37] Canada, *Handbook for Conducting Environmental Assessments of Trade Negotiations*, pp. 8–9.

which is equivalent to the 'scoping' phase as explained above; (3) initial EA report, issued during the negotiations and identifying potential environmental impacts; (4) where likely significant impacts are identified, a draft EA will be prepared and more detailed assessment will be made; (5) the final EA report is issued with the conclusion of the negotiations; and (6) follow-up and monitoring will be performed following the conclusion of the negotiations.

Although offering the right balance between public participation and innovation, one limitation in this Canadian EA methodology is that it focuses only on the environmental impacts within Canada, without explicitly requiring the assessment of social and developmental concerns. Furthermore, this procedure eschews any investigation of the environmental impacts on the trading partner or potential implications on a global level.[38] The Canadian EA was used, *inter alia*, as part of the trade negotiations with the Andean Community (2008) and with Panama (2009). In both cases it was concluded that the environmental consequences for Canada resulting from the trade flow and foreign investment in Canada would be negligible.[39] Also, the assessments did not consider the effects of the negotiations on either Panama or the Andean Community, nor was a more regional approach to the EA considered. With regard to public participation, although it is still limited, it nonetheless provides members of civil society with insights into at least the economic rationale of trade liberalisation negotiations.[40]

c **United States** In practice, environmental reviews (ERs) have been performed in the United States since 1992 when the NAFTA was negotiated and reviewed.[41] However, it was only in 1999 that President Clinton signed an executive order codifying ERs as an internally binding assessment obligation for trade negotiations.[42] Like the Canadian EAs, US ERs

---

[38] Gehring, 'Impact Assessments of Investment Treaties', p. 158.

[39] See 'Initial Environmental Assessment Report of the Canada–Andean Community Free Trade Negotiations', available at: www.international.gc.ca/trade-agreements-accords-commerciaux/assets/pdfs/andea-eaapr2008-en.pdf; 'Initial Environmental Assessment Report of the Canada–Panama Free Trade Negotiations', available at: www.international.gc.ca/trade-agreements-accords-commerciaux/agr-acc/ea-panama.aspx?lang=eng&view=d.

[40] Gehring, 'Impact Assessments of Investment Treaties', p. 159.

[41] See US Environmental Protection Agency, 'Environmental Reviews of Trade and Investment Agreements', available at: www.epa.gov/international/trade/reviews.html.

[42] Executive Order No. 13141, 16 November 1999, 'Environmental Reviews of Trade Agreements', National Environmental Policy Act, available at: http://ceq.hss.doe.gov/nepa/regs/eos/eo13141.html.

are conducted as *ex ante* procedures and are laden with public participation requirements.[43] Indeed, there is evidence that ERs engage with parts of civil society, particularly academia, and some recommendations made in the ERs are carefully evaluated and considered by negotiators.

Similarly to Canadian EAs, US ERs look mainly to domestic impacts and foreign impacts that may affect the United States. It should be noted, however, that where 'appropriate and prudent', ERs may also assess global and transboundary environmental impacts.[44] Again, like Canadian EAs, US ERs are concerned primarily with environmental issues. ERs have been used for the Central American Free Trade Agreement (CAFTA), the US–Andean FTA, the US–Panama FTA and the US–Chile FTA.

d **European Union** In the EU, the scope of assessment of investment chapters of FTAs is broader than in the United States and Canada, both in terms of subject matter and jurisdiction. The EU has established SIA mechanisms seeking to identify potential social, economic and environmental impacts, placing these SIAs at the vanguard of impact assessment tools, being a fully integrated instrument which also includes recommendations for enhancement and mitigation, if relevant.[45] SIAs also include an important public participation component. Indeed, the establishment of SIA mechanisms by the EU Trade Commissioner at the time, Pascal Lamy, was explained as a response to civil society pressure and growing suspicions towards economic globalisation, as was demonstrated in the negotiations over the OECD Multilateral Agreement on Investment and the 1999 WTO Ministerial Conference in Seattle.[46]

SIAs consist of the following phases: screening, scoping, preliminary sustainability assessment, and mitigation and enhancement analysis.[47] As already mentioned, these phases include opportunities for public participation and consultation with civil society organisations.[48] Unlike the Canadian and US impact assessment mechanisms, the SIA methodology

---

[43] See United States Trade Representative and Council on Environmental Quality, 'Guidelines for implementation of Executive Order 13141, Environmental Review of Trade Agreements', Office of the United States Trade Representative, December 2000, available at: www.ustr.gov/sites/default/files/guidelines%20for%2013141.pdf.

[44] Executive Order No. 13141, Art. 5(b).

[45] Gehring, 'Impact Assessments of Investment Treaties', p. 164.

[46] Thomas F. Ruddy and Lorenz M. Hilty, 'Impact Assessment and Policy Learning in the European Commission', *Environmental Impact Assessment Review* 28(2/3) (2008): 90, p. 94.

[47] EU Commission, 'Handbook for Sustainability Impact Assessment', p. 8.

[48] EU Commission, 'Handbook for Sustainability Impact Assessment', p. 49.

is not limited to the impact within the EU, but aims at exploring the impact within trading partners as well. According to some, about 80 per cent of the impacts studied by European SIAs are expected to take place outside the EU.[49] SIAs were used, *inter alia*, in the ambit of the EU–Mercosur trade negotiations and EU–Mediterranean FTAs.

2 The dispute resolution process

a Overview Another procedural aspect that can be relevant for the promotion of the green economy is the body of procedural rules according to which investor–state arbitrations are held. The investor–state dispute settlement mechanism is often criticised for being held out of the public eye.[50] The chosen dispute settlement model adopted by most investment agreements – the commercial arbitration model – indeed opts for a discrete method of adjudication. The reasons for this choice are understandable: the commercial arbitration model, at least theoretically, ensures an efficient, non-politicised, professional and easily enforceable form of dispute settlement. Additionally, this model allows investors to distance disputes from the control of host states and the reach of biased, or simply overly-patriotic, domestic courts.

It is argued, however, that the public nature of investment disputes,[51] and the possibility of improving the quality and legitimacy of investment awards, require certain modifications to this model. The following section explains that through increased open process and by adhering to the sustainable development principle of public participation, wider perspectives, such as those that go beyond the immediate commercial dispute, can be assimilated into this process.

b Public participation in investment disputes The concept of public participation in decision-making processes has been recognised in many international documents.[52] In 1992, this concept was declared a

---

[49] Ruddy and Hilty, 'Impact Assessment and Policy Learning in the European Commission', p. 91.

[50] See, e.g., Jan Wouters and Nicolas Hachez, 'The Institutionalization of Investment Arbitration and Sustainable Development', in Cordonier Segger *et al.* (eds), *Sustainable Development in World Investment Law*, p. 627; 'Public Statement on the International Investment Regime', 31 August 2010, available at: www.osgoode.yorku.ca/public_statement.

[51] Gus van Harten and Martin Loughlin, 'Investment Treaty Arbitration as a Species of Global Administrative Law', *European Journal of International Law* 17(1) (2006): 121.

[52] See, e.g., Art. 21(1) of the Universal Declaration of Human Rights, GA Resolution 217(III), UN GAOR, 3rd Sess., Supp. No. 13, UN Doc. A/810, 1948; Art. 5 of the UN Declaration on

'principle' in international sustainable development law by the Rio Declaration on Environment and Development ('the Rio Declaration').[53] In essence, the principle of public participation includes: (a) the public's right to participate in decision-making processes in which sustainable development issues are involved, and (b) effective access to information so as to ensure the quality of the public's participation.[54] This principle is mostly derived from the public's right to actively participate in decisions that affect their lives, and as part of the people's right to express their opinion. More recently, this principle has also been regarded as a means to ensure good governance and high quality decision-making.[55] Although designed for decision-making processes and not for adversarial forms of adjudication, it is argued that this principle can, and should, be assimilated into investor–state dispute settlement mechanisms.

Investment disputes are often public in nature. The measures scrutinised by investment tribunals are mostly administrative,[56] and can involve subject matter such as financial, social or environmental regulation. For example, in numerous cases filed against Argentina investors have challenged emergency measures put in place by the state in order to address the catastrophic financial crisis it endured during the early 2000s. This crisis, it should be remembered, involved, *inter alia*, questions of poverty, security and public health.[57] These issues, as argued by some, were not always adequately addressed by investment tribunals.[58]

Moreover, the compensation claimed by investors is paid from taxpayers' money. Considering the high sums involved in these cases (it was estimated that Argentina's potential liability in investment cases litigated against it was, at a certain point in time, to be as high

---

Social Progress and Development, UN GAOR, 24th Sess., UN Doc. A/RES/24/2542, 1969, available at: www.un-documents.net/a24r2542.htm; UNCSD, 'The Future We Want', paras 43, 76(h), 99.

[53] Rio Declaration on Environment and Development, UN GAOR, UN Doc. A/CONF.151/26,1992, available at: www.un.org/documents/ga/conf151/aconf15126–1annex1.htm.

[54] Usually, this principle also includes a requirement to enable access to judicial and administrative procedures in order to enable claims for compensation. This part, however, is less relevant for this chapter.

[55] See, e.g., the Aarhus Convention on Access to Information, below, n. 62.

[56] See relevant critique in van Harten and Loughlin, 'Investment Treaty Arbitration as a Species of Global Administrative Law'.

[57] See review of these issues in *LG&E* v. *Argentine Republic*, ICSID Case No. ARB/02/1, Decision on Liability, 3 October 2006 (United States–Argentina BIT), paras 232–5.

[58] See critique by Jorge Daniel Taillant and Jonathan Bonnitcha, 'International Investment Law and Human Rights', in Cordonier Segger *et al.* (eds), *Sustainable Development in World Investment Law*, pp. 67–8.

as US$8 billion),[59] and the effect this can have on a state's budget, the public interest in these cases is obvious.

It can be seen, therefore, that investment disputes potentially affect the public's living reality. But where the public is not entitled to follow, critique, participate or even to know about the existence of these disputes,[60] serious questions of legitimacy and accountability should be raised. This fact has indeed been emphasised by several investment tribunals.[61] It is important, therefore, to ensure that the dispute settlement process does not overlook non-commercial interests, especially where either states or investors ignore them.

Implementing the principle of public participation can help in this respect. It can ensure that all stakeholders will be heard, and enforce standards of transparency in tribunals in which public matters are being deliberated. Moreover, public participation in investment disputes can also improve the quality of investment awards.[62] Public participation can present arbitrators with wider perspectives or information that were not available or known to them. It can also bring to arbitrators' attention the voices of unrepresented stakeholders, whose interests may not coincide with those of the state. Decision-making processes in which effective public participation is permitted, therefore, are likely to be more accurate and comprehensive.[63]

---

[59] Estimation made by Gabriel Bottini from the Office of the Attorney-General, Republic of Argentina, as quoted in William Burke-White and Andreas von Staden, 'Investment Protection in Extraordinary Times: The Interpretation and Application of Non-precluded Measures Provisions in Bilateral Investment Treaties', *Virginia Journal of International Law* 48(2) (2008): 307, at p. 311. Burke-White and von Staden mention that other estimates regarding Argentina's potential liability total up to US$80 billion.

[60] In 2008, among known UNCITRAL arbitrations (not all investor–state arbitrations are known to the public), a quarter of the awards were not released to the public. See Federico Ortino, 'External Transparency of Investment Awards', Society of International Economic Law (SIEL), Inaugural Conference Paper, 2008, available at: http://papers.ssrn.com/sol3/papers.cfm?abstract_id=1159899> [Ortino].

[61] *Biwater Gauff (Tanzania) Ltd* v. *United Republic of Tanzania (Procedural Order No. 5)*, ICSID Case No ARB/05/22, 2007, para. 51; *Suez, Sociedad General de Aguas de Barcelona SA and Vivendi Universal SA* v. *Argentine Republic*, ICSID Case No. ARB/03/19, Order in Response to a Petition for Transparency and Participation as *Amicus Curiae*, 19 May 2005, para. 22.

[62] The notion according to which public participation improves the quality of decisions was recognised, *inter alia*, in the preamble to the Aarhus Convention on Access to Information, Public Participation in Decision Making and Access to Justice in Environmental Matters, UN Doc. ECE/CEP43, 25 June 1998.

[63] Indeed, for these reasons 'public participation' has been recognised as a principle in sustainable development law on more than one occasion. See, e.g., Principle 10 of the Rio Declaration on Environment and Development and Principle 5 of the ILA, 'New Delhi Declaration'.

c   Investor–state arbitration procedural rules on public participation

It should be remembered in this respect that arbitrators are permitted to hear and consider only those issues and claims that were requested and presented to them by the parties. The focus of this discussion, therefore, should concentrate on the arbitration procedural rules and the ways in which these have been read by investment tribunals. These rules, in general, allow some space for public participation. Mostly, rules of arbitration permit arbitrators to accept *amicus curiae* briefs from the public.[64] Access to information (to the arbitration's documents, for example), however, is still largely restricted, and in most cases depends on the parties' consent to make such information public. Similarly, access to arbitration hearings is also often restricted.[65] On several occasions, third parties have also requested the right to actively participate in the dispute by raising legal claims and to defend their interests before the tribunal.[66] These requests, however, were all denied.

Although in recent years some changes have been made in order to improve aspects like transparency and public participation,[67] the full application of the public participation principle is still far from a reality. For example, effective access to arbitration documents or hearings is relatively restricted,[68] despite the fact that allowing such access can enhance the

---

[64] See, e.g., the ICSID Rules of Arbitration as amended in 2006 or the practice of investment tribunals under the UNCITRAL Rules of Arbitration, as demonstrated in several NAFTA cases. See, e.g., *United Parcel Services of America Inc.* v. *Canada*, Decision of the Tribunal on Petitions for Intervention and Participation as *Amici Curiae*, 2001, UNCITRAL; *Methanex Corporation* v. *United States of America*, Decision of the Tribunal on Petitions from Third Persons to Intervene as '*Amici Curiae*', 2001, UNCITRAL, (NAFTA). See also a statement made by the NAFTA Free Trade Commission in this respect, NAFTA Free Trade Commission, 'Statement of the Free Trade Commission on Non-disputing Party Participation', 2003, available at: www.international.gc.ca/trade-agreements-accords-commerciaux/assets/pdfs/Nondisputing-en.pdf.

[65] See, e.g., Rule 32 of the ICSID Rules of Arbitration and Art. 28 of the UNCITRAL Rules of Arbitration.

[66] See, e.g., *Aguas del Tunari SA* v. *Republic of Bolivia*, ICSID Case No. ARB/02/3, Petition of La Coordinadora para la defensa del Agua y Vida and others to the Arbitral Tribunal, available at: http://ita.law.uvic.ca/documents/Aguaaboliviapetition.pdf; *United Parcel Services of America Inc.* v. *Canada*, see above n. 64.

[67] See, e.g., the 2006 amendments made in the ICSID Arbitration Rules or Arts 10.20–10.21 of the Central America–Dominican Republic–United States FTA (CAFTA-DR).

[68] Regarding access to hearings, see Art. 28 of the UNCITRAL Arbitration Rules (as revised in 2010), and Rule 32 of the ICSID Arbitration Rules. Regarding access to documents, ICSID tribunals have denied such access on several occasions; see, e.g., *AES Summit Generation Ltd and AES-Tisza Erömü Kft* v. *Republic of Hungary*, ICSID Case No. ARB/07/22, Award, 23 September 2010, para. 3.22. See also UNCITRAL tribunals, e.g.,

quality of submitted *amicus curiae* briefs. Moreover, measures such as making investment disputes known to the public, publishing arbitration documents or allowing public access to hearings are also often denied.

To conclude, it is argued that the principle of public participation should be, if not completely assimilated into investment treaties, at least better balanced against other rationales of the investor–state dispute settlement mechanism. It is believed that the measures suggested above, if refined and adjusted to the context of investment arbitration, will undermine conflicting values such as efficiency only to a certain extent (if at all). In light of their potential advantages, they should be considered by states.

B   Substantive dimension

The effects of FDIs, as mentioned before, are complex and multi-faceted. Their impact touches such matters as trade, services, intellectual property, industrial policies, labour issues, movement of personnel and environmental concerns. Furthermore, FDIs can both promote and frustrate sustainable development goals. The challenge faced by treaty negotiators, therefore, is to balance the conflicting interests present in the essence of foreign investments. Treaty negotiators, for example, must design tools that will promote the transition to a green economy by providing a secure and stable business environment. On the other hand, they also need to secure ample regulatory flexibility so that states will be able to reform and adapt their policies.

Although increasing,[69] the explicit presence of sustainable development objectives in investment treaties remains relatively low.[70] The following section discusses some of the examples offered by the substantive rules of IIAs in order to address sustainable development objectives.

V. G. Gallo v. *Government of Canada*, UNCITRAL, Procedural Order No. 1, 4 June 2008, para. 38. The one exception for this rule is the *Piero Foresti* arbitration (under ICSID rules), in which the tribunal allowed access to information. The case, however, was discontinued before the non-disputing parties had the chance to view these documents, see *Piero Foresti, Laura de Carli and others* v. *Republic of South Africa* (2009), ICSID Case No ARB/05/22, Letter from the Tribunal to the Parties, 5 October 2009, para. 2.2–3.

[69] Kathryn Gordon and Joachim Pohl, 'Environmental Concerns in International Investment Agreements: A Survey', OECD Working Papers on International Investment, No. 2011/1, 2011, available at: www.oecd.org/dataoecd/50/12/48083618.pdf, p. 8.

[70] See Kathryn Gordon, 'International Investment Agreements: A Survey of Environmental, Labour and Anti-corruption Issues', in *International Investment Law: Understanding Concepts and Tracking Innovations* (Paris: OECD, 2008), available at: www.oecd.org/dataoecd/3/5/40471550.pdf, Annex 3.A1.

It should be mentioned that this is not an exhaustive list of possible solutions. In fact, the complex nature of concepts such as the green economy or sustainable development requires many different approaches for the numerous issues embedded in this concept. Indeed, what is right for climate change will not necessarily work for smoking prevention or biodiversity. However, the following section can be used as a point of departure, from which more complex solutions can be developed.

1 Preambular language

One, albeit uncommon, solution adopted by states is the inclusion of references to sustainable development objectives in preambles to IIAs.[71] The importance of preambular language can be understood from Article 31(2) of the 1969 Vienna Convention on the Law of Treaties (VCLT), according to which the context and the purpose of a treaty is to be derived, *inter alia*, from the treaty's preamble.[72] In light of the different interpretations given to legal terms such as 'expropriation', 'legitimate expectations' and 'like circumstances', and the effects these can have on sustainable development objectives,[73] the role the preambular language can fulfil is significant.[74]

Preambular references can be made either directly to the concept of the green economy, or to sustainable development as a whole, or to a specific issue such as climate change, labour standards, health or human rights. There are several ways in which states refer to sustainable development objectives in their preambles. First, states can declare the transition to a green economy, or sustainable development, to be a specific objective of the treaty. For example, the Canadian Model Foreign Investment Protection Agreement (Canadian Model FIPA) states in its preamble that:

> the promotion and the protection of investments of investors of one Party in the territory of the other Party will be conducive to the stimulation of mutually beneficial business activity, to the development

---

[71] Andrew Newcombe, 'Sustainable Development and Investment Treaty Law', *Journal of World Investment and Trade* 8 (2007): 357.

[72] Article 31(2) of the Vienna Convention on the Law of Treaties, 23 May 1969, *UNTS* 1980, vol. 1155.

[73] For a review of these terms and their relations to sustainable development, see Cordonier-Segger *et al.* (eds), *Sustainable Development in World Investment*.

[74] Marie-Claire Cordonier Segger and Andrew Newcombe, 'An Integrated Agenda for Sustainable Development in International Investment Law', in Cordonier Segger *et al.* (eds), *Sustainable Development in World Investment Law*, p. 126.

of economic cooperation between them and to the promotion of sustainable development.[75]

Similarly, the parties to the North American Free Trade Agreement (NAFTA) express in its preamble both their determination to promote sustainable development in general, and to address many of the topics that are included under this definition, such as environmental objectives and economic development.[76] Similar examples can be found in the preamble to the Common Market for Eastern and Southern Africa (COMESA) investment agreement[77] and several Canadian IIAs.[78] Some agreements also refer to more specific issues, such as the promotion of objectives dealing with climate change.[79]

A second type of preambular language, while not referring to sustainable development as a treaty objective *per se*, imposes an obligation upon parties to behave consistently with this principle. This type of language can be found in US IIAs. The preamble to the US–Rwanda IIA, for example, defines as treaty objectives, *inter alia*, the promotion of economic cooperation, the stimulation of private investment and the creation of a stable business environment. It continues, however, by stating that the parties are: '*Desiring* to achieve these objectives in a manner consistent with the protection of health, safety, and the environment, and the promotion of internationally recognised labor rights.'[80]

A third example of preambular language can be defined as 'non-derogation' language. This language can be found in many of the IIAs signed by states such as Finland, the Netherlands, Japan and the United States.[81] According to these references, the treaty's objectives (often

[75] Canada Model Foreign Investment Promotion and Protection Agreement, 2004, available at: www.international.gc.ca/trade-agreements-accords-commerciaux/agr-acc/fipa-apie/index.aspx (Canada Model FIPA).

[76] North American Free Trade Agreement, 17 December 1992, Can TS 1994 No. 2, 32 *ILM* 1480 (1994), entered into force 1 January 1994).

[77] Common Market for Eastern and Southern Africa, Investment Agreement for the COMESA Common Investment Area, 2007 (COMESA).

[78] See, e.g., the Canada–Peru IIA (2006) and the Canada–Jordan IIA (2009).

[79] See, e.g., the preamble to the Japan–Switzerland FTA (2009).

[80] See similar language in the US Model BIT (2204), and the US–Uruguay BIT (2006) (emphasis added).

[81] See, e.g., Finland–Ethiopia BIT (2006); Finland–Armenia BIT (2004); the Netherlands–Suriname BIT (2005); the Netherlands–Burundi BIT (2007); US–Mozambique BIT (1998); US–Jordan BIT (2003); US–Bahrain BIT (2001); Japan–Korea BIT (2002); Japan–Vietnam BIT (2003).

economic in nature) are to be achieved without relaxing regulatory standards in fields such as the environment, health or safety.

Lastly, on very rare occasions, references to sustainable development treaties can be found in the preamble to IIAs. Such references can be found in model treaties that are not in use, such as the Model BIT of the International Institute for Sustainable Development (IISD Model BIT), in which references to numerous treaties have been made,[82] or the Norway Model BIT (2007),[83] in which reference to the United Nations Charter and the Universal Declaration of Human Rights can be found. More relevant examples can be found in the preamble to the Singapore–EFTA FTA (which includes investment protection), in which the parties reaffirm 'their commitment to the principles set out in the United Nations Charter and the Universal Declaration of Human Rights',[84] and in the Energy Charter Treaty, in which the parties state that they are 'recalling the United Nations Framework Convention on Climate Change, the Convention on Long-Range Transboundary Air Pollution and its protocols, and other international environmental agreements with energy-related aspects'.[85]

2 Exceptions and reservations

Another way in which states attempt to promote sustainable development and green economy objectives is the use of exceptions and reservations in IIAs. IIAs, like almost any international agreement, impose certain restraints on states' regulatory flexibility. Through the use of exceptions, states ensure that their ability to regulate certain fields will not be restricted by investment treaties.

Exceptions in IIAs appear in several forms. First, some IIAs include provisions that allow for treaty reservations, which are sector-specific carve-outs from treaty obligations. For example, Annex I of the Canada–Peru FIPA includes a list of sectors that are exempted from the IIA's substantive rules.[86] Second, a few IIAs have adopted general exceptions

---

[82] The IISD Model BIT includes, *inter alia*, references to the 1992 Rio Declaration on Environment and Development, the 2002 World Summit on Sustainable Development and the Millennium Development Goals, and the OECD Guidelines for Multinational Enterprises. See Howard Mann *et al.* 'IISD Model International Agreement on Investment for Sustainable Development', 2005, available at: http://italaw.com/documents/investment_model_int_agreement.pdf (IISD Model BIT).

[83] Norway Draft Model BIT (2007), available at: www.asil.org/ilib080421.cfm#t1.

[84] Free Trade Agreements between the EFTA states and Singapore (2002).

[85] Energy Charter Treaty, opened for signature 17 December 1994, 34 *ILM* 360, 385.

[86] See. e.g., Art. 9 of the Canada–Peru FIPA (2003).

provisions, modelled on Article XX of the General Agreement on Tariffs and Trade (GATT). These general exceptions exclude from the scope of IIAs measures relating to the protection of, *inter alia*, 'human, animal, or plant life or health', or to the conservation of exhaustible natural resources. As in Article XX of the GATT, these exceptions are subject to non-discriminatory treatment and should not be used as disguised restrictions for investment or trade.[87]

Third, some IIAs include what was described by some as 'non-precluded measures' (NPMs).[88] NPMs are intended to exempt certain subject areas (e.g., public health, public security, morality) from the scope of the treaty or from specific treaty obligations. For example, the protocol following the Germany–Bangladesh BIT states: 'Measures that have to be taken for reasons of public security and order, public health or morality shall not be deemed "treatment less favourable" within the meaning of Article 2.'[89]

Exceptions, at least in theory, can promote sustainable development objectives. Their main contribution in this respect is in preventing conflicts between investment rules and sustainable development regulation. The recent claims by Philip Morris made against Australia and Uruguay following their anti-smoking regulations (mainly plain packaging rules) is an excellent example of a case in which general exceptions would have been helpful.[90] However, the authors believe that the use of exceptions should be made with care. First, exceptions should not be overly inclusive. While they may be useful in certain cases of public health, human rights or treatment granted to indigenous peoples, they may actually frustrate the objectives of fields such as climate change in which private investment is badly needed. Alternatively, as stated by Newcombe, in several cases tribunals have already approved that

---

[87] For examples and detailed discussion, see Andrew Newcombe, 'General Exceptions in International Investment Agreements', in Cordonier Segger *et al.* (eds), *Sustainable Development in World Investment Law*, p. 358.

[88] Burke-White and von Staden, 'Investment Protection in Extraordinary Times'; Newcombe, 'General Exceptions in International Investment Agreements', p. 358

[89] Germany–Bangladesh BIT (1981), See, e.g., general exclusion in Art. X in the US–Panama BIT (1982).

[90] FTR Holding SA, *Philip Morris Products SA and Abal Hermanos SA* v. *Oriental Republic of Uruguay*, ICSID Case No. ARB/10/7, Regarding Philip Morris' claim against Australia, 2010; see report by Luke E. Peterson, 'Philip Morris puts Australia on notice of treaty claim, but both parties decline to release documents; claim over tobacco regulation would be third treaty-based investor–state claim filed by Philip Morris since 2010', *IAReporter*, 30 June 2011, available at: www.iareporter.com/articles/20110630_5.

measures aimed at the protection of public policy objectives do not breach investment treaty obligations. Providing a closed list of protected areas will, therefore, simply limit the scope of what can be considered as *bona fide* public policy objectives.[91]

3 Language clarifications

A third tool available to states in order to promote the transition to a green economy can be described as 'language clarification' provisions or 'improved definitions'. The field of international investment law relies on several standards of protection, most notably 'fair and equitable treatment', non-discriminatory treatment (including 'national treatment' and 'most-favoured-nation treatment') and protection from unlawful expropriation. The definition of each of these standards includes many legal tests, most of which rely on the interpretation of legal terms. For example, the 'national treatment' standard relies on arbitrators' interpretation of what may constitute 'like circumstances'. Similarly, the 'fair and equitable treatment' standard relies, among other things, on the tribunal's interpretation of what investors may 'legitimately expect' when making their investment. Other questions that tribunals dispute, include the role of a state's intentions (whether *bona fide* or *mala fide*) when expropriating an investor's property.

All these questions, and the manner in which tribunals choose to answer them, can affect sustainable development.[92] For example, by deciding that carbon footprints are irrelevant for what may constitute 'like circumstances', states' attempts to differentiate between low-carbon and carbon-intensive producers (e.g., by imposing carbon taxes) can be viewed as a violation of the non-discrimination rules. By clarifying the language used in treaties, states can avoid such conflicts.

Indeed, in recent years states have become aware of these potential conflicts and have aimed to clarify legal terms.[93] Most notably, some states have made clarifications with respect to the terms 'expropriation' and 'indirect expropriation', perhaps due to the wide meaning some

---

[91] Newcombe, 'General Exceptions in International Investment Agreements', pp. 357–8.

[92] For a detailed review of all the potential issues that may arise out of these questions, see Cordonier Segger, *et al.* (eds), *Sustainable Development in World Investment Law.*

[93] See examples in Mahnaz Malik, 'Recent Developments in International Investment Agreements: Negotiations and Disputes', IV Annual Forum for Developing Country Investment Negotiators, Background Papers, 2010, available at: www.iisd.org/pdf/2011/dci_2010_recent_developments_iias.pdf, pp. 4–5.

tribunals have read into them.[94] The ASEAN–Australia–New Zealand FTA, for example, emphasises with respect to 'expropriation' that:

> Non-discriminatory regulatory actions by a Party that are designed and applied to achieve legitimate public welfare objectives, such as the protection of public health, safety, and the environment do not constitute expropriation of the type referred to in Paragraph 2(b).[95]

Similar clarifications can also be found, *inter alia*, in Canadian and US IIAs, and the COMESA investment agreement.[96] With respect to the term 'indirect expropriation', under the US–Uruguay BIT it is stressed that:

> Except in rare circumstances, non-discriminatory regulatory actions by a Party that are designed and applied to protect legitimate public welfare objectives, such as public health, safety, and the environment, do not constitute indirect expropriations.[97]

Language clarifications can also be found more generally. As mentioned above, commitment to rules of international law implies a certain loss of regulatory flexibility. In some cases, states provide clarifications as to what is included in this 'loss' of regulatory flexibility, and what is not. Article 10.12 of the US–Chile FTA ('Investment and Environment'), for instance, clarifies that environmental regulation shall not be limited by the investment rules prescribed in the agreement. It states that:

> Nothing in this Chapter shall be construed to prevent a Party from adopting, maintaining, or enforcing any measure otherwise consistent with this Chapter that it considers appropriate to ensure that investment activity in its territory is undertaken in a manner sensitive to environmental concerns.[98]

---

[94] The Metalclad tribunal, e.g., has stated that: 'expropriation under NAFTA includes not only open, deliberate and acknowledged takings of property, such as outright seizure or formal or obligatory transfer of title in favour of the host State, but also covert or incidental interference with the use of property which has the effect of depriving the owner, in whole or in significant part, of the use or reasonably-to-be-expected economic benefit of property even if not necessarily to the obvious benefit of the host State'. *Metalclad Corporation* v. *Mexico*, ICSID Case No. ARB(AF)97/1, 2000, (NAFTA), para. 103.

[95] Annex on Expropriation and Compensation, Art. 4, ASEAN–Australia–New Zealand FTA.

[96] See in COMESA, Art. 20(8); Annex 811 ('Indirect Expropriation') of the Canada–Colombia FTA (2008). For US IIAs, see, below, n. 97.

[97] Annex B, Art. 4(b) of the US–Uruguay BIT. See also Annex 10-D, ch. 10, Art. 4(b) of the US–Chile FTA.

[98] US–Chile FTA, Art. 10.12.

Similar language concerning the term 'expropriation' can also be found in IIAs signed by other states.[99] Other potential language clarifications could also be made in future treaties. For example, it could be emphasised that a specific state commitment is needed in order to establish investors' 'legitimate expectations',[100] and that the mere change in regulation (subject to good faith and non-discrimination) should not be considered as a breach of such. Furthermore, it could also be clarified that environmental issues, human rights or social considerations, when applied in order to protect such interest, should be considered as part of the 'like circumstances' legal test.

Language clarifications can also be made with respect to the term 'investment'. The *Salini* test, for example, requires 'contribution, a certain duration of performance of the contract and participation in the risks of transaction' in order to establish 'investment'.[101] Recently, it was doubted by a certain prominent scholar whether investment in cigarettes should be considered as 'investment'.[102] This suggestion was made following the recent Philip Morris investment claims, and the doubts concerning whether investment in cigarettes actually promoted states' development. While this proposition is certainly appealing, it is not without fault. Most notably, this proposition leaves investors in doubt as to whether their investment is, or is not, covered by the investment treaty, until such a time as an investment tribunal makes the determination. The term 'contribution' is wide and vague, and by itself does not allow investors to know in advance whether their investment is to be considered as 'contributing' (and thus covered by the IIA) or not. While agreeing with the general idea, according to which only investments that promote sustainable development should be covered

---

[99] See, e.g., Art. VII(4) of the Luxembourg/Luxembourg–Colombia BIT (2009); Art. G-14 of the Canada–Chile FTA (1996).

[100] This approach was adopted by several investment tribunals. See, e.g., *Total SA* v. *Argentine Republic*, ICSID Case No. ARB/04/01, Decision on Liability, 27 December 2010, para. 117; *Grand River Enterprises Six Nations Ltd et al.* v. *United States of America*, UNCITRAL (NAFTA), Award, 12 January 2011, para. 141; *Glamis Gold Ltd* v. *United States of America*, UNCITRAL (NAFTA), Award, 8 June 2009, paras 766–7; *Joseph Charles Lemire* v. *Ukraine*, ICSID Case No. ARB/06/18, Decision on Jurisdiction and Liability, 14 January 2010, para. 284.

[101] *Salini Costruttori SpA and Italstrade SpA* v. *Morocco*, ICSID Case No. ARB/00/4, Decision on Jurisdiction, 23 July 2001, para. 52.

[102] This remark was made by one of the senior speakers in a conference held at Leiden University, 'The Interaction of International Investment Law with Other Fields of Public International Law', 8–9 April 2011.

by investment agreements, the authors believe that such a determination should be made *ex ante*, before the investment is made, and not *ex post facto* only after a dispute has arisen. This is required for reasons of predictability and transparency. Furthermore, decisions as to the investment's contribution should be made by professional bodies and not by arbitrators, who are not suited to making such determinations. It is argued, therefore, that decisions as to the contributing nature of an investment should be made by impact assessment mechanisms or any other pre-investment examination.

To conclude this section, a word of caution is required. States should not forget that private investments are crucial for sustainable development, and that a stable legal and business environment is essential for their promotion. States should, therefore, be wary of turning language clarifications into overly sweeping exclusions. States should identify those legal tests that could potentially effect sustainable development goals, and refine them so as to achieve a delicate balance between the need to provide a stable business environment, on the one hand, and to allow sufficient regulatory flexibility, on the other.

4   Corporate social responsibility

Another layer in which IIAs can promote the transition to a green economy is by the use of corporate social responsibility (CSR). The modern concept of CSR can be traced back to the 1950s, when CSR was defined as 'obligations of businessmen to pursue those policies, to make those decisions, or to follow those lines of action which are desirable in terms of the objectives and values of our society'.[103] Although nowadays some debate still takes place on the exact definition of CSR,[104] for the purposes of this chapter the words of Judge Gontheir will suffice:

> [CSR] generally embodies the notion that a corporation must act in a responsible manner with regard to the environment, community and the society in which it operates. In its most basic form, CSR emphasizes an approach to corporate governance and operations that integrates and

---

[103] H. R. Bowen, *Social Responsibility and Accountability* (New York: Harper & Row, 1953), as cited in Archie B. Carroll, 'Corporate Social Responsibility: Evolution of a Definitional Construct', *Business and Society* 38(3) (1999): 268, at p. 270.

[104] Peter T. Muchlinski, *Multinational Enterprises and the Law* (New York: Oxford University Press, 2007), p. 101.

balances the self-interests of the corporation, and those of its investors, with the concerns and interests of the public.[105]

The promotion of CSR norms was called for on numerous occasions, most recently in 'The Future We Want' declaration, following the Rio+20 Summit.[106] Perhaps the most eminent example of a CSR code is the OECD Guidelines for Multinational Enterprises (OECD Guidelines), which have been described by Muchlinski as an 'emerging consensus on the social obligations of MNEs'.[107] The OECD Guidelines represent a comprehensive code of conduct, including voluntary standards for the environment, employment, combating bribery, science, competition and taxation.[108] A more recent example, albeit one that focuses exclusively on human rights, is the 2011 'principles for responsible contracts' that were formulated by John Ruggie, the Special Representative of the Secretary-General on the issue of human rights and transnational corporations and other business enterprises.[109] These principles include, *inter alia*, the planning and management of potential adverse impacts on human rights, project operating standards, community engagement and grievance mechanisms.

The vast majority of CSR norms can be considered as 'soft law', as they are voluntary and rely on self-governance. This, however, does not make them ineffective. Soft law mechanisms often include other 'sticks and carrots' besides the threat of legal action.[110] In some cases CSR 'soft law' norms have indeed proven to be successful in enforcing higher standards of social responsibility.[111]

---

[105] Hon. Charles Doherty Gonthier, 'Foreword', in Michael Kerr, Richard Janda and Chip Pitts (eds), *Corporate Social Responsibility: A Legal Analysis* (Ontario: LexisNexis, 2009), as cited in Jarrod Hepburn and Vuyelwa Kuuya, 'Corporate Social Responsibility and Investment Treaties', in Cordonier Segger *et al.* (eds), *Sustainable Development in World Investment Law*, p. 585.

[106] UNCSD, 'The Future We Want', para. 46.

[107] Muchlinski, *Multinational Enterprises and the Law*, p. 103.

[108] OECD, 'Guidelines for Multinational Enterprises', available at: www.oecd.org/daf/investment/guidelines.

[109] UN Human Rights Council, 'Report of the Special Representative of the Secretary-General on the issue of human rights and transnational corporations and other business enterprises', UN GAOR, 17th Sess., Agenda Item 3, UN Doc. A/HRC/17/31/Add.3, 2011, available at: UN www.ohchr.org/Documents/Issues/Business/A.HRC.17.31.Add.3.pdf.

[110] Roya Ghafele and Angus Mercer, 'Not Starting in Sixth Gear: An Assessment of the UN Global Compact's Use of Soft Law as a Global Governance Structure for Corporate Social Responsibility', *University of California Davies Journal of International Law and Policy* 17 (2010): 41.

[111] John Conley and Cynthia Williams, 'Global Banks as Global Sustainability Regulators?: The Equator Principles,' *Law and Policy* 33(4) (2011): 542.

The activity of foreign investors, as discussed above, can impact social, economic and environmental issues. But while some governments are equipped with the means to regulate and control these effects, others are not. This situation can be aggravated where states are eager to attract foreign investment and, consequently, are willing to ignore the adverse effects on issues like human rights or the environment. Furthermore, the existence of governmental corruption, or the mere inability to enforce high standards of regulation, can result in the exploitative behaviour of foreign multinationals. All these scenarios are the result of inefficient enforcement of high standards of corporate social 'behaviour' on foreign investors. The role that CSR can play in this respect is evident. By adhering to external norms on top of, or in place of, the norms imposed by host states, higher standards of behaviour can be achieved. Furthermore, following CSR principles such as those proposed by John Ruggie, will assist foreign investors to plan and avoid potential conflicts and enhance their acceptance by the local community.

CSR norms can be imported into IIAs in several ways. First, several of the provisions already discussed in this chapter are designed to enforce (as 'hard law') higher standards of social activity.[112] With respect to self-governed 'soft law' norms, these can be mentioned in the preambles to IIAs and serve as a source for treaty interpretation. The preamble to the Canada–Peru FTA, for example, 'encourages' enterprises to respect CSR norms. A more comprehensive example can be found in the preamble to the IISD Model BIT, where one of its aims is described as:

> Affirming the progressive development of international law and policy on the relationships between multinational enterprises and host governments as seen in such international instruments as the ILO Tripartite Declaration on Multinational Enterprises and Social Policy; the OECD Guidelines for Multinational Enterprises; and the United Nations' Norms and Responsibilities of Transnational Corporations and Other Business Enterprises with Regard to Human Rights.[113]

Furthermore, IIAs can also include more specific treaty provisions with respect to CSR. The IISD Model BIT, for example, includes a CSR provision (Article 16), according to which foreign investors must adhere to a list of CSR codes and guidelines. Another possibility is an *ex ante* review of the investors' CSR policies and their suitability for designated

---

[112] See a review in Hepburn and Kuuya, 'Corporate Social Responsibility and Investment Treaties', pp. 599–600.
[113] IISD Model BIT.

projects. The implementation of such a review may be prescribed as a precondition for certain types of investments, especially for those that were identified as sensitive by SIAs. Alternatively, as implied by Article 13.6(2) of the EU–Korea FTA (which specifically refers also to FDI), states can also grant preferential treatment to investors that comply with CSR obligations.[114] If such a strategy is to be adopted, states should adjust other treaty provisions, such as the non-discrimination provisions, for example, in order to ensure that CSR-based preferential treatment will not be considered as a treaty violation.

Interesting developments in this respect can be found in the evolving EU policy of international investment law. Pursuant to the entry into force of the Treaty of Lisbon, FDI had been integrated into the EU common commercial policy. While the formulation of the EU's future investment policy is still ongoing, it may be predicted that the inclusion of CSR in this policy is highly likely. First, the EU's latest FTAs with Korea and with Colombia and Peru, mention CSR standards as a means of promoting sustainable development goals.[115] Second, in several recent documents the European Parliament has expressed its will to see CSR provisions incorporated into future investment and trade agreements.[116] Most notably, in its Resolution on the Future European International Investment Policy it was stated that the Parliament called 'for a corporate social responsibility clause and effective social and environmental clauses to be included in every FTA the EU signs'.[117] Similar recognition was also made by the European Council in 2010 in its 'conclusion on a comprehensive European international investment policy'.[118]

---

[114] Hepburn and Kuuya, 'Corporate Social Responsibility and Investment Treaties', p. 609.

[115] In both cases, FDI are specifically mentioned. See Art. 13.6 of the EU–Korea FTA and Art. 271 of the EU–Colombia Peru FTA.

[116] European Parliament, Resolution of 25 November on Corporate Social Responsibility in International Trade Agreements, 2010, available at: /www.europarl.europa.eu/sides/get-Doc.do?type=TA&language=EN&reference=P7-TA-2010-0446; European Parliament, Resolution of 6 April 2011 on the Future European International Investment Policy, 2011, available at: www.europarl.europa.eu/sides/getDoc.do?type=TA&reference=P7-TA-2011-0141&language=EN; EU Commission, Statement of the European Union and the United States on Shared Principles for International Investment, 10 April 2012, para. 6, available at: http://trade.ec.europa.eu/doclib/docs/2012/april/tradoc_149331.pdf.

[117] European Parliament, Resolution on the Future European International Investment Policy.

[118] Council of the European Union, Conclusion on a Comprehensive European International Investment Policy, 3041st Foreign Affairs Council Meeting, Luxembourg, 25 October 2010, available at: www.consilium.europa.eu/uedocs/cms_data/docs/pressdata/EN/foraff/117328.pdf, para. 16.

5   Interaction with sustainable development treaties

Another aspect that should be addressed in future IIAs in order to promote sustainable development is the interaction between IIAs and multilateral environmental agreements. As mentioned above, FDIs interact with numerous other subject matter. Investors' activity can, therefore, both promote and frustrate the objectives of other treaties. International relations (IR) scholars refer to this situation as 'institutional interaction'.[119] Gehring and Oberthür, for example, identify 'behavioural interaction' as a situation under which the rules of one institution[120] impose behavioural changes on its members, which consequently affect the effectiveness of other institutions. The phenomenon of 'regulatory chill' can serve as an example in this respect, as restrictions imposed by investment treaties can 'chill' states from promoting the objectives of other institutions (climate change objectives, for example).[121] Similarly, 'impact level' interaction is a situation in which externalities created by one institution affect the ultimate target of another institution. For example, increased low-carbon investments and the enhanced transfer of technologies that they bring can be seen as externalities of IIAs, which in turn promote the ultimate target of the United Nations Framework Convention on Climate Change (UNFCCC).

The main challenge in this respect is to ensure that IIAs will promote the objectives of sustainable development treaties (i.e., environmental treaties, human rights treaties, etc.). Currently, IIAs hardly ever explicitly address the objectives of other treaties. Rare examples can be found, *inter alia*, in the preamble to the ECT, Article 104 of the NAFTA, Article I(6)

---

[119] See, e.g., Thomas Gehring and Sebastian Oberthür, 'The Causal Mechanisms of Interaction between International Institutions', *European Journal of International Relations* 15 (2009): 125; Olav Schram Stokke, 'The Interplay of International Regimes: Putting Effectiveness Theory to Work', *Fridtjof Nansen Institute(FNI) Report* 14/2001, 2001, available at: www.fni.no/doc&pdf/FNI-R1401.pdf.

[120] The reader should note that the IR definition of 'institutions' is perhaps comparable to what lawyers often (mistakenly) define as 'regimes', a definition that is wider, and much less formal than that of 'organisations' such as the World Trade Organization or the United Nations. An often sited definition of institutions was provided by Keohane: 'a persistent and connected set of rules (formal or informal) that prescribe behavioural roles, constrain activity, and shape expectations'. See Robert Keohane, 'International Institutions: Two Approaches', *International Studies Quarterly* 32(4) (1988): 379, at p. 383.

[121] See review by Freya Baetens, 'Foreign Investment Law and Climate Change: Legal Conflicts Arising from Implementing the Kyoto Protocol Through Private investment', Sustainable Development Law on Climate Change Working Paper Series (Rome: IDLO, 2010), p. 11.

of the Belgium/Luxembourg–Colombia BIT and in model treaties like the IISD Model BIT.[122] Implicitly, however, it can be argued that the above discussed measures (exceptions, reservations, language clarifications, etc.) are also aimed at ensuring that the ability of states to promote the objectives of sustainable development treaties shall not be frustrated by the rules of IIAs.

Although IIAs have not yet posed fundamental challenges to other regimes, there has been a certain amount of dispute, both at the WTO and in investment law arbitration, directly related to environmental issues. For example, in *Vattenfall v. Germany*[123] the Swedish state-owned company Vattenfall challenged regulations imposed on its coal-fired power plant located near Hamburg, which imposed more onerous measures on the plant compared to those originally guaranteed. These measures were enacted after the 2008 elections, when the Green Party entered power in a coalition in the Hamburg municipal government, and were partly justified by the fact that coal-fired plants affected climate change. Vattenfall claimed violation of the Energy Charter Treaty[124] (which mandates that investments be accorded fair and equitable treatment, and not suffer unreasonable impairment) and sought €1.4 billion in damages.

Following Vattenfall's legal actions, the German federal government agreed to a settlement according to which the required permits for Vattenfall's operation would be granted. Furthermore, Vattenfall was released from earlier commitments to reduce environmental damage.[125] While the exact reasons for the government's motivation to settle this case are not known to the authors, it can be assumed that the prospect of paying €1.4 billion in compensation has 'chilled' the government's desire to stop the construction and the operation of this power plant. This case represents an example of climate-related disputes that could become

---

[122] The preamble to the Energy Charter Treaty includes reference to the UNFCCC, the Convention on Long-Range Transboundary Air Pollution and other international environmental agreements with energy-related aspects. Article 104 of the NAFTA includes references to Convention on International Trade in Endangered Species of Wild Fauna and Flora, the Montreal Protocol on Substances that Deplete the Ozone Layer, and the Basel Convention on the Control of Transboundary Movements of Hazardous Wastes and Their Disposal; Article I(6) of the Belgium/Luxembourg–Colombia BIT includes reference to the International Labour Organization Declaration on Fundamental Principles and Rights at Work.

[123] *Vattenfall AB et al. v. Federal Republic of Germany.*   [124] See n. 85, above.

[125] *Vattenfall AB et al. v. Federal Republic of Germany.*

popular in the future, and it may demonstrate that it is possible for IIA provisions to frustrate the objectives of climate change treaties.

What kind of treaty measures are being applied by states in order to address institutional interactions? Largely, as can be seen from the above reviewed, states have focused their attention on avoiding conflicts. This can be viewed as a 'defensive' strategy, according to which states mainly attempt to ensure that one treaty will not frustrate the objectives of another. For example, Article 104 of the NAFTA instructs that in the event of legal conflicts between the NAFTA and a list of environmental treaties, the later shall prevail. More commonly, as stated above, exceptions and reservation provide the same solution, as they exclude certain fields from the scope of IIAs and *de facto* prioritise such subject matter over the need to protect foreign investments. States' motivation to apply this 'defensive' strategy is obvious; such action prevents future legal claims by investors.

It should be noted, however, that institutional interaction can also result in synergies, that is, the promotion of one treaty's objectives through the provisions of another. States, it is argued, should devote more attention to creative investment provisions, such that may actually promote sustainable development objectives, rather than just ensure the avoidance of future conflicts. In trade law, for example, the concept of 'green goods and services' prescribes that by reducing tariffs for specific goods and services, states can promote climate change objectives. This is an example of how one treaty's provisions can actively promote the objectives of another. In light of the potential embedded in FDI for the promotion of sustainable development objectives, similar concepts should also be developed within IIAs.

III   Conclusion

Modern IIAs offer greater possibilities to balance different public policy objectives. This is mainly due to the growing concern of the parties involved in the negotiation of the agreements regarding the widespread impact that these instruments can have not only on the environment, but also on trade, labour conditions, health issues, etc. This chapter reviewed some of the tools states may find useful when attempting to incorporate the green economy's objectives into their IIAs. It was explained that the challenge faced by treaty drafters is multi-layered, as states must strike a balance between the need to secure ample regulatory flexibility, on the one hand, and to create a stable, transparent and inviting business environment, on the other. These tools, it was emphasised, should be developed and refined in order to maximise the potential embedded in FDI for supporting the transition to a green economy.

In conclusion, three last remarks should be made. First, the essence of the terms 'sustainable development' and 'green economy' lies in the desired balance between economic, social and environmental concerns. All three pillars are important, and all should be taken into consideration. This is what distinguishes 'sustainable development' or 'green economy' from pure environmental or economic approaches. Following this view, it is argued that states should apply some of the discussed measures with caution, and only after a careful review of their *full* implications. For example, it may be that the easiest way to prevent future conflicts actually frustrates potential synergies. The use of exceptions, for example, may hinder foreign investment and thus frustrate technology transfer or the creation of new jobs.

Second, the concept 'green economy' includes numerous interests, with almost everyone requiring different balances and different treatment. IIAs should, therefore, avoid using a 'one size fits all' solution that will address 'sustainable development' or 'green economy' as a whole. For example, it would be wrong to address the interaction between economic development and climate change mitigation with the same legal tools used for the interaction between human rights and economic development. More detailed IIAs should therefore be promoted.

Lastly, IIAs should focus more on potential synergies with other treaties. At the moment, IIAs (where these actually refer to other treaties or policies) apply a 'defensive' strategy, according to which emphasis is made on preventing conflicts and avoiding future claims by investors. There are hardly any IIAs in which the ultimate goals of another treaty are actively promoted.[126] It could be that this is due mainly to the tool often applied by IIAs – investment protection – in which the potential to promote certain types of investment is rather limited (although not non-existent). Perhaps a conceptual change should be made and other tools, which are based on incentives such as those applied by the Kyoto Protocol flexible mechanism, for example, should also be developed in order to prioritise certain types of investments.

---

[126] A very limited implementation of this concept can be found in the Energy Charter Protocol on Energy Efficiency and Related Environmental Aspects, Annex 3 to the Final Act of the European Energy Charter Conference.

9

The role of international investment agreements in fostering sustainable development

WOLFGANG ALSCHNER AND ELISABETH TUERK[*]

1 Introduction

Foreign investment is an important source of finance for development, especially in low-income countries. If managed properly, foreign investment can improve access to essential services such as water, education and health care, which, in turn, can contribute to achieving the Millennium Development Goals (MDGs). Foreign investment can also facilitate the generation and dissemination of knowledge and technology, support entrepreneurship, job creation and attendant spill-over effects. Through all of this, foreign investment can pave the way for long-term, sustainable and inclusive growth.

However, these benefits from foreign investment are not automatic. More often than not, reaping these benefits requires a carefully tailored policy response at the national and international level to make foreign investment conducive to sustainable development. One of the policy tools typically aimed at attracting foreign investment has been the conclusion of international investment agreements (IIAs), notably bilateral investment treaties (BITs) and free trade agreements (FTAs) with investment provisions (so-called 'other IIAs'). As of June 2011, the IIA regime consisted of 2,830 BITs and 314 'other IIAs'.[1]

However the link between IIAs, foreign investment and sustainable development is a complex one. Not only does the mere conclusion of an IIA not necessarily lead to more foreign investment, but foreign investment does not automatically contribute to sustainable development. Instead, a host state's political and legal framework (of which IIAs are

---

[*] The views expressed in this chapter are those of the authors and do not reflect the views of the UNCTAD Secretariat or its member states.

[1] UNCTAD, *World Investment Report 2011: Non-Equity Modes of International Production and Development* (New York and Geneva: UNCTAD, 2011), available at: www.unctad-docs.org/files/UNCTAD-WIR2011-Full-en.pdf.

part) is only one of several elements that impact a company's decision where to make an investment.[2] And once an investment is made, regulatory action by host governments plays a crucial role in order to maximise the positive and minimise the negative effects of foreign investment.

The challenge of harnessing foreign investment to sustainable development is compounded by the fact that investment protection obligations in IIAs may constrain host countries' policy space necessary to regulate foreign investment in the public interest. From a sustainable development angle, therefore, IIAs raise complex issues in terms of their impact, touch upon sensitive public policy concerns and affect a wide range of stakeholders. Addressing the highly intricate challenges raised by IIAs requires a considerate and sophisticated policy response.

Over time, UNCTAD has worked to strengthen the development dimension of IIAs. This chapter gives a brief overview of recent UNCTAD research on the nexus between IIAs and sustainable development. After sketching the historic evolution and current trends in IIA treaty practice, it explores the linkages between IIAs and three areas of public policy-making that have been at the centre of UNCTAD's research and policy analysis with respect to IIAs and sustainable development. These include: (1) combating climate change; (2) integrating investment and industrial policy; and (3) promoting responsible corporate behaviour. The chapter concludes on the need for more inter-state cooperation to address the various challenges facing the IIA regime today and to enhance its sustainability dimension. In this context, UNCTAD's recently released Investment Policy Framework for Sustainable Development (IPFSD) can provide helpful guidance for the formulation of a new generation of more sustainable investment policy-making.

2 Historic and current IIA practice and sustainable development

The principle rationale behind the conclusion of IIAs was (and still is to a large extent) the protection of foreign investment abroad. Capital-exporting countries sought to ensure a certain level of treatment for their

---

[2] A host country's legal and policy framework affects investment decisions, as do economic determinants for FDI and possible investment incentives. IIAs alone can, therefore, never be a sufficient policy tool to attract FDI. UNCTAD, *The Role of International Investment Agreements in Attracting Foreign Direct Investment to Developing Countries*, UNCTAD Series on International Investment Policies for Development (Geneva: UNCTAD, 2009), available at: www.unctad.org/en/docs/diaeia20095_en.pdf.

investors in host countries, such as fair and equitable treatment and protection against expropriation. Capital-importing countries, in turn, hope that assurances of this very treatment will promote and attract foreign investment in their territory.

In more than fifty years since the conclusion of the first BIT in 1959, the IIA regime has evolved into a highly fragmented and complex universe of more than 3,000 treaties. Today's universe of IIAs is atomised (consisting of thousands of individual agreements that lack any system-wide coordination and coherence), multi-layered (with IIAs existing at the bilateral, regional, intra-regional, inter-regional, sectoral, plurilateral and multilateral level) and multi-faceted (with IIAs differing widely in terms of their content).

Adding a further layer of complexity to the system, IIAs started to include provisions on investor–state dispute settlement (ISDS) in the 1960s. They were deemed as substitutes for what were considered weak or unreliable legal institutional frameworks in host countries. After lying dormant for many years, such treaty-based ISDS mechanisms started to be used more frequently in the late 1990s. In 2011, the number of new ISDS cases peaked with forty-six new known claims filed against host states before international arbitration. This brought the total number of known treaty-based cases to 450 at the end of 2011.[3] Often involving millions of dollars of claimed damages, these cases have started to have a considerable impact on IIA policy-making.

The wave of ISDS claims in recent years has highlighted that investment protection can conflict with other policy objectives, including those related to sustainable development. Protective standards enshrined in IIAs were not only used to challenge grossly unfair or manifestly arbitrary conduct by states and their organs, but also to file claims against measures aimed at achieving legitimate public policies, such as the preservation of the environment,[4] the promotion of social equality[5] or the protection of public health.[6] As warning signs for policy-makers,

---

[3] UNCTAD, 'Latest Developments in Investor–State Dispute Settlement', IIA Issue Note No. 1, 2012, available at: www.unctad.org/en/PublicationsLibrary/webdiaeia2012d10_en. pdf.

[4] For example, *Vattenfall AB, Vattenfall Europe AG, Vattenfall Europe Generation AG* v. *Federal Republic of Germany*, ICSID Case No. ARB/09/6.

[5] For example, *Piero Foresti, Laura de Carli & others* v. *The Republic of South Africa*, ICSID Case No. ARB(AF)/07/01.

[6] For example, *FTR Holding SA, Philip Morris Products SA and Abal Hermanos SA* v. *Oriental Republic of Uruguay*, ICSID Case No. ARB/10/7.

these cases demonstrate the need for more balanced and far-sighted IIA drafting to align IIAs with sustainable development considerations.

In response, some states have started refining their treaties with a view to harmonising the protection of investors abroad with other public policy objectives. The approach followed by these states consisted of a combination of various means that can be grouped into four categories.

First, states have sought to re-balance their rights and obligations under IIAs.[7] Standards of investment protection traditionally found in IIAs are supplemented by tools to preserve policy flexibilities, such as affirmations of the right to regulate or the insertion of public-policy exceptions.[8] This allows a state to guarantee protection to foreign investors, while, at the same time, respecting its obligations under human rights or environmental treaties, as well as preserving the policy space needed to pursue its development agenda. Such fine-tuning of rights and obligations does not necessarily weaken the protective force of an agreement or lead to a loss of a competitive advantage. On the contrary, the general trend displayed in recent US and Canadian treaties suggests that more flexibility goes hand in hand with more protective obligations.

Second, states have begun to re-assert control over their treaties vis-à-vis the discretion exercised by arbitral tribunals. At the drafting stage of IIAs, states clarify treaty language so as to foster predictability and reduce the discretion of arbitrators in potential ISDS proceedings, for example, by defining terms like 'indirect expropriation'. At the implementation stage, more and more treaties contain institutional arrangements that allow states to monitor the application of the agreement or have a say on interpretation issues brought before arbitral tribunals.[9]

Third, the coverage of issues addressed by IIAs is widening. From issues of 'transparency'[10] to 'not lowering environmental standards',[11] 'corporate social responsibility'[12] or 'corruption',[13] new provisions – often in the form of state obligations – are being introduced in IIAs to

---

[7] See also UNCTAD, *World Investment Report 2010. Investing in a Low-carbon Economy* (New York and Geneva: UNCTAD, 2010), ch. III, available at: www.unctad.org/en/docs/wir2010_en.pdf.

[8] For example, see recently concluded Japanese, Canadian and US BITs on UNCTAD's online IIA database, available at: unctad.org/iia.

[9] UNCTAD, 'Interpretation of IIAs: What States Can Do', IIA Issues Note No. 3, 2011, available at: www.unctad.org/en/docs/webdiaeia2011d10_en.pdf.

[10] US–Uruguay BIT (2005), Art. 11.   [11] Belgium–Tajikistan BIT (2009), Art. 5.

[12] Canada–Peru FTA (2008), Art. 810.   [13] Colombia–Japan BIT (2011), Art. 8.

enhance their good governance promoting function. They complement traditional investment protection and react to current policy challenges.

Fourth, responding to the looming threats of ISDS claims, states have strengthened the defensive characters of their treaties. This is done, for example, by inserting limitation periods for filing a notice of arbitration, making it easier to reject frivolous claims or restricting the type of remedy available or the amount of damages.[14] These efforts seek to mitigate the asymmetry prevalent in the current ISDS system where states tend to occupy the respondent's bench, while investors act exclusively as claimants.

In sum, the IIA regime is going through a period of re-balancing aimed at aligning investment protection with other policy objectives. Any such re-balancing has to be done with care, so as to avoid the abyss of investment protectionism. The following sections address three policy areas – climate change, industrial policy and responsible corporate conduct – where this re-balancing has become particularly evident.

3 Harnessing foreign investment for combating climate change

Effectively preventing and mitigating climate change is among the most pressing challenges of our time. While efforts to reach a multilateral agreement with binding targets for greenhouse gas emissions continue, the gradual transition to a low-carbon economy requires, first and foremost, technology and financing. New policy responses, with a view to attracting foreign investment to low-carbon areas can play an important role in this regard.[15]

When it comes to combating climate change, IIAs are a double-edged sword. On the one hand, they can help to promote investment in green technologies, on the other hand, they may be used to challenge regulatory efforts aimed at reducing greenhouse gases.

With regard to their positive role, IIAs, through the reduction of political and regulatory risk, are considered to play a general investment promotion role that can contribute to attracting low-carbon investments. Since investment in renewable energies and low-carbon activities is often reliant on public incentives and government promises of support, the stabilising effect of IIAs, for example, through protection from expropriation, the commitment to fair and equitable treatment or

---

[14] See, e.g., US Model BIT (2012).
[15] This section draws heavily on UNCTAD, *World Investment Report 2010*, ch. IV.

the existence of umbrella clauses, is considered particularly important for fostering investment in these sectors.[16]

At the same time, these very protective standards in IIAs can also constrain states' regulatory prerogatives when they are used to challenge countries' regulatory initiatives aimed at combating climate change. For instance, investors engaged in resource extraction might see their business prospects diminished by regulations regarding the use of land or policies requiring a particular way of managing forest areas. Similarly, investors in industrial production processes could face considerable increases in manufacturing costs in situations where host countries impose a border carbon tax adjustment on carbon-intensive imports. It cannot be ruled out that under those or similar circumstances, foreign investors may consider seeking relief by bringing an ISDS claim under an IIA.[17]

In response to these concerns, a number of states have started adjusting their international investment policies, and have recently concluded IIAs that contain provisions designed to address the unintended effect stemming from the potential ISDS-related challenge and that offer adequate policy space for climate change regulation. States have used different tools in this regard.

One option is to put investment protection in its broader policy context, for example, by including a reference to the objective of combating climate change in the preamble of the agreement.[18] Another option is

---

[16]   See Anatole Boute, 'Combating Climate Change and Securing Electricity Supply: The Role of Investment Protection Law', *European Environmental Law Review* 16(8) (2007): 227–48. Anatole Boute, 'The Potential Contribution of International Investment Protection Law to Combat Climate Change', *Journal of Energy and Natural Resources Law* 27(3) (2009): 333–76.

[17]   The possibility of potential investors' claims against domestic climate change measures has been discussed by numerous commentators, including: Lise Johnson, 'International Investment Agreements and Climate Change: The Potential for Investor–State Conflicts and Possible Strategies for Minimizing It', *Environmental Law Reporter: News and Analysis*, 39 (12) (2009): 11147–60; Fiona Marshall and Deborah Murphy (2009), 'Climate Change and International Investment Agreements: Obstacles or Opportunities?' IISD Draft for Discussion, 2009, available at: www.iisd.org/pdf/2009/bali_2_copenhagen_iias.pdf; Jacob Werksman, Kevin A. Baumert and Navroz K. Dubash, (2001), 'Will International Investment Rules Obstruct Climate Protection Policies?', World Resources Institute, Climate Notes, 2001.

[18]   Japan–Switzerland FTA (2009), Preamble: 'Desiring to promote and reciprocally protect investments, including low-carbon investments, with a view to benefitting from its beneficial impact on the sustainable development of home and host countries, the pursuance of the millennium goals, the combating of climate change, the transfer of technology and the development of human capacity.' See also Austria–Kosovo FTA (2010), Preamble.

to include climate change-related exceptions, exclusions or carve-outs in the treaty text. For example, a number of treaties specify that general *bona fide* regulation designed and applied to protect public welfare objectives, such as protecting the environment, which would arguably include climate change measures, would not amount to an indirect expropriation.[19] Others carve out environmental regulation, such as climate change-related measures, from the scope of ISDS or otherwise qualify the application of ISDS.[20] Finally, some treaties have references to multinational environmental agreements, a practice aimed at fostering a harmonised reading of potentially conflicting international obligations and promoting coherence in international law.[21]

While the above can be considered useful steps in the right direction, the evident link between IIAs and climate change, as well as the magnitude of the global policy challenge, suggests that addressing the interaction between the two regimes through a treaty by treaty piecemeal approach may not be the most efficient response. Instead, as suggested by UNCTAD's 2010 World Investment Report, one could consider an interpretative declaration on investment protection and climate change. Such a *'multilateral declaration* could help enhance coherence between the IIA and the climate change regimes. By clarifying that IIAs do not constrain climate change measures enacted in good faith, such an instrument could help ensure that the IIA framework is in line with multilaterally agreed global priorities.'[22]

4 Foreign investment and its role in industrial policy

In recent years, policy-makers from both developing and developed countries have shown a new interest in industrial policy and brought to light a more proactive role of governments in guiding industrial

---

[19] See, among others, India–Korea CEPA (2009), Annex 10-A, para. 3(b); COMESA Common Investment Area (2007), Art. 20(8).

[20] Some of Belgium's more recent BITs contain examples of this emerging trend (e.g., BITs with Barbados, Colombia, Panama, Tadjikistan and Togo signed in 2009). Such an approach would also address the concern that ISDS tribunals – with their specific expertise in IIA and investment-related issues – might not be the institutions best suited to decide cases that involve complex issues at the interface between environmental protection/sustainable development and investment, and the respective legal regimes/obligations.

[21] Belgium–Barbados BIT (2009), Art. 11(3); Belgium–Tadjikistan BIT (2009), Art. 5(3); Belgium–Togo BIT (2009), Art. 5(3).

[22] UNCTAD, *World Investment Report 2010*, p. 138.

development. The (re)discovery of industrial policy tools by states has been prompted, among other things, by disappointment with the results of a laissez faire policy; the desire to support and protect national champions in light of growing international competition; and the interventions by governments during the recent financial and economic crisis. For developing countries, in particular, industrial policy concerns are often part of their larger development strategies, including those focusing on sustainable development outcomes. Foreign investment is often an element of, and interacts with, industrial policies.[23]

Similar to the climate change context, IIAs exhibit a dual nature, both potentially supporting and potentially constraining industrial policies. First and foremost, IIAs can be important tools to attract FDI, for example, by creating a stable legal framework or by liberalising investment flows. IIAs can channel FDI into specific sectors, for example, by taking the form of sector-specific agreements such as the Energy Charter Treaty. The attractive function of an IIA can be further enhanced if the agreement contains mechanisms for specific investment-promotion activities.[24]

However, IIAs can also constrain industrial policy to the extent that countries may not want to attract, but to shield domestic industries from foreign investors (e.g., states may perceive foreign investments as running counter to industrial policy goals, such as the nurturing of a national champion in a selected industry). Pre-establishment IIAs containing liberalisation commitments may then constrain such investment restrictions. In response, some countries have claimed national security reasons for restricting FDI, hoping to benefit from a security exception found in many pre-establishment IIAs.[25] This has fuelled worries of a rise of investment protection, and hence a careful balance must be struck to preserve policy space, on the one hand, and avoid unjustified investment protectionism, on the other hand.

In addition to issues arising with respect to the entry of foreign investment into a host country, IIAs may come into play with respect to behind-the-border regulation in pursuit of industrial policy objectives. For example, IIAs may prevent the provision of incentives solely to

---

[23] This section builds on UNCTAD, *World Investment Report 2011*, ch. III.

[24] UNCTAD, *Investment Promotion Provisions in International Investment Agreements*, UNCTAD Series on International Investment Policies for Development (Geneva: UNCTAD, 2008), available at: www.unctad.org/en/docs/iteiit20077_en.pdf.

[25] UNCTAD, *The Protection of National Security in IIAs*, UNCTAD Series on International Investment Policies for Development (Geneva: UNCTAD, 2008), available at: www.unctad.org/en/docs/diaeia20085_en.pdf.

domestic investors by mandating unconditional, unqualified national treatment of foreign investors. Moreover, some IIAs also contain prohibitions on performance requirements and, hence, can limit a state's capacity to reap the full development benefits from foreign investment for industrial policy (e.g., by prohibiting transfer of technology obligations imposed on foreign investors).[26]

In response to these concerns, IIA signatories have taken action to safeguard policy space in this regard. For example, some countries have excluded certain industrial policy tools, such as taxation, subsidies or government procurement, from the scope of the treaty or individual provisions;[27] or they have balanced the investment protection commitments in their treaties with fine-tuned flexibilities. A sophisticated way of preserving policy space is to include reservations for selected policies, sectors and industries. These non-conforming measures are typically listed in the annex to an IIA and exempt the indicated measures from a number of treaty obligations, such as national treatment (NT), most-favoured-nation (MFN) treatment and prohibitions on performance requirements. To address the need for adapting industrial policies and thus reservations to new policies in the future, these agreements sometimes provide for the possibility of enacting new non-conforming measures in already specified sectors.[28] The drawback of such a reservation approach is its complexity. Some developing countries may not have sufficient capacity to identify sectors and measures vital for industrial policy purposes or to ensure that its scheduled reservation is consistent within their IIA network.

In sum, the interaction between investment and industrial policies is increasing, and so is the challenge of how to best manage this interaction so as to enhance the contribution of IIAs to countries' industrial development strategies.

5 Fostering responsible investor behaviour

Balancing investment protection and policy flexibility in IIAs is but one challenge in making the investment regime work for sustainable development. Another issue relates to investors as such. Most current IIAs

---

[26] See also box on WTO TRIMs Agreement in UNCTAD, *World Investment Report 2011*, pp. 107–8.

[27] For example, Egypt Model BIT, Art. 2.

[28] An alternative approach found in the Norway Model BIT, Annex A, allows for a change of scheduled reservation if compensatory adjustments are offered so as to maintain the overall level of commitments.

provide investors with rights, for example, to bring claims against the host state before international arbitration. Yet they do not confer independent obligations on investors. As a result, IIAs do little to ensure that states get the development contribution they seek from foreign investment in return for tying their hands in an international agreement. Even more so, in some cases, investment may have a negative impact on sustainable development if investors fail to act responsibly, for example, by not respecting core environmental or labour standards. Acknowledging that not only states, but also investors should act responsibly is an important step towards ensuring that investment is conducive to sustainable development.[29]

Of course, investors are bound by the domestic laws of the country in which they operate. In addition, many IIAs provide that investments have to be made in accordance with local laws and regulations in order to benefit from treaty protection.[30] Yet these mechanisms may not always be enough to ensure a positive contribution of investment to host state development. Some countries may not have sufficient administrative capacities to monitor investor behaviour or to enforce domestic law. In other cases, investors may wilfully circumvent or co-opt national regulators through corrupt practices. Finally, foreign investment is often directed at sectors that have a particularly strong impact on their ecological and social environment, such as the extractive industry, large-scale infrastructure projects or the provision of public services (e.g., water distribution, sewage or public transportation). Against this background, it is all the more important that investors are enticed through international mechanisms to act responsibly.

Recent years have seen the emergence of international corporate social responsibility (CSR) standards. Most of these standards are of a voluntary nature and vary in form, scope and monitoring or reporting mechanisms. This expanding body of soft law is important in order to provide guidelines for the self-regulation of industries and individual companies.[31] Furthermore, these standards can inspire and complement national regulations. IIAs can play an important role in promoting responsible corporate behaviour, including through CSR references.

---

[29] This section builds on UNCTAD, *World Investment Report 2011*, ch. III.
[30] See, e.g., China–Cuba BIT (1995), Art. 1(1). Such requirement is typically linked to entry or establishment, but does not include the ongoing operations of a company.
[31] UNCTAD, *World Investment Report 2011*, ch. III.

While CSR-specific clauses do not feature prominently in IIAs, recent treaty practice outlines four ways in which states can promote CSR. First, states may encourage a CSR-friendly reading of the entire treaty by including a reference to socially responsible investment in the IIA's preamble. Some agreements mention the concept of CSR explicitly;[32] others refer to international standards, such as the OECD Guidelines for Multinational Enterprises[33] or the UN Global Compact.[34]

A second type of CSR-specific clause includes treaties that call on the contracting states – through best endeavour commitments – to promote the adoption of CSR standards by companies. These provisions can be found mostly in FTAs with investment chapters.[35] At the forefront of these efforts are recent Canadian FTAs that contain a provision specifically entitled 'Corporate Social Responsibility'.[36] Similarly, some FTAs concluded by the United States refer to the principle of corporate stewardship, and recognise the importance of implementing policies that seek to ensure coherence between social, economic and environmental objectives.[37]

Also European FTAs with investment chapters address the issue of the social responsibility of investors, and call on the contracting states to enact necessary investor-related measures to fight corruption, to promote compliance with international and national environmental and labour standards, and to foster liaison with local communities.[38] Aside from these 'best effort' commitments to promote CSR, some IIAs also provide for the establishment of a committee that, among other things, is charged with considering CSR-related issues arising under the IIA.[39] Such an institutional mechanism facilitates consultations over CSR, allows the adjustment of CSR policies over time, and helps to prevent CSR-related misunderstandings and disputes.[40]

A more far-reaching third development already envisaged in model BITs, but not yet established in treaty practice, is the imposition of CSR

---

[32] Norway Draft Model BIT (2007), Preamble and Art. 32.
[33] Austria Model BIT (2008), Preamble.   [34] EFTA–Colombia FTA (2008).
[35] An exception is Art. 32 of the Norway Draft Model BIT (2007).
[36] Canada–Peru FTA (2008), Art. 810; Canada–Colombia FTA (2008), Art. 816.
[37] US–Singapore FTA (2003), Art. 18.9.
[38] EC–CARIFORUM Economic Partnership Agreement (2008), Art. 72.
[39] Canada–Colombia FTA (2008), Art. 815(3); Canada–Peru FTA (2008), Art. 817; Norwegian Draft Model BIT (2007), Art. 23.
[40] UNCTAD, *Investor–State Disputes: Prevention and Alternatives to Arbitration*, UNCTAD Yellow Series (New York and Geneva: UNCTAD, 2010), p. 96.

obligations directly on investors. This would mark a departure from the current practice of IIAs that confer rights on individual investors, but do not impose obligations. These model treaties oblige foreign investors to comply with relevant international CSR standards, and stipulate that foreign investors shall contribute to the socioeconomic development of host state communities by encouraging 'human capital formation, local capacity building through close cooperation with the local community, create employment opportunities and facilitate training opportunities for employees, and the transfer of technology'.[41] Whether or not the introduction of such investor obligations into actually negotiated treaties is politically and legally feasible or even desirable remains open to debate.

A fourth way, which stops short of imposing direct obligations on investors, consists of a screening procedure of incoming investors. Found in a number of recent IIAs, such a mechanism enables the potential host state to seek information on potential investors, including on their corporate governance history and their practices as investors in their home state.[42] Based on such information, the host state can make an informed decision whether or not to admit an investment. Investors with a questionable CSR record or those that are merely interested in treaty shopping can thus be rejected from the start.

In sum, CSR may not yet be part of what is considered 'IIA mainstream', but it is finding its way into an increasing number of treaties. Current deliberations at the EU level on the future European investment policy have addressed CSR-related issues, which may point to a growing importance of the concept in the IIA context.[43] Furthermore, innovative approaches pursued in model agreements may further inspire IIA negotiators to include innovative CSR provisions in their treaties.

---

[41] Ghana Model BIT (2008), Art. 12. Similarly, Botswana Model BIT (2008), Art. 11.
[42] Azerbaijan–Croatia BIT (2007), Art. 3. Similarly, India–Japan EPA (2011), Art. 91.
[43] Following the competency shift on international investment matters from the EU Member States to the EU through the Lisbon Treaty, the EU is currently devising a comprehensive European international investment policy. The European Parliament Resolution on CSR in trade agreements is likely to have an impact on the formulation of this policy. European Parliament, Resolution on Corporate Social Responsibility in International Trade Agreements, 2009/2201(INI), 25 November 2010. For recent developments on the EU FDI policy, see UNCTAD, *Investment Policy Monitor*, No. 5, 5 May 2011 and No. 6, 12 October 2011. available at: www.unctad.org/en/Pages/Publications/Investment-Policy-Monitor.aspx.

6 Towards a new generation of more sustainable IIAs

The three issues discussed above – climate change, industrial policy and responsible investor behaviour – are but three examples of the broader nexus between investment treaties and sustainable development. They demonstrate, however, how complex international investment policy-making has become in the twenty-first century. Just as trade regulation is not only about trade, investment regulation is not only about investment. Therefore, new ways need to be found to accommodate health, environmental and social concerns in IIAs to make them more sustainable and development friendly.

For each of the three examples, this chapter has given a sketch of recent efforts to balance investment protection with other public policy objectives in new IIAs. Together with the innovative approaches adopted in model BITs, recent treaty practice can have a guiding function for policy-makers and negotiators of future investment treaties. Yet encouraging as this development may be, it has important limitations if it remains piecemeal.

The overwhelming majority of the IIAs in existence were concluded following the traditional approach with a focus exclusively on investment protection. Even if new, balanced treaties are signed, investors may still be able to circumvent development-friendly provisions by using unqualified MFN clauses to claim the 'more favourable treatment' afforded to investors under older treaties. So what are the alternatives? The renegotiation of old treaties may pose considerable demands on countries' capacity. Also the termination of a particular IIA may be of limited use, since IIAs typically provide for survival clauses that lock-in the protective effect of the treaty for ten, or sometimes even twenty, years after termination takes effect.[44]

These challenges are compounded by the fact that investment stakeholders are increasingly dissatisfied with the system. The multi-layered, multi-faceted and highly atomised nature of the current IIA regime is prone to create inconsistencies between and within investment treaty networks. Divergent findings by investment tribunals on similarly worded provisions form but one expression of the lack of coherence in the investment law architecture that seriously undermines legal

---

[44] UNCTAD, *Denunciation of the ICSID Convention and BITs: Impact on Investor–State Claims*, IIA Issue Note No. 2, 2010, available at: www.unctad.org/en/docs/web-diaeia20106_en.pdf.

predictability. In short, the IIA regime has become too large for states to handle, too complicated for firms to take advantage of, and too complex for stakeholders at large to monitor.[45]

Hence, as an issue a specific piecemeal approach may find its limits in effectively aligning international investment law with sustainable development, states need to be more proactive and comprehensive in fostering a more sustainable investment law system. This can be done through inter-state, cooperative solutions on three levels.

First, on the bilateral level, contracting states can be more active in re-asserting their authority over the application and interpretation of investment treaties through cooperative efforts. As masters of their treaties, the contracting parties have a number of common tools at their disposal to guide arbitral tribunals, such as the possibility of issuing binding inter-pretations. Treaty-based institutions are particularly important in this respect, since they provide a framework for inter-state deliberations throughout the life time of a treaty. Moreover, through a non-disputing party's intervention in investment disputes, technical cooperation or investment promotion, the investor's home state can also do its share to make its IIAs work better for sustainable development.[46]

Second, on the regional level, investment rule-making is picking up speed. The traditional largely bilateral structure of the IIA system is increasingly giving way to regionally concentrated investment areas. Recently concluded agreements such as the trilateral investment agreement between China, Japan and the Republic of Korea or the Central America–Mexico Free Trade Agreement, as well as the ongoing negotiations on a Trans-Pacific Partnership (TPP) Agreement, are cases in point.[47] Regional investment rule-making on such an unprecedented scale provides new opportunities for concerted efforts to promote sustainable development in IIAs.

Third, on the multilateral level, issue-specific negotiations and deliberations are taking place, for instance, on the question of transparency in investor–state dispute settlement based on UNCITRAL arbitration rules,[48] or on the nexus between IIAs and human rights through the

---

[45] At the same time, the regime is still inadequate to cover all possible investment relationships, since full coverage would require another 14,100 bilateral treaties. See UNCTAD, *World Investment Report 2011*.

[46] UNCTAD, 'Interpretation of IIAs: What States Can Do'.

[47] UNCTAD, *World Investment Report 2012*, ch. III.

[48] Note by the UNCITRAL Secretariat, 'Settlement of Commercial Disputes: Preparation of a Legal Standard on Transparency in Treaty-based Investor–State Arbitration', United

2011 UN Guiding Principles on Business and Human Rights.[49] These efforts can help to strengthen the sustainable development dimension of IIAs, and point to the need to tackle some of the IIA regime's systemic challenges multilaterally.

On all three levels, investment policy-makers can take guidance from UNCTAD's recently released Investment Policy Framework for Sustainable Development (IPFSD).[50] The IPFSD consists of a set of core principles for investment policy-making, guidelines for national investment policies and guidance for policy-makers on how to engage in the international investment policy regime, in the form of options for the design and use of international investment agreements. This framework aims to assist countries in aligning their investment policy with their individual development strategy fostering a 'new generation' of IIAs where inclusive growth and sustainable development take centre stage.

Nations Commission on International Trade Law, Working Group II (Arbitration and Conciliation), A/CN.9/WG.II/WP.169, 13 December 2011.

[49] The Principles were adopted by the UN Human Rights Council in May 2011 and are aimed at the implementation of the 'Protect, Respect and Remedy' Framework presented by the UN Special Representative John Ruggie. The text of the Guiding Principles on Business and Human Rights can be found at: www.business-humanrights.org/media/documents/ruggie/ruggie-guiding-principles-21-mar-2011.pdf.

[50] See Investment Policy Framework for Sustainable Development, available at: ipfsd.unctad.org.

10

Reservations, corporate social responsibility and other mechanisms in support of sustainable development in Canada's Model Foreign Investment Promotion and Protection Agreement

PIERRE-OLIVIER SAVOIE*

I Introduction: Canada's FIPA programme

This chapter examines so-called 'reservations' and other treaty provisions that allow for the promotion of sustainable development under Canada's bilateral investment treaties (officially known as foreign investment promotion and protection agreements or FIPAs).

Canada has twenty-three FIPAs currently in force,[1] and another seven have been signed or recently concluded.[2] Canada has also been

---

* Any position expressed in this chapter does not necessarily represent the position of the government of Canada. This chapter is up to date as at 4 August 2012.

[1] Canada has FIPAs with the following countries that entered into force at the date in parentheses: Argentina (29 April 1993), Armenia (29 March 1999), Barbados (17 January 1997), Costa Rica (29 September 1999), Croatia (29 September 1999), the Czech Republic (9 March 1992), Ecuador (6 June 1997), Egypt (3 November 1997), Hungary (21 November 1993), Jordan (14 December 2009), Latvia (27 July 1995), Lebanon (19 June 1999), Panama (13 February 1998), the Philippines (13 November 1996), Poland (22 November 1990), Romania (11 February 1997), the Russian Federation (27 June 1991), the Slovak Republic (9 March 1992), Thailand (24 September 1998), Trinidad and Tobago (8 July 1996), Ukraine (24 June 1995), Uruguay (2 June 1999), and Venezuela (28 January 1998). A listing of Canada's FIPAs is available at: www.international.gc.ca/trade-agreements-accords-commerciaux/agr-acc/fipa-apie/fipa_list.aspx?lang=en. The Canada–Peru FIPA (20 June 2007) is suspended as long as the Canada–Peru Free Trade Agreement (1 August 2009) (Canada–Peru FTA) is in force. See Canada–Peru FTA, Art. 845.

[2] Canada has recently concluded or signed FIPAs with Bahrain, Bénin, China, India, Kuwait, Madagascar and Mali. 'Concluded' treaties refer to those where the negotiations have been concluded, but have not yet been signed. Between conclusion and signature, a legal drafting review (or legal scrub) is conducted for the purpose of ensuring conformity with treaty drafting practice and between different linguistic versions.

re-negotiating FIPAs with several European countries.[3] Twelve more FIPAs are under negotiation,[4] while Canada is at the exploratory discussion stage with four other countries.[5] The government of Canada has received standing authority to negotiate further FIPAs.[6]

There are three generations of Canadian FIPAs. The first generation of FIPAs, concluded between 1989 and 1991, is loosely based on the 1967 OECD model.[7] The second generation of FIPAs, concluded between 1994 and 1999, incorporates some particularities of the investment chapter of the North American Free Trade Agreement (NAFTA). The third generation of FIPAs, based on the 2004 model,[8] continues to resemble the NAFTA's investment chapter, but also contains some additions discussed below.[9] Canada is also a party to four free trade agreements (FTAs) in force that provide investor–state dispute settlement.[10] Another has been signed and another has been concluded, though not yet signed,[11] and Canada is currently negotiating another seven.[12]

---

[3] There have been negotiations to update the FIPAs, leading to the entry into force of updated FIPAs with the Czech Republic (22 January 2012), Latvia (24 November 2011), Romania (23 November 2011) and the Slovak Republic (14 March 2012). Negotiations are ongoing with Hungary and Poland.

[4] Canada is currently negotiating FIPAs with Burkina Faso, Cameroon, Côte d'Ivoire, Ghana, Indonesia, Kazakhstan, Mongolia, Pakistan, Tanzania, Tunisia, Vietnam and Zambia.

[5] Exploratory discussions are being held with Azerbaijan, Cuba, Guinea and Senegal.

[6] See Canada's 'Policy on Tabling Treaties in Parliament', available at: www.treaty-accord.gc. ca/procedure.asp: 'Before entering into treaty negotiation, the initiating department or agency should ensure that it has a policy mandate to begin negotiations. In most cases, the department or agency will submit a Memorandum to Cabinet (MC) to obtain this negotiating mandate ... The MC may seek blanket policy authority to enter into negotiation of a number of similar treaties, rather than a separate submission for each one ... Such blanket authority now exists for: Foreign Investment Protection Agreements.'

[7] OECD Draft Convention on the Protection of Foreign Property, 7 *ILM* 117 (1968).

[8] The 2004 FIPA Model (Model FIPA) is available at: www.international.gc.ca/trade-agreements-accords-commerciaux/assets/pdfs/2004-FIPA-model-en.pdf.

[9] See, e.g., Model FIPA, Art. 11 ('Health, Safety and Environmental Measures') and Annex B.13(1) ('Expropriation').

[10] Such FTAs in force are the Canada–Chile FTA (5 July 1997), Canada–Colombia FTA (15 August 2011), Canada–Peru FTA (1 August 2009) and the North American Free Trade Agreement (Mexico, United States) (NAFTA) (1 January 1994).

[11] Canada has signed an FTA with Panama that is not yet in force and has concluded negotiations with Honduras.

[12] FTA negotiations are ongoing with the Caribbean Community, the European Union, India, Japan, Korea, Morocco and Ukraine.

FIPAs negotiated today are based on Canada's investment arbitration experience, gained primarily under the NAFTA's investment chapter. Canada has been a respondent in thirty-one NAFTA cases, including ten cases that have been concluded and six that are ongoing.[13] Moreover Canada has participated as a third party in some nine NAFTA cases against the United States and Mexico.[14]

II Sustainable development and Canada's FIPAs

Canada's approach to investment treaties is aimed at achieving a careful balance between the legitimate regulatory role of the state and the concerns of investors. Canada's most recent FIPAs and FTAs contain at least seven mechanisms that allow for the regulatory flexibility necessary to achieve these objectives, which include sustainable development. We briefly list the first five and examine in more detail the sixth and seventh, being the so-called 'reservations' and the corporate social responsibility clause.

A Five mechanisms in support of sustainable development

First, FIPAs contain an annex clarifying the meaning of indirect expropriation.[15] The annex clarifies the circumstances in which governments can regulate in areas such as health, safety and the environment without such measures being considered an expropriation. Second, FIPAs require that the parties must promptly publish laws, regulations, procedures and administrative rulings of general application regarding matters covered by the FIPA.[16] The FIPA also encourages the parties to publish in

---

[13] A list of the NAFTA Chapter 11 ('Investment') cases filed against Canada is available at: www.international.gc.ca/trade-agreements-accords-commerciaux/disp-diff/gov.aspx.

[14] Canada made submissions in *ADF Group Inc.* v. *United States of America*, ICSID Case No. ARB(AF)/00/1; *Grand River et al.* v. *United States of America* (UNCITRAL); *Loewen Group, Inc. and Raymond L. Loewen* v. *United States of America*, ICSID Case No. ARB (AF)/98/3; *Methanex Corporation* v. *United States of America* (UNCITRAL); *Marvin Roy Feldman Karpa* v. *United Mexican States*, ICSID Case No. ARB(AF)/99/1; *Fireman's Fund Insurance Company* v. *United Mexican States*, ICSID Case No. ARB(AF)/02/01; *Metalclad Corporation* v. *United Mexican States*, ICSID Case No. ARB(AF)/97/01; *International Thunderbird Gaming Corporation* v. *United Mexican States* (UNCITRAL); *Waste Management Inc.* v. *United Mexican States*, ICSID Case No. ARB(AF)/98/2.

[15] Model FIPA, Annex B.13(1); Canada–Peru FIPA, Annex B.13(1); Canada–Jordan FIPA, Annex B.13(1).

[16] Model FIPA, Art. 19(1); Canada–Peru FIPA, Art. 19(1); Canada–Jordan FIPA, Art. 19(1).

advance measures that it proposes to adopt and to provide interested persons with a reasonable opportunity to comment on such proposed measures.[17]

Third, FIPAs contain a clause that recognises that it is inappropriate to encourage investment by relaxing domestic health, safety or environmental measures.[18] In the event that a party has offered such encouragement, the other party may request consultations. Fourth, FIPAs include general exceptions that allow a party to take measures necessary to protect human, animal or plant life or health, the environment and safety, or measures primarily aimed at the conservation of exhaustible natural resources, provided that these measures are not applied in an arbitrary or unjustifiable manner and are not disguised restrictions on trade or investment.[19]

Fifth, FIPAs contain provisions that seek to bring more transparency to the investor–state dispute settlement process. For example, Canada's Model FIPA explicitly provides for the public availability of documents and making hearings open to the public. While these FIPA provisions have not yet been used, an important number of documents submitted in Canada's NAFTA Chapter Eleven cases are publicly available,[20] pursuant to similar rules established by the NAFTA parties pursuant to the 31 July 2001 Note of Interpretation of the NAFTA parties.[21] The sixth and seventh examples of provisions that help achieve sustainable development objectives are 'reservations' and the corporate social responsibility provision.

B   So-called 'reservations' to FIPAs

The mechanism of 'reservations' allows for the exclusion of existing and future non-conforming measures, from the application of four substantive obligations: (1) national treatment; (2) most-favoured-nation (MFN) treatment; (3) senior management and board of directors requirements; and (4) performance requirements.[22] Existing and future non-conforming

---

[17] Model FIPA, Art. 19(2); Canada–Peru FIPA, Art. 19(2); Canada–Jordan FIPA, Art. 19(2).

[18] Model FIPA, Art. 11; Canada–Peru FIPA, Art. 11; Canada–Jordan FIPA, Art. 11.

[19] Model FIPA, Art. 10, Canada–Peru FIPA, Art. 10; Canada–Jordan FIPA, Art. 10.

[20] Available at: www.international.gc.ca/trade-agreements-accords-commerciaux/disp-diff/gov.aspx?lang=eng&view=d.

[21] Notes of Interpretation of Certain Chapter 11 Provisions, NAFTA Free Trade Commission, 31 July 2001, para. 1.

[22] 'Reservations' have been at issue before, including in the NAFTA Chapter 20 (State to State) case *In the Matter of Cross-Border Trucking Services*, Secretariat File No. USA-MEX-98-2008-01, Final Report of the Panel, 6 February 2001.

measures cannot be excluded from obligations pertaining to the minimum standard of treatment or expropriation.

It is important to note that FIPA 'reservations' are not 'reservations' of the type referred to in Articles 2(1)(d) and 19–23 of the Vienna Convention on the Law of Treaties. This is because FIPA 'reservations' are negotiated and listed in the annexes, and therefore do not form 'unilateral statements' under the definition of Article 2(1)(d).[23] The annexes, according to the FIPA itself, are 'an integral part' of the treaty.[24]

1   'Reservations' for existing non-conforming measures

In practice, Canada uses two different approaches for the listing of existing non-conforming measures. The first is the 'list or lose' approach,[25] as reflected by a 'long form' or a 'short form' annex. It is

---

[23] See also *Iran* v. *United States*, Case B-1, Full Tribunal, Award No. 382-B1-FT, signed 31 August 1988, Iran–US CTR 273, at p. 287, para. 48: 'The Tribunal notes, in this context, that the proviso inserted in Paragraph 9 is part of the text agreed upon by both Parties to the General Declaration, and is not, as argued by Iran, a reservation within the meaning of Article 19(c) of the Vienna Convention as defined in Article 2(1)(d) of that Convention. See *supra* para. 35. According to Article 2(1)(d), a reservation is a "unilateral statement ... made by a State" after adoption of the text of the treaty. A sentence included in the text of the General Declaration obviously is not a reservation in this sense. Article 19(c) of the Convention, therefore, is irrelevant.'; J. M. Ruda, 'Reservations to Treaties', *Recueil des Cours* 146 (1975): 95, at p. 105, stating that 'a reservation is a declaration made outside the treaty, not within it' and that 'the way in which the reservation is entitled or described has no importance at all'. The negotiators of the failed Multilateral Agreement on Investments (MAIs) were also of the opinion that the equivalent of FIPA 'reservations', which originated in NAFTA, were not real public international law reservations, but rather 'exceptions' since such 'reservations' failed to have a reciprocal effect: OECD, Negotiating Group on the Multilateral Agreement on Investment, Multilateral Agreement on Investment: Draft Consolidated Text, DAFFE/MAI(98)7/REV1, 22 April 1998, at p. 89, fn. 1: 'It is generally agreed to replace the term "reservations" by the term "exceptions".' Under treaty law, 'reservations normally have reciprocal effect unless otherwise specified. This is clearly not intended to be the case with respect to Country Schedules. Any possible confusion with the general exceptions could be taken care of by the qualification of "country-specific". The use of the term "exception" would not prevent the listing of a measure with a reciprocity requirement. It would help avoid confusion in the case of any genuine "reservations" in the treaty law sense were to be made and called as such.'

[24] Model FIPA, Art. 52(1).

[25] Model FIPA, Art. 9(1): 'Articles 3 (national treatment), 4 (MFN), 6 (performance requirements) and 7 (senior management and board of directors) *shall not apply to*: (a) *any existing non-conforming measure* that is maintained by (i) a Party at the national level, *as set out in its Schedule to Annex I*, or (ii) a sub-national government; (b) the continuation or prompt renewal of any non-conforming measure referred to in subparagraph (a); (c) an amendment to any non-conforming measure referred to in

Canada's preferred approach and is used in FTAs. The 'long form' has been used in the Canada–Peru FIPA,[26] while the 'short form' has been used in the Canada–Jordan FIPA.[27] Under the 'short form', each party must list all its existing non-conforming measures and provide a description of the reserved measure.[28] Under the 'long form' annex, more information is provided, including a more detailed description of the reserved measure.[29]

There are special rules of interpretation for 'reservations' of existing non-conforming measures under FIPAs and FTAs. Such rules can vary from one treaty to another.[30] The advantage of the 'list or lose' approach is its high level of transparency because non-conforming measures are identified and described. One of the disadvantages of this approach is that it requires extensive examination of all the law on the books.

The second approach Canada uses is called 'grandfathering' of all existing non-conforming measures. A provision simply excludes all existing non-conforming measures without listing them. The advantage of this approach is its simplicity. One variant Canada is currently exploring in ongoing negotiations is a list of existing non-conforming measures, but only for transparency purposes. Such a list is not as detailed as the 'long form' annex. Nevertheless, it allows investors and other interested persons to know what existing measures the treaty partners believe may be non-conforming.

---

subparagraph (a) to the extent that the amendment does not decrease the conformity of the measure, as it existed immediately before the amendment, with Articles 3, 4, 6 and 7.'

[26] Canada–Peru FIPA, Annex I ('Reservations for Existing Measures and Liberalization Commitments').

[27] Canada–Jordan FIPA, Annex I ('Reservations for Existing Non-Conforming Measures and Liberalization Commitments').

[28] See, e.g., Canada–Jordan FIPA.

[29] Canada–Peru FIPA, Headnote to Annex I, para. 2 establishes that reservations contain six elements (sector, subsector, industry classification, type of reservation, measures and description). By contrast, para. 2 of the Headnote to NAFTA's, Annex I establishes that reservations contain eight elements (sector, subsector, industry classification, type of reservation, level of government, measures, description and phase out).

[30] Canada–Peru FIPA, Headnote to Annex I, para. 3 contains rules of priority regarding which element of the reservation prevails. Paragraph 3 of the Headnote to Annex I of the NAFTA contains slightly different rules of priority. By contrast, para. 2 of the Headnote of the Canada–Jordan FIPA provides that the measure prevails in the event of a discrepancy with the description. With respect to NAFTA, see the submissions of Canada, Mexico, and the United States in *Mobil Investments Canada Inc. and Murphy Oil Corporation* v. *Canada*, ICSID Case No. ARB(AF)/07/4, available at: www.international.gc.ca/trade-agreements-accords-commerciaux/disp-diff/mobil_archive.aspx?lang=en.

2 'Reservations' for future measures

'Reservations' are also allowed for future measures.[31] In that case, the parties set out at least the sectors and subsectors excluded from national treatment, MFN treatment, performance requirements, and/or the obligations of senior management and board of directors after the entry into force of the treaty.[32] For example, one standard 'reservation' Canada makes for future measures relates to social services, including public education and health care.[33] There are also special rules of interpretation for 'reservations' for future measures under FIPAs and FTAs, which differ from existing special rules for 'reservations' to existing nonconforming measures.[34]

C The corporate social responsibility provision

Another mechanism that can support sustainable development objectives is the provision on corporate social responsibility. It has been included in the investment chapters of the Canada–Peru and Canada–Colombia FTAs,[35] and there is no reason why it should not be included in FIPAs as well.

For example, Article 810 of the Canada–Peru FTA provides that:

> Each Party should encourage enterprises operating within its territory or subject to its jurisdiction to voluntarily incorporate internationally recognized standards of corporate social responsibility in their internal policies, such as statements of principle that have been endorsed or are supported by the Parties. These principles address issues such as labour, the

---

[31] Model FIPA, Art. 9(2): 'Articles 3, 4, 6 and 7 shall not apply to any measure that a Party adopts or maintains with respect to sectors, subsectors or activities, as set out in its schedule to Annex II.'

[32] See, e.g., Canada–Jordan FIPA. By contrast, para. 2 of the Headnote to Annex II ('Reservations for Future Measures') of the Canada–Peru FIPA and para. 2 of the Headnote to Annex II ('Reservations for Future Measures') of the NAFTA establish that reservations contain six elements (sector, subsector, industry classification, type of reservation, description and existing measures).

[33] Canada–Peru FIPA, Annex II, II-C-10; Canada–Jordan FIPA, Annex II; NAFTA, Annex II, II-C-9.

[34] Under both para. 3 of the Headnote to Annex II ('Reservations for Future Measures' of the Canada–Peru FIPA and para. 3 of the Headnote to Annex II ('Reservations for Future Measures') of the NAFTA, the description element prevails in the event of a discrepancy between elements. The Canada–Jordan FIPA does not contain special rules of interpretation.

[35] Canada–Peru FTA, Art. 810; Canada–Colombia FTA, Art. 816.

environment, human rights, community relations and anti-corruption. The Parties remind those enterprises of the importance of incorporating such corporate social responsibility standards in their internal policies.

This provision is a new avenue to promote corporate social responsibility. The standards referred to would include, for example, the OECD Guidelines for Multinational Enterprises.[36] It also remains to be seen whether the provision will be invoked one day as a relevant context within which to interpret other substantive obligations.

III   Conclusion

A few years ago, Professor Céline Lévesque wrote that 'the [Canadian and US bilateral investment treaty] models also have in common their length and complexity'.[37] Another of the FIPA's more salient characteristics is its sophistication. The FIPA's detailed provisions offer increased predictability, for example, with respect to procedural issues in investor–state dispute settlement. The sophistication of the substantive obligations and annexes is also necessary to ensure adequate regulatory flexibility, including with respect to sustainable development.

Some states have more bilateral investment treaties than Canada. This may be because their treaties are shorter and require less negotiation or because these states started their treaty programme decades before Canada, which did so only in 1989. In any event, one of the goals of Canada's Global Commerce Strategy is to significantly increase the number of FIPAs by 2014. This would also entail an increase in the number of investment treaties while taking care to maintain a careful balance between the concerns of investors and legitimate regulatory objectives, such as sustainable development.

---

[36] OECD Guidelines for Multinational Enterprises, Recommendations for Responsible Business Conduct in a Global Context, OECD Ministerial Meeting, 25 May 2011, p. 5: 'As at 25 May 2011 adhering governments are those of all OECD members, as well as Argentina, Brazil, Egypt, Latvia, Lithuania, Morocco, Peru and Romania', available at: www.oecd.org/dataoecd/43/29/48004323.pdf.

[37] 'Influences on the Canadian FIPA model and US model BIT: NAFTA Chapter 11 and Beyond', *Canadian Yearbook of International Law* 44 (2006): 249, at p. 249.

11

Deciding international investment agreement applicability: the development argument in investment

DIANE A. DESIERTO

"Sustainable development" is a well-entrenched norm of international law,[1] defined as "development which meets the needs of the present without compromising the ability of future generations to meet their own needs."[2] This concept has been scarcely treated in international investment arbitrations,[3] and neither has any investment arbitral award to date referred to a specific definition of "sustainable development."

The silence of international investment awards on "sustainable development" is perplexing. After all, the concept of development figures in two highly polemical questions that have become a staple in contemporary investment arbitral disputes. The first question asks whether development should be treated as an essential element or criterion (rather than simply a descriptive feature) to establish the existence of an "investment" to which the international investment agreement (IIA) would apply.[4]

---

[1] Nico Schrijver, *The Evolution of Sustainable Development in International Law: Inception, Meaning, and Status* (The Hague: Martinus Nijhoff, 2008), at pp. 33 *et seq.*

[2] Markus Gehring and Andrew Newcombe, "An Introduction to Sustainable Development in World Investment Law," in Marie-Claire Cordonier Segger, Markus W. Gehring, and Andrew Paul Newcombe (eds.), *Sustainable Development in World Investment Law* (Alphen aan den Rijn: Kluwer Law, 2011), pp. 3–12, at p. 6.

[3] See *Biwater Gauff (Tanzania) Ltd* v. *Tanzania*, ICSID Case No. ARB/05/22, Procedural Order No. 5 (*Amicus Curiae*), 2 February 2007, paras. 50–54, 65, 70 (where the arbitral tribunal agreed to permit written submissions by the petitioning non-governmental organizations in view of the public interest and sustainable development concerns raised in the dispute, but did not authorize the petitioners to have access to key arbitration documents nor attend hearings unless authorized by the actual disputing parties); *Methanex Corporation* v. *United States*, UNCITRAL (*Ad hoc*), Decision on *Amicus Curiae*, 15 January 2001, para. 47.

[4] Diane A. Desierto, "Development as an International Right: Investment in the New Trade-Based IIAs," *Trade Law and Development* 3(2) (2011): 296, available at www.

Development advocates contend that investments that have not significantly contributed to a host state's national economy (the famous *Salini* test)[5] should not be covered by the IIA and its dispute settlement mechanism enabling investors direct recourse against the host state for alleged injuries to investment. The second question inquires if the state's regulatory prerogative to pursue development objectives forms part of subject matter that can be deemed excluded from the applicability of an IIA, allegedly through "measures not precluded" or "essential security interests" clauses within the IIA.[6] While some development advocates may find purchase in arguments favoring the interpretation of "essential security interests" or "measures not precluded" clauses as those that portend the complete inapplicability of an IIA to host state policy matters, to date this interpretive outcome has rarely been upheld in current investment arbitral tribunal practice.[7] Admittedly, both questions involve intricate processes of IIA interpretation of variant treaty texts and complex interwoven facts in different cases. Nevertheless, these questions speak to a much broader *problématique* about the extent of applicability of an IIA to an investor–state dispute when the host state has to contend with challenging adverse development situations arising during the life of an investment.

tradelawdevelopment.com/index.php/tld/article/viewFile/3%282%29%20TRADE.%20L%20%26%20DEV.%20296%20%282011%29/110, accessed July 1, 2012.

[5] *Salini Costruttori SpA and Italstrade SpA* v. *Kingdom of Morocco*, ICSID Case No. ARB/00/4, Decision on Jurisdiction, para. 52: "doctrine generally considers that investment infers: contributions, a certain duration of performance of the contract and a participation in the risks of the transaction ... In reading the Convention's preamble, *one may add the contribution to the economic development of the host State of the investment as an additional condition*" (emphasis added).

[6] See, among others, Jose Alvarez and Kathryn Khamsi, "The Argentine Crisis and Foreign Investors: A Glimpse into the Heart of the Investment Regime," in Karl Sauvant and Lisa Sachs (eds.), *Yearbook on International Investment Law and Policy 2008-2009* (New York: Oxford University Press, 2009), pp. 379–478; Howard Mann, "The Right of States to Regulate and International Investment Law: A Comment," United Nations Conference on Trade and Development, The Development Dimension of FDI: Policy and Rule-Making Perspectives, Proceedings of the Expert Meeting held in Geneva from November 6–8, 2002, 2003, pp. 211–223 available at: http://unctad.org/en/docs/iteiia20034_en.pdf, accessed July 1, 2012.

[7] Diane A. Desierto, *Necessity and National Emergency Clauses: Sovereignty in Modern Treaty Interpretation, International Litigation in Practice* (Leiden: Martinus Nijhoff, 2012), vol. 3, pp. 145–236. See also William J. Moon, "Essential Security Interests in International Investment Agreements," *Journal of International Economic Law* 15 (2012): 481–502.

The academic literature is profuse on all the doctrinal, interpretive, and policy issues attendant to both questions.[8] For the purposes of this brief contribution, however, I will not focus on the detailed argumentative valences behind each question. Rather, I propose to invite attention to the emerging phenomenon of IIA inapplicability as a somewhat surprising *ex post* method for achieving a host state's development objectives. The jurisprudence on IIA inapplicability provides a useful heuristic for the analysis of potential interpretive impediments to mediating the concept of sustainable development within IIA rule-making and adjudication.

Arbitral reasoning on the matter of IIA applicability *qua* interpretation has been uneven and inconsistent. By contrast, *ex ante* rule-making by host states demonstrates through new IIAs that host states might prefer to carve out particular subject matter that would be expressly insulated from the applicability of the IIA, as well as its investor–state dispute settlement mechanism. The disparate experiences in IIA adjudication and IIA rule-making on the matter of IIA applicability should give pause to reassess the suitability of each mechanism to accomplish a host state's development objectives. Both *ex post* arbitral interpretation and *ex ante* IIA rule-making contend with difficulties arising from the inherent fluidity of the concept of "sustainable development." Unlike the accepted use of "sustainable development" in international trade law as an "interstitial" norm[9] that is increasingly harmonized through common treaty instruments adjudication mechanisms, there is some resistance to grafting this norm onto IIA interpretation. The "resistance," I submit, could be explained by inherent limitations in the IIA texts, as well as in the reticence of arbitral tribunals to any untoward broad use of their

---

[8] See, in particular, Julien Davis Mortenson, "The Meaning of Investment: ICSID's Travaux and the Domain of International Investment Law," *Harvard International Law Journal* 51 (2010): 1, at pp. 257–318; Antoine Martin, "The Definition of 'Investment': Could a Persistent Objector to the Salini Tests be Found in ICSID Arbitral Practice?" *Global Jurist* 11 (2011): 2, at pp. 1934–2640; Nathalie Bernasconi-Osterwalder and Lise Johnson (eds.), *International Investment Law and Sustainable Development: Cases from 2000–2010*, available at: www.iisd.org/pdf/2011/int_investment_law_and_sd_key_cases_2010.pdf, accessed July 1, 2012; Desierto, *Sovereignty in Modern Treaty Interpretation*, pp. 145–236.

[9] Markus W. Gehring and Marie-Claire Cordonier Segger (eds.), *Sustainable Development in World Trade Law* (The Hague: Kluwer Law, 2005), pp. 5–7: "a commitment to promote sustainable development, in international law, requires a balanced reconciliation or integration between economic growth, social justice, and environmental protection objectives, towards participatory improvement in … collective quality of life that can meet the needs of the present without compromising the needs of future generations."

mandate. Unless the individual mandates of arbitral tribunals in the universe of IIAs are correspondingly revolutionized and reconceptualized, "sustainable development" could remain lost in translation within international investment arbitral reasoning.[10]

Contribution to "development" and the establishment of an "investment" for purposes of IIA applicability

The "double-barrel" test in International Centre for the Settlement of Investment Disputes (ICSID) arbitrations requires a claimant to meet the definition of investment in both the IIA and Article 25(1) of the ICSID Convention.[11] In interpreting the latter definition of "investment" in Article 25, the development genealogy from *Fedax*[12] in 1997 seems relatively straightforward. Among the basic features of an investment, the *Fedax* tribunal enumerated: "a certain duration, a certain regularity of profit and return, assumption of risk, a substantial commitment *and a significance for the host State's development.*"[13] In 2002, the tribunal in *Mihaly v. Sri Lanka* emphasized that:

> in the absence of a generally accepted definition of investment for the purpose of the ICSID Convention, the Tribunal must examine the current and past practice of ICSID and the practice of States as evidenced in multilateral and bilateral treaties and agreements binding on States … It is for the Tribunal to determine the meaning or definition of 'investment' for this purpose as a question of law.[14]

Thereafter, it appeared that the *Fedax* feature of "significance to the host State's development" had subsequently been accepted as a formal

---

[10] On the interactions between international human rights law, international environmental law, and international trade law, see, among others, Christina Voigt, *Sustainable Development as a Principle of International Law: Resolving Conflicts between Climate Measures and WTO Law* (Oxford: Blackwell, 2009); Francesco Francioni (ed.), *Environment, Human Rights and International Trade* (Oxford: Hart, 2001); Dire Tladi, *Sustainable Development in International Law: An Analysis of Key Enviro-Economic Instruments* (Pretoria: Pretoria University Law Press, 2007).

[11] Convention on the Settlement of Investment Disputes between States and Nationals of Other States, 575 *UNTS* 159 (1965), Preamble, first paragraph, available at: http://icsid. worldbank.org/ICSID/ ICSID/RulesMain.jsp, accessed July 1, 2012 (ICSID Convention).

[12] *Fedax NV v. Valenzuela*, ICSID Case No. ARB/96/3, Decision on Jurisdiction, IIC 101 (1997), (2002) 5 *ICSID Reports* 183.

[13] *Fedax* (emphasis added).

[14] *Mihaly International Corporation v. Democratic Socialist Republic of Sri Lanka*, ICSID Case No. ARB/00/2, Award, 2002.

condition – indeed, determinative of the existence of an investment in *Consortium RFCC*[15] and *Salini*.[16] Other tribunals followed suit, including those in *Joy Mining* v. *Egypt* in 2004,[17] *Saipem SpA* v. *Bangladesh* in 2009,[18] and *Phoenix* v. *Czech Republic* in 2009.[19]

The 2009 annulment decision in *Malaysian Salvors*,[20] however, broke from previous cases, casting the concept of "contribution to the host State's development" as a mere *characteristic* of "investment," and not a formal condition or independent criterion for determining the existence of "investment." In this case, the annulment committee examined the legislative history behind Article 25(1) of the ICSID Convention and failed to find any explicit acceptance of the notion of "contribution to host state development" in the *travaux préparatoires*. The annulment committee instead endorsed the liberal treatment of the *Salini* criteria in the 2008 award in *Biwater* v. *Tanzania*,[21] and declared that the sole arbitrator in *Malaysian Salvors* had exceeded his powers by failing to exercise jurisdiction through, among other things, elevating the *Salini* criteria into "jurisdictional conditions ... exigently interpret[ing] the alleged condition of a contribution to the economic development of the host State so as to exclude small contributions."[22] This decision, which clearly departs from any sense of *jurisprudence constante*[23] insofar as the status of the concept of "contribution to host state development" is concerned, exemplifies the continuing ambiguity of the normative role of sustainable development in deciding IIA applicability.

The element of "contribution to host state development" remains robustly argued as an essential condition of "investment" under Article 25(1) of the ICSID Convention, particularly in the realm of financial investment assets. The 2011 *Abaclat and others* v. *The Argentine Republic*

---

[15] *Consortium RFCC* v. *Morocco*, ICSID Case No. ARB/00/6, Award, 2003.

[16] *Salini Costruttori SpA and Italstrade SpA* v. *Jordan*, ICSID Case No. ARB/02/13, Award, 2006.

[17] *Joy Mining Machinery* v. *Egypt*, ICSID Case No. ARB/03/11, Award on Jurisdiction, 2004.

[18] *Saipem SpA* v. *The People's Republic of Bangladesh*, ICSID Case No. ARB/05/07, Decision on Jurisdiction, 2009.

[19] *Phoenix Action Ltd* v. *Czech Republic*, ICSID Case No. ARB/06/5, Award, 2009.

[20] *Malaysian Historical Salvors Sdn Bhd* v. *Government of Malaysia*, ICSID Case No. ARB/05/10, Decision on the Application for Annulment, 2009.

[21] *Malaysian Salvors*, paras. 78–80.   [22] *Malaysian Salvors* para. 80(b).

[23] See Jose E. Alvarez, Karl P. Sauvant, Kamil Gerard Ahmed, and Gabriela Vizcaino (eds.), *The Evolving International Investment Regime: Expectations, Realities, Options* (New York: Oxford University Press, 2011).

Decision on Jurisdiction and Admissibility found that the security entitlements of the mass claimants to Argentine bonds fell within the definition of an "investment" under the IIA in question (Article 1(1) of the 1990 Argentina–Italy bilateral investment treaty (BIT)), as well as Article 25(1) of the ICSID Convention.[24] The majority of the tribunal concluded in particular that the security entitlements could still be deemed "made in Argentina":

> there is no doubt that the funds generated through the bonds issuance process were ultimately made available to Argentina, and served to finance Argentina's economic development. Whether the funds were actually used to repay pre-existing debts of Argentina or whether they were used in government spending is irrelevant. In both cases, it was used by Argentina to manage its finances, and as such must be considered to have contributed to Argentina's economic development and thus to have been made in Argentina.[25]

The famous October 28, 2011 dissenting opinion of Professor Georges Abi-Saab (who thereafter resigned his appointment as arbitrator) challenged the *Abaclat* majority's finding of the existence of an investment. Professor Abi-Saab declared that:

> the investment that the Convention seeks to encourage by providing it with an international procedural guarantee is that which contributes to the economic development of the host country, i.e. to the expansion of its productive capacity, a contribution that presupposes a commitment to this task not only of economic resources, but also in terms of duration in time and the taking of risk, with the expectation of reaping profits and revenue in return.[26]

He then stressed a teleological approach to interpreting "investment" under Article 25(1) of the ICSID Convention:

> It is worth recalling that the object and purpose of the Convention was to encourage the flow of private foreign investment into developing countries, by making available an additional international facility or guarantee that counter-balances the host State's regulatory authority over

---

[24] *Abaclat and others* v. *The Argentine Republic*, ICSID Case No. ARB/07/5, August 4, 2011, paras. 352–362.

[25] *Abaclat and others*, para. 378.

[26] *Abaclat and others* v. *The Argentine Republic*, ICSID Case No. ARB/07/5, Dissenting Opinion of Professor Georges Abi-Saab, October 28, 2011, para. 50, available at: www.italaw.com/documents/Abaclat_Dissenting_Opinion.pdf, accessed July 1, 2012.

investment and economic activities in its territory; in other words, by providing a neutral international forum in case of dispute, as an alternative to submitting to the jurisdiction of the tribunals of the host State.[27]

He found that there was no such "investment made in the territory of Argentina" as required under the IIA, since

> the financial securities instruments that constitute the alleged investment, i.e. the security entitlements in Argentinean bonds, have been sold in international financial markets, outside of Argentina, with choice of law and forum selection clauses subjecting them to laws and fora foreign to Argentina. In fact, they were intentionally situated outside Argentina and out of reach of its laws and tribunals.[28]

Professor Abi-Saab's Dissenting Opinion thus directly repudiated the restrictive interpretation of "investment" conferred by the *Malaysian Salvors* annulment committee in 2009 to "investment" under Article 25(1) of the ICSID Convention, and favored a return to the *Salini* test and its use of "development" as a criterion, and not just a descriptive feature, of "investment" for purposes of determining IIA applicability. Noticeably, both the *Abaclat* majority and its dissenting arbitrator appeared to accept "contribution to economic development" as an element of investment, but differed as to the status of this element (e.g., descriptive feature for the majority, strict condition for the dissenting arbitrator) and the definition of "economic development." For the *Abaclat* majority, the existence of a contribution to economic development was sufficiently shown by the availability of fiscal resources raised to the Argentine Government through the sovereign bond issue, whereas the dissenting arbitrator sought a clear nexus between the investment asset (whether private direct investment or financial portfolio investment) and the economic benefit to a host state.

Significantly, neither the *Abaclat* majority nor its dissenting arbitrator included any definition of "development" as an international legal standard, much less the legal norm of "sustainable development." Similar to the practice of many tribunals that refused to view "contribution to economic development" as a hard criterion under the *Salini* test, the ultimate result in the *Abaclat* decision was to view "development" expansively so as to find in favor of the existence of an "investment." The IIA

---

[27] *Abaclat and others*, Dissenting Opinion, para. 53.
[28] *Abaclat and others*, Dissenting Opinion, para. 78.

and its investor–state dispute settlement clause would usually be found applicable, and only very rarely deemed inapplicable.[29]

Finally, it bears observing that the fluidity of the norm of "sustainable development" may, ironically, also pose difficulties for even the *subjects* of sustainable development protection to hurdle the jurisdictional issue of IIA/treaty applicability through the definition of "investment." In its January 2011 Award in *Grand River Enterprises Six Nations Ltd et al. v. United States of America*,[30] the NAFTA tribunal held that the claimants – members of the Six Nations of the Iroquois Confederacy/ Haudenosaunee – failed to prove that their reservation activities of tobacco production and cigarette manufacturing amounted to an enterprise as defined in NAFTA, Article 1139 in relation to Article 1101.[31] While the tribunal significantly acknowledged that it was "respectful of Seneca law and custom, and does not question that the written or unwritten customary laws of indigenous peoples could be the basis for establishing an enterprise for the purposes of NAFTA," the tribunal declared that the evidence submitted by the claimants was insufficient, being "mere assertions of the existence of Seneca law and custom."[32] The tribunal omitted to state the quality or degree of evidence acceptable in order to prove such customary laws as being a possible source of meaning on the definition of "investment" or "enterprise" for purposes of invoking the applicability of the IIA to their reservation activities.

The question of the status of "contribution to economic development," in relation to the meaning of "investment" triggering the applicability of an IIA, in reality, side-steps the conceptual definition of "development" and particularly ignores the international legal standard of "sustainable development." Divergent strands of arbitral reasoning continue to contest the *Salini* test's use of "development" as an essential element or criterion to determine the existence of an "investment" to which an IIA would apply. What is profoundly interesting from this ongoing controversy is that to date, arbitral tribunals have not yet elucidated a clear definition of "economic development" in order to differentiate actual

---

[29] Desierto, "Development as an International Right," p. 313: "The irony in debating the use of development as either a criterion or a mere descriptive characteristic is that, in actual arbitral practice, the majority of arbitral tribunals to date have had little difficulty finding that a given transaction, operation, or activity indeed contributes to a host State's economic development."

[30] *Grand River Enterprises Six Nations Ltd et al. v. United States of America*, NAFTA/ UNCITRAL, Award, January 12, 2011.

[31] *Grand River Enterprises*, paras. 85–106.   [32] *Grand River Enterprises*, para. 103.

"contributions" to a host state's development that merit protection through IIA applicability, from those remotely beneficial economic transactions that could not have been contemplated by states parties to an IIA. Tribunals assume an understanding of "development" that may not necessarily adhere to the international legal standard of "development"[33] or "sustainable development."[34]

A self-judged "development carve-out": interpreting "measures not precluded" and "essential security interests clauses" toward complete IIA inapplicability

Turning now to the issue of "essential security interests" or the "measures not precluded" clauses in the older generation of IIAs (pre-2004), there are emergent attempts seeking to mediate regulatory prerogatives over host state development through the extreme effect of making the IIA wholly *inapplicable* when a host state invokes an "essential security interests" or "measures not precluded" clause.

The United Nations Conference on Trade and Development (UNCTAD) observes that most BITs signed between 1995 and 2006 show a "worldwide"[35] trend of "general treaty *exceptions* ... cover[ing] a broad range of issues, including taxation, essential security interests and public order, protection of human health and natural resources, protection of culture and prudential measures for financial services."[36] UNCTAD notes that most of these BITs "include a clause on protection for losses due to situations of war, insurrection, riot, rebellion or other civil disturbance," as well as "clauses whose scope is not clear ... provid[ing] that protection shall be granted in situations of *national emergency*,"[37] with such protection usually assuming the form of compensation in the event of losses from these disturbances and emergencies. On the other hand, the Organisation for Economic Co-operation and Development (OECD) has reported that there have been broad and narrow usages of "essential security interests," "necessity," or

---

[33] See definition of the international right to development under the 1986 Declaration on Development, Declaration on the Right to Development, GA Resolution 41/128, UN Doc. A/RES/41/128, December 4, 1986, Art. 1(1).

[34] Declaration on Development, fn. 1.

[35] United Nations Conference on Trade and Development (UNCTAD), *Bilateral Investment Treaties 1995–2006: Trends in Investment Rulemaking* (New York and Geneva: UNCTAD, 2007), p. 142.

[36] UNCTAD, p. xiii ('Executive Summary').   [37] UNCTAD, pp. 52–53.

"emergency" by OECD members.[38] The IIAs surveyed, however, generally do not expressly provide for the effect of treaty inapplicability.

Until the 2008 Award in *Continental Casualty* v. *Argentine Republic*,[39] these types of clauses had never been interpreted as resulting in wholesale treaty *inapplicability* upon invocation by the host state.[40] The Democratic Republic of Congo (DRC) attempted to advance this precise argument to annul the award in *Mitchell* v. *Democratic Republic of Congo*, but the DRC did not succeed in persuading the ICSID annulment committee in *Mitchell* that a similarly worded "measures not precluded" or "essential security interests" clause could result in treaty inapplicability.[41] In 2010, the annulment decision in *Sempra* embraced the *Continental Casualty* interpretation, giving the effect of IIA/treaty inapplicability to "measures not precluded" or "essential security interests" clauses.[42] The 2010 annulment decision in *Enron*, however, did not reach a similar interpretation of IIA/treaty inapplicability for such clauses. Rather, the *ad hoc* committee in *Enron* was careful not to make any pronouncement on the effect of the "essential security interests" clause, instead confining its finding of annullable error to the tribunal's decision that Argentina was altogether precluded from relying on the clause.[43] Subsequent awards involving "measures not precluded" or "essential security interests" clauses, such as *Total SA* v. *Argentina*[44] and *Impregilo SpA* v. *Argentine Republic*,[45] did not adopt the interpretation of IIA inapplicability made by the *Continental Casualty* tribunal.

---

[38] Organisation for Economic Co-operation and Development (OECD), *International Investment Perspectives: Freedom of Investment in a Changing World* (Paris: OECD, 2007), pp. 93–134 ("Essential Security Interests Under International Investment Law") (OECD 2007 Report).

[39] *Continental Casualty Company* v. *Argentine Republic*, ICSID Case No. ARB/03/9, Award, September 5, 2008.

[40] Diane A. Desierto, "Necessity and Supplementary Means of Interpretation of Non-Precluded Measures in Bilateral Investment Treaties," *University of Pennsylvania Journal of International Law* 31(3) (2010): 827.

[41] *Mitchell* v. *Democratic Republic of Congo*, ICSID Case No. ARB/99/7, Decision on the Application for Annulment of the Award, 2006.

[42] *Sempra Energy International* v. *Argentine Republic*, ICSID Case No. ARB/02/16, Decision on the Argentine Republic's Application for Annulment of the Award, paras. 200 and 204.

[43] *Enron Creditors Recovery Corporation Ponderosa Assets LP* v. *Argentine Republic*, ICSID Case No. ARB/01/3, Decision on the Application for Annulment of the Argentine Republic, July 31, 2010, para. 405.

[44] *Total SA* v. *Argentina*, ICSID Case No. ARB/04/1, Decision on Liability, December 21, 2010, paras. 482–484.

[45] *Impregilo SpA* v. *Argentine Republic*, ICSID Case No. ARB/07/17, Final Award, June 21, 2011, paras. 336–360.

The main difficulty with the attempted use of "measures not pre-cluded" or "essential security interests" clauses as a form of self-judged development carve-out mechanism for host states lies with the silence of current treaty texts. Article XI of the Argentina–United States BIT – the "measures not precluded" clause at issue in numerous cases involving the 2001–2002 Argentina financial crisis – does not indicate the effect of IIA inapplicability.[46] The absence of any treaty definition of the legal standard of "development" or "sustainable development," supposedly justifying a host state's "essential security interest" measure, further makes the intended result of IIA inapplicability an apocryphal conclusion expectedly avoided by arbitral tribunals.[47]

Explaining "resistance": obstacles to the acceptance of "sustainable development" in international investment arbitrations

While arbitrators increasingly confront host states' invocations of devel-opment, they have not yet been fully receptive to its pragmatic force toward the (re)interpretation of current formulations of "investment" provisions and "essential security interests" clauses within BITs. There could be several explanations for the "resistance" toward reading in "sustainable development." First, the nebulous and porous usage of the concept of "development" within the context of an investor–state dispute might make the norm too unwieldy and imprecise for purposes of concrete adjudication.[48] Second, arbitral tribunals might analogously

---

[46] Desierto, *Sovereignty in Modern Treaty Interpretation*, p. 170: "the trend in investment treaty practice implies that when contracting States do contemplate situations where the entire treaty is inapplicable, they purposely define, delimit, and qualify these situations in the treaty language of exceptions or necessity clauses. Absent this explicit or detailed language, it is the more reasonable presumption that contracting States intend to ensure continuous observance of all their treaty obligations in accordance with *pacta sunt servanda*. The rarity of exceptions that cause total treaty inapplicability bolsters this presumption, since in fact, 'most [BITs] do not [even] contain express exceptions for measures necessary for national security or the protection of essential security interests (security exceptions).'"

[47] An IIA can also expressly rule out the applicability of the investor–state dispute settle-ment mechanism for certain subject matter. See Article 18 of the 2000 Mexico–Sweden BIT: "The dispute settlement provisions of this Section shall not apply to the resolutions adopted by a Contracting Party which, in accordance with its legislation, and for national security reasons, prohibit or restrict the acquisition by investors of the other Contracting Party of an investment in the territory of the former Contracting Party, owned or controlled by its nationals."

[48] Desierto, "Development as an International Right," pp. 302–315.

adopt preferences for "judicial parsimony" in their own adjudicative methodology, resulting in a narrow resolution of issues only according to the terms of reference submitted by the parties.[49] Finally, the textual limitations of the IIA provisions being interpreted on the matter of "sustainable development" and the effect of IIA inapplicability could likewise justify arbitral tribunals' reticence to identify any operative customary international law norms on development.[50] Where the matter is of fundamental jurisdictional importance as to decide whether an IIA applies or not to a dispute,[51] it is not unexpected that arbitral reasoning would hearken somewhat conservatively toward IIA text, leaving other matters to the merits phase, such as using the international legal standard of "sustainable development" as a potential argument for the host state.

Most importantly, because development is frequently argued within the lexicon of subject-matter jurisdiction (whether through the meaning of "investment" or "measures not precluded" clauses in IIAs), regardless of their inclinations arbitral tribunals are thus inevitably drawn into some degree of review over host states' asserted demarcation of their regulatory freedoms or policy spaces to vindicate the public interest.

Notably, recent practice does demonstrate a promising sensitivity toward the host state's regulatory freedom to effectuate "sustainable development" objectives. The 2012 Award in *Unglaube and Unglaube v. Costa Rica*[52] is one such example. This case involved a claim of alleged IIA breaches of an expropriatory and non-expropriatory nature in relation to the investors' beachfront property, which had also been the subject of the Costa Rican Government's attempt to establish a national reserve and nesting habitat for the endangered species of leatherback turtles, consistent with its environmental obligations under the Costa Rica Constitution and the Inter-American Convention for the Protection and Conservation of Sea Turtles. While the *Unglaube* tribunal found that

---

[49] Guillermo Aguilar Alvarez and W. Michael Reisman, "How Well are Investment Awards Reasoned?" in Guillermo Aguilar Alvarez and W. Michael Reisman (eds.), *The Reasons Requirement in International Investment Arbitration: Critical Case Studies* (Leiden: Martinus Nijhoff, 2008), pp. 1–33, at p. 30.

[50] Desierto, "Development as an International Right," pp. 301–315, 332.

[51] Tribunals restrict jurisdictional review to a *prima facie* standard of review. See Audley Sheppard, "The Jurisdictional Threshold of a Prima Facie Case," in Peter Muchlinski, Federico Ortino and Christoph Schreuer (eds.), *Oxford Handbook in International Investment Law* (Oxford University Press, 2008), pp. 932–961, at pp. 941–954.

[52] *Unglaube and Unglaube v. Costa Rica*, ICSID Case Nos ARB/08/1 and ARB/09/20, Award, May 16, 2012.

expropriation had been committed,[53] it laudably declined to find any violation of the IIA's fair and equitable treatment standard arising from the regulatory procedures and processes observed by the Costa Rican Government in the establishment of the national reserve:

> the Tribunal understands that the workings of the courts and administrative agencies of Costa Rica surely involve noticeable differences from those with which the Claimants may be more familiar. But because governments are accorded a considerable degree of deference regarding the regulation or administration of matters within their borders, such differences are not significant ... unless they involve or condone arbitrariness, discriminatory behaviour, lack of due process or other characteristics that shock the conscience, are clearly "improper or discreditable" or which otherwise blatantly defy logic or elemental fairness.[54]

While "sustainable development" was not deployed as a distinct argument in this arbitration, this could have been one feasible instance in which to examine an additional "interstitial" role for this norm written into the international environmental obligations of the Costa Rican Government on the protection of such endangered species.

Conclusion: revolutionizing arbitral mandate toward sustainable development by reconceptualizing IIAs

Deciding the issue of IIA applicability using the argument of development certainly requires better explication of this argument, particularly the normative role of "sustainable development." The paradox exists because arbitral tribunals derive their mandate from the terms of consent of states parties under the IIA. Where the IIA is silent on the effect of treaty inapplicability, arbitral tribunals cannot be expected to supply this effect, even when the same is invoked for benevolent developmental purposes. Because every investor–state dispute will almost always implicate the host state's regulatory prerogative over development objectives in relation to foreign private investment, it is up to host states to cure the situation by revolutionizing the arbitral mandate through IIAs that are distinctly reconceptualized toward concretely effectuating sustainable development.

Lacking any clarification from the IIA itself, arbitral tribunals will rightly tend to decline defining an iron-clad conceptual content when

---

[53] *Unglaube*, paras. 221–223.   [54] *Unglaube*, para. 258.

determining "contribution to development" of a supposed "investment." The result is to expansively view "investment" for purposes of establishing IIA applicability (and subject-matter jurisdiction in an investor–state dispute), as virtually any transaction that redounds to the economic benefit of a host state is equated with the concept of "economic development." As noted in this contribution, very few awards have actually denied the existence of an investment due to its failure to contribute to a host state's economic development.[55] IIA inapplicability due to the non-existence of an "investment" means that investors seek recourse to the IIA's dispute settlement mechanism. But this remains an infrequent conclusion among arbitral awards.[56] The challenge lies in how to use the concept of "development" and "sustainable development" as distinct legal standards that can operate as feasible jurisdictional gate-keeping mechanisms against investments that do not meet these legal standards, and thus do not merit IIA protection, without incurring the moral hazard of pretextual invocations of development by host states bent on avoiding obligations toward foreign investors.

The same may be said of other IIA clauses that states parties may design to deliberately carve out from development regulatory areas from the investor–state dispute settlement mechanism. Many tribunals' interpretations of "measures not precluded" or "essential security interests" clauses rightly reject the notion of complete IIA inapplicability simply for the reason that the IIAs do not provide for this effect. Tribunals are loathe to stretch the interpretation of a "measures not precluded" clause in an IIA as some kind of catch-all development carve-out triggered at any time by a host state that wants to avoid any *ex post* finding of IIA breach.[57]

---

[55] Desierto, "Development as an International Right," p. 313.

[56] See *Joy Mining Machinery Ltd* v. *Egypt*, ICSID Case No. ARB/03/11, Award on Jurisdiction, July 30, 2004; *Mitchell* v. *The Democratic Republic of the Congo*, ICSID Case No. ARB/99/7, Decision on the Application for Annulment of the Award, October 27, 2006; *Romak SA* v. *Uzbekistan*, Award, PCA Case No. AA280, November 26, 2009; *Global Trading Resource Corp. and Globex International Inc.* v. *Ukraine*, ICSID Case No. ARB/ 09/11, Award, November 23, 2010; *F-W Oil Interests Inc.* v. *Trinidad and Tobago*, ICSID Case No. ARB/01/14, Award, February 20, 2006; *Alps Finance and Trade AG* v. *Slovakia*, Award (*Ad hoc* arbitration), March 5, 2011.

[57] *Continental Casualty Company* v. *Argentine Republic*, ICSID Case No. ARB/03/9, Award, September 5, 2008 (affirmed in Decision on Annulment, September 16, 2011, where the ICSID tribunal favored Argentina's interpretation that "necessary measures" in Art. XI would preclude the applicability of all obligations in the entire treaty so as to prevent a breach from arising); *Sempra Energy International* v. *Argentine Republic*, ICSID Case No. ARB/02/16, Decision on the Argentine Republic's Application for Annulment of the Award, June 29, 2010.

As long as IIAs remain silent on the normative parameters of "sustainable development" or "economic development," arbitral tribunals will continue to exhibit a common reluctance to engage this norm to decide the critical issue of IIA applicability. Investment tribunals will continue to err on the side of prudence, and will prefer to resolve a dispute according to a narrow construction of the arbitral mandate as defined by the terms of consent of states as expressed in the IIA. Unless the issue of "sustainable development" is unavoidably put in issue in a case due to an IIA clause that specifically refers to this norm for purposes of determining subject-matter jurisdiction or IIA applicability, few international investment awards will include this norm in arbitral reasoning. One need go no further to illustrate this point than to recall how the ponderous attempt of the sole arbitrator in *Malaysian Salvors* to inductively specify the content of "contributions to economic development"[58] was given short shrift by the ad hoc committee during the annulment phase of proceedings.[59]

Finally, it should be noted that the porousness of "development" as an international legal standard also makes it difficult to stabilize its conceptual content for purposes of consistent IIA interpretation among arbitral tribunals. The strict adherence to arbitral mandate, when combined with the ambiguity in the concept of "development," plausibly explains the rejection by arbitral tribunals of "development" as a strict precondition or essential element of "investment" within the meaning of an IIA or Article 25 of the ICSID Convention,[60] and, concomitantly, their refusal to expansively treat the open-textured[61] "measures not precluded" or

---

[58] See *Malaysian Historical Salvors Sdn Bhd* v. *Malaysia*, ICSID Case No. ARB/05/10, Decision on the Application for Annulment, Dissenting Opinion of Judge Mohamed Shahabuddeen, April 16, 2009, B, para. 21; *Malaysian Historical Salvors Sdn Bhd* v. *Malaysia*, ICSID Case No. ARB/05/10, Award on Jurisdiction, May 10, 2007, paras. 123–124, 138.

[59] *Malaysian Historical Salvors Sdn Bhd* v. *Malaysia*, ICSID Case No. ARB/05/10, Decision on the Application for Annulment, February 28, 2009, paras. 57–81.

[60] See, among others, *Inmaris Perestroika Sailing Maritime Services GmbH and others* v. *Ukraine*, ICSID Case No. ARB/08/8, Decision on Jurisdiction, paras. 131–132; *Bureau Veritas, Inspection, Valuation, Assessment and Control, BIVAC BV* v. *Paraguay*, ICSID Case No. ARB/07/9, Decision on Objection to Jurisdiction, May 29, 2009, paras. 94, 96; *Pantechniki SA Contractors and Engineers* v. *Albania*, ICSID Case No. ARB/07/21, Award, July 28, 2009, paras. 36 and 43; *Fakes* v. *Turkey*, ICSID Case No. ARB/07/20, Award, July 12, 2010, para. 111; *Alpha Projektholding GMBH* v. *Ukraine*, ICSID Case No. ARB/07/16, Award, October 20, 2010, paras. 312–313.

[61] On the resort to open-textured language in the earliest BITs, see Kenneth J. Vandevelde, "A Brief History of International Investment Agreements," in Karl P. Sauvant and Lisa E.

"essential security interests" clauses in IIAs as some kind of self-judging development carve-out for the host state in economic crisis. While these deliberative outcomes are indeed well justified under the prescribed process of interpretation under law of treaties,[62] they provide cold comfort to those seeking to elicit substance from "international cooperation for economic development, and the role of private international investment therein."[63]

The comparably stable definition and widespread acceptance of sustainable development as an operative norm of international trade law has not always found an easy counterpart in international investment law. The key to disentangling this Gordian knot, in my view, might be discerned from how proponents of "sustainable development" in the international trade law regime succeeded over time in calling upon states themselves to clarify and reform treaty language, as well as to carefully empower and authorize their designated agents and adjudicators in the dispute settlement process toward feasibly mediating "sustainable development" within the interpretive architecture. Despite being the situs of many public policy controversies, the argument for "sustainable development" has become a well-established axiom within the dialogic processes of the international trade law regime.[64]

By contrast, institutional efforts to reform the new generations of international investment treaties have only begun to crystallize of late, particularly with the promising release of UNCTAD's proposed Investment Policy Framework for Sustainable Development (IPFSD).[65] Mediating the concept of sustainable development could gain more traction

Sachs (eds.), *The Effect of Treaties on Foreign Direct Investment: Bilateral Investment Treaties, Double Taxation Treaties, and Investment Flows* (Oxford University Press, 2009), pp. 3–35.

[62] Desierto, "Development as an International Right"; Desierto, "Necessity and Supplementary Means of Interpretation," pp. 827–934.

[63] ICSID Convention, Preamble, first paragraph, available at: http://icsid.worldbank.org/ICSID/ ICSID/RulesMain.jsp, accessed July 1, 2012.

[64] See Ernst-Ulrich Petersmann, "Human Rights and International Trade Law: Defining and Connecting the Two Fields," and Christine Breining-Kaufmann, "The Legal Matrix of Human Rights and Trade Law: State Obligations versus Private Rights and Obligations," both in Thomas Cottier, Joost Pauwelyn, and Elisabeth Bürgi (eds.), *Human Rights and International Trade* (Oxford University Press, 2005), pp. 29–94 and pp. 95–135, respectively; Joost Pauwelyn, *Conflict of Norms in Public International Law: How WTO Law Relates to Other Rules of International Law* (Cambridge University Press, 2003), pp. 25–88.

[65] See suggested reforms of UNCTAD, specifically the proposed Investment Policy Framework for Sustainable Development (IPFSD). United Nations Conference on Trade and Development, 2012 World Investment Report, pp. 99–161.

when coursed through reforms to IIA rule-making, rather than through induced (re)interpretations of "investment" or "measures not precluded clauses" in IIAs in international investment arbitrations. Ushering in reforms to define IIA applicability through rule-making attracts less opposition because rule-making reforms represent *ex ante* jurisdictional planning strategies consensually determined by states parties to the IIAs. On the other hand, advancing *ex post* novel interpretations in arbitral reasoning provokes more contestation among IIA parties when both treaty text and the *travaux préparatoires* are clearly silent on the purported effect of treaty inapplicability. For "sustainable development" to be regarded as an essential element and jurisdictional condition when deciding the issue of IIA applicability (or inapplicability), states must deliberately and carefully legislate this norm's conceptual content and bases for assessment into the IIA itself, along with the rules of interaction between this norm and rest of the obligations under the IIA. States cannot, and should not, abdicate the decision on IIA applicability based on the argument of development to future individual arbitrator discretion.

PART IV

International investment, trade and
developing countries

12

International investment law and trade: the relationship that never went away

MARY E. FOOTER

I Introduction

This contribution maintains that the relationship between international investment law and trade has been a constant, if not a consistent, one throughout the history of international economic relations. Arguably, the relationship is stronger today than at any time previously when various treaty instruments sought to establish the ground rules for the reciprocal protection of their nationals' commercial interests abroad. This is because a foreign investor or trader is seeking specific terms and conditions for commercial access to overseas markets, combined with certain guarantees as to the level of treatment that may reasonably be expected from that access. The investor or trader is therefore not indifferent to the protection that the rule of law in international investment law and trade provides.[1]

My aim is to explore this premise with a view to understanding the historical and contextual antecedents of the relationship between international investment law and trade, and the similarities and differences in the approaches towards the multilateralisation of both areas of international economic activity. A further aim is to offer some perspectives on the contemporary jurisprudential nexus between investment and trade, and finally to reflect on the future prospects of this enduring relationship.

---

[1] In fact, the rule of law is essential for participation in the global economy, see Susan D. Franck, 'The Legitimacy Crisis in Investment Treaty Arbitration: Privatizing Public International Law Through Inconsistent Decisions', *Fordham Law Review* 73 (2004/5): 1521, at p. 1524, cited in L. Yves Fortier, 'Investment and the Rule of Law: Change or Decline', in Robert McCorquodale (ed.), *The Rule of Law in International and Comparative Context* (London: British Institute of International and Comparative Law, 2010).

II Historical and contextual background to the investment law and trade nexus

This section examines the historical and contextual background to the relationship between investment and trade. The story begins with bilateral treaties of friendship, commerce and navigation (FCN treaties) and moves through the attempt at multilateralising the relationship between investment law and trade in the stillborn Havana Charter for an International Trade Organization (ITO),[2] followed by some further cursory attempts at multilateralism in the General Agreement on Tariffs and Trade (GATT).[3] Only belatedly has this linkage been more fully taken up in the World Trade Organization (WTO).[4] Along the way the relationship between investment law and trade has been strengthened by developments at the Organisation for International Economic Co-operation and Development (OECD),[5] in the UN General Assembly and at the UN Conference on Trade and Development (UNCTAD).[6] Running alongside the emergence of the GATT/WTO trade regime, international investment law has developed from a body of customary international law rules, through protection under FCN treaties and finally emerged as a regime of bilateral investment treaties (BITs). Where international investment law and trade have regained a closer relationship is in the inclusion of investment chapters in regional integration agreements, such

---

[2] For details of the stillborn International Trade Organization (ITO), see John H. Jackson, *The World Trading System* (Cambridge, MA: MIT Press, 1997), pp. 36–7; see below, n. 18, for details of the proposed ITO Charter.

[3] Final Act Adopted at the Conclusion of the Second Session of the Preparatory Committee of the United Nations Conference on Trade and Development, 30 October 1947, 55 *UNTS* 188 (1947), containing the General Agreement on Tariffs and Trade and the Protocol of Provisional Application, entered into force 1 January 1948 (GATT 1947).

[4] The World Trade Organization's founding instrument is the Agreement Establishing the World Trade Organization, done at Marrakesh, 15 April 1994, 1867 *UNTS* 154, 33 *ILM* 1144 (1994), entered into force 1 January 1995 (WTO Agreement).

[5] The Organisation for Economic Co-operation and Development (OECD) was established in 1961 as a successor to the Organisation for European Economic Co-operation (OEEC), which was founded in 1948, on the basis of the Convention on the Organisation for Economic Co-operation and Development, done at Paris, 14 December 1960, 888 *UNTS* 179, entered into force 30 September 1961, as subsequently amended.

[6] The United Nations Conference on Trade and Development (UNCTAD) was established pursuant to UNGA Resolution 1785, 17 UN GAOR, Supp. 17, p. 14, UN Doc A/5217, 1963 and UNCTAD Final Act, UN Doc. E/Conf. 46/141, vols 6–8, 1964. It became an official organ of the UN General Assembly by means of GA Resolution 1995, 19 UN GAOR, Supp. 15, p. 1, UN Doc. A/5815, 1965.

as the North American Free Trade Agreement (NAFTA),[7] or functional integration agreements like the Energy Charter Treaty (ECT).[8]

A   Degrees of bilateralism and multilateralism in the investment and trade relationship: from FCN treaties to the GATT

The story of the complex relationship between investment and trade proceeds by twists and turns through the development of international investment law by means of bilateral treaties, as opposed to the multi-lateralisation of international trade law.

The post-war era of bilateralism in international investment law

It has long been recognised that FCN treaties and similar types of bilateral treaty instruments, which are commercial in the broadest sense of the word, can provide a basis for agreement between states. Although the content of FCN treaties has changed over time, typically they have been the focus of the exercise of foreign relations in the domestic sphere.[9] Above all, they are treaties of establishment designed to protect natural and legal persons, their interests and their properties in a country other than their own.[10] The basic principles on access, non-discrimination, security and due process, which existed in FCN treaties, have all retained their place in modern BITs.[11]

---

[7] North American Free Trade Agreement between the Government of Canada, the Government of the United States of Mexico and the Government of the United States of America (NAFTA), 13 December 1993, (1993) 32 *ILM* 289.

[8] Final Act of the European Energy Charter Conference, 12 December 1994, AF/EECH, reprinted in (1995) 34 *ILM* 373 (Energy Charter Treaty or ECT). For an extensive discussion of the provisions of the Energy Charter Treaty, see Thomas W. Wälde (ed.), *The Energy Charter Treaty: An East–West Gateway for Investment and Trade* (London: Kluwer Law, 1996).

[9] Some of the earliest examples in the post-Westphalia period include the Treaty of Amity and Commerce between the United States and France, 6 February 1778, 8 St. 12, TS No. 83; the Treaty of Friendship and Alliance between His Britannic Majesty and the Prince Regent of Portugal, signed at Rio de Janeiro, 19 February 1810, 61 Cons. Treaty Ser. 41; and Treaty of Friendship, Commerce and Navigation between Paraguay and the Zollverein, 1 August 1860, 122 Cons. Treaty Ser. 283.

[10] Herman Walker, Jr, 'Modern Treaties of Friendship, Commerce and Navigation', *Minnesota Law Review* 42 (1957/8): 805–24, at p. 805.

[11] Kenneth J. Vandevelde, *Bilateral Investment Treaties* (Oxford University Press, 2010), p. 21.

As a former American diplomat, Herman Walker, stated a half century ago, what these treaties share is their 'similarity of subject matter molded into concrete provisions', and their durability requiring reasonable commitments. Their lengthy subject matter coverage calls for 'rules framed in terms of principles that remain valid regardless of an unpredictable future'.[12] Since foreign investment is essentially grounded in principles of equity and fair treatment, there was no place for the trading of concessions and the type of bargaining found in international commerce[13] that came to dominate the GATT/WTO trading system.

Even so, when it comes to treaty-making, what both international investment law and trade share is a reconciliation between the need for 'positive, universally tenable rules' and the need to provide some 'moderation and a spirit of accommodation'.[14] A more detailed consideration of this point is taken up in the next section, where the similarities and differences in the multilateralisation of international investment law and trade are examined.

The post-war era of multilateralism in trade

Immediately after the Second World War it had been the grand aim of the United States and its European allies to establish favourable conditions for economic recovery on a multilateral basis with investment and trade being closely linked. The Bretton Woods Conference of 1944,[15] which resulted in the establishment of the International Monetary Fund (IMF) and the International Bank for Reconstruction and Development (World Bank), was a first step on the road to post-war economic recovery and future stability. It was followed in 1946 by a proposal for an International Conference on Trade and Employment at the first meeting of the United Nations Economic and Social Council (ECOSOC).[16]

Already by the following year the Preparatory Committee (Prepcom) of the UN Conference on Trade and Employment had completed work on a charter for an ITO,[17] which was presented to a specially convened

---

[12] Walker, 'Modern Treaties of Friendship, Commerce and Navigation', pp. 806 and 809.
[13] Walker, 'Modern Treaties of Friendship, Commerce and Navigation', pp. 809–10.
[14] Walker, 'Modern Treaties of Friendship, Commerce and Navigation', p. 810.
[15] *Proceedings and Documents of the United Nations Monetary and Financial Conference*, Bretton Woods, New Hampshire, 1–22 July 1944, vol. 1 (Washington, DC: US Department of State, 1947), p. 941.
[16] 1 UN ECOSOC Resolution 13, UN Doc. E/22, 1946.
[17] *Report of the Second Session of the Preparatory Committee of the United Nations Conference on Trade and Employment*, UN Doc. E/PCT/186 (Geneva: UNCTAD, 1947).

conference in Havana at the end of 1947.[18] From the very beginning rules on investment and competition policy were to exist alongside those for trade in goods. It is not surprising then to find chapter III of the Havana Charter for an ITO titled 'International Investment for Economic Development and Reconstruction'. However, a brief perusal of the language of the chapter reveals a tension in the relationship between international investment and trade, centred on the issue of economic sovereignty.[19]

Article 12 of the Havana Charter specifically recognised that 'international investment, both public and private can be of great value in promoting economic development and reconstruction'.[20] At the same time it made clear that future ITO members would retain the right to take safeguarding measures to ensure that inward foreign investment would not interfere in their internal affairs and domestic policies. It further upheld the principle of economic sovereignty by recognising that ITO members would be free to determine the terms and conditions for the entry of foreign direct investment (FDI).[21] It also explicitly recognised that bilateral and multilateral agreements on investment could promote and protect investment by the nationals of capital-exporting members in other capital-importing members so as 'to promote their economic development or reconstruction'.[22] When it came to admitting foreign investment ITO members would undertake the dual obligation to 'provide reasonable opportunities ... and adequate security for existing and future investments' and 'give due regard to the desirability of avoiding discrimination as between foreign investments'.[23]

Had the Havana Charter come into force, this would have paved the way for the co-existence of a treaty-based system of bilateral and multilateral treaties on foreign investment alongside members trade obligations. It would not, however, have promoted the specific integration and development of international investment in the ITO. As the tide of

---

[18] The Final Act and Related Documents of the United National Conference on Trade and Employment, Havana, Cuba, 21 November 1947–24 March 1948 (Final Act of the Havana Conference), included the draft Charter for the International Trade Organisation (ITO), UN Doc. ICITO/1/4 (1948) (Havana Charter).

[19] Report by the Secretariat of the UNCTAD, 'The Outcome of the Uruguay Round: an Initial Assessment: Supporting Papers to the Trade and Development Report', 1994, UNCTAD/TDR/14 (Supplement), p. 135, at pp. 136 et seq. for an overview of foreign investment and the trading system under the Havana Charter (UNCTAD Secretariat Report).

[20] Havana Charter, section III, Art. 12.1(a). [21] Havana Charter, Art. 12.1(c)(i) and (ii).

[22] Havana Charter, Art. 12.1(d). [23] Havana Charter, Art. 12.2(a) (i) and (ii).

history reveals, international investment and trade were about to enter
into what in some societies is termed a 'Living Apart Together', or 'LAT',
relationship.[24] In other words, the two areas of economic activity
were related to one another, but each maintained its separate domain.
The development of this LAT relationship had effectively begun in the
late 1940s when an unparalleled exercise in tariff cutting in manufactures
heralded the end of the natural alliance between investment and trade,
which had survived for so long in FCN treaties.

Following the completion of negotiations on wide-ranging tariff reductions, the GATT entered into force in 1948 as a temporary arrangement,
to be replaced by the ITO. However, due largely to the intransigence of
the US Congress, the Havana Charter never entered into force,[25] and
neither did the ITO. One reason for this intransigence arose from the
investment protection provisions in the charter. American businessmen
had lobbied Congress, believing that the provisions, as drafted, had been
weakened at the insistence of developing countries.[26]

Following the failure of the Havana Charter to enter into force and
various attempts to revive the stillborn ITO in the 1950s, the international community was left with the GATT 1947 and its annexed tariff
schedules. While the GATT 1947 marks the successful conclusion of an
unparalleled exercise in tariff cutting, combined with rules to protect the
value of those bound tariffs, it was bereft of any specific rules on foreign
investment. Not only did the GATT represent a paradigm shift from
bilateral to multilateral treaty-making in trade regulation, but it also
signalled the end of the alliance between investment and trade that had
previously existed under the system of FCN treaties.

---

[24] The term 'Living Apart Together', or 'LAT', relationship has been used to describe the
circumstances in which two people consider themselves to be a couple, or nuclear family,
and others recognise this but both partners maintain a separate home. It originated in
the Netherlands in 1978, where the term is still commonly used; see Irene Levin, 'Living
Apart Together: A New Family Form' *Current Sociology*, 52(2) (2004): 223–40, at
pp. 226–7.

[25] Richard N. Gardner, *Sterling–Dollar Diplomacy in Current Perspective* (New York:
Columbia University Press, 1980), pp. 369–80, for a detailed historical account of the
issues the US administration faced.

[26] Vandevelde, *Bilateral Investment Treaties*, p. 41; see also Todd S. Shenkin, 'Comment:
Trade-related Investment Measures in Bilateral Investment Treaties and the GATT:
Moving Toward a Multilateral Investment Treaty', *University of Pittsburgh Law Review*
55 (1993/4): 451–606, at p. 556, with reliance on William Diebold, Jr, *The End of the ITO*,
Princeton Essays in International Finance No. 16 (Princeton University Press, 1952),
pp. 1–11, at p. 9.

Meanwhile, over the next six decades, and despite the lack of a tangible link between international investment law and trade, the multilateral trading system dealt with specific aspects of this LAT relationship. There were a few sporadic decisions adopted by the GATT contracting parties in the 1950s dealing with investment issues, as, for example, with the resolution aimed at encouraging donor and recipient countries to conclude bilateral and multilateral investment agreements to stimulate the international flow of capital.[27]

Investment in the GATT 1947

Throughout the 1960s and 1970s the relationship between international investment and trade at the multilateral level remained a distant one. Then in 1981, a broader-based GATT policy initiative, known as the Consultative Group of Eighteen,[28] took up the challenge of dealing with 'investment performance requirements and incentives', both of which were closely linked to export and import substitution requirements. However, the Consultative Group of Eighteen failed to reach consensus on their trade-related effects.[29] This was hardly surprising given that the GATT was primarily concerned with the reduction of tariffs and the removal of non-tariff barriers rather than FDI flows.

Evidence of this can be seen in the *Canada–Foreign Investment Review Agreement (FIRA)* decision of 1984,[30] relating to a complaint by the United States against Canada's Foreign Investment Review Act or FIRA.[31] The FIRA required foreign investors to give written undertakings that they would favour the purchase of Canadian goods over imported goods, in the form of local purchasing requirements. Foreign investors

---

[27] Resolution of the Contracting Parties, 4 March 1955, on 'International Investment for Economic Development' (1955) *BISD* 3S/49, p. 50; see UNCTAD Secretariat Report, p. 136.

[28] The Consultative Group of Eighteen was established by Decision of the GATT Council of 11 July 1975, GATT Doc. L/4204, *BISD* 22S/15, later confirmed by means of a further Decision of the Contracting Parties, 22 November 1979, being the 'Mandate of the Consultative Group of Eighteen', GATT Doc. L/4869, *BISD* 26S/289–90; see further Note by the GATT Secretariat, 9 June 1987, GATT Doc. MTN.GNG/NG14/W/5 and Mary E. Footer, *An Institutional and Normative Analysis of the World Trade Organization* (Leiden: Martinus Nijhoff, 2006), pp. 122–3.

[29] Report of the Consultative Group of Eighteen to the Council of Representatives, GATT Doc. No. L/5210, 1981, reprinted in *BISD* 28S/71, pp. 75–6.

[30] GATT Panel Report, *Canada–Administration of the Foreign Investment Review Act*, L/5504, adopted 7 February 1984, *BISD* 30S/140 (*Canada–FIRA*).

[31] Canada, Foreign Investment Review Act, 1973, 1st Sess., 29th Parliament, 21 Elizabeth II, 1973. The House of Commons of Canada, BILL C-132, (1973) 12(5) *ILM* 1136–53.

also had to fulfil certain export performance requirements, thereby contravening Articles III and XI of the GATT 1947.[32]

At the time the GATT Council established the Panel several delegates doubted its competence to deal with the matter, since it involved investment. They presumed that the Panel would limit itself to dealing only with those investment issues that fell within the 'four corners of the GATT'.[33] As parties to the dispute, the United States and Canada agreed that the matter concerned neither the FIRA nor Canada's right to regulate the entry and expansion of FDI, but the consistency of the required purchase and export undertakings under the FIRA.[34]

The Panel subsequently found that the local purchasing requirements violated the national treatment standard under Article III:4 of the GATT 1947 (and also Article III:5 of the GATT 1947),[35] but not the prohibition on quantitative restrictions in Article XI:1 of the GATT 1947 because they did 'not prevent the importation of goods as such'.[36] It did not find that Canada had acted inconsistently with its GATT obligations in allowing certain foreign investments to be subject to the export of specific amounts in proportion to production, that is, product mandating. There was quite simply 'no provision in the General Agreement which [forbade] requirements to sell goods in foreign markets in preference to the domestic market'.[37]

The *FIRA* Panel concentrated on just two trade-related investment measures (TRIMs), namely, local purchasing requirements and product mandating, and left unaddressed other undertakings required by the Canadian legislation for foreign investors. These included the requirements to: (a) set up a purchasing division in a Canadian subsidiary; (b) manufacture goods and components locally that would otherwise be imported; and (c) require Canadian participation in the investment enterprise.[38]

B   The emergence of a BITs regime, soft law instruments on investment and ICSID

Following the demise of the Havana Charter in the immediate post-war era, and any possibility that international investment law would find its

---

[32] Articles III and XI, GATT 1947.   [33] *Canada–FIRA*, Panel Report, para. 1.4.
[34] *Canada–FIRA*, Panel Report para. 3.3; see further Shenkin, 'Comment', p. 562.
[35] *Canada–FIRA*, Panel Report, paras 5.12 and 5.13.
[36] *Canada–FIRA*, Panel Report, para. 5.14.   [37] *Canada–FIRA*, Panel Report, para. 5.18.
[38] UNCTAD Secretariat Report, n. 176, p. 138.

place in a multilateral trade agreement, there followed a number of further developments in which initially investment and trade went their separate ways.

The 1950s and 1960s: BITs and the protection of foreign property

From the 1950s onwards, owing to the absence of an obvious relationship between investment and trade at the multilateral level, international investment law evolved through a range of reciprocal, mutually enforcing FCN-type BITs. The trend was paralleled by the adoption of a series of international investment contracts between foreign investors and host state governments, often in the form of concession agreements for the exploitation of oil, gas and mineral resources, and the emergence of soft law instruments on investment. Further developments took place within the OECD and by means of resolutions of the UN General Assembly, but arguably it was the work of UNCTAD[39] that was the most supportive of the LAT relationship between international investment and trade, particularly where it concerned developing countries.

The end of colonialism in many parts of the world, and the emergence of a large number of newly independent but economically underdeveloped states,[40] provided the impetus for many capital-exporting countries to enter into 'newer-style' FCN treaties with developing, capital-importing states. These bilateral treaties were premised on the underlying assumption that an increase in FDI would provide a reasonable return to the investor, while the developing host state would benefit from the 'multiplier effect' that an injection of capital, human resources and transfer of technology would bring.[41] Post-war FCN treaties typically addressed diverse aspects of the trade and investment relationship that emphasised 'favourable conditions' and 'non-discrimination', embodied in the most-favoured-nation (MFN) and

---

[39] See, above, n. 6 for details of the origins of UNCTAD.

[40] Vandevelde, *Bilateral Investment Treaties*, pp. 42–3; examples include the FCN treaty practice of the United States with countries like China, Ethiopia, Iran, Israel and a host of European countries, details of which are found in Walker, 'Modern Treaties of Friendship, Commerce and Navigation', pp. 805–6 and 809–12, where he discusses the scope and coverage of FCN treaties.

[41] W. Michael Reisman and Robert D. Sloane, 'Indirect Expropriation and its Valuation in the BIT Generation', 74 *British Yearbook of International Law*, 74 (2003): 115–50, at p. 116.

national treatment standards. They also imposed on host states the obligation not to expropriate without compensation.[42]

One of the first capital-exporting states to forge ahead with its own treaty programme, designed to protect investments made by its nationals in accordance with the laws of the host states in which they operated, was the Federal Republic of Germany (FRG).[43] The FRG signed its first BIT with Pakistan on 25 November 1959.[44] Other European countries, including Switzerland, the Netherlands and Italy,[45] soon followed suit and the era of BITs treaty-making had begun.

However, the Pakistan–FRG BIT of 1959 was more like an earlier FCN treaty than a modern BIT. While it contained all the usual investor protection guarantees, its dispute settlement provisions only foresaw inter-state resolution of an investment dispute.[46] Failing such resolution, parties could agree to submit their dispute to the International Court of Justice (ICJ)[47] or make a unilateral submission to arbitration, but an individual investor would have to rely on its state of nationality to espouse a claim by way of diplomatic protection.

There were attempts in the late 1950s by Herman J. Abs, a German banker, to form a multilateral treaty, known as a 'Magna Carta for the Protection of Foreign Property', with specific standards on foreign investment and a permanent arbitral tribunal,[48] and a later attempt to establish a 'Convention on Investments Abroad'.[49] However, it was not until the OECD adopted a soft law instrument, known as the Convention on the

---

[42] Vandevelde, *Bilateral Investment Treaties*, pp. 50–1.

[43] Rudolf Dolzer and Christoph Schreuer, *Principles of International Investment Law*, 2nd edn (Oxford University Press, 2012), pp. 6–7.

[44] Treaty between Pakistan and the Federal Republic of Germany for the Promotion and Protection of Investments, 25 November 1959, (1963) 457 *UNTS* 23 (1963), entered into force 28 November 1962 (Pakistan–FRG BIT, 1959).

[45] Andrew Newcombe and Luís Paradell, *Law and Practice of Investment Treaties: Standards of Treatment* (Alphen aan den Rijn: Kluwer Law, 2009), pp. 42–3.

[46] FRG–Pakistan BIT, Art. 11.

[47] An example of an investment dispute submitted to the ICJ, which was based on an FCN treaty was the American claim on behalf of shareholders, Raytheon Company and Machlett Laboratories, Inc., in Elettronica Sicula SpA, against the government of Italy in the *Case Concerning Elettronica Sicula SpA (ELSI) (United States of America v. Italy)*, *ICJ Reports* 1989, 15, at pp. 48–51 (United States–Italy FCN, 1948).

[48] Dolzer and Schreuer, *Principles of International Investment Law*, p. 8.

[49] Dolzer and Schreuer, *Principles of International Investment Law*, p. 8; see generally, A. Vaughan Lowe, 'Changing Dimensions of International Investment Law', in W. Shan, P. Simons and D. Singh (eds), *Collected Courses of the Xiamen Academy of International Law* (Leiden: Martinus Nijhoff, 2008), pp. 395–475.

Protection of Foreign Property, in 1967[50] that there were new developments. This OECD Convention was a novel instrument. It gave investors from OECD member states the right to take up any complaint involving FDI against a host state before an international arbitration tribunal without recourse to the diplomatic protection of their home state.

Similar OECD instruments followed, which sought to liberalise capital movements[51] and so-called 'invisible transactions', that is, revenues, or income, derived from services, intellectual property rights, including licences, and exchange transactions,[52] and to regulate investment incentives.[53] Normative activity at the OECD left its mark on the LAT relationship between international investment law and trade from the 1960s onwards. It extended through the Uruguay Round Multilateral Trade Negotiations (MTN) and the negotiations on trade in services,[54] and ultimately in the first, albeit unsuccessful, attempt to draft multilateral rules on investment.[55]

The post-colonialist era: FDI, developing countries and ICSID

At the UN General Assembly other developments, which to some extent paralleled activities at the OECD, focused on the role of developing countries in the investment and trade context. It began with the inauguration of the UN Development Decade, which, in operative paragraph 2(b) of the supporting UN General Assembly Resolution, called upon

---

[50] OECD, Convention on the Protection of Foreign Property, 1967, reproduced in 7 *ILM* 117 (1968); see further Newcombe and Paradell, *Law and Practice of Investment Treaties*, p. 30.

[51] Code of Liberalisation of Capital Movements, OECD/C(61)96, adopted by the Council on 12 December 1961, as updated through 2010, available at: www.oecd.org/dataoecd/10/62/39664826.pdf.

[52] Code of Liberalisation of Current Invisible Operations, OECD/C(61)95, adopted by the Council on 12 December 1961, available at: www.oecd.org/dataoecd/41/21/2030182.pdf.

[53] The OECD Council Decision on International Investment Incentives and Disincentives forms part of the OECD Declaration on International Investment and Multinational Enterprises, 26 June 1976, OECD/C(76)99, reprinted in 15 *ILM* 967, 977 (1976); see further Norbert Horn, 'International Rules for Multinational Enterprises: The ICC, the OECD, and the ILO Initiatives', *American University Law Review* 30 (1981): 923–40, at pp. 924–5

[54] Mary E. Footer and Carol George, 'The General Agreement on Trade in Services', in Patrick MacRory, Arthur Appleton and Michael Plummer (eds), *The World Trade Organization: Legal, Economic and Political Analysis* (Aspen: Springer, 2005), ch. 19, pp. 799–953, at pp. 805–6.

[55] See below, at section II.C, for further details concerning the draft OECD Multilateral Agreement on Investment (MAI).

states: 'to pursue policies designed to ensure to the developing countries an equitable share of earnings from the extraction and marketing of their natural resources by foreign capital, in accordance with the generally accepted reasonable earnings on invested capital'.[56] It was followed by the convening of an international conference that eventually led to the creation of UNCTAD,[57] which remains supportive of the relationship between international investment and trade to this day.

A further UN General Assembly Resolution 1803 concerning Permanent Sovereignty over Natural Resources[58] was also significant in recognising the right of states to permanent sovereignty over their 'natural wealth and resources' in the interests of national development and the well-being of their people. It also established a common understanding that inward capital investment should be in conformity with the rules and conditions of the host state and international law, with an equitable sharing of the benefits between the investor and the beneficiary host state.[59]

Contemporaneously, the idea of investor–state arbitration emerged as one of the key provisions in the adoption of the Convention on the Settlement of Investment Disputes between States and Nationals of Other States of 1965 (the ICSID Convention),[60] which had entered into force in 1966. For the first time in the history of FDI, investors had an effective remedy against the wrongful acts of host states, such as unlawful expropriation, and no longer needed to rely on local courts in the host state or the diplomatic protection of their home state in any investment dispute.[61] Spurred on by the adoption of the 1967 OECD Convention on the Protection of Foreign Property,[62] capital-exporting states were increasingly prepared to conclude BITs that provided *ex ante* for host state consent to investor–state arbitration of investment disputes. This standing offer to arbitrate in many BITs, and some host state foreign investment laws, meant the investor only had to accept the offer, that is, start proceedings, to establish the basis of consent to the arbitral

---

[56] UN GA Resolution 1710 (XVI), 19 December 1961, on the UN Development Decade.
[57] For details about the formation of UNCTAD, see, above, n. 6.
[58] UN GA Resolution 1803 (XVII), 14 December 1962, Permanent Sovereignty over Natural Resources.
[59] UN GA Resolution 1803, para. 3.
[60] Convention on the Settlement of Investment Disputes Between States and Nationals of Other States, 18 March 1965, 575 *UNTS* 159, 4 *ILM* 524 (1965), entered into force 14 October 1966.
[61] Vandevelde, *Bilateral Investment Treaties*, p. 58.
[62] OECD Convention on the Protection of Foreign Property.

process.[63] A choice of alternative fora for resolving investment disputes, using ICSID, ICC Arbitration Rules[64] or *ad hoc* arbitration based on UNCITRAL Arbitration Rules,[65] became commonplace in many BITs.

This was followed by a period in the 1970s and 1980s that saw the rise of transnational corporations (TNCs) or multinational enterprises (MNEs), which became prominent actors in the investment and trade relationship. It led to a call by developing countries in the UN General Assembly for a new international economic order[66] that would, *inter alia*, regulate their activities. The UN Centre on Transnational Corporations tried, albeit unsuccessfully, to intermediate and to secure international agreement on a code of conduct for transnational corporations.[67] Then, in 1976, the OECD adopted its first set of Guidelines for Multinational Enterprises, which has recently completed its second full revision.[68] A year later, the International Labour Organization (ILO) completed its Tripartite Declaration of Principles concerning Multinational Enterprises and Social Policy.[69] All these non-binding or 'soft law' instruments, which are arguably 'short and precise public codes' that form part of a set of specific, transnational corporate constitutions,[70] were

---

[63] Christoph Schreuer, 'The Dynamic Evolution of the ICSID System', in Rainer Hofmann and Christian Tams (eds), *The International Convention on the Settlement of Investment Disputes (ICSID): Taking Stock after 40 Years*, Schriften zur Europäischen Integration und Internationalen Wirtschaftsordnung, 7 (Baden-Baden: Nomos, 2007), pp. 15–30, at p. 20.

[64] International Chamber of Commerce (ICC), Rules of Arbitration, in force from 1 January 1998, available at: www.iccarbitration.org.

[65] United Nations Commission on International Trade Law (UNCITRAL), Arbitration Rules, adopted by UN GA Resolution 31/98, 15 December 1976.

[66] Declaration on the Establishment of a New International Economic Order, UN GA Resolution 3201 (S-VI), 1 May 1974.

[67] Draft UN Code of Conduct for Transnational Corporations, UN Doc. E/1990/94, 12 June 1990, an earlier example of which can be found at 23 *ILM* 626 (1984).

[68] OECD Guidelines on Multinational Enterprises, adopted in 1976, revised in 2000 and most recently in 2011, being: the OECD Guidelines on Multinational Enterprises: Recommendations for Responsible Business Conduct in a Global Environment, May 2011, available at: www.oecd.org/dataoccd/43/29/48004323.pdf.

[69] ILO Tripartite Declaration of Principles Concerning Multinational Enterprises and Social Policy (MNE Declaration), adopted by the ILO Governing Body, 204th Sess., November 1977, as amended 279th Sess., November 2000 and 295th Sess., March 2006, available at: www.ilo.org/wcmsp5/groups/public/@ed_emp/@emp_ent/@multi/documents/publication/wcms_094386.pdf.

[70] Gunther Teubner, 'Self-constitutionalizing TNCs? On the Linkage of "Private" and "Public" Corporate Codes of Conduct', *Indiana Journal of Global Legal Studies*, 18(2) (2011): 617–38, at pp. 618 and 620–1.

indirectly instrumental in supporting the LAT relationship between international investment law and trade.

C   Multilateral approaches to investment law and trade redux: WTO, a failed MAI and a new era for the GATT/WTO

It was not until the mid-1990s that the LAT relationship between investment law and trade was revisited at the multilateral level. This happened in more formal terms by means of two separate but related developments. One was the establishment of the WTO in 1995 with new annexed agreements,[71] known as the 'multilateral trade agreements', some of which addressed the investment and trade relationship in varying degrees. The other was an abortive attempt at the OECD to negotiate a multilateral agreement regulating FDI between states, which would have led to a parallel multilateral initiative on investment alongside the WTO. Following the breakdown of the negotiations for this multilateral investment instrument in 1998, it was anticipated that the initiative would be taken up more fully within the multilateral trading system.

Investment issues in the WTO: services

Taking the first, and more significant, of these two developments, the establishment of the WTO witnessed the introduction of a major agreement on the services trade into the multilateral trading system. Traditionally, governments recorded their international trade in services in terms of balance of payment statistics, wherein services transactions between resident and non-resident transactions were listed alongside other foreign exchange receivables, such as returns from foreign investment, royalties and other non-resident transactions, or so-called 'invisibles'.[72] When it came to the negotiation of an agreement on trade in services during the Uruguay Round, the basis for the provision of services in terms of resident/non-resident transactions also included enterprises that supply services internationally through a foreign affiliate or a commercial presence abroad.

Mode 3 of the General Agreement on Trade in Services (GATS)[73] defines this means of supply as the supply of a service 'by a service

---

[71] WTO Agreement, with annexes.

[72] Footer and George, 'General Agreement on Trade in Services', pp. 823–6.

[73] General Agreement on Trade in Services, done at Marrakesh, 15 April, 1994, 1869 *UNTS* 183, 33 ILM 1167, entered into force 1 January 1995 (GATS) is taken up in Annex 1B to the WTO Agreement.

supplier of one Member, through commercial presence in the territory of any other Member'.[74] In fact, the definition of 'commercial presence' is 'any type of business or professional establishment', which might include either 'the constitution, acquisition or maintenance of a juridical person', including, but not limited to, 'the creation or maintenance of a branch or a representative office' in the territory of a member for the purpose of supplying a service.[75]

The reference to 'a commercial presence' as a means of delivering international services is an innovation of the GATS, which requires the proximity of the supplier and the consumer. From a balance of payments perspective, such supply of a service by an entity resident in the consumer's territory is a transaction between residents and is therefore *not* recorded as a trade transaction.[76] Instead, its characterisation is more readily that of an investment. Not surprisingly then, the provision of services abroad usually requires some sort of commercial presence. Whatever form the commercial presence takes, be it through a subsidiary or branch of a company, or through an agency, it will be a form of FDI in a WTO member that is effectively the host state.

In fact, the close relationship between investment and trade becomes even more apparent when one looks at those GATS provisions under which members have made specific commitments with respect to market access and national treatment.[77] They have done so in order to liberalise market access. This is coupled with a guarantee as to the type of treatment to be accorded in respect of all measures 'affecting' the supply of services in the sectors inscribed in their schedules of services commitments. The only restrictions on that access may be conditions, or qualifications, that are set out in those schedules. Additionally, some of the general obligations under the GATS, such as the MFN principle and the principle of transparency,[78] apply to the treatment provided by a WTO member in any services sector, irrespective of what it has chosen to list in its individual schedule of services commitments.[79]

Taken collectively, we can see that the conditions on which access to a particular market is granted and the type of treatment that is guaranteed,

---

[74] GATS, Art. I:2(c).   [75] GATS, Art. XXVIII(d).
[76] Footer and George, 'General Agreement on Trade in Services', p. 825.
[77] GATS, Arts XVI (market access) and XVII (national treatment).
[78] GATS, Arts II:1 and III, respectively.
[79] Footer and George, 'General Agreement on Trade in Services', pp. 846 and 856.

is exactly the same kind that is covered by investor protection clauses under many BITs. The latter, as we have noted above in section II, specifically control the entry and/or establishment of foreign investors and investment.[80] It would even be fair to say that there is a considerable overlap between some BITs and the GATS, an issue that became apparent immediately after the conclusion of the Uruguay Round and the entry into force of the GATS. Many WTO members chose to list specific sectoral commitments with limitations in their schedules of services commitments, in accordance with their existing national laws on foreign investment and/or their bilateral and multilateral treaty obligations.[81]

In many cases WTO members either bound an existing treaty obligation on market access, on the basis of their national law on foreign investment (so-called 'standstill'), or else they removed certain existing restrictions on market access ('rollback').[82] Some WTO members did this while maintaining 'permitted' limitations that were inconsistent with Article XVI:2 of the GATS (so-called 'market access limitations').[83] The latter included such matters as limitations on the type of legal entity through which a service could be supplied or limitations on equity participation in a corporate or business entity, 'in accordance with [a Member's] laws and regulations'. It was also possible for a WTO member to list other territorial limitations and restrictions on the basis of nationality for both services and service suppliers. Both types of limitation are usually found in relation to the 'controlled entry' model of admission and establishment of foreign investment and investors, which is common to the majority of BITs and some regional free trade agreements (FTAs) with investment chapters,[84] collectively known as 'international investment agreements' or 'IIAs'.

---

[80] Jeswald W. Salacuse, *The Law of Investment Treaties* (Oxford University Press, 2010), p. 102.

[81] Rudolf Adlung, Peter Morrison, Martin Roy and Weiwei Zang, 'FOG in GATS Commitments: Boon or Bane', World Trade Organization: Staff Working Paper No. ERSD-2011-04, March 2011, pp. 10–11. The Working Paper is significant in that the analysis deals only with Mode 3 supply, i.e., commercial presence, which is the mode of supply most analogous to FDI.

[82] Footer and George, 'General Agreement on Trade in Services', pp. 859–60.

[83] GATS, Art. XVI:2.

[84] *Admission and Establishment*, UNCTAD Series on Issues in International Investment Agreements (New York and Geneva: UNCTAD, 2002), pp. 6–14.

Investment issues in the WTO: TRIMs

Another link between investment and trade is the Agreement on Trade-Related Investment Measures (TRIMs Agreement),[85] which was negotiated in the Uruguay Round. It seeks to prevent the trade-restrictive and distorting effects that some investment measures may have on trade in goods. Strongly influenced in its conception by the GATT Panel decision in *Canada–Foreign Investment Review Act (FIRA)*,[86] Article 2.1 of the TRIMs Agreement[87] bans any TRIM that is inconsistent with the national treatment standard of Article III of the GATT 1994[88] or the prohibition on quantitative restrictions in Article XI of the GATT 1994.[89] The Agreement uses an 'illustrative list' approach to define what is meant by TRIMs. Broadly summarised, they include what are known as 'performance requirements', that is, local purchasing and local content requirements, trade balancing requirements, foreign exchange restrictions and export performance requirements.[90]

Some states, such as the United States and Canada, favour the admission and establishment of FDI on the basis of the national treatment standard or MFN, including pre- and post-establishment.[91] What amounts to 'a right of admission, albeit limited in scope',[92] may nevertheless be subject to the right of each party to the BIT to adopt or maintain certain exceptions falling within certain sectors, subsectors or activities, which are listed in a separate annex.[93] These two states have also specifically dealt with performance requirements both in the context of their individual model BITs[94] and in the trilateral relationship with Mexico under Chapter Eleven of NAFTA.[95]

---

[85] Agreement on Trade-Related Investment Measures, done at Marrakesh, 15 April 1994, 1868 *UNTS* 186, entered into force 1 January 1995 (the TRIMs Agreement or TRIMs) is taken up in Annex 1A to the WTO Agreement.

[86] *Canada–FIRA* Panel Report, above n. 30.   [87] TRIMs Agreement, Art. 2.1.

[88] Article III of the General Agreement on Tariffs and Trade 1994 (GATT 1994) is contained in Annex 1A to the WTO Agreement.

[89] GATT 1994, Art. XI.   [90] TRIMs Agreement, Art. 2.2 and Annex.

[91] Treaty between the Government of the United States of America and the Government of [Country] Concerning the Encouragement and Reciprocal Protection of Investment, 2012, Arts 3 and 4 (2012 US Model BIT), available at: www.ustr.gov/sites/default/files/BIT%20text%20for%20ACIEP%20Meeting.pdf; Agreement between Canada and [Country] for the Promotion and Protection of Investments, 2012, Arts 3 and 4 (Canada Model FIPA), available at: www.international.gc.ca/trade-agreements-accords-commerciaux.

[92] Dolzer and Schreuer, *Principles of International Investment Law*, p. 89.

[93] 2012 US Model BIT, Art. 14 and Canada Model FIPA, Art. 7.

[94] 2012 US Model BIT, Art. 8 and Canada Model FIPA, Art. 7.

[95] See Art. 1106 in Chapter Eleven, NAFTA, which can be found at 32 *ILM* 639 *et seq.* (1993).

Investment issues in the WTO: the WGTI

Early on in the life of the WTO the LAT relationship between international investment law and trade was re-visited when it was decided at the First Ministerial Conference held in Singapore in 1996 to establish 'a working group to examine the relationship between trade and investment'.[96] However, the task of the Working Group on the relationship between Trade and Investment (WGTI) was limited to being merely analytical and exploratory. No new rules or commitments were to be negotiated without agreement by consensus from the WTO membership. Trade ministers also recognised the ongoing work in the UNCTAD[97] and other international organisations, such as the OECD,[98] which could contribute to an examination of this relationship.

Negotiations for an MAI

Parallel with this development a group of OECD members, spurred on by developments in the Uruguay Round and the conclusion of the tripartite NAFTA, with a section on investment (Chapter Eleven),[99] began negotiations for a multilateral agreement on investment (MAI).[100] The intention was to create a comprehensive multilateral framework for all types of international investment with high standards for liberalising investment protection.[101] It also sought to establish effective dispute settlement procedures with both state-to-state procedures, modelled on the WTO and NAFTA trade panel system, as well as investor–state arbitration. However, MAI panels under inter-state investment dispute settlement, unlike WTO panels, would be allowed to grant direct, pecuniary compensation or restitution in kind.

[96] First WTO Ministerial Conference, Singapore, 9–13 December 1996, Ministerial Declaration, WT/MIN(96)/DEC, 18 December 1996, para. 20.

[97] Specifically, the work of the UNCTAD Division on Investment, Technology and Enterprise Development (known as the DITE).

[98] For references to some of the work of the OECD Investment Committee, see above n. 50 for the OECD Convention on the Protection of Foreign Property, n. 51 for the OECD Code of Liberalisation of Capital Movements, n. 52 for the OECD Code of Liberalisation of Current Invisible Operations and n. 53 for the OECD Council Decision on International Investment Incentives and Disincentives.

[99] For details of Chapter Eleven NAFTA, see, above, n. 95.

[100] Details about the draft Multilateral Agreement on Investment, and the draft text up until 1998, are available at: www.oecd.org/document/35/0,3343,en_2649_33783766_1894819_1_1_1_1,00.html.

[101] Sol Picciotto, 'Linkages in International Investment Regulation: The Antinomies of the Draft Multilateral Agreement on Investment', *University of Pennsylvania Journal of International Economic Law* 19 (1998): 731–68, at pp. 742–3.

Consistent with the practice of BIT treaty-making, investor–state dispute settlement under the MAI would provide for investment arbitration using ICSID, UNCITRAL Arbitration Rules or the ICC Arbitration Rules. While only OECD member countries, all of which were developed at the time, were involved in the negotiation of the MAI, it was the intention that the final agreement would be open for ratification and acceptance by *all* states, irrespective of whether they were OECD members.

Despite producing a series of drafts, the MAI negotiations stalled when the French Government, which was hosting negotiations at the OECD, withdrew its support in 1998 and any attempt to negotiate further was abandoned. It did so pursuant to a report by French MEP Catherine Lalumière,[102] which criticised the negotiations for their infringement on state sovereignty, especially in the cultural and audiovisual sector, their secrecy, and their failure to take into account public opinion over social and environmental concerns. The latter two aspects were at the forefront of a vocal civil society movement, spurred on by the rapid dissemination of 'leaked' negotiating texts over the Internet. The French Government was also opposed to the potential reach of extraterritorial legislation from investors' home states, the potential economic disequilibrium that EU member states faced vis-à-vis the United States, and the proposed investor–state dispute settlement provisions. There was also principal disagreement among other OECD members on matters such as the overly broad definitions of both 'investor' and 'investment', and protection against expropriation.

A further aspect of the MAI negotiations exercise was its asymmetrical character. OECD member states backed the development of strong pro-investor rules on FDI, which were largely negotiated without adequate consideration of host states, many of whom were non-OECD members and often developing countries. The latter felt that they would eventually be forced to abide by rules on foreign investment in which they had had no hand in making. Thus, while they felt duty bound to attend the negotiating sessions, as observers, they could not actively participate nor could they influence the course of negotiations.

---

[102] 'Rapport sur l'accord multilatéral sur l'investissement (AMI)', Rapport intérimaire, Mme Catherine Lalumière, Députée européenne, et M Jean-Pierre Landau, Inspecteur général des Finances, September 1998, details of which are available in the report of the National Assembly EU Delegation to the French parliament (Assemblée nationale), No. 1150, 23 October 1998, pp. 20–22, available at: www.assemblee-nationale.fr/europe/rap-info/2fdi1150.pdf.

Failure of the MAI negotiations: back to
investment in the WTO

The failure of the draft MAI, which was due in no small part to the nature of the internationally coordinated campaign against it,[103] saw the matter of negotiating multilateral rules on investment shift temporarily from the OECD to the heart of the multilateral trading system, as proposed by France,[104] where the topic had already made landfall at the WTO. At the Doha Ministerial Conference in 2001, ministers recognised that there was a case to be made for having a multilateral framework for trade and investment. It would secure 'transparent, stable and predictable conditions for long-term cross-border investment, particularly foreign direct investment'.[105] It was therefore agreed that negotiations would take place *after* the Fifth Ministerial Conference 'on the basis of a decision to be taken, by explicit consensus, at that Session on modalities of negotiations'.[106]

However, following the Doha Ministerial Conference the WGTI could not agree on how to address the concerns of developing country members who did not want to see their right to regulate investment curtailed. This included the right to apply TRIMs and other performance measures, which they considered essential to fulfil their development needs.[107] Due in part to a group of developing country members, who firmly rejected the launch of negotiations on investment and other so-called 'Singapore issues', the matter became polarised at the Cancún Ministerial Conference.[108] The meeting concluded without any consensus on taking the work of the WGTI forward in the form of a multilateral agreement on trade and investment.[109]

Incorporating investment provisions into regional
trade and sectoral agreements

Shaken but not stirred, the LAT relationship between international investment law and trade had suffered a set-back at the multilateral level,

---

[103] Picciotto, 'Linkages in International Investment Regulation', p. 749.
[104] Assemblée nationale, No. 1150, pp. 21–2.
[105] Fourth WTO Ministerial Conference, Doha, 9–14 November 2001, Ministerial Declaration, WT/MIN(01)/DEC, 20 November 2001, para. 20.
[106] Fourth WTO Ministerial Conference, Doha.
[107] Peter T. Muchlinski, *Multinational Corporations and the Law*, 2nd edn (Oxford University Press, 2007), pp. 669–73; Martha Lara de Sterlini, 'The Agreement on Trade-related Investment Measures', in MacRory, Appleton and Plummer (eds), *The World Trade Organization*, ch. 10, pp. 437–83, at pp. 477–8.
[108] Fifth WTO Ministerial Conference, Cancún, 10–14 September 2003, with no mention being made of the matter in the Ministerial Declaration.
[109] Sterlini, 'The Agreement on Trade-related Investment Measures', p. 478.

but it was not an irrevocable one. Instead, a closer relationship has developed not because, but in spite, of multilateralism. Since the late 1980s there has been a movement among some states to desert the classical BIT, which addresses only foreign investment issues, for the negotiation of investment provisions in the context of FTAs.[110] The first of these was the US–Canada FTA of 1988,[111] which formed the basis for conclusion of the NAFTA in 1993 and Chapter Eleven[112] with its own investment regime and system of investment arbitration.

The trend towards the incorporation of investment provisions in FTAs has continued unabated, beginning with the United States, which has entered into a number of FTAs with Israel,[113] Jordan,[114] Bahrain,[115] Chile[116] and Singapore,[117] all with investment treaty chapters. Japan has adopted a similar policy course, with a series of economic partnership agreements (EPAs),[118] and other Asian countries have followed Japan's lead.[119] Besides this, older forms of regional economic integration, such as the Association of Southeast Asian Nations, more commonly known as ASEAN,[120] have developed fully-fledged multilateral investment instruments at a regional level.[121] At the end of 2010 there were reportedly some 309 different sorts of

---

[110] Dolzer and Schreuer, *Principles of International Investment Law*, p. 14.

[111] US–Canada FTA, 4 October 1988, 27 *ILM* 281 (1988).

[112] Chapter Eleven, NAFTA.

[113] Agreement on the Establishment of a Free Trade Area between the United States and Israel, 22 April 1985, entered into force 19 August 1985.

[114] Agreement on the Establishment of a Free Trade Area between the United States and Jordan, 24 October 2000, entered into force 17 December 2001.

[115] Agreement on the Establishment of a Free Trade Area between the United States and Bahrain, 14 September 2004, entered into force 1 August 2006.

[116] Agreement on the Establishment of a Free Trade Area between the United States and Chile, 6 June 2003, entered into force 1 January 2004.

[117] Agreement on the Establishment of a Free Trade Area between the United States and Singapore, 6 May 2003, entered into force 1 January 2004.

[118] See, e.g., the Agreement between Japan and the Republic of Indonesia for an Economic Partnership, 20 August 2007, entered into force 1 July 2008.

[119] Salacuse, *The Law of Investment Treaties*, p. 103.

[120] The Association of Southeast Asian Nations (ASEAN) was established on 8 August 1967 in Bangkok, Thailand, with the signing of the Bangkok Declaration by Indonesia, Malaysia, Philippines, Singapore and Thailand, since when Brunei Darussalam, Vietnam, Laos PDR, Myanmar (Burma) and Cambodia have joined. For details of the ASEAN Charter, including revisions, see: www.asean.org/21861.htm.

[121] ASEAN Comprehensive Investment Agreement (ACIA), Cha-am, Thailand, 26 February 2009, available at: www.asean.org/22244.htm.

regional or sectoral agreements, primarily aimed at trade, with either a substantive investment chapter or with an additional protocol on investment.[122]

Another multilateral treaty that has important chapters on both investment and trade is the Energy Charter Treaty (ECT),[123] which has a sectoral rather than a regional focus. It creates a legal framework designed to 'encourage the development of a secure international energy supply through liberalised trade and investment among member states'.[124] Part III of the ECT, titled 'Investment Promotion and Protection', is effectively an investment instrument within this broader East–West Energy Treaty regime, which 'has been profoundly influenced by the language of the various European and American BITs in its structure, content and drafting'.[125] It should be noted that while the ECT incorporates WTO rules by reference, with respect to trade in goods in the energy sector, these rules apply only to trade between ECT contracting parties, *at least one of which* is a WTO member.

Seemingly, then, the link between investment law and trade is beginning to turn full circle. While the LAT relationship may have weakened at the multilateral level, it has been strengthened in some regions in the face of deeper economic integration or economic functionalism. Over the course of time the relationship itself has been instructive: from the attempts to incorporate a chapter on investment in the Havana Charter, to the treatment of investment in the GATT 1947 (and later in the context of the GATS), as well as the failed attempt to start negotiations on a multilateral agreement on trade and investment at the WTO Ministerial Conference in Cancún. The essential conflict centres on the fact that sovereign states remain determined to exercise their right to regulate foreign investment on their own terms, and to do so through reciprocal and mutually beneficial bilateral agreements. The reasons for doing this are explored more fully in section III, below, when considering the similarities and the differences in approaches towards what appears to be the 'multilateralisation' of international investment law and trade.

---

[122] UNCTAD, *World Investment Report 2011: Non-Equity Modes of International Production and Development* (Geneva: UNCTAD, 2011), p. 100.

[123] ECT, see, above, n. 8.   [124] Salacuse, *The Law of Investment Treaties*, p. 102.

[125] Salacuse, *The Law of Investment Treaties*, p. 102.

III Similarities and differences in the 'multilateralisation' of international investment law and trade

Over the course of the past sixty years there has been a paradigm shift from customary international law to treaty-making in many areas of international economic activity, not least in the promotion and regulation of FDI. We have already traced this development in the preceding sections of this chapter in terms of both investment and trade. The trend is perhaps best exemplified by the modern BITs regime that now accounts for some 3,000 such treaties between 176 states, of which approximately 1,800 are in force.[126] We have also noted that over the past decade the BIT landscape has been reinforced by a number of regional economic and free trade agreements with investment chapters or additional protocols on investment. Therefore, currently we can speak of a broader variety of IIAs than was previously the case.

A Notions about customary international law and/or uniform governing structures for foreign investment

It may be true that the extraordinary number of BITs in force today constitutes a special juridical regime, which is

> designed to re-state, in treaty form, international minimum standards of treatment of foreign investors as accepted by the capital-exporting states, and to merge these with established, treaty-based, standards of commercial conduct that do not possess the character of customary international law, despite their widespread usage over many centuries, notably, the MFN standard and the national treatment standard.[127]

Previously some scholars went further in claiming that the conclusion of hundreds of similar bilateral treaty instruments supported the creation of customary international law in the field of foreign investment.[128] Others argued that many existing BITs resembled one another, given that they were 'broadly similar in character, content and standards', even

---

[126] Reference is made here to the UNCTAD database, which records details of all BITs, including whether such treaties are in force between the parties, and is available at: www.unctad.org/Templates/Page.asp?intItemID=3775&lang=.

[127] International Law Association (ILA), Toronto Conference, First Report of the Committee on International Law on Foreign Investment, 2006, p. 11, available at: www.ila-hq.org.

[128] See, e.g., F. A. Mann, 'British Treaties for the Promotion and Protection of Investments', *British Yearbook of International Law* 52 (1981): 241–54, at p. 249.

if there were some important national differences between them in terms of emphasis and detail.[129] There was even a group of scholars who were of the view that BITs represented the codification of existing practice, which could create customary international law principles in the future.[130]

In fact, many BITs may have a similar structure, but they nevertheless differ when it comes to the details.[131] Some scholars have suggested that each BIT represents a *lex specialis*, which only operates between the parties to it. This has been necessary due to the lack of multilateral rules and established principles of customary international law in the field.[132] Others have pointed to the fact that even clearly established provisions in BITs, which have their origin in customary international law, such as the 'Hull' standard of prompt, adequate and effective compensation for expropriation, do not find their exact same counterpart in every BIT.[133]

While it is possible that, where there is 'concordance of standards in ... bilateral investment treaties such standards on which there is consistent agreement evidenced by such treaties could become international law',[134] the idea that all BITs basically have the same content is tenuous. Closer examination reveals that many of them 'vary as to detail to such an extent that it would be difficult to argue that they are capable of giving rise to

---

[129] Eileen Denza and Shelagh Brooks, 'Investment Protection Treaties: The United Kingdom Experience', *International and Comparative Law Quarterly* 36 (1987): 908–23, at p. 913.

[130] Gillian White, 'The New International Economic Order: Principles and Trends', in Hazel Fox (ed.), *International Economic Law and Developing States* (London: British Institute of International and Comparative Law, 1992), pp. 45–46, summarising the debate in the early part of the 1990s; see also *Restatement (Third) of Foreign Relations Law of the United States* (Philadelphia, PA: American Law Institute, 1986), § 102, Comment I, in the sense that a 'wide network of similar bilateral arrangements may constitute practice and ... result in customary law'.

[131] M. Sornarajah, *The International Law on Foreign Investments*, 3rd edn (Cambridge University Press, 2010), p. 253, seeks to disprove this point, based on the notion of investment. He claims that under some BITs investment is permitted in a host state only if it is an 'approved investment'. Alternatively, it may qualify for protection only if it is made 'in accordance with the laws and regulations of the host state'.

[132] Jeswald W. Salacuse, 'BIT by BIT: The Growth of Bilateral Investment Treaties and their Impact on Foreign Investment in Developing Countries', *International Lawyer*, 24 (1990): 655–75, at p. 660, referring to the fact that BITs were intended to create 'specific legal rules' between parties. See also Bernard Kishoiyian, 'The Utility of Bilateral Investment Treaties in the Formulation of Customary International Law', *Northwestern Journal of International Law and Business*, 14 (1994): 327–75, at p. 329.

[133] Sornarajah, *The International Law on Foreign Investments*, p. 233.

[134] M. Sornarajah, 'State Responsibility and Bilateral Investment Treaties', *Journal of World Trade*, 20 (1986): 79–98.

customary international law'.[135] Moreover, the mere repetition by states in their individual BITs of particular provisions, such as certain investor protection standards,[136] does not amount to a general, uniform practice over a period of time, nor is there any evidence that other states feel bound to follow this practice.[137] The tribunal in *Asian Agricultural Products Ltd (AAPL)* v. *Sri Lanka* found that the provisions of a BIT, being *lex specialis*, supersede any general principle of international law, which might otherwise govern the issues at stake.[138] It came to the conclusion that 'in the absence of a specific rule provided for in the Treaty itself as *lex specialis*, the general international law rules have to assume their role as *lex generalis*'.[139]

As Sornarajah points out, the failure of states to reach agreement on an MAI led to new attempts to use investment treaties, together with their interpretation, 'to construct the belief that a widely accepted body of customary principles has been created on the basis of the treaties and the arbitral awards based on them'.[140] It has also led some scholars, like Stephan Schill, to go a step further and claim that the network of BITs forms a 'unitary treaty-overarching legal framework that is based on largely uniform principles of international investment law and arbitration, and whose functions are analogous to a truly multilateral system for investment'.[141]

Schill's concept of multilateralism rests on the idea that the rules and standards of investment protection, found in a plethora of BITs and similar investment instruments, that is, the full spectrum of IIAs, have become generalised and apply equally to all participating actors, irrespective of their two-party provenance in a BIT or another investment

---

[135] Sornarajah, *The International Law on Foreign Investments*, p. 81.

[136] The most common ones are the relative standards of MFN and national treatment, and the absolute standards of fair and equitable treatment and of full protection and security; see Muchlinski, *Multinational Corporations and the Law*, pp. 621–49. It could be argued that certain of these concepts represent 'general principles of law', for which see Jeswald W. Salacuse, 'The Treatification of International Investment Law', *Law and Business Review of the Americas*, 13(1) (2007): 155–66, at p. 165.

[137] Sornarajah, *The International Law on Foreign Investments*, pp. 81, 174 and 232–3.

[138] *Asian Agricultural Products Ltd (AAPL)* v. *Republic of Sri Lanka*, ICSID Case No ARB/87/3, Award and Dissenting Opinion, 27 June 1990, 30 *ILM* 577 (1990), para. 31.

[139] *AAPL* v. *Sri Lanka*, para. 54.

[140] Sornarajah, *The International Law on Foreign Investments*, p. 81.

[141] Stephan W. Schill, 'The Multilateralisation of International Investment Law: Emergence of a Multilateral System of Investment Protection on Bilateral Grounds', *Trade Law and Development*, 2(1) (2010): 59–86, at p. 61.

treaty instrument.[142] This notion of the operation of 'generalised principles', as exemplified by international investment law, is reminiscent of the earlier arguments for the codification of existing practice. As already stated above, it could carry any weight only if there was evidence of a consistent, uniform and generalised practice of states in the matter, coupled with the belief by states that this practice is binding upon them in the absence of a treaty provision.[143]

Unlike some earlier commentators, who thought that because BITs resemble one another closely, in terms of their character, content and standards, they represented a codification of existing practice,[144] Schill suggests that international investment treaties inevitably conform to an archetype. This arises from the convergence in the wording of many BITs, which have developed a surprisingly uniform structure, scope and content in terms of the standards they encompass, that is, MFN, national treatment, fair and equitable treatment, and full protection and security combined with prohibitions on direct and indirect expropriation and grant-free capital transfers.[145] He would even have us believe that the way in which BITs function is analogous to 'a truly multilateral system', because they establish 'uniform principles' in investor–state relations.[146]

It means that international investment law, instead of being prone to infinite fragmentation, is developing into 'a uniform governing structure for foreign investment' through a process of convergence, based on 'investment treaties [that] follow uniform rationales'.[147] Compare and contrast this approach with the development of so-called 'standard form contracts' in the field of international commercial law where the 'unification of the law of international trade' has proceeded by means of the development of uniform and model legislation,[148] rather than the

---

[142] Stephan W. Schill, *The Multilateralization of International Investment Law* (Cambridge University Press, 2009), p. 9, relying on the work of John G. Ruggie, 'Multilateralism: The Anatomy of an Institution', *International Organization* 46(3) (1992): 561–98.

[143] Peter T. Muchlinski, 'Corporations and the Uses of Law: International Investment Arbitration as a "Multilateral Legal Order"', *Oñati Socio-Legal Series* 1(4) (2011): 11.

[144] See for further details, Mann, 'British Treaties for the Promotion and Protection of Investments'.

[145] Schill, *The Multilateralization of International Investment Law*, p. 65.

[146] Muchlinski, 'Corporations and the Uses of Law', p. 9.

[147] Schill, *The Multilateralization of International Investment Law*, p. 16.

[148] 'Unification of the Law of International Trade: Note by the Secretariat', Record of the 20th Sess., UN GA, annexes, agenda item 92, UN Doc. A/C.6/L.572, reproduced in *Yearbook of the United Nations Commission on International Trade Law* (Vienna: UNCITRAL, 1970), vol. 1, pp. 13–17.

spontaneous (and somewhat spurious) development of uniform law by means of convergence, as suggested by Schill.

Where Schill's notion of the multilateralisation of international investment law fails is precisely in its comparison with developments in the field of international trade. As Salacuse explains, while states were busy developing a global regime for investment they had simultaneously developed one for international trade. We have already traced this development in section II, on the basis of the LAT relationship between investment and trade that has endured more than half a century. The difference between the two regimes is as follows. The trade regime was developed 'on a *multilateral* basis through a succession of multilateral negotiating rounds' (MTNs) that led to the conclusion of multilateral treaties (first the GATT and then the WTO).[149] The investment regime was 'built largely on a *bilateral* basis as numerous pairs of countries have negotiated similar rules and enforcement mechanisms',[150] with the resulting BITs, or other IIAs, applying to each others' nationals and investments in each others' territories. This idea of differing treaty regimes governing international investment law and trade is discussed more fully below.

B The organising principles for investment and trade

A further difference between the two forms of multilateralisation is that if one is to place reliance on the emergence of multilateralism in the field of international investment law there must be some form of generalised ordering principle. In the case of international trade, the main organising or ordering principle has been 'the economic theory underlying a liberal trade order, that is the principle of comparative advantage',[151] which is operationalised through MFN treatment. In particular, the adherence of the collectivity of the GATT contracting parties (and later the WTO membership) to the MFN norm has rendered the multilateral trading system an indivisible whole. So, too, has its reliance on diffuse reciprocity, which is the belief by its participants that the system will yield roughly equivalent benefits in terms of increased trade.[152]

---

[149] Salacuse, *The Law of Investment Treaties*, p. 3 (emphasis added).
[150] Salacuse, *The Law of Investment Treaties*, p. 3 (emphasis added).
[151] Donald M. McRae, 'The WTO in International Law: Tradition Continued or New Frontier?' *Journal of International Economic Law* 3(1) (2000): 27–41, at p. 29.
[152] Muchlinski, 'Corporations and the Uses of Law', p. 10 with reliance on Ruggie, 'Multilateralism', p. 571.

By contrast, if international investment law has a generalised organising principle it probably comes closer to what Donald McRae has
identified as the organising principle for general international law, and
that is the concept of sovereignty.[153] But while the global investment
regime may be built on the same fundamental construct as international
law, that is, on a 'community of sovereign states',[154] it differs significantly
from the latter. This is because states have undertaken in their bilateral
(and occasionally multilateral) treaty-making to protect foreign investors
and investments in their territories alongside, rather than in preference
to, their own citizens. At first sight, then, the organising principle of
international investment law appears closer to that of the liberal trade
order, but this is not so.

C   The reciprocal nature of investment and trade obligations

One reason for the divergence between international investment law and
trade lies in the manner in which market access/establishment is granted.
Whereas in the case of the multilateral trading system this is assured
through the operation of MFN, which guarantees full liberalisation, in
the case of the majority of BITs it is 'controlled entry that reserves the
right of the host state to regulate the entry of foreign investments into its
territory'.[155] It means that the entry of FDI is conditional upon host state
approval, which usually requires that such investment be in accordance
with its domestic laws. This is at odds with any multilateral system of
investment precisely because it reinforces the territorial sovereignty
of individual host states.

Similarly, there is a variety of approaches to the inclusion of investment protection standards in BITs that suggest they fail 'to meet Ruggie's
requirement of "indivisibility among members of a collectivity with
respect to the range of behaviour in question"'.[156] This stems both from
the BITs themselves as well as the manner in which they are concluded.
What international investment law and trade do have in common is that,
at the outset, both proceed with negotiations that are bilateral in character. While this is obvious for the negotiation of a BIT, the GATT/WTO

---

[153] McRae, 'The WTO in International Law', p. 29.
[154] McRae, 'The WTO in International Law', p. 29.
[155] Muchlinski, 'Corporations and the Uses of Law', p. 11.
[156] Muchlinski, 'Corporations and the Uses of Law', p. 13, drawing on Ruggie, 'Multilateralism', p. 571.

MTN process also operates on an 'offer and request' basis. Thus, tariff concessions and specific services commitments are negotiated, usually in country pairs, and eventually lead to the conclusion of a set of reciprocal promises.

However, where international investment law and trade differ from one another is that international investment law is left with clusters of individual BITs, which bind only the two states that are parties, while the WTO process ensures that trade obligations 'while binding on *one* Member "also represent a common agreement among *all* Members"'.[157] Besides, WTO obligations 'remain a collection of reciprocal or bilateral obligations, which are synallagmatic in character' even though the treaty rules are mutually dependent on each other and they thereby acquire an integral and intra-dependent character.[158] This process of multilateralisation, which is at the heart of the multilateral trading system, is absent in international investment law, which remains uniquely bilateral. Thus, whereas the GATT/WTO evolved 'on a multilateral basis through a succession of multilateral negotiating rounds the investment regime has been built on a bilateral basis as numerous pairs of countries have negotiated similar rules and enforcement mechanisms that apply to their nationals in each others' territory'.[159]

It is also clear that the regime of BITs and other international investment instruments does not 'meet Ruggie's criterion of "diffuse reciprocity"'[160] in the way that the multilateral trading system is conceived and operates. Instead, bilateralism in the field of international investment law is characterised by 'the process of specific reciprocity, coupled with, "a simultaneous balancing of specific quid-pro-quos by each party with every other at all times"'.[161] While it may have been true in an earlier period of FCN treaty-making, or for the first and second generation

---

[157] Footer, *An Institutional and Normative Analysis of the World Trade Organization*, p. 193, with reference to the Appellate Body in *United States–Measures Affecting the Cross Border Supply of Gambling and Betting Services*, Appellate Body Report, DS/285/AB/R, adopted 20 April 2005 (*US–Gambling*), para. 159.

[158] Footer, *An Institutional and Normative Analysis of the World Trade Organization*, p. 194, with reliance on Joost Pauwelyn, 'A Typology of Multilateral Treaty Obligations: Are WTO Obligations Bilateral or Collective in Nature?' *European Journal of International Law* 14(5) (2003): 907–51, at pp. 931–2.

[159] Salacuse, 'The Treatification of International Investment Law', p. 164.

[160] Muchlinski, 'Corporations and the Uses of Law', p. 14 with reference to Ruggie, 'Multilateralism', p. 572.

[161] Muchlinski, 'Corporations and the Uses of Law', p. 14 with reference to Ruggie, 'Multilateralism', p. 572.

BITs,[162] that the negotiation and drafting of substantive provisions, embodying absolute, non-contingent standards such as 'equity' and 'fair treatment', simply did not lend themselves to 'the trading of concessions or the bargaining for an array of tangible *quid pro quos*',[163] the situation is changing. Currently many model BITs and other IIAs contain a broader range of permissive and exceptive clauses that mirror those contained in some multilateral trade agreements. Some of these permissive and exceptive clauses cover environmental and social matters, and have even been phrased along similar lines to the general exception clause of Article XX of the GATT 1994, as is clear from the US Model BIT 2012.[164] A better way to describe this spread of BITs and other IIAs is what Salacuse calls 'treatification', which has 'increased the importance of international investment law in international relations among states to levels that it never enjoyed before'.[165]

D   The treaty regimes governing investment and trade

Perhaps more importantly, it has resulted in 'an emerging global regime for international investment'.[166] Even so, this emergent international investment regime is different in many respects from the GATT/WTO trade regime. Previously, I have analysed the GATT/WTO in terms of regime theory,[167] in much the same way as Salacuse does in his work on the law of investment treaties,[168] to support the premise that 'the [WTO] is better understood in terms of a regime, which continues the tradition of the former semi-institutionalised GATT treaty regime alongside, and even within, the overall organisational and institutional framework of the *WTO Agreement*, and its Annexes'. This exercise led to a reading of the multilateral WTO regime as 'a dynamic and evolving institution, which

---

[162] First generation BITs refer to those international investment treaties that were founded upon, or contained very similar provisions, to the earlier FCN treaties, and often with no specific provision for investor-state dispute settlement, e.g., the Pakistan–Federal Republic of Germany BIT. Second generation BITs refer to those investment treaty instruments that have been included within, or attached to, a broader framework treaty governing trade relations between the parties, such as Chapter Eleven, NAFTA.

[163] Walker, 'Modern Treaties of Friendship, Commerce and Navigation', p. 809.

[164] See Arts 12 and 13 of the US Model BIT 2012 dealing with, respectively, 'Investment and Environment' and 'Investment and Labor'.

[165] Salacuse, 'The Treatification of International Investment Law', pp. 156–7 and 163.

[166] Salacuse, 'The Treatification of International Investment Law', pp. 156–7 and 163.

[167] Footer, *An Institutional and Normative Analysis of the World Trade Organization*, ch. II.

[168] Salacuse, *The Law of Investment Treaties*, pp. 6–11.

operates in a more complex regime of norms, decision-making activities and procedures than … its predecessor, the GATT'.[169] Put simply, the WTO is in many ways much more than the sum of its parts.

The same cannot be said for the relatively uncoordinated system of bilateral, regional and plurilateral instruments in the field of international investment law that 'represent something less than a fully-fledged multilateral regime'.[170] Moreover, international investment law, aside from a clear organising principle, lacks any overarching organisational structure or institutional basis. It displays a relatively simple and unsophisticated set of norms governing investor–state relations and 'lacks any developed institutional form other than a privately ordered system of dispute settlement based on a variety of distinctive dispute settlement clauses'.[171]

IV   Some thoughts on the contemporary jurisprudential nexus in the investment and trade relationship

The current LAT relationship between international investment and trade is undergoing further change, brought about by developments within the two regimes. As Nicholas DiMascio and Joost Pauwelyn explain, the contemporary relationship between trade and investment law has developed with 'different, but complementary, objectives and interests'.[172] Whereas 'the sophisticated interstate trading system embodied in the WTO … focused on liberalizing market access for foreign goods … to improve the aggregate welfare of nations … BITs have sought to protect individual investor rights … [and] to stimulate' FDI flows into host states 'eager to boost their economic development'.[173] Not surprisingly this has led to different approaches to interpreting some of the basic standards, as, for example, with the principle of non-discrimination, which is articulated through MFN and the national treatment standard in various BITs and IIAs, as well as the GATT/WTO trading system.

---

[169] Salacuse, *The Law of Investment Treaties*, p. 79.
[170] Muchlinski, 'Corporations and the Uses of Law', p. 7.
[171] Muchlinski, 'Corporations and the Uses of Law', p. 7.
[172] Nicholas DiMascio and Joost Pauwelyn, 'National Treatment in Trade and Investment: Worlds Apart or Two Sides of the Same Coin?' *American Journal of International Law* 102(1) (2008): 48–89, at p. 58.
[173] DiMascio and Pauwelyn, 'National Treatment in Trade and Investment', p. 59, with particular reference to the national treatment standard in international trade law and foreign investment.

A   Institutional design: procedure and remedies

A divergence in interpretative approaches in the investment and trade regimes could be put down to the different institutional antecedents. This may be explained on the basis of the different stances adopted by the negotiators of BITs and IIAs, as opposed to the trade diplomats in the GATT/WTO. Or else it could be based on the differing role of practitioners and decision-makers in the world of de-localised investor–state arbitration compared with the established WTO dispute settlement system with its panels and Appellate Body. Even the remedy arising out of a dispute is premised on a different basis. In the field of international investment law this is normally compensation (and occasionally restitution) for a wrongful act. In WTO dispute settlement the remedy sought is compliance with decisions of the Dispute Settlement Body, following the rulings and recommendations of a panel or the Appellate Body, as a means of re-dressing the imbalance of rights and obligations caused by a member's breach of its WTO obligations.

B   Treatment of substantive provisions

With respect to specific MFN and national treatment provisions, which are common to both international investment law and the international trade agreements, they are more commonly disputed under BITs and similar IIAs than previously, especially before NAFTA Chapter Eleven tribunals. This has led to investment arbitration tribunals having to grapple with 'the tension between preventing discrimination against foreign investors and respecting a nation's sovereign right to regulate'.[174] In some cases, arbitral tribunals have made reference to GATT/WTO case law, as in the NAFTA cases of *S. D. Myers* v. *Canada*,[175] *Pope & Talbot* v. *Canada*[176]

---

[174] DiMascio and Pauwelyn, 'National Treatment in Trade and Investment', p. 59.

[175] *S. D. Myers* v. *Canada*, First Partial Award, 13 November 2000, 40 *ILM* 1408 (2001), paras 243–6, with reliance on the Appellate Body's reasoning over 'like products' in *Japan–Alcoholic Beverages II*, WT/DS38/AB/R, 1 November 1996.

[176] *Pope & Talbot* v. *Canada*, Award on Merits, 10 April 2001, 22 *ILR* 352 (2002), paras 45–63 and 68–9, with reliance on the WTO Panel Reports in *EC–Bananas III*, WT/DS27/R, 22 May 1997 and *EC–Asbestos*, WT/DS135/R, 18 September 2000, as well as the GATT Panel Reports in *US–Alcoholic and Malt Beverages*, 19 June 1992, DS23/R, *BISD* 39S/206 and *US–Section 337 of the Tariff Act 1930*, 7 November 1989, L/6439, *BISD* 36S/345. The tribunal noted that in the GATT context national treatment was reviewed for its effect on the 'modification of conditions of competition' rather than 'less favourable treatment', as applied in the investment context.

and *Feldman* v. *Mexico*,[177] where a 'like circumstances' test was developed even though the test is fundamentally different to the 'like products' test under the GATT.[178]

Some commentators have applauded these early NAFTA decisions for their extensive referencing of WTO jurisprudence on national treatment.[179] Others have been more circumspect,[180] noting that national treatment jurisprudence by investment arbitration tribunals has moved 'from an originally intrusive construction to a more recent, hands-off interpretation'.[181] Moreover, this national treatment jurisprudence favours host state regulation and the regulatory context is important, given the impact that it has on society in the host state.[182]

This is clearly demonstrated by some other investment arbitration tribunals that have reversed this earlier jurisprudence, as, for example, with the ICSID award in *Occidental* v. *Ecuador*.[183] The tribunal in *Occidental* v. *Ecuador* explicitly rejected the argument put forward by the claimant that WTO jurisprudence was relevant in interpreting the national treatment provision in the Ecuador–US BIT. It even went as far as to state that 'the purpose of national treatment in this dispute is the opposite of that under the GATT/WTO'.[184] This was because the purpose of investment arbitration is 'to avoid exporters being placed at a disadvantage in foreign markets because of the indirect taxes paid in the country of origin' (in this case Ecuador). Instead, 'in the GATT/WTO the purpose is to avoid imported products being affected by a distortion of competition with similar domestic products because of taxes and other regulations in the country of destination'.[185]

Soon thereafter, the arbitral tribunal in the NAFTA case of *Methanex* v. *US*[186] declared itself opposed to the competition-based reading of

---

[177] *Marvin Roy Feldman Karpa* v. *United States of Mexico*, ICSID Case No. Arb(AF)/99/1, Award, 16 December 2002, *ICSID Review: Foreign Investment Law Journal* 18 (2003): 488, para. 165, with reference to Art. III of the GATT concerning the issue of 'like circumstances'.

[178] DiMascio and Pauwelyn, 'National Treatment in Trade and Investment', pp. 71–2.

[179] Jürgen Kurtz, 'The Use and Abuse of WTO Law in Investor–State Arbitration: Competition and its Discontents', *European Journal of International Law* 20(3) (2009): 749–71, at p. 763.

[180] DiMascio and Pauwelyn, 'National Treatment in Trade and Investment', p. 78.

[181] DiMascio and Pauwelyn, 'National Treatment in Trade and Investment', p. 81.

[182] DiMascio and Pauwelyn, 'National Treatment in Trade and Investment', p. 81.

[183] *Occidental Exploration and Production Co.* v. *The Republic of Ecuador*, Award, 1 July 2004, 12 *ICSID Reports* 59.

[184] *Occidental* v. *Ecuador*, para. 175.   [185] *Occidental* v. *Ecuador*, para. 175.

[186] *Methanex* v. *United States of America*, Award, 3 August 2005, 44 *ILM* 1345 (2005), Pt V, ch. B, paras 30–5.

national treatment[187] as set out in those earlier NAFTA awards. Providing a literal interpretation, clause by clause, of the treaty text of Article 1102 of NAFTA, the tribunal was at pains to point out that the text of the provision used different language in different parts, besides which the parties to NAFTA were aware of such differences when negotiating Chapter Eleven and had deliberately referred to 'like circumstances' as opposed to 'like goods'.[188]

C   Burden of proof

One of the often cited reasons for this reversal is that WTO jurisprudence requires the respondent WTO member government to bear the burden of proving that its policy is not discriminatory or that it otherwise fulfils a legitimate purpose, which is an approach that has been considered inappropriate for investment arbitration.[189] The approach was also explicitly rejected in *Thunderbird* v. *Mexico*,[190] where the tribunal stated that the burden of proof to show less favourable treatment remains with the investor claiming the discrimination. Unlike WTO dispute settlement, where once an affirmative claim has been made by a complainant member, the burden of proof shifts[191] and then it is up to the respondent member to rebut the presumption of discrimination that has been raised.

D   Interpretative cross-fertilisation

There has also been a cross-fertilisation of WTO jurisprudence into investor–state arbitral jurisprudence when it comes to interpreting exceptive clauses in a BIT. In the case of *Continental Casualty* v. *Argentina*,[192] the tribunal placed reliance on interpreting the concept of 'state

---

[187] Kurtz, 'The Use and Abuse of WTO Law in Investor–State Arbitration', p. 766.

[188] *Methanex* v. *US*, paras 33–4.

[189] Dolzer and Schreuer, *Principles of International Investment Law*, p. 205, with reliance on Don Regan, 'Further Thoughts on the Role of Regulatory Purpose under Article III of the General Agreement on Tariffs and Trade', *Journal of World Trade* (2003) 37(4): 737–60, at p. 752.

[190] *International Thunderbird Gaming Corporation* v. *United States of Mexico*, Award, 26 January 2006, paras 176–8. For a contrary view, see the separate opinion of Arbitrator Thomas Wälde, at para. 2, where he differs from his fellow arbitrators over the burden of proof in this national treatment claim.

[191] Dolzer and Schreuer, *Principles of International Investment Law*, p. 205.

[192] *Continental Casualty Company* v. *The Argentine Republic*, ICSID Case No. ARB/03/9, Award, 5 September 2008.

of necessity', as it appeared in Article XI of the Argentina–US BIT and in customary international law, on the basis of the necessity test imported from Article XX of the GATT jurisprudence.[193] Rather than interpreting the customary international law rule on the state of necessity, as codified by the ILC in its works on state responsibility – specifically Article 25 of the ILC Articles on State Responsibility[194] – the tribunal took the view that Article XI of the Argentina–US BIT was derived from a parallel model clause in US FCN treaties, which in turn reflected the formulation in Article XX of the GATT 1947.

It therefore considered it more appropriate to have reference to GATT/WTO case law that had dealt extensively with 'the concept and requirements of necessity in the context of economic measures derogating to ... obligations contained in GATT, rather than [referring] to the requirement of necessity under customary international law'.[195] The tribunal drew in particular on *Korea–Beef*[196] in determining that the word 'necessary' in Article XX(d) of the GATT 1994 was not 'limited to that which is "indispensable" or "of absolute necessity" or "inevitable"'. Instead, other measures might fall within its ambit and, in fact, the term 'necessary' referred to 'a range of degrees of necessity that could be measured along a continuum'.[197] Additionally, in determining whether a measure, which is 'not necessary' may nevertheless be 'indispensable', it applied the process of 'weighing and balancing' various factors, again on the basis of *Korea–Beef* and confirmed in later WTO jurisprudence.[198] Finally, the tribunal in *Continental Casualty* v. *Argentina*, basing itself on *US–Gambling*[199] and *Brazil–Retreaded Tyres*,[200] determined that a measure is not necessary if another treaty consistent, or less inconsistent, measure is 'reasonably available' as an alternative measure.[201] This

---

[193] *Continental Casualty* v. *Argentina*, paras 192–5.

[194] Responsibility of States for Internationally Wrongful Acts, 2001, text adopted by the International Law Commission at its 53rd Session, 2001, reproduced as an annex to General Assembly Resolution 56/83, 12 December 2001 (ILC Articles on State Responsibility).

[195] *Continental Casualty* v. *Argentina*, para. 192.

[196] *Korea–Measures Affecting Imports of Fresh, Chilled and Frozen Beef*, Appellate Body Report, WT/DS161/AB/R, adopted 10 January 2001.

[197] *Continental Casualty* v. *Argentina*, para. 193, with reliance on *Korea–Beef*, para. 161.

[198] *Continental Casualty* v. *Argentina*, para. 194.

[199] *US–Gambling*, Appellate Body Report, para. 308 (with reference to GATS, Art. XIV).

[200] *Brazil–Measures Affecting Imports of Retreaded Tyres*, Panel Report, WT/DS332/R, para. 7.211.

[201] *Continental Casualty* v. *Argentina*, para. 195.

approach to interpretation, involving the importation of the concept of necessity under Article XX of the GATT into investor–state arbitration, has proven to be controversial. It has been criticised for the way in which the tribunal in *Continental Casualty* v. *Argentina* applied it, as well as more generally in relation to its transposition into investment treaty arbitration.[202]

Many of the standards in BITs, or similar investment treaty instruments, are designed to protect either the investor or the investment, or both, and as in the case of the fair and equitable treatment standard, they can be interpreted and applied only by reference to the specific circumstances applicable to a particular investment. In terms of their scope, some of these provisions have more in common with the negotiation of substantive obligations designed to protect matters relating to the economic rights of individuals, such as intellectual property or consumer health and safety protection.

In this respect, the design of BITs and similar investment instruments in free trade agreements has something in common with the Agreement on Trade-Related Intellectual Property Rights (TRIPS),[203] the Agreement on Sanitary and Phytosanitary Measures[204] and the Agreement on Technical Barriers to Trade.[205] These agreements, negotiated during the Uruguay Round, with the exception of the TBT Agreement, all represent a normative shift in rule-making. They represent a move away from rules designed mostly to discipline state behaviour in protecting tariff reductions, and instead are focused on the need for the protection of particular societal values or consumer protection in the legal orders of WTO members.[206]

---

[202] José E. Alvarez and Tegan Brink, 'Revisiting the Necessity Defence: *Continental Casualty* v. *Argentina*', in Karl P. Sauvant (ed.), *Yearbook on International Investment Law and Policy, 2010–2011* (Oxford University Press, 2011), ch. 8.

[203] Agreement on Trade-Related Intellectual Property Rights, done at Marrakesh 15 April, 1994, 33 *ILM* 1197, entered into force 1 January 1995 (TRIPS) is taken up in Annex 1C to the WTO Agreement.

[204] Agreement on Sanitary and Phytosanitary Measures, done at Marrakesh 15 April 1994, 33 *ILM* 1125, entered into force 1 January 1995 (SPS Agreement or SPS), is taken up in Annex 1A to the WTO Agreement.

[205] Agreement on Technical Barriers to Trade done at Marrakesh, 15 April 1994, 33 *ILM* 1144, entered into force 1 January 1995 (TBT Agreement or TBT), is also to be found in Annex 1A to the WTO Agreement.

[206] Footer, *An Institutional and Normative Analysis of the World Trade Organization*, p. 192, with discussion of the change in regulatory philosophy that underpins these agreements.

It is therefore not surprising to find an investment arbitration tribunal like *Chemtura* v. *Canada*[207] conducting something akin to an SPS enquiry into the 'restricted use' of a pesticide, known as 'lindane', by the Canadian Government. It may only be a matter of time before we begin to see other similar cases in investor–state arbitration arising out of consumer health and safety protection provisions in various BITs, some of which have been modelled on the WTO SPS Agreement, or which take account of the TRIPs Agreement.

Finally, the cross-fertilisation is a two-way process in the LAT relationship between international investment law and trade. This is perhaps less obvious in the case of investment law being taken up, or referenced, in WTO dispute settlement proceedings before either a panel or the Appellate Body. Nevertheless, in *United States–Stainless Steel*[208] the Appellate Body referred to the importance of 'the legal interpretation embodied in adopted panel and Appellate Body reports' that 'becomes part and parcel of the *acquis* of the WTO dispute settlement system', notwithstanding the lack of a doctrine of precedent. The Appellate Body cited with approval the arbitral tribunal's pronouncement in *Saipem* v. *Bangladesh*[209] in support of the notion that the WTO dispute settlement system ensures 'security and predictability', and that 'absent cogent reasons, an adjudicatory body will resolve the same legal question in the same way in a subsequent case'.[210]

It also drew attention to a lengthy passage in the *Saipem* v. *Bangladesh* decision in which the tribunal recorded that it was not bound by previous decisions. Nevertheless, it found itself duty bound to consider earlier decisions of international tribunals and to adopt a consistent line of jurisprudence. The decision would thereby 'contribute to the harmonious development of investment law and … meet the legitimate expectations of the community of States and investors towards certainty of the rule of law'.[211]

It may also be asked whether WTO panels and the Appellate Body could learn any lessons from investment arbitration tribunals in matters

---

[207] *Chemtura Corporation (formerly Crompton Corporation)* v. *Government of Canada*, NAFTA *ad hoc* arbitration under UNCITRAL Rules, Award, 2 August 2010.
[208] *United States–Final Anti-Dumping Measures on Stainless Steel from Mexico*, Appellate Body Report, WT/DS344/AB/R, adopted 20 May 2008.
[209] *Saipem SpA* v. *The People's Republic of Bangladesh*, ICSID Case No. ARB/05/07, Decision, 21 March 2007, *IIC* 280 (2007), p. 20, para. 67.
[210] *United States–Stainless Steel*, para. 160, fn. 313.
[211] *United States–Stainless Steel*, para. 160.

such as the application of the principle of proportionality or the doctrine of state responsibility, especially the rules on attribution. Indeed, there might be other areas of substantive or procedural investment law, or matters such as evidence and proof that WTO law could usefully draw upon.

V   Some concluding remarks and future prospects for the investment and trade relationship

What the foregoing sections of this contribution have sought to establish is that the LAT relationship between international investment law and trade is as strong as ever. It is clear from the historical and contextual background in section II that these two areas of economic activity have been intertwined for nigh on a century and a half. Whether enshrined in bilateral or multilateral instruments, the relationship between investment law and trade has ebbed and flowed.

From the early nineteenth century with the rise of FCN treaties, which were the market access instruments of their day, foreign investment and trade were frequently bargained for in a single instrument. With the advent of large regional or sectoral agreements, such as NAFTA[212] and the ECT,[213] respectively, we have come full circle; in both cases investment treaty instruments have been taken up in stand-alone chapters or sections of the framework treaty.

In between times the idea of bringing international investment law more fully within the realm of multilateral trade has been attempted in the stillborn ITO, under the Havana Charter and again with the failure by WTO members at the Cancún Ministerial Meeting in 2003 to take the work of the WGTI forward. This is particularly poignant in light of the failed MAI negotiations just five years earlier, and could have seen the LAT relationship abandoned for a more integrated approach towards investment and trade. Instead, it seems as the economist, DeAnne Julius, pointed out two decades ago, that foreign direct investment appears doomed to remain the 'neglected twin of trade'[214] – at least in terms of its multilateral regulation. However, this would be to deny the importance that international investment law has acquired since the beginning of the twenty-first century, due in no small part to the vast increase in

---

[212] Chapter Eleven, NAFTA.   [213] ECT, see, above n. 8.

[214] DeAnne Julius, 'Foreign Direct Investment: The Neglected Twin of Trade', Occasional Paper No. 30, Group of Thirty, Washington, DC, 1991.

cross-border investment flows between countries on the basis of both international investment contracts and treaty-based investment.

What does all of this mean for the relationship between international investment law and trade? Currently, in international relations we are seeing the emergence of different but interconnected treaty regimes in these two fields of economic activity, the most important of which is undoubtedly the further development of more regional trade agreements, with stand-alone investment treaty instruments.

The real challenge may lie not so much in determining whether a single multilateral instrument can ever be forged around this particular LAT relationship, but more precisely in the extent to which the inter-action between international investment law and trade is leading to either a greater convergence, or a possible divergence, in rule-making and dispute settlement between them. In terms of the latter element, we have already seen that there has been some cross-fertilisation between dispute settlement organs operating in the WTO and certain investment arbitration tribunals, even though this has not been without controversy as in *Continental Casualty* v. *Argentina*.[215] Whether this trend will continue is uncertain. What we can be sure of is that the LAT relationship between international investment law and trade looks set to continue for the foreseeable future.

---

[215] *Continental Casualty* v. *Canada*, for which see the contribution by Alvarez and Brink, 'Revisiting the Necessity Defence'.

13

Reviewing the administration of domestic regulation in WTO and investment law: the international minimum standard as 'one standard to rule them all'?

ANASTASIOS GOURGOURINIS[*]

A Introduction

This study seeks to demonstrate how essentially the same minimum standards of treatment protecting foreign traders/investors are established by the World Trade Organization (WTO) multilateral trade regime, on the one hand, and international investment law, which comprises the web of international investment agreements (IIAs),[1] as well as Free-Trade Agreements containing provisions on investment,[2] on the other. While trade and investment, indeed, constitute distinct regimes, with different goals, processes, actors and institutional mechanisms,[3] both provide for international adjudication with regard to the review of domestic governmental practices.[4] It will be analysed herein how WTO and IIA provisions on standards of 'fair and equitable

---

[*] The present study is an updated and revised version of a paper, 'Intersections: Dissemblance or Convergence between International Trade and Investment Law', *TDM* 3 (2011), available at: www.transnational-dispute-management.com/article.asp?key=1731.

[1] Most notably, over 2,750 concluded bilateral investment treaties (BITs) as at the end of 2008. UNCTAD, 'Recent Developments in International Investment Agreements (2008– June 2009)', *IIA Monitor* No. 3 (2009): 2.

[2] Such as the North American Free Trade Agreement (NAFTA), 32 *ILM* 289 (Pts 1–3); 32 *ILM* 605 (Pts 4–8). NAFTA Chapter Eleven provides protection for investors and investments in NAFTA countries.

[3] For example, see with regard to the differences between the two regimes in the context of countermeasures, M. Paparinskis, 'Equivalent Primary Rules and Differential Secondary Rules: Countermeasures in WTO and Investment Protection Law', in T. Broude and Y. Shany (eds), *Multi-Sourced Equivalent Norms in International Law* (Oxford: Hart, 2011), p. 259.

[4] For example, T. Ginsburg, 'Judicialization of Administrative Governance: Causes, Consequences and Limits', *Nottingham Law Review*, 3 (2008): 14–17.

treatment', for foreign traders/investors with regard to the administration of domestic regulation, interact under the influence of the
international minimum standard: 'one standard to rule them all'. In
other words, whether on the basis of the same or similar facts norms
derived from different regimes lead to the same or similar juridical
consequences, thus leading to a certain degree of regime harmonisation
via harmonised arrangements.[5] A study juxtaposing national treatment
provisions in trade and investment concluded that 'investors cannot
assume that they will prevail on a national treatment claim before an
investment tribunal even if their country has earlier prevailed on the
same claim at the WTO, and vice versa'.[6] However, it is submitted here
that the juxtaposition of equitable treatment provisions in WTO law
and IIAs leads to the opposite conclusion, so that the same set of facts
regarding the administration of domestic regulation can give rise to
successful challenges brought before either the WTO or investment
arbitration tribunals.

Hence, before entering the merits of the above proposition via an
examination of the due process prescriptions of WTO and investment
protection law against the background of the international minimum
standard of treatment of aliens, it is first necessary to briefly discuss the
potential dual capacity of aliens as both foreign traders and as investors,
and vice versa, in contemporary international economic law.

B   The potential dual capacity of foreign traders as investors, and vice versa

International trade and investment law, albeit distinct specialised
regimes, cannot be viewed in isolation from each other and are interconnected and concomitant in the context of the globalised economy.[7]
Accordingly, while the close relationship between the two disciplines
can be explained in terms of trade theory, it can also be traced in the

---

[5] To paraphrase from *Emilio Agustín Maffezini* v. *Spain*, ICSID Case No. ARB/97/7, Decision on Objections to Jurisdiction, 25 January 2000, *IIC* 85 (2000), para. 62.

[6] N. DiMascio and J. Pauwelyn, 'Nondiscrimination in Trade and Investment Treaties: Worlds Apart or Two Sides of the Same Coin?' *American Journal of International Law* 102 (2008): 48, at p. 88. Similarly, see J. Kurtz, 'The Use and Abuse of WTO Law in Investor–State Arbitration: Competition and its Discontents', *European Journal of International Law* 20 (2009): 749.

[7] See WTO, Doha Ministerial Declaration, adopted 14 November 2001, WT/MIN(01)/DEC/1, 41 *ILM* 746 (2002), paras 20–2.

texts of the WTO-covered agreements themselves.[8] International trade regulation on goods, services and intellectual property rights (IP rights) impinge upon issues of investment protection to the extent that it directly affects trade, as reflected in the WTO Agreement,[9] the 1994 General Agreement on Tariffs and Trade (GATT),[10] the Subsidies and Countervailing Measures (SCM) Agreement,[11] the Trade-Related Aspects of Intellectual Property Rights (TRIPs) Agreement,[12] the Agreement on Trade-Related Investment Measures (TRIMs),[13] the Agreement on Sanitary and Phytosanitary Measures[14] and the General Agreement on Trade in Services (GATS).[15]

One cannot ignore the important different characteristics of the WTO and the investment protection regimes.[16] While the WTO prescribes solely for inter-state dispute settlement, with little or no visible role for private parties, dispute settlement under IIAs mostly operates on an investor versus host state adjudicative basis. While the WTO dispute

---

[8] See, e.g., M. Trebilcock and R. Howse, *The Regulation of International Trade*, 3rd edn (Abingdon: Routledge, 2005), pp. 442–6, 452–61; M. Sornarajah, *The International Law on Foreign Investment* (Cambridge University Press, 2004), pp. 397–402.

[9] Agreement Establishing the World Trade Organization, Marrakesh. WTO, *The Legal Texts: The Results of the Uruguay Round of Multilateral Trade Negotiations* (Cambridge University Press, 1994) (*Legal Texts*), p. 3.

[10] General Agreement on Tariffs and Trade, 1994, Annex 1A of the Marrakesh Agreement, see WTO, *Legal Texts*, p. 17.

[11] Agreement on Subsidies and Countervailing Measures, Annex 1A of the Marrakesh Agreement, see WTO, *Legal Texts*, p. 231.

[12] Agreement on Trade-Related Aspects of Intellectual Property Rights, Annex 1C of the Marrakesh Agreement, see WTO, *Legal Texts*, p. 321.

[13] Agreement on Trade-Related Investment Measures, Annex 1A of the Marrakesh Agreement, see WTO, *Legal Texts*, p. 143.

[14] Agreement on the Application of Sanitary and Phytosanitary Measures, Annex 1A of the Marrakesh Agreement, see WTO, *Legal Texts*, p. 59.

[15] General Agreement on Trade in Services, Annex 1B of the Marrakesh Agreement, see WTO, *Legal Texts*, p. 284. So despite the fact that a multilateral agreement dealing specifically with investment in the WTO ambit is lacking, service suppliers under GATS Mode 3 are rather likely to qualify as foreign investors.

[16] For example, T. Brewer and S. Young, 'Investment Issues at the WTO: The Architecture of Rules and the Settlement of Disputes', *Journal of International Economic Law* 1 (1998): 459–64; M. Molinuevo, 'Can Foreign Investors in Services Benefit from WTO Dispute Settlement? Legal Standing and Remedies in WTO and International Arbitration', NCCR Trade Working Paper No. 2006/17 (2006), available at: www.nccr-trade.org; P. Gugler and J. Chaisse, 'Foreign Investment Issues and WTO Law: Dealing with Fragmentation while Waiting for a Multilateral Framework', in J. Chaisse and T. Balmelli (eds), *Essays on the Future of the World Trade Organization, vol. 1: Policies and Legal Issues* (Lugarno: Edis, 2008), pp. 140–62.

settlement aims at the removal of WTO-incompatible measures or, in the alternative, compensation and suspension of concessions (retaliation) *pro futuro*, investor–state adjudication under IIAs focuses on reparation, that is, retrospective remedies awarded to private parties themselves (i.e., investors) without a duty to withdraw the illegal measure. Also, while in the WTO adjudication there is no requirement of legal or economic interest for complainants,[17] in investor–state adjudication under IIAs claimants must prove the existence of a causal link between the acts or omissions complained of and the injury suffered.[18]

But crucially, what both the trade and investment regimes feature in common are the eventual beneficiaries of the standards of protection under both disciplines, that is, private parties. While foreign investors are afforded direct protection by IIAs, the goal of the WTO agreements, to use the formulation featured on the WTO website, 'although negotiated and signed by governments … is to help producers of goods and services, exporters, and importers conduct their business'.[19] This has been reiterated by WTO adjudicators: hence, a panel has noted that 'predictability in the intellectual property regime is indeed essential for the nationals of WTO Members when they make trade and investment decisions in the course of their businesses'.[20] Similarly, WTO arbitrators, addressing a suggestion that suspension of commitments or other obligations under the GATS in principal service sectors other than distribution services

---

[17] For example, Appellate Body Report, *European Communities–Regime for the Importation, Sale and Distribution of Bananas*, WT/DS27/AB/R, adopted 25 September 1997, DSR 1997:II, 591, paras 132–8; Panel Report, *Korea–Definitive Safeguard Measure on Imports of Certain Dairy Products*, WT/DS98/R and Corr. 1, adopted 12 January 2000, as modified by Appellate Body Report WT/DS98/AB/R, DSR 2000:I, 49, paras 7.13–7.14; Panel Report, *Colombia–Indicative Prices and Restrictions on Ports of Entry*, WT/DS366/R, adopted 20 May 20 2009, paras 7.325–7.330.

[18] For example, *CME Czech Republic BV* v. *Czech Republic*, Partial Award, *Ad hoc* UNCITRAL Arbitration Rules, *IIC* 61 (2001), para. 615; *Link-Trading Joint Stock Company* v. *Moldova*, Final Award, 18 April 2002, *Ad hoc* UNCITRAL Arbitration Rules; *IIC* 154 (2002), para. 87; *Occidental Exploration and Production Company* v. *Ecuador*, LCIA Case No. UN 3467, Award, 1 July 2004, *IIC* 202 (2004), paras 201–3; *Biwater Gauff (Tanzania) Ltd* v. *Tanzania*, ICSID Case No ARB/05/22, Award, and Concurring and Dissenting Opinion, 18 July 2008, *IIC* 330 (2008), para 779.

[19] Available at: www.wto.org/english/thewto_e/whatis_e/tif_e/fact1_e.htm. Cf. S. Charnovitz, 'Economic and Social Actors in the World Trade Organization', *ILSA Journal of International and Comparative Law* 7 (2000/1): 261–5.

[20] Panel Report, *India–Patent Protection for Pharmaceutical and Agricultural Chemical Products, Complaint by the United States*, WT/DS50/R, adopted 16 January 1998, as modified by Appellate Body Report WT/DS50/AB/R, DSR 1998:I, 41, para. 7.30.

would not be 'practicable or effective' under Article 22.3(b) of the Dispute Settlement Understanding (DSU),[21] accepted the possible detrimental impact on the foreign direct investment.[22] Perhaps the most pertinent illustration of the above considerations can be traced in the so-called NAFTA 'spaghetti-bowl', where the trade and investment obligations of the United States, Canada and Mexico under both the NAFTA and the WTO-covered agreements have been premised on the overlap of provisions on trade and investment protection.[23]

Ergo, as a working hypothesis, foreign traders (producers or service providers or holders of IP rights) will be taken, for the purposes of the present study, to also qualify as foreign investors under IIAs, and vice versa. One could point to instances where the former have established their own distribution network in the importing member, or have otherwise established a subsidiary in the importing country so as to facilitate the flow and provision of goods and services in the given foreign market, thus eventually rendering them capable of qualifying as foreign investors as well foreign traders. Still, for a given foreign trader to qualify also as a foreign investor certain requirements must be met.

More specifically, in the field of international investment protection, and given that the qualification of 'investors' is linked with the definition of 'foreign investment',[24] often a distinction is drawn between, on the one hand, 'foreign direct investments', which are accorded IIAs' remedies, and, on the other hand, 'portfolio investments', which are sometimes not included in the protection.[25] What is more, no precise or uniform definition of the term 'investment' exists in international law, to the extent that Article 25(1) of the Convention on the Settlement of

---

[21] Understanding on Rules and Procedures Governing the Settlement of Disputes, Annex 2 of the Marrakesh Agreement, see WTO, *Legal Texts*, p. 354.

[22] Decision by the Arbitrators, *European Communities–Regime for the Importation, Sale and Distribution of Bananas–Recourse to Arbitration by the European Communities under Article 22.6 of the DSU*, WT/DS27/ARB/ECU, 24 March 2000, DSR 2000:V, 2237, paras 108–14.

[23] See J. Pauwelyn, 'Adding Sweeteners to Softwood Lumber: The WTO–NAFTA "Spaghetti Bowl" is Cooking', *Journal of International Economic Law* 9 (2006): 197; J. Dunoff, 'The Many Dimensions of Softwood Lumber', *Alberta Law Review* 45 (2007): 319; L. Reif, 'Desperate Softwood Lumber Companies?: The Canada–US Softwood Lumber Dispute and NAFTA Chapter 11', *Alberta Law Review* 45 (2007): 357.

[24] For example, *Bayview Irrigation District No. 11 and others v. Mexico*, ICSID Case No. ARB(AF)/05/1, Award, 19 June 2007, *IIC* 290 (2007), paras 90–122.

[25] See for the distinction, Sornarajah, *The International Law on Foreign Investment*, pp. 7–18, 227–8.

Investment Disputes between States and Nationals of Other States (ICSID Convention)[26] does not purport to define it.[27] Hence, it is essentially reserved for state parties to IIAs to define in detail what constitutes an 'investment' for the purposes of their *inter se* international legal relations.[28] Still, certain generic criteria seem to have prevailed with regard to the notion of 'investments' in ICSID arbitration, often seen as reflected in the so-called *Salini* test: (i) a contribution of money or other assets of economic value; (ii) a certain duration; (iii) an element of risk; and (iv) a contribution to the host state's development, in addition to a fifth element of regularity of profit and return as noted in the earlier case of *Fedax NV* v. *Venezuela*.[29] More recently, the *Phoenix Action* Tribunal, building on the *Plama Consortium* Award,[30] identified two further requirements: (v) assets invested according to host state laws and regulations;[31] and (vi) assets invested *bona fide*.[32] Nonetheless, it cannot be ignored that the merits of the *Salini* test have been subject to criticism;[33]

---

[26] Convention on the Settlement of Investment Disputes Between States and Nationals of Other States, 40 *ILM* 577.

[27] Note that any given ICSID tribunal must satisfy itself that the claimant has made an 'investment' under both the BIT *in casu* (or any other instrument containing the consent to arbitrate) as well as the ICSID Convention. See *Salini Construtorri SpA and Italstrade SpA* v. *Morocco*, ICSID Case No. ARB/00/4, Decision on Jurisdiction, 23 July 2001, 30 *ILM* 577, para. 44; *Joy Mining Machinery Ltd* v. *Egypt*, ICSID Case No. ARB/03/11, Award on Jurisdiction, 30 July 2004, *IIC* 147 (2004), *ICSID Review: Foreign Investment Law Journal* 19 (2004): 486, para. 50. The definition of investments in IIAs can confirm or restrict the generic ICSID definition, but they cannot expand it in order to have access to arbitration under the ICSID facilities. Equally, the Energy Charter Treaty or the UNCITRAL Rules do not contain a definition of 'investment'.

[28] See, respectively, *Mihaly International Corporation* v. *Sri Lanka*, ICSID Case No. ARB/00/2, Award, 15 March 2002, *IIC* 170 (2002), para. 33: 'the definition [of investment] was left to be worked out in the subsequent practice of States, thereby preserving its integrity and flexibility and allowing for future progressive development of international law on the topic of investment'.

[29] *Salini* v. *Morocco*, para. 52 and *Fedax NV* v. *Venezuela*, ICSID Case No. ARB/96/3, Decision on Jurisdiction, *IIC* 101 (1997), 37 *ILM* 1378, para. 43.

[30] *Plama Consortium Ltd* v. *Bulgaria*, ICSID Case No. ARB/03/24, Award, 27 August 2008, *IIC* 338 (2008), paras 138–46.

[31] Cf. *Fraport AG Frankfurt Airport Services Worldwide* v. *Republic of the Philippines*, ICSID Case No. ARB/03/25, Award, 16 August 2007, *IIC* 299 (2007), paras 346–7 on possible issues of estoppel.

[32] *Phoenix Action Ltd* v. *Czech Republic*, ICSID Case No. ARB/06/5, Award, 9 April 2009, *IIC* 367 (2009), paras 82–3, 101–15.

[33] See, e.g., Z. Douglas, *The International Law of Investment Claims* (Cambridge University Press, 2009), pp. 198–202, as well as *Biwater* v. *Tanzania*, paras 310–18; *Pantechniki SA Contractors and Engineers* v. *Albania*, ICSID Case No. ARB/07/21, Award, 28 July 2009, *IIC* 383 (2009), paras 36–43; *Toto Costruzioni Generali SpA* v. *Lebanon*, ICSID Case No.

for instance, the *Abaclat* Tribunal questioned the adequacy of the criteria and refused to decline jurisdiction should the claimants' investments *in casu* (Argentinean sovereign bond-holders) fail to satisfy them, insofar as:

> the *Salini* criteria may be useful to further describe what characteristics contributions may or should have. They should, however, not serve to create a limit, which the Convention itself nor the Contracting Parties to a specific BIT intended to create.[34]

One could also refer to the *Romak* Tribunal (UNCITRAL), which interpreted the term 'investment' in the respective BIT in accordance with its ordinary meaning, that is, as generally pertaining to expenditures or contributions, as well as for the purpose of obtaining an economic benefit (by definition, uncertain), to conclude that that 'the term "investments" under the BIT has an inherent meaning (irrespective of whether the investor resorts to ICSID or UNCITRAL arbitral proceedings) entailing a contribution that extends over a certain period of time and that involves some risk'.[35]

In any case, one should always keep in mind the authoritative observation by a leading commentator according to which the abovementioned elements 'should not necessarily be understood as jurisdictional requirements but merely as typical characteristics of investments under the [ICSID] Convention'.[36] Crucially for the purposes of the present

---

ARB/07/12, Decision on Jurisdiction, 8 September 2009, *IIC* 391 (2009), paras 81–5. Favourably towards the *Salini* test, see *Joy Mining*, para. 53; *Jan de Nul NV and Dredging International NV* v. *Egypt*, ICSID Case No. ARB/04/13, Decision on Jurisdiction, 16 June 2006, *IIC* 144 (2006), para. 91.

[34] *Abaclat and others* v. *Argentina*, ICSID Case No. ARB/07/5, Decision on Jurisdiction and Admissibility, 4 August 2011, *IIC* 504 (2011), para. 364. Cf. regarding the *Salini* test, *Alpha Projektholding GMBH* v. *Ukraine*, ICSID Case No. ARB/07/16, Award, 20 October 2010, *IIC* 464 (2010), para. 314: 'To cite the classic example, a simple contract for the sale of goods, without more, would not constitute an investment within the meaning of Article 25(1) [of the ICSID Convention], even if a BIT or a contract defined it as one.'

[35] *Romak SA* v. *Uzbekistan*, PCA Case No. AA280, Award, 26 November 2009, *IIC* 400 (2009), para. 207.

[36] C. Schreuer *et al.*, *The ICSID Convention: A Commentary* (Cambridge University Press, 2009), pp. 128, 140. Cf. *Inmaris Perestroika Sailing Maritime Services GmbH and others* v. *Ukraine*, ICSID Case No. ARB/08/8, Decision on Jurisdiction, 8 March 2010, *IIC* 431 (2010), para. 131, stating that the *Salini* criteria could provide guidance 'in the event that a tribunal were concerned that a BIT or contract definition of investment was so broad that it might appear to capture a transaction that would not normally be characterized as an investment under any reasonable definition'. Further in the ongoing debate over the proper definition of 'investments' for the purposes of investment arbitration, see, e.g.,

study, it indeed appears that, in view of the analysis above, it is in principle feasible for foreign traders to qualify simultaneously as foreign investors in the state to which they export their products or provide their services abroad. What, in fact, foreign traders and investors share in common, from a normative point of view, is that both in principle benefit from the protection afforded by the customary minimum standard for the treatment of aliens, which is to be discussed below.

C   The international minimum standard of treatment of aliens as a 'floor'

The debate on the existence and content of an international minimum standard for the treatment of aliens dominated international legal discourse in late 1930s. On one side of the spectrum, the Latin American states appeared as the main advocates of the so-called 'Calvo Doctrine', according to which the principle of non-intervention in the domestic *domaine réservé* of states dictated that aliens could not claim treatment more favourable than that reserved for nationals.[37] On the other, the view shared by Western states was early capitalised by Elihu Root in 1910:

> There is a standard of justice, very simple, very fundamental, and of such general acceptance by all civilized countries as to form a part of the international law of the world. The condition upon which any country is entitled to measure the justice due from it to an alien by the justice which it accords to its own citizens is that its system of law and administration shall conform to this general standard. If any country's system of law and administration does not conform to that standard, although the people of the country may be content or compelled to live under it, no other country can be compelled to accept it as furnishing a satisfactory measure of treatment to its citizens.[38]

J. Fellenbaum, '*GEA* v. *Ukraine* and the Battle of Treaty Interpretation Principles Over the Salini Test', *Arbitration International* 27 (2011): 249; J. D. Mortenson, 'The Meaning of "Investment": ICSID's Travaux and the Domain of International Investment Law', *Harvard International Law Journal* 51 (2010): 257.

[37]   See, among many, A. Roth, *The Minimum Standard of International Law Applied to Aliens* (Leiden: Sijthoff, 1949); D. Shea, *The Calvo Clause: A Problem of Inter-American and International Law and Diplomacy* (Minneapolis, MN: University of Minnesota Press, 1955); R. Lillich, *The Human Rights of Aliens in Contemporary International Law* (Manchester University Press, 1984), pp. 14–17.

[38]   E. Root, 'The Basis of Protection to Citizens Residing Abroad', *American Journal of International Law* 4 (1910): 521–2.

Contemporary international law has seemingly resolved the issue in favour of the latter view: an international minimum standard of treatment of non-nationals has indeed prevailed irrespective of the treatment afforded to nationals.[39] To use the formulation of an authoritative treatise, there exist 'general requirements of customary international law, such as those which impose on a state international responsibility for denial of justice to aliens, or which require it to observe in its treatment of aliens certain minimum international standards'.[40]

The above proposition perhaps echoes, *inter alia*, the long-standing ruling of the Permanent Court of International Justice (PCIJ) in the *Upper Silesia* case, where the existence of an international (customary) minimum standard of treatment of aliens was acknowledged by making reference to 'limits set by the generally accepted principles of international law' conditioning the treatment of non-nationals by host states.[41] It is also in this spirit that the International Court of Justice (ICJ) has subsequently remarked in the *Barcelona Traction* case that, 'when a State admits into its territory foreign investments or foreign nationals, whether natural or juristic persons, it is bound to extend to them the protection of the law and assumes obligations concerning the treatment to be afforded them'.[42] In a later passage, the Court then explained that this standard of treatment of aliens is in fact 'guaranteed by general international law'.[43] Reference to the international minimum standard was made in 2004 by the Eritrea–Ethiopia Claims Commission

---

[39] Cf. G. Sacerdoti, 'Bilateral Treaties and Multilateral Instruments on Investment Protection', *Recueil des Cours* 269 (1997): 342: 'National treatment should be considered to satisfy "prima facie" the requirements of the international minimum standard. Invocation of the latter can be still considered relevant whenever national law does not provide, generally or in a specific instance, for adequate guarantees of fair treatment in accordance with generally shared values of substantial and procedural fairness and justice in respect of the enjoyment of property and the normal conduct of business operations.'

[40] R. Jennings and A. Watts (eds), *Oppenheim's International Law, vol. 1: Peace, Parts 2 to 4*, 9th edn (London: Longman, 1992), p. 909. Similarly, see M. Shaw, *International Law*, 6th edn (Cambridge University Press, 2008), pp. 824–7. Discussing the scope of the term 'general international law' as encompassing international legal norms binding *erga omnes*, contrary to treaty (or other) norms binding only *inter partes*, see A. Gourgourinis, 'General/ Particular International Law and Primary/Secondary Rules: Unitary Terminology of a Fragmented System', *European Journal of International Law* 22 (2011): 1110–16.

[41] *Case Concerning Certain German Interests in Polish Upper Silesia (Germany v. Poland)*, Merits, Judgment, PCIJ Series A, No. 7 (1926), 22.

[42] *Case Concerning the Barcelona Traction, Light and Power Company Limited (Belgium v. Spain)*, Judgment, *ICJ Reports* 1970, para. 33.

[43] *Barcelona Traction*, para. 87.

when discussing Ethiopia's failure to provide reasonable notice regarding the collection of tax liabilities of Eritrean expellees; as stated: 'international law did not prohibit Ethiopia from requiring that expellees settle their tax liabilities, but it required that this be done in a reasonable and principled way ... Viewed overall, the tax collection process was approximate and arbitrary and failed to meet the minimum standards of fair and reasonable treatment necessary in the circumstances.'[44] In late 2010, the ICJ in the *Ahmadou Diallo* case reiterated that treatment of aliens should not fall below customary standards, by stating that 'there is no doubt ... that the prohibition of inhuman and degrading treatment is among the rules of general international law which are binding on States in all circumstances, even apart from any treaty commitments'.[45] Accordingly, it is today safely maintained that a certain international minimum standard of treatment of aliens is concretely entrenched in public international law.

The normative content of the minimum standard of treatment, characterised as a 'contingent standard',[46] has traditionally been linked with wrongful deaths of aliens,[47] cruel and inhumane treatment,[48] abusive

---

[44] *Civilians Claims, Eritrea's Claims 15, 16, 23 & 27–32 (The State of Eritrea v. The Federal Democratic Republic of Ethiopia)*, Eritrea–Ethiopia Claims Commission, Partial Award, 17 December 2004, Permanent Court of Arbitration, 44 *ILM* 601, 26 *RIAA* 197, para. 144.

[45] *Ahmadou Sadio Diallo (Republic of Guinea v. Democratic Republic of the Congo)*, Judgment, 30 November 2010, available at: www.icj-cij.org, accessed 1 January 2011, para. 87 *in fine*. Further, see A. Alvarez-Jimenez, 'Minimum Standard of Treatment of Aliens, Fair and Equitable Treatment of Foreign Investors, Customary International Law and the Diallo Case before the International Court of Justice', *Journal of World Investment and Trade*, 9 (2008): 52.

[46] See A. Falsafi, 'The International Minimum Standard of Treatment of Foreign Investors' Property: A Contingent Standard', *Suffolk Transnational Law Review* 30 (2006/7): 317.

[47] See, e.g., *J. W. & N. L. Swinney (USA) v. United Mexican States*, General Claims Commission, Convention of 8 September 1923 (United Mexican States, United States of America), 16 November 1926, 4 *RIAA* 98, at p. 100: 'It is not clear from the record why Swinney [a US national] looked like a smuggler or a revolutionary at that time and place, and how the Mexican officials could explain and account for their act of shooting under these circumstances, even when they considered him committing an unlawful act in crossing from one bank to another (a fact they did not see). Human life in these parts, on both sides, seems not to be appraised so highly as international standards prescribe.'

[48] For example, *Harry Roberts (USA) v. United Mexican States*, General Claims Commission, Convention of 8 September 1923 (United Mexican States, United States of America), 2 November 1926, 4 *RIAA* 77, at p. 80: 'That test is, broadly speaking, whether aliens are treated in accordance with ordinary standards of civilization. We do not hesitate to say that the treatment of Roberts was such as to warrant an indemnity on the ground of cruel and inhumane imprisonment.'

expulsion of aliens,[49] taking of property[50] and, most notably, denial of justice.[51] In fact, it is often that references to the minimum standard of treatment of aliens relate to the administration of justice at the domestic level affecting the rights and interests of aliens. Denial of justice, as a standard that 'can hardly be defined in a purely rationalistic way',[52] according to Jan Paulsson is always procedural, though 'there may be extreme cases where the proof of the failed process is that the substance of a decision is so egregiously wrong that no honest or competent court could possibly have given it. Such cases would sanction the state's failure to provide a decent system of justice.'[53]

That said, it bears noting that the pertinent observation that 'the adjective "minimum" does not mean that the standard itself is low, i.e., an easy test to meet. Instead, the standard is something below which no government conduct can fall without triggering a successful claim for compensation'.[54] In fact, the threshold required for the ascertainment of

[49] See *Boffolo* case, Mixed Claims Commission (Italy–Venezuela), 13 February and 7 May 1903, 10 *RIAA* 528, at p. 532: 'there may be a broad difference between the right to exercise a power [i.e., expulsion of aliens] and the rightful exercise of that power'.

[50] See, *inter alios*, E. Borchard, 'Minimum Standard of the Treatment of Aliens', 38 *Michigan Law Review* (1939/40): 445, at pp. 458–60.

[51] See, *inter alia*, *Laura M. B. Janes et al. (USA)* v. *United Mexican States*, General Claims Commission, Convention of 8 September 1923 (United Mexican States, United States of America), 16 November 1926, 4 *RIAA* 82, at p. 88. As Charles de Visscher wrote in 1935: 'le déni de justice n'est plus désormais le seul fait générateur de la responsabilité internationale. Celle-ci peut être engagée par des actes ou par des omissions imputables à l'Etat et qui 'sont sans connexion avec l'administration de la justice. Tel est le cas, par exemple, si la législation locale prive les étrangers du minimum de droits auquel le droit international leur permet de prétendre.' C. de Visscher, 'Le deni de justice en droit international', *Recueil des Cours*, 52 (1935): 419–20.

[52] H. Spiegel, 'Origin and Development of Denial of Justice', *American Journal of International Law* 32 (1938): 80. Similarly, see the previously published relevant analysis in O. Lissitzyn, 'The Meaning of the Term Denial of Justice in International Law', *American Journal of International Law* 30 (1936): 632.

[53] J. Paulsson, *Denial of Justice in International Law* (Cambridge University Press, 2005), p. 98. Cf. A. Adede, 'A Fresh Look at the Meaning of the Doctrine of Denial of Justice under International Law', *Canadian Yearbook of International Law* 14 (1976): 90–3. On the relationship between denial of justice and access to justice, see F. Francioni, 'Access to Justice, Denial of Justice and International Investment Law', *European Journal of International Law* 20 (2009): 729, and at p. 731: 'in its historical evolution, access to justice is inseparable from the "minimum standard of treatment of aliens"'.

[54] See, referring to NAFTA, Art. 1105, T. Weiler, 'NAFTA Article 1105 and the Principles of International Economic Law', *Columbia Journal of Transnational Law* 42 (2003/4): 75. Note that in 2001, after the merits award and before the award on damages in the *Pope & Talbot* Chapter Eleven investment dispute, the NAFTA Free Trade Commission pursuant to NAFTA, Art. 2001(2)(c) issued an interpretation binding on NAFTA tribunals,

breach of the international minimum standard of treatment of aliens is rather demanding. In this respect, it is commonplace to refer to the *Neer* claim before the US–Mexican Claim Commission as the landmark case, where it was stated that:

> the treatment of an alien, in order to constitute an international delinquency should amount to an outrage, to bad faith, to wilful neglect of duty, or to an insufficiency of governmental action so far short of international standards that every reasonable and impartial man would readily recognize its insufficiency. Whether the insufficiency proceeds from the deficient execution of a reasonable law or from the fact that the laws of the country do not empower the authorities to measure up to international standards is immaterial.[55]

In the same fashion, the ruling on the *Chattin* case equated the breach of the customary minimum standard with the treatment of aliens as 'far below international standards of civilization'.[56] In the *Salem* case, the tribunal opted for an equally stringently high threshold and stated that:

> international law has from the beginning conceived under the notion of 'denial of justice' forming base of political claims only exorbitant cases of judicial injustice. Absolute denial of justice; inexcusable delay of proceedings; obvious discrimination of foreigners against natives; palpable and malicious iniquity of a judgment – these are the cases which, one after another, have been included into the notion of 'denial of justice'.[57]

Put differently, if 'considerable efforts' of the state concerned can be traced, then a 'broad and general view of the steps taken rather than on

---

according to which 'fair and equitable treatment' and 'full protection and security' in NAFTA, Art. 1105(1) do not require treatment in addition to or beyond that which is required by the customary international law minimum standard of treatment of aliens. Further on fair and equitable treatment provisions in IIAs, see, below, section E.

[55] *L. F. H. Neer and Pauline Neer (USA)* v. *United Mexican States*, General Claims Commission, Convention of 8 September 1923 (United Mexican States, United States of America), 15 October 1926, 4 *RIAA* 60, 61–2. For an identical reasoning, see *Louis B. Gordon (USA)* v. *United Mexican States*, General Claims Commission, Convention of 8 September 1923 (United Mexican States, United States of America), 8 October 1930, 4 *RIAA* 586, 590.

[56] *B. E. Chattin (USA)* v. *United Mexican States*, General Claims Commission, Convention of 8 September 1923 (United Mexican States, United States of America), 23 July 1927, 4 *RIAA* 282, 292. Similarly, see, e.g., *Daniel Dillon (USA)* v. *United Mexican States*, General Claims Commission, Convention of 8 September 1923 (United Mexican States, United States of America), 3 October 1928, 4 *RIAA* 368, 369.

[57] *Salem* case (Egypt, USA), *Agreement between the United States of America and Egypt regarding arbitration of the claim of George J. Salem*, signed at Cairo, 20 January 1931, Award, 8 June 1932, 2 *RIAA* 1161, 1202.

a criticism of some particular point' may suffice for the acknowledgement that the treatment of aliens did not fall below customary standards.[58]

The same high threshold for the violation of the minimum standard appears to have also been endorsed in the much later *ELSI* case, where the ICJ interpreted 'full protection and security required by international law' under the 1948 Treaty of Friendship, Commerce and Navigation between the United States and Italy as corresponding to the international minimum standard.[59] The ICJ held that: 'arbitrariness is not so much something opposed to a rule of law, as something opposed to the rule of law ... It is a wilful disregard of due process of law, an act which shocks, or at least surprises, a sense of juridical propriety.'[60]

For the purposes of the present discussion, it is important to note as an interim conclusion that it is exactly the customary character of the minimum standard as a part of general international law (that is, binding *erga omnes*) that verifies its relevance with regard to the treatment afforded to aliens independently of their capacity as investors or traders, or both. In this sense, it indeed prescribes for generic minimum guarantees as a 'floor'. In the following sections of this study it will be shown how the customary standard has in fact permeated the international trade and investment regimes by contextually underlying their provisions dealing with the proper administration of domestic regulation vis-à-vis aliens.

D   WTO due process standards and administration of domestic regulation

The WTO-covered agreements focus on trade in goods, services and IP rights. While it is rather common that these three are regulated as such in the WTO texts (i.e., as products, services or rights), a closer look reveals

---

[58] *A. L. Harkrader (USA) v. United Mexican States*, General Claims Commission, Convention of 8 September 1923 (United Mexican States, United States of America), 3 October 1928, 4 *RIAA* 371, 372–3. Cf. G. Fitzmaurice, 'The Meaning of the Term "Denial of Justice"', *British Yearbook of International Law* 13 (1932): 110–11: 'the merely erroneous or unjust decision of a court, even though it may involve what amounts to a miscarriage of justice, is not a denial of justice, and, moreover, does not involve the responsibility of the state. To involve the responsibility of the state the element of bad faith must be present, and it must be clear that the court was actuated by bias, by fraud, or by external pressure, or was not impartial; or the judgment must be such as no court which was both honest and competent could have delivered.'

[59] *Elettronica Sicula SpA (ELSI) (United States of America v. Italy)*, Judgment, *ICJ Reports* 1989, para. 111.

[60] *ELSI*, para. 128.

that a number of provisions also provide for standards of protection for natural or legal persons benefiting from inter-state trade, that is, foreign traders, producers, service providers and IP rights' holders. As a result, what follows is an overview of WTO provisions concerning minimum due process standards that can possibly benefit foreign investors in their capacity as foreign traders.

1 Minimum standards for transparency and procedural fairness in the administration of domestic trade regulations

As a necessary prerequisite for the preservation of the basic principles and to further the objectives underlying the multilateral trading system, members of the WTO have a general duty to maintain WTO-compliant domestic legislation. According to Article XVI:4 of the WTO Agreement, 'each Member shall ensure the conformity of its laws, regulations and administrative procedures with its obligations as provided in the annexed Agreements'. Nevertheless, in reality not only the content, but also the *modus* of administering domestic legislation, which has to be reasonable and transparent, is crucial for the observance of the rights and obligations stemming from the 'Single Undertaking'.[61] As a result, the covered agreements are equipped with provisions relating to the administration of otherwise WTO-consistent domestic regulation affecting international trade, providing for certain minimum due process and transparency self-standing standards benefiting foreign traders. These standards have been inserted in the WTO agreements as fundamental protective guarantees infused with considerations relating to justice, fairness and equity.[62]

To start with, in the GATT context, Article X of the GATT, titled 'Publication and Administration of Trade Regulations', is designed so as to afford protective guarantees mainly for private parties, that is, traders.[63]

---

[61] For example, see W. Davey, 'GATT Article X: Transparency and Proper Administration', in W. Davey (ed.), *Enforcing World Trade Rules: Essays on WTO Dispute Settlement and GATT Obligations* (London: Cameron May, 2006), pp. 300–1; F. Weiss and S. Steiner, 'Transparency as an Element of Good Governance in the Practice of the EU and the WTO: Overview and Comparison', *Fordham International Law Journal* 30 (2006/7): 1571–85.

[62] *Accord*, A. von Bogdandy, 'Law and Politics in the WTO: Strategies to Cope with a Deficient Relationship', *Max Planck Yearbook of UN Law* 5 (2001): 669.

[63] *Argentina–Measures Affecting the Export of Bovine Hides and Import of Finished Leather*, Panel Report, WT/DS155/R and Corr. 1, adopted 16 February 2001, DSR 2001:V, 1779, para. 11.68.

As has been held by a panel, Article X of the GATT is a 'due process theme', whose title and content is 'aimed at ensuring that due process is accorded to traders when they import or export'.[64] *Ergo*, Article X of the GATT deals rather with the *publication* and *administration* of laws, regulations, judicial decisions and administrative rulings of general application; whether the former are themselves discriminatory is a matter of conformity with the substantive provisions of the GATT.[65]

Under Articles X:1 and X:2 of the GATT, 'laws, regulations, judicial decisions and administrative rulings of general application' must be published and cannot be enforced prior to their official publication.[66] According to the Appellate Body, Article X:2 is expressive of the transparency principle, which 'has obviously due process dimensions' and dictates that:

> Members and other persons affected, or likely to be affected, by governmental measures imposing restraints, requirements and other burdens, should have a reasonable opportunity to acquire authentic information about such measures and accordingly to protect and adjust their activities or alternatively to seek modification of such measures.[67]

Moreover, under Article X:3 of the GATT WTO members must administer their domestic legislation of general application relating to trade in goods in a 'uniform, impartial and reasonable manner'. Further, they must institute 'independent judicial, arbitral or administrative tribunals or procedures' made available to interested private parties to have recourse for prompt and effective review of measures affecting trade

---

[64] *European Communities–Selected Customs Matters*, Panel Report, WT/DS315/R, adopted 11 December 2006, as modified by Appellate Body Report, WT/DS315/AB/R, DSR 2006: IX–X, 3915, para. 7.107.

[65] For example, *EC–Bananas*, Appellate Body Report, para. 200 *in fine*; *EC–Poultry*, WT/DS69/AB/R, para. 115.

[66] Measures of 'general application' are those whose restraint affects 'an unidentified number of economic operators, including domestic and foreign producers'. *United States–Restrictions on Imports of Cotton and Man-made Fibre Underwear*, Panel Report, WT/DS24/R, adopted 25 February 1997, as modified by Appellate Body Report, WT/DS24/AB/R, DSR 1997:I, 31, para. 7.65.

[67] *United States–Restrictions on Imports of Cotton and Man-made Fibre Underwear*, Appellate Body Report, WT/DS24/AB/R, adopted 25 February 1997, DSR 1997:I, 11, para. 21. As noted by Steve Charnovitz, this was the first instance where 'the connection [was made] between information transparency for the public and the ability of the affected individual to act on the information by participating in a government's administrative review process'. S. Charnovitz, 'Transparency and Participation in the World Trade Organization', *Rutgers Law Review* 56 (2003/4): 935.

not in conformity with the above standards. It is in this spirit, that Article X:3 of the GATT establishes 'certain minimum standards for transparency and procedural fairness in the administration of trade laws',[68] encompassing 'notions such as notice, transparency, fairness and equity'.[69] Uniformity, impartiality and reasonableness are not cumulative requirements, so that, for instance, a WTO member may be found to administer domestic regulation in an unreasonable manner, even if not in a non-uniform or impartial manner.[70] Reasonableness has, thus, been interpreted as corresponding to 'notions such as "in accordance with reason", not "irrational or absurd", "proportionate", "having sound judgement", "sensible", "not asking for too much", "within the limits of reason, not greatly less or more than might be thought likely or appropriate", "articulate"',[71] or as a process that 'inherently contains the possibility of revealing confidential business information'.[72] On the other hand, 'uniformity' has been envisaged as requiring consistency and predictability in the administration of domestic law,[73] resulting in 'an actual or possible future adverse impact on the trading environment',[74] but still not requiring 'identical results where relevant facts differ'.[75] Per the Appellate Body, the lack of uniformity of administrative processes (as contrasted to their application) does not necessarily entail a violation of Article X:3(a) of the GATT;[76] for, importantly,

> the term 'administer' in Article X:3(a) refers to putting into practical effect, or applying, a legal instrument of the kind described in Article X:1. Thus, under Article X:3(a), it is the application of a legal instrument

---

[68] *United States–Import Prohibition of Certain Shrimp and Shrimp Products – Recourse to Article 21.5 of the DSU by Malaysia,* Appellate Body Report, WT/DS58/AB/RW, adopted 21 November 2001, DSR 2001:XIII, 6481, para. 183.

[69] *EC–Selected Customs Matters,* Panel Report, para. 7.134. Further, see D. Erskine, 'The US–EC Dispute over Custom Matters: Trade Facilitation, Customs Unions, and the Meaning of WTO Obligations', *Florida Journal of International Law* 18 (2006): 431–57.

[70] *Dominican Republic–Measures Affecting the Importation and Internal Sale of Cigarettes,* Panel Report, WT/DS302/R, adopted 19 May 2005, as modified by Appellate Body Report, WT/DS302/AB/R, DSR 2005:XV, 7425, para. 7.383.

[71] *Dominican Republic–Cigarettes,* Panel Report, paras 7.385–7.388.

[72] *Argentina–Hides and Leather,* Panel Report, para. 11.94.

[73] *Argentina–Hides and Leather,* Panel Report, para. 11.83.

[74] *EC–Selected Customs Matters,* Panel Report, para. 7.154.

[75] *United States–Anti-Dumping Measures on Stainless Steel Plate in Coils and Stainless Steel Sheet and Strip from Korea,* Panel Report, WT/DS179/R, adopted 1 February 2001, DSR 2001:IV, 1295, paras 6.50–6.51.

[76] *European Communities–Selected Customs Matters,* Appellate Body Report, WT/DS315/AB/R, adopted 11 December 2006, DSR 2006:IX, 3791, paras 224–6.

of the kind described in Article X:1 that is required to be uniform, but not the processes leading to administrative decisions, or the tools that might be used in the exercise of administration.[77]

Finally, the requirement of impartiality would not be met in cases where administrative procedures permit private parties with a competitive interest, but lacking relevant legal interest *in casu*, to gain access to otherwise confidential information.[78] What would then seem to be a core element for a violation is 'the uncertainty created as the result of non-uniformity, i.e. where application of a policy varies across time and locations'.[79]

Noteworthy also is that in *EC–Customs* the Appellate Body had emphatically noted that:

> while the substantive content of the legal instrument being administered is not challengeable under Article X:3(a), we see no reason why a legal instrument that regulates the application or implementation of that instrument cannot be examined under Article X:3(a) if it is alleged to lead to a lack of uniform, impartial, or reasonable administration of that legal instrument.[80]

Hence, it has been observed that the above dictum signalled the abandonment of the substantive–administrative dichotomy previously followed by panels, and potentially brings substantial aspects of domestic regulation into the scope of Article X:3 of the GATT.[81] In any event, claims under Article X of the GATT generally require a high threshold of 'solid evidence' which the complaining member must adduce, reflecting 'the gravity of the accusations inherent in [Article X GATT] claims'.[82]

---

[77] *European Communities–Selected Customs Matters*, Appellate Body Report, para. 224. Cf. the critique in A. Mitchell and E. Sheargold, 'Global Governance: The World Trade Organization's Contribution', *Alberta Law Review* 46 (2008/9): 1071–72.

[78] *Argentina–Hides and Leather*, Panel Report, para. 11.100.

[79] B. Hoekman and P. Mavroidis, 'Nothing Dramatic (… Regarding Administration of Customs Laws): A Comment on the WTO Appellate Body Report: EC Selected Customs Matters', *World Trade Review* 8 (2009): 39.

[80] *European Communities–Selected Customs Matters*, Appellate Body Report, para. 200.

[81] P. Ala'i, 'The WTO and the Anti-Corruption Movement', *Loyola University of Chicago International Law Review* 6 (2008/9): 270–1.

[82] *United States–Sunset Reviews of Anti-Dumping Measures on Oil Country Tubular Goods from Argentina*, Appellate Body Report, WT/DS268/AB/R, adopted 17 December 2004, DSR 2004:VII, 3257, para. 217. Cf. *Egypt–Definitive Anti-Dumping Measures on Steel Rebar from Turkey*, Panel Report, WT/DS211/R, adopted 1 October 2002, DSR 2002:VII, 2667, para. 7.429.

Almost identical is the coverage of Article VI of the GATS as a matter of both substance and language,[83] while the threshold of evidence also remains high.[84] In the TRIPS ambit, Articles 41.2, 42 and 63 of the TRIPS form 'an internationally-agreed minimum standard which Members are bound to implement in their domestic legislation' for the protection of nationals of other members.[85] WTO members are obligated to establish domestic IP rights' enforcement procedures that are 'fair and equitable', 'not unnecessarily complicated or costly, or entail unreasonable time limits or unwarranted delays', providing adequate effective procedural due process guarantees to interested private parties, that is, IP rights' holders as well as defendants. What is more, Article 63 of the TRIPS on 'Transparency of Dispute Prevention and Settlement', similarly to Article X:1 of the GATT and Article III of the GATS,[86] establishes transparency requirements.

One could further point to Article 1.3 of the Licensing Agreement, which according to the Appellate Body, 'by its very terms' establishes 'neutral … fair and equitable' *administration* and *application* of import licensing procedures in a way identical to Article X:3(a) of the GATT.[87] *Mutatis mutandis*, the 'minimum standards' of fairness established by Article X:3(a), and applied in the administration of domestic trade regulation, must be observed in the area of anti-dumping and safeguards measures, given that they would fall into the scope of Article X:1 of the GATT as measures of general application,[88] and thus are to be read in conformity with the disciplines of Article X of the GATT.

---

[83] See P. Delimatsis, 'Due Process and "Good" Regulation Embedded in the GATS: Disciplining Regulatory Behaviour in Services Through Article VI of the GATS', *Journal of International Economic Law* 10 (2006): 20–1. On the general relevance of GATT provisions for the interpretation of GATS, see, e.g., *EC–Bananas*, Appellate Body Report, para. 231.

[84] See *United States–Measures Affecting the Cross-Border Supply of Gambling and Betting Services*, Panel Report, WT/DS285/R, adopted 20 April 2005, as modified by Appellate Body Report, WT/DS285/AB/R, DSR 2005:XII, 5797, paras 6.430–6.437.

[85] *United States–Section 211 Omnibus Appropriations Act of* 1998, Appellate Body Report, WT/DS176/AB/R, adopted 1 February 2002, DSR 2002:II, 589, paras 206–7, 215, 219, 221.

[86] Note that GATT, Art. X has been referred to in the interpretation of TRIPS, Art. 63. See *India–Patent Protection for Pharmaceutical and Agricultural Chemical Products, Complaint by the United States*, Panel Report, WT/DS50/R, adopted 16 January 1998, as modified by Appellate Body Report, WT/DS50/AB/R, DSR 1998:I, 41, para.7.48, reversed on appeal as not falling within the panel's terms of reference, but not in its substance.

[87] *EC–Bananas*, Appellate Body Report, paras 197, 203.

[88] *US–Stainless Steel*, Panel Report, para. 4.36.

As a result, it has been found, for example, in *Mexico–Steel Pipes*, that 'positive evidence' must be 'inherently reliable and creditworthy', an 'objective examination' can take place only if the anti-dumping investigation is conducted 'in an unbiased manner, without favouring the interests of any interested party, or group of interested parties, in the investigation', and be accompanied by 'even-handed' identification, investigation and evaluation of the relevant factors.[89] In the same spirit, in *Argentina–Imports of Footwear*, the panel held that in the absence of explanations relating to the selection of one set of data to the exclusion of others during a safeguards investigation, the findings and conclusions reached on the basis of such data could not be 'reasoned'.[90]

In sum, the minimum due process guarantees of the administration of domestic trade regulations enshrined in Article X of the GATT appear to permeate substantially all facets of WTO regulation. Overall, it appears that the scope of Article X of the GATT can feasibly extend beyond customs duties to all trade rules, as further evidenced by various provisions of other WTO agreements,[91] so that eventually, and 'after being neglected for over 50 years, GATT Article X has a bright future ahead of it'.[92] This is to be rendered even more evident by the relevance of Article X:3 of the GATT in the interpretation of the chapeau of Article XX of the GATT, as the Appellate Body recognised in *US–Shrimp*.[93]

In effect, the analysis of the non-arbitrariness element in Article XX of the GATT, as well as Article XIV of the GATS, and Articles 2.3 and 5.5 of the SPS, that follows in the next section, reveals that almost identical considerations have also prevailed in the interpretation of the above provisions by WTO organs, thus fully confirming the preponderant role of Article X of the GATT 1994 as an 'umbrella' requirement safeguarding domestic compliance with WTO rules. In this sense, equitable considerations relating to minimum due process and transparency requirements

---

[89] *Mexico–Anti-Dumping Duties on Steel Pipes and Tubes from Guatemala*, Panel Report, WT/DS331/R, adopted 24 July 2007, paras 7.213–7.214.

[90] *Argentina–Safeguard Measures on Imports of Footwear*, Appellate Body Report, WT/DS121/AB/R, adopted 12 January 2000, DSR 2000:I, 515, para. 8.218.

[91] P. van den Bossche, *The Law and Policy of the World Trade Organization: Text, Cases and Materials* (Cambridge University Press, 2005), p. 474.

[92] Pauwelyn, 'Nothing Dramatic', pp. 45, 48.

[93] *United States–Import Prohibition of Certain Shrimp and Shrimp Products*, Appellate Body Report, WT/DS58/AB/R, adopted 12 October 1998, DSR 1998:VII, 2755, paras 182–4.

will equally re-appear as dominant, forming an emerging element of good governance in and under WTO law.[94]

2   The 'non-arbitrariness' requirement under Article XX of the GATT, Article XIV of the GATS and Articles 2.3 and 5.5 of the SPS

Article XX of the GATT 1994 and Article XIV of the GATS, paradoxically titled 'General Exceptions', operate as non-precluded measures clauses defining the limits of WTO members' regulatory autonomy to address non-trade societal concerns, but still without engaging in protectionist practices in trade in goods and services. Overall, and given the fact that they feature very similar structures and formulations, both provisions have been harmoniously interpreted by WTO organs, so that eventually the conditions for their invocation have become almost identical as a matter of principle.[95]

Hence, Article XX of the GATT 1994 has long been viewed as 'a limited and conditional exception from obligations under other [GATT] provisions',[96] but still 'not a positive rule establishing obligations in itself'.[97] Since the Appellate Body Report in *US–Gasoline*, the invocation of Article XX of the GATT 1994 as a defence for a measure has been deemed to entail a two-tiered analysis consisting, first, of the 'provisional justification' by reason of characterisation of the measure under Article XX, paragraphs (a)–(j), and, second, 'further appraisal of the same measure under the introductory clauses of Article XX', with the burden of proof lying with the WTO member invoking the exception.[98] In effect, while the measures resulting in discrimination must fall within the scope of paragraphs (a)–(j), thus encompassing a wide range of domestic regulatory concerns, the chapeau additionally requires a further determination of whether the *modus* of application of the measure in question

---

[94] See P. Ala'i, 'From the Periphery to the Center?: The Evolving WTO Jurisprudence on Transparency and Good Governance, *Journal of International Economic Law* 11 (2008): 779.

[95] *United States–Measures Affecting the Cross-Border Supply of Gambling and Betting Services*, Appellate Body Report, WT/DS285/AB/R, adopted 20 April 2005, DSR 2005: XII, 5663, Corr. 1, DSR 2006:XII, 5475, paras 291–2.

[96] *United States–Customs User Fee*, GATT Panel Report, L/6264, adopted 2 February 1988, BISD 35S/245, para. 5.9.

[97] *United States–Restrictions on Imports of Tuna*, GATT Panel Report, DS21/R, 3 September 1991, unadopted, BISD 39S/155, para. 5.22.

[98] *United States–Standards for Reformulated and Conventional Gasoline*, Appellate Body Report, WT/DS2/AB/R, adopted 20 May 1996, DSR 1996:I, paras 3, 22–3.

results in 'arbitrary' or 'unjustifiable' discrimination between countries where the same conditions prevail, or otherwise constitute a 'disguised restriction on international trade'.[99] From these three requirements dictated by the chapeaux, the reference to 'arbitrariness' in its plain meaning probably denotes the most apparent case of insertion of equitable considerations relating to the successful utilisation of the general exceptions of Article XX of the GATT 1994 and Article XIV of the GATS.[100]

Accordingly, the Appellate Body in US–Shrimp has specifically identified 'arbitrariness', under the chapeau of Article XX of the GATT, in the administration of the US Section 609 certification process due to, *inter alia*, the lack of transparency, predictability, any formal opportunity for an applicant country to be heard, or to respond to any arguments that may be made against it, in the course of the certification process before a decision to grant or to deny certification was made. Moreover, crucial was the rigidity of the application of the measure without due regard to its appropriateness according to the conditions prevailing in the various exporting members, as well as the fact that no formal, written, reasoned decision was actually provided in the course of the certification process, so that WTO members whose applications were denied did not receive notice of such denial (other than by omission from the list of approved applications) nor were they given reasons for the denial.[101] Later the panel in the Article 21.5 DSU compliance dispute referred to the ordinary meaning of the word 'arbitrary' in the context of the chapeau as 'capricious, unpredictable, inconsistent',[102] to be later followed by the Panel in *Brazil–Retreaded Tyres*.[103]

In the context of the chapeau of Article XIV of the GATS, the Appellate Body in US–Gambling provided some guidance on instances where the application of measures takes place in an arbitrary way by referring to 'facially neutral measures, [where] there may nevertheless be

---

[99] *United States–Gasoline*, Appellate Body Report.

[100] See D. Lovric, *Deference to the Legislature in WTO: Challenges to Legislation* (Alphen aan den Rijn: Kluwer Law, 2010), 184–5.

[101] *US–Shrimp*, Appellate Body Report, paras 177–84.

[102] *United States–Import Prohibition of Certain Shrimp and Shrimp Products - Recourse to Article 21.5 of the DSU by Malaysia*, Panel Report, WT/DS58/RW, adopted 21 November 2001, as upheld by Appellate Body Report, WT/DS58/AB/RW, DSR 2001: XIII, 6529, para. 5.124 (footnote omitted).

[103] *Brazil–Measures Affecting Imports of Retreaded Tyres*, Panel Report, WT/DS332/R, adopted 17 December 2007, as modified by Appellate Body Report, WT/DS332/AB/R, paras 7.257–7.258, approvingly referred to by the Appellate Body, though reversed on its merits in WT/DS332/AB/R, para. 231.

situations where the selective prosecution of persons rises to the level of discrimination', but only when they are accompanied by (high-threshold) evidence concerning 'the *overall* number of suppliers, and on *patterns* of enforcement, and on the reasons for particular instances of non-enforcement'.[104] Similar is the effect of Articles 2.3 and 5.5 of the SPS which, read together, essentially reproduce the structure and aims of the chapeaux of Article XX of the GATT 1994 and Article XIV of the GATS.

Nonetheless, note that, while Article XX of the GATT 1994 and Article XIV of the GATS are *exceptions*, the SPS Agreement rather creates *obligations* to be met so that sanitary or phytosanitary measures are introduced or maintained, that is, different obligations not already imposed by GATT 1994, because 'nowhere is consistency with GATT presumed to be consistency with the SPS Agreement'.[105] In effect, Articles 2.3 and 5.5, read together, prohibit 'arbitrary or unjustifiable' discrimination in different but comparable situations concerning the appropriate levels of sanitary or phytosanitary protection. Again, 'arbitrariness' under Articles 2.3 and 5.5 of the SPS has been found in cases where justification of different levels of protection in comparable or identical situations was lacking and scientific evidence pointed to contrary conclusions;[106] while lack of arbitrariness was identified in cases of difference in the levels of protection concerning hormones used for growth promotion purposes, as distinct from hormones used for therapeutic and zootechnical purposes.[107] Overall, it would appear that the requirement for 'non-arbitrariness' under Article XX of the GATT 1994, Article XIV of the GATS, and Articles 2.3 and 5.5 of the SPS is very much influenced by the disciplines of the grandfathered Article X of the GATT 1994, and, hence, also reflecting a minimum standard of administration of domestic trade regulation to be observed by WTO members.

---

[104] *US–Gambling*, Panel Report, paras 354, 356 (original emphasis).

[105] *EC–Measures Concerning Meat and Meat Products (Hormones), Complaint by the United States*, Panel Report, WT/DS26/R/USA, adopted 13 February 1998, as modified by Appellate Body Report, WT/DS26/AB/R, WT/DS48/AB/R, DSR 1998:III, 699, paras 8.42–8.45.

[106] *Australia–Measures Affecting Importation of Salmon*, Appellate Body Report, WT/DS18/AB/R, adopted 12 October 1998, DSR 1998:VIII, 3327, paras 234–6.

[107] *EC–Measures Concerning Meat and Meat Products (Hormones)*, Appellate Body Report, WT/DS26/AB/R, WT/DS48/AB/R, adopted 13 February 1998, DSR 1998:I, 135, para. 225.

The insertion of such equitable considerations in the WTO agreements has been considered, *in passim*, by a commentator as recasting the customary international law minimum standard of treatment of aliens.[108] This is further reinforced by the Appellate Body's remark in *EC–Bananas* that Article 1.3 of the Licensing Agreement, making explicit reference to the 'fair and equitable manner' of administration has identical coverage with Article X of the GATT.[109] Hence, support is indeed provided for the view supported herein that Article X of the GATT 1994, and the other relevant provisions of the covered agreements, have actually incorporated the customary minimum standard, insofar as protecting foreign traders from arbitrary discrimination in practice may necessitate identical guarantees to those traditionally recognised for foreign investors; and which are analysed below.

E 'Fair and equitable treatment' under IIAs and administration of domestic regulation

In the previous section, an overview of WTO provisions relating to the administration of domestic trade regulations showed that equity principles, such as due process, procedural fairness, transparency and so on, enjoy a central role. This section aims to demonstrate that these provisions of the WTO agreements as minimum standards of treatment of foreign traders are essentially identical to the (customary) international minimum standard of treatment of foreign investors. As a result, the analysis that follows will seek to address whether the guarantees of fair and equitable treatment provided by IIAs to foreign investors, often seen as reflecting the customary minimum standard of treatment of aliens, could also afford the same degree of protection to investors as traders on the basis of facts, giving rise, for example, to a breach of Article X:3(a) of the GATT 1994.

The 'fair and equitable treatment' standard for foreign investors was first inserted into the 1948 Havana Charter for an International Trade Organization,[110] which was never ratified. Since then, it has featured in a

---

[108] See F. Weiss, 'From Havana to Marrakesh: Treaty Making for Trade', in J. Klabbers and R. Lefeber (eds), *Essays on the Law of Treaties: A Collection of Essays in Honour of Bert Vierdag* (The Hague: Martinus Nijhoff, 1998), p. 163.

[109] *EC–Bananas*, Appellate Body Report, para. 203. Cf. also M. Ewing-Chow, 'Thesis, Antithesis and Synthesis: Investor Protection in Bits, WTO and FTAS', *University of NSW Law Journal* 30 (2007): 567.

[110] Havana Charter for an International Trade Organization, Final Act of the UN Conference on Trade and Development, Art. 11(2)(a)(i).

number of earlier international instruments on investment protection,[111] but contemporarily is included in almost every IIA in force, albeit occasionally under different formulations.[112] For instance, the requirement of fair and equitable treatment of foreign investors is also prescribed by Article 1105(1) of the NAFTA and Article 10(1) of the ECT, as well as Article 5(1) of the 2012 US Model BIT.[113]

As is obvious from the formulation of the standards, fair and equitable treatment is rooted in considerations of fairness and equity,[114] and is thus inherently vague, so that resorting to dictionary definitions can become somewhat circular.[115] This is further understandable given the scope of application of the concept: marking the dividing line between legitimate domestic regulation and administration, on the one hand, and unfair or inequitable treatment of foreign investors, on the other, is undoubtedly a rather sensitive issue in the field of investment protection, especially given the fact that it is different from cases of direct or indirect expropriatory takings of alien property. The quest for a proper definition of the standard as included in a vast number of international instruments on investment protection has thus focused on the appropriate yardstick by reference to which host state measures are to be scrutinised. Accordingly, when arbitral tribunals established under IIAs are called to assess whether a provision related to fair and equitable treatment has been breached, they will either regard the relevant treaty stipulation as referring to the minimum standard of treatment of aliens under customary international law or as referring to all sources of international law, or, alternatively, view it as an independent, autonomous and self-contained treaty standard.[116] This is understandable to the extent that, at the end of

---

[111] On the origins of the concept, see, e.g., K. Yannaca-Small, 'Fair and Equitable Treatment Standard in International Investment Law', OECD Working Papers on International Investment, 2004/3, pp. 3–7.

[112] See M. Klein Bronfman, 'Fair and Equitable Treatment: An Evolving Standard', *Max Planck Yearbook of UN Law* 10 (2006): 625–37.

[113] Available at: www.ustr.gov/sites/default/files/BIT%20text%20for%20ACIEP%20Meeting.pdf.

[114] For example, S. Vasciannie, 'The Fair and Equitable Treatment Standard in International Investment Law and Practice', *British Yearbook of International Law* 70 (2000): 145–7; P. Muchlinski, '"Caveat Investor"?: The Relevance of the Conduct of the Investor under the Fair and Equitable Treatment Standard', *International and Comparative Law Quarterly* 55 (2006): 531–3; A. Orakhelashvili, 'The Normative Basis of "Fair and Equitable Treatment": General International Law on Foreign Investment?', *Archiv des Völkerrechts* 46 (2008): 92–3.

[115] R. Dolzer, 'Fair and Equitable Treatment: A Key Standard in Investment Treaties', *International Law* 39 (2005): 88.

[116] See, e.g., C. Schreuer, 'Fair and Equitable Treatment in Arbitral Practice', *Journal of World Investment and Trade* 6 (2005): 357.

the day, investment tribunals only have jurisdiction to hear claims based on alleged violations of specific IIAs' provisions.

As a result, a process of interpretation of any given fair and equitable treatment IIA clause is necessary in every instance, given that in some cases the standard is explicitly linked to the customary minimum standard, or international law, while in other occasions it appears self-standing without any qualification. Thus, what could safely be said is that a violation of fair and equitable treatment would depend largely on the treaty instrument in which it is contained, hence, leaving no room for generalisations, but allowing only for *ad hoc* conclusions.[117] So, while there indeed exists a debate on the relationship between fair and equitable treatment, on the one hand, and the minimum standard as well as customary international law, on the other, it bears noting that on a number of occasions, even when tribunals viewed the fair and equitable treatment in IIA provisions either as referring to the customary minimum or as self-standing treaty clauses, they nevertheless held that both were in essence contextually identical,[118] to the extent that 'this precision is more theoretical than real ... the treaty standard of fair and equitable treatment is not materially different from the minimum standard of treatment in customary international law'.[119]

---

[117] For example, *Lauder* v. *Czech Republic, Ad hoc* UNCITRAL Arbitration Rules, Final Award, 3 September 2001, *IIC* 205 (2001), para. 292; *Continental Casualty Co.* v. *Argentina*, ICSID Case No. ARB/03/9, Award, 5 September 2008, *IIC* 336 (2008), para. 254. Note that BIT provisions prescribing that fair and equitable treatment afforded to foreign investors 'shall in no case be accorded treatment less than that required by international law' have been interpreted so that 'actions or omissions of the Parties [to the IIA in question] may qualify as unfair and inequitable, even if they do not amount to an outrage, to wilful neglect of duty, egregious insufficiency of State actions, or even in subjective bad faith'. See *Lemire* v. *Ukraine*, ICSID Case No. ARB/06/18, Decision on Jurisdiction and Liability, 14 January 2010, *IIC* 424 (2010), paras 253–4.

[118] See, e.g., *Duke Energy Electroquil Partners and Electroquil SA* v. *Ecuador*, ICSID Case No. ARB/04/19, Award, 12 August 2008, *IIC* 333 (2008), paras 333–7; *Chevron Corporation and Texaco Petroleum Corporation* v. *Ecuador, Ad hoc* UNCITRAL Arbitration Rules, Interim Award, 1 December 2008, *IIC* 355 (2008), para. 233; *Jan de Nul NV and Dredging International NV* v. *Egypt*, ICSID Case No. ARB/04/13, Award, 24 October 2008, *IIC* 356 (2008), paras 187–95. Cf. A. Gourgourinis, '*Lex Specialis* in WTO and Investment Protection Law', *German Yearbook of International Law* 53 (2010): 591: 'One can also trace an explicit derogation from *lex specialis derogat legi generali* in the various investment treaty provisions stipulating that the fair and equitable standard they themselves contain (i.e. as *lex specialis*) simply reflect and go no further than the customary law minimum standard of treatment of aliens (i.e. the relevant *lex generalis*), which as a result becomes, even indirectly via *renvoi*, the prevalent standard.'

[119] *Rumeli Telekom AS and Telsim Mobil Telekomikasyon Hizmetleri AS* v. *Kazakhstan*, ICSID Case No. ARB/05/16, Award, 21 July 2008, *IIC* 344 (2008), para. 611. Cf.

Nevertheless, the *Neer* and *ELSI* cases should not be read as enshrining the minimum standard as a contemporary customary rule. Custom evolves through the passage of time, it is not static. As the *Mondev* Tribunal noted, the international minimum standard cannot considered 'as meaning no more' than the *Neer* claim, nor should the *ELSI* case be seen as undoubtedly conclusive; for, in view of the emergence of a vast number of international instruments on investment protection providing for 'fair and equitable treatment' and 'full protection and security':

> in the end the question is whether, at an international level and having regard to generally accepted standards of the administration of justice, a tribunal can conclude in the light of all the available facts that the impugned decision was clearly improper and discreditable, with the result that the investment has been subjected to unfair and inequitable treatment.[120]

In this respect, the *Waste Management* Tribunal, referring to the earlier *S. D. Myers*, *Mondev*, *ADF* and *Loewen* cases, identified the breach of the minimum standard in cases of conduct attributable to the host state as:

> arbitrary, grossly unfair, unjust or idiosyncratic, is discriminatory and exposes the claimant to sectional or racial prejudice, or involves a lack of due process leading to an outcome which offends judicial propriety – as might be the case with a manifest failure of natural justice in judicial proceedings or a complete lack of transparency and candour in an administrative process.[121]

Other arbitral tribunals have followed this line of reasoning, envisaging the customary minimum standard as evolving over time, for example,

---

T. Gazzini, 'The Role of Customary International Law in the Field of Foreign Investment', *Journal of World Investment and Trade* 8 (2007): 698–701; I. Tudor, *The Fair and Equitable Treatment Standard in the International Law of Foreign Investment* (Oxford University Press, 2008), pp. 67–85; C. McLachlan, 'Investment Treaties and General International Law', *International and Comparative Law Quarterly* 57 (2008): 380–3.

[120] *Mondev International Ltd* v. *United States*, ICSID Case No. ARB(AF)/99/2, Award, 11 October 2002, *IIC* 173 (2002), para. 127.

[121] *Waste Management, Inc.* v. *Mexico*, ICSID Case No. ARB(AF)/00/3, Award, 30 April 2004, *IIC* 270 (2004), para. 98. Similarly, *International Thunderbird Gaming Corporation* v. *Mexico*, *Ad hoc* UNCITRAL/NAFTA Rules, Award, 26 January 2006, *IIC* 136 (2006), para. 194. Cf. J. Stone, 'Arbitrariness, the Fair and Equitable Treatment Standard, and the International Law of Investment', *Leiden Journal of International Law* 25 (2012): 106: 'The value of arbitrariness as an individual basis for claim notwithstanding, an allegation of arbitrariness may also be useful in terms of buttressing a claim based on other elements of the fair and equitable treatment standard.'

not contemporarily requiring bad faith conduct so as to trigger a violation of fair and equitable treatment.[122]

Hence, the *ADF* Tribunal stated that 'both customary international law and the minimum standard of treatment of aliens it incorporates, are constantly in a process of development'.[123] According to the *Glamis* Award, while substantiating a change in the content of a customary norm is rather cumbersome, the minimum standard has been modified with regard to what today (as opposed to in 1926) is considered as 'shocking' and 'outrageous', despite the fact that the minimum standard as such does not appear to have moved beyond the *Neer* formulation.[124] In the same spirit, the *Merrill & Ring Forestry LP* v. *Canada* NAFTA Chapter Eleven Tribunal, when applying Article 1105 of the NAFTA, opined that:

> the applicable minimum standard of treatment of investors is found in customary international law and that, except for cases of safety and due process, today's minimum standard is broader than that defined in the *Neer* case and its progeny. Specifically this standard provides for the fair and equitable treatment of alien investors within the confines of reasonableness. The protection does not go beyond that required by customary law, as the FTC has emphasized. Nor, however, should protected treatment fall short of the customary law standard.[125]

Overall, a violation of the fair and equitable treatment standard, similarly to the international minimum standard for the treatment of aliens and WTO case law analysed earlier, essentially entails 'an outright and unjustified' repudiation of domestic regulation, evidenced by 'the record as a whole – not dramatic incidents in isolation'.[126] To use the words of the *AES* Tribunal, the fair and equitable treatment standard

---

[122] See, e.g., *Occidental* v. *Ecuador*, Award, para. 186; *Siemens AG* v. *Argentina*, ICSID Case No ARB/02/8, Award, 6 February 2007, *IIC* 227 (2007), para. 300; *Jan de Nul* v. *Egypt*, Award, para. 184.

[123] *ADF Group Inc* v. *United States*, ICSID Case No. ARB(AF)/00/1, Award, 9 January 2003, *IIC* 02 (2003), para. 179.

[124] *Glamis Gold Ltd* v. *United States*, Ad hoc UNCITRAL Arbitration Rules, Award, 8 June 2009, *IIC* 380 (2009), paras 611–16.

[125] *Merrill & Ring Forestry LP* v. *Canada*, Ad hoc UNCITRAL Arbitration Rules, Award, 31 March 2010, *IIC* 427 (2010), para. 173.

[126] *GAMI Investments, Inc.* v. *Mexico*, Ad hoc UNCITRAL Arbitration Rules, Final Award, 15 November 2004, *IIC* 109 (2004), para. 103. Cf. *Helnan International Hotels AS* v. *Egypt*, ICSID Case No. ARB/05/19, Decision on the Application for Annulment, 29 May 2010, *IIC* 440 (2010), para. 50: 'A single aberrant decision of a low-level official is unlikely to breach the standard unless the investor can demonstrate that it was part of

is not one of perfection. It is only when a state's acts or procedural omissions are, on the facts and in the context before the adjudicator, manifestly unfair or unreasonable (such as would shock, or at least surprise a sense of juridical propriety) ... that the standard can be said to have been infringed.[127]

Ergo, according to the grain of the practice of investment tribunals, fair and equitable treatment provisions in IIAs have been envisaged as encompassing,[128] *inter alia*, 'legal security', that is, 'the quality of the legal system which implies certainty in its norms and, consequently, their foreseeable application';[129] 'stability of the legal and business framework';[130] 'treatment in an even-handed and just manner';[131] failure to accord due process resulting in denial of justice;[132] transparency 'as a significant element for the protection of both the legitimate expectations of the Investor and the stability of the legal framework'.[133] It is perhaps mindful of this 'polyphony' of interpretations that the

a pattern of state conduct applicable to the case or that the investor took steps within the administration to achieve redress and was rebuffed in a way which compounded, rather than cured, the unfair treatment.'

[127] *AES Summit Generation Ltd and AES-Tisza Erömü Kft* v. *Hungary*, ICSID Case No. ARB/07/22, Award, 17 September 2010, *IIC* 455 (2010), para. 9.3.40.

[128] Cf. *Lemire* v. *Ukraine*, Decision on Jurisdiction and Liability, para. 258: 'An inquiry into the ordinary meaning of the expression "fair and equitable treatment" does not clarify the meaning of the concept. "Fair and equitable treatment" is a term of art, and any effort to decipher the ordinary meaning of the words used only leads to analogous terms of almost equal vagueness.'

[129] *Siemens* v. *Argentina*, Award, para. 303. Also, *LG&E Energy Corp. and others* v. *Argentina*, ICSID Case No. ARB 02/1, Decision on Liability, 3 October 2006, *IIC* 152 (2006), 46 *ILM* 36 (2007), para. 125.

[130] *Occidental* v. *Ecuador*, Award, para. 183. Similarly, *Duke Energy* v. *Ecuador*, Award, para. 338; *Continental* v. *Argentina*, Award, para. 258.

[131] *Azurix Corp.* v. *United States*, ICSID Case No. ARB/01/12, Award, 14 July 2006, *IIC* 24 (2006), para. 360.

[132] *Waguih Elie George Siag and Clorinda Vecchi* v. *Egypt*, ICSID Case No. ARB/05/15, Award, 11 May 2009, *IIC* 374 (2009), para. 452.

[133] *Plama Consortium* v. *Bulgaria*, Award, para. 178; See also, *Waguih* v. *Egypt*, Award, para. 450; *Rumeli* v. *Kazakhstan*, Award, para. 617; *Biwater* v. *Tanzania*, Award, and Concurring and Dissenting Opinion, para. 602; *Toto Costruzioni Generali SpA* v. *Lebanon*, ICSID Case No. ARB/07/12, Decision on Jurisdiction, 8 September 2009, *IIC* 391 (2009), paras 169–73; *EDF (Services) Ltd* v. *Romania*, ICSID Case No. ARB/05/13, Award, 2 October 2009, *IIC* 392 (2009), para. 286. See also C-S. Zoellner, 'Transparency: An Analysis of an Evolving Fundamental Principle in International Economic Law', *Michigan Journal of International Law* 27 (2005/6): 604–24. As the *Walter Bau* Tribunal explained, 'the Treaty promised FET and "legitimate expectations" come within FET's parameters'. *Walter Bau AG* v. *Thailand*, Ad hoc UNCITRAL Arbitration Rules, Award, 1 July 2009, *IIC* 429 (2009), para. 11.7.

Total v. *Argentina* favoured the conduct of 'a comparative analysis of what is considered generally fair or unfair conduct by domestic public authorities in respect of private firms and investors in domestic law' so as to ascertain the content of the fair and equitable treatment provision in the respective BIT.[134]

Lastly, a word of caution: one should always remain mindful of the fact that the international minimum standard is indeed a *minimum* standard.[135] It is, for example, the investor–claimant who bears the burden of exhausting all effective judicial remedies provided within the host state's legal system in order to successfully allege a denial of justice, as a violation of fair and equitable treatment, suffered,[136] apart from convincing the given investment tribunal that the high threshold of violation is met.

F   The WTO and IIA standards for the administration of domestic regulation as two sides of the customary 'coin'

In view of the discussion in the previous section, it is readily apparent that both the trade and the investment regimes have been influenced by the common customary 'core' of the international minimum standard that, independently of treaty dictates, benefits private parties in their dual capacity as foreign traders and investors. As the foregoing survey has demonstrated, WTO provisions prescribing minimum due process requirements in the administration of domestic trade regulation converge with the fair and equitable treatment protection afforded by IIAs. In the context of trade and investment disputes regarding the administration of domestic regulation, the international minimum standard as *lex generalis* could, then, possibly be relevant in the interpretation of the concordant (i.e., not conflicting) WTO or IIA provisions on minimum due process requirements as a 'relevant rule of international law'

---

[134] *Total SA* v. *Argentina*, ICSID Case No. ARB/04/1, Decision on Liability, 21 December 2010, *IIC* 484 (2010), para. 111.

[135] *Genin and others* v. *Estonia*, ICSID Case No. ARB/99/2, Award, 25 June 2001, *IIC* 10 (2001), para. 367.

[136] 'Failure' to exercise rights within a legal system or 'unwise' exercise of these rights do not constitute unfair and inequitable treatment, for in this case the investor would 'pass his own responsibility for the outcome to the administration of justice, and from there to the host State in international law'. *AMTO LLC* v. *Ukraine*, SCC Case No. 080/2005, Final Award, 26 March 2008, *IIC* 346 (2008), para. 76. Similarly, *Chevron Corporation and Texaco Petroleum Corporation* v. *Ecuador*, Interim Award, paras 234–5.

(applicable, as general custom, in the legal relations of all WTO members and IIA parties) under Article 31(3)(c) of the Vienna Convention on the Law of Treaties.[137] One could even wait to eventually see a WTO Panel ruling on a GATT, Article X:3 complaint, for example, to authoritatively refer not only to *lex generalis*, but also to the *lex specialis* from the investment protection regime, and vice versa.[138] Furthermore, and notwithstanding the distinct, in principle, objectives and operation of both disciplines, there exists room to argue that under the same set of facts parallel proceedings before the WTO panels as well as investment tribunals could be both and equally fruitful. Both deal with facets of administration of domestic regulation, both do not necessitate proof of bad faith on behalf of the domestic authorities, and both seek to establish minimum standards of treatment for foreign business.

To take the example of the *ADF* v. *USA* investment dispute in the NAFTA context: in this case the Canadian investor challenged on the basis, *inter alia*, of Article 1105(1) of the NAFTA the public procurement process by the Commonwealth of Virginia. The tribunal did not entertain the claim on a number of grounds: the relevant domestic content and performance requirements could not be characterised as 'idiosyncratic or aberrant and arbitrary', the legitimate expectations arising from US case law were unfounded and not based on any misleading representations by US officials, while there was no proof

---

[137] On Article 31()3(c), see, e.g., C. McLachlan, 'The Principle of Systemic Integration and Article 31(3)(c) of the Vienna Convention', *International and Comparative Law Quarterly* 54 (2005): 279. Still note that 'it is one thing to invoke a "relevant rule of international law applicable in the relations between the parties" to a treaty and (interpretatively) apply it so as to clarify the meaning of a treaty term, and quite another to *lato sensu* apply this other relevant rule independently of interpretation: the juridical results arising out of interpretative application are far more limited than those resulting from *lato sensu* application proper'. A. Gourgourinis, 'The Distinction between Interpretation and Application of Norms in International Adjudication', *Journal of International Dispute Settlement* 2 (2011): 51.

[138] While investment tribunals have not hesitated to authoritatively refer to WTO case law (e.g., see, among many instances, *Continental* v. *Argentina*, Award, para. 187, fn. 281; *Mobil Corporation Venezuela Holdings BV and others* v. *Venezuela*, ICSID Case No. ARB/07/27, Decision on Jurisdiction, 10 June 2010, *IIC* 435 (2010), para. 170), WTO panels and the Appellate Body appear rather reluctant to do so. In any case, a few examples of cross-citation may be found: see Appellate Body Report, *United States–Anti-Dumping Act of 1916*, WT/DS136/AB/R, WT/DS162/AB/R, adopted 26 September 2000, DSR 2000:X, 4793, para. 54, fn. 30; Appellate Body Report, *United States–Final Anti-Dumping Measures on Stainless Steel from Mexico*, WT/DS344/AB/R, adopted 20 May 2008, para. 160, fn. 313.

of discrimination in favour of other bidders situated in like circumstances.[139] The resemblance of the above criteria with those established by Articles X, XIX and XX of the plurilateral WTO Procurement Agreement[140] is striking, also in view of the overall panel and Appellate Body jurisprudence on minimum due process requirements for the administration of domestic trade regulations.

In essence, it would not be unfeasible to suggest that if the facts of the *ADF* case had been different, that is, in case of 'unfair', 'discriminatory' and 'partial' selection of suppliers in a procurement process in US territory, the option of WTO adjudication would also be open for Canada to challenge (possibly, successfully) under Article XXII of the plurilateral Procurement Agreement (the United States is also a member) the arbitrariness of the procurement process. Put differently, had there been a 'non-discriminatory, timely, transparent and effective and generally available' procedures for review of the relevant Commonwealth of Virginia measures, apart from the investor–state route under NAFTA chosen by *ADF*, the WTO adjudication route would also be open for Canada to challenge (possibly, successfully) under Article XXII of the plurilateral Procurement Agreement the arbitrariness of the procurement process.

Similarly, recall that according to the facts of the *Argentina–Hides and Leather* WTO dispute, under Argentinean customs laws, the representatives of the domestic Association of Industrial Producers of Leather, Leather Manufacturers and Related Products (ADICMA) were entitled, upon request, to be present in the export clearance process of bovine hides along with the individual exporters of hides and their customs clearance agents. The WTO Panel there found a violation of Article X:3 (a) of the GATT 1994 on the basis of the unreasonableness and the impartiality of the process: the only private parties with a relevant legal interest in the process were the domestic exporter (and his agent) and the foreign buyer. Conversely, the representatives of ADICMA would lack a specific legal interest in the case, but, moreover, they would have 'an adverse commercial interest' being competitors of the foreign buyers, so that obtaining access to otherwise confidential business information relating to the names of the exporters, prices and details of exporting deals, would run counter to due process and impartiality in the export

---

[139] *ADF* v. *USA*, Award, paras 188–91.
[140] Agreement on Government Procurement, Annex 4 of the Marrakesh Agreement, see WTO, *Legal Texts*, p. 383.

clearance process.[141] Assuming *arguendo* that the European buyers could qualify as investors under the Argentinean IIAs (which would not be unlikely, if, for instance, they maintained a subsidiary in Argentina), it would then appear that, apart from the WTO complaint launched by the EC (now EU), they themselves could resort to arbitration against Argentina; for they could also invoke, *inter alia*, the fair and equitable treatment protective standard that they enjoy as foreign investors on the basis of the same relevant facts, so as to challenge the clearance process and seek compensation for damage sustained because of the inherent impartiality of the process, and the detrimental flow of confidential information related to their business activities.

G   Conclusions

The present study has attempted to demonstrate how the provisions of WTO and investment law on the administration of domestic regulation, and more specifically the treatment afforded to foreign traders/investors, have both been influenced by the international minimum standard as two sides of the customary 'coin'. On the basis of the potential dual capacity of aliens as foreign traders or as investors in contemporary international economic law, this chapter discussed the international minimum standard of treatment of aliens as a 'floor' for the protection of foreign traders/investors vis-à-vis, on the one hand, due process standards regarding the administration of domestic regulation under WTO law, and, on the other hand, fair and equitable treatment standards prescribed by the various IIAs. The last section eventually suggested that a triangular normative relationship regarding the administration of domestic regulation between the customary rule as *lex generalis* and the provisions of the trade and investment regimes as *leges speciales* can be attained, thus enforcing the proposition advanced herein that, based on the same set of facts, investors can assume that they will prevail on a fair and equitable treatment claim if their country has earlier prevailed, for example, on a GATT, Article X:3 claim at the WTO, and vice versa.

---

[141] Panel Report, *Argentina–Hides and Leather*, paras 11.86–11.101. Further, see A. Alvarez-Jimenez, 'Emerging WTO Competition Jurisprudence and its Possibilities for Future Development', *Northwestern Journal of International Law and Business* 24 (2003/4): 480–5.

14

Are investment treaty standards flexible enough to meet the needs of developing countries?

URSULA KRIEBAUM*

I Introduction

UN Secretary General Kofi Annan opened his preface to the 2003 World Investment Report with the following statement:

> With its enormous potential to create jobs, raise productivity, enhance exports and transfer technology, foreign direct investment is a vital factor in the long-term economic development of the world's developing countries …
>
> While national policies are the most important consideration in attracting such investment and benefiting more from it, they are increasingly being affected by rule-making at the international level. The challenge is to find a development-oriented balance.[1]

There are multiple interactions between policy-making at the national level and international investment rules. These start with the definition of an 'investor' and an 'investment', which has an impact on the assets that are covered and therefore on the policy tools available for the host country to deal with particular types of investments.[2] They involve the issue of protection standards as well the clauses against expropriation without compensation and their interpretation. They end with different dispute settlement clauses, which are available in many different

---

* This contribution is based on a presentation at the conference in April 2011 on 'The Interaction of International Investment Law with Other Fields of Public International Law'. For a more comprehensive analysis of the relevance of economic and political conditions for the protection under investment treaties see: U. Kriebaum, 'The Relevance of Economic and Political Conditions for the Protection under Investment Treaties', *The Law and Practice of International Courts and Tribunals* 10 (2011): 383–404.

[1] UNCTAD, *World Investment Report 2003* (Geneva: UNCTAD, 2003), p. iii, available at: www.unctad.org/en/docs/wir2003light_en.pdf.

[2] See on the issue of development and investment, e.g.: D. A. Desierto, 'Development as an International Right: Investment in the New Trade-based IIAs', *Trade, Law and Development* 3 (2011): 296–333.

forms,[3] and have implications on the interplay between national and international methods of dispute settlement. Furthermore, interactions are possible not only between national and international policy-making, but also between the different fields of international law.

In recent years, with an ever increasing number of investment cases being brought before investor–state arbitral tribunals, the discussion about the balance between regulatory state functions and investor protection has gained momentum. Much of the debate in this context concerns indirect expropriation, especially in the form of regulatory takings, and how to balance the interests of investors and host states.[4] This discussion is often driven by developed countries that suddenly find themselves in the role of respondent. Developing countries and NGOs have argued that investment protection treaties do not satisfy the needs of developing countries.

It is inherent to some treaty standards, such as national treatment and most-favoured-nation (MFN), that the treatment that they ensure may vary: they depend upon standards granted to the host state's nationals or to investors from third states. By contrast, standards like

---

[3] For example, broad or narrow jurisdictional clauses, waiting periods, fork-in-the-road clauses, exhaustion of local remedies requirements, requirements to waive the further use of local remedies, etc.

[4] On indirect expropriation see, e.g., V. Lowe, 'Regulation or Expropriation?' *Current Legal Problems* 55 (2002): 447–66; R. Dolzer, 'Indirect Expropriations: New Developments?' *NYU Environmental Law Journal* 11 (2003): 64–93; W. M. Reisman and R. D. Sloane, 'Indirect Expropriation and its Valuation in the BIT Generation', *British Year Book of International Law* 74 (2003): 115–50; G. H. Sampliner, 'Arbitration of Expropriation Cases Under US Investment Treaties: A Threat to Democracy or the Dog That Didn't Bark?', *ICSID Review: Foreign Investment Law Journal* 18 (2003): 1–43; J. Paulsson and Z. Douglas, 'Indirect Expropriation in Investment Treaty Arbitration', in N. Horn and S. Kröll (eds), *Arbitrating Foreign Investment Disputes: Procedural and Substantive Legal Aspects* (The Hague: Kluwer Law, 2004), pp. 145–58; L. Y. Fortier and S. L. Drymer, 'Indirect Expropriation in the Law of International Investment: I Know It When I See It, or Caveat Investor', *ICSID Review: Foreign Investment Law Journal* 19 (2004): 293–327; D. Clough, 'Regulatory Expropriations and Compensation under NAFTA', *Journal of World Investment and Trade* 6 (2005): 553–84; A. Newcombe, 'The Boundaries of Regulatory Expropriation in International Law', *ICSID Review: Foreign Investment Law Journal* 20 (2005): 1–57; U. Kriebaum, 'Regulatory Takings: Balancing the Interests of the Investor and the State', *Journal of World Investment and Trade* 8 (2007): 717–44; S. Ratner, 'Regulatory Takings in Institutional Context: Beyond the Fear of Fragmented International Law', *American Journal of International Law* 102 (2008): 475–528; M. Paparinskis, 'Regulatory Expropriation and Sustainable Development', in M-C. Cordonier Segger and M. W. Gehring and A. Newcombe (eds), *Sustainable Development in World Investment Law* (Alphen aan den Rijn: Kluwer Law, 2011), pp. 299–327.

fair and equitable treatment (FET) and full protection and security provide fixed reference points.

The question arises as to whether these fixed reference points are the same for all states regardless of their level of development and their economic, social and political circumstances at the time of the investment.[5] Only the Investment Agreement for the Common Market for Eastern and Southern Africa (COMESA) Common Investment Area[6] in Africa provides explicitly for the taking into account of the different levels of development in certain investment protection standards such as fair and equitable treatment.[7]

The protection standards in investment law are flexible enough to take the different development standards across nations into account. Have tribunals made use of this flexibility? What are the advantages and disadvantages of allowing for such flexibility?

II The practice of investor–state arbitral tribunals

Most tribunals have not systematically examined the economic and political circumstances prevailing in host states when examining compliance with treaty standards. Only a limited number of tribunals have

---

[5] See N. Gallus, 'The Influence of the Host State's Level of Development on International Investment Treaty Standards of Protection', *Journal of World Investment and Trade* 6 (2005): 711–29; J. Tudor, *The Fair and Equitable Treatment Standard in the International Law of Foreign Investment* (Oxford University Press, 2008), pp. 127, 130, 131, 132, 150, 165, 223.

[6] See, e.g., Investment Agreement for the COMESA Common Investment Area 2007, Art. 14(3), available at: www.givengain.com/cause_data/images/1694/Investment_agreement_-for_the_CCIA.pdf. See also P. Muchlinski, 'The COMESA Common Investment Area: Substantive Standards and Procedural Problems in Dispute Settlement', SOAS School of Law Research Paper No. 11/2010, available at: http://papers.ssrn.com/sol3/papers.cfm?abstract_id=1698209; D. A. Desierto, 'Development as an International Right: Investment in the New Trade-based IIAs', *Trade, Law and Development* 3 (2011): 296, 324–7.

[7] Article 14 – Fair and Equitable Treatment: 1. Member States shall accord fair and equitable treatment to COMESA investors and their investments, in accordance with customary international law. Fair and equitable treatment includes the obligation not to deny justice in criminal, civil, or administrative adjudicatory proceedings in accordance with the principle of due process embodied in the principal legal systems of the world. 2. Paragraph 1 of this Article prescribes the customary international law minimum standard of treatment of aliens as the minimum standard of treatment to be afforded to covered investments and does not require treatment in addition to or beyond what is required by that standard. 3. For greater certainty, Member States understand that different Member States have different forms of administrative, legislative and judicial systems and that Member States at different levels of development may not achieve the same standards at the same time. Paragraphs 1 and 2 of this Article do not establish a single international standard in this context.

considered factors such as the level of development or political stability. In some cases economic and political conditions prevailing in the host state were discussed in a general way without being linked to a particular standard. At times, considerations of this kind have played a certain role in decisions that dealt with indirect expropriations. Most often tribunals have discussed these issues in the context of the fair and equitable treatment and the full protection and security standard.

Tribunals have considered these factors in two different phases of the arbitral proceedings: in some cases, tribunals have discussed economic and political conditions in their decisions on liability.[8] In these cases, the existence of a treaty violation depended, *inter alia*, on the particular circumstances of the state. In another group of cases, tribunals took these circumstances into consideration when they assessed the amount of compensation due for a violation of one or more of the investment protections standards.[9]

The cases in which tribunals took these factors into account in their decision on liability related to three different situations. One group of awards concerned ex-communist countries in transition.[10] Another group concerned host states confronted with economic and financial crises.[11] The third group involved host states with ongoing political disturbances.[12]

---

[8] *Genin, Eastern Credit Ltd, Inc. and A. S. Baltoil* v. *The Republic of Estonia*, Award, 25 June 2001, 6 *ICSID Reports* 241; *Olguín* v. *Republic of Paraguay*, Award, 26 July 2001, 6 *ICSID Reports* 164; *Nagel* v. *Czech Republic*, Award, 9 September 2003, 13 *ICSID Reports* 33; *Generation Ukraine Inc.* v. *Ukraine*, Award, 16 September 2003, 10 *ICSID Reports* 240; *LG&E Energy Corp.* v. *Argentine Republic*, Award, 3 October 2006; *Parkerings* v. *Lithuania*, Award, 11 September 2007; *Duke Energy Electroquil Partners & Electroquil S.A.* v. *Republic of Ecuador*, Award, 18 August 2008; *Continental Casualty* v. *Argentina*, Award, 5 September 2008; *Pantechniki* v. *Albania*, Award, 30 July 2009; *Bayindir Insaat Turizm Ticaret ve Sanayi* v. *Pakistan*, Award, 27 August 2009; *Toto* v. *Lebanon*, Decision on Jurisdiction, 11 September 2009.

[9] *American Manufacturing & Trading, Inc.* v. *Republic of Zaire*, Award, 21 February 1997, 5 *ICSID Reports* 14; *CMS Gas Transmission Company* v. *Argentine Republic*, Award, 12 May 2005.

[10] *Genin, Eastern Credit Ltd, Inc. and A. S. Baltoil* v. *The Republic of Estonia*, Award, 25 June 2001, 6 *ICSID Reports* 241; *Nagel* v. *Czech Republic*, Award, 9 September 2003, 13 *ICSID Reports* 33; *Generation Ukraine Inc.* v. *Ukraine*, Award, 16 September 2003, 10 *ICSID Reports* 240; *Parkerings* v. *Lithuania*, Award, 11 September 2007.

[11] *Olguín* v. *Republic of Paraguay*, Award, 26 July 2001, 6 *ICSID Reports* 164; *LG&E Energy Corp.* v. *Argentine Republic*, Award, 3 October 2006; *Duke Energy Electroquil Partners & Electroquil SA* v. *Republic of Ecuador*, Award, 18 August 2008; *Continental Casualty* v. *Argentina*, Award, 5 September 2008.

[12] *Bayindir Insaat Turizm Ticaret ve Sanayi* v. *Pakistan*, Award, 27 August 2009; *Toto* v. *Lebanon*, Decision on Jurisdiction, 11 September 2009; *Pantechniki* v. *Albania*, Award, 30 July 2009.

A   *The impact of the host state's level of development on liability*

1   Ex-communist countries in transition

A number of cases were directed against countries that had made a recent transition from communist centrally planned economies to democratic market-oriented systems. Tribunals took this fact into account either in general remarks or as part of their analysis of the individual protection standards. When they discussed it in connection with an individual standard they often linked it to the legitimate expectations of the investor.

The tribunal in *Genin* v. *Estonia*[13] is an example of the first approach. Before assessing the individual standards of protection contained in the bilateral investment treaty (BIT), it made some general remarks about the fact that Estonia was a country in transition from a communist to a market economy. It found that shortcomings in administrative procedures did not lead to a violation of FET, which it considered to be a minimum standard.

The tribunal in *Parkerings* v. *Lithuania*[14] did not find a violation of FET despite a lack of predictability of the legal environment.[15] The tribunal held that the investor had not been deprived of any legitimate expectations leading to a breach of the fair and equitable treatment standard.[16] The tribunal pointed out that Lithuania was a country in transition:

> 335 ... At the time of the Agreement, the political environment in Lithuania was characteristic of a country in transition from its past being part of the Soviet Union to candidate for the European Union membership. Thus, legislative changes, far from being unpredictable, were in fact

---

[13] *Genin, Eastern Credit Ltd, Inc. and A. S. Baltoil* v. *The Republic of Estonia*, Award, 25 June 2001, 6 *ICSID Reports* 241; See also paras 348 and 358: 'No notice was ever transmitted to EIB to warn that its licence was in danger of revocation unless certain corrective measures were taken, and no opportunity was provided to EIB to make representations in that regard.'

[14] *Parkerings-Compagniet AS* v. *Lithuania*, Award, 11 September 2007.

[15] The tribunal in *Kardassopoulos and Fuchs* v. *Georgia*, Award, 3 March 2010, did not consider the economic and political circumstances prevailing in the host state even though the host state invoked the economic and political situation prevailing in the country and expressly relied on the award in *Parkerings* for that purpose (para. 420).

[16] *Parkerings-Compagniet AS* v. *Lithuania*, paras 306, 335, 338, 345, 346: '306. ... In fact, it would have been foolish for a foreign investor in Lithuania to believe, at that time, that it would be proceeding on stable legal ground, as considerable changes in the Lithuanian political regime and economy were undergoing.'

to be regarded as likely … The circumstances surrounding the decision to invest in Lithuania were certainly not an indication of stability of the legal environment. Therefore, in such a situation, no expectation that the laws would remain unchanged was legitimate.[17]

2   Host states in economic crisis

In cases involving Latin American countries suffering from economic crises some tribunals seem to have been influenced in their decisions on the legitimacy of investors' expectations by the condition of the economies of the host countries.[18] Here again, tribunals used legitimate expectations as a trigger mechanism to take the host state's economic and social situation into consideration. Two examples are discussed below.

In *LG&E* v. *Argentina*[19] the tribunal found that an unspecified reduced FET standard was applicable. However, even that reduced standard had not been met by Argentina.[20]

The tribunal in *Duke Energy* v. *Ecuador*[21] linked the stability requirement for the legal and business environment in the host state directly to the justified expectations of the investor.[22] It found that the political, social and economic conditions prevailing in the host state have to be taken into account when assessing the reasonableness of the investor's expectations.[23] Nevertheless, the tribunal found a violation of the fair and equitable treatment clause of the treaty.

---

[17] *Parkerings-Compagniet AS* v. *Lithuania*, para. 335.
[18] *Olguín* v. *Republic of Paraguay*, Award, 26 July 2001, 6 *ICSID Reports* 164, paras 65, 70, 75; *LG&E Energy Corp.* v. *Argentine Republic*, Decision on Liability, 3 October 2006, para. 139; *Continental Casualty* v. *Argentina*, Award, 5 September 2008.
[19] *LG&E Energy Corp.* v. *Argentine Republic*, Decision on Liability, 3 October 2006.
[20] *LG&E.* v. *Argentina*, para. 139: 'Certainly, LG&E was aware of the risks inherent in investing in a foreign State. But here, the Tribunal is of the opinion that Argentina went too far by completely dismantling the very legal framework constructed to attract investors.'
[21] *Duke Energy Electroquil Partners & Electroquil SA* v. *Republic of Ecuador*, Award, 18 August 2008.
[22] *Duke Energy* v. *Ecuador*, para. 340.
[23] *Duke Energy* v. *Ecuador*, para. 340 (footnotes omitted): 'To be protected, the investor's expectations must be legitimate and reasonable at the time when the investor makes the investment. The assessment of the reasonableness or legitimacy must take into account all circumstances, including not only the facts surrounding the investment, but also the political, socioeconomic, cultural and historical conditions prevailing in the host State. In addition, such expectations must arise from the conditions that the State offered the investor and the latter must have relied upon them when deciding to invest.'

The same approach was adopted by the tribunal in *El Paso* v. *Argentina*.[24] It held that the fair and equitable treatment standard involves considerations of reasonableness and proportionality, and that due regard has to be given to all surrounding circumstances:[25]

> There can be no legitimate expectation for anyone that the legal framework will remain unchanged in the face of an extremely severe economic crisis. No reasonable investor can have such an expectation unless very specific commitments have been made towards it or unless the alteration of the legal framework is total.[26]

The tribunal still found a violation of the fair and equitable treatment clause of the treaty.

In *National Grid* v. *Argentina*[27] the tribunal rejected Argentina's plea of necessity, but took the difficult economic circumstances under which Argentina had implemented the measures at issue into account.[28] As a consequence, it found that Argentina was not liable for losses incurred by *National Grid* during the first six months of the crisis.

These cases show that some arbitral tribunals were prepared to consider the economic situation of the host states, especially when assessing the legitimacy of investors' expectations.

3   Ongoing political disturbances in host states

Two tribunals, *Bayindir* v. *Pakistan*[29] and *Toto* v. *Lebanon*,[30] were confronted with ongoing political disturbances in host states. Both tribunals denied the reasonableness of expectations given the political

---

[24] *El Paso Energy International Company* v. *Argentina*, Award, 31 October 2011.
[25] *El Paso* v. *Argentina*, para. 373.   [26] *El Paso* v. *Argentina*, para. 374.
[27] *National Grid* v. *Argentina*, Award, 3 November 2008.
[28] *National Grid* v. *Argentina*, paras 179, 180: '180. ... The Tribunal's conclusion that the Respondent has been in breach of the Treaty [FET] cannot ignore the context in which the Measures were taken. The determination of the Tribunal must take into account all the circumstances and in so doing cannot be oblivious to the crisis that the Argentine Republic endured at that time. What is fair and equitable is not an absolute parameter. What would be unfair and inequitable in normal circumstances may not be so in a situation of an economic and social crisis. The investor may not be totally insulated from situations such as the ones the Argentine Republic underwent in December 2001 and the months that followed. For these reasons, the Tribunal concludes that the breach of the fair and equitable treatment standard did not occur at the time the Measures were taken on January 6, 2002 but on June 25, 2002 when the Respondent required that companies such as the Claimant renounce to the legal remedies they may have recourse as a condition to re-negotiate the Concession' (footnote omitted).
[29] *Bayindir Insaat Turizm Ticaret ve Sanayi A.S.* v. *Pakistan*, Award, 27 August 2009.
[30] *Toto* v. *Lebanon*, Decision on Jurisdiction, 11 September 2009.

circumstances prevailing in the host states. They did so when evaluating the reasonableness and legitimacy of investors' expectations with regard to the functioning of the executive and judicial systems and the stability of legislation in these states. *Bayindir* v. *Pakistan* concerns the functioning of the executive under circumstances of rapidly changing governments with opposing views on the investment project. In such a situation an investor cannot expect stable and predictable decision-making on the part of the government.[31] In *Toto* v. *Lebanon* the tribunal said that in a situation of severe political disturbances an investor cannot expect a smooth functioning of the judiciary.[32] Furthermore, the tribunal held in its award on the merits that in a post-civil war situation an investor does not have a legitimate expectation that tax laws and customs duties would not be changed:

> the post-civil war situation in Lebanon, with substantial economic challenges and colossal reconstruction efforts, did not justify legal expectations that custom duties would remain unchanged.[33]

The approach in *Pantechniki* v. *Albania*[34] was different. In that case the Greek investor sought to recover losses sustained during the widespread civil strife that shook Albania in 1997. In commenting on the relevance of the level of development of a host state, the sole arbitrator addressed the issue not in the context of fair and equitable treatment, but with regard to full protection and security. He drew a distinction between denial of justice and protection against violence. The threshold for a denial of justice should be absolute and not be influenced by a host state's level of development. By contrast, protection against physical violence would depend on the state's resources. The sole arbitrator, Paulsson, concluded that 'the Albanian authorities were powerless in the face of social unrest

---

[31] *Bayindir Insaat Turizm Ticaret ve Sanayi A.S.* v. *Pakistan*, Award, 27 August 2009, paras 192–5, 197–9: '192. A second question concerns the circumstances that the Tribunal must take into account in analyzing the reasonableness or legitimacy of Bayindir's expectations at the time of the revival of the Contract. In doing so, it finds guidance in prior decisions ... which relied on "all circumstances, including not only the facts surrounding the investment, but also the political, socioeconomic, cultural and historical conditions prevailing in the host State." 197. ... in the light of the political changes of the preceding years, the Claimant could not reasonably expect that no further political changes would occur ... 199. Therefore, the Tribunal is of the opinion that Bayindir's claim relating to the frustration of its legitimate expectations cannot be sustained' (footnotes omitted).

[32] *Toto* v. *Lebanon*, Decision on Jurisdiction, 11 September 2009, paras 139–44.

[33] *Toto* v. *Lebanon*, Award, 7 June 2012, para. 245.

[34] *Pantechniki* v. *Albania*, Award, 30 July 2009.

of this magnitude'.[35] He stated that protection against physical violence emanating from private sources would have to be judged differently with respect to a powerful state and one that is poor and fragile. The sole arbitrator denied a violation of the full protection and security standard given the general situation prevailing in the country. He added that his assessment of the claim might have been different in the presence of police refusing to intervene.[36]

B   The impact of the host state's level of development on compensation

Another approach to taking the host state's development into account is to do so in the decision on compensation by awarding reduced damages. Some tribunals, having found a violation of substantive standards, took account of the host states' state of development or economic, social and political circumstances in their decisions on the amount of compensation. Such was the case, for example, in *AMT* v. *Zaire*[37] and *CMS* v. *Argentina*.[38]

In *AMT* v. *Zaire* the investor had incurred losses as a result of looting and destruction of its property during riots and acts of violence. The tribunal found Zaire responsible for failing to fulfil its obligation of protection and security.[39] It did not mention that the difficult security situation would alter the standard of full protection and security as applied to Zaire. However, when calculating compensation the tribunal took the unstable political and business environment into account. It held that especially lost profits and interest could not be awarded in the same manner as if the investment had been made in a country with a stable investment environment.[40]

In *CMS Gas Transmission Company* v. *Argentina*[41] the respondent had given guarantees for price adjustments for the transportation of natural gas in various legal instruments. Subsequently, during the economic crisis Argentina first suspended and then terminated these guarantees. The tribunal referred to the economic situation of the country when

---

[35] *Pantechniki* v. *Albania*, para. 82.   [36] *Pantechniki* v. *Albania*, para. 82.
[37] *American Manufacturing & Trading, Inc.* v. *Republic of Zaire*, Award, 21 February 1997, 5 *ICSID Reports* 14, para. 7.17.
[38] *CMS Gas Transmission Company* v. *Argentina*, Award, 12 May 2005, available at: http://ita.law.uvic.ca/ documents/CMS_FinalAward.pdf.
[39] *AMT* v. *Zaire*, paras 6.04–6.11.   [40] *AMT* v. *Zaire*, paras 7.14, 7.15.
[41] *CMS Gas Transmission Company* v. *Argentina* , Award, 12 May 2005, available at: http://ita.law.uvic.ca/ documents/CMS_FinalAward.pdf.

assessing the fair and equitable treatment standard. It found that the crisis in and of itself was not severe enough to exclude liability or to preclude the wrongfulness of Argentina's measure. However, the tribunal decided to consider the crisis when determining the amount of compensation. It discussed how to 'weigh the significance of a legal guarantee in the context of a collapsing economic situation'.[42] It adopted a balanced approach, and held that while the economic circumstances do not eliminate the requirement to comply with the law they 'do have a perceptible influence on the manner in which the law can be applied'.[43] It found that both parties to the dispute should share some of the costs of the crisis in a reasonable manner.[44] 'While not excusing liability or precluding wrongfulness from the legal point of view they [certain consequences stemming from the crisis] ought nevertheless to be considered by the Tribunal when determining compensation.'[45]

III   Concluding remarks

Confronted with a need to take into account the special situation prevailing in a developing country, a tribunal should first investigate whether it can do so in the decision on liability by using the existing flexibility in the substantive standards. If this is not possible, it can still address this need at the level of compensation.

Standards like fair and equitable treatment and full protection and security provide fixed reference points. But they are not inherently inflexible with regard to the economic and political situation prevailing in the host state. Fair and equitable treatment allows for a balance between investment protection and the host state's public interest. One of the tools to achieve this is the concept of legitimate expectations.[46]

---

[42] *CMS Gas* v. *Argentina*, para. 165.   [43] *CMS Gas* v. *Argentina*, para. 240.
[44] *CMS Gas* v. *Argentina*, para. 248.   [45] *CMS Gas* v. *Argentina*, para. 356.l.
[46] Generally on the significance of legitimate expectations, see: C. Schreuer, 'Fair and Equitable Treatment in Arbitral Practice', *Journal of World Investment and Trade* 6 (2005): 357, at pp. 374–80; E. Snodgrass, 'Protecting Investors' Legitimate Expectations: Recognizing and Delimiting a General Principle', *ICSID Review: Foreign Investment Law Journal* 21 (2006): 1; S. Fietta, 'The "Legitimate Expectations" Principle under Article 1105 NAFTA – International Thunderbird Gaming Corporation v. The United Mexican States', *Journal of World Investment and Trade* 7 (2006): 423; A. Walter, 'The Investor's Expectations in International Investment Arbitration', in A. Reinisch and Ch. Knahr (eds), *International Investment Law in Context* (The Hague: Eleven International Publishing, 2008), p. 173; C. Brown, 'The Protection of Legitimate Expectations as a "General Principle of Law": Some Preliminary Thoughts', *Transnational Dispute Management*,

On the other hand, going too far with a relativistic approach would act as a disincentive to progress in fields like good governance and the rule of law. Development could raise the demands on the countries concerned and would hence punish them for making progress in economic and political affairs. States that do not strive for good governance and the implementation of the rule of law would be measured against lower standards than countries that try to live up to those principles.

Therefore, as indicated in *Pantechniki*, there should be no flexibility with regard to denial of justice. Due process standards, such as the right to be heard or to an independent and impartial judiciary, should not depend on the economic or political situation prevailing in a country. The situation might be different with regard to delay of procedures unless this amounts to a denial of justice.

With regard to full protection and security: violence stemming from state organs or a refusal to intervene on the part of the official forces to stop violence by private groups is not subject to the mitigating effect of the host state's stage of development. The situation is different in the case of violence emanating from a private source where the state is incapable of putting an end to the violence because of a lack of resources.

January 2008; I. Tudor, *The Fair and Equitable Treatment Standard in the International Law of Foreign Investment* (Oxford University Press, 2008), p. 163. Tudor argues, however, that the balancing should take place exclusively at the compensation phase (p. 205).

15

Relevance of the host state's development status in investment treaty arbitration

MARIA GRITSENKO*

I Introduction

The purpose of this contribution is to provide a brief overview of the recent decisions dealing with the host state's development status in the context of investment treaty arbitrations. Indeed, certain states have attempted to invoke circumstances arising from their 'underdeveloped' or 'developing' status as part of their defence against investor claims. The expressions 'level of development' or 'development status' are used here as including not only the economic development, but also the political and legal conditions prevailing in developing countries. Indeed, there is no universally acceptable definition of a 'developing' country; for the purposes of this chapter we would roughly adopt the classification of the UN Statistical Office,[1] with the addition of the so-called 'economies in transition'.

In general public international law, the International Court of Justice (ICJ) seems to have settled the matter in its *Continental Shelf* decision (*Libya* v. *Malta*), when it declined to take into account the different economic positions of the states for the purposes of delimiting

---

* Any views expressed in this chapter are personal to the author and do not purport to represent those of the Skadden, Arps, Slate, Meagher & Flom (UK) LLP.
[1] According to the UN Statistical Office, 'there is no established convention for the designation of "developed" and "developing" countries or areas in the United Nations system. In common practice, Japan in Asia, Canada and the United States in northern America, Australia and New Zealand in Oceania, and Europe are considered "developed" regions or areas. In international trade statistics, the Southern African Customs Union is also treated as a developed region and Israel as a developed country; countries emerging from the former Yugoslavia are treated as developing countries; and countries of eastern Europe and of the Commonwealth of Independent States (code 172) in Europe are not included under either developed or developing regions [those are considered by the United Nations as 'economies in transition'].' See 'Composition of Macro Geographical (continental) Regions, Geographical Sub-regions, and Selected Economic and other Groupings', revised 20 September 2011, available at: http://unstats.un.org/unsd/methods/m49/m49regin.htm#ftnc, accessed 28 June 2012.

continental shelf, stating that 'such considerations are totally unrelated to the underlying intentions of the applicable rules of international law'.[2]

In international investment law, however, several arbitral decisions have suggested that the respondent state's level of development could affect the application of the bilateral investment treaty (BIT) provisions at all main stages of arbitral proceedings: jurisdiction, merits and damages.

II   Jurisdiction of the tribunal

The jurisdiction phase may not be the obvious stage where one would look at how developed the host state is; such considerations are unlikely to come into play when considering jurisdiction *ratione temporis* or *ratione personae*. This analysis may, however, become relevant for the purposes of finding jurisdiction *ratione materiae*, in particular, for arbitrations initiated under the Convention on the Settlement of Investment Disputes between States and Nationals of Other States (ICSID Convention).

Indeed, some ICSID tribunals, for the purposes of determining whether an investment has been made, have adopted the so-called *Salini* test, which was first stated in the *Salini* v. *Morocco* case and since then reiterated, sometimes with slight variations, in a number of awards. This test requires the arbitrators to look at the following criteria: a contribution, certain duration of the operation, a risk and a contribution to the host state's development.[3] This last criterion is potentially significant in terms of the interplay between international development and investment treaty law. The 'contribution to development' condition, however, has been subject to heavy criticism in recent awards, and several tribunals have declined to take it into consideration when ruling on the existence of an investment.[4]

---

[2] *Continental Shelf (Libya v. Malta)*, 1985 ICJ 13, at p. 41. The ICJ went on to declare that 'It is clear that neither rules determining the validity of legal entitlement to the continental shelf, nor those concerning delimitations between neighbouring countries, leave room for any considerations of economic development of the States in question.'

[3] *Salini Costruttori SpA and Italstrade SpA* v. *Kingdom of Morocco*, ICSID Case No. ARB/00/4, Decision on Jurisdiction, 31 July 2001, para. 52.

[4] *Saba Fakes* v. *Republic of Turkey*, ICSID Case No. ARB/07/20, Award, 12 July 2010, para. 111; *Phoenix Action Ltd* v. *Czech Republic*, ICSID Case No. ARB/06/5, Award, 15 April 2009, para. 85.

Another element of the *Salini* test that is relevant for our purposes is the requirement of 'risk' to be assumed by the investor. In *Alpha Projectholding GmbH* v. *Ukraine*,[5] the tribunal was faced with a dispute arising out of certain commercial arrangements involving the renovation of a hotel against monthly payments. The ownership of the hotel changed hands and payments to the claimant were suspended. The respondent state argued that the investment did not satisfy the *Salini* criteria and, in particular, that the claimant had not assumed any risk when entering into the venture with the hotel.

In response, the claimant emphasised the inherent riskiness of the venture, noting that, especially in light of the turmoil in Ukraine in the years following the collapse of the Soviet Union, there was no guarantee that the joint activities would realise returns. Although the tribunal did not specifically rely on the *Salini* test, it agreed that claimant's participation in the venture with the hotel carried commercial risks:

> The Claimant was investing in Ukraine at a time of great political, legal and commercial uncertainty. Ukraine's economy was experiencing negative growth, and the Hotel could not find other investors apart from Alpha. All of these elements demonstrate the riskiness of Claimant's investments.[6]

At this stage of the proceedings, the 'developing' status actually appears to facilitate the finding of jurisdiction against the state by an ICSID tribunal and therefore plays to the state's disadvantage. However, it is worth noting that the finding above did not prevent the *Alpha* tribunal from ruling that the claimant 'did possess a legitimate expectation that the government would not interfere with the contractual relationship between Claimant and the Hotel, and that the agreements would be honoured'.[7] The claimant therefore prevailed in its claims on the merits.

III Merits of the case

At the merits stage, the host state's developing status has most often been considered when assessing an investor's legitimate expectations or an alleged failure by the state to ensure full security and protection. The arbitrators, however, have not been consistent in their approach.

---

[5] *Alpha Projectholding GmbH* v. *Ukraine*, ICSID Case No. ARB/07/16, Award, 8 November 2010.
[6] *Alpha* v. *Ukraine*, paras 319–20.   [7] *Alpha* v. *Ukraine*, para. 422.

A   Legitimate expectations

Legitimate expectations of an investor are key when analysing potential breaches by the state of the fair and equitable treatment standard or of prohibition of expropriation without compensation. This is precisely the context where we find most cases involving discussion of the conditions prevailing in a developing state. Indeed, it is often argued that the host state's stage of development is particularly relevant when assessing the investor's legitimate expectations; that is, the foreign investor's expectations should vary depending on the host state's resources and experience in implementing its policies.

1   Host state's developing status as part of legitimate expectations

The legitimacy of an investor's expectations has been frequently evaluated against various factors relating to the host state's 'level of development'.

For example, in *Alex Genin* v. *Estonia*,[8] a case relating to the revocation of a bank licence, the tribunal criticised the revocation process, but noted that:

> it considered it imperative to recall the particular context in which the dispute arose, namely, that of a renascent independent state, coming rapidly to grips with the reality of modern financial, commercial and banking practices and the emergence of state institutions responsible for overseeing and regulating areas of activity perhaps previously unknown. This is the context in which Claimants knowingly chose to invest in an Estonian financial institution, EIB.[9]

The tribunal in *X* v. *Central European Republic*[10] dismissed the claim for other reasons, but also noted, in relation to the factual background, that Mr X may 'not have taken sufficient account that the country was still in a state of transition, in which the Government and public authorities were labouring to develop the newly born democratic system and to create a well-functioning market economy'.[11]

---

[8] *Alex Genin, Eastern Credit Limited, Inc. and A. S. Baltoil* v. *Republic of Estonia*, ICSID Case No. ARB/99/2, Award, 25 June 2001.

[9] *Alex Genin* v. *Estonia*, para. 348.

[10] *X* v. *Central European Republic*, SCC Case 49/2002, Award, 2003, reprinted in Stockholm Arbitration Report, 2004, pp. 161, 179.

[11] Stockholm Arbitration Report, 2004, p. 156.

According to the *Duke* v. *Ecuador*[12] tribunal, the reasonableness and legitimacy of the investor's expectations must be assessed by taking into account 'all circumstances, including not only the facts surrounding the investment, but also the political, socioeconomic, cultural and historical conditions prevailing in the host State'.[13]

In *Generation Ukraine* v. *Ukraine*,[14] a dispute arising out of the state's alleged interference with a construction project, the arbitrators considered 'the vicissitudes of the economy of the state' and specifically noted the speculative character of the claimant's investment: 'The Claimant was attracted to the Ukraine because of the possibility of earning a rate of return on its capital in significant excess to the other investment opportunities in more developed economies. The Claimant thus invested in the Ukraine on notice of both the prospects and the potential pitfalls. Its investment was speculative.'[15]

Any 'bureaucratic incompetence' would have to be measured against the claimant obtaining 'a leasehold over a prime property in central Kiev without even participating in a tender'. The tribunal therefore concluded that failure of the state administration to produce revised lease agreements did not amount to an indirect expropriation.

A number of further holdings were made in the context of an economic crisis, but their reasoning remains relevant for the purposes of the present study as well. For example, the *Olguín* v. *Paraguay*[16] tribunal felt 'that prudence would have prompted a foreigner arriving in a country that had suffered severe economic problems to be much more conservative in his investments'.[17] The claims were denied because the claimant must have been aware of the situation in Paraguay, and it was not reasonable to seek compensation for the losses on a speculative, or at best, a not very prudent investment.

In *AWG* v. *Argentina*,[18] the tribunal examined the claimant's expectations from an 'objective and reasonable point of view', declaring that the

[12] *Duke Energy Electroquil Partners and Electroquil SA* v. *Ecuador*, ICSID Case No. ARB/04/19, Award, 18 August 2008.
[13] *Duke* v. *Ecuador*, para. 340.
[14] *Generation Ukraine, Inc.* v. *Ukraine*, ICSID Case No. ARB/00/9, Award, 16 September 2003.
[15] *Generation Ukraine* v. *Ukraine*, para. 20.37.
[16] *Olguín* v. *Paraguay*, ICSID Case No. ARB/98/5, Award, 26 July 2001.
[17] *Olguín* v. *Paraguay*, para. 75.
[18] *AWG Group Ltd* v. *Argentina*, UNCITRAL Arbitration Rules, Award, 30 July 2010.

state was required to respect only those expectations that are 'legitimate and reasonable in the circumstances'.[19] 'In the circumstances' meant taking into account the country's history and its political, economic and social conditions.[20]

None of the above rulings, however, was based on the definition of a 'developing country' as such (according to either UN or other classification); the arbitrators in these cases have instead integrated in their analysis various characteristics (mostly economic) specific to developing countries.

2   Awards disregarding the respondent state's developing status

It is worth noting from the outset that a large number of awards rendered against developing countries did not include a discussion on how the host country's stage of development could be a possible justification for not performing its obligations vis-à-vis foreign investors.[21]

In *GAMI* v. *Mexico*,[22] the tribunal had to deal with a dispute arising out of GAMI's investment in Mexican sugar mills and Mexican regulation of the sugar cane industry. Mexico adopted a view to which many developing countries would subscribe, and argued that proper implementation of the regulation was too difficult in light of the country's circumstances. The tribunal rejected the Mexican defence in the following terms:

> The duty of NAFTA tribunals is rather to appraise whether and how pre-existing laws and regulations are applied to the foreign investor. It is no excuse that regulation is costly. Nor does a dearth of able administrators or a deficient culture of compliance provide a defence. Such is the challenge of governance that confronts every country. Breaches of NAFTA are assuredly not to be excused on the grounds that a government's compliance with its own law may be difficult. Each NAFTA Party

---

[19] *AWG* v. *Argentina*, para. 229.   [20] *AWG* v. *Argentina*, para. 228.

[21] *American Manufacturing & Trading, Inc.* v. *Zaire*, ICSID Case No. ARB/93/1, Award and Separate Opinion, 11 February 1997; *SwemBalt AB* v. *Latvia*, UNCITRAL Arbitration Rules, Award, 23 October 2000; *MTD Equity Sdn Bhd and MTD Chile SA* v. *Chile*, ICSID Case No. ARB/01/7, Award, 25 May 2004; *Técnicas Medioambientales Tecmed SA* v. *Mexico*, ICSID Case No. ARB(AF)/00/2, Award, 29 May 2003; *Metalclad Corporation* v. *The United Mexican States*, ICSID Case No. ARB(AF)/97/1, Award, 30 August 2000.

[22] *GAMI Investments, Inc.* v. *Mexico*, UNCITRAL Arbitration Rules, Final Award, 15 November 2004.

must to the contrary accept liability if its officials fail to implement or implement regulations in a discriminatory or arbitrary fashion.[23]

There are also limits to the acceptance by tribunals of 'the political, socio-economic, cultural and historical conditions prevailing in the host State' (as directed in the *Duke Energy* v. *Ecuador* Award). For example, in *World Duty Free* v. *Kenya*, the claimant alleged that 'donations' to the president were 'routine practice', which had 'cultural roots' and were 'regarded as a matter of protocol by the Kenyan people'. The tribunal was unmoved by these arguments and plainly considered such payments to be bribes which stripped the resulting investment of the BIT protections.[24]

In *Tokios Tokelés*[25] and *Lemire*,[26] there was no express rejection of the 'developing status' argument. However, the arbitrators, after portraying the developing background of the respondent state, did not consider the implications thereof when assessing whether Ukraine breached its obligations under the investment treaties. The *Tokios Tokelés* v. *Ukraine* decision, in particular, described the political background and economic situation in Ukraine at some length, but did not expressly consider these factors when assessing whether Ukraine had breached its obligations.

In *Lemire* v. *Ukraine*, the tribunal noted an admission by Ukraine that 'in the initial years of independence, constant political battles and economic instability caused a lack of coordination in the activities of state bodies and hampered their ability to create an effective system of government'.[27] The tribunal nevertheless held that 'on a general level, Claimant could expect a regulatory system for the broadcasting industry which was to be consistent, transparent, fair, reasonable, and enforced without arbitrary or discriminatory decisions'.[28]

In *Pantechniki* v. *Albania*,[29] the sole arbitrator heard a dispute arising out of riots damaging a road works project and the government's failure to pay the agreed compensation. The decision contains an *obiter dictum* suggesting that states would not be held liable for denial of justice because of their lack of resources, but as a result of assessment of 'the

---

[23] *GAMI* v. *Mexico*, para. 94.
[24] *World Duty Free Company Ltd* v. *Kenya*, ICSID Case No. ARB/00/7, Award, 25 September 2006, paras 110, 120.
[25] *Tokios Tokelés* v. *Ukraine*, ICSID Case No. ARB/02/18, Award, 26 July 2007.
[26] *Lemire* v. *Ukraine*, ICSID Case No. ARB/06/18, Decision on Jurisdiction, 14 January 2010.
[27] *Lemire* v. *Ukraine*, para. 239.   [28] *Lemire* v. *Ukraine*, para. 267.
[29] *Pantechniki SA Contractors and Engineers* v. *Albania*, ICSID Case No. ARB/07/21, Award, 30 July 2009.

human factor of obedience to the rule of law'. Foreign investors in any country are entitled to a 'decision-making which [is] neither xenophobic nor arbitrary'. The arbitrator further expressed a view that assessing a state's compliance with international law on an ad hoc basis, given its capacity at a particular moment of its development, would procure no incentive for that state to improve.[30]

B   Full protection and security

Arguably, the *Pantechniki* v. *Albania* Award did not apply the reasoning above to the full protection and security claims. It is generally accepted that full security and protection entails an obligation of due diligence by the state as 'as reasonable under circumstances'.[31]

The arbitrator in *Pantechniki* held that the standard of due diligence is a 'modified objective standard' depending on the circumstances and resources of the state in question.[32] As stated in Newcombe and Paradell

---

[30] See *Pantechniki* v. *Albania*, para. 76: 'This issue recalls a similar problem that arises with respect to claims of denial of justice. Should a state's international responsibility bear some proportion to its resources? Should a poor country be held accountable to a minimum standard which it could attain only at great sacrifice while a rich country would have little difficulty in doing so? No such proportionality factor has been generally accepted with respect to denial of justice. Two reasons appear salient. The first is that international responsibility does not relate to physical infrastructure; states are not liable for denial of justice because they cannot afford to put at the public's disposal spacious buildings or computerised information banks. What matters is rather the human factor of obedience to the rule of law. Foreigners who enter a poor country are not entitled to assume that they will be given things like verbatim transcripts of all judicial proceedings – but they are entitled to decision-making which is neither xenophobic nor arbitrary. The second is that a relativistic standard would be none at all. International courts or tribunals would have to make ad hoc assessments based on their evaluation of the capacity of each state at a given moment of its development. International law would thus provide no incentive for a state to improve. It would in fact operate to the opposite effect: a state which devoted more resources to its judiciary would run the risk of graduating into a more exacting category.'

[31] *Lauder* v. *Czech Republic*, Ad hoc UNCITRAL Arbitration Rules, Final Award, 3 September 2001; *Asian Agricultural Products Ltd* v. *Republic of Sri Lanka*, ICSID Case No. ARB/87/3, Award, 27 June 1990; *CME Czech Republic BV* v. *Czech Republic*, UNCITRAL Arbitration Rules, Partial Award and Separate Opinion, 13 September 2001.

[32] *Pantechniki* v. *Albania*, para. 77: 'To apply the same reasoning with respect to the duty of protection and security would be parlous. There is an important distinction between the two in terms of the consciousness of state behaviour in each case. A legal system and the dispositions it generates are the products of deliberate choices and conduct developed or neglected over long periods. The minimum requirement is not high in light of the great value placed on the rule of law. There is warrant for its consistent application. A failure of

(cited in *Pantechniki*): 'An investor investing in an area with endemic civil strife and poor governance cannot have the same expectation of physical security as one investing in London, New York or Tokyo.'[33] The *Pantechniki* Award relied on the witnesses' testimony describing 'an environment of desolation and lawlessness' encountered by the investor's team upon arrival. It was therefore held that 'the Claimant cannot say today that it felt entitled to rely on a high standard of police protection'.[34]

The *FPS* v. *Czech Republic*[35] Decision applied the duty of protection and security in the context of legal protection (and not protection against public violence as in *Pantechniki*).[36] The allegations raised by the investor included, in particular, a flawed process by the bankruptcy judges and non-intervention by the Czech authorities to remedy the treatment being received by the claimant. The *FPS* Tribunal expressly disagreed with *Pantechniki*:

> In *Pantechniki*, the tribunal applied a modified objective standard of due diligence in a situation of public violence. It found that liability in a situation involving civil strife depended on the host state's resources. However, there are no authorities which indicate that other situations, not involving violence, would warrant the application of a relative standard.[37]

Therefore, we find ourselves in the presence of two standards depending on the scope of the full protection and security obligation (i.e., depending on whether it extends beyond physical protection).

IV Damages

The discussion on damages brings us back to the concept of risk assumed by the claimant when investing in a developing state. Several tribunals have accepted that a voluntary assumption of risk by the investor should be factored into the amount of compensation for breaches by the state.

protection and security is to the contrary likely to arise in an unpredictable instance of civic disorder which could have been readily controlled by a powerful state but which overwhelms the limited capacities of one which is poor and fragile. There is no issue of incentives or disincentives with regard to unforeseen breakdowns of public order; it seems difficult to maintain that a government incurs international responsibility for failure to plan for unprecedented trouble of unprecedented magnitude in unprecedented places. The case for an element of proportionality in applying the international standard is stronger than with respect to claims of denial of justice.'

[33] *Pantechniki* v. *Albania*, para. 81.   [34] *Pantechniki* v. *Albania*, para. 82.
[35] *Frontier Petroleum Services* v. *Czech Republic*, PCA – UNCITRAL Arbitration Rules, Final Award, 12 November 2010.
[36] *FPS* v. *Czech Republic*, para. 263.   [37] *FPS* v. *Czech Republic*, para. 271.

The *AMT* v. *Zaire*[38] Tribunal, when assessing compensation for damage caused by riots and looting by Zairian soldiers, did not consider local conditions for the purposes of its finding that Zaire failed to provide the required standard of treatment, but reduced damages nevertheless on the basis that an investor should bear the high political and business risk of investing in a country like Zaire:

> AMT would have liked to adopt a method of calculating compensation ... practicable in the normal circumstances prevailing in an ideal country where the climate of investment is very stable, such as Switzerland or the Federal Republic of Germany.[39]

On the issue of interest, the tribunal opted

> for a method that is most plausible and realistic in the circumstances of the case, while rejecting all other methods of assessment which would serve unjustly to enrich an investor who, rightly or wrongly, has chosen to invest in a country such as Zaire, believing that by so doing the investor is constructing a castle in Spain or a Swiss chalet in Germany, without any risk, political or even economic or financial or any risk whatsoever.[40]

In *Alpha* v. *Ukraine*, the tribunal modified the proposed interest rate to update the damages claim, because it believed that the revised rate 'better reflected the opportunity cost associated with Claimant's losses, adjusted for the risks of investing in Ukraine'.[41] In *Himpurna* v. *PLN*, noting 'the fact that it is riskier to enter into a 30-year venture in Indonesia than in more mature economies', the tribunal increased the discount rate to 19 per cent (from 8.5 per cent) to establish the present value of lost profits.[42]

In *Lemire* v. *Ukraine*,[43] the claimant proposed a methodology developed by the US National Association of Valuators and Analysts, in order to determine the discount rate to be applied in the discounted cash flow (DCF) model.[44] The tribunal rejected this proposition on the basis that such method was 'domestic' and, while 'appropriate to value

---

[38] *AMT* v. *Zaire*, Award and Separate Opinion, 21 February 1997.
[39] *AMT* v. *Zaire*, para. 7.13.   [40] *AMT* v. *Zaire*, paras 7.14–7.15.
[41] *Alpha* v. *Ukraine*, para. 514.
[42] *Himpurna California Energy Ltd* v. *PT (Persero) Perusahaan Listruik Negara*, Ad hoc UNCITRAL Arbitration Rules, Final Award, 4 May 1999, para. 358.
[43] *Joseph Charles Lemire* v. *Ukraine*, ICSID Case No. ARB/06/18, Award, 28 March 2011.
[44] DCF analysis is a method of valuing an investment by using future cash flow projections and discounting them to arrive at a present value. The discount rate usually reflects risk (the discount rate will be higher if the risk of the cash flows is estimated to be significant).

companies in the US and possibly in other developed nations', it did not 'reflect country risk, i.e. the fact that the same company, situated in the US or in Ukraine, is subject to different political and regulatory risks'. The tribunal ruled that the discount rate should therefore be higher, and the valuations lower, than in the United States.[45]

Two further aspects of the *Lemire* Tribunal's analysis on damages are particularly noteworthy. The arbitrators had to test the amount of damages (established applying a DCF model developed 'on a number of assumptions') against other parameters in order to confirm the reasonableness of the calculation. With regard to one of those parameters – the 'risk environment' – the tribunal stated that Mr Lemire 'had the courage to venture into a transitional State and to create from scratch a completely new business'. According to the tribunal, 'transitional economies need such investors, who take considerable risks and commit themselves with great energy, notwithstanding the absence of clear recovery horizons'.[46]

The tribunal then had to consider whether compensation ought to be proportional to the investment. In this respect, it was noted that Mr Lemire could not be compared with a 'passive' investor. The tribunal found that there was adequate proportionality – 'not in cash alone but in a combination of cash, risk-taking, personal commitment, and the essential contribution of a path-breaker'.[47] Although the tribunal did not consider Ukraine's development status at the merits stage of *Lemire*, it did take it into account at the damages stage. Note the change in tone compared with *Genin* and *Generation Ukraine*: no longer was the claimant an investor who should have been mindful of the host state's conditions, but he was a 'path breaker'.

There seems to be a divergence of approaches among arbitrators when faced with a defence arising out of the host state's developing status; it remains to be seen whether future decisions will seek to harmonise the varying strands. In practice, absent a generally recognised 'level of development' standard, parties will likely continue to make the argument that the conditions prevailing in the host state should be factored into the arbitrators' decision, to an extent depending on the factual circumstances of the case.

---

[45] *Lemire* v. *Ukraine*, para. 280.   [46] *Lemire* v. *Ukraine*, para, 303.
[47] *Lemire* v. *Ukraine*, para. 306.

PART V

International investment and the European Union

16

The investment regime under Article 207 of the TFEU – a legal conundrum: the scope of 'foreign direct investment' and the future of intra-EU BITs

FRIEDL WEISS AND SILKE STEINER

I Introduction

The increased importance of internationalisation – that is, of foreign-owned production and distribution facilities in most countries – is not a new phenomenon. It is rather tangible evidence of globalisation.[1] Owing to further trade liberalisation, policy shifts in favour of foreign ownership in many countries and leaps in telecommunication technologies have accelerated in past decades. Foreign direct investment (FDI) and the formation of transnational corporations (TNCs) have been at the centre of this process.[2] Already in the mid-1990s estimated sales of foreign affiliates of TNCs exceeded the value of world trade in goods and services,[3] though local knowledge advantage appears to explain why nine-tenths of world production is still under domestic ownership.[4] The purposes driving FDI,[5] the economic welfare gains through economic growth, and also the link between TNC activities and home and host country employment and distributional concerns, among other things, have been widely studied. Given the high stakes involved, it is scarcely surprising that the design and development of a new

[1] See, e.g., WTO, *Trade and Foreign Direct Investment, Annual Report 1996*, vol. 1 (Geneva: WTO, 1997), p. 44.
[2] Philippe Maystadt, Preface, 'The Internationalisation of Production in Europe: Causes and Effects of Foreign Direct Investment and Non-equity Forms of International Production', *EIB Papers* 9(1) (2004): 5.
[3] UNCTAD, *World Investment Report: Transnational Corporations and Competitiveness* (Geneva: UNCTAD, 1995).
[4] K. Uppenberg and A. Riess, 'Determinants and Growth Effects of Foreign Direct Investment, *EIB Papers* 9(1) (2004): 53–84, at p. 54.
[5] Uppenberg and Riess, 'Determinants and Growth Effects of Foreign Direct Investment, p. 53.

Common EU Investment Policy (CEIP) and of its normative framework has given rise to much controversial debate.[6]

Generally, it remains an evergreen truism to say that treaties are not made by lawyers, but by politicians through diplomacy pursuant to specific negotiating mandates. Lawyers, legal advisers or independent academic experts and practitioners rarely, if ever, play a central role in the drafting process. Criticism of certain aspects of treaties after their ratification may, therefore, appear all the more trenchant. This would appear to be the case with respect to the exclusive competence for the conclusion of 'trade agreements relating to ... foreign direct investment' conferred upon the EU by virtue of Article 207 of the Treaty on the Functioning of the EU (TFEU), introduced by the Treaty of Lisbon.

Previously, the inclusion of a general investment provision in EU free trade agreements (FTAs) was considered to be hampered by the fact that competence for investment resided with the EU member states. Indeed the Multilateral Agreement on Investment (MAI) was – albeit not successfully – negotiated by member states, as was the more ambitious EU–Chile FTA. Yet even more ambitious investment provisions will be called for – for instance, in ongoing FTA negotiations with Canada, Singapore, India and MERCOSUR – so as to match the comprehensive investment rules in all US FTAs, which contain separate chapters for cross-border supply of services and investments.[7] Be that as it may, far from providing greater coherence and predictability, it would appear that the addition of 'foreign direct investment' to the EU's exclusive competence for the common commercial policy (CCP) to be conducted in the context of the principles and objectives of the EU's external action, has created a significant amount of uncertainty, controversy and debate. Indeed, as

---

[6] Suffice it to refer to some selected academic writings from an abundant and diverse variety of publications: Armand de Mestral C.M., 'The Lisbon Treaty and the Expansion of EU Competence Over Foreign Direct Investment and the Implications for Investor–State Arbitration', in K. P. Sauvant (ed.), *Yearbook on International Investment Law and Policy* (New York: Oxford University Press, 2009/10), pp. 365–95; see also contributions in Marc Bungenberg, Jörn Griebel, Steffen Hindelang (eds), *European Yearbook of International Economic Law, Special Issue: International Investment Law and EU Law* (Heidelberg: Springer, 2011); Nikos Lavranos, 'New Developments in the Interaction between International Investment Law and EU Law', *Law and Practice of International Courts and Tribunals* 9 (2010): 409–41; Joachim Karl, 'The Competence for Foreign Direct Investment: New Powers for the European Union?' *Journal of World Investment and Trade* 5 (2005): 413 ff.

[7] Stephen Woolcock, 'European Union Policy towards Free Trade Agreements', ECIPE Working Paper No. 03, 2007, p. 8.

mentioned, a host of legal problems relating to this new CEIP has come in for severe criticism, mainly by investment lawyers, rattled by what they consider to constitute a grievously ill-conceived new policy, conceptually and in terms of consequential practical difficulties.

What are the problems arising from the exclusive EU competence in FDI, introduced by the Treaty of Lisbon, that have attributed to the EU? In this chapter, we will analyse the challenges with regard to not only the scope of FDI in the sense of Article 207 of the TFEU, but also the question of the future of intra-EU BITs.

II   General situation before and after the Treaty of Lisbon

1   Situation before the Treaty of Lisbon

Before the entry into force of the Treaty of Lisbon on 1 December 2009, the European Community (EC) did not have exclusive competence in international investment matters, but only competence shared with member states. In Opinion 2/92 (OECD),[8] for instance, the European Court of Justice (ECJ) held that the national treatment rule, which was basically a rule on FDI activities, related only partially to international trade with non-member countries, so that ex Article 113 of the TEC (later Article 133 of the TEC, now Article 207 of the TFEU) could not be used as the legal basis for the Community's exclusive competence. Member states themselves prolifically concluded foreign investment protection agreements,[9] though since the establishment of EU freedoms in 1957 seemingly only a few between them.

Notable practice under the regime of shared competence includes the 2006 Minimum Platform on Investment for EU Free Trade Agreements (MPoI).[10] Adopted 'with a view to develop an ambitious investment

---

[8]   Opinion 2/92 regarding the competence of the Community to participate in the Third Revised Decision of the OECD on national treatment, Decision of 24 March 1995 [1995] ECR I-52. The Court confirmed its case law on the limits of the CCP and on the exclusivity of implied competences as previously laid down in Opinions 2/91 (ILO) and 1/94 (WTO).

[9]   There are 1,300 BITs between EU Member States and third countries; some 190 intra-EU BITs, particularly with the twelve new Member States since their accession to the EU in 2004 and 2007, respectively, see de Mestral, 'The Lisbon Treaty and the Expansion of EU Competence', p. 366.

[10]   This document, though never officially issued, was originally drafted by DG Trade as 'Note for the Attention of the 133 Committee: Minimum Platform on Investment for EU FTAs – Provision on Establishment in Template for a Title on "Establishment, Trade in Services and e-commerce"', 28 July 2006, D (2006) 9219, available at: www.iisd.org/pdf/2006/itn_ecom.pdf, accessed 7 November 2011.

policy, an objective supported by member states',[11] it represents, conceivably, a kind of partial model EU BIT, though primarily focused on establishment and trade in financial services providing investment services. It contains guidance to negotiators of EU trade agreements having a mandate to include provisions relating to investment.[12] Practice also encompasses three important cases[13] before the ECJ involving pre-accession BITs between EU member states and third states (extra-EU BITs) and before investment arbitration tribunals relating to BITs between different EU member states (intra-EU BITs).

Practice concerning intra-EU BITs – that is, BITs concluded between EU member states – has surged since the EU enlargement of 2004, from two to 190.[14] While the EU Commission has called for the termination of intra-EU BITs, it has for some time taken the view that certain provisions in extra-EU BITs between EU member states and non-EU countries are problematic. Following the terrorist attacks of 9/11, restrictions of the free movement of capital and payments, including the freezing of funds, became an instrumental necessity to thwart terrorist activities.[15] In the light of this development, the Commission insisted that BITs of EU member states with third countries, which did not permit such restrictions, were incompatible with EU law, particularly with its right to restrict capital flows in extraordinary circumstances.[16] As Finland, Austria and Sweden had neither re-negotiated nor denounced or suspended a number of their pre-accession BITs with non-European countries, nor had they invoked a fundamental change of circumstances,[17] the Commission initiated infringement proceedings in the ECJ against them,

---

[11] Minimum Platform on Investment for EU FTAs, p. 1.

[12] Armand de Mestral, 'Is a Model EU BIT Possible – or even Desirable?' *Columbia FDI Perspectives*, 21 24 March 2010. Reprinted with permission from the Vale Columbia Center on Sustainable International Investment.

[13] For further details, see, below, n. 19.

[14] Only Germany had concluded two intra-EU BITs, one with Greece (1961) and one with Portugal (1980), but none ever in dispute; Angelos Dimopoulos, 'The Validity and Applicability of International Investment Agreements between EU Member States under EU and International Law', *Common Market Law Review* 48 (2011): 63–93, at p. 63.

[15] For EU freezing measures, both implementing UN Security Council sanctions and adopted autonomously, see http://eeas.europa.eu/cfsp/sanctions/index_en.htm.

[16] Article 75 of the TFEU (ex Art. 60 of the TEC) for financial restrictions and Art. 215 of the TFEU (ex Art. 301 of the TEC) for economic and financial sanctions for the reduction or interruption of economic relations with a third country.

[17] See Arts 56 (denunciation or withdrawal), 57 (suspension), 62 (fundamental change of circumstances, '*clausula rebus sic stantibus*') of the Vienna Convention on the Law of Treaties; see also, e.g., the *Open Skies* cases C-466–469, C-471–472, C-475–476/98,

claiming a breach of ex Article 307(2) of the TEC (now Article 351(2) of the TFEU).[18] In 2009, the ECJ found that Austria, Sweden and Finland were in breach of Article 307 of the TEC[19] due to their failure to revise BITs with certain non-EU countries. [20]

2 Situation after the Treaty of Lisbon

According to Article 207(1) of the TFEU, the CCP also includes trade in services, commercial aspects of intellectual property, as well as FDI as exclusive competences of the EU:

> 1. The common commercial policy shall be based on uniform principles, particularly with regard to changes in tariff rates, the conclusion of tariff and trade agreements relating to trade in goods and services, and the commercial aspects of intellectual property, foreign direct investment.

This provision constitutes a substantial *extension* of *EU competence* in the area of the CCP, by which FDI has become an exclusive EU competence.[21] The current legal framework for FDI is a comprehensive one: it consists of 1,200 BITs between EU member states and third countries.[22] The EU Council has expressed the view that the EU can develop, in the

---

Commission v. *UK, Denmark, Sweden, Finland, Belgium, Luxembourg, Austria and Germany* [2002] ECR I-9519.

[18] Article 315(2) of the TFEU states that 'To the extent that such agreements are not compatible with the Treaties, the Member State or States concerned shall take all appropriate steps to eliminate the incompatibilities'.

[19] Article 351 of the TFEU (ex Art. 307 of the TEC): 'The rights and obligations arising from agreements concluded ... for acceding States, before the date of their accession, between one or more Member states on the one hand, and one or more third countries on the other, shall not be affected by the provisions of the Treaties' (para. 1). 'To the extent that such agreements are not compatible with the Treaties, the Member State or States concerned shall take all appropriate steps to eliminate the incompatibilities established. Member States shall, where necessary, assist each other to this end and shall, where appropriate, adopt a common attitude' (para. 2).

[20] Case C-205/06, *Commission v. Austria (Re Provisions on the Free Transfer of Investment Related Payments in Bilateral Investment Agreements)* [2009] ECR I-1301; Case C-249/06, *Commission v. Sweden* [2009] ECR I-1335; Case C-118/07, *Commission v. Finland* [2009] ECR I-10889; and case notes on these cases cited in Lavranos, 'New Developments in the Interaction between International Investment Law and EU Law', pp. 409–41, at p. 410, fn. 2.

[21] Articles 3(1)(e), 206 and 207 of the TFEU.

[22] Also compared with approximately 2,600 BITs worldwide, this means an enormous number; see Hanno Wehland, 'Intra-EU Investment Agreements and Arbitration: Is European Community Law an Obstacle?' *International and Comparative Law Quarterly* 58 (2009): 297–320, at p. 298.

framework of its external action, a comprehensive investment policy. Such a policy, possibly articulated in the form of some kind of EU model BIT, could replace the disparate efforts of the twenty-seven EU member states. In July 2012, the Commission published a progress report thereon.[23] A major step forward for EU investment policy was made by the adoption of Regulation 1219/2012 establishing transitional arrangements for bilateral investment agreements between member states and third countries.

III   Scope and interpretation of the term 'FDI'

1   FDI in EU law

In EU law all restrictions on capital movement between member states, and between them and third countries are prohibited (Article 63(1) of the TFEU).[24] The material scope of 'capital movement' undoubtedly comprises 'direct investment', by implication of the express provision of exceptions for, *inter alia*, national measures on 'direct investment' with respect to third countries (Article 64(1) of the TFEU). The ECJ, moreover, considered Article 64(1) of the TFEU to be 'precisely worded, with the result that no latitude is granted to the member states or the Community legislature regarding … the categories of capital movements which may be subject to restrictions'.[25] The term FDI is nowhere defined, neither in the Treaty provisions on capital and payments (Article 64 of the TFEU), nor in those defining the remit of the CCP (Articles 206 and 207 of the TFEU). Nevertheless, 'that concept has been defined in Community law in the nomenclature of the capital movements set out in Annex I to Council Directive 88/361/EEC of 24 June 1988 … which

---

[23] European Commission, 'External Sources of Growth: Progress Report on EU Trade and Investment Relationship with Key Economic Partners', Commission Staff Working Document, 18 July 2012. Additionally, a proposal for a regulation establishing a framework for managing financial responsibility linked to investor–state dispute settlement tribunals established by international agreements to which the European Union is party, COM(2012) 335 final, 21 June 2012, has been published by the Commission.

[24] Regulation (EU) No. 1219/2012 of the European Parliament and of the Council, 12 December 2012, establishing transitional arrangements for bilateral investment agreements between member states and third countries, OJ 2012 L351, 40.

[25] Joined Cases C-163/94, C-165/94 and C-250/94, *Criminal Proceedings against Lucas Emilio Sanz de Lera, Raimundo Diaz Jiménez and Figen Kapanoglu* [1995] ECR I-4821, para. 44.

sets out 13 categories of capital movements'.[26] The Court also observed that since Article 63 of the TFEU substantially reproduced the content of Article 1 of the EC Capital Movements Directive, that provision and the nomenclature at the Annex to it, while not defining the concept of FDI either, retains its indicative value as interpretative guidance by virtue of an illustrative list of 'direct investment',[27] described as a concept that must be understood 'in its widest sense'.[28] This includes so-called 'foreign portfolio investment' (FPI). FDI investors take both ownership and control positions in the domestic firms, are in effect the managers of the firms under their control, whereas FPI investors, who gain ownership without control of domestic firms, must delegate decisions to managers.[29] However, the question of when an investment will turn from a portfolio into a direct investment certainly eludes abstract determination,[30] but possibly also arbitrarily established numerical thresholds, such as that of the OECD Benchmark Definition of FDI requiring a holding of '10 percent or more of the ordinary shares or voting power',[31] which would not necessarily justify the conclusion that in the individual case the investor is actually in a position to exercise control over the entrepreneurial activities of the investment.[32]

2   Positions on FDI taken by EU institutions

a   Interpretation by the ECJ

As already mentioned, EU law lacks a definition of the term FDI (Articles 206 and 207 of the TFEU). However, in the case *Test Claimants in the FII*

---

[26] See Case C-446/04, *Test Claimants in the FII Group Litigation* v. *Commissioners of Inland Revenue* [2006] ECR I-11753, para. 178.

[27] *FII Group Litigation* v. *Commissioners of Inland Revenue*, para. 179.

[28] Directive 88/361/EEC, see especially Annex I containing a nomenclature of the capital movements referred to in Art. 1 of the Directive. Accordingly, 'direct investment' refers to 'investments of all kinds by natural persons or commercial, industrial or financial undertakings, and which serve to establish or to maintain lasting and direct links between the person providing the capital and the entrepreneur to whom or the undertaking to which the capital is made available in order to carry on an economic activity'.

[29] Goldstein Itay and Assaf Razin, 'Foreign Direct Investment v. Foreign Portfolio Investment', National Bureau of Economic Research, Working Paper No. 11047, January 2005, p. 2.

[30] Steffen Hindelang, *The Free Movement of Capital and Foreign Direct Investment: The Scope of Protection in EU Law* (Oxford University Press, 2009), p. 66.

[31] OECD, *OECD Benchmark Definition of Foreign Direct Investment* (Paris: OECD, 2008), pp. 7 ff.

[32] Hindelang, *The Free Movement of Capital and Foreign Direct Investment*, p. 66.

Group Litigation the ECJ specified its understanding of FDI on the basis of the following three criteria: first, it should be a long-lasting investment; second, it should represent at least 10 per cent of the affiliated company's equity capital/shares; and, third, it should provide the investor with managerial control over the affiliated company's operations.[33] This definition is in line with those of the IMF and the OECD and is *opposed*, in particular, to the inclusion of portfolio investments, debt obligations on the part of enterprises and intellectual property rights. This definition by the ECJ is also referred to by the European Parliament in the Arif Report.[34]

b European Commission

According to the European Commission, FDI 'is generally considered to include any foreign investment which serves to establish lasting and direct links with the undertaking to which capital is made available in order to carry out an economic activity'. In the case of investments taking the form of a shareholding, this objective requires that the shares enable the shareholder to participate effectively in the management of that company or in its control. This contrasts with foreign investments where there is no intention on behalf of the investor to influence the management and control of an undertaking. Such investments, which are often of a more short-term and sometimes speculative nature, are commonly referred to as 'portfolio investments'.[35] Portfolio investments are consequently not included in the Commission's concept of FDI.[36]

The Commission warned that overlap between European Community law and BITs between EU member states would create 'legal uncertainty'. It had already raised its concern with the EU's Economic and Financial Committee (EFC)[37] in 2006, when it cautioned that 'investors could try

---

[33] ECJ Case C-446/04, *Test Claimants in the FII Group Litigation* [2006] ECR, I-11753.

[34] For further details on this report, see below, section III.2.c.

[35] Communication from the Commission to the Council, the European Parliament, the Economic and Social Committee and the Committee of the Regions, 'Towards a Comprehensive European International Investment policy', COM(2010) 343 final, pp. 2–3.

[36] This category of investments could, however, be included on the basis of other treaty provisions, meaning in particular the provisions on the free movement of capital, see 'From the Board', *Legal Issues of Economic Integration* 37(4) (2010): 261–73, at p. 263.

[37] The Treaty of Maastricht provided for an Economic and Financial Committee to be set up at the start of the third stage of the Economic and Monetary Union (EMU), which began on 1 January 1999. Its tasks are: to keep under review the economic and financial situation of the Member States and the Community and to report regularly to the Council and the Commission on this subject, in particular on financial relations with third

to practice forum shopping by submitting claims to BIT arbitration instead of – or additionally to – national courts. This could lead to BIT arbitration taking place without relevant questions of EC law being submitted to the ECJ, with unequal treatment of investors among member states a possible outcome.'[38]

c European Parliament

In the recent Arif Report[39] the European Parliament asked the Commission to provide a clear definition of the investments to be protected, including both FDI and portfolio investment.[40] However, it considered that speculative forms of investment, as defined by the Commission, should not be protected. The European Parliament insisted that where intellectual property rights are included in the scope of the investment agreement,[41] the provisions should avoid negatively impacting the production of generic medicines and must respect the TRIPS exceptions for public health.[42]

Furthermore, the European Parliament expressed the view that the fact that the Treaty of Lisbon made FDI an exclusive EU competence necessitates striking a delicate *balance* between protecting investors' rights and the right of public authorities to regulate.[43] This approach, in turn, requires clear definitions of what type of investors and investments will be protected.

The Arif Report of the European Parliament's International Trade Committee proposed not to extend the same level of protection to

countries and international institutions; and to contribute to the preparation of the work of the Council, particularly as regards recommendations required as part of multilateral surveillance and decisions required as part of the excessive deficit procedure. The preparatory work of the Economic and Financial Committee for the Council of the European Union includes the economic and financial situation, the euro exchange rate and relations with third countries and international institutions. This advisory committee also provides the framework for preparing and pursuing the dialogue between the Council and the European Central Bank.

[38] Damon Vis-Dunbar, 'EU Member States Reject the Call to Terminate Intra-EU Bilateral Investment Treaties', *Investment Treaty News* March 2009.

[39] European Parliament, Committee on International Trade, 'Report on the Future European International Investment Policy', 2010/2203(INI), Rapporteur Kader Arif (Arif Report), 23 March 2011.

[40] By this statement, the European Parliament refers to the definition by the ECJ.

[41] In this scope of investment agreements, agreements where draft mandates have already been proposed should also be included.

[42] European Parliament, Committee on International Trade, Arif Report, paras 11–14.

[43] Arif Report, para. 17.

portfolio investments and intellectual property rights, to define 'investor' strictly to avoid 'abusive' practices, to exclude sensitive sectors from the scope of the agreement, and to explicitly ensure the right to regulate in the public interest. Additionally, Rapporteur Arif proposed to include legally binding social and environmental clauses, to exclude umbrella clauses, to ensure greater transparency with respect to investor–state arbitration, to provide the opportunity for parties to appeal and the obligation 'to exhaust local judicial remedies'.

These recommendations lead to the conclusion that the views of the Commission and the European Parliament diverge on some substantive issues.

The European Parliament noted with concern that negotiating a broad variety of investments would lead to the mixing of exclusive and shared competences and called for the introduction of the term 'EU investor'. Reflecting the spirit of Article 207 of the TFEU, an 'EU investor' would underline the significance of promoting investors from all member states on equal terms and ensure them conditions of functioning and protection of their investments on an equal footing. Furthermore, the European Parliament recalled that the standard EU Member State BIT uses a broad definition of 'foreign investor' and asked the Commission to assess where this has led to. Additionally, a number of member states have used broad definitions, with a simple postal address deemed sufficient to determine the nationality of an enterprise. Such practices clearly must not be permitted, as they have enabled some enterprises to bypass the national legal mechanisms of their own countries.[44] Besides, the so-called 'umbrella clause', which enables the integration into the scope of a BIT of all private law contracts concluded between an investor and the signatory state of the BIT, should be excluded from future agreements.[45] Subsequently, the European Parliament asked the Commission to provide a clear definition of a foreign investor based on this assessment and drawing on the latest OECD benchmark definition of FDI.[46]

According to the opinion of Rapporteur Arif, not all kinds of investments require the same high level of protection: short-term

---

[44] By using their branches abroad, these enterprises have been able to file suits against their own countries by means of a BIT signed by a third country, and investors have exploited this technique to select the BITs most conducive to filing a complaint.

[45] Arif Report, 'Explanatory Statement'.

[46] Arif Report, paras 11–14. See *OECD Benchmark Definition of Foreign Direct Investment*, 3rd edn (OECD: Paris, 1996).

speculative investments, for example, do not deserve the same level of protection as long-term investments.[47] The Rapporteur therefore recommended that the scope of future European agreements should be limited to FDI only. If the member states chose to give the Commission a mandate to negotiate on a broad range of investments, this could create a risk of important European concessions in the field of investments, since the EU's extremely open economy leaves few other levers in international trade negotiations. In order to balance private investor protection and public regulation prerogatives, the Arif Report emphasised that the Commission should focus not only on investor protection, but 'better address the right to protect the public capacity to regulate and meet the EU's obligation to exercise policy coherence for development'.[48]

It was also argued that future investment agreements should include the following three precisely defined standards: (1) non-discrimination among foreign and national investors; (2) fair and equitable treatment; and (3) the protection against direct and indirect expropriation. Since EU treaties do not explicitly define 'foreign direct investment', the European Parliament's Trade Committee also stressed the need for a *'clear definition* of the investments to be protected', and insisted that 'speculative forms of investment, as defined by the Commission, shall not be protected'.[49] In addition, the Arif Report asked for an assessment of past instances in which the broad definition of 'foreign investor' might have led to abusive practices – such as domestic investors using BITs to sue their regulators in their own countries – and urged that the term should be clearly defined.[50]

---

[47] Arif Report, 'Explanatory Statement', p. 10.

[48] It called on the Commission to include specific clauses in all future investment agreements that would lay down the rights of parties to regulate in the name of 'national security, the environment, public health, workers' and consumer rights, industrial policy and cultural diversity', Arif Report, para 25.

[49] Arif Report, para. 11.

[50] According to Rapporteur Kader Arif, the report 'sends a strong signal to both the Council and the Commission, which is about to start investment negotiations with third countries such as Canada, India, and, in the near future, China. Therefore it is crucial for the Parliament to ensure the responsible behaviour of European investors abroad, while at the same time protecting the EU's right to regulate in the public interest', European Parliament, Press Release, 'EU Investment Policy needs to Balance Investor Protection and Public Regulation, says International Trade Committee', available at: www.europarl. europa.eu/sides/getDoc.do?pubRef=-//EP//TEXT+IM-PRESS+20110314IPR15476+0+DOC +XML+V0//EN.

d   Council of the European Union

As a reaction to the Commission's Communication 'Towards a Comprehensive European International Investment Policy', the Council requested that the new European legal framework should not negatively affect investor protection and guarantees enjoyed under the existing agreements. The Council also saw – as did the European Parliament – a need to identify best practices.[51]

Given that the bilateral investment agreements concluded by the member states with third parties are, so far, the main source of protection and legal security for the European investor abroad, the Council stressed that the new legal framework should not negatively affect investor protection and guarantees enjoyed under the existing agreements. This priority is expected to be met in the recently adopted Regulation on transitional arrangements for bilateral investment agreements between member states and third countries. In accordance with Article 351 of the TFEU, bilateral investment agreements concluded by member states should continue to afford protection and legal security to investors until they are replaced by at least equally effective EU agreements.[52] The Council called for a pragmatic and realistic approach by ensuring a legal framework that empowers member states to negotiate and conclude bilateral investment agreements with third parties when no EU investment agreement is envisaged in the near future. The procedures in this legal framework should be light, quick and efficient, and carried out by member states and the Commission in a spirit of good cooperation.

In particular, the Council stressed the need for an effective investor-to-state dispute settlement mechanism in the EU investment agreements, and asked the Commission to carry out a detailed study on the relevant issues concerning international arbitration systems. This study should, *inter alia*, include the legal and political feasibility of EU membership in international arbitration institutions, as well as the question of liability arising from arbitration procedures and the responsibilities of the member states in this respect.[53]

---

[51] Council of the European Union, 'Conclusions on a Comprehensive European International Investment Policy', 3041st Foreign Affairs Council Meeting, Luxembourg, 25 October 2010, para. 15.

[52] Cf. Marc Bungenberg, 'Going Global? The Common Commercial Policy after Lisbon', in Christoph Herrmann and Jörg Terhechte (eds), *European Yearbook of International Economic Law* (Berlin: Springer, 2010), pp. 123–51, at p. 145.

[53] Council of the European Union, 'Conclusions on a Comprehensive European International Investment Policy', para. 18.

Most of the individual member states, however, oppose the Commission's wide interpretation of FDI to some extent, since they do not share the Commission's concern with regard to arbitration risks and discriminatory treatment of investors. Therefore, a clear majority of member states prefer to maintain the existing agreements.[54]

IV   Intra-EU BITs

In recent years, the validity and applicability of BITs concluded between EU member states (intra-EU BITs) have been the subject of much debate, particularly as regards their relationship to the fundamental freedoms under the TEC and later under the TFEU, and with respect to the exclusive jurisdiction of the ECJ to interpret EU law according to Article 344 of the TFEU.[55]

The question of the inapplicability of intra-EU BITs with the TFEU was first raised in the *Eastern Sugar* v. *Czech Republic* arbitration proceedings,[56] which were commenced under the BIT between the Czech and Slovak Republic and the Netherlands. So far, the validity and applicability of intra-EU BITs have not been dealt with by the ECJ in either infringement proceedings under Article 258 of the TFEU or as a result of a submission for a preliminary ruling. The ECJ, however, indirectly addressed this issue in the cases against Austria, Sweden and Finland, in which it ruled that they had breached ex Article 307(2) of the TEC[57] by failing to remove the provisions in their BITs with non-EU member states (extra-EU BITs) that were incompatible with EU law.[58] Even though the ECJ ruling related to extra-EU BITs, its conclusions are *mutatis mutandis* applicable to intra-EU BITs, as the only difference between them being the legal consequences that result from the argued incompatibility of the treaties: in the case of extra-EU BITs, the removal of the given

---

[54] For further information on the position of the Member States, see section IV.3, below.

[55] Article 344 of the TFEU provides that: 'Member States undertake not to submit a dispute concerning the interpretation or application of the Treaties to any method of settlement other than those provided for therein.'

[56] *Eastern Sugar BV* v. *Czech Republic*, *Ad hoc* UNCITRAL Arbitration Rules, Partial Award, 27 March 2007, Final Award, 12 April 2007.

[57] Now Art. 351(2) of the TFEU.

[58] For further details on these cases, see section II.1, above.

provisions pursuant to Article 351 of the TFEU; and in the case of intra-EU BITs, the automatic inapplicability of the contested provisions.[59]

In the *Mox Plant* case the ECJ concluded that:

> an international agreement cannot affect the allocation of responsibilities defined in the Treaties and, consequently, the autonomy of the Community legal system … That exclusive jurisdiction of the Court is confirmed by Article 292 EC [now Article 344 of the TFEU], by which Member States undertake not to submit a dispute concerning the interpretation or application of the EC Treaty to any method of settlement other than those provided for therein …[60] The act of submitting a dispute of this nature to a judicial forum such as the Arbitral Tribunal involves the risk that a judicial forum other than the Court will rule on the scope of obligations imposed on the Member States pursuant to Community law.[61]

This decision undoubtedly implies that in cases where controversy arises as to the application and interpretation of EU law, arbitration tribunals are not entitled to decide if, or to what extent, EU law and the respective international treaty (e.g., BITs) are to be applied. This would mean that tribunals are not entitled to decide that certain parts of BITs are to be applied while other parts are not.

An important difference, however, is that intra-EU investment arbitration takes place not between two member states, but between a Member State and an investor – ex Article 292 of the TEC (now Article 344 of the TFEU), which was relied on in the *MOX Plant* case, only mentions disputes submitted by member states. Nevertheless, apart from the fact that *MOX Plant* relates to a dispute between two states, and not between an individual and a state, an arbitration arising from a BIT would not significantly differ so as to justify an assumption of an ECJ approach different to that it had adopted in *MOX Plant*.

At the same time, we can argue that this decision does not imply that the tribunals are not entitled to resolve disputes that do not relate to EU law or where the interpretation and application of EU law is not disputed.

---

[59] For details on the interpretation of Art. 351 of the TFEU, see Jörg Philipp Terhechte, 'Art. 351 TFEU, the Principle of Loyalty and the Future Role of the Member States' Bilateral Investment Treaties', in Marc Bungenberg, Jörg Griebel and Steffen Hindelang (eds), *European Yearbook of International Economic Law, Special Issue: International Investment Law and EU Law* (Heidelberg: Springer, 2011), pp. 79–94.

[60] ECJ Case C-459/03, *MOX Plant* [2006] ECR I-4635, para. 123.

[61] *MOX Plant*, para. 177.

The arbitration clause itself is a legal enactment binding two states, both of which are obliged to follow Articles 344 and 267 of the TFEU and guarantee the uniform interpretation of EU law.[62] Therefore, the application of these obligations is supreme, and the investor is in a diagonal relationship with regard to the state and is not entitled to invoke the arbitration clause.

1 The position of the European Commission

The Commission strongly opposes the application of BITs between EU member states. An example demonstrating the Commission's negative attitude towards intra-EU BITs is the *Eureko* v. *Slovakia* arbitration case.[63] In this case, where Eureko initiated a claim against the Slovak Republic based on the Netherlands–Slovakia BIT, the Commission cast 'serious doubts' on the jurisdiction of the tribunal to hear a claim based on an intra-EU BIT.

The question of the applicability of an intra-EU BIT had already been raised previously in the *Eastern Sugar* v. *Czech Republic* arbitration case. In this case, two letters from the Commission were considered by the tribunal. These included statements such as: 'where the EC Treaty or secondary legislation are in conflict with some of these BITs' provisions ... Community law will automatically prevail over the non-conforming BIT provisions'; 'intra-EU BITs should be terminated insofar as the matters under the agreements fall under Community competence'; or 'that member states [should] exchange notes to the effect that such BITs are no longer applicable, and also formally rescind such agreements'. The Commission therefore considered that intra-EU BITs should be rescinded because they were superseded by EU law (notwithstanding the fact that EU law does not confer access to international arbitration upon investors).[64]

In September 2008, the Commission intervened directly in two ICSID arbitration proceedings against Hungary (*AES* v. *Hungary*[65] and *Electrabel* v. *Hungary*[66]) by filing an *amicus curiae* brief. It has been reported

---

[62] For further details, see Wehland, 'Intra-EU Investment Agreements and Arbitration', pp. 297–320, at pp. 301 ff.

[63] Award of 26 October 2010.

[64] See also Lavranos, 'New Developments in the Interaction between International Investment Law and EU Law', pp. 409–41.

[65] *AES Summit Generation Ltd and AES-Tisza Erömü Kft* v. *Republic of Hungary*, ICSID Case No. ARB/07/22, Award, 23 September 2010.

[66] *Electrabel SA* v. *Republic of Hungary*, ICSID Case No. ARB/07/19.

that the Commission took Hungary's side by stating that the power purchase agreements between the investors and a Hungarian state-owned entity violated EC law as they could restrict competition, thereby not taking account of the protection granted to the investors by the investment treaty at stake. The Commission's view, based on the supremacy of EC law over investment treaties, seems to leave little room for the application of investment treaties between member states.[67]

The Commission's views have also been expressed in more informal settings.[68] International law specialists hold a different position, according to which questions relating to conflicts between treaties must be resolved by the application of the Vienna Convention on the Law of Treaties, including Article 59 which sets out conditions for a treaty to be terminated by the conclusion of a later treaty.[69]

2   The Commission's reasons for its position

An analysis of the relevant Commission documents and statements points to the following reasons behind the position of the European Commission.

The Commission argued that 'the application of intra-EU BITs could lead to a more favourable treatment of investors and investments between the parties covered by the BITs and consequently discriminate against other member states, a situation which would not be in accordance with the relevant Treaty provisions'.[70] What does this difference of treatment amount to? One element of BITs comes to mind: the right of investors to have recourse to international arbitration. Indeed, only EU investors whose state of origin has entered into a BIT with the host state would have access to international arbitration.

---

[67] With regard to intra-EU BITs, it actually seems highly likely that ICSID awards rejecting the 'European law defence' of a respondent EU Member State will also be challenged before national courts, see Thomas Eilmansberger, 'Bilateral Investment Treaties and EU Law', *Common Market Law Review* 46 (2009): 383–429, at p. 428.

[68] During a conference on investment law and the European Union in Paris in April 2009, the Commission reiterated its views on the supremacy of EC law over intra-EU BITs.

[69] Wehland, 'Intra-EU Investment Agreements and Arbitration', pp. 303 ff; Christopher von Krause, 'The European Commission's Opposition to Intra-EU BITs and its Impact on Investment Arbitration', Kluwer Law Arbitration Blog, 28 September 2010, available at: http://kluwerarbitrationblog.com/blog/2010/09/28/the-european-commissions-opposition-to-intra-eu-bits-and-its-impact-on-investment-arbitration, accessed 28 November 2011.

[70] See von Krause, 'The European Commission's Opposition to Intra-EU BITs'.

Furthermore, the Commission states that investors starting international arbitration proceedings based on intra-EU BITs 'could lead to arbitration taking place without relevant questions of EC law being submitted to the ECJ, with unequal treatment of investors among member states as a possible outcome'.[71] These statements lead to the conclusion that the Commission seems to consider the application of intra-EU BITs, including the access to arbitration, as a potential source of inequality between EU citizens, as well as a hindrance to the harmonised development of EU law.

Internationally, the Commission's position has frequently been criticised. In the – so far few – investment arbitration cases on this issue, arbitral tribunals have determined that intra-EU BITs were not implicitly terminated when those countries acceded to the EU. The arbitral tribunal in the case *Eastern Sugar* v. *Czech Republic*, for instance, rejected the Czech Republic's argument that all of its BITs with other EU member states were implicitly terminated when it acceded to the EU.[72] It stated that the BIT in question was not superseded by EC law because this was not expressly set out in the treaties marking the Czech Republic's accession to the EU nor in the BIT, and because the conditions set out in Article 59 of the Vienna Convention were not satisfied. Also, in the *AES* v. *Hungary* award,[73] the tribunal stated that EC law, 'once introduced in the national legal orders ... is part of these legal orders' and that 'a state may not invoke its domestic law as an excuse for alleged breaches of its international obligations'.[74]

3 The position of member states

The majority of the EU member states want to maintain the network of BITs that exist between them. A report by the Economic and Financial Committee of 2008 highlighted that a clear majority of member states

---

[71] *Eastern Sugar BV* v. *Czech Republic*, Partial Award, 27 March 2007, para. 126. See also Markus Burgstaller, 'The Future of Bilateral Investment Treaties of EU Member States', in Marc Bungenberg, Jörg Griebel and Steffen Hindelang (eds), *European Yearbook of International Economic Law, Special Issue: International Investment Law and EU Law* (Heidelberg: Springer, 2011), pp. 55–78, at pp. 73–4.

[72] *Eastern Sugar BV* v. *Czech Republic*, Partial Award, 27 March 2007, paras 143–75.

[73] Award, 23 September 2010.

[74] See also Wenhua Shan and Sheng Zhang, 'The Treaty of Lisbon: Half Way toward a Common Investment Policy', *European Journal of International Law* 21 (2010): 1049–73, at pp. 1055 ff.

prefer to maintain the existing intra-EU BITs, in particular with a view to the provisions on investor–state dispute settlement.[75]

However, some of the member states, including in particular those that acceded in 2004 and 2007, seem to support the Commission's view as several of the latter member states have announced their plans to terminate their intra-EU BITs. The Czech Republic, for example, announced already in 2005 its intention to terminate all its BITs with other EU member states. The Italy–Czech Republic BIT has already been terminated, while the termination of Denmark–Czech Republic BIT is on the way. Recently, Slovenia and Malta declared that they intended to terminate their own BITs. In addition to the new member states, Italy too has indicated the same intention. Nevertheless, some of the EU member states – including, for instance, Belgium, Germany, the Netherlands and the United Kingdom – do not agree with the Czech Republic's approach.[76]

As already mentioned above, the Commission recently successfully applied to intervene in two investment treaty arbitration cases, both relating to power generation in Hungary (*AES* v. *Hungary* and *Electrabel* v. *Hungary*). Both claims were targeted at Hungarian Government requirements that the Hungarian purchasers of electricity make changes to long-term contracts ('power purchase agreements') entered into before Hungarian accession to the EU. Part of the Hungarian defence was that it had to make the changes required under EU law, since the Commission had determined that such agreements were illegal under EU law. In both cases, the Commission was granted permission to file non-party submissions. While the submissions have not yet been made public, it is generally understood that the Commission intervened to defend Hungary's actions as being required by EU law. The Commission also reportedly sought to challenge the jurisdiction of the tribunal on the ground that some aspects of the dispute and the underlying contract from which the dispute arose were subject to EU law, and therefore within the competence of the Commission.[77]

---

[75] See Vis-Dunbar, 'EU Member States Reject the Call to Terminate Intra-EU Bilateral Investment Treaties', p. 3.

[76] Interestingly, many of the disputes recently brought against the Czech Republic arose under BITs with those countries, Shan and Zhang, 'The Treaty of Lisbon', p. 1056; see also Marinn Carlson, Jennifer Haworth McCandless and Geoffrey Antell, 'The European Commission and Investment Treaties', *European and Middle Eastern Arbitration Review* (2010): 20–2, at p. 21.

[77] Shan and Zhang, 'The Treaty of Lisbon', p. 1056.

It should, however, be recalled that the Treaty of Lisbon neither provides for a transition period, nor contains a right of member states to keep in place their existing agreements.[78]

V   Conclusion

By the inclusion of FDI into the scope of the EU's CCP, the Treaty of Lisbon has considerably extended EU competence in this area. As Article 207 of the TFEU, however, does not provide a definition of the meaning and scope of FDI, the current transition period is characterised by considerable uncertainty.

This uncertainty is aggravated by the fact that the EU institutions hold different positions with regard to the interpretation of the scope of FDI. Only the Commission supports a broad definition of FDI, including indirect investment, a position vigorously and persistently criticised by experts in investment law. They also point out that the Commission, understandably, has not yet been in a position to acquire the necessary expertise and experience to conduct comprehensive negotiations with third countries. This situation may perhaps be compared with the one faced by the Commission at the beginning of the Uruguay Round of multilateral trade negotiations in the 1980s, when Commission representatives lacked the necessary experience in the area of trade in services, a new area which had not then formed part of the EC's exclusive negotiating competence.

Not only the scope of FDI in the sense of Article 207 of the TFEU, but also the question of the future of intra-EU BITs is still to be solved, since even the member states themselves do not have a common position. The Commission, which strongly opposes the continuing application of intra-EU BITs, apparently aims to avoid the situation where already existing BITs discriminate between EU citizens and consequently violate the fundamental EU principle of non-discrimination.

Although the extensive interpretation of the scope of FDI has been heavily criticised by experts, the strict attitude of the Commission regarding the necessary termination of intra-EU BITs seems to be in line with the ECJ's case law. Already in 1973, the ECJ decided in the case *French Merchant Seamen*[79] that the mere possibility of violating

---

[78] Cf. also Burgstaller, 'The Future of Bilateral Investment Treaties of EU Member States', p. 67.

[79] ECJ Case 167/73, *Commission v. French Republic (French Merchant Seamen)* [1974] ECR 359.

EC law (even by a national provision which has not been applied) is enough to constitute a breach of EC law.[80]

For all these reasons one is left wondering why the unsettling impact of an abrupt and profound overhaul of EU investment law potentially involving the simultaneous failure of two types of BITs could not have been mitigated. Thus, with regard to intra-EU BITs, an extended and staged transition period would have been in order. With regard to extra-EU BITs, conceptual clarity with respect to the definition and scope of FDI under Article 207 of the TFEU would have gone a long way towards enhancing legal certainty. Hopefully, an opportunity to amend the treaty accordingly might present itself shortly, in conjunction with the envisaged treaty amendment to deal with the Eurozone sovereign debt crisis.

---

[80] The Court did not accept the defending argument that administrative practices ensure that the national law in breach of Community is not applied in fact.

17

International investment and the European Union: an uneasy relationship

THOMAS HENQUET*

1 Introduction

As the world's largest economy, the EU is both 'the world's leading host and source of [foreign direct investment]' according to the European Commission.[1] Foreign investment requires a stable business environment and investment protection forms an important part thereof. Accordingly, one might expect the EU to pursue state-of-the-art investment protection for EU investors investing abroad and foreign investors investing in the EU. This holds particularly true at this time of financial crisis, when investment is much needed in the EU. That reality also underscores the need to protect EU investors investing within the EU.

However, developments at EU level with regard to investment protection under bilateral investment treaties (BITs) between EU member states and third states (extra-EU BITs) and among EU member states (intra-EU BITs) give rise to concerns.[2]

Section 2 below first discusses the latter. Intra-EU BITs have been in place, in particular, between older EU member states and the Central and Eastern European member states that have acceded to the EU in recent years. According to one estimate, there are about 150 such intra-EU BITS

---

* The opinions in this chapter are solely the author's and do not necessarily represent those of the Kingdom of the Netherlands. This chapter is based in part on T. Henquet, 'Dutch Bilateral Investment Treaties and Investment Protection in the European Union: Some Observations on Non-Discrimination and Investment Restructuring', in *Hague Yearbook of International Law* (2011).
[1] Communication from the Commission to the Council, the European Parliament, European Economic and Social Committee and the Committee of the Regions, 'Towards a comprehensive European international Investment Policy', 7.7.2010, COM(2010)343 final (Commission Communication on Investment).
[2] All BITs referred to in this chapter are available at: www.unctadxi.org/templates/ Search____97.aspx?quicksearchquery=bits, accessed 20 July 2012.

in force.[3] In practice, these treaties are valuable to investors as evidenced by the mere fact that investment arbitration on the basis of such treaties continues to take place.[4] Nonetheless, the European Commission and several EU member states oppose such treaties allegedly since they contravene EU law. However, both the legal reasoning (see section 2.1) relied on and the underlying policy objectives (see section 2.2) are questionable.

Section 3 below discusses developments with regard to extra-EU BITs. Under Article 207(1), in conjunction with Article 3(1)(e) of the Treaty on the Functioning of the European Union (TFEU), the EU has become exclusively competent in the area of 'foreign direct investment' (FDI), as part of the EU's common commercial policy. The aim of the European Commission (see section 3.1), largely endorsed by the Council,[5] is to gradually replace extra-EU BITs with agreements between the EU and third states. To that end, EU policy will be developed on the basis of 'best available practices' of member states. It is important to provide for high standards of protection and a broad scope of protection, such as under the broad definitions of the terms 'investment' and 'national' in Dutch BITs (see section 3.2). Furthermore, rather than guarding the respective competences of the EU and member states, the Commission, the European Parliament and the member states should jointly address the implications and challenges that arise for investment arbitration (see section 3.3).

Section 4 contains concluding remarks.

2   Intra-EU BITs

2.1   Legal arguments

The legal validity of intra-EU BITs has been challenged in investment arbitration. For example, in the UNCITRAL investment arbitration case *Eastern Sugar* v. *Czech Republic*, the state challenged the jurisdiction of

---

[3] *Eastern Sugar BV (Netherlands)* v. *The Czech Republic*, Ad hoc UNCITRAL Arbitration, SCC No. 088/2004, Partial Award, 27 March 2007 (*Eastern Sugar* v. *Czech Republic*, Partial Award), para. 126.

[4] See, e.g., the case mentioned in n. 2, above. For further references, see at: www.iareporter.com/categories/20090724_12.

[5] See the EU Council, 'Conclusions on a Comprehensive European International Investment Policy', 3041st Foreign Affairs Council meeting, Luxembourg, 25 October 2010 (EU Council Conclusions).

the arbitral tribunal on the ground, *inter alia*, that the Netherlands–Czech BIT had terminated in accordance with Article 59 of the 1969 Vienna Convention on the Law of Treaties.[6] In this respect it contended that the BIT and EU rules concern the same subject matter, that the parties to the BIT intended that the BIT be governed by EU law (i.e., the later treaty), and that the BIT and EU law could not be applied at the same time since this would result in discrimination of investors who are not covered by a BIT, discrimination being prohibited under EU law.[7]

The tribunal rejected each of these arguments. As to the respective subject matter of the BIT and EU rules, according to the tribunal, the difference is that EU law concerns the free movement of capital, that is, it confers the right to make an investment in an EU state, as well as the right to take the investment, and profits, out of that state. By contrast, the BIT confers rights during the investment and it includes an arbitration clause.[8] Furthermore, in the view of the tribunal, the parties to the BIT did not intend that EU law should prevail.[9]

The tribunal also held that the BIT and EU law are not incompatible, dismissing the discrimination argument by the Czech Republic. According to the tribunal, investors who are not covered by a BIT with the host state should 'claim their equal rights'.[10] This would mean that investors of EU member states that have not entered into a BIT with the investment host state would claim vis-à-vis such a state the protection that that state has guaranteed to investors from states with which it has entered into a BIT. However, this leads to complex questions in connection with the requirement of consent in arbitration.

One may, in fact, challenge the discrimination argument on other grounds. Arguably, it is true that the BIT does result in discrimination insofar as investors covered by a BIT are in a better position than those that are not. After all, while both types of investors can resort to the domestic courts of the investment host state, only the investor covered by a BIT has the additional right to commence investment arbitration against that state before an international tribunal. The question, however, is whether such difference contravenes the

---

[6] 1155 *UNTS* 331, 8 *ILM* 679 (1969).
[7] *Eastern Sugar* v. *Czech Republic*, Partial Award, paras 101, 102, 106.
[8] *Eastern Sugar* v. *Czech Republic*, Partial Award, paras 159–66.
[9] *Eastern Sugar* v. *Czech Republic*, Partial Award, para. 167.
[10] *Eastern Sugar* v. *Czech Republic*, Partial Award, para. 170.

prohibition of discrimination in EU law. The ECJ has merely sanctioned member states for violating the discrimination prohibition in cases in which they favoured *their own nationals* over nationals of other EU member states. This is not the case here: the nationals of the investment host state are as much disadvantaged as investors of third EU member states.

2.2   Policy arguments

The European Commission has been mounting a political campaign against intra-EU BITs. However, the policy rationale underlying the Commission's stance against intra-EU BITs is questionable. That rationale seems to be to preserve the integrity of EU law under the control of the Court of Justice of the European Union (CJEU). However, this is not necessarily at odds with investment arbitration. After all, in arbitrations under the New York Convention, within certain limits, both in annulment and enforcement proceedings national courts may and, in final instance, must request the ECJ for a preliminary ruling concerning the validity and interpretation of EU law in arbitral awards.[11]

A policy reason *against* terminating intra-EU BITs is that this would result in a more favourable treatment of investors from third states making investments in the EU compared with EU investors investing within the EU. The former enjoy protection under extra-EU BITs or future EU investment agreements with third states, while the latter do not enjoy treaty protection. Why should the option to resort to investor–state arbitration be limited to an investor from outside the EU? This inequality with EU investors might lead EU investors to relocate to a third state in order to protect their investments under an extra-EU BIT or in a future EU investment agreement. In this respect, investment arbitration tribunals generally accept investment restructuring, provided the restructuring is done before the dispute arises.

Whether such relocation is worthwhile depends on the contents of the future EU investment agreements, discussed next. The level of protection under such agreements is, of course, no less relevant to EU investors investing abroad.

---

[11] See, e.g., *European Court of Justice: Eco Swiss China Time Ltd* v. *Benetton International NV*, No. C-126/97, 1 June 1999.

3   Extra-EU BITs

3.1   The position of the Commission

With regard to the newly acquired powers of the EU under the Lisbon Treaty, the European Commission released two documents: (i) the Commission Communication on Investment; and (ii) a 'Proposal for a Regulation of the European Parliament and of the Council establishing transitional arrangements for bilateral investment agreements between member states and third countries'[12] (EU draft Regulation).[13] According to the Commission, 'in accordance with Article 2(1) of the TFEU, only the Union may legislate and adopt legally binding acts in an area where exclusive competence is conferred upon the Union'.[14] Preambular paragraph 4 of the Draft Regulation explicitly stated that BITs of EU member states 'will be progressively replaced by future agreements of the Union relating to the same subject matter'.

Pending the development of this EU investment policy, the Commission has proposed transitional arrangements. At the time of writing, these proposals had not yet resulted in the adoption of a regulation. The proposals are illustrative of the Commission's rather dismissive approach towards investment protection. Briefly put, these transitional arrangements authorise EU member states' BITs with third states to remain in force. However, during a period of five years after entry into force of the Regulation, the Commission will review these BITs for their compatibility with EU law, EU agreements with third countries and EU policies relating to investment, and this may lead to the authorisation being withdrawn. Presumably, in case of such withdrawal, the member state in question could attempt to re-negotiate the BIT with the third state to make the BIT acceptable to the Commission, or it must terminate the agreement.[15] Likewise, EU member states must obtain authorisation from the Commission to enter into negotiations to amend an existing BIT or to conclude a new one with a third country. As part of its authorisation, the Commission may put forward appropriate clauses

---

[12] Brussels, COM(2010)344 final, 2010/0197, 7 August 2010.

[13] Furthermore, reference is made to European Parliament Resolution of 6 April 2011 (2010/2203(INI)) on the future European international investment policy.

[14] EU Draft Regulation, Explanatory Memorandum, p. 2.

[15] However, the Council of the EU has already concluded that extra-EU BITs 'should continue to afford protection and legal security to investors till they are replaced by at least equally effective EU agreements'. See EU Council Conclusions, para. 9.

and/or request to participate in the negotiations. Before signing an agreement, the member state must once more obtain the approval of the Commission. Finally, member states have to cooperate with the Commission in dispute settlement procedures under BITs with third states.

One of the issues with respect to the proposed transitional arrangements that gives rise to concern is the Commission's stance on the compatibility of extra-EU BITs with EU law. The Commission has previously determined that provisions in BITs that guarantee unhampered capital transfers by investors contravene EU law, insofar as EU law prohibits such transfers in certain cases, for example, restrictive measures imposed by the EU on third states or certain persons. In practice, a clash between EU law and a BIT over this matter has never arisen, but in 2006 and 2007, the Commission nonetheless decided to bring proceedings against Austria, Sweden and Finland on this basis. The CJEU ruled in favour of the Commission, holding that the provisions were incompatible with Articles 57(2), 59 and 60 of the EC Treaty (now Articles 64, 66 and 215 of the TFEU). For a BIT to be compatible with EU law, thus, it needs to allow for certain capital transfer restrictions. This is, of course, subject to the agreement of the other state party. That party can be expected to insist on amending the clause in such a way as to allow for the capital transfer restrictions to apply reciprocally. This threatens the stability of the business environment for EU investors abroad, since they may be precluded from transferring capital in connection with their investment out of the investment host state. Thus, from the perspective of investment protection one may question the wisdom of the CJEU ruling secured by the Commission.

Returning to the future EU agreements with third states, the effect of these agreements in lieu of national BITs will be the creation of a level playing field between the EU and third countries with which the EU has concluded such agreements. This means that for an investor of such a state the investment protection will be the same throughout the EU irrespective of the Member State in which the investment is made. Likewise, to benefit from investment protection in a third state with which the EU has concluded an investment agreement, it is not relevant in which Member State a company is incorporated.

For the EU to remain attractive, for both inbound and outbound investments, EU investment agreements will need to guarantee a high level of protection. After all, reduced investment protection may lead to companies reconsidering their incorporation in the EU or their investment in the EU. Therefore, to ensure that the EU offers a competitive investment protection regime, the European Commission will need to study carefully the experience of member states. EU investment agreements should adopt the highest standards of protection in BITs between member states and third states. These include broad definitions of 'investment' and 'investor', as discussed next.

3.2 Contents of EU investment treaties

With well over ninety BITs entered into with states across the globe, the Netherlands ranks fourth among EU member states in terms of the number of BITs concluded.[16] These treaties derive their popularity in particular from the broad definitions of 'investment' and 'investor', though these provisions are not unique to Dutch BITs.

3.2.1 'Investment'

As to the definition of 'investment', Dutch BITs typically define the term 'investment' as 'every kind of asset', followed by a non-exhaustive enumeration, including, for example, 'rights derived from shares'. This while the definition of 'investment' in other investment instruments is sometimes restricted, for example, to investments that are made in certain industry sectors.[17]

The broad definition in Dutch BITs has been upheld in the case law. For example, in *Fedax* v. *Venezuela*,[18] the tribunal ruled that promissory notes acquired through endorsement constituted an investment under the Netherlands–Venezuela BIT. According to the tribunal, this is because the issuer (Venezuela) enjoys a continuous credit until the notes become due; it does not matter that the holder of the notes changes. In *Eureko* v. *Poland*,[19] the tribunal held that certain rights that the foreign investor obtained in addition to shareholding qualified as an investment, since these rights had 'some economic value'.[20] The tribunal in *Saluka* v. *Czech Republic*[21] held that under the Netherlands–Czech Republic BIT, a

---

[16] Commission Communication, Annex, p. 12.
[17] See, e.g., the Energy Charter Treaty, 34 *ILM* 360, 385 (1995).
[18] *Fedax NV* v. *Republic of Venezuela*, ICSID Case No. Arb/96/3, Decision of the Tribunal on Objections to Jurisdiction, 11 July 1997.
[19] *Eureko BV* v. *Republic of Poland*, Partial Award and Dissenting Opinion, *Ad hoc* UNCITRAL Arbitration Rules, IIC 98, 19 August 2005 (*Eureko* v. *Poland*, Partial Award and Dissenting Opinion).
[20] *Eureko* v. *Poland*, para. 145.
[21] *Saluka Investments BV* v. *The Czech Republic*, Partial Award, 17 March 2006 (*Saluka* v. *Czech Republic*, Partial Award).

mere shareholding qualified as an investment, and that it is not relevant whether such shareholding involves 'making a substantial contribution to the local economy or to the well-being of a company operating within it'.[22]

The tribunal in *Mobil* v. *Venezuela*[23] held that an investment under the broad generic definition thereof in the Netherlands–Venezuela BIT can be either direct or indirect. In that case, the investment was made, *inter alia*, by a Dutch holding company. Rather than itself investing directly in the oil sector in Venezuela, the Dutch company did so through a string of foreign companies incorporated in Delaware and the Bahamas. The tribunal held that this did not detract from the protection that the investment enjoyed under the Netherlands–Venezuela treaty. Investments are, in fact, often made indirectly; investment host states sometimes even require that investments be channelled through a local company. It is important that the EU agreements, too, extend protection to indirect investments. In this respect, there may be cause for confusion in light of the term 'foreign direct investment' under Article 207 of the TFEU. A literal reading may be taken to suggest that the term covers only *direct* investments and, *a contrario*, that it does not cover *indirect* investments. To avoid any ambiguity it would be advisable to stipulate in the agreement that the definition of 'investment' covers both kinds of investments.

Another consequence of the wording of Article 207 of the TFEU arguably is that only *direct* investments are part of the exclusive competence of the EU in this field, and that *indirect* investments presumably remain part of the competence of the EU member states. The implication would be that in order for EU investment agreements to cover also indirect investments, by necessity these agreements would need to be mixed, that is, they must be concluded by both the Commission on behalf of the EU and by the member states.

3.2.2 'Investor'

A different matter for attention in connection with future EU investment agreements is the definition of 'investor'. In the Dutch Model BIT, and indeed in many BITs entered into by the Netherlands, the 'national' entitled to protection under the BIT is defined as: (i) a natural person

---

[22] *Saluka* v. *Czech Republic*, Partial Award, para. 211.
[23] *Mobil Corporation, Venezuela Holdings BV; Mobil Cerro Negro Holdings Ltd; Mobil Venezolana de Petróleos Holdings, Inc.; Mobil Cerro Negro Ltd; and Mobil Venezolana de Petróleos, Inc.* v. *Bolivarian Republic of Venezuela*, ICSID Case No. ARB/07/27, Decision on Jurisdiction, 10 June 2010 (*Mobil* v. *Venezuela*, Decision on Jurisdiction).

as defined by national law of the respective state; (ii) a legal person constituted under the law of the respective state; or (iii) a legal person controlled, directly or indirectly, by an aforementioned natural or legal person. There are no additional requirements for a legal person to qualify for protection. Thus, for example, as to (ii), in *Saluka* v. *Czech Republic*, the state challenged the jurisdiction *ratione personae* of the tribunal on the basis that Saluka was a mere shell company without 'real and continuous links to the Netherlands'.[24] The tribunal dismissed this challenge as the definition of 'national' in the Netherlands–Czech Republic BIT simply does not require any such links.[25] The tribunal in *Rompetrol Group* v. *Romania* decided along similar lines.[26] While this definition of investor is not unique to Dutch BITs, BITs of other countries may contain more restrictive tests. For example, a company may qualify as a 'national' of a BIT contracting state party only if, in addition to being incorporated in that country, it has 'real economic activities'.[27]

As to the control test under (iii) above, this leads to a particularly broad scope of protection. In *Mobil* v. *Venezuela*, for example, Dutch companies had full ownership of their foreign (Delaware and Bahamian) subsidiaries that were investing in Venezuela. The tribunal considered these subsidiaries to qualify as Dutch nationals, because of the Dutch company's 100 per cent ownership, regardless of whether 'genuine control' was exercised by the Dutch company.[28]

3.3   Competences within the EU and investment arbitration

We return to the issue of the distribution of competences within the EU in the field of investment protection. Rather than merely guarding their respective competences, the member states and the Commission on

---

[24] *Saluka* v. *Czech Republic*, Partial Award, para. 239.

[25] *Saluka* v. *Czech Republic*, Partial Award, paras 240–1.

[26] *Rompetrol Group NV* v. *Romania*, ICSID Case No. ARB/06/3, Decision on Respondent's Preliminary Objections on Jurisdiction and Admissibility, 18 April 2008.

[27] See, e.g., Art. 1(2)(b) of the Thailand–Korea BIT, which cumulatively requires the company to be incorporated, to have its seat and to have real economic activities in the state.

[28] However, the *ultimate ownership* of a claimant may be determinative in terms of jurisdiction. For instance, in *TSA Spectrum de Argentina SA* v. *Argentine Republic*, the tribunal denied jurisdiction under Art. 25(2)(b) of the ICSID Convention on the basis that the Argentinean claimant TSA, while 100 per cent owned by a Dutch company, was ultimately owned by an Argentinean citizen. See *TSA Spectrum de Argentina SA* v. *Argentine Republic*, ICSID Case No. ARB/05/5, Award, 19 December 2008, para. 162.

behalf of the EU should carefully consider the complex issues that arise in this regard. Important questions are: who acts as defendant in an investment arbitration?; who bears responsibility for violations of the investment agreement?; and who ultimately pays the bill?

A logical starting point might be that the responsibility and financial burden lie with the EU and/or the Member State depending on whether their respective competences are at stake in a given case. Thus, insofar as a dispute in connection with the treatment of an investment in the EU concerns a measure taken at the EU level, this would be the responsibility of the EU. In such a case, it would also seem logical for the Commission to defend the action in the arbitration proceedings. In most cases, however, the dispute will concern actions taken by national authorities. Insofar as the action strictly involves implementing EU law by the Member State, also in this case the EU would be responsible and the Commission would be best placed to defend the action.

But in practice a dispute is likely to regard actions by national authorities that concern the competence of both the Member State and the EU. In such a case, the dividing line between these competencies and, consequently, the attribution of responsibility and the allocation of the financial burden may not be readily apparent. The same would apply in cases where the Member State and the Commission disagree as to whether the former acted pursuant to EU law, whether the Member State did so correctly or whether it acted within a margin of appreciation left to it. It may be for the CJEU in proceedings between the Commission and the Member State to settle any disagreement in this regard. However, the investor would suffer potentially significant delays in obtaining an award if the CJEU would first need to rule on any disagreement between Commission and Member State. Therefore, the internal division of responsibility and the allocation of financial burden must be dealt with subsequent to the arbitration. Meanwhile, in the investment arbitration the investor will want to be able to sue the party or parties that can be held legally responsible for all alleged violations of the agreement and against whom the award can be enforced.

One possible scenario would be that the EU is the sole party to the investment agreement and the sole defendant in the arbitration. In that scenario, from the perspective of the investor, the Commission should not be able to defend against the claim on the basis that it is not the EU, but the Member State that is responsible. To this end, the investment agreement would need to stipulate that the EU assumes full responsibility for any and all violations of the agreement. An award in favour of the claimant would be rendered against the EU. The Commission would subsequently seek redress against the Member State for any responsibility that relates to that state's competence, to which end a legal basis would presumably need to be created under EU law.

From the perspective of the Member State, however, the problem is that insofar as that state bears ultimate responsibility, it will want to be able to partake in the defence in the investment arbitration. This would be particularly the case if the Commission and the Member State disagree as to the division of competences or with regard to the legality of the impugned action by the Member State under EU law. After all, in the latter case the Commission would need to defend an action that it would itself believe to be illegal, and the Member State may not feel confident that the Commission is acting in its interest.

An alternative scenario would be that both the Member State and the EU are parties to the investment agreement and both are co-defendants in the arbitration.[29] This would allow the Member State to control its defence. The investor would want to be able to claim performance of the award irrespective of the subsequent internal division of the financial burden between the EU and the Member State. Unless the Commission is willing to accept sole responsibility, in order not to delay implementation or enforcement of the award, the investor would want the agreement to stipulate that the EU and the Member State are jointly and severally responsible for all potential violations thereof. Enforcement of the award does not seem merely theoretical, since voluntary compliance may not be forthcoming as long as the EU's internal burden-sharing remains unresolved. Enforcement might be disadvantageous for the Member State, insofar as its non-governmental assets typically do not enjoy immunity from execution. This while under Article 1 of the Protocol (No. 7) on the Privileges and Immunities of the European Union,

> the property and assets of the Union shall not be the subject of any administrative or legal measure of constraint without the authorisation of the Court of Justice.

These are but some of the complex issues that arise in connection with the EU's competences under Article 207 of the TFEU. The Commission

---

[29] Inspiration could be drawn from the negotiations concerning the accession of the EU to the European Convention on Human Rights, as well as the practice of the EU and the Member States with regard to WTO dispute settlement.

and the member states would do well to focus their attention thereon
before entering into negotiations with third states.

4   Conclusion

Proper investment protection must be in place to retain and attract
investors and investment, and this is needed for the EU to safeguard its
position as the world's leading economy. Both the legal reasoning and the
policy rationale underlying the Commission's stance against intra-EU
BITs are questionable, and the Commission should reconsider this. It is
also necessary for the EU to urgently bring its house in order in the field
of extra-EU BITs. In doing so, it must build on the experiences of the
member states and face the technical complications inherent in the
relationship between the EU and its member states. The current financial
challenges facing the EU underscore that the EU must make investment
protection a serious priority.

18

The new EU competence in foreign direct investment and intra-EU investment treaties: does the emperor have new clothes?

RUMIANA YOTOVA

Introduction

The focus of this chapter is the interaction of intra-EU bilateral investment treaties (BITs) with European Union (EU) law following the entry into force of the Lisbon Treaty, which constitutes the first explicit conferral of exclusive competence to the EU in the area of foreign direct investment (FDI), so as to assess whether the conflict of norms is indeed the most appropriate narrative. As the new FDI development generated a broad debate within both practice and academia,[1] this work analyses only the position of intra-EU BITs from the perspective of general international law, including the law of treaties, international organisations, and investment law and practice. The starting point is the interpretation of the current EU legal framework on the matter, with a historical discourse on whether and how it has changed with the Lisbon Treaty. The second source of interpretation is the official opinions and the evolving practice of EU member states and institutions, including the regulation of intra-EU investment relations, their positions expressed in investment treaty arbitrations and in the context of ongoing EU negotiations, so as to assess whether a new general practice has emerged reshaping the area of intra-EU FDI. Finally, the chapter will analyse the approaches on the interaction between EU law

---

[1] See W. Shan, *The Legal Framework of EU-China Investment Relations* (Portland, OR: Hart, 2005); S. Hindelang, *The Free Movement of Capital and Foreign Direct Investment: the scope of protection in EU law* (Oxford University Press, 2009); M. Bungenberg, J. Griebel and S. Hindelang (eds), *International Investment Law and EU Law, Special Issue of the European Yearbook of International Economic Law* (Heidelberg: Springer, 2011); and A. Dimopoulos, *EU Foreign Investment Law* (Oxford University Press, 2012).

and investment law adopted by the Court of Justice of the European
Union (CJEU), on the one side, and by investment arbitral tribunals, on
the other.

The intra-EU investment treaties debate was stirred, but not resolved,
by the entry into force of the Lisbon Treaty and the legislative proposals
that followed. It is both academically and practically significant, as even
though intra-EU BITs are approximately six times fewer than extra-EU
ones (according to the Commission's latest calculations of 2011 presented before the EFC, there are around 170 intra-EU BITs and approximately six times more, i.e. 1,200 BITs between EU member states and
third states), the proportions are reversed with respect to investment
treaty arbitrations involving an EU party: around 70 per cent of the ICSID
cases involving EU nationals or member states arise under intra-EU BITs
and only 30 per cent are based on BITs with third countries. Of the 148
cases currently pending before the International Centre for Settlement of
Investment Disputes (ICSID), thirteen have been brought by EU investors against EU member states, or a bit less than 10 per cent of the overall
case load.[2] The proportion of intra-EU investment arbitrations currently
pending before the Permanent Court of Arbitration (PCA) is even bigger:
six of the thirty-five pending investment arbitrations are based on intra-
EU BITs, that is, 20 per cent of the overall case load.[3] For these reasons,
the present analysis looks both at the possible frameworks for conceptualising the interaction between EU law and investment law in the area of
intra-EU FDI, as well as at the practical consequences of choosing one
framework over the other.

The Lisbon Treaty and the EU competence in FDI

The distinction between the intra- and the extra-EU FDI competence
should be stressed at the outset. It has particular importance to this
analysis as it has direct bearing on whether international investment
law as between EU member states is, and can be, in conflict with EU

---

[2] Available at: http://icsid.worldbank.org/ICSID/FrontServlet?requestType=GenCaseDtlsR-
H&actionVal=ListPending, accessed 1 July 2012.

[3] The author wishes to thank Ms Jara Minguez Almeida from the PCA for kindly supplying
these statistics. Two of these intra-EU investment cases are publicly available: *Achmea BV
(formerly known as 'Eureko BV')* v. *The Slovak Republic* and *European American Investment Bank AG (Austria)* v. *The Slovak Republic*. Another recent intra-EU case was decided
in 2011 between *HICEE BV* v. *The Slovak Republic*. For the PCA docket, see www.pca-cpa.
org/showpage.asp?pag_id=1029, accessed 15 July 2012.

law, or whether their parallel existence has interpretative consequences only.[4]

The Lisbon Treaty, as consolidated in the Treaty on the Functioning of the European Union (TFEU), determines and delimits the competences of the EU vis-à-vis its member states.[5] The treaty is an international agreement, which was signed and ratified by the twenty-seven EU member states, as well as signed by the presidents of the European Council, Commission and Parliament, and approved by a vote of the latter, constituting the EU as a party to it. Accordingly, the general international law rules of interpretation of treaties as codified in Articles 31–33 of the Vienna Convention on the Law of Treaties between States and International Organisations (VCLTIO)[6] apply to its interpretation.

While Article 207 constitutes the first explicit conferral of a new exclusive FDI competence to the EU to regulate relations with third states, the question of EU competence with respect to intra-EU FDI remains much less straightforward. Article 207 is included in the common commercial policy (CCP) of the EU, along with trade, tariff rates and the commercial aspects of intellectual property. The CCP is part of the 'Union's action on the international scene',[7] including, in particular, the exclusive competence to negotiate and conclude international agreements with third (non-EU) countries and international organisations in the specified areas,[8] such as bilateral investment treaties (BITs) with non-EU states. Notably, Article 207 makes clear that its conferral of competences in the area of the CCP does not otherwise affect 'the delimitation of competences between the Union and the member states'.[9] This provision should be borne in mind when interpreting the scope of other areas of more limited conferral of EU competence, such as those shared with its member states in the area of internal market regulation. It is also important in answering the contention that since FDI is now part of the exclusive CCP, intra-EU FDI should be naturally constituted as an implied power of the EU, in line with the maxim *qui magis potest, minus potest*. The TFEU expressly precludes such an interpretation.

---

[4] See ILC, 'Report on Fragmentation of International Law: Difficulties Arising from the Diversification and Expansion of International Law' (2006) A/61/10, para. 251(2).

[5] TFEU, Art. 1, C 115/51 *Official Journal of the European Union*, 9 May 2008.

[6] Vienna Convention on the Law of Treaties between States and International Organisations or between International Organisations, 21 March 1986, A/CONF.129/15, not yet in force.

[7] See TFEU, Art. 205, Pt V, External Action by the Union.

[8] TFEU, Arts 3(2) and 207(3) and (4).   [9] TFEU, Art. 207(5).

According to the Commission's interpretative communications in the area of intra-EU investment, the provisions regulating the free movement of capital and freedom of establishment, set out in Articles 63 and 49 of TFEU, respectively, form the legal basis of the EU competence on intra-EU FDI.[10] The Commission is of the opinion that while the freedom of capital movements applies to all forms of FDI, including portfolio investments, the freedom of establishment, including the principle of national treatment, applies only to the acquisition of controlling stakes in a domestic company by an EU investor.[11] The legal value of the Commission's interpretation is limited as it constitutes the *opinio juris* of only one of the institutions of the EU and parties to the TFEU, be it the main executive, in the application of the Treaty, in accordance with Article 31 (3)(b) of the VCLTIO. As it will be discussed in the next section, the Commission's position is not fully shared by the member states or, indeed, by the other institutions.

From a systematic point of interpretation, it should be noted that Article 63 of the TFEU regulates both the movement of capital between member states and between them and third countries, following the Commission's interpretation, it confers to the EU competences with respect to extra-EU FDI too. Still, the drafters of the TFEU felt it necessary to regulate extra-EU FDI expressly and in a different section, while omitting to include such conferral of competence to the EU with respect to intra-EU investment, when presented with an optimal negotiation opportunity in the context of the reforms introduced by the Lisbon Treaty. One could recall the Latin maxim of interpretation *expressio unius est exclusio alterius* to observe that such an omission to regulate intra-EU FDI competences, coupled with the restriction on a broad interpretation of Article 207 of the TFEU discussed above, may well constitute the exclusion of intra-EU FDI regulation by the organisation.

Finally, there is an important contextual distinction to be drawn between, on the one hand, the provisions on the freedoms of capital movement and establishment, which form part of the internal market regulation in the TFEU, and the provisions on the external EU

---

[10] Communication of the Commission on Certain Legal Aspects concerning Intra-EU Investment, C 220, *Official Journal of the European Economic Community*, 19 July 1991, p. 16, paras 3–4. See also s. 2, Commission Communication on Intra-EU Investment in the Financial Services Sector, C 293/2, *Official Journal of the European Union*, 25 November 2011.

[11] Commission Communication on Intra-EU Investment in the Financial Services Sector.

competence in FDI, which form part of the Common Commercial Policy, on the other. This is significant, because while the latter is an area of exclusive competence of the EU, the former is a shared one. With respect to the difference between EU exclusive and shared competences, Article 2(2) of the TFEU clarifies that:

> When the Treaties confer on the Union a competence shared with the Member States in a specific area, the Union and the Member States may legislate and adopt legally binding acts in that area. The Member States shall exercise their competence to the extent that the Union has not exercised its competence.

In contrast, according to Article 2(1) of the TFEU, 'when the Treaties confer on the Union the exclusive competence in a specific area, only the Union may legislate and adopt legally binding acts', that is, conclude BITs or indeed adopt binding secondary legislation such as regulations or directives.

Given that the EU has not so far purported to regulate intra-EU investment or investors in the comprehensive and targeted way in which intra-EU BITs encourage and protect FDI, it can be concluded that the member states may continue to adopt legally binding treaties in the area in exercise of their shared competence with the EU, to the extent that this does not contravene the treaty freedoms. Given that the object and purpose of BITs is to encourage capital flows, it is difficult to conceive how would they contravene the TFEU capital freedoms. In line with this is the fact that the Commission has never identified intra-EU BITs as one of the existing restrictions to Articles 49 and 63 of the TFEU.[12] Notably, the accession agreements concluded by the EU with member states, including the latest one with Croatia of April 2012,[13] nowhere regulate the matter of the purported conflict between EU law and intra-EU BITs either, even though their very purpose is to set out the conditions of accession, including the ability to assume the obligations stemming from EU law and policies.[14] Apparently, the termination of

---

[12] Communication of the Commission on Certain Legal Aspects concerning Intra-EU Investment, paras 6–8 and Commission Communication on Intra-EU investment in the financial services sector, ss 6 and 7.

[13] See L112/21, *Official Journal of the European Union*, 24 April 2012. All accession agreements are available at: http://eur-lex.europa.eu/en/treaties/index.htm#accession, accessed 15 July 2012.

[14] See TEU, Art. 49 and 1993 Copenhagen Criteria, p. 15 available at: http://ue.eu.int/ueDocs/cms_Data/docs/pressdata/en/ec/72921.pdf, accessed 15 July 2012.

intra-EU BITs was not considered to be an impediment to that objective and, accordingly, never included as a condition for accession.

The practice of the Commission and of EU member states in the regulation of intra-EU FDI

The interpretation of the TFEU with reference to the internal rules of the organisation, including its established practice, is of particular relevance in general international law. The VCLTIO specifies that the rules of the organisations include its constituent instruments, decisions and the established practice of the organisation.[15] Furthermore, the International Court of Justice (ICJ) has given special weight to such practice in interpreting the constituent treaties of international organisations.[16] In the *Legality of Use by a State of Nuclear Weapons* Advisory Opinion, referred to it by the World Health Organisation (WHO), the Court approached the question of whether nuclear weapons fell within the competence of the organisation by assessing both its constituent treaty and its subsequent practice, reasoning that:

> the constituent instruments of international organizations are also treaties of a particular type ... Such treaties can raise specific problems of interpretation owing, *inter alia*, to their character which is conventional and at the same time institutional; the very nature of the organization created, the objectives which have been assigned to it by its founders, the imperatives associated with the effective performance of its functions, as well as its own practice, are all elements which may deserve special attention when the time comes to interpret these constituent treaties.[17]

The Court went on to interpret the WHO treaty by reference to its ordinary meaning, context, object and purpose and 'the practice followed

---

[15] VCLTIO, Art. 2(1)(j). See also VCLTIO, Art. 31(3)(c).

[16] See *Certain Expenses of the United Nations (Article 17, Paragraph 2, of the Charter)*, Advisory Opinion, *ICJ Reports* 1962, p. 151, at pp. 160–2, 165; and *Legal Consequences for States of the Continued Presence of South Africa in Namibia (South West Africa) Notwithstanding Security Council Resolution 276 (1970)*, Advisory Opinion, *ICJ Reports* 1971, p. 16, at p. 22, para. 22, where the Court adopted a broad interpretation of Art. 27 of the UN Charter by reference to the consistent and uniform practice of the Security Council, extending over a long period of time, which it qualified as evidence of a general practice of the organisation.

[17] *Legality of the Use by a State of Nuclear Weapons in Armed Conflict*, Advisory Opinion, *ICJ Reports* 1996, p. 66, at p. 75.

by the Organisation'.[18] The Court assessed, *inter alia*, the relevance of WHO resolutions as practice, taking into account that they were:

> adopted not without opposition, as soon as the question of the legality of the use of nuclear weapons was raised at the WHO, could not be taken to express or to amount on its own to a practice establishing an agreement between the members of the Organization to interpret its Constitution as empowering it to address the question of the legality of the use of nuclear weapons.[19]

The Court accordingly concluded that 'such a practice cannot be inferred from isolated passages of certain resolutions of the World Health Assembly'.[20]

When applying the so identified general international law approach towards constituent treaty interpretation to the question of the intra-EU FDI competence, one cannot help noting that the Commission has so far not initiated regulation of intra-EU FDI with secondary legislation or international agreements, but only with 'isolated passages' of certain non-binding communications, 'adopted not without opposition' by the majority of member states.

For instance, in the Communication on Certain Legal Aspects Concerning Intra-EU Investment of 1997,[21] the Commission took note of the increased importance of intra-EU investment and of the corresponding measures adopted by member states to monitor and control it, recommending a harmonious interpretation of the treaty provisions on capital movement and the right to establishment.[22] It went on to identify certain types of discriminatory measures incompatible with the internal market provisions and proposed to 'enter into a continuing dialogue with member states in order to identify difficulties which could create obstacles to the free movement of capital as well as the freedom of establishment'.[23] What the Commission did not do was make a legislative proposal to positively regulate intra-EU FDI or, indeed, to identify intra-EU BITs as measures incompatible with the treaty freedoms. Instead, it

---

[18] *Legality of the Use by a State of Nuclear Weapons in Armed Conflict*, Advisory Opinion, p. 76.
[19] *Legality of the Use by a State of Nuclear Weapons in Armed Conflict*, Advisory Opinion, p. 81.
[20] *Legality of the Use by a State of Nuclear Weapons in Armed Conflict*, Advisory Opinion, p. 81.
[21] Communication on Certain Legal Aspects Concerning Intra-EU Investment, C 220, *Official Journal of the European Communities*, 19 July 1997, pp. 15–18.
[22] Communication on Certain Legal Aspects Concerning Intra-EU Investment, p. 15, paras 1–2.
[23] Communication on Certain Legal Aspects Concerning Intra-EU Investment, p. 18, paras 9–10.

called for negotiations and further harmonisation,[24] both mechanisms being typical in the areas of shared competences absent regulation at the EU level.

In a later 2005 Communication on Intra-EU Investment in the Financial Services Sector,[25] the Commission noted the 'lack of cross-border consolidation in the financial sector ... suggesting obstacles to investment' and in response suggested 'carrying out an open consultation with Member States and the financial sector in order to identify other possible obstacles ... that could hinder the cross-border consolidation in the EU financial sector'.[26] Similarly to the 1997 Communication, the Commission did not initiate an EU-level positive regulation or discuss intra-EU BITs. Finally, the most recent Commission Communication on a Comprehensive European International Investment Policy specifies in footnote 11 that it does not purport to cover intra-EU BITs.[27] The same approach is adopted in the Commission's Proposal for a Regulation establishing transitional arrangements for bilateral investment agreements between member states and third countries, whose scope is expressly limited to 'bilateral agreements with third countries related to investment'.[28] The Preamble states unequivocally in paragraph 15 that: 'Agreements between Member States relating to investment should not be covered by this Regulation.'[29]

It is true that there exists some secondary legislation purporting to regulate issues related to intra-EU FDI, however, the majority of it concerns the gathering of statistical data on investment projects by the Commission.[30] There are very few acts governing aspects of FDI,

---

[24] Communication on Certain Legal Aspects Concerning Intra-EU Investment, p. 17, paras 6–8.

[25] Communication on Intra-EU Investment in the Financial Services Sector, C 293/2, *Official Journal of the European Communities*, 25 November 2005.

[26] Communication on Intra-EU Investment in the Financial Services Sector, s. 6.

[27] Communication from the Commission to the Council, the European Parliament, the European Economic and Social Committee and the Committee of the Regions, 'Towards a Comprehensive European International Investment Policy', 7 July 2010, COM (2010) 343 final, p. 4, fn. 11, *in fine*.

[28] Proposal for a Regulation of the European Parliament and of the Council establishing transitional arrangements between Member States and third countries, 7 July 2010, COM (2010) 344 final, Art. 1.

[29] Proposal establishing transitional arrangements between Member States and third countries, p. 9, para. 15.

[30] See Council Directive 64/475 EEC concerning Co-ordinated Annual Surveys of Investment Industry, 30 July 1964, 2193/64, *Official Journal of the European Communities*; Council Regulation (Euratom) 2587/1999 Defining the Investment Projects to be

with very specific subject matter limited to investment aid for pig production or to collective investment in transferable securities,[31] both aiming at establishing restrictive regimes rather than promoting investment, that is, by endowing investors with rights additional to the treaty freedoms, such as fair and equitable treatment or full protection and security.

The annual reports of the Economic and Financial Committee (EFC) of the Council of the EU are another important source for assessing whether the practice and opinions of the EU and the member states in the area of internal market freedoms has evolved into a general practice establishing an agreement on the matter of intra-EU BITs. In addition, the EFC reports give a historical discourse on the gradual shift of the Commission's interpretation of the freedoms, indicating the factors that may have influenced, if not motivated, it. The EFC consists of members of the competent national administrations, the national central banks, of the European Commission and the European Central Bank.[32] It is mandated under the TFEU to examine annually the situation and all measures regarding the freedom of capital movements, and to report to the Commission and the Council.[33] In its reports it summarises and

---

Communicated to the Commission in accordance with Article 41 of the Treaty Establishing the European Atomic Energy Community, 2 December 1999, L 315/1, *Official Journal of the European Communities*; Directive 2004/39/EC of the European Parliament and the Council as regards Record-keeping Obligations for investment firms, transaction reporting, market transparency, admission of financial instruments to Trading, and Defined Terms as Implemented by Commission Regulation (EC) 1287/2006, 10 August 2006, L 241/1, *Official Journal of the European Union*; Council Regulation 617/2010 concerning Notification to the Commission of Investment Projects in Energy Infrastructure within the EU, as implemented by Commission Regulation (EU, Euratom) 833/2010, 21 September 2010, L 248/36, *Official Journal of the European Union*; Regulation (EC) 184/2005 of the European Parliament and of the Council on Community Statistics concerning Balance of Payments, International Trade in Services and Foreign Direct Investment, as regards the Update of Data Requirements and Definitions, as amended by Commission Regulation (EU) 555/2012, 22 June 2012, L 166/22, *Official Journal of the European Union*.

[31] Council Regulation (EEC) 1945/81, Restricting Investment Aid for Pig Production, L197/31, *Official Journal of the European Communities*, followed by an implementing Commission Regulation and Directive 2009/65/EC of the European Parliament and of the Council on the Coordination of Laws, Regulations and Administrative Provisions relating to Undertakings for Collective Investment in Transferable Securities, 13 July 2009, L 302/32, *Official Journal of the European Union*.

[32] Article 4 of the Statutes of the Economic and Financial Committee, L 158/59, *Official Journal of the European Union*, 27 June 2003, as amended.

[33] TFEU, Art. 134(2).

assesses the positions taken by all relevant EU institutions on these matters, as well as the responses of the member states.

Notably, it was not until 2006 that the Commission raised the issue of intra-EU BITs and their potential partial overlap with EU law before all member states in the context of the EFC.[34] The 2005 EFC Annual Report on the Movement of Capital and Freedom of Payments discussed the intra-EU investment flows and obstacles to FDI, and called for the abolition of the restrictions identified by the Commission without any mention of intra-EU BITs constituting a restriction to the treaty freedoms.[35]

The shift in the Commission's position on intra-EU BITs first became evident in the 2006 EFC Report, where it noted the existence of about 150 BITs in force between EU member states, and took the view that 'while part of their content has been superseded by community law upon accession', 'in order to avoid legal uncertainties and unnecessary risks for Member States in the unclear situation', it invited them to 'review the need for such BITs agreements and inform the Commission about the actions taken in this context' by 2007.[36] This shift in the Commission's approach towards intra-EU BITs coincided, on the one hand, with the intensified negotiations just before the signing of the Lisbon Treaty in October 2007 (including the extension of the EU competences to FDI with third states), and, on the other hand, probably more importantly, with the post-enlargement period in 2004 when ten new member states, traditionally viewed as capital-importers, became part of the EU. Until then, there were very few intra-EU BITs, that is, those between Germany and Greece and Germany and Portugal,[37] none of which has so far given rise to an investment treaty arbitration. However, there was one signifi-cant example of a multilateral investment treaty – the Energy Charter Treaty[38] – which was signed as a mixed agreement, that is, by both the EU and the member states in 1998. The Council's and Commission's act

---

[34] See EFC, 'Report to the Commission and the Council on the Movement of Capital and Freedom of Payments', 2006, available at: http://register.consilium.europa.eu/pdf/en/07/st05/st05044.en07.pdf, accessed 15 July 2012.

[35] EFC, 'Report to the Commission and the Council on the Movement of Capital and Freedom of Payments', 21 December 2005, paras 3 and 11.

[36] 2006 EFC, 'Report to the Commission and the Council on the Movement of Capital and Freedom of Payments', para. 16.

[37] See UNCTAD, 'International Investment Agreements Compendium', available at: www.unctadxi.org/templates/DocSearch____780.aspx, accessed 15 July 2012.

[38] Energy Charter Treaty, 2080 *UNTS* 95, 17 December 1994.

on the conclusion of the ECT expressly acknowledged that 'the decisions to be taken by the Energy Charter Conference concern areas of mixed competence, the European Communities and the member states are to cooperate with a view to achieving a common position'.[39]

The Commission's arguments against intra-EU BITs evolved further in the 2007 EFC Report, now specifying that there were 'arbitration risks and discriminatory treatment of investors if intra-BITs are maintained',[40] while also noting that the number of intra-EU BITs had increased with the accession of Bulgaria and Romania.[41] The EFC Report, however, also noted the reaction of the member states to the Commission's opinion, being that:

> Most Member States do not share the Commission's concern about arbitration risks and discriminatory treatment of investors. *A clear majority of Member States prefers to maintain the existing agreements*, in particular with view to the provisions on expropriation, compensation, protection of investments and investor-to-state dispute settlement. Still, a few Member States are seeking a solution for this issue.[42]

The Commission's first serious attempt at putting an end to existing intra-EU BITs was met with widespread resistance by the 'clear majority of Member States'; accordingly, it can hardly be constitutive of a new general practice, let alone an agreement between the organisation and its members. In fact, it is evidence as to the lack of such practice and agreement on intra-EU BITs.

The 2009 EFC Report shows further evolution of the opinion of the Commission against the maintaining of intra-EU BITs, concerning 'the proper application of Community law, also in respect of state aid rules, and potential discrimination between investors from different Member States and between Member States, as investment in BIT Member States may be more attractive', with particular reference to the 'increasing number of arbitration procedures where investors based in one Member State invoke a BIT in order to claim damages from another Member State'.[43]

---

[39] 98/181/EC/ECSC/Euratom, Council and Commission Decision of 23 September 1997 on the Conclusion, by the European Communities, of the Energy Charter Treaty and the Energy Charter Protocol on Energy Efficiency and Related Environmental Aspects, Preamble.

[40] EFC, 'Report to the Commission and the Council on the Movement of Capital and Freedom of Payments', 2007, para. 14.

[41] 2007 EFC Report.   [42] 2007 EFC Report, para. 15 (emphasis added).

[43] EFC, 'Report to the Commission and the Council on the Movement of Capital and the Freedom of Payments', 10 December 2009, para. 18, available at: http://register.consilium. europa.eu/pdf/en/09/st17/st17446.en09.pdf, accessed 15 July 2012.

The so expressed concerns of the Commission acknowledge that the incompatibility between existing intra-EU BITs and the treaty freedoms is only of a 'potential' character, and that investment treaties are more attractive to investors than the mere treaty-based protections, but still dismisses that higher level of protection of investment flows rather than fostering it by requiring member states to include MFN clauses in all intra-EU BITs so as to generate a level playing field of highest standards. Such an approach is hardly in line with the purposes of consolidation of the internal market and the increase in intra-EU capital flows. In fact, it puts investors from third countries in a better position to invest in the EU than EU investors would be in absent the protection of BITs. The report also indicates that a main concern of the Commission, underlying its position, is the increased number of arbitrations brought against EU member states and paid for by EU taxpayers, which was not the case before the fourth and fifth enlargements of the organisation.

The 2010 EFC Report confirms that the Commission's intra-EU BITs concerns are very closely related to the increased number of intra-EU investment arbitrations following the accession of the twelve new member states. It notes specifically the 'increasing number of arbitration procedures going on where investors based in one Member State invoke a BIT in order to claim damages from another (normally EU-12) Member State'.[44] According to the Commission, 'intra-EU BITs *seem not to be compatible* with the EU single market', '*may conflict* with the principles of EU law' and create '*the risk* that EU law is ignored or wrongly applied by arbitration panels without a review by the CJEU'.[45] Again, all the so formulated concerns are based on speculative future dangers, rather than on the text of the primary treaties or, indeed, the jurisprudence of the CJEU. Notably, none of the Commission's arguments against intra-EU BITs is based on the new exclusive external competence of the EU in the area of FDI under the Lisbon Treaty.

Finally, the latest EFC Report of 2011 observes that:

> After the recent termination of some intra-EU BITs, there were 176 intra-EU BITs in February 2011 … The EFC acknowledges that some Member States still consider that intra-EU BITs are needed in order to maintain protection of their investors, though at the same time an increasing

---

[44] EFC, 'Report to the Commission and the Council on the Movement of Capital and the Freedom of Payments', 14 December 2010, available at: http://register.consilium.europa.eu/pdf/en/10/st17/st17870.en10.pdf, accessed 15 July 2012, para. 22.

[45] 2010 EFC Report (emphasis added).

number of Member States have expressed the view that intra-EU BITs are inapplicable, due to the supremacy of EU law.[46]

The report reaffirmed that 'the Commission is especially concerned about ongoing investor-to-state arbitration proceedings', mentioning in particular the case of *Eureko* v. *Slovak Republic*.[47]

The recent termination of fourteen of over 190 intra-EU BITs can hardly be interpreted as evidence of an agreement between the EU member states and the Commission on the compatibility between BITs and EU law. Quite the contrary, it affects less than 8 per cent of the existing intra-EU BITs and is mostly in relation to two of the twenty-seven EU member states; notably the Czech Republic,[48] whose intra-EU BITs coincidentally have given rise to eleven out of a total of fifteen publicly reported investment treaty arbitrations against it.[49] It is note-worthy that the Czech Republic raised an intra-EU jurisdictional objec-tion in only two of these cases.[50] It can be concluded that its practice is hardly indicative of a general shift in the position of EU member states and, furthermore, that it is more likely motivated by the practical conse-quences of maintaining the intra-EU BITs, rather than by the potential conflict between EU and BIT obligations proclaimed by the Commission.

On the basis of the so observed practice of the Commission from the past six years on the question of the EU competence on intra-EU BITs, and the continuing opposition of the vast majority of the EU member states to it, it can be concluded that while there are isolated instances of non-binding Commission communications claiming such competence, there is no general 'subsequent practice in the application of the treaty which establishes the agreement of the parties regarding its interpret-ation' within the meaning of Article 31(3)(c) of the VCLTIO. There is, however, a consistent practice by the majority of the member states to regulate intra-EU investment by concluding intra-EU BITs and keeping them in force *inter se*. Finally, if the Commission is indeed convinced

---

[46] EFC, 'Report to the Commission and the Council on the Movement of Capital and the Freedom of Payments', 13 December 2011, available at: http://register.consilium.europa. eu/pdf/en/11/st18/st18451.en11.pdf, accessed 15 July 2012, paras 22–3.

[47] 2011 EFC Report, para. 23.

[48] Available at: www.iareporter.com/articles/20090719_2, accessed 15 July 2012.

[49] Available at: http://italaw.com/cases-by-respondent?field_case_respondent_tid=150, accessed 15 July 2012.

[50] *Binder* v. *Czech Republic*, Award on Jurisdiction, 6 June 2007, reportedly upheld at national court review on 22 June 2009; and *Eastern Sugar BV* v. *Czech Republic*, Partial Award, 27 March 2007.

that intra-EU BITs and resulting arbitrations are in conflict with the EU treaties, of which it is the guardian,[51] it is difficult to understand why it has not brought infringement proceedings against any of the EU member states retaining their intra-EU BITs, in accordance with Article 258 of the TFEU, six years after it identified for the first time the potential conflict and eight years after the 2004 enlargement, as it did in 2007 with respect to extra-EU BITs against Austria, Sweden and Finland.[52]

The interpretation of EU law and intra-EU BITs in international dispute settlement

The arbitral and judicial decisions discussing the interaction between EU law and intra-EU BITs can serve as another interpretative discourse, given their character of subsidiary source of international law.[53] They are the focus of the majority of the scholarly writings on the matter.[54]

The CJEU, which according to the Commission should have exclusive jurisdiction over intra-EU FDI, has not yet been seised with the question of the compatibility of intra-EU BITs with EU law, either by the Commission or by a EU Member State. This omission itself is telling. In contrast, the Commission did bring three infringement proceedings before the CJEU against Austria, Sweden and Finland, challenging the compatibility of their extra-EU BITs with EU law obligations.[55] And indeed, the Court found partial incompatibility of certain provisions regarding the free transfer of capital connected with an investment with the power of the Council to restrict such movements of capital between

---

[51] See Art. 17 (1), Consolidated Version of the Treaty on European Union (TEU), C 83/15, *Official Journal of the European Union*, 30 March 2010.

[52] See C-205/06, *Commission* v. *Austria* and C-249/06, *Commission* v. *Sweden*, 3 March 2009, and C-118/07, *Commission* v. *Finland*, 19 November 2009.

[53] Article 38(1)(d) of the Statute of the International Court of Justice, 892 *UNTS* 119, 26 June 1945.

[54] See, e.g., H. Wehland, 'Intra-EU Investment Agreements and Arbitration: Is European Community Law an Obstacle?' *International and Comparative Law Quarterly* 58 (2009): 297; M. Wierzbowski and A. Gubrynowicz, 'Conflict of Norms Stemming from Intra-EU BITs and EU Legal Obligations: Some Remarks on Possible Solutions', in Ch. Binder *et al* (eds), *International Investment Law for the 21st Century* (Oxford University Press, 2009), pp. 544–60; A. Reinisch, 'Articles 30 and 59 of the Vienna Convention on the Law of Treaties in Action: The Decisions on Jurisdiction in *Eastern Sugar* and *Eureko* Investment Arbitrations', *Legal Issues of Economic Integration* 39(2) (2012): 157.

[55] C-205/06, *Commission* v. *Austria* and C-249/06, *Commission* v. *Sweden*, 3 March 2009, and C-118/07, *Commission* v. *Finland*, 19 November 2009.

member states and third countries under the treaty, even though it had not purported to exercise it.[56] The Court ruled that member states had an obligation to ensure the immediate effectiveness of this future possibility by inserting a provision to that effect in their BITs. Notably, however, the CJEU expressly ruled out 'the possibility ... of taking other steps made available under international law such as the suspension or the denunciation of the agreement at issue or of certain provisions of that agreement [as being] too uncertain in its effects'.[57] Indeed, in practice, the way to remedy this incompatibility has now been established: it simply requires the insertion of a regional economic international organisation (REIO) clause into the relevant BITs, rather than their termination as a whole by all EU member states. One example of such clause can be found in the UK Model BIT of 2005, which lists among the exceptions to the standards of treatment:

> any requirements resulting from the United Kingdom's membership of the European Union including measures prohibiting, restricting or limiting the movement of capital to or from any third country.[58]

When dealing with the three infringement proceedings, the Court did not make any pronouncements on the issue of compatibility of intra-EU BITs with EU law. This is not surprising, given that the legal basis for its judgments was Article 307(2) of the Treaty (now Article 351 of the TFEU), which is a conflict provision defining the relationship between the TFEU and international law where:

> The rights and obligations arising from agreements concluded before 1 January 1958 or, for acceding States, before the date of their accession, between one or more Member States on the one hand, and one or more third countries on the other, shall not be affected by the provisions of the Treaties.
>   To the extent that such agreements are not compatible with the Treaties, the Member State or States concerned shall take all appropriate steps to eliminate the incompatibilities established.[59]

The provision makes clear that it does not apply to *inter se* international agreements between the member states, but only to their agreements with third countries. Accordingly, it cannot serve as a basis for interpreting the interaction between intra-EU BITs and EU law. This is why

---

[56] *Commission* v. *Finland*, para. 43.   [57] *Commission* v. *Finland*, para. 32.
[58] See, e.g., Art. 7(1)(c), UK Model BIT, 2005 (as amended in 2006).   [59] TFEU, Art. 351.

the Commission's attempts to invoke the three extra-EU BITs judgments of the CJEU as an argument by analogy against intra-EU BITs[60] is legally flawed.

The Commission was unsuccessful in bringing infringement proceedings against Slovakia, alleging its discriminatory treatment of EU investors due to the fulfilment of international obligations stemming from a BIT with Switzerland, the Energy Charter Treaty and an investment contract.[61] The CJEU chose to limit its compatibility analysis to the BIT only, even though Slovakia's main arguments were based on the Energy Charter Treaty,[62] given that the EU is also a party to it. After noting that 'it is not for the Court to interpret the Investment Protection Agreement, it is none the less appropriate to examine the factors which make it possible to determine whether that agreement imposes an obligation on the Slovak Republic which cannot be affected by the EC Treaty, within the terms of the first paragraph of Article 307 EC',[63] it went on to interpret the BIT by reference to the Vienna Convention on the Law of Treaties and to conclude that the contract in question was an investment contract protected under the BIT and that its annulment, as suggested by the Commission, would breach the substantive treaty provisions against expropriation. The CJEU accordingly upheld both the continued existence of the extra-EU BIT and the contract.[64] This case is an important precedent as the Court having engaged in the interpretation of a BIT to assess its compatibility with EU primary and secondary law on non-discriminatory access for EU nationals, upheld the preferential access as a protected investment under the BIT.[65] This approach confirms that the CJEU is able and willing to interpret BITs when necessary to assess their compatibility with EU law, and that it can do so with due regard to the international obligations assumed by the member states.

---

[60] See EFC, 'Annual Report to the Commission and the Council on the Movement of Capital and Freedom of Payments', 2008, para. 18, available at: http://register.consilium.europa.eu/pdf/en/08/st17/st17363.en08.pdf, accessed 15 July 2012.

[61] C-264/09, *Commission* v. *Slovak Republic*, 15 September 2011.

[62] *Commission* v. *Slovak Republic*, Opinion of Advocate General Jääskinen, 15 March 2011, paras 60–7.

[63] *Commission* v. *Slovak Republic*, Judgment, para. 40.

[64] *Commission* v. *Slovak Republic*, Judgment, paras 47–51.

[65] *Commission* v. *Slovak Republic*, Judgment, paras 51–3. See also CJEU cases upholding intra-EU double taxation treaties, which alike investment treaties grant preferential treatment on reciprocal basis, discussed in J. Klabbers, *Treaty Conflict and the European Union* (Cambridge University Press 2009), pp. 207–11.

On the plane of international dispute settlement, all positions expressed by the Commission regarding the incompatibility between intra-EU BITs and EU law and the resulting lack of jurisdiction of investment treaty tribunals, have been unanimously rejected by all such tribunals and by all arbitrators sitting on them.

In *Eastern Sugar*, the Czech Republic raised intra-EU jurisdictional objections under the Czech and Slovak Republic–Netherlands BIT. The dispute arose in relation to the changes of the Czech regulatory regime on sugar at the time of its accession to the EU and its protectionist agrarian system. The respondent challenged the jurisdiction of the tribunal and the applicability of the BIT on the basis that the latter was superseded by the EU legal framework, which addressed the same subject matter.[66] In support of its position, the Czech Republic submitted to the tribunal its correspondence with the European Commission's Directorate General Internal Market and Services, taking the view that EU law prevailed automatically over the conflicting provisions of the BIT as of the date of accession, as the BIT application 'could lead to a more favourable treatment of investors and investments between the parties covered by the BIT and consequently discriminate against other member states, a situation which would not be in accordance with the relevant Treaty provisions'.[67] The Commission did concede, however, that 'residual matters, such as diplomatic representation, expropriation and eventually investment promotion, would appear to remain in question',[68] that is, are not covered by EU law.

Notably, with respect to the BIT arbitration clause, the Commission noted that since the obligation 'not to submit a dispute concerning the interpretation or application of the Treaties to any method of settlement other than those provided for therein', under ex Article 292 TEU (now Article 344 of the TFEU) was addressed to member states only 'if the dispute concerns an investor-to-state claim under a BIT, the legal situation is more complex'.[69] The Commission concluded that in such cases, investors could continue to rely on the BIT dispute settlement provisions with respect to claims that arose prior to the date of accession, and, very importantly, that 'the primacy of Community law should in such instances be considered by the arbitration instance'.[70] In other words,

---

[66] *Eastern Sugar BV* v. *The Czech Republic*, Partial Award, 27 March 2007, paras 104–8.
[67] *Eastern Sugar* v. *Czech Republic*, para. 119.
[68] *Eastern Sugar* v. *Czech Republic*, para. 119.
[69] *Eastern Sugar* v. *Czech Republic*, para. 119.
[70] *Eastern Sugar* v. *Czech Republic*, para. 119.

the Commission seemed to acknowledge that since investors are not granted direct standing before EU courts, they may continue to rely on intra-EU BIT arbitration clauses; however, with a temporal limitation for claims arising up to the time of the host state's accession to the EU. Such a position is internally inconsistent and legally unsatisfactory.

The arbitral tribunal rejected the proposition that the EU Treaty covered the same subject matter as the BIT and thus prevailed over it.[71] It reasoned that while the EU guarantees the free movement of capital outwards, 'by contrast, the BIT provides for fair and equitable treatment of the investor during the investor's investment in the host country, prohibits expropriation and guarantees full protection and security and the like'.[72] The tribunal concluded accordingly that 'free movement of capital and protection of investment are different, but complimentary things',[73] not incompatible with each other and, as such, not triggering the successive treaties conflict rules codified in Articles 30 and 59 of the VCLT.[74] The arbitrators also upheld the applicability of the arbitration clause, underlying its significance by qualifying it as 'the best guarantee that the investor will be protected against potential undue infringements by the host state', and noting that such procedures are not provided for in EU law.[75] It accordingly upheld its jurisdiction unanimously.[76]

Two additional aspects of the award merit consideration for the purposes of the present analysis. First, that the tribunal identified at the outset the novelty of the intra-EU jurisdictional objection and the fact that it had not been raised in prior investment treaty arbitrations involving the very same BIT, either by the Commission or by the Czech Republic.[77] Second, the Commission's letter itself specified that 'the general question ... concerns the compatibility of BITs concluded between Member States ... almost exclusively (apart from agreements between Germany and Portugal and Germany and Greece) BITs concluded between the 10 new Member States'.[78] This observation is telling with regard to the motivation of the Commission in raising

---

[71] *Eastern Sugar v. Czech Republic*, para. 159.
[72] *Eastern Sugar v. Czech Republic*, para. 164.
[73] *Eastern Sugar v. Czech Republic*, para. 169.
[74] *Eastern Sugar v. Czech Republic*, paras 179–81.
[75] *Eastern Sugar v. Czech Republic*, para. 165, *in fine*.
[76] There was a Partial Dissenting Opinion of Voltera on the merits of the award.
[77] *Eastern Sugar v. Czech Republic*, para. 155.
[78] *Eastern Sugar v. Czech Republic*, para. 119.

incompatibility objections against intra-EU BITs only after the fourth EU enlargement when the new, capital-importing EU member states started to be respondents in investment treaty arbitrations. However, it is hard to see how this factual development could change the legal relationship between international investment law and EU law, which co-existed happily before the 'baby boom of treaty-based arbitration'.[79] For instance, the Germany–Portugal BIT mentioned by the Commission was concluded in 1980, at a time when both states were members of the EU and twenty-six years before the Commission started considering the compatibility of intra-EU BITs with the EU internal market provisions, which were set out in general by Council Directive 88/361/EEC, 24 June 1988, removing the restrictions on capital movements between residents of the member states, and comprehensively in the Treaty of Maastricht of 1992. However, the Commission never raised a similar compatibility concern in the two and a half decades that followed.

The tribunal in *Eureko* v. *Slovak Republic* refined further the international law-based perspective on the interaction between intra-EU BITs and EU law. The dispute arose under the same BIT between the Netherlands and the Czech and Slovak Republic of 1992, and related to regulatory changes in the health insurance market. The European Commission was formally invited to submit written observations on the intra-EU jurisdictional objection raised by the Slovak Republic. In addition to the arguments already submitted in *Eastern Sugar*, the Commission went on to purport that intra-EU BITs are incompatible with 'mandatory provisions of EU law and with the EU's judicial system', describing them as an 'anomaly within the EU internal market'.[80] With respect to the investor–state arbitration clauses, the Commission retreated from its partially pro-arbitration position expressed in *Eastern Sugar* and instead took the extreme view that 'under the EU judicial system, investors must either address a national court (which may or must refer questions of interpretation to the ECJ) or alternatively call on the Commission to initiate infringement proceedings'.[81] It elaborated its arbitration concerns further, stating that investment treaty arbitration would 'inevitably promote competing judicial and arbitral mechanisms, increase "forum shopping" by

---

[79] See S. Alexandrov, 'The "Baby Boom" of Treaty-Based Arbitrations and the Jurisdiction of ICSID Tribunals: Shareholders as 'Investors' under Investment Treaties', *Law and Practice of International Courts and Tribunals* 4 (2005): 19.

[80] *Eureko BV* v. *The Slovak Republic*, Award on Jurisdiction, 26 October 2010, para. 177.

[81] *Eureko* v. *Slovak Republic*, para. 179.

litigants and contribute to the further fragmentation of international law',[82] as well as reveal mistrust in the courts of EU member states, which had 'no place in the current post-enlargement context'.[83]

The practical post-enlargement concern was raised again, along with the strengthening anti-arbitration bias of the Commission, purportedly concealed behind concerns for the fragmentation of international law. With regard to the competition between judicial and arbitral proceedings, it should be recalled that the Commission has never raised such concerns with respect to commercial arbitrations, which are abundant within the EU. Furthermore, the Commission's position that the arguments in favour of maintaining investor–state mechanisms 'are not persuasive from an internal EU law perspective',[84] is difficult to reconcile with the fact that the EU itself is a party to the Energy Charter Treaty, which in Article 26 offers investors no less than four options for recourse to investor–state arbitration.

Furthermore, in that particular instance, Eureko had in fact filed a complaint with the Commission in 2008, which was ongoing; but according to the investor, it had limited influence on the progress of the procedure and, more importantly, 'ancillary proceedings in the European Court of Justice can by their very nature not result in a damages award'.[85] This factual background makes it clear why EU investors continue to invoke BIT arbitral clauses rather than having recourse to the EU Treaty procedures.

The Commission's solution to the identified inconsistency is simply untenable under any standard of international law, as it went as far as to assert that 'where there is a conflict with EU law, the rule of *pacta sunt servanda* does *not* apply to agreements between EU Member States' due to the principle of supremacy established by the jurisprudence of the CJEU.[86] According to the Commission, this was the relevant internal conflict rule, defining the relationship between EU law and intra-EU BITs. One should recall, however, that according to the VCLTIO, the internal rules of the organisation may not be invoked to justify a failure to comply with an international obligation, pursuant to Article 27. Furthermore, the rule of supremacy defines the relationship between EU law and the national law of the member states, it is not a rule of conflict applicable to international obligations.

---

[82] *Eureko* v. *Slovak Republic*, para. 185.   [83] *Eureko* v. *Slovak Republic*, para. 185.
[84] *Eureko* v. *Slovak Republic*, para. 185.   [85] *Eureko* v. *Slovak Republic*, paras 55–6.
[86] *Eureko* v. *Slovak Republic*, para. 180.

The tribunal, again unanimously, dismissed both lines of the Commission's argumentation. It adopted a reverse *Kadi* reasoning, holding that as the CJEU held in *Kadi* that its perspective was dictated by the treaties establishing it, 'so the perspective of this Tribunal must begin with the instrument by which the legal order within which consent originated', that is, the frameworks of the BITs and international law 'including applicable EU law'.[87] On the argument of conflict of norms, the tribunal affirmed that, 'EU law does not provide substantive rights for investors that extend as far as those provided by the BIT. There are rights that may be asserted under the BIT that are not secured by EU law',[88] and that 'there is no reason why those rights should not be fulfilled and upheld in addition to the rights protected by EU law',[89] thus resolving the apparent conflict purported by the Commission in favour of the parallel applicability of both regimes.

With respect to the challenge against the arbitration clause, the tribunal asserted that 'consensual arbitration under well-established arbitration rules adopted by the United Nations, in a neutral place and with a neutral appointing authority, cannot be equated simply with the legal right to bring legal proceedings before the national courts of the host state',[90] and also that there is 'no rule of EU law that prohibits investor–state arbitration', noting that transnational, that is, commercial arbitration, is a commonplace throughout the EU and that the CJEU has in fact given guidance on how to interpret certain mandatory rules of EU law within the meaning of the public policy exception in Article V of the New York Convention on Foreign Arbitral Awards in *Eco Swiss*.[91] It concluded that 'far from being precluded from considering and applying EU law the Tribunal is bound to apply it to the extent it is part of the applicable law(s)'.[92] The question of the applicability of EU law in investment treaty arbitration is the more important and interesting one than the conflict of norms purported by the Commission. According to the *Eureko* Tribunal, EU law applied as international law and as part of the *lex loci arbitri*.[93] However, due to the supranational nature of EU law, conferring rights directly upon individuals and forming part of the national laws of the member states with supremacy over conflicting provisions, it may be argued that it also qualifies as part of the law of

---

[87] *Eureko v. Slovak Republic*, para. 228.   [88] *Eureko v. Slovak Republic*, para. 262.
[89] *Eureko v. Slovak Republic*, para. 263.   [90] *Eureko v. Slovak Republic*, para. 264.
[91] *Eureko v. Slovak Republic*, para. 274.   [92] *Eureko v. Slovak Republic*, para. 281.
[93] *Eureko v. Slovak Republic*, para. 225.

the host member state, be it a supreme part, which as such is subject to the corrective function of the applicable principles of international law, as well as the standards of the BIT.

The approach of the *Eureko* Tribunal and the validity of its award were upheld by the Higher Regional Court of Frankfurt – the competent court at the seat of the arbitration – when challenged by the respondent on the basis that the arbitration clause in the intra-EU BIT was incompatible with EU law. The Court rejected this reiterating that Article 344 of the TFEU applies only to inter-state dispute settlement, not to investor–state mechanisms, and that, in any event, like commercial arbitral awards, investment awards are also subject to the control of national courts if in conflict with EU law, which in turn can submit the question to the CJEU. The Court disregarded the Slovak Republic's request for a preliminary ruling referral to the CJEU, reasoning that the case did not give rise to any serious doubts.[94]

A very different approach to the applicability of EU law in investment treaty arbitration was adopted by the arbitrators in *AES* v. *Hungary*, arising under the Energy Charter Treaty, who treated it as a matter of fact rather than law due to the express agreement between the parties to that effect.[95] The tribunal went on to approximate it to national laws,[96] reasoning that:

> once introduced in the national legal orders, it is part of these legal orders. It is common ground that in an international arbitration, national laws are to be considered as facts. Both parties having pleading that the Community competition law regime should be considered as a fact, it will be considered by this Tribunal as a fact, always taking into account that a state may not invoke its domestic law as an excuse for alleged breaches of its international obligations.[97]

Setting aside the debate as to whether national law is indeed to be treated as a fact in investment treaty arbitration, the approach of this tribunal in approximating the interaction between EU law and investment law to that of national law and investment law is not without merit. Further qualifications would be needed, given that some of the EU law obligations operate on an inter-state level only, as acknowledged by the *Eureko*

---

[94] 26 SchH 11/10 Oberlandesgericht Frankfurt am Main, 10 May 2012, available at: www.italaw.com/sites/default/files/case-documents/ita0931.pdf, accessed 15 July 2012.

[95] *AES Summit Generation Ltd* v. *The Republic of Hungary*, Award, 23 September 2010, para. 7.5.2.

[96] *AES* v. *Hungary*, para. 7.6.6.   [97] *AES* v. *Hungary*, para. 7.6.6.

Tribunal. The tribunal in this case, however, did not end up applying EU law as a fact or otherwise, it avoided the question by concluding that the dispute was not about a conflict between the EU competition law and the Energy Charter Treaty, but about the compliance of Hungary's measures with the latter.[98]

In similar vein, the tribunal in *ADC* v. *Hungary* avoided the question of EU law, which was raised as a defence to the respondent's actions, on the basis that the Directive in question was never mentioned as a reason for the expropriation prior to the proceedings, and further that in any case EU law did not mandate 'the steps actually taken' by Hungary.[99] Similar reluctance to engage in EU law interpretation can be seen in *Telenor* v. *Hungary*, where 'the tribunal remain[ed] unclear as to why the duty of Hungary to secure compatibility with EU legislation is relevant to the present case'.[100] In conclusion, it remains to be seen whether, and how, investment tribunals would interpret and apply EU law in the intra-EU disputes before them, but it seems that so far they have been reluctant to engage with it due to the institutional and constitutional uncertainties involved.

Finally, one non-investment dispute involving areas of shared EU competence should be mentioned, namely, the *Iron Rhine* Arbitration. Even though often quoted in the discussions of intra-EU BITs, the *MOX Plant* (*Commission* v. *Ireland*) dispute is not as pertinent to this discussion because, while it involved an area of shared competence between the EU and its member states in the protection of the marine environment, the EU had arguably exercised its regulatory option by becoming a party to an international agreement in the area – the UN Convention on the Law of the Sea – as well as by appending a declaration on the delimitation of competences between it and the member states upon accession. There is no such mixed agreement regulating in general the area of intra-EU investment and delimiting the respective shared competences between the EU and its members. However, concluding a general intra-EU BIT might be one way of resolving the complex legal situation and the surrounding uncertainties for all parties involved, including the investors. Furthermore, such a negotiated and mutually accepted agreement by all EU member states and by the EU could constitute a successive treaty

---

[98] *AES* v. *Hungary*, paras 7.6.8–7.6.9.

[99] *ADC Affiliate Ltd* v. *The Republic of Hungary*, Award, 2 October 2006, paras 268–72.

[100] *Telenor Mobile Communications* v. *The Republic of Hungary*, Award, 13 September 2006, para. 50.

relating to the same subject matter and including all parties to the intra-
EU BITs within the meaning of Article 59 of the VCLTIO, which would
thus prevail, provided, of course, that it covers all substantive and
procedural investment protections set out in the existing intra-EU BITs.

Turning back to the dispute between Belgium and the Netherlands
over the Iron Rhine, where the tribunal was asked to decide the claims
'on the basis of international law, including European Union law if
necessary, while taking into account the Parties' obligations under Article
292 of the EC Treaty'.[101] Even though none of the parties raised an intra-
EU jurisdictional objection, nor did the Commission take a position on
the matter after being notified about it by letter of the parties, the tribunal
considered it *proprio motu*.[102] The *Iron Rhine* dispute arose under the
1839 Treaty of Separation between Belgium and the Netherlands, which,
like intra-EU BITs, was a treaty signed by EU member states prior to
their accession to the Union and partly regulating matters that later fell
within the EU shared competence, namely, the system of trans-European
rail networks under Articles 154–6 of the EC Treaty (now Articles 170–1
of the TFEU, part of the EU Social Policy), implemented by secondary
legislation,[103] as well as within the EC environmental regulation, particularly the Habitats and the Birds directives.[104]

In order to decide the question of whether it had jurisdiction over the
so defined dispute and by reference to Article 292 of the EC Treaty, the
tribunal found itself:

> in a position analogous to that of a domestic court within the EC … if the
> Tribunal arrived at the conclusion that it could not decide the case before
> it without engaging in the interpretation of rules of EC law which
> constitute neither *actes clairs* nor *actes éclairés*, the Parties' obligations
> under Article 292 would be triggered in the sense that the relevant
> question of EC law would need to be submitted to the European Court
> of Justice.[105]

The tribunal applied the same national court analogy in determining its
approach to the applicability of EU law to the dispute before it, namely,

---

[101] *Belgium* v. *the Netherlands, Iron Rhine* Arbitration, PCA, Award, 24 May 2005, para. 4.
[102] *Iron Rhine*, Award, ch. III.
[103] That is, Council Regulation (EC) 2236/95, 15 September 1995, as amended by Regulation (EC) 807/2004, European Parliament and the Council, 21 April 2004.
[104] Council Directive 92/43/EEC, 21 May 1992, on the Conservation of Natural Habitats
and of Wild Flora and Fauna; Council Directive 79/409/EEC, 2 April 1979, on Conservation of Wild Birds.
[105] *Iron Rhine*, Award, para. 103.

by using the criteria as to whether the question of interpretation of EC law 'is necessary to enable it to give judgment'.[106] After assessing the primary and secondary EU legislation on the matter, the tribunal concluded that, 'the questions of EC law debated by the Parties are not determinative, or conclusive for the Tribunal'.[107] This seems to be the most in-depth analysis so far on the applicability of EU law in intra-EU arbitration, and could serve as a starting point in future instances, particularly on the points regarding *actes clairs*, already authoritatively clarified by the CJEU and on the *CILFIT* criteria as to whether the EU law question would affect the outcome of the case. This approach allows for the application of EU law by investment tribunals, while avoiding encroaching upon the CJEU interpretative monopoly over it. The domestic court analogy, however, remains controversial, as the CJEU has specified on more than one occasion that arbitral tribunals are not to be equated to national courts.[108]

The arbitral case law is consistent in showing that the question of the interaction between EU law and international law in the assessment of intra-EU international agreements is not one of conflict resulting in lack of jurisdiction, but rather one of the applicability of EU law and of the modalities of its application by arbitral tribunals. Tribunals have been unanimous in accepting jurisdiction under their constituent instrument governed by international law, but have differed in their approaches for qualifying the EU legal order as a *quasi* domestic one, as a specialised regime under international law, as a fact and, finally, as a *sui generis* regime displaying characteristics of both national and international law. In practice, both the CJEU and arbitral tribunals display the inclination not to apply the legal orders outside their constituent one, which is in line with their jurisdictional limitations. However, when called upon by the parties, both the CJEU and arbitral tribunals have engaged in such interpretation in passing while refraining from an actual application. Notably, however, neither the CJEU nor investment treaty tribunals have

---

[106] *Iron Rhine*, Award, paras 104–5, quoting Case 283/81, *Srl CILFIT and Lanificio di Gavardo SpA* v. *Ministero della Sanità* [1982] ECR 3415, paras 10–11 and Lord Denning in *H. P. Bulmer Ltd* v. *J. Bollinger SA* [1974] 2 CMLR 91, 2 All ER 1226.

[107] *Iron Rhine*, Award, para. 137.

[108] See Case 102/81, *Nordsee Deutsche Hochseefischerei GmbH* v. *Reederei Mond Hochseefischerei Nordstern AG & Co. KG, and Reederei Friedrich Busse Hochseefischerei Nordstern AG & Co. KG*, Judgment, 23 March 1982, paras 10 and 13; see also Case 126/97, *EcoSwiss China Time Ltd* v. *Benetton International NV*, Judgment, 1 June 1999, paras 33–8.

so far established a genuine conflict in the interaction between international investment law and EU law, leading to the complete non-application of one of the regimes in favour of the other.

Instead of using the prism of conflict of norms, endorsed and imposed not too long ago by the European Commission, the question of the interaction between EU law and investment law could be better discussed from the perspectives of interpretation and of applicable law. The CJEU has consistently defined the EU as 'a new legal order of international law', but also one whose 'subjects comprise not only Member States but also their nationals'.[109] Not surprisingly, EU law contains numerous rules on its interaction with the national laws of the member states, including the CJEU-developed principles of direct effect and supremacy, but very few rules on its interplay with international law, including Article 21 of the TEU concerning the EU's external action and Article 351 of the TFEU concerning extra-EU agreements concluded prior to accession. On this basis one could argue that EU law applies in investment treaty arbitration mostly as part of the national law of the host state or the investor, where it regulates investor rights and Member State direct obligations towards the individuals, as well as in its own right as an international legal regime when it regulates the rights and obligations of member states *inter se*. Such an approach could to a certain extent avoid the narrative of genuine conflict of norms, while maintaining the primacy of the investment treaty standards of protection and preserving the corrective function of international law in investment treaty arbitration.

Conclusions and prospects *de lege ferenda*

According to the opinions expressed by the European Commission in intra-EU investment treaty arbitrations and before the Economic and Financial Committee, FDI within the EU is already regulated as part of the internal market, in particular, by the provisions on the free movement of capital, freedom of establishment and the principle of non-discrimination. Accordingly, the Commission concludes that there is a conflict between EU law and investment law in the relations between EU member states, which should be resolved in favour of the primacy of the European legal order. This contention was analysed from a few interpretative perspectives of general international law. First and foremost, an

---

[109] Case 26/62, *Van Gend en Loos v. Nederlandse Administratie der Belastingen* [1963] ECR 1.

interpretation of the EU legal framework, in accordance with the general rules of treaty interpretation codified in Articles 31–33 of the Vienna Convention on the Law of Treaties between States and International Organisations, showed that the Lisbon Treaty provides no basis for an extension of the EU's FDI competence to intra-EU relations. Second, the practice of the EU institutions and the member states is in accordance with the shared character of the intra-EU investment competence and is exercised by the member states concluding BITs as opposed to the EU, which has not so far purported to regulate intra-EU FDI as such. Finally, the Commission's position with regard to the incompatibility between EU law and intra-EU BITS has not been endorsed by any of the international investment treaty tribunals it was presented to, and in fact was most recently rejected by the Court of Appeal of Frankfurt. It can be observed from a practical perspective that EU investors operating within the EU continue invoking their rights of international arbitration under existing intra-EU BITs, rather than relying on the fundamental capital movement freedoms under the TFEU before national courts or the Commission.

Last, but not least, in light of the lack of legislative initiative by the Commission to regulate comprehensively the shared EU competence in intra-EU investment capital flows, in contrast to all the acts produced in relation to the newly acquired external competence in FDI, it is possible to conclude that the Commission does not intend to initiate more detailed pro-investment regulation now that twenty years have passed since the Treaty of Maastricht incorporating the capital freedoms for the first time. The legal consequences of the Commission's approach, motivated mainly by the fourth and fifth EU enlargements and the resulting increase in investment treaty arbitrations against EU member states (mostly the twelve new ones), would include not only the non-availability of investor–state arbitration for intra-EU investment disputes, but also a considerable lowering of the currently available substantive standards of intra-EU investment protection, including fair and equitable treatment, full protection and security, and indirect expropriation. These would be reduced to the principles prohibiting discrimination and protecting the free movement of capital and the freedom of establishment,[110] the latter excluding portfolio investments.[111] In practice, this would create an

---

[110] See *Eureko* v. *Slovak Republic*, para. 247, chart.
[111] See Commission Communication on Intra-EU Investment in the Financial Services' Sector, C 293/2, *Official Journal of the European Union*, 25 November 2005, s. 2.

un-level playing field between EU investors operating within and outside
the Union. This may potentially have the effect of channelling intra-EU
investment flows outside the EU to countries where the full substantive
protections and arbitration guarantees of international investment law
apply. Such a development is both unnecessary and undesirable from the
perspectives of the EU and of the member states.

Proposals for an alternative course of action by the Commission so as
to better accommodate intra-EU BITs in the EU legal order could
include referral of the question of compatibility between intra-EU BITs
and EU law to the CJEU; the issuing of recommendations to include
special 'EU MFN' clauses in existing and future BITs so as to ensure the
harmonisation of their substantive and procedural standards by reference to the highest available ones in intra-EU BITs; and, finally, the
drafting of a model intra-EU BIT, containing REIO compatibility
clauses, as well as authoritative guidance on the applicability of EU
law in investment treaty arbitration.

PART VI

Outlook: international investment in the
twenty-first century

19

International investment dispute settlement in the twenty-first century: does the preservation of the public interest require an alternative to the arbitral model?

NICOLAS HACHEZ AND JAN WOUTERS

1 Arbitration in the international investment legal regime

While the international legal regime on foreign direct investment (FDI) is unique in many respects, its most peculiar characteristic is the arbitral model which has become an 'institution' for solving disputes between investors and host states.[1] Even though this model cannot (yet) be said to have become part of customary international law for regulating the relations between investors and host states,[2] the presence of clauses allowing investors to directly sue the host State before an *ad hoc* arbitral tribunal in case of dispute is a recurrent feature of international investment agreements (IIAs), be they investment contracts governing the relationship of an investor and the host state regarding one investment, or investment treaties governing the relationship of the investors of a state (the 'home state') with one or several other states in which the investor has an investment (the 'host state'). There are, however, notable exceptions to this legal trend.[3] The role of

---

[1] Jan Wouters and Nicolas Hachez, 'The Institutionalization of Investment Arbitration and Sustainable Development', in Marie-Claire Cordonier Segger, Markus Gehring and Andrew Newcombe (eds), *Sustainable Development in World Investment Law* (Alphen aan den Rijn: Kluwer Law, 2011), p. 616. On the reasons for the increasing recourse to arbitration to solve investment disputes, see Jeswald Salacuse, 'Explanations for the Increased Recourse to Treaty-based Investment Dispute Settlement: Resolving the Struggle of Life against Form?' in Karl P. Sauvant (ed.), *Appeals Mechanism in International Investment Disputes* (Oxford University Press, 2008), pp. 105–26.

[2] Bernard Kishoiyian, 'The Utility of Bilateral Investment Treaties in the Formulation of Customary International Law', *Northwestern Journal of International Law and Business* 14 (1994): 327, at p. 368.

[3] The US–Australia free trade agreement's investment chapter does not contain a dispute settlement clause, possibly because both developed countries are inclined to trust each other's judicial system. See Free Trade Agreement between Australia and the United

arbitral tribunals in shaping the international investment regime has been decisive,[4] and there is every reason to believe that investor disputes will continue to be a main driver in the emergence and evolution of international norms on FDI. Therefore, it seems fitting to evaluate how arbitration is faring in its role as promoter of the general interest.

Arguably, the reason for having such a peculiar dispute settlement mechanism has to do with the credence that, in order to attract FDI, a host state has to display a 'friendly investment climate' through the development of an effective rule-based regime governing its relations with investors.[5] Next to a number of substantive protections in favour of investors (fair and equitable treatment, full protection and security, protection against (indirect) expropriation, etc.), the existence of a dispute settlement mechanism separate from domestic judicial and administrative procedures is thought to contribute to such friendly investment climate in the host state. *A contrario*, host states would also be induced into accepting the arbitral model so as not to be seen, among capital-importing countries, as having an 'unfriendly' investment climate for being one of the only countries not allowing such remedy.[6] The perceived advantages of arbitration for investors are multiple. First, domestic judicial institutions are generally bypassed (at least after some time of trying them out – see below), and with them their supposedly lengthy procedures and their possibly corrupt, biased or incompetent judges. As distrust

---

States, done at Washington, DC, 18 May 2004, available at: http://203.6.168.65/fta/ausfta/final-text/. Similarly, China was for many years very cautious regarding the inclusion of arbitration clauses into international investment instruments, notably by limiting the jurisdiction of tribunals to certain issues or requiring prior recourse to domestic remedies. However, it seems to have relaxed its practice in the last decade. See Monika Heymann, 'International Law and the Settlement of Investment Disputes Relating to China', *Journal of International Economic Law* 11 (2008): 507; Dan Wei, 'Bilateral Investment Treaties: An Empirical Analysis of the Practices of Brazil and China', *European Journal of Law and Economics* (2010), Online First, DOI:10.1007/s10657-010-9157-z.

4 See UNCTAD, 'Investor–State Dispute Settlement and Impact on Investment Rulemaking', 2007 (Investor–State Dispute Settlement, 2007), available at: www.unctad.org/en/docs/iteiia20073_en.pdf.

5 As opposed to the 'gunboat diplomacy' that used to prevail, according to which a foreign investor had to rely on the diplomatic efforts and power of its home state if it had to have its investment protected against abuse by the host state. See Susan D. Franck, 'Challenges Facing Investment Disputes: Reconsidering Dispute Resolution in International Investment Agreements, in Karl Sauvant (ed.), *Appeals Mechanism in International Investment Disputes* (Oxford University Press, 2008), p. 149.

6 See Andrew Guzman, 'Why LDCs Sign Treaties that Hurt Them: Explaining the Popularity of Bilateral Investment Treaties', *Virginia Journal of International Law* 38 (1998): 639.

towards domestic judicial institutions is thus at the root of investor–state arbitration. Second, having recourse to arbitration directly between the foreign investor and the host state for breach of an international obligation by the latter[7] also allows the disadvantages and uncertainties of the customary diplomatic protection process, in which a foreign investor is entirely dependent on the goodwill and power of its home state in order to get a wrong redressed, to be circumvented.[8] Third, international arbitration, despite its sometimes staggering cost (counsel, arbitrator and expert fees, travel and administrative costs, secretarial costs, etc.[9]), is thought to be more effective than domestic judicial processes, as its procedures are more flexible, and as the awards are final and not subject to appeal, save in a limited number of 'annulment' instances.

As one can see, the benefits of arbitration for investors are direct, whereas for host states, the advantages are indirect, as by giving up the jurisdiction of their own courts they hope to send a favourable message to potential investors, perhaps resulting in a growth in incoming capital.[10] While the positive effect on investment flows is yet to be demonstrated,[11] investors have not refrained from using

---

[7] As we shall see below, the host state is in 99 per cent of the cases the respondent in investment arbitration.

[8] Stephan Schill, 'Private Enforcement of International Investment Law: Why We Need Investor Standing in BIT Dispute Settlement', in Michael Waibel, Asha Kaushal, Kyo-Hwa Liz Chung and Claire Balchin (eds), *The Backlash against Investment Arbitration: Perceptions and Reality* (Alphen aan den Rijn: Kluwer Law, 2010), pp. 36–45.

[9] Even though transparent data are often lacking to evaluate the true cost of arbitration in most of the cases. See Susan D. Franck, 'Empirically Evaluating Claims about Investment Treaty Arbitration', *North Carolina Law Review* 86 (2006/7): 1 at pp. 66–70. A 2010 UNCTAD survey, however, claims that '*costs involved in investor–State arbitration have skyrocketed* in recent years. This refers not only to the damages States must pay to foreign investors in the case of a violation of a treaty provision, but the costs for conducting arbitration procedures are extremely high, with legal fees amounting to an average of 60 per cent of the total costs of the case … In addition to legal fees, there are arbitrator's fees, administration fees of arbitration centres and additional costs for the involvement of experts and witnesses', UNCTAD, 'Investor–State Disputes: Prevention and Alternatives to Arbitration', *UNCTAD Series on International Investment Policies for Development*, 2010, available at: http://unctad.org/en/docs/diaeia200911_en.pdf, pp. 16–17 (emphasis in original, references omitted). The report gives example of cases in which a party's legal fees and other arbitration costs sometimes amounted to more than US$10,000,000.

[10] Olivia Chung, 'The Lopsided International Investment Law Regime and its Effect on the Future of Investor–State Arbitration', *Virginia Journal of International* Law 47 (2007): 953.

[11] See, e.g., Mary Hallward-Driemeier, 'Do Bilateral Investment Treaties Attract Foreign Direct Investment? Only a Bit … And They Could Bite', World Bank Policy Research Working Paper No. 3121, August 2003, available at: http://econ.worldbank.org/external/default/main?pagePK=64165259&piPK=64165421&theSitePK=469372&menuPK=64216926

arbitration to vindicate their rights under international investment instruments, especially over the last decade.[12] A number of phenomena, such as a race for capital by host states, the supposedly uncritical signing by host states of some 'model agreements' containing arbitration clauses and presented by capital-exporting states, the unequal bargaining positions inducing host states to sign BITs with arbitration clauses, or simply a phenomenon of imitation and replication operating throughout the investment legal regime, have made arbitration a *fait accompli* in international investment instruments. To be sure, the outcomes of a number of these proceedings have at times proven bitter for respondent host states, as the latter were condemned to paying steep damages to claimant investors.[13] As the number of awards concerning investment disputes kept growing, scrutiny and criticism simultaneously intensified towards investment arbitration, leading to what some have called a 'backlash against investment arbitration'.[14] A number of points in the design and operation of investment tribunals have polarised the debate.

In the following sections, we first give an overview of the main criticisms against investor–state arbitration. We then briefly present the steps that have recently been taken to reform the arbitral institution in order to respond to the critique. We finally turn to more radical

&entityID=000094946_03091104060047; and Jason Webb Yackee, 'Bilateral Investment Treaties, Credible Commitment, and the Rule of (International) Law: Do BITs Promote Foreign Direct Investment?', *Law and Society Review* 42 (2008): 805; Jeswald Salacuse and Nicholas Sullivan, 'Do BITs Really Work? An Evaluation of Bilateral Investment Treaties and their Grand Bargain', *Harvard International Law Journal* 46 (2005): 67.

[12] At the end of 2011, the number of known arbitration cases was 450. The number of filed claims before investment tribunals has been growing exponentially since the mid-1990s. In 2011, forty-six new cases were started, which constitutes the highest number of known treaty-based disputes filed in one year. See UNCTAD, 'Latest Developments in Investor–State Dispute Settlement', *IIAs Issues*, Note No. 1, April 2012, available at: http://unctad.org/en/PublicationsLibrary/webdiaeia2012d10_en. pdf, p. 1. Statistics in this regard are, however, quite volatile, since 2010, with 'only' twenty-five new cases, had 'the lowest number of known treaty-based disputes filed annually since 2001', see, UNCTAD, 'Latest Developments in Investor–State Dispute Settlement', *IIAs Issues*, Note No. 1, April 2012, available at: www.unctad.org/en/docs//webdiaeia20113_en.pdf, pp. 1–2.

[13] For a review of some of the highest damages awarded as at 2005, see UNCTAD, 'Investor–State Disputes Arising from Investment Treaties: A Review', 2006, available at: www.unctad.org/en/docs/iteiit20054_en.pdf, pp. 9–12.

[14] See Michael Waibel *et al.* (eds), *The Backlash against Investment Arbitration: Perceptions and Reality* (Alphen aan den Rijn: Kluwer Law, 2010).

proposals for reform, some of which even suggest doing away with arbitration altogether, and we evaluate these proposals for alternatives to the arbitral model.

2   Criticism of the arbitral model

2.1   Commercial process versus the public interest: democracy and the rule of law

The main criticism levelled at the arbitral model is that it fails to live up to the basic precepts of democracy and the rule of law.[15]

First of all, since investment arbitrations are one-off proceedings, and since the various arbitral tribunals do not share an organic link in the form of a *stare decisis* rule, or an appeals mechanism, arbitration has produced a number of inconsistent decisions, reaching different outcomes in similar situations.[16] A visible stream of inconsistencies have resulted from the dozens of claims that have been filed against Argentina following the economic crisis that struck the country in 2000/1, in which international investors challenged Argentina's anti-crisis measures as breaching a number of investment protections. Whereas some arbitral panels accepted Argentina's defence of necessity and reliance on the 'non-precluded measures' clause to justify these measures,[17] others rejected it, even though the factual context was the same in all cases.[18] Other well-known instances of

---

[15] See, e.g., Barnali Choudhury, 'Recapturing Public Power: Is Investment Arbitration's Engagement of the Public Interest Contributing to the Democratic Deficit?', *Vanderbilt Journal of Transnational Law* 41 (2008): 775; and Gus van Harten, *Investment Treaty Arbitration and Public Law* (Oxford University Press, 2007).

[16] August Reinisch, 'The Issues Raised by Parallel Proceedings and Possible Solutions', in Michael Waibel *et al.* (eds), *The Backlash against Investment Arbitration: Perceptions and Reality* (Alphen aan den Rijn: Kluwer Law, 2010), pp. 115–17, classifies the cases of inconsistency in three categories: (1) divergent views on legal issues; (2) divergent assessment of identical facts; and (3) conflicting results in the same dispute.

[17] See *LG&E* v. *Argentine Republic*, ICSID Case No. ARB/02/1, Award, 25 July 2007; *Continental Casualty Company* v. *Argentine Republic*, ICSID Case No. ARB/03/9, Award, 5 September 2008.

[18] See *CMS Gas Transmission Company* v. *Argentine Republic*, ICSID Case No. ARB/01/8, Award, 12 May 2005; *Sempra Energy International* v. *Argentine Republic*, ICSID Case No. ARB/02/16, Award, 28 September 2007; *Enron Corporation and Ponderosa Assets LP* v. *Argentine Republic*, ICSID Case No. ARB/01/3, Award, 22 May 2007. All three awards were subsequently annulled by ICSID *ad hoc* committees, e.g., for wrongful application of the customary rules on necessity and of the Non-Precluded Measures (NPM) clause contained in the US–Argentina BIT, on which all three claims were based. On the

inconsistencies can be found in the *Lauder* v. *Czech Republic* and *CME* v. *Czech Republic* cases, in which two tribunals reached radically different verdicts while judging the same parties and the same facts in parallel proceedings, the former rejected the claimant's case while the latter awarded it several hundred million dollars in damages and interest.[19]

Even though according to UNCTAD cases of blatant contradiction are scarce,[20] the very possibility that inexplicable inconsistencies[21] can arise cultivates an impression that arbitration might at times rhyme with arbitrariness and that states, in accepting that they should submit themselves to arbitration, would in a sense be 'gambling' with the general interest.[22] Depending on to whom the dispute is submitted, the outcome of the case can be radically different, and there is no appeals mechanism to correct erratic awards. True, there are marginal review mechanisms attached to the arbitral institution, either before international bodies or before domestic courts. But these are reserved for a limited number of hypotheses.[23] The

application of the NPM clauses in the Argentina awards, see generally William Burke-White and Andreas von Staden, 'Investment Protection in Extraordinary Times: The Interpretation and Application of Non-Precluded Measures Provisions in Bilateral Investment Treaties', *Virginia Journal of International Law* 48 (2008): 307.

[19] See Lauder v. *Czech Republic*, UNCITRAL, Final Award, 3 September 2001; and *CME Czech Republic BV* v. *Czech Republic*, UNCITRAL, Partial Award, 13 September 2001 and Final Award, 14 March 2003.

[20] See UNCTAD, Investor–State Dispute Settlement, 2007, p. 91. See also Reinisch, 'The Issues Raised by Parallel Proceedings and Possible Solutions', p. 115: Jan Paulsson, 'Avoiding Unintended Consequences', in Karl Sauvant, (ed.), *Appeals Mechanism in International Investment Disputes* (Oxford University Press, 2008), pp. 241 ff., who insist that one should distinguish *obiter dicta* and *ratio decidendi* before concluding that it is a case of inconsistency.

[21] Some apparent inconsistencies can arguably be explained by the nuances in the wording of treaties for the same kind of protection. See the example of the various versions of the 'fair and equitable treatment' standard in various BITs in Anna Joubin-Bret, 'The Growing Diversity and Inconsistency in the IIA System', in Karl Sauvant (ed.), *Appeals Mechanism in International Investment Disputes* (Oxford University Press, 2008), p. 138.

[22] See Susan D. Franck, 'The Legitimacy Crisis in Investment Treaty Arbitration: Privatizing Public International Law through Inconsistent Decisions', *Fordham Law Review* 73 (2005): 1521, at p. 1523: 'Tribunals have applied [investor protection] standards differently and made divergent findings on liability. Rather than creating certainty for foreign investors and Sovereigns, the process of resolving investment disputes through arbitration is creating uncertainty about the meaning of those rights and public international law.'

[23] See ICSID Convention on the Settlement of Investment Disputes between States and Nationals of Other States, done at Washington, DC 18 March 1965, entered into force 14 October 1966, amended 10 April 2006, Art. 52(1) (ICSID Convention), providing that: 'Either party may request annulment of the award by an application in writing addressed

CMS v. *Argentina* Award, for example, was partially annulled by an International Centre for the Settlement of Investment Disputes (ICSID) *ad hoc* Committee, even though the latter insisted that grounds for reviewing the legal reasoning contained in an arbitral award had to amount to a 'manifest' error nearing an excess of powers.[24] The only ground for annulment in such a case is when a tribunal fails to apply the proper law, but not when it errs in applying it.[25] Annulment procedures are not, therefore, an appeals mechanism, and are aimed only at removing manifest and grossly unfair anomalies from the body of arbitral case law. They are not as such capable of preserving unity in this case law.[26] In other words, legal certainty is not guaranteed in international investment law.[27]

A second and more foundational line of criticism concerns the fact that international arbitration is traditionally a commercial instrument of dispute settlement, while investor–state disputes do not have that character. First, an investment tribunal has jurisdiction to review state acts, and thus the exercise of sovereign authority by organs of the host state that allegedly go against obligations contained in an international agreement.[28] Investor–state arbitration is therefore a public/administrative

to the Secretary-General on one or more of the following grounds: (a) that the Tribunal was not properly constituted; (b) that the Tribunal has manifestly exceeded its powers; (c) that there was corruption on the part of a member of the Tribunal; (d) that there has been a serious departure from a fundamental rule of procedure; or (e) that the award has failed to state the reasons on which it is based.' For awards rendered by tribunals constituted under other rules than those of the ICSID, the Convention on the Recognition and Enforcement of Foreign Arbitral Awards, done at New York 10 June 1958, entered into force 7 June 1959, the so-called 'New York Convention', provides in its Art. V that domestic courts can refuse recognition and enforcement of an arbitral award only for a limited number of reasons.

[24] *CMS Gas Transmission Company* v. *Argentine Republic*, ICSID Case No. ARB/01/8, Annulment Decision, 25 September 2007, paras 51 and 136.

[25] *MTD Equity Sdn Bhd & MTD Chile SA* v. *Chile*, ICSID Case No. ARB/01/7, Decision on Annulment, 21 March 2007, para. 47. See also Christina Knahr, 'Annulment and its Role in the Context of Conflicting Awards', in Michael Waibel *et al.* (eds), *The Backlash against Investment Arbitration: Perceptions and Reality* (Alphen aan den Rijn: Kluwer Law, 2010), p. 155.

[26] See Knahr, 'Annulment and its Role in the Context of Conflicting Awards', p. 160: 'Although committees regularly harshly criticize the performance and the reasoning of arbitration tribunals, in the end they tend not to qualify the deficiencies as severe enough to lead to an annulment of the award.'

[27] See Reinisch, 'The Issues Raised by Parallel Proceedings and Possible Solutions', p. 115: 'Where investment tribunals produce inconsistent or even conflicting awards, one of the central values of any rule-based system of law, that is, predictability, is lost.'

[28] See, e.g., the growing number of cases openly challenging high-profile public policies in host states, such as the Australian policy against tobacco use (see pending case *Philip Morris* v. *Australia*, UNCITRAL), or Germany's phasing out of nuclear energy (see

law mechanism, yet it is removed from the democratic constitutional realm.[29] Second, investment disputes typically oppose a state and its (supposedly) public interest-oriented policies to the commercial interests of a private corporation.[30] Third, the outcome of the review may have serious consequences for the citizens of the host state, be it because the latter is condemned to pay damages using taxpayers' money or because as a result of the award the host state is forced to amend some of its policies which were judged contrary to the provisions of an investment instrument. The commercial and private nature of arbitration is said to be at odds with the public character of investor–state disputes, and this, it is said, amounts to a 'democratic deficit'.

From a procedural point of view, critics of arbitration fustigate the lack of transparency in investment arbitral proceedings, which copy the confidentiality that is consubstantial with commercial arbitration. Procedural rules applicable in arbitral disputes are often the same as those applicable to regular commercial arbitration between private parties: the UNCITRAL Arbitration Rules; the Rules of Arbitration of the International Chamber of Commerce (ICC); the Arbitration Rules of the Stockholm Chamber of Commerce, etc. The Permanent Court of Arbitration also developed rules that are to be used for 'disputes between two parties of which only one is a State',[31] but the arbitration rules of the ICSID[32] are the only set of arbitral rules designed specifically for investment arbitration. Despite a reform in 2006 (see below), they remain very much influenced by the commercial model, and confidentiality remains the rule rather than the exception. The influence of confidentiality in

pending case *Vattenfall AB, Vattenfall Europe AG, Vattenfall Europe Nuclear Energy GmbH, Kernkraftwerk BrunsbüttelGmbH und Co. oHG, Kernkraftwerk Krümmel GmbH und Co. oHG v. Federal Republic of Germany*, ICSID Case No. ARB/12/12).

[29] See generally Gus van Harten and Martin Loughlin, 'Investment Treaty Arbitration as a Species of Global Administrative Law', *European Journal of International Law* 17 (2006): 121.

[30] On the difficult question of the public–private divide in international investment law, see Alex Mills, 'Antinomies of Public and Private at the Foundations of International Investment Law and Arbitration', *Journal of International Economic Law* 14 (2011): 469.

[31] See the 1993 Permanent Court of Arbitration Optional Rules for Arbitrating Disputes between Two Parties of Which Only One is a State, available at: www.pca-cpa.org/upload/files/1STATENG.pdf.

[32] See Rules of Procedure for Arbitration Proceedings (ICSID Arbitration Rules), available at: http://icsid.worldbank.org/ICSID/StaticFiles/basicdoc/CRR_English-final.pdf, pp. 99 ff.; ICSID Additional Facility Rules, available at: http://icsid.worldbank.org/ICSID/Static-Files/facility/AFR_English-final.pdf, governing certain disputes falling outside the scope of the ICSID Convention. The ICSID rules are the most commonly used set of rules in investment arbitration.

investment arbitration makes it difficult to have a clear view of the arbitral reality, as it is impossible to have a precise knowledge of how many investment disputes are ongoing, between which states and which investors. This may make it difficult for democratic accountability processes to play out with regard to the issues being arbitrated and with regard to the way in which host governments are defending the public interest in the framework of arbitral proceedings.

From a substantive point of view, critics emphasise that panels tend to view investment disputes as regular commercial litigation between equals, without taking into account the special position of the host state, the public nature of the issues at stake or the legal basis of their jurisdiction,[33] the investment agreement (treaty or contract). This approach manifests itself in awards through an emphasis on the sanctity of contract[34] or through the application of strict, non-public, standards of review of state policies, according no deference whatsoever to the latter.[35] This contributes to reducing the 'policy space' of the state and to encroaching on the democratic choices of citizens and on the right to regulate in the public interest.[36]

This is why critics call for taking into account the public character of investor–state relations and for reforming investment dispute

---

[33] In this regard, see William Park, 'Arbitrator Integrity', in Michael Waibel *et al.* (eds), *The Backlash against Investment Arbitration: Perceptions and Reality* (Alphen aan den Rijn: Kluwer Law, 2010), p. 246: 'One must be cautious about unselective attempts to transplant judicial standards into the world of arbitration. Given a judge's clear obligations to the citizenry as a whole, the calculus of judicial duties will differ from what might be expected of arbitrators who remain principally (albeit not exclusively) creatures of the litigants' contracts.'

[34] See Louis Wells, 'Backlash to Investment Arbitration: Three Causes', in Michael Waibel *et al.* (eds), *The Backlash against Investment Arbitration: Perceptions and Reality* (Alphen aan den Rijn: Kluwer Law, 2010), pp. 342–7.

[35] William Burke-White and Andreas von Staden, 'Private Litigation in a Public Law Sphere: The Standard of Review in Investor-State Arbitration', *Yale Journal of International Law* 35 (2010): 283. According to these authors' review, this not in line with the practice of other international institutions entitled to review acts of states, such as the European Court of Human Rights or the WTO Dispute Settlement Body. See recently for a more relaxed standard of review, according considerable deference to state decisions: *Joseph Charles Lemire* v. *Ukraine*, ICSID Case No. ARB/06/18, Decision on Jurisdiction and Liability, 14 January 2010, para. 283, stating, e.g.: 'A claim that a regulatory decision is materially wrong will not suffice [to find a violation of the BIT]. It must be proven that the State organ acted in an arbitrary or capricious way.'

[36] See, in relation with the case law on regulatory takings, UNCTAD, 'FDI Policies for Development: National and International Perspectives', *World Investment Report 2003*, available at: www.unctad.org/en/docs/wir2003light_en.pdf, p. 111.

settlement accordingly. In the words of Burke-White and von Staden, to remedy the rule of law and democracy deficits, 'it is time to recognize that contemporary investor–State arbitrations are not merely another form of private commercial arbitration, with one party now being a State, but that they are more fittingly understood as a form of dispute settlement that, like many domestic judicial proceedings, also operates in a public law context'.[37]

2.2   Which standard of justice in investment arbitration?

The second line of criticism is also connected with the value of the rule of law and has to do with the functional suitability of arbitrators as judges in public law disputes. Arbitration is accused of structurally leaving the door open to arbitrators' conflicts of interest, lack of independence and partiality.[38] Arbitrators could be biased in two ways, which we examine in turn below.

2.2.1   Independence of arbitrators

Independence for a judge means that he must not be personally interested in the outcome of the case before him, financially, emotionally or otherwise. An independent judiciary is one of the fundamental features of the rule of law, and therefore in domestic judiciaries a number of mechanisms are typically put in place in order to guarantee such independence, notably the granting of tenure to judges and the setting of a list of functions or positions that are 'incompatible' with being a judge.

Arbitrators do not have tenure. They are typically appointed for a specific case,[39] generally by the parties themselves, and are remunerated by the latter as well. Since the parties get to choose the arbitrators who are going to hear their case, they will likely be tempted to elect arbitrators

---

[37] Burke-White and von Staden, 'Private Litigation in a Public Law Sphere', p. 285.

[38] Choudhury, 'Recapturing Public Power', p. 820.

[39] An exception to the punctual appointment of arbitrators, connected to a specific stream of events, is the Iran–US Claims Tribunal, for which nine arbitrators are permanently appointed to rule on pending claims of US or Iranian nationals, as a means of resolving the crisis between the two countries that arose as a result of the events of November 1979. See Declaration of the Government of the Democratic and Popular Republic of Algeria Concerning the Settlement of Claims by the Government of the United States of America and the Government of the Islamic Republic of Iran (Claims Settlement Declaration), 19 January 1981, available at: www.iusct.org/claims-settlement.pdf.

whose past decision-making record seems to suit their position.[40] Starting from there, arbitrators may be induced to adopt pro-investor or pro-host state stances in order to improve their chances of being appointed by one side or the other. This 'competition' within a profession whose members are appointed on a case by case basis seems difficult to reconcile with the aforementioned requirement of independence.[41]

Moreover, there are no structural incompatibilities for arbitrators (except, of course, being a party to the dispute[42]). Admittedly, arbitrators must disclose any information that might put their independence in doubt,[43] and certain indicative lists resembling incompatibilities have been developed,[44] as well as a 'jurisprudence of ethical standards' applicable to arbitrators.[45] However, dubious relationships and uneasy situations may not be so uncommon, as it is a fact that the practice of investment arbitration sees many of the same faces, and arbitrators are often practising lawyers, sitting as judges in some cases, and defending parties in other cases. Some of those lawyer-arbitrators defend

---

[40] For a discussion of the fact that arbitrators are appointed by the parties has a significant influence on their decisions, see Jan Paulsson, 'Moral Hazard in International Dispute Resolution', Inaugural Lecture as Holder of the Michael R. Klein Distinguished Scholar Chair, University of Miami School of Law, 29 April 2010, available at: www.arbitration-icca.org/media/0/12773749999020/paulsson_moral_hazard.pdf, pp. 8 ff., revealing the 'uncomfortable fact' that 'dissenting arbitrators are nearly always those who have been appointed by the party aggrieved by the majority decision'.

[41] See Aaron Cosbey, Howard Mann, Luke Eric Peterson and Konrad von Molkte, *Investment and Sustainable Development: A Guide to the Use and Potential of International Investment Agreements* (Winnipeg: International Institute for Sustainable Development (IISD), 2004), available at: www.iisd.org/pdf/2004/investment_invest_and_sd.pdf, p. 6.

[42] See also the conditions of nationality, ICSID Arbitration Rules, rr. 1–3.

[43] See ICSID Arbitration Rules, r. 6; and UN General Assembly, UNCITRAL Arbitration Rules as Revised in 2010, Resolution 65/22, 6 December 2010, UN Doc. A/RES/65/22, Art. 11.

[44] See International Bar Association, 'IBA Guidelines on Conflicts of Interest in International Arbitration', 22 May 2004, available at: www.int-bar.org/images/downloads/guidelines%20text.pdf. The Guidelines non-exhaustively list situations that are relevant to evaluating the arbitrators' independence and impartiality, and classify them in three lists. The Red List contains situations that normally preclude a person from being an arbitrator in a dispute (save with the express consent of the parties for waivable conflicts arising from such situations). The Orange List contains situations that may raise doubts as to the arbitrator's independence and impartiality, which must then be disclosed; the parties are deemed to accept the appointment of the arbitrator failing a timely objection after disclosure. The Green List contains a list of situations that should normally not pose problems for the independence or impartiality of arbitrators and that do not have to be disclosed, such as previously expressed legal opinions.

[45] Park, 'Arbitrator Integrity', p. 231.

indifferently states or investors. In order to keep doing so, it would be natural that, when acting as arbitrators, they try to stay as neutral as possible so as not to alienate either category of parties to investment disputes. However, it seems that a majority of lawyer-arbitrators are active in the defence of investors' interests.[46] In this regard, it was pointed out that many lawyer-arbitrators are members of business law firms whose services are hired by corporations investing in various parts of the world. Those corporations are therefore likely to have recourse, at some point in time, to investor–state arbitration. As a result, certain lawyer-arbitrators have a direct interest in adopting extensive interpretations of investor protections so as to please their clients and defend their present or future interests. An author suggests that this state of facts is partly responsible for the ever greater scope of investor protection that one can find in the developing case law.[47] Again, this sits rather uneasily with the principle of independence.[48]

2.2.2   Impartiality of arbitrators

This aspect of the critique against investment arbitration has to do with impartiality, that is, with the assurance that arbitrators have not made up their minds before they decide on the case.

---

[46] OECD, 'Scoping Paper for the Public Consultation on Investor–State Dispute Settlement', 2012, available at: www.oecd.org/dataoecd/61/29/50291642.pdf, p. 43, stating that: 'over 50% of [Investor–State Dispute Settlement (ISDS)] arbitrators have acted as counsel for investors in other ISDS cases, while it has been estimated about 10% of ISDS arbitrators have acted as counsel for States in other cases. It does not appear that government ISDS defense counsel (for example, from those countries with sizable in-house litigation departments that defend ISDS claims) have been selected as arbitrators for cases involving other States' (references omitted).

[47] Howard Mann, 'Transparency and Consistency in International Investment Law: Can the Problems Be Fixed by Tinkering?', Karl Sauvant (ed.), *Appeals Mechanism in International Investment Disputes* (Oxford University Press, 2008), p. 216, noting that arbitrators are often 'lawyers who come from major law firms that generally represent large corporations who are themselves foreign investors. In this circumstance, it is readily arguable that the arbitrators have clients that have a specific interest in the expansion of the scope of investor protection.' On such expansionary trends, see Muthucumaraswamy Sornarajah 'A Coming Crisis: Expansionary Trends in Investment Arbitration', in Karl Sauvant (ed.), *Appeals Mechanism in International Investment Disputes* (Oxford University Press, 2008), pp. 39–80.

[48] See generally Gus van Harten, 'Perceived Bias in Investment Treaty Arbitration?', in Michael Waibel *et al.*, *The Backlash against Investment Arbitration: Perceptions and Reality* (Alphen aan den Rijn: Kluwer Law, 2010), pp. 433–54.

2.2.2.1   Are arbitrators biased towards investor interests?   A frequent criticism against investment arbitration is that arbitral panels would suffer from a structural bias in favour of investors. It is a fact that investment instruments – and hence the dispute settlement mechanisms they contain – were originally intended to reassure and protect investors, their property and their profits so as to, possibly, foster investment flows into host states. The whole philosophy of the regime is meant to be favourable to investor interests.[49] While arbitrators are required to apply the law, some critics point to elements indicating that the scales may have a better chance of being tipped in the direction of investors' claims.

In practice, an overwhelming majority of claims are brought by investors: only five known claims out of several hundred have reportedly been brought by host states.[50] In this connection, it is a commonly expressed fear that the corporation of arbitrators could favour investors' interests in order to induce the latter to file claims and thus increase the size of the arbitration business.[51] The legal culture from which most arbitrators come may also be suspected of creating a 'professional' bias, given that most arbitrators are practising lawyers active in the field of business law, and rarely in areas of public law in which a host state could find defences, such as human rights law or

---

[49]   See Muthucumaraswamy Sornarajah, 'A Law for Need or a Law for Greed? Restoring the Lost Law in the International Law of Foreign Investment', *International Environmental Agreements* 6 (2006): 329, p. 342.

[50]   Mehmet Toral and Thomas Schultz, 'The State, a Perpetual Respondent in Investment Arbitration? Some Unorthodox Considerations', in Michael Waibel *et al.* (eds), *The Backlash against Investment Arbitration: Perceptions and Reality* (Alphen aan den Rijn: Kluwer Law, 2010), pp. 589–90. All these cases were introduced under investment contracts and not treaties. This can partly be explained by the fact that investors are not parties to investment treaties, and therefore their express consent is required before arbitration can be mounted against them. (*ibid.*, p. 579). This may also be explained by the fact that BITs and other investment treaties usually confer very few litigable rights to host states. See Salacuse, 'Explanations for the Increased Recourse to Treaty-based Investment Dispute Settlement', p. 111. On host state claims, see generally Gustavo Laborde, 'The Case for Host State Claims in Investment Arbitration', *Journal of International Dispute Settlement* 1 (2010): 97, at pp. 99 ff. More generally, an explanation for this imbalance may be that states prefer having recourse to their domestic judicial institutions, or to resort to non-judicial or non-arbitral means to settle disputes with investors.

[51]   See van Harten, 'Perceived Bias in Investment Treaty Arbitration?', p. 445 and references cited: 'Where only one class of parties (here, investors) can bring the claims against the other class (States), and not vice-versa, arbitrators have an apparent interest to interpret the law in a way that encourages claims (albeit without undermining the political basis for the system's existence).'

environmental law.[52] For instance, the ICSID Convention provides only that arbitrators 'shall be persons of ... recognized competence in the fields of law, commerce, industry, or finance'.[53] Moreover, the fact that arbitrators are often practising lawyers, whose clients may possibly be involved in other arbitration cases, can also have an (un)conscious influence on those arbitrators' impartiality. It is, indeed, not really inconceivable that an arbitrator would decide in a certain way on an issue if he or she has defended or is defending the opposite point of view as counsel in another case. His or her mind, on those issues, is already set.[54] Admittedly, this is to some extent applicable to any judge who previously practised as a lawyer and, of course, host states also get to nominate arbitrators that they think will be sympathetic to their arguments.

However, even when the arbitrator(s) must, for some reason, be appointed by the default appointing authority in the place of the parties, a sort of 'institutional bias' favourable to investors is said to be at play.[55] In ICSID arbitrations, arbitrators are, if need be, appointed by the Chairman of ICSID's Administrative Council,[56] who is also the President of the World Bank, and who has to date always been a US national, the largest capital-exporting country. The World Bank is also an organisation that is strongly dominated by donor – that is, developed – states, from whence come most foreign investors. As a result of this supposed 'institutional bias',[57] some have expressed the concern that this mechanism could result in the appointment of pro-investor arbitrators.[58] In ICC

---

[52] See Sornarajah, 'A Law for Need or a Law for Greed?' p. 357; Burke-White and von Staden, 'Private Litigation in a Public Law Sphere', pp. 330–2.

[53] See ISCID Convention, Art. 14 (1).

[54] See Mann, 'Transparency and Consistency in International Investment Law', p. 216: 'the average person cannot expect an arbitrator to rule against the very arguments he or she is making in a second case on the same issues, knowing that his or her participation in such a decision will undercut his or her client's interest in the other arbitration'.

[55] See generally van Harten, 'Perceived Bias in Investment Treaty Arbitration?', pp. 443–5.

[56] See ICSID Arbitration Rules, r. 4.

[57] The notion that the World Bank generally, and ICSID in particular, could be vehicles of a neo-liberal ideology favourable to liberalising and protecting investment, is at the basis of the ongoing distrust against the ICSID in certain Latin American countries. In 2007, Bolivia denounced the ICSID Convention. See Antonios Tzanakopoulos, 'Denunciation of the ICSID Convention under the General International Law of Treaties', in Rainer Hoffman and Christian Tams (eds), *International Investment Law and General International Law: From Clinical Isolation to Systemic Integration* (Baden Baden: Nomos, 2011), pp. 75–93.

[58] van Harten, 'Perceived Bias in Investment Treaty Arbitration?', p. 443.

arbitrations, the default appointing authority is the ICC's International Court of Arbitration,[59] whose members are chosen by the ICC World Council.[60] The ICC brands itself as 'the world business organisation'.[61] This is not to say that arbitrators are all dishonest and biased in favour of investors and against host states. Actually, the statistics are in favour of host states: out of 220 concluded cases at the end of 2011, about 40 per cent were decided in favour of the state, 30 per cent in favour of the investor, with the remaining 30 per cent being settled.[62] However, the aforementioned structural elements of arbitration admittedly entertain a legitimate doubt as to whether the institution is perfectly independent and impartial. In other words, no matter how often justice is done, it is not seen to be done, and this produces understandable criticism.

2.2.2.2 Are arbitrators biased towards the application of international investment law in isolation of other branches of international law ('fragmentation' critique)?

The 'fragmentation' critique comes from the observation that certain arbitral tribunals have tended to view and apply the body of international investment law in isolation of other relevant fields of international law.[63] This has led to awards in which investment obligations somehow took precedence over other international obligations in other fields, such as, for example, environmental protection, or awards in which the whole of the international legal

---

[59] See International Chamber of Commerce, Arbitration and ADR Rules, effective 1 January 2012, available at: www.iccwbo.org/uploadedFiles/Court/Arbitration/other/2012_Arbitration%20and%20ADR%20Rules%20ENGLISH.pdf, Art. 12.

[60] See ICC, Arbitration and ADR Rules, Appendix I (Statutes of the International Court of Arbitration), Art 2. Moreover, see Art. 11(4) of the Arbitration and ADR Rules, which reads: 'The decisions of the Court as to the appointment, confirmation, challenge or replacement of an arbitrator shall be final, and the reasons for such decisions shall not be communicated.'

[61] See www.iccwbo.org.

[62] See UNCTAD, 'Latest Developments in Investor–State Dispute Settlement', *IIAs Issues*, Note No. 1, April 2012, p. 3.

[63] A general definition of 'fragmentation' in the international legal order was given in 2006 by the International Law Commission. Fragmentation occurs where 'specialized law-making and institution-building tends to take place with relative ignorance of legislative and institutional activities in the adjoining fields and of the general principles and practices of international law. The result is conflicts between rules or rule-systems, deviating institutional practices and, possibly, the loss of an overall perspective on the law.' See UN General Assembly, International Law Commission, 'Fragmentation of International Law: Difficulties Arising from the Diversification and Expansion of International Law', Report of the Study Group of the International Law Commission, 13 April 2006, UN Doc. A/CN.4/L.682, p. 11.

environment was overlooked in favour of a strict application of international investment disciplines as if the latter were a sort of 'self-contained regime'.

The following well-known paragraph in the *Santa Elena* v. *Costa Rica* Award epitomises this perceived problem:

> While an expropriation or taking for environmental reasons may be classified as a taking for a public purpose, and thus may be legitimate, the fact that the Property was taken for this reason does not affect either the nature or the measure of the compensation to be paid for the taking. That is, the purpose of protecting the environment for which the Property was taken does not alter the legal character of the taking for which adequate compensation must be paid. The international source of the obligation to protect the environment makes no difference.[64]

In such situations, host states find themselves caught between the hammer and the anvil, as they may have to choose between abiding by one or the other of their international obligations. As indicated above, this also reduces their policy space as they cannot implement international agendas to which they may be deeply committed. This topic has attracted much attention from researchers in the recent past. While some have openly doubted the reality of the fragmentation problem from the outset,[65] others have actively looked for solutions. One way to redress the imbalance could lie in an interpretative discipline[66] through which arbitrators would be encouraged to overcome their pro-investor bias and to interpret investment treaty obligations of host states in the light of, for example, Article 31(3)(c) of the Vienna Convention on the Law of Treaties, which commands that, in interpreting a particular treaty: 'there shall be taken into account, together with the context ... any relevant rules of international law applicable in the relations between the parties'.[67] Reference to general principles

---

[64] *Compañía del Desarrollo de Santa Elena SA* v. *Republic of Costa Rica*, ICSID Case No. ARB/96/1, Final Award, 17 February 2000, para. 71.

[65] See, with regard to the relationship between international investment law and human rights, James Fry, 'International Human Rights Law in Investment Arbitration: Evidence of International Law's Unity', *Duke Journal of Comparative and International Law* 18 (2007): 77.

[66] See generally Anne van Aaken, 'Defragmentation of Public International Law Through Interpretation: A Methodological Proposal', *Indiana Journal of Global Legal Studies* 16 (2009): 483.

[67] Anne van Aaken, 'Fragmentation of International Law: The Case of International Investment Protection', *Finnish Yearbook of International Law* 17 (2008): 91; Moshe Hirsch, 'Interactions between Investment and Non-Investment Obligations', in Peter Muchlinski,

of law was also designated as helpful guidance for the interpretation of the relevant legal rules.[68] Other authors emphasise the need to reconsider the way investment agreements are drafted in order to relocate the obligations they contain within the wider framework of the host state's policies and obligations.[69]

Whether the fragmentation problem is real or not, recent years have witnessed an evolution in investment practice concerning the relationship of international investment law with the rest of international law.[70] First of all, some arbitral awards now tread more lightly when discussing investment obligations with regard to other international obligations, and explicitly make the balancing exercise.[71] Also, a new generation of international investment agreements is emerging, which tend to balance the interests of investors against other agendas.[72] However, such a widespread change in drafting practices is proving difficult to achieve

---

Federico Ortino and Christoph Schreuer (eds), *The Oxford Handbook of International Investment Law* (Oxford University Press, 2008), pp. 154–81; Jan Wouters and Nicolas Hachez, 'When Rules and Values Collide: How Can a Balanced Application of Investor Protection Provisions Be Ensured?', *Human Rights and International Legal Discourse* 3 (2009): 301.

[68] Campbell McLachlan, 'Investment Treaties and General International Law', *International and Comparative Law Quarterly* 57 (2008): 361.

[69] See Schill, 'Private Enforcement of International Investment Law', p. 50; Wouters and Hachez, When Rules and Values Collide', pp. 334 ff.

[70] See, with regard to the relationship between the international investment regime and the worldwide sustainable agenda, Marie-Claire Cordonier Segger and Avidan Kent, 'Promoting Sustainable Investment through International Law', in Marie-Claire Cordonier Segger *et al.* (eds), *Sustainable Development in World Investment Law* (Alphen aan den Rijn: Kluwer Law, 2011), pp. 771–92.

[71] See *Suez, Sociedad General de Aguas de Barcelona SA and InterAguas Servicios Integrales del Agua SA* v. *Argentine Republic*, ICSID Case No. ARB/03/19, Decision on Liability, 30 July 2010, which considers the interaction with the human right to water at para. 262, even though it denies the *amici curiae*'s opinion that 'Argentina's human rights obligations to assure its population the right to water somehow trumps its obligations under the BITs and that the existence of the human right to water also implicitly gives Argentina the authority to take actions in disregard of its BIT obligations'. See also *S. D. Myers, Inc.* v. *Canada*, UNCITRAL, First Partial Award, 13 November 2000, which weighs the provisions of NAFTA Chapter Eleven (see, below, n. 77) with the obligations of Canada under the Basel Convention on the Control of Transboundary Movements of Hazardous Wastes and Their Disposal (see paras 209 ff.). The tribunal, nonetheless, found a breach of NAFTA, Art. 1102 (national treatment), because there were other measures that could have complied with Canada's obligations under the Basel Convention while not being contrary to NAFTA (see para. 255).

[72] For an analysis of this 'new generation' of investment treaties, see Wouters and Hachez, 'When Rules and Values Collide', pp. 336 ff.

and the traditional tenets of investor protection can prove to be resistant, as was shown by the failure of the new Norwegian Model BIT.[73]

2.3   Interim conclusion

As the current natural way to settle investor–state disputes, arbitration is under fire. This is even though cases are more often won by host states than not (see above). However, a number of dubious awards evidence a lack of unity in the case law, and host states' interests may be threatened by the philosophy of the system. There is a feeling that going to arbitration, for a host state, can be like playing Russian roulette when public interest is involved. Regardless of how many awards are well balanced, apply the law sensibly and take the public interest into account, the arbitral system cannot hide the fact that real chances also exist for an award that contradicts other awards and that is supported by odd legal reasoning, with dire consequences for the host state's budget. In such cases, hardly any recourse is open to the host state for getting a second examination of the case. This risk associated with investor–state arbitration is unfortunately the result of the way in which the institution was designed, and to the extent that arbitration can be said to be at odds with democracy and the rule of law, it must be alleviated.

Arbitration works well most of the time because of the personal integrity of arbitrators, their legal skills and reasoning, and ventures into strange territory are scarce and random. The purpose of the above paragraphs was thus certainly not to tarnish the general reputation of honesty and competence that arbitrators enjoy. However, in view of the requirements of the rule of law and in light of the public interest, 'working well most of the time' is not enough. Any rule of law- and democracy-abiding dispute settlement system needs to comprise structural guarantees that it is going to work effectively and that interests will be weighed against each other in a balanced manner according to legal rules. In the next sections, we analyse reforms that have been introduced in the recent past to address this critique, and what is being proposed on top of these reforms to go even further.

---

[73] See Damon Vis-Dunbar, 'Norway Shelves its Draft Model Bilateral Investment Treaty', 8 June 2009, available at: www.iisd.org/itn/2009/06/08/norway-shelves-its-proposed-model-bilateral-investment-treaty.

3   Current reforms of the arbitral model: too little, too late?

In the face of the above critique, and in particular in response to the democracy- and rule of law-based criticism, investor–state arbitration has attempted to reform itself in recent years. More precisely, procedural rules have been adapted, and states have adopted new interpretations of investment agreements in order to bring more transparency into arbitral proceedings and to facilitate the participation of civil society in disputes engaging the public interest.

The ICSID reformed its rules of procedures in 2006, while UNCITRAL has been in the process of doing so for quite a while, although still unsuccessfully on transparency and participation issues.[74] Concerning transparency, the emphasis has been on facilitating the publication of awards and other documents, such as parties' submissions, and on rendering certain hearings public. If they were to be made a general rule in investment arbitration, these changes would shake the foundations of the whole system, which is still premised on the paradigm of commercial arbitration and on its seal of confidentiality. Confidentiality may be precious not only for businesses: for some governments seeking to escape public accountability in relation to investment claims, it may also be convenient. Therefore, the dose of publicity that these reforms have tried to instil, though welcome, is insufficient insofar as they remain very dependent upon the parties' consent.[75]

Awards (or legally relevant parts of them) may be published by ICSID,[76] but there is no practice of systematic publication for UNCITRAL awards or for awards rendered under the rules of other institutions such as chambers of commerce.[77] Regarding the other arbitration documents, such as submissions of the parties, they may be released only with

---

[74] See UN General Assembly, UNCITRAL, 'Settlement of Commercial Disputes: Preparation of a Legal Standard of Transparency in Treaty-based Investor–State Arbitration: Note by the Secretariat', 29 July 2011, UN Doc. A/CN.9/WG.2/WP.166.

[75] J. Anthony VanDuzer, 'Enhancing the Procedural Legitimacy of Investor–State Arbitration through Transparency and *Amicus Curiae* Participation', *McGill Law Journal/Revue de droit de McGill* 52 (2007): 681, at p. 706.

[76] ICSID Arbitration Rules, r. 48(4), reads: 'The Centre shall not publish the award without the consent of the parties. The Centre shall, however, promptly include in its publications excerpts of the legal reasoning of the Tribunal.'

[77] See North American Free Trade Agreement (NAFTA), done at San Antonio, 17 September 1992, effective 1 January 1994, Art. 1137 and Annex 1137.4, which allows parties to publish awards.

the consent of the parties.[78] In the framework of NAFTA, however, a much higher standard of transparency applies.[79] In a 2001 Statement,[80] the Free Trade Commission clarified that 'nothing in the relevant arbitral rules imposes a general duty of confidentiality or precludes the Parties from providing public access to documents submitted to, or issued by, Chapter Eleven tribunals, apart from the limited specific exceptions set forth expressly in those rules'. Therefore, the NAFTA parties agreed:

> to make available to the public in a timely manner all documents submitted to, or issued by, a Chapter Eleven tribunal, subject to redaction of:
>
> 1. confidential business information;
>
> 2. information which is privileged or otherwise protected from disclosure under the Party's domestic law; and
>
> 3. information which the Party must withhold pursuant to the relevant arbitral rules, as applied.

The above applies only to NAFTA, but it appears to have affected treaty practice in a certain way, in that the 'new generation of BITs' seems to be commanding more transparency in arbitral proceedings along the lines described above.[81] Hearings under ICSID Arbitration Rules are normally in public only if parties agree,[82] as under the UNCITRAL Rules.[83] However, the NAFTA parties have issued statements to the effect of systematically consenting to holding hearings in public, save to protect legitimate confidentiality interests.[84] The practice of open hearings is not systematic outside NAFTA, though.

Concerning the participation of the public in arbitral proceedings, rules have been relaxed to give more leeway to arbitral tribunals for

---

[78] See ICSID, 'Administrative and Financial Regulations', 10 April 2006, reg. 22(2), available at: https://icsid.worldbank.org/ICSID/FrontServlet?requestType=CasesRH&actionVal= OpenPage&PageType=AnnouncementsFrame&FromPage=Announcements&pageName= Archive_%20Announcement30_PressRelease1.

[79] For a comparison between the trade and investment provisions of NAFTA with regard to transparency, see Hugo Perezcano Díaz, 'Transparency in International Dispute Settlement Proceedings on Trade and Investment, in Karl Sauvant (ed.), *Appeals Mechanism in International Investment Disputes* (Oxford University Press, 2008), pp. 193–200.

[80] See NAFTA Free Trade Commission, 'Notes of Interpretation of Certain Chapter Eleven Provisions', 31 July 2001, available at: www.international.gc.ca/trade-agreements-accords-commerciaux/disp-diff/nafta-interpr.aspx?lang=en&view=d.

[81] See Wouters and Hachez, 'When Rules and Values Collide', pp. 339–40.

[82] ICSID Arbitration Rules, r. 32(2).   [83] UNCITRAL Arbitration Rules, Art. 28(3).

[84] See NAFTA Free Trade Commission, Joint Statement, 'Decade of Achievement', San Antonio, 16 July 2004, available at: www.international.gc.ca/trade-agreements-accords-commerciaux/agr-acc/nafta-alena/js-sanantonio.aspx?lang=en&view=d.

admitting what are called '*amicus curiae* briefs', which are submissions presented to the tribunal by a third party to the dispute to inform the latter of a particular interest or to present it with a particular legal position. This avenue is especially used by civil society organisations in defence of public interest positions, such as the protection of the environment. Prior to the modification of arbitral rules, the door had already been opened by progressive tribunals,[85] which mirrored their practice on the example set by the WTO Dispute Settlement Body.[86] Certain states have now expressly accepted the practice of *amicus curiae* briefs,[87] though under certain conditions inspired by the case law on the matter. For example, under NAFTA, tribunals have the authority to accept *amicus curiae* briefs under the following conditions:

> In determining whether to grant leave to file a non-disputing party submission, the Tribunal will consider, among other things, the extent to which:
>
> (a) the non-disputing party submission would assist the Tribunal in the determination of a factual or legal issue related to the arbitration by bringing a perspective, particular knowledge or insight that is different from that of the disputing parties;
>
> (b) the non-disputing party submission would address matters within the scope of the dispute;
>
> (c) the non-disputing party has a significant interest in the arbitration; and
>
> (d) there is a public interest in the subject-matter of the arbitration ...
>
> The Tribunal will ensure that:
>
> (a) any non-disputing party submission avoids disrupting the proceedings; and
>
> (b) neither disputing party is unduly burdened or unfairly prejudiced by such submissions.[88]

---

[85] See *Methanex v. United States*, UNCITRAL, Decision on *Amici Curiae*, 15 January 2001; *United Parcel Service of America Inc. v. Government of Canada*, UNCITRAL, Decision on *Amici Curiae*, 17 October 2001.

[86] World Trade Organization (WTO), *United States–Import Prohibition of Certain Shrimp and Shrimp Products*, Report of the Appellate Body, 12 October 1998, WTO Doc. No. WT/DS58/AB/R, para. 99 (arbitration).

[87] See United States Model BIT, 2012, available at: www.state.gov/documents/organization/188371.pdf, Art. 28(3).

[88] See also NAFTA Free Trade Commission, 'Statement of the Free Trade Commission on Non-disputing Party Participation, "Notes of Interpretation"', 7 October 2003, available at: www.international.gc.ca/trade-agreements-accords-commerciaux/assets/pdfs/Nondisputing-en.pdf.

ICSID Rules were also modified to provide for the admission of *amicus curiae* briefs under similar conditions.[89] UNCITRAL Rules are still silent on the subject, even though there have been intense discussions on how to increase transparency in treaty-based investment arbitration.[90]

These changes were made – by tribunals themselves or by arbitration institutions and states – explicitly in order to remedy the perceived legitimacy deficit of the arbitration institution[91] and to provide the public with more understanding of arbitral processes.[92] In the words of the *Methanex* Tribunal, a pioneer in this regard:

> [The investor–state arbitral] process could benefit from being perceived as more open or transparent; or conversely be harmed if seen as unduly secretive. In this regard, the Tribunal's willingness to receive *amicus* submissions might support the process in general and this arbitration in particular; whereas a blanket refusal could do positive harm.[93]

However, these reforms are unlikely to resolve the legitimacy crisis by themselves. As indicated above, the transparency reforms remain subject to the consent of the parties and therefore do not institutionalise transparency *per se*. Furthermore, the ability of NGOs and other third parties

---

[89] ICSID Arbitration Rules, r. 37(2): 'After consulting both parties, the Tribunal may allow a person or entity that is not a party to the dispute (in this Rule called the "nondisputing party") to file a written submission with the Tribunal regarding a matter within the scope of the dispute. In determining whether to allow such a filing, the Tribunal shall consider, among other things, the extent to which: (a) the non-disputing party submission would assist the Tribunal in the determination of a factual or legal issue related to the proceeding by bringing a perspective, particular knowledge or insight that is different from that of the disputing parties; (b) the non-disputing party submission would address a matter within the scope of the dispute; (c) the non-disputing party has a significant interest in the proceeding. The Tribunal shall ensure that the non-disputing party submission does not disrupt the proceeding or unduly burden or unfairly prejudice either party, and that both parties are given an opportunity to present their observations on the non-disputing party submission.' It is not a requirement that issues of public interest be involved.

[90] The 2010 reform does not address this. For relevant proposals now being discussed, see UN General Assembly, UNCITRAL, 'Settlement of Commercial Disputes', paras 43–51.

[91] Amokura Kawharu, 'Participation of Non-governmental Organizations in Investment Arbitration as *Amici Curiae*', in Michael Waibel *et al.* (eds), *The Backlash against Investment Arbitration: Perceptions and Reality* (Alphen aan den Rijn: Kluwer Law, 2010), p. 284.

[92] See *Suez, Sociedad General de Aguas de Barcelona and Vivendi Universal SA v. Argentine Republic*, ICSID Case No. ARB/03/19, Order in Response to a Petition for Transparency and Participation as *Amicus Curiae*, 19 May 2005, para. 22.

[93] *Methanex v. United States*, Decision on *Amici Curiae*, para. 49.

to submit *amicus curiae* briefs does not guarantee that the public interest will be taken into account. Several arguments to the contrary can actually be formulated. First, the tribunal remains free to rely on the arguments of the *amicus* or not. Second, *amici* are not themselves necessarily accountable to the public and they may not always be capable of representing the general interest.[94] Third, authors have underlined that it is unlikely that they can make a meaningful input in their briefs if they cannot have access to the documents of the proceedings, which as a general rule remain confidential.[95] Fourth, admitting non-disputing parties to participate clearly disrupts the natural timeline of arbitration and can severely slow down the proceedings, even though measures as to this (such as a maximum number of pages or the submission of a joint brief by several NGOs) are taken by parties and tribunals and are foreseen in arbitration rules.[96] Yet it will force parties to respond to such arguments[97] and inevitably disorganise their defence, on top of inevitably raising costs (which, for the host state, may not be in the general interest). Finally, one cannot fail to note that, for a significant number of judicial traditions, be they domestic, regional or international, the admission of *amicus curiae* briefs coming from civil society organisations is not necessarily a widespread practice, as the general interest is supposed to be protected by the guarantees of independence and impartiality of the judge, by his or her legal competence (*iura novit curia*) or by the adjunction to the court of a publicly appointed *amicus*, such as the advocates general at the European Court of Justice.[98] The International Court of Justice, for instance, is yet to admit a single civil society *amicus curiae* brief.

[94] Kawharu, 'Participation of Non-governmental Organizations in Investment Arbitration as *Amici Curiae*', pp. 285–6, and generally Peter J. Spiro, 'New Global Potentates: Nongovernmental Organisations and the "Unregulated" Marketplace', *Cardozo Law Review* 18 (1996): 957.

[95] Nigel Blackaby and Caroline Richard, '*Amicus Curiae*: A Panacea for Legitimacy in Investment Arbitration?' in Michael Waibel *et al.* (eds), *The Backlash against Investment Arbitration: Perceptions and Reality* (Alphen aan den Rijn: Kluwer Law, 2010), p. 266.

[96] See NAFTA Free Trade Commission, 'Statement of the Free Trade Commission on Non-disputing Party Participation', r. B(2).

[97] Even though, as submitted by an arbitral tribunal, 'the role of an *amicus curiae* is not to challenge arguments or evidence put forward by the Parties. This is the Parties' role. The role of the Petitioners in their capacity as *amicus curiae* is to provide their perspective, expertise, and arguments to help the court.' *Suez, Sociedad General de Aguas de Barcelona SA and Vivendi Universal SA* v. *Argentine Republic*, ICSID Case No. ARB/03/19, Order in Response to *Amicus* Petition, 12 February 2007, para. 25.

[98] See Esther Kentin, 'Sustainable Development in International Dispute Settlement: The ICSID and NAFTA Experience', in Nico Schrijver and Friedl Weiss (eds), *International*

The above observations indicate that, whereas states seem to be aware of the legitimacy crisis, the recent reforms are hardly sufficient to redress the flaws of the investor–state arbitral model. This is why some authors and critics have for some time been advocating more radical departures from the current dispute settlement institution in international investment law. We study these proposals below.

4 Doing away with arbitration? A critical overview of possible alternatives to the commercial arbitral model

Despite the criticism levied against the arbitral model, the awareness that it should be reformed in a way or another and the suspicion that the ongoing transparency and participation reform will fall short of the objective, many authors hesitate before taking the leap and suggesting a fundamental change in investment dispute settlement. Some argue that, given the structure of the international investment legal regime and the missing political will on the part of (home) states, any fundamental reform is an unrealistic prospect.[99] Others argue that the system is actually healthy and that its deficiencies will cure themselves naturally once it becomes more mature.[100] What is certain is that, should there be a radical overturn, the new system should be carefully designed so as not to prove worse than its predecessor.[101]

Other authors, while recognising the difficulty of the task, do not shy away from making ambitious and creative suggestions to move towards a less uncertain dispute settlement system or even to do away with arbitration altogether. We discuss these suggestions briefly here.

The idea of reinstating the customary requirement of the exhaustion of local remedies is sometimes put forward.[102] Exhaustion of local remedies is most often required when international institutions are mandated to

---

Law and Sustainable Development: Principles and Practice, (Leiden: Martinus Nijhoff, 2004), p. 323, stating that NGOs may be gaining more rights to participate in investment dispute settlement proceedings than they do under most other domestic or international mechanisms.

[99] See Barton Legum, 'Options to Establish an Appellate Mechanism in Investment Disputes', in Karl Sauvant (ed.), Appeals Mechanism in International Investment Disputes (Oxford University Press, 2008), pp. 231–40.

[100] See Paulsson, 'Avoiding Unintended Consequences'.

[101] Franck, 'Challenges Facing Investment Disputes', p. 157.

[102] On the customary status of the exhaustion of local remedies rule, see International Court of Justice, Interhandel Case (Switzerland v. USA, Preliminary Objections), Judgment, 21 March 1959, p. 27.

review acts of a state, as this gives the state whose exercise of regulatory power is challenged a chance to remedy the wrong without seeing its international responsibility engaged.[103] However, in IIAs, notwithstanding rare exceptions, this customary requirement is waived.[104] The suggestion that, as a rule, there be a requirement to use local courts again is very bold, because many IIAs do not provide for the exhaustion of local remedies for the very reason that they want to avoid confronting investors with local courts, whose competence, integrity and independence is subject to doubt and whom they fear may be biased against foreigners.[105] Also, resorting to arbitration without having to make the local detour would speed up the dispute settlement process. A departure from this situation could disrupt the economy of the system and shake investors' confidence.[106]

However, critics have argued that bypassing at all times local remedies somehow shows prejudice,[107] and in any case was likely to disempower local institutions, notably in developing countries where such institutions need to be strengthened and taken seriously.[108] This would undermine

---

[103] See, e.g., Council of Europe, Convention for the Protection of Human Rights and Fundamental Freedoms, done at Rome, 4 November 1950, effective 3 September 1953, Art. 35(1).

[104] Ralph Lorz, 'Local Remedies Rule in Public International Law and in Investment Protection Law', in ILA German Branch, Subcommittee on Investment, *General Public International Law and International Investment Law: A Research Sketch on Selected Issues*, December 2009, available at: http://telc.jura.uni-halle.de/sites/default/files/BeitraegeTWR/Heft%20105.pdf, p. 45. Recently, see the analysis of the very clear waiver contained in the US–Ukraine BIT in *Joseph Charles Lemire* v. *Ukraine*, Decision on Jurisdiction and Liability, paras 274 ff.

[105] See Salacuse, 'Explanations for the Increased Recourse to Treaty-based Investment Dispute Settlement', p. 121. See in practice the *Loewen* case's analysis of the perceived anti-Canadian and pro-American bias of a Mississippi local court and its jury, at the end of which the tribunal concluded that: 'By any standard of measurement, the trial involving O'Keefe and Loewen was a disgrace … By any standard of evaluation, the trial judge failed to afford Loewen the process that was due.' *Loewen Group, Inc. and Raymond L. Loewen* v. *United States*, ICSID Case No. ARB(AF)/98/3, Award on Merits, 26 June 2003, para 119.

[106] See *Helnan International Hotels A/S* v. *Arab Republic of Egypt*, ICSID Case No. ARB/05/19, Decision on the Application for Annulment, 14 June 2010, paras 52–3.

[107] Sornarajah, 'A Law for Need or a Law for Greed?', pp. 349–50.

[108] The reverse argument is also made in that the availability of arbitration could emulate state courts to do better and get the 'business' of investment dispute settlement anyway. Susan D. Franck, 'Foreign Direct Investment, Investment Treaty Arbitration, and the Rule of Law', *McGeorge Global Business and Development Law Journal* 19 (2007): 337, at p. 367.

the local rule of law. A recent study shows that such suspicion is not necessarily without foundations:

> Under certain circumstances, the presence of international alternatives might undermine the quality of the local legal system … If governments and foreign investors can turn to external sources of dispute resolution, they have little incentive to make marginal investments in improving local judicial quality. In some circumstances, this dynamic might allow domestic court structures to become captured by corrupt local coalitions. Unless domestic judiciaries internalize the benefits of institutional quality, they will not be concerned with the loss of 'business' to international competitors such as arbitral bodies. The availability of international alternatives, then, may perpetuate poor domestic institutions by allowing powerful actors to exit.[109]

In light of the above, recognising to a certain extent the jurisdiction of local courts in investment disputes could have several advantages. First, it could equip the system with several degrees of jurisdiction. On the one hand, this would perhaps slow down the process and run counter to the sought after 'finality' of arbitration, but, on the other hand, a generalised right to appeal may all in all be favourable to investors themselves, who seem to lose their non-appealable arbitral cases more often than not.[110] Second, it would allow the local situation to be better taken into account, to better appraise the motives (and good faith) of government measures, and to have a better understanding of the host state's international obligations. In any event, the embeddedness of local courts in the host state's socioeconomic context would endow such courts with more legitimacy to review the acts of the host government.[111]

---

[109] Tom Ginsburg, 'International Substitutes for Domestic Institutions: Bilateral Investment Treaties and Governance', *International Review of Law and Economics* 25 (2005): 109, at p. 121.

[110] See, above, n. 62.

[111] See Burke-White and von Staden, 'Private Litigation in a Public Law Sphere', pp. 332–3: 'Generally, the greater embeddedness of a tribunal in a State's socio-political context justifies and supports the application of more strict scrutiny by the tribunal. In contrast, lack of embeddedness suggests the need for greater deference to decisions made by institutions that are more culturally, legally, and politically embedded. Such embeddedness and proximity to the issues at stake serves certain functions that cannot be easily replicated … The application of strict scrutiny in effect authorizes a tribunal to fully evaluate all aspects of a case up to the point of substituting any assessments made by the governmental actors in the case with its own. At the international level, especially in the case of temporary, free-floating ad hoc tribunals, such an approach is generally inappropriate and will likely result in a reduction of perceived legitimacy, at least from the perspective of respondent states.'

Some states are therefore reconsidering their outright and absolute rejection of the local remedies rule. The requirement that local courts must be resorted to for a minimal period of time before an arbitral complaint can be lodged has been included in investment agreements for some time. Moreover, some states have included in their BITs certain features of fairness and certainty that the host state courts have to show, as an obligation towards foreign investors, pointing to the fact that this avenue should not be automatically overlooked by investors.[112] An emerging line of arbitral case law has also qualified the principle that investors are free of any obligation to have recourse to local courts.[113] In *Chevron v. Ecuador*, the tribunal stated, in response to Ecuador's submission that resort to local remedies is necessary where mechanisms appear to be available:

> While reiterating its view that strict exhaustion of local remedies is not necessary, the Tribunal agrees with the Respondent that a claimant is required to make use of all remedies that are available and might have rectified the wrong complained of … Moreover, a high likelihood of success of these remedies is not required in order to expect a claimant to attempt them. In the case of undue delay, the delay itself usually evidences the general futility of all remedies except those that specifically target the delay. Resort to these remedies may also be excused if another

---

[112] See US Model BIT, Art. 11(6) and (7).

[113] An author systematically reviewed the recent case law dealing with local remedies and observed that the thrust of the local remedies rule was actually quite far-reaching in arbitral case law, in that: 'several distinct propositions of law are distillable from the Local Remedies Cases, including: 1. An investor cannot establish a treaty breach based on judicial conduct if there exists a reasonably available domestic legal mechanism for having such conduct reviewed and corrected, which the investor failed to invoke. 2. The same may also be true with regard to claims based on reviewable administrative conduct. 3. A treaty claim may be defective on the merits if it is predicated in part on a breach of contract by the host State but the investor has not sought a ruling on the contractual issues in a domestic forum. 4. If the investor does pursue a local remedy, the tribunal in a subsequent treaty-based arbitration should defer to the findings of the local court absent a "denial of justice." 5. The pursuit of local remedies may preclude the investor from asserting a treaty claim having the same "fundamental basis," if the relevant BIT contains a "fork-in-the-road" clause.' The author then goes on to argue that, while the relevance of the local remedies rule for certain claims, it should not be stretched to the point where investors have to go to unreasonable lengths to pursue them or where absolute deference is given to domestic courts. See George K. Foster, 'Striking a Balance Between Investor Protections and National Sovereignty: The Relevance of Local Remedies in Investment Treaty Arbitration', *Columbia Journal of Transnational Law* 49 (2010/11): 201, at pp. 238–9.

traditional exemption applies, such as if these remedies were shown to be ineffective or futile in resolving delay.[114]

Whether this kind of interpretation will provide for a re-birth of the local remedies rule – at least to the extent that the investor should try in good faith to have its wrong redressed by local courts – remains to be seen, as contrary case law also exists.[115] For example, an award that decided that a ministerial decision could not be seen as a breach of a BIT (not requiring exhaustion of local remedies), failing a challenge before the host state's administrative courts,[116] was annulled by an *Ad hoc* ICSID Committee.[117]

Other suggestions propose that going to arbitration be avoided, and also that local courts should be bypassed, notably by using 'alternative dispute resolution' mechanisms, that is, non-adversarial ways to resolve a difference between an investor and a host state.[118] The variety of such mechanisms is considerable,[119] and analysing all of them here would take us too far. However, such mechanisms have already proven their efficacy

---

[114] *Chevron Corporation (USA) and Texaco Petroleum Company (USA)* v. *Republic of Ecuador*, UNCITRAL, PCA Case No. 34877, Partial Award on the Merits, 30 March 2010, paras 325–6. The US–Ecuador BIT contains the following in Art. II(7): 'Each Party shall provide effective means of asserting claims and enforcing rights with respect to investment, investment agreements, and investment authorizations.' No exhaustion of local remedies was, however, required by the BIT. *In casu*, the claim had to do with delays that Chevron had to suffer before Ecuadorian courts.

[115] See *Plama Consortium Ltd* v. *Bulgaria*, ICSID Case No. ARB/03/24, Decision on Jurisdiction, 8 February 2005, para. 224, in which the tribunal characterised a treaty requirement to try an investment dispute in domestic courts for the first eighteen months as 'curious' and 'nonsensical from a practical point of view'. Another tribunal allowed an investor to disregard a similar requirement of the Italy–Argentina BIT for the reason that Argentine courts would not have been able to solve the dispute within eighteen months, and that therefore, given that 'Argentina was not in a position to adequately address the present dispute within the framework of its domestic legal system … Argentina's interest in pursuing this local remedy does not justify depriving Claimants of their right to resort to arbitration for the sole reason that they decided not to previously submit their dispute to the Argentinean courts'. See *Abaclat and Others* v. *Argentine Republic*, ICSID Case No. ARB/07/5, Decision on Jurisdiction and Admissibility, 4 August 2011, para. 588.

[116] See *Helnan International Hotels A/S* v. *Arab Republic of Egypt*, ICSID Case No. ARB/05/19, Award, 3 July 2008, para. 148.

[117] See *Helnan* v. *Egypt*, Award, paras 42 ff.   [118] See UNCTAD, above, n. 9, pp. 22 ff.

[119] See generally Franck, 'Challenges Facing Investment Disputes'; UNCTAD, 'Investor-State Disputes: Prevention and Alternatives to Arbitration II', *Proceedings of the Washington and Lee University and UNCTAD Joint Symposium on International Investment and Alternative Dispute Resolution*, Lexington, 29 March 2010, available at: www.unctad.org/en/docs/webdiaeia20108_en.pdf.

in some cases and have for some time expressly been mentioned in a number of investment agreements, sometimes as a prerequisite to arbitration. Article 23 of the US Model BIT, for example, provides the following:

> In the event of an investment dispute, the claimant and the respondent should initially seek to resolve the dispute through consultation and negotiation, which may include the use of nonbinding, third-party procedures.

The much publicised issue of the inconsistency of certain awards has also prompted students of the international investment regime to reflect upon possible solutions. Whereas a system of preliminary references *à la* the European Union has been evoked,[120] as well as procedures for the consolidation of parallel claims,[121] the possibility of setting up a degree of appeal in investor–state dispute settlement has been the most popular subject of debate. The suggestions considered concern a proper appeals system and not the existing marginal annulment procedures, which exist to cure the regime from gross errors and unfairness, but which are by no means a guarantee of cohesion in the case law (see above).[122]

The ICSID itself contributed to the debate in a 2004 Discussion Paper containing a section titled 'An ICSID Appeals Facility?' with a detailed discussion of what such a facility would look like and how it would function.[123] The Appeals Facility was seen as a means of overcoming the potential for inconsistencies which was growing with the number of cases. This study by ICSID was inspired by the increasing number of BITs which were considering an appellate mechanism in their dispute settlement provisions, mostly at the behest of the United States, whose former (2004) Model BIT contained the following Annex D:

> Within three years after the date of entry into force of this Treaty, the Parties shall consider whether to establish a bilateral appellate body or similar

---

[120] See Christoph Schreuer, 'Preliminary Rulings in Investment Arbitration', in Karl Sauvant (ed.), *Appeals Mechanism in International Investment Disputes* (Oxford University Press, 2008), pp. 207–12.

[121] See Reinisch, 'The Issues Raised by Parallel Proceedings and Possible Solutions', pp. 119–20.

[122] For a well thought-out proposal to establish an 'Investment Arbitration Appellate Court', see Franck, 'The Legitimacy Crisis in Investment Treaty Arbitration', pp. 1617–25.

[123] See ICSID Secretariat, 'Possible Improvements of the Framework for ICSID Arbitration', Discussion Paper, 22 October 2004, available at: http://icsid.worldbank.org/ICSID/FrontServlet?requestType=ICSIDPublicationsRH&actionVal=ViewAnnouncePDF&AnnouncementType=archive&AnnounceNo=14_1.pdf, p. 14 and Annex 1.

mechanism to review awards rendered under Article 34 in arbitrations commenced after they establish the appellate body or similar mechanism.[124]

This would, admittedly, not solve inconsistency issues in the whole regime since it would be a bilateral mechanism. And, indeed, the new (2012) US Model BIT no longer provides for the possibility of establishing a bilateral appellate body, but still considers the possibility that a multilateral appeals facility might come about in its Article 28(10):

> In the event that an appellate mechanism for reviewing awards rendered by investor–State dispute settlement tribunals is developed in the future under other institutional arrangements, the Parties shall consider whether awards rendered under Article 34 should be subject to that appellate mechanism. The Parties shall strive to ensure that any such appellate mechanism they consider adopting provides for transparency of proceedings similar to the transparency provisions established in Article 29.

The possibility of adjoining an appeals mechanism to the currently disparate arbitral system has attracted an avalanche of critique, notably on feasibility grounds,[125] and because it would dismiss the existing arbitration paradigm based on the principles of finality and expediency. But the elephant in the room is the question of what sort of institution would be appropriate as the appeals mechanism. In this regard, proposals for a permanent arbitral institution were advanced. It was argued that such an institution's mandate should be that of an appeals mechanism for the decisions of *ad hoc* arbitral tribunals, along the lines of the WTO Appellate Body.[126] Some authors go even further and argue that it should be a free-standing institution replacing altogether the current arbitral practice. Such institution would therefore be competent in first instance jurisdiction for all cases, but also possibly equipped with a second degree of jurisdiction.[127] Without even trying to guess what such an institution would look like, and in full recognition of the far-fetched character of

---

[124] See United States Model BIT, 2004, available at: www.state.gov/documents/organization/117601.pdf, Annex D.

[125] See generally Legum, 'Options to Establish an Appellate Mechanism in Investment Disputes'.

[126] Even though it is underlined that this might be quite difficult, since an investment appeals mechanism would be interpreting thousands of free-standing agreements and not a coherent legal ensemble. See Donald McRae, 'The WTO Appellate Body: A Model for an ICSID Appeals Facility?', *Journal of International Dispute Settlement* 1 (2010): 371.

[127] Gus van Harten, 'A Case for an International Investment Court', Society of International Economic Law (SIEL) Inaugural Conference 2008 Paper, 30 June 2008, available at: http://papers.ssrn.com/sol3/papers.cfm?abstract_id=1153424&rec=1&srcabs=916351.

such a proposal (politically as well as legally), let us recount some of the advantages it may have. Whether an appeals chamber or a court of full jurisdiction, a permanent institution would, on top of everything, provide a solution to the independence and impartiality problems that are encountered with the system of scattered arbitration, as judges could be tenured and statutorily excluded from other functions. Moreover, balance in legal expertise could be ensured and the appointment authorities could see to it that the domination of business lawyers in the arbitration corporation is not replicated on the bench of an international investment court. Finally, nothing in the nature of such a court would prevent provision for the degree of openness, transparency and participation which is required from judicial institutions under the rule of law and which we see emerging in the arbitral system.

5   Conclusion

Whereas dispute settlement is a necessary feature of the international investment legal regime, its current design leaves much to be desired. It applies commercial procedural standards to issues which, given their public law nature, should benefit from the guarantees of administrative review mechanisms.

So far, reforms have been adopted or are underway to the effect of opening up arbitral proceedings and providing opportunities for the participation of public interest groups. As indicated above, these changes are unlikely to soothe the worries caused by investor–state arbitration. More ambitious, practically and intellectually seductive proposals have been put forward, notably the idea of setting up a permanent institution that could hear cases in first instance or play the role of an appeals mechanism for arbitral proceedings.

Unfortunately, the current model seems to suit the interests of investors, and there is no reason to believe that capital-exporting countries, the main law-givers in international investment law, will soon experience a change of heart regarding arbitration.[128] The European Union, which since 1 December 2009 has had exclusive competence regarding foreign direct investment as part of its common

---

[128] See Katia Yannaca-Smal, 'Improving the System of Investor–State Dispute Settlement: The OECD Governments' Perspective', in Karl Sauvant (ed.), *Appeals Mechanism in International Investment Disputes* (Oxford University Press, 2008), pp. 223–9.

commercial policy,[129] could, however, be a game-changer in the near future. The introduction of a new powerful player in the investment legal regime could, indeed, be a good occasion to reconsider the rules of the game, especially given the fact that the system itself is not really prepared for the EU's joining it, as is shown by the fact that the ICSID Convention does not provide for accession by an international organisation.

In its 2010 'Communication Concerning a Future European International Investment Policy',[130] the European Commission reflected on what type of dispute settlement mechanism it envisioned for 'enforcing' the 'investment commitments' made under its forthcoming investment policy. Whereas in the view of the Commission the EU should 'build on Member State practices to arrive at state-of-the-art investor–state dispute settlement mechanisms', it does not seem to question the suitability of arbitration as such (and even less as it announces that it will explore the possibility of the EU seeking to accede to the ICSID Convention). Nonetheless, the Commission may have some ambition for reforming the arbitral model a bit further, as it insists on the necessary transparency that the investment dispute settlement mechanism has to guarantee and on the fact that a solution must be found for the 'atomisation of disputes and interpretations', possibly by way of establishing an appellate mechanism.[131] No word, however, is to be found concerning the requirement to exhaust domestic remedies,[132] or the possibility viz. desirability of establishing a permanent body for adjudicating investor–state disputes.

In conclusion, it seems that despite a pressing need for (r)evolution, conservatism firmly holds the international investment legal regime, especially on the part of capital-exporting countries, as their corporations

---

[129] See Article 207 of the Treaty on the Functioning of the European Union and, generally, Jan Asmus Bischoff, 'Just a Little *Bit* of "Mixity"? The EU's Role in the Field of International Investment Protection Law', *Common Market Law Review* 48 (2011): 1527.

[130] 7 July 2010, EU Doc. No. COM(2010) 343 final.

[131] EU Doc. No. COM(2010) 343 final, pp. 9–10.

[132] Contrary to the European Parliament Report on the matter, which expressly mentions that 'changes must be made to the present dispute settlement regime, in order to include greater transparency, the opportunity for parties to appeal, *the obligation to exhaust local judicial remedies where they are reliable enough to guarantee due process*, the possibility to use *amicus curiae* briefs and the obligation to select one single place of investor-state arbitration' (emphasis added). See European Parliament, Committee on International Trade, Report on the Future European International Investment Policy, 22 March 2011, EU Doc. No. 2010/2203(INI), para. 31.

value highly the possibility of resorting to arbitration.[133] One would hope that, in the absence of a sea change, small tides of reform will, in the course of the twenty-first century, progressively shape a fairer and more open dispute settlement system that is more concerned with the general interest.

[133] See Timothy Nelson, "'History Ain't Changed": Why Investor–State Arbitration Will Survive the "New Revolution"', in Michael Waibel *et al.* (eds), *The Backlash against Investment Arbitration: Perceptions and Reality* (Alphen aan den Rijn: Kluwer Law, 2010), pp. 555–76.

20

Non-investment obligations in investment treaty arbitration: towards a greater role for states?

VID PRISLAN*

I Introduction

The growth of investment jurisprudence that has been witnessed in the past two decades has brought about a certain maturation of the field of foreign investment law, and with it an ever-increasing interaction with other fields of international law. Until recently, the study of this inter-action received only scant attention, but with the growing impact of international investment law, scholarly interest has now turned to con-sidering more closely the interface between investment and other areas of international regulation.[1] Undoubtedly, the need for studying and reflecting upon this interaction is not only academic, but also practical. Not only can developments in other fields of international law contribute to the development of international investment law, as attested to by the occasional instances of 'judicial borrowing' when investment tribunals rely upon legal solutions developed in other treaty regimes, such as the World Trade Organization (WTO) or human rights systems.[2] These

---

* The author would like to thank Freya Baetens, Eric de Brabandere, Robert Heinsch and Yannick Radi of Leiden Law School for their valuable comments on an earlier draft. The responsibility for any errors remains with the author.

[1] The emerging literature seeks to capture different aspects of this interface, focusing on the role of human rights (see, e.g., the various contributions in P-M. Dupuy, E-U. Petersmann and F. Francioni (eds), *Human Rights in International Investment Law and Arbitration* (Oxford University Press, 2009)), environmental protection standards (see, e.g., J. E. Viñuales, *Foreign Investment and the Environment in International Law* (Cambridge University Press, 2012)) or European law (see, e.g., M. Bungenberg, J. Griebel and S. Hindelang (eds), *International Investment Law and EU Law* (Heidelberg: Springer, 2011)), to mention a few examples.

[2] See, e.g., *Pope & Talbot Inc.* v. *Government of Canada*, UNCITRAL, Award on the Merits of Phase 2, 10 April 2001, paras 45–82 (where the tribunal relied in its reasoning upon WTO jurisprudence), or *Mondev International Ltd* v. *United States of America*, ICSID Case No. ARB(AF)/99/2, Award, 11 October 2002, paras 143–4, and *Saipem SpA* v. *People's Republic of Bangladesh*, ICSID Case No. ARB/05/07, Decision on Jurisdiction

'other' fields of international law also directly enter investor–state disputes, as norms and rules originating from other subsystems of international law are now increasingly invoked and relied upon by both claimants and respondents in investment arbitration, often in conjunction with competing claims to priority and supremacy.

The increased complexity of the legal issues that, as a result, are facing investment tribunals calls for a theoretical examination of the relationship between investment law and its broader normative environment. On the one hand, issues have occasionally arisen about the concurrent application of protection standards offered by separate, albeit complementary, treaty regimes, as when investors sought to rely upon guarantees provided under human rights treaties to broaden the protections available to their investments under international investment agreements (IIAs).[3] On the other hand, there is also a growing perception of investment protection standards as potentially encroaching upon and conflicting with other areas of international regulation. And it is the problem of 'normative conflicts', potential and real, that has generated most scholarly debate. This problem started to manifest itself when foreign investors began to challenge legislative and administrative measures adopted by the host state in pursuance of public policy objectives – such as those aimed at the realisation of basic human rights, promotion of public health or protection of the environment – on the ground that these regulatory measures violated investment protection standards.[4] Expectedly, this has given rise to concerns that the standards of behaviour prescribed by international investment treaties might be unduly restraining the

---

and Recommendation on Provisional Measures, 21 March 2007, paras 130–2 (where the tribunals found support for their reasoning in the jurisprudence of the European Court of Human Rights).

[3] See, e.g., *Spyridon Roussalis* v. *Romania*, ICSID Case No. ARB/06/1, Award, 7 December 2011 (where the claimant not only alleged breaches of the respondent's international obligations under the Greece–Romania BIT, but also Art. 1 of the First Additional Protocol to the European Convention on Human Rights).

[4] For some earlier cases, see, e.g., *Aguas del Tunari SA* v. *Republic of Bolivia*, ICSID Case No. ARB/02/3 (concerning host state interference with water concession rights allegedly pursued in the realisation of the citizen's right to water) or *Metalclad Corporation* v. *Mexico*, ICSID Case No. ARB(AF)/97/1 (arising out of the refusal by the local authorities of Mexico to issue a waste disposal permit and the subsequent adoption of an environmentally protected area). More recent examples include *Philip Morris Asia Ltd* v. *Australia*, UNCITRAL (arising out of the adoption by Australia of stringent tobacco legislation) or *Vattenfall* v. *Federal Republic of Germany* ICSID Case No. ARB/09/6 (arising out of Germany's decision regarding its nuclear phase-out).

host states' regulatory space.[5] At the same time, it has also pointed to potential incompatibilities between obligations arising under investment treaties and host states' other international obligations, given that the adoption of disputed domestic regulatory measures was often dictated by specific international instruments.[6] Recently, the problem of normative conflicts has also arisen in relation to the EU legal order, where the (in)compatibility of obligations under IIAs and under EU treaties is increasingly becoming an issue.[7]

In light of these developments, the present chapter examines some of the legal avenues that investment tribunals can use to consider arguments based on sources of obligations other than the investment treaty, and take them into account in adjudicating investor–state disputes. Section II touches upon the problems concerning the limited jurisdictional competence of investment tribunals, and the discrepancy between that jurisdiction and the applicable law. It essentially argues that, while investment

---

[5] See, especially 'Business and Human Rights: Towards Operationalizing the "Protect, Respect and Remedy" Framework', Report of the Special Representative of the UN Secretary General on the Issue of Human Rights, Transnational Corporations and Other Business Enterprises, UN Doc. A/HRC/11/13, 22 April 2009, para. 30.

[6] See, e.g., *Piero Foresti, Laura de Carli & Others* v. *Republic of South Africa*, ICSID Case No. ARB(AF)/07/01 (concerning Black Economic Empowerment laws enacted by South Africa pursuant to the Convention on the Elimination of All Forms of Racial Discrimination); *S. D. Myers, Inc.* v. *Canada*, UNCITRAL, First Partial Award, 13 November 2000 (concerning an export ban on PCBs which was adopted by Canada pursuant to its obligations under the Basel Convention on the Control of Transboundary Movements of Hazardous Waste and Their Disposal); or *Compañía del Desarrollo de Santa Elena SA* v. *Republic of Costa Rica*, ICSID Case No. ARB/96/1, Award of the Tribunal, 17 February 2000 (concerning an expropriation of an investor's territory for the purpose of adding it to a national park, in pursuance of Costa Rica's obligations under the UNESCO World Heritage Convention).

[7] On the one hand, see Case C-205/06, *EC Commission* v. *Austria* [2006] OJ C165; Case C-249/06, *EC Commission* v. *Sweden* [2006] OJ C178; Case C-118/07, *EC Commission* v. *Finland* [2007] OJ C95, in which the European Court of Justice found the unrestricted transfer of funds clauses present in some EU Member States' BITs to be incompatible with EU law measures taken in the context of the fight against terrorism. On the other hand, the issue of incompatibility has also arisen with regard to the 190 or so BITs that still exist between some of the EU Member States (the so-called intra-EU BITs). The European Commission has steadily opposed such BITs, on the ground that their continued existence could lead to discrimination between EU investors that enjoy the benefits of such BITs and other EU investors. This has even led to the Commission's involvement in some ongoing investment arbitrations, beginning with *Eastern Sugar BV* v. *Czech Republic*, SCC Case No. 088/2004, Partial Award, 27 March 2007. See on these issues generally, M. Potestà, 'Bilateral Investment Treaties and the European Union: Recent Developments in Arbitration and Before the ECJ', *Law and Practice of International Courts and Tribunals* 8 (2009): 225–45.

tribunals generally enjoy considerable latitude with regard to the scope of legal rules that they are entitled to apply to a particular dispute, jurisdictional limitations may prevent them from considering claims based on obligations other than the jurisdiction-endowing treaties (section II.A). It also argues, on the other hand, that investment treaties cannot be applied in isolation of international law, and that tribunals are always bound to resort to rules other than the investment treaty (section II.B). Section III then suggests that some of these limitations may be overcome by taking account of non-investment obligations in the process of interpreting the provisions of the investment treaty. To that end, it proposes three interpretative techniques that could more often be applied by investment tribunals (sections III.A–C). It also acknowledges, however, that there are limits as to what can be achieved through the interpretative process. Therefore, section IV suggests that the problem ought to be resolved primarily through the political process. For that purpose, some practical ways are examined through which states could address problems concerning normative conflicts by improving the language of their investment treaties. Lastly, the chapter concludes with some final observations in section V.

II Choice-of-law provisions as the obvious entry point for considering obligations other than the investment treaty

One can think of a number of different settings in which non-investment obligations could potentially feature in investment treaty arbitration. On the one hand, it is perfectly possible that non-investment obligations are invoked by an investor as part of its principal or subsidiary claims.[8] In the more likely situation, however, they will be relied upon by the host state in defence of its liability. The latter may argue that a specific measure said to be in breach of investment obligations was in furtherance of obligations undertaken in non-investment instruments, as in the case of the adoption of regulatory measures aimed at the realisation of basic human rights, the establishment of an environmentally protected area

---

[8] See, e.g., the dispute between a Canadian investor and Barbados concerning the former's investment in an eco-tourism facility in one of Barbados' natural wetlands areas, where the claimant contended that the government of Barbados had violated its international obligations under the Canada–Barbados BIT by refusing to enforce its environmental laws, in defiance of Barbados' obligations under the RAMSAR Convention on Wetlands of International Importance and the United Nations Convention on Biological Diversity. Notice of Dispute, available at: http://graemehall.com/legal/papers/BIT-Complaint.pdf.

pursuant to an international environmental agreement or, say, the implementation of EU regulations. Alternatively, the respondent state may argue that the investor's conduct was undermining the state's obligations under non-investment instruments and that its intervention was necessary to fulfil these obligations. This might, for example, be contended in the case of a refusal to issue a permit due to the danger of pollution or of interference with a water supply concession. But this is not to say that non-investment obligations could not also influence the outcome of investment proceedings in other, incidental ways. For instance, they could importantly affect the tribunal's jurisdiction by making the whole investment treaty inapplicable, or be indirectly determinative for defining the scope of protected assets or the legality of a given investment.[9] In all such situations, investment tribunals may thus be bound to take account of non-investment obligations in the adjudicative process, either as part of the principal or incidental determinations. And the most obvious and direct way to do so is to consider them as part of applicable law.

While not always oblivious of host state's obligations other than those under the investment treaty,[10] investment tribunals have generally shown a rather reluctant attitude when it came to considering and applying external, non-investment rules in the context of an investor-state dispute, thus fuelling the perception of arbitrators being inclined to apply investment law in isolation of other fields of law.[11] As some

---

[9] This is particularly the case with EU law, which may operate in several distinct ways. See on this, *Eureko BV* v. *Slovak Republic*, PCA Case No. 2008–13, Award on Jurisdiction, Arbitrability and Suspension, 26 October 2010, para. 229.

[10] See, e.g., *Southern Pacific Properties (Middle East) Ltd* v. *Arab Republic of Egypt*, ICSID Case No. ARB/84/3, Award, 20 May 1992, paras 154ff. (where account was taken of Egypt's obligations under the 1972 UNESCO Convention for the Protection of World Cultural and Natural Heritage in determining the quantum of compensation); *S. D. Myers*, paras 201–21 (where consideration was given to Canada's obligations under the 1989 Basel Convention on the Control of Transboundary Movements of Hazardous Waste and Their Disposal); *Maffezini* v. *Spain*, ICSID Case No. ARB/97/7, Award on the Merits, 13 November 2000, para. 67 (where account was taken of the obligation to conduct an environmental impact assessment procedure as required by Spanish and European law, as well as by the 1991 Espoo Convention on Environmental Impact Assessment in a Transboundary Context); or *Parkerings-Compagniet AS* v. *Lithuania*, ICSID Case No. ARB/05/8, Award, 11 September 2007, paras 377–97 (where the differential treatment of the claimant's investment was found to be legitimate considering the location of the latter in a UNESCO-protected area).

[11] See generally on this M. Hirsch, 'Conflicting Obligations in International Investment Law: Investment Tribunals' Perspective', in T. Broude and Y. Shany (eds), *The Shifting Allocation of Authority in International Law: Considering Sovereignty, Supremacy and Subsidiarity* (Oxford: Hart, 2008), pp. 321–43. See also E. de Brabandere, 'Human Rights

have suggested, this may have to do with the general inclination of investment arbitrators to adopt the private, *inter partes* model of dispute settlement that is prevalent in commercial arbitration, which makes investment tribunals less likely to take into account wider public policy considerations in the settlement of specific disputes.[12] It may also have to do with arbitrators' lack of acquaintance with other specialised fields of international law.[13] At least partly, however, it may be attributed to the limited jurisdictional competence of investment tribunals.[14]

A   Jurisdictional constraints

Surely, investment tribunals are not tribunals of unqualified, general jurisdiction. Like other international tribunals, they are creatures of state consent, which means that their jurisdiction is not only based on the consent of the parties, but also limited by the scope of such consent. Their jurisdiction is usually confined to a particular type of dispute (e.g., disputes concerning an investment)[15] or to disputes arising under a particular instrument (e.g., disputes concerning the application or interpretation of an investment treaty or disputes concerning violations

Considerations in International Investment Arbitration', in M. Fitzmaurice and P. Merkouris (eds), *Critical Essays on the European Convention on Human Rights* (Leiden: Nijhoff, 2012) regarding the relative reluctance of investment tribunals to engage with human rights arguments.

[12] See, e.g., B. Simma, 'Foreign Investment Arbitration: A Place for Human Rights?', *International and Comparative Law Quarterly* 60 (2011): 573–96, at p. 576. For an example of this inclination, see *Glamis Gold Ltd* v. *United States of America*, UNCITRAL, Award, 8 June 2009, para. 3. That investment tribunals are, indeed, 'dispute-oriented' has also been statistically demonstrated by O. K. Fauchald, 'The Legal Reasoning of ICSID Tribunals: An Empirical Analysis', *European Journal of International Law* 19 (2008): 301–64, at p. 357.

[13] See, e.g., E. Kentin, 'Sustainable Development in International Investment Dispute Settlement: The ICSID and NAFTA Experience', in N. J. Schrijver and F. Weiss (eds), *International Law and Sustainable Development: Principles and Practice* (Leiden: Nijhoff, 2004), pp. 309–38, at p. 324.

[14] See, e.g., B. Simma and T. Kill, 'Harmonizing Investment Protection and International Human Rights: First Steps Towards a Methodology', in C. Binder, U. Kriebaum and A. Reinisch (eds), *International Investment Law for the 21st Century: Essays in Honour of Christoph Schreuer* (Oxford University Press, 2009), pp. 678–707, at p. 679, who contend that 'affirmative claims based on international human rights law are well outside the jurisdiction of arbitration tribunals convened pursuant to BIT dispute settlement clauses'.

[15] See, e.g., Germany Model BIT 2008, Art. 10; Netherlands Model BIT 2004, Art. 9; or France Model BIT 2006, Art. 7.

of the substantive rights under the treaty).[16] Ignoring the jurisdictional limits can have important consequences, insofar as the exercise by an investment tribunal of jurisdiction that it does not have can potentially be sanctioned by the annulment of an award due to an excess of power – just like the failure to apply the proper law to the arbitration.[17] What must not be forgotten, however, is that limitations to jurisdictional competence do not necessarily restrict the scope of the law applicable to the dispute; for, the latter is a different matter than the scope of jurisdiction. Even the jurisdiction of the International Court of Justice (ICJ), which is otherwise directed to apply the sources of international law laid down in Article 38 of its Statute, is necessarily limited by the instrument upon which the Court's jurisdiction is founded in each case.

At least as far as the clauses on applicable law that are typically found in investment treaties are concerned, these do not necessarily prevent an investment tribunal from considering and applying international obligations other than those arising under an investment treaty. In fact, a large number of IIAs do not even identify the scope of the law applicable to the resolution of disputes.[18] But when they nonetheless do, investment treaties almost invariably provide for the application of international law, in addition to the treaty in question and/or the domestic law of the host state.[19] To the same extent, neither do default choice of law clauses in the ICSID Convention or other arbitral rules prevent the application of non-investment obligations by an investment tribunal. As regards the former, the second part of Article 42(1) of the ICSID Convention, which applies in case there is no party agreement on the applicable law, directs the tribunal to apply, in addition to the national laws of the party to the dispute, 'such rules of international law as may be applicable'.[20] The

---

[16] See, e.g., UK Model BIT, Art. 8(1); NAFTA, Art. 1116(1); or ECT, Art. 26.

[17] See generally, C. Schreuer *et al.* (eds), *The ICSID Convention: A Commentary*, 2nd edition (Cambridge University Press, 2009), pp. 943 ff.

[18] For an analysis, see E. Gaillard and Y. Banifatemi, 'The Meaning of "and" in Article 42(1), Second Sentence, of the Washington Convention: The Role of International Law in the ICSID Choice of Law Process', *ICSID Review: Foreign Investment Law Journal* 18 (2003): 375–411, at pp. 376–8, claiming that the majority of BITs entered into by countries such as the United States, the United Kingdom, France or Germany do not contain a clause on the applicable law regarding investor–state disputes. This is also the case with BITs of the Netherlands, which are generally silent on applicable law.

[19] See, e.g., NAFTA, Art. 1131; ECT, Art. 26(6); US Model BIT 2004, Art. 30; Canada Model BIT 2004, Art. 40(1); Chinese Model BIT 2003, Art. 9(3).

[20] Convention on the Settlement of Investment Disputes between States and Nationals of Other States, Establishing the International Centre for the Settlement of Investment

reference to the language 'as may be applicable' must not be understood as in any way conditioning the application of international law, but 'as making reference, within international law, to the competent rules to govern the dispute at issue'.[21] The pertinence of the rule to the dispute at issue generally depends on the question of whether the rule is intended to bestow the parties to the proceedings with certain rights or obligations and whether it relates to an investment.[22] With regard to other arbitration rules, these generally provide investment tribunals with even greater latitude in deciding upon the scope of applicable law. For example, pursuant to Article 35(1) of the UNCITRAL Arbitration Rules (as revised in 2010), an investment tribunal established in accordance with those rules will apply, in the absence of a designation by the parties of rules applicable to the substance of the dispute, 'the law which it determines to be appropriate'.[23] Neither ICSID nor non-ICSID tribunals will thus be *a priori* precluded from considering arguments relating to non-investment obligations in view of the broad discretion that they will generally enjoy in determining the law applicable to the dispute.[24] To a certain extent, they may even be bound to consider non-investment obligations, in the event that investment protection guarantees conflict with *jus cogens* norms[25] or other types of prevailing obligations.[26]

Disputes, Washington, 18 March 1965, entered into force 14 October 1966, 575 *UNTS* 159, 4 *ILM* 532 (1965) (ICSID Convention).

[21] *LG&E* v. *Argentina*, ICSID Case No. ARB/02/1, Decision on Liability, 3 October 2006, para. 88.

[22] The frame of reference in this regard is Art. 25(1) of the ICSID Convention, which requires the dispute to be a 'legal dispute arising directly out of an investment'.

[23] UNCITRAL Arbitration Rules as revised in 2010, UN Doc. A/RES/65/22, 6 December 2010. Similarly, the 1976 UNCITRAL Arbitration Rules provide in Art. 33(1) that: 'the arbitral tribunal shall apply the law designated by the parties as applicable to the substance of the dispute'. UNCITRAL Arbitration Rules, UN Doc. A/31/17 (1976). Similar provisions can also be found in arbitral rules of different chambers of commerce.

[24] In fact, even where the applicable law clause would provide only for the application of domestic laws, international non-investment obligations may still be applicable indirectly, to the extent they are explicitly incorporated in the national law of the host state.

[25] Pursuant to Art. 53 of the Vienna Convention on the Law of Treaties (VCLT), an investment treaty will also be void, if it conflicts with a peremptory norm of general international law. As appropriately observed in this respect by an investment tribunal, 'nobody would suggest that ICSID protection should be granted to investments made in violation of the most fundamental rules of protection of human rights, like investments made in pursuance of torture or genocide or in support of slavery or trafficking of human organs'. *Phoenix Action Ltd* v. *Czech Republic*, ICSID Case No. ARB/06/5, Award, 15 April 2009, para. 78.

[26] Important in this category are especially the obligations under the UN Charter, which shall prevail, by virtue of Art. 103 of the UN Charter, in the event of a conflict with obligations under any other international agreement. In the context of the investment

The matter is in principle not any different when it comes to considering and applying European law in an investor–state dispute; in fact, as properly noted by the tribunal in *Eureko* v. *Slovakia*, 'far from being precluded from considering and applying EU law the Tribunal is bound to apply it to the extent that it is part of the applicable law(s)'.[27] This can be either as a matter of international law or as a matter of domestic law, given that EU law may operate at the level of international law as between the parties to an investment treaty (if these are both member states of the EU), but also as part of the domestic legal order of the host state (when the latter is an EU member).[28] Alternatively, it may even be taken into account as a relevant *fact* when determining the respondent's compliance with its investment treaty obligations, particularly in situations where the applicable law clauses exclude the application of domestic law.[29] In any event, there is nothing that would suggest that European law could not be interpreted and applied by an investment tribunal, nor that the European Court of Justice (ECJ) would have exclusive jurisdiction over investor–state disputes. The jurisdiction of the latter may be exclusive with regard to certain categories of disputes between two EU member states, but certainly not with regard to all disputes that arise between an EU member state and an individual investor.[30]

To be sure, the possibility of applying international (or European) law as such to an investment dispute does not automatically extend the competence of an investment arbitral tribunal to the consideration of *claims* based on others' non-investment instruments. The extent to which an investment tribunal may be capable of pronouncing – as an independent head of claim – upon, say, the host state's violations of investors' rights under a human rights convention or breaches by the host state of its obligations under an environmental agreement, very much depends on the specific language of the instruments from which the tribunal

---

regime, this could play a role, e.g., in the event of smart sanctions adopted by the Security Council, as the measures demanding the freezing of funds which could conflict with unlimited transfer of funds clauses in a BIT. Furthermore, non-ICSID tribunals will have to take account of constraints potentially imposed by the mandatory rules of the *lex loci arbitri* and by considerations of transnational public policy, insofar as a failure to respect these rules may be ground for annulment of an award or later inhibit its enforcement.

[27] *Eureko*, para. 281.

[28] See, e.g. *Eureko*, para. 225; *AES Summit Generation Ltd and AES-Tisza Erömü Kft* v. *Republic of Hungary*, ICSID Case No. ARB/07/22, Award, 23 September 2010, para. 7.6.6.

[29] *AES*, paras 7.6.6–7.6.9.   [30] See on this *Eureko*, paras 276 and 283.

derives its authority, and the source of the rights and obligations in issue. So far, international courts and tribunals have generally refused to pronounce upon claims other than those falling within the ambit of the compromissory clause, even if the clause on applicable law directed them to apply a broader set of rules than those contained in the jurisdiction-conferring instrument.[31] In this regard, one could argue that an investment tribunal may not be able to pronounce upon claims based on non-investment instruments in case its jurisdiction is limited to disputes concerning the interpretation or application of a particular investment treaty – unless, of course, the treaty itself includes a direct *renvoi* to other instruments. The latter would be the case, for example, with various 'preservation of rights' clauses providing that other obligations under international law potentially prevail to the extent that they are more favourable than the protections provided for in the investment treaty.[32] It would also be the case where the treaty provides that the investor has to comply with domestic legislation in order to be protected, and this legislation would be the implementation of obligations under international instruments.[33]

---

[31] This has been the case in many situations where the jurisdiction was confined to disputes 'concerning the interpretation or application' of a particular instrument. See, e.g., *Dispute Concerning Access to Information Under Article 9 of the OSPAR Convention between Ireland and the United Kingdom of Great Britain and Northern Ireland*, Final Award, 2 July 2003, 23 *RIAA* 59, para. 85; *MOX Plant Case (Ireland v. United Kingdom)*, Order No. 3, 24 June 2003, 126 *ILR* 310, para. 19; *The Channel Tunnel Group Limited/France-Manche SA v. The Secretary of State for Transport of the Government of the United Kingdom of Great Britain and Northern Ireland/Le ministre de l'équipement, des transports, de l'aménagement du territoire, du tourisme et de la mer du Gouvernement de la République française*, Partial Award, 30 January 2007, 132 *ILR* 1, paras 144–51; or *Case concerning Pulp Mills on the River Uruguay (Argentina v. Uruguay) ICJ Reports* 2010, p. 14, paras 52 ff. For an informative study on the jurisdiction–applicable law distinction, see L. Bartels, 'Jurisdictions and Applicable Law Clauses: Where does a Tribunal find the Principal Norms Applicable to the Case before it?' in T. Broude and Y. Shany (eds), *Multi-sourced Equivalent Norms in International Law* (Oxford: Hart, 2011), pp. 115–42.

[32] See, e.g., US Model BIT 2004, Art. 16 or Dutch Model BIT 2004, Art. 3(5). However, as demonstrated by *Spyridon Roussalis*, para. 312, the existence of such clauses may not necessarily induce an investment tribunal to pronounce upon claims based upon those other obligations. The tribunal in that case, while not excluding the possibility that obligations deriving from the European Convention of Human Rights and its Additional Protocol No.1 could provide for 'more favourable' rules, refused to actually consider claims based upon the latter by arguing that the issue was moot, given the higher and more specific level of protection offered by the BIT to the investors compared with the more general protections offered to them by the human rights instruments.

[33] See, e.g., *Maffezini*, para. 71.

But in case an investment treaty provides for arbitration with regard to *any dispute concerning an investment*, there appears to be no bar, in principle, for an investment tribunal to consider (at least, in conjunction with a breach of an investment protection standard) claims arising under other instruments as well, to the extent that such claims indeed 'concern' an investment. This has been practically demonstrated in *Biloune* v. *Ghana*, where the tribunal did not deem itself debarred from considering the alleged violations of the investor's human rights resulting from his alleged arbitrary detention and expulsion by the government of Ghana to the extent that these violations 'may be relevant in considering the investment dispute under arbitration'. It must also be noticed, though, that the tribunal at the same time found itself without competence to pronounce upon these human rights violations 'as an independent cause of action', since its jurisdiction was limited to disputes 'in respect of' a foreign investment.[34]

Admittedly, pronouncing upon breaches of a non-investment instrument as an independent head of claim is not the same as considering such breaches for the purpose of making a principal determination under the investment treaty. In the latter case, the issue may not be considered as one of expanding the jurisdiction of the arbitral tribunal to claims under other instruments, but as one of determining a legal fact which is relevant for the purpose of applying the jurisdiction-conferring treaty. The point appears to have been well accepted by the Permanent Court of International Justice (PCIJ), which as far back as in the *Upper Silesia* judgment of 1925 was able to observe that 'the interpretation of other international agreements is indisputably within the competence of the Court if such interpretation must be regarded as incidental to a decision on a point in regard to which it has jurisdiction'.[35] Be that as it may, one can also expect that investment tribunals are likely to refrain, as far as possible, from making determinations on such incidental matters. Thus, the tribunal in *Eureko* v. *Slovakia* rejected the possibility that it would have jurisdiction to rule on alleged breaches of EU law as such; instead,

---

[34] *Biloune* v. *Ghana Investments Centre*, Award on Jurisdiction and Liability, 27 October 1989, 95 *ILR* 183, p. 203.

[35] *Case concerning Certain German Interests in Polish Upper Silesia* (*Germany* v. *Poland*), Preliminary Objections, *PCIJ Reports*, Series A, No. 6, p. 18. The Permanent Court made this observation after noting that the application of the 1922 Convention between Germany and Poland relating to Upper Silesia (9 *LNTS* 466), upon which its jurisdiction was founded in that case, was hardly possible without giving an interpretation of Art. 256 of the Treaty of Versailles and several other international agreements invoked by Poland.

its jurisdiction was 'confined to ruling upon alleged breaches of the BIT', notwithstanding the fact that investment treaty in question provided for the arbitration of all disputes 'concerning an investment'.[36] In the end, it would be reasonable to expect investment tribunals to at least *consider* the obligations that the host state may have under other instruments as questions preliminary, or incidental, to the application of the investment treaty, to the extent that is necessary to pronounce upon claims based on the investment treaty itself. All the more so, since it is precisely the application of these other instruments that often gives rise to issues under the investment treaty.

B   The 'clinical isolation' problem

Notwithstanding the potentially limited scope of jurisdictional clauses, it is obvious that an investment tribunal cannot be oblivious to other rules of international law, nor entirely exclude their application, even in cases where the clause governing applicable law may only direct it to apply the investment treaty as such. For the provisions of an investment treaty, like any other treaty, cannot be interpreted and applied in a vacuum, but against the normative background of the legal order to which the treaty belongs; that is, public international law.[37] Already in *AAPL* v. *Sri Lanka*, the first ICSID case based on a jurisdictional clause in a BIT, the tribunal cogently observed that:

> the Bilateral Investment Treaty is not a self-contained closed legal system limited to provide for substantive material rules of direct applicability, but it has to be envisaged within a wider juridical context in which rules from other sources are integrated through implied incorporation methods, or by direct reference to certain supplementary rules, whether of international law character or of domestic law nature.[38]

---

[36] *Eureko*, para. 290.

[37] Arbitral and judicial bodies in other treaty regimes have already demonstrated that they will not be oblivious to systemic considerations, even where their jurisdiction is circumscribed to the interpretation and application of the instrument, upon which their jurisdiction is founded. See, e.g., the statements to such effect by the European Court of Human Rights in *Banković and others* v. *Belgium and others*, No. 52207/99, para. 57, or *Al-Adsani* v. *United Kingdom*, No. 35763, para. 60, as well as by the WTO Appellate Body in *US–Standards for Reformulated and Conventional Gasoline*, WT/DS2/AB/R. 29 April 1996, p. 18.

[38] *Asian Agricultural Products Ltd (AAPL)* v. *Democratic Socialist Republic of Sri Lanka*, ICSID Case No. ARB/87/3, Award, 27 June 1990, para. 21. In a similar way, the tribunal in *Phoenix Action Ltd* v. *Czech Republic*, ICSID Case No. ARB/06/5, Award, 15 April

In practice, investment tribunals have regularly resorted to other rules of international law in order to determine matters not governed by the investment treaty. Today, one could practically not imagine an investment tribunal not applying the customary rules governing the interpretation of treaties as codified in Articles 31 and 32 of the 1969 Vienna Convention on the Law of Treaties (VCLT).[39] Nor could one imagine a tribunal not resorting to the customary rules on state responsibility when it comes to issues of attribution, circumstances precluding wrongfulness or reparation.[40] Last, but not least, tribunals have never considered themselves debarred from resorting, independently from any treaty provision, to certain general principles of law, such as the principle of good faith or estoppel, in analysing investors' claims.[41]

Of course, the recourse to such *secondary* rules of international law may not be considered at all problematic, for these are to be considered applicable by default in the absence of specific rules prescribed by the investment treaties themselves. Being confined in their content to a set of primary rules on investment protection, investment treaties were certainly never intended to function as self-contained regimes. What does give rise to problems, however, is the applicability of other *primary* rules of international law – be they of customary or conventional character. In principle, other primary rules remain operative in the absence of any treaty provisions that had the effect of excluding them, which means that an investment tribunal may apply them, unless and to the extent that the investment treaty providing the tribunal's jurisdictional basis has created

---

2009, para. 78, emphasised that 'the ICSID Convention's jurisdictional requirements – as well as those of the BIT – cannot be read and interpreted in isolation from public international law, and its general principles'.

[39] The customary rules of interpretation embodied in Arts 31 and 32 of the VCLT have regularly been applied to the interpretation of treaties that were concluded even before the VCLT's entry into force, such as the ICSID Convention. See, e.g., *Malaysian Historical Salvors Sdn Bhd* v. *Malaysia*, ICSID Case No. ARB/05/10, Decision on the Application for Annulment, 16 April 2009, para. 56, where the ICSID Annulment Committee 'consider[ed] itself on firm ground in resorting to the customary rules on interpretation of treaties as codified in the Vienna Convention'.

[40] See, e.g., *Sempra Energy International* v. *Argentine Republic*, ICSID Case No. ARB/02/16, Award, 28 September 2007, para. 378; *Enron Corporation and Ponderosa Assets LP* v. *Argentine Republic*, ICSID Case No. ARB/01/3, Award, 22 May 2007, para. 334, where the tribunals resorted to the customary law rules governing the invocation of a state of necessity.

[41] See, respectively, *Inceysa Vallisoletana SL* v. *Republic of El Salvador*, ICSID Case No. ARB/03/26, Award, 2 August 2006, paras 179–81; *Fraport AG Frankfurt Airport Services Worldwide* v. *Philippines*, ICSID Case No. ARB/03/25, Award, 16 August 2007, para. 346.

a *lex specialis*.[42] This relationship of specialty can be defined by way of exception to the general rule, the typical example being 'the inalienable right of all States freely to dispose of their natural wealth and resources in accordance with their national interests' as an element of the customary international law principle of permanent sovereignty over natural resources,[43] the operation of which is affected by investment treaty provisions governing the legality of expropriations. Alternatively, specialty can also be established through elaboration of the general rules, as in the case of the minimum standard of treatment of aliens under customary international law, which may be modified by more specific standards of treatment contained in investment treaties. Essentially, the principle of *lex specialis* can therefore have a bearing on the determination of other primary rules that could be applied by an investment tribunal in adjudicating the claim under the investment treaty.

At the same time, the principle is of limited usefulness for resolving normative conflicts between the investment treaty and other primary rules. For, it is well known that the application of *lex specialis* may face difficulties when one needs to determine the relationship between two different normative orders or rules deriving from different areas of law, such as investment law, on the one hand, and human rights law or environmental law, on the other.[44] Being an interpretative rule without substantive content, *lex specialis* cannot in fact provide guidance in determining which of the subsystems is general and which specific, and which thus shall prevail over the other. Therefore, it cannot resolve a conflict potentially arising between the application of investment protection guarantees and the implementation of states' obligation under customary international law to ensure that activities within their jurisdiction or control do not cause damage to the environment of other states or of areas beyond the limits of national jurisdiction,[45] if measures relating to the implementation of this obligation were to negatively affect an investor and breach its rights under an investment treaty.

---

[42] See, e.g., *Sempra*, para. 378, and *Enron*, para. 334, for the acknowledgement that 'a treaty regime specifically dealing with a given matter will prevail over more general rules of customary law'. Cf. *OSPAR* Arbitration, para. 84.

[43] Permanent Sovereignty over Natural Resources, UN GA Resolution 1803 (XVII), 14 December 1962.

[44] See A. Lindroos, 'Addressing Norm Conflicts in a Fragmented Legal System: The Doctrine of *Lex Specialis*', *Nordic Journal of International Law* 74 (2005): 27–66, at pp. 41–2.

[45] Cf. *Legality of the Threat or Use of Nuclear Weapons*, *ICJ Reports* 1996, p. 26, para. 29.

Nor can it resolve normative conflicts where the standards of behaviour prescribed by the investment treaty appear to be inconsistent with the obligations arising under other conventional instruments to which the host state is a party.

But, in fact, neither can other treaty-conflict rules successfully resolve the tensions between investment and non-investment rules.[46] As regards, for example, the *lex posterior derogat anteriori* rule as expressed in Article 30 of the VCLT, it is well known that its application is conditioned upon not only identity of the parties to the successive treaties, but requires the latter to relate to 'the same subject matter'.[47] Yet to establish that the provisions of an investment treaty relate 'to the same subject matter' as provisions, say, in a human rights convention, an environmental agreement or provisions under EU law may often require a considerable effort in creativity. Indeed, as demonstrated by a few recent decisions involving questions on the relationship between investment treaties and EU treaties, arbitral tribunals may not easily accept that provisions under different treaties indeed relate to the same subject matter.[48]

Be that as it may, in the end, it cannot be disputed that obligations under customary and conventional international law will remain in force for the host state and may continue to govern the relationship of the latter with the other party to the investment treaty and/or third states.[49] And to the extent that they may be relevant to the dispute between an investor and the host state, they can – and should – be considered in the process of treaty interpretation.

---

[46] On the inadequacy of traditional conflict rules for resolving conflicts between different branches of international law, see generally J. Klabbers, *Treaty Conflict and the European Union* (Cambridge University Press, 2009); R. Michaels and J. Pauwelyn, 'Conflict of Norms or Conflict of Laws? Different Techniques in the Fragmentation of International Law', in T. Broude and Y. Shany (eds), *Multi-sourced Equivalent Norms in International Law* (Oxford: Hart, 2011), pp. 19–44.

[47] Cf. Art. 30(1) and (3) of the VCLT.

[48] See *Eastern Sugar*, para. 160, and *Eureko*, paras 258 ff.

[49] Thus, the ICJ in the *Gabčíkovo-Nagymaros Project*, while considering that the relationship between Slovakia and Hungary was governed by a disputed treaty of 1977, appositely added that the 'relationship [between the Parties] is also determined by the rules of other relevant conventions to which the two States are party, by the rules of general international law and, in this particular case, by the rules of State responsibility; but it is governed, above all, by the applicable rules of the 1977 Treaty as a *lex specialis*'. *Gabčíkovo-Nagymaros Project* (*Hungary* v. *Slovakia*), *ICJ Reports* 1997, p. 7, para. 132.

III   Consideration of non-investment obligations through the process of treaty interpretation

The legal framework for considering non-investment rules in the analysis of investment treaty claims is not only determined by the clauses on applicable law, but is also laid down in the general rules of treaty interpretation, in accordance with which an investment treaty, like any other treaty, must be interpreted. Hence, notwithstanding the jurisdictional limitations potentially preventing an investment tribunal from directly applying other rules of international law in adjudicating investors' claims, there is no impediment for investment tribunals to consider these rules when constructing the meaning of the substantive protections laid down in an investment treaty.[50] There are three techniques in particular that can be employed by an investment tribunal for the purpose of considering external, non-investment rules in the interpretative process and each of these will be briefly dealt with below.[51]

A   Principle of systemic integration

It is beyond doubt that the starting point of any interpretative exercise must be the ordinary meaning of the terms of the treaty, in their context and in the light of the treaty's object and purpose, in accordance with Article 31(1) of the VCLT. Yet it is obvious that the search for the ordinary meaning is sometimes bound to bear few results. A typical case is the notion of 'fair and equitable treatment', the ordinary meaning of which, as has once been noted, 'can only be defined by terms of almost equal vagueness'.[52] In such cases, resort to Article 31(3)(c) of the VCLT – which directs the interpreter to take account of 'any relevant rules of international law applicable in the relations between the parties' – may provide a useful technique for determining the meaning of open-ended standards of protection.

---

[50] In *Pulp Mills*, paras 63–66, the ICJ expressly noted that the taking into account in the interpretative process of other relevant rules applicable in the relations between the parties had no bearing on the scope of the jurisdiction conferred on the Court.

[51] On these mechanisms of incorporation generally, see D. French, 'Treaty Interpretation and the Incorporation of Extraneous Legal Rules', *International and Comparative Law Quarterly* 55 (2006): 281–314.

[52] *Saluka Investments BV (the Netherlands)* v. *Czech Republic*, UNCITRAL, Partial Award, 17 March 2006, para. 297.

In view of its usefulness, it is rather surprising that the importance of Article 31(3)(c) of the VCLT has long been neglected, and that it was only in its 2006 Report on Fragmentation that the International Law Commission (ILC) rediscovered and even embraced it – together with the principle of 'systemic integration' to which the provision is said to give expression – as a means of harmonising the disparate and ever-fragmenting fields of international law.[53] Indeed, accepted today as a codification of customary international law,[54] Article 31(3)(c) of the VCLT definitely bears the capacity to also promote coherence between investment and non-investment obligations in investment treaty arbitration, inasmuch as it requires the adjudicator to interpret international obligations by reference to their normative environment.[55] But aside from the practical usefulness of resorting to other relevant rules of international law when the ascertainment of the ordinary meaning proves impossible, it must not be forgotten that the application of Article 31(3)(c) of the VCLT is in fact a *mandatory* part of the interpretation process. Unlike the resort to supplementary means of interpretation, which in accordance with Article 32 of the VCLT 'may' be referred to when the meaning of treaty terms is ambiguous, obscure, absurd or unreasonable, Article 31(3)(c) of the VCLT clearly demands from the interpreter that such rules 'shall' be taken into account. In fact, recourse to 'any relevant rules of international law applicable in the relations between the parties' is part and parcel of the same interpretative process, which starts, but does not stop, with the ordinary meaning of the terms of the treaty in accordance with Article 31(1) of the VCLT. All in all, it is well known that Article 31 of the VCLT lays down a single, general rule of interpretation, the provisions of which form one

---

[53] See 'Fragmentation of International Law: Difficulties Arising from the Diversification and Expansion of International Law', Report of the Study Group of the International Law Commission, UN Doc. A/CN.4/L.682, 13 April 2006.

[54] *Certain Questions of Mutual Assistance in Criminal Matters (Djibouti v. France) ICJ Reports* 2008, p. 177, para. 112.

[55] On systemic interpretation of investment treaties, see generally C. McLachlan, 'Investment Treaties and General International Law', *International and Comparative Law Quarterly* 57 (2008): 361–401, at pp. 369 ff. See also Simma and Kill, 'Harmonizing Investment Protection and International Human Rights', pp. 695–707, who demonstrate that international human rights law may well be taken into account through the application of Art. 31(3)(c) of the VCLT; or J. E. Viñuales, 'Foreign Investment and the Environment in International Law: An Ambiguous Relationship', *British Yearbook of International Law* 80 (2009): 244–332, who emphasises the importance of this provision for considering environmental obligations in investment treaty arbitration.

integrated whole, and that therefore the process of interpretation 'is ultimately a holistic exercise that should not be mechanically subdivided into rigid components'.[56]

Against this backdrop, one may wonder why references to Article 31(3)(c) of the VCLT have not figured more often in the reasoning of investment tribunals; at least explicitly. Surely, resort has sometimes been made in the interpretative process to other relevant rules of international law, particularly of a customary law nature, but without expressly mentioning Article 31(3)(c) of the VCLT. Thus, the tribunal in *ADF Group Inc.* v. *USA* seems to have relied on the rule implicitly when considering 'that any general requirement to accord "fair and equitable treatment" and "full protection and security" must be disciplined by being based upon State practice and judicial or arbitral case law or other sources of customary or general international law'.[57] In contrast, the award in *Saluka* v. *Czech Republic* (2006) appears to be one of the rare instances so far where Article 31(3)(c) of the VCLT was explicitly relied upon in interpreting one of the treaty's substantive investment protection standards. At the same time, it was also one of the more odd instances of the use of the rule. Namely, the tribunal in that case did not interpret the concept of 'deprivation' as this was used in the investment treaty's expropriation clause by reference to the respondent's non-investment obligations. Instead, it relied upon Article 31(3)(c) of the VCLT for the purpose of importing into the treaty the customary international law exception that a deprivation could be justified if it resulted from the exercise of regulatory actions aimed at the maintenance of public order, in which case the host state was not liable to pay compensation to a foreign investor.[58] Be that as it may, the precedent retains importance for its acknowledgement that the host state's sovereign powers to regulate are implicitly preserved under customary international law, and that an exception for the exercise of these powers can be imported into an investment treaty through the process of interpretation. This is a reaffirmation that will undoubtedly have important consequences considering that currently the large majority of investment treaties do not expressly acknowledge the host state's right to regulate in pursuit of policy objectives other than the promotion and

---

[56] *EC–Customs Classification of Frozen Boneless Chicken Cuts*, WT/DS269/AB/R and WT/DS286/AB/R, 12 September 2005, para. 176. See generally also *ILC Yearbook* 1966, vol. II, at pp. 219–20, para. 8.
[57] *ADF Group Inc.* v. *USA*, ICSID Case No. ARB(AF)/00/1, Award, 9 January 2003, para. 184.
[58] *Saluka*, paras 254–5.

protection of investments.[59] Furthermore, *Saluka*'s importance is also in implicitly acknowledging that the scope of regulatory powers, inasmuch as their content would follow the evolution of customary international law, may now well encompass measures aimed at the preservation of the environment or the attainment of basic human rights.[60] This was later demonstrated in *Chemtura* v. *Canada*, where the tribunal, by expressly referring to the *Saluka* decision, considered that the respondent's measures, which led to the cancellation of the registrations of a group of products based on the lindane pesticide (and which resulted from Canada's obligations under the Aarhus Protocol to the Long-Range Transboundary Air Pollution Convention), constituted a valid exercise of the respondent's police powers.[61]

But while the tribunal in *Saluka* – and the few other investment tribunals that have actually referred to Article 31(3)(c) in their reasoning[62] – have used that provision as a gateway to interpreting by reference to rules of customary international law, it needs to be emphasised that the wording of

[59] See generally on this S. A. Spears, 'The Quest for Policy Space in a New Generation of International Investment Agreements', *Journal of International Economic Law* 13 (2010): 1037–75. See *ADC Affiliate Ltd and ADC & ADMC Management Ltd* v. *The Republic of Hungary*, ICSID Case No. ARB/03/16, Award, 2 October 2006, para. 423, for one of the few instances where a tribunal expressly, reaffirmed 'the basic international law principle' that 'a sovereign state possesses the inherent right to regulate its domestic affairs' (albeit adding that the exercise of such right is not unlimited and has its boundaries in the rule of law).

[60] See for a similar reasoning the considerations of the ICJ in the *Dispute Regarding Navigational and Related Rights*, where the Court – after acknowledging that Nicaragua, as sovereign over the San Juan River, had the inherent power to regulate Costa Rica's right to freedom of navigation; a right that was granted to the latter under a boundary treaty of 1858 – considered that 'over the course of the century and a half since the 1858 Treaty was concluded, the interests which are to be protected through regulation in the public interest may well have changed in ways that could never have been anticipated by the Parties at the time: protecting the environment is a notable example'. *Case concerning the Dispute Regarding Navigational and Related Rights (Costa Rica* v. *Nicaragua) ICJ Reports* 2009, p. 213, at paras 87–9.

[61] *Chemtura Corporation* v. *Government of Canada*, UNCITRAL, Award, 2 August 2010, para. 266. However, the principle that a non-discriminatory regulation for a public purpose may not be deemed expropriatory and compensable (i.e., 'police powers' exception) had previously already been upheld by the arbitral tribunals in *S. D. Myers*, paras 281–2, and *Methanex* v. *United States*, UNCITRAL, Final Award, 3 August 2005, paras 7ff, both of which also concerned environment-related cases. The principle had also been recognised by the Iran–US Claims Tribunal in *SEDCO, Inc., et al.* v. *National Iranian Oil Company and the Islamic Republic of Iran* (1985) 9 IUSCTR 248, para. 275.

[62] See *Ioannis Kardassopoulos* v. *Republic of Georgia*, ICSID Case No. ARB/05/18, Decision on Jurisdiction, 6 July 2007, paras 207 ff.; *Veteran Petroleum Ltd (Cyprus)* v. *Russian Federation* and *Hulley Enterprises Ltd (Cyprus)* v. *Russian Federation*, UNCITRAL, Interim Award on Jurisdiction and Admissibility, 30 November 2009, para. 309, all relying on Art. 31(3)(c) of the VCLT when referring to the rules of customary international law relating to the provisional application of an investment treaty.

Article 31(3)(c) is not restricted to 'general international law', but extends to 'any relevant rules of international law applicable in the relations between the parties'. This includes other treaties too, to the extent that they are 'applicable'.[63] In fact, interpreting a bilateral investment treaty by reference to other conventional rules gives rise to fewer problems than interpreting the provisions of a multilateral convention by reference to other conventional rules, given that in a bilateral context it is easier to take account of the rules applicable between *all* the parties to the treaty under interpretation.[64] And there are good reasons, too, for investment tribunals to take account of other conventional obligations in the interpretation of the investment treaty. For one, it is difficult to contend that an investment treaty could have been intended to discharge the parties to it *inter se* from obligations that they may have assumed under other international instruments.[65] Furthermore, it is even more difficult to contend that the obligations in an investment treaty were assumed *a priori* to override other conventional obligations, such as those under labour conventions, international environmental agreements, human rights treaties or EU law. But, needless to say, these other conventional rules need also to be 'relevant' to the interpretation of a treaty term, which in the end depends upon the appreciation of them as such by the arbitral tribunal.[66] As suggested by the tribunal in *RosInvest*, relevance must be taken to mean those rules that 'condition the performance of the specific rights and obligations stipulated in the treaty'.[67] Then again, the scope of such 'relevant' rules may be considerably broad and not necessarily limited to obligations dealing with the same subject matter.[68]

---

[63] Cf. *Pulp Mills*, para. 66.

[64] On the limitations of Art. 31(3)(c) in this respect, see M. Samson, 'High Hopes, Scant Resources: A Word of Scepticism about the Anti-Fragmentation Function of Article 31(3) (c) of the Vienna Convention on the Law of Treaties', *Leiden Journal of International Law* 24 (2011): 701–14.

[65] Cf. *OSPAR* Arbitration, para. 85.

[66] Arguably, investment tribunals will have discretion in determining the 'relevance' of a particular rule. See, e.g., *Klöckner Industrie-Anlagen GmbH and others* v. *United Republic of Cameroon and Société Camerounaise des Engrais*, ICSID Case No. ARB/81/2, Decision of the *Ad hoc* Committee, 3 May 1985, para. 91, for the proposition that 'within the dispute's "legal framework", arbitrators must be free to rely on arguments which strike them as the best ones, even if those arguments were not developed by the parties (although they could have been).'

[67] *RosInvest* v. *Russian Federation*, SCC Case No. V 079/2005, Award on Jurisdiction, 1 October 2007, para. 39.

[68] Thus, in *Djibouti* v. *France*, para. 113, the ICJ considered the provisions of the 1977 Treaty of Friendship and Cooperation between the two parties as relevant for the purpose of

In practice, investment tribunals have already demonstrated their ability to take account of host states' conventional obligations (even those not directly relating to the treatment of investments) in the interpretation of key investment protection standards, albeit without expressly referring to Article 31(3)(c). Thus, the tribunal in *Parkerings-Compagniet* had no problem with considering the respondent's obligations under the UNESCO World Heritage Convention in the assessment of whether the investor was 'in like circumstances' for the purpose of pronouncing upon an alleged breach of the national treatment standard.[69]

However, key to considering other 'relevant rules' in the process of interpretation is that these are also 'applicable in the relations between the parties', which requires the relevant instrument to be in force for *both* parties to the investment treaty.[70] This eventually points to the limits of Article 31(3)(c) as a means of considering non-investment obligations through the interpretative process, given that it cannot be used as a gateway for interpreting provisions by reference to instruments that are concluded by only one of the parties to the investment treaty. This has the potential to give rise to problems, particularly in the context of investment treaties concluded between EU member states and third states, where only one of the contracting parties will be bound by obligations under EU treaties. Nor can Article 31(3)(c) be used for the purpose of allowing other rules of international law to be applied directly to the facts in the context of which the treaty is being considered.[71] For interpreting by reference to 'relevant rules' does not mean to defer to the scope and effect of those rules – save perhaps to the extent that the 'relevant rules' are of a higher hierarchical status – but to clarify the

---

interpreting the 1986 Convention on Mutual Assistance in Criminal Matters, even though the former did not deal at all with cooperation in criminal matters and contained only rules that were 'formulated in a broad and general manner, having an aspirational character'.

[69] *Parkerings-Compagniet*, paras 377–97.

[70] See on this problem, Simma and Kill, 'Harmonizing Investment Protection and International Human Rights', pp. 696–702.

[71] Though, admittedly, there may sometimes be only a fine line between applying non-investment rules directly and considering them indirectly through the process of interpretation. On this, see J. Klabbers, 'Reluctant Grundnormen: Articles 31(3)(c) and 42 of the Vienna Convention on the Law of Treaties and the Fragmentation of International Law', in M. Craven, M. Fitzmaurice and M. Vogiatzi (eds), *Time, History and International Law* (Leiden: Brill, 2007), pp. 141–61, at p. 161. See also A. Gourgourinis, 'The Distinction between Interpretation and Application of Norms in International Arbitration', *Journal of International Dispute Settlement* 2 (2011): 31–57, who extensively discusses the differences between the normative processes of interpretation and application.

content of the provisions being interpreted.[72] For the 'relevant rules' to prevail, the treaty under interpretation would have to be open to being interpreted as allowing these other rules to prevail, which can be the case where the treaty under interpretation contains specific language on its relation with other agreements.[73] This may not necessarily be an issue of treaty interpretation, though, but probably one concerning the application of parallel or successive treaties, as provided for in Article 30(2) of the VCLT.

B   Interpretation of 'generic' terms of an evolving character

In resolving conflicts between divergent obligations, investment tribunals shall also make use of the interpretative flexibility that is inherent in provisions that may be deemed to have an 'evolving character'. While it is one of the general axioms of treaty interpretation that the terms used in a treaty must be interpreted in light of what is determined to have been the parties' common intention at the time of the treaty's conclusion,[74] it is also well established that international courts and tribunals shall not be oblivious to later developments of international law in the interpretation of treaty terms that could be characterised as 'conceptual' or 'generic'.[75]

---

[72] See R. K. Gardiner, *Treaty Interpretation* (Oxford University Press, 2008), p. 271; A. Orakhelashvili, 'Restrictive Interpretation of Human Rights Treaties in the Recent Jurisprudence of the European Court of Human Rights', *European Journal of International Law* 14 (2003): 529–68, at p. 537.

[73] See, e.g., ECT, Art. 16 or NAFTA, Art. 104. But this could arguably also be the case with some recent Dutch BITs, which affirm in their preamble that the treaty objective of encouragement and reciprocal protection of investments 'can be achieved without compromising health, safety and environmental measures of general application'.

[74] This has often been seen as requiring the interpreter to ascertain the meaning of a treaty term at the time when the treaty was drafted, in accordance with Judge Huber's famous dictum 'that a juridical fact must be appreciated in the light of the law contemporary with it, and not of the law in force at the time when a dispute in regard to it arises or falls to be settled'. *Island of Palmas Case (Netherlands v. United States of America)* (1928) 2 *RIAA* 829, at p. 846. Hence, the ICJ found it justified in a few cases to adhere to the original meaning of a term, even where that meaning had evolved since the conclusion of the treaty at issue. See, in particular, the *Case concerning Rights of Nationals of the United States of America in Morocco (France v. United States of America) ICJ Reports* 1952, p. 176, at p. 189, or the *Case concerning Kasikili/Sedudu Island (Botswana v. Namibia) ICJ Reports* 1999, p. 1062, para. 25.

[75] Already in the *Namibia* Advisory Opinion, the ICJ considered that where the terms used in the treaty are 'not static, but were by definition evolutionary', their interpretation cannot remain unaffected by the subsequent development of law. *Legal Consequences for States of the Continued Presence of South Africa in Namibia (South West Africa)*

In the *Dispute Regarding Navigational and Related Rights*, the ICJ even considered that, when using such terms, the contracting parties must be presumed, as a general rule, to have intended those terms to have an evolving meaning, so as to make allowance for developments in international law.[76] Surely, there is no indication as to which terms may indeed be considered 'generic'. In the circumstances of that same case, the relevant term was the word 'commerce', which the ICJ interpreted as covering not only the purchase and sale of physical goods, but also services such as passenger transport, although this was certainly not what the signatories had contemplated when the treaty was drafted in 1858.[77] On the basis of similar reasoning, in the *Pulp Mills* case the ICJ interpreted the obligation 'to protect and preserve' the aquatic environment, which was laid down in the 1975 Statute of the River Uruguay, as entailing the obligation to undertake an environmental impact assessment, which in view of the Court had developed into a requirement under general international law since the conclusion of the 1975 treaty.[78]

Following the reasoning of the ICJ, one could say that many of the terms used in current IIAs potentially qualify as 'generic', and that their interpretation should make allowance for developments in international law. The more so, since IIAs are certainly not static instruments. While originally concluded for a fixed period of years, many of them have actually remained in force, through tacit extensions, for several decades.[79] In view of such practice, therefore, there is nothing to suggest that the parties to an IIA shall have intended its terms always to have a fixed meaning, particularly when it comes to concepts like 'discriminatory' or 'fair and equitable' treatment, the exact meaning of which will always have to be determined by reference to the specific circumstances of

---

notwithstanding *Security Council Resolution 276 (1970) ICJ Reports* 1971, p. 16, para. 53. A similar approach was later adopted in *Aegean Sea Continental Shelf* (*Greece* v. *Turkey*) *ICJ Reports* 1978, p. 3, para. 77, and *Gabčíkovo-Nagymaros Project*, paras 67–8. As for other tribunals, see *Iron Rhine* ('*IJzeren Rijn*') *Railway* Arbitration (*Belgium* v. *the Netherlands*), Award, 24 May 2005, 27 *RIAA* 35, para. 79; *US–Import Prohibition of Certain Shrimp and Shrimp Products*, WT/DS58/AB/R, 12 October 1998.

[76] *Case concerning the Dispute Regarding Navigational and Related Rights* (*Costa Rica* v. *Nicaragua*) *ICJ Reports* 2009, p. 213, paras 64–6.

[77] *Costa Rica* v. *Nicaragua*, paras 70–1.   [78] *Pulp Mills*, paras 203–4.

[79] For example, a number of agreements on economic (and technical) cooperation that the Netherlands started to conclude with developing countries in the second half of the 1960s, and that already contained investment protection rules, are still in force today. See, e.g., the 1965 treaties with the Ivory Coast (*Tractatenblad*, 173 (1965)) and Cameroon (*Tractatenblad*, 208 (1965)).

application. The same may be said when the IIA uses generic terms that have a recognised meaning in customary international law, such as 'full protection and security', 'expropriation' or 'deprivation'.[80] Thus, already in its 1926 judgment on the merits in *Upper Silesia*, the PCIJ considered it 'reasonable to suppose' that, in using the word 'expropriation' in the relevant treaty, the intention of the parties was to convey the meaning that this word had under customary international law.[81] The scope of 'expropriation' would then also depend upon the developments in customary international law. As hinted at by the tribunal in *Saluka*, the same would also be the case with the meaning of the term 'deprivation'. This would depend upon the development of international law, particularly insofar as international law had 'yet to draw a bright and easily distinguishable line between non-compensable regulations, on the one hand, and, on the other, measures that have the effect of depriving foreign investors of their investment and are thus unlawful and compensable in international law'.[82] Inevitably, it would fall upon the adjudicator to determine the content of these obligations in the particular circumstances of each case.

C Presumption in favour of coherence

Lastly, in constructing specific treaty provisions, investment tribunals may more often resort to the interpretative presumption that there is no *a priori* conflict between the obligations accruing to a state under the applicable investment treaty and its other international legal obligations – a presumption which is now a well-accepted rule of treaty interpretation.[83] Paradoxical as this may sound, this may entail first

---

[80] On the use of customary international law for the purpose of interpreting such terms of art, see M. Paparinskis, 'Investment Treaty Interpretation and Customary Investment Law: Preliminary Remarks', in C. Brow and K. Miles (eds), *Evolution in Investment Treaty Law and Arbitration* (Cambridge University Press, 2011), pp. 65–96, who also argues that the use of customary international law in this way is a different technique than that of Art. 31(3)(c) of the VCLT.

[81] *Case concerning Certain German Interests in Polish Upper Silesia (Germany v. Poland)*, Merits, *PCIJ Reports*, Series A, No. 7, p. 21.

[82] *Saluka*, para. 263.

[83] See R. Jennings and A. Watts (eds), *Oppenheim's International Law*, 9th edn (London: Longman, 1992), p. 1275. According to the ICJ, 'it is a rule of interpretation that a text emanating from a Government must, in principle, be interpreted as producing and intended to produce effects in accordance with existing law and not in violation of it'.

establishing an incompatibility between the two sources of obligations, only for such an incompatibility subsequently to be 'interpreted away'.[84] Yet, save for the few arbitral tribunals that were willing to pronounce upon the issue of compatibility of respondents' obligations under intra-European BITs with their obligations under EU treaties,[85] investment tribunals have generally preferred to avoid deciding issues of compatibility of investment treaties with other instruments. For example, some have done so on the ground that the matter was not fully argued.[86] Others have sought to reframe the problem by changing the focus from the issue of compatibility to the examination of whether the respondent state had any alternative way to comply with investment obligations without impinging upon its non-investment obligations.[87]

The interpretative presumption in favour of coherence with existing international legal obligations of the host state is especially justified in cases where the parties to an investment treaty do not appear to have intended to alter their pre-existing obligations under conventional and customary international law. This may not always be easy to discern, considering the inherent nature of treaties as *leges speciales*, which can be

---

Right of Passage over Indian Territory (*Portugal* v. *India*) *ICJ Reports* 1957, p. 125, para. 141. Though, admittedly, the fiction of the unitary law-maker is becoming increasingly implausible in view of the growth in size and complexity of modern governmental bureaucracies.

[84] This is why the ILC considered that 'conflict-resolution and interpretation cannot be distinguished from each other. Whether there is a conflict and what can be done with *prima facie* conflicts depends on the way the relevant rules are interpreted. This cannot be stressed too much. Interpretation does not intervene only once it has already been ascertained that there is a conflict. Rules appear to be compatible or in conflict *as a result of interpretation*.' ILC, 'Report on Fragmentation of International Law: Difficulties Arising from the Diversification and Expansion of International Law' (2006) A/61/10 (ILC, Report on Fragmentation), para. 412. On this, see also C. McLachlan, 'The Principle of Systemic Integration and Article 31(3)(c) of the Vienna Convention', *International and Comparative Law Quarterly* 54 (2005): 279–320, at p. 286.

[85] See *Eastern Sugar*, paras 168–9, and *Eureko*, paras 263–6. For a broader discussion of EU law compatibility issues, see H. Wehland, 'Intra-EU Investment Agreements and Arbitration: Is European Community Law an Obstacle?', *International and Comparative Law Quarterly* 58 (2009): 297–320.

[86] See, e.g., *Azurix* v. *Argentine Republic*, ICSID Case No. ARB/01/12, Award, 14 July 2006, para. 261; or *Siemens AG* v. *Argentine Republic*, ICSID Case No. ARB/02/8, Award, 17 January 2007, para. 354.

[87] *Sempra Energy International* v. *Argentine Republic*, ICSID Case No. ARB/02/16, Award, 28 September 2007, paras 331–2. That decision was, however, annulled in its entirety due to a manifest excess of powers.

intended to derogate from general international law.[88] Nonetheless, it is also not warranted to adopt the assumption that the relationship between investment and non-investment obligations is necessarily contradictory (and certainly not when an investment treaty itself stipulates that its goal is not to undermine other public policy objectives).[89] In the end, it would be difficult to contend that IIAs were purposefully developed as a tool for derogating from human rights obligations or obligations aimed at the protection of the environment. Of course, as with the case of Article 31(3)(c), the presumption in favour of coherence remains an interpretative tool, which is not intended to serve as a means for deferring to the scope and effect of host states' other obligations. But the same presumption is also not a technique to avoid the applicability of non-investment obligations altogether; what it entails is actual harmonisation of obligations arising under IIAs with those arising under non-investment instruments.

IV The limits of legal technique

In the end, however, what needs to be recognised is that the different interpretative tools that were briefly discussed in the previous sections can be used only for resolving particular normative conflicts as they arise – and, indeed, investment tribunals should not shy away from resorting to these tools in order to bring broader, non-investment considerations into their process of deliberation. At the same time, it must be kept in mind that interpretative tools are obviously not intended to establish definite relationships of priority between investment law and other subsystems of international law. As carefully noted in this respect by the ILC in its 2006 Report on Fragmentation:

> Normative conflicts do not arise as technical 'mistakes' that could be 'avoided' by a more sophisticated way of legal reasoning. New rules and legal regimes emerge as responses to new preferences, and sometimes out

[88] Yet, as noted by McLachlan, 'Investment Treaties and General International Law', p. 372, the framers of investment treaties often consciously sought not to go beyond obligations that were thought to reflect the current state of international law. Arguably, rather than extending investors' rights themselves, the purpose of investment treaties was to enhance the mechanisms for the protection of those rights.

[89] For example, a number of Dutch BITs of the latest generation now expressly provide that the treaty objectives of encouragement and reciprocal protection of investments 'can be achieved without compromising health, safety and environmental measures of general application'.

of conscious effort to deviate from preferences as they existed under old regimes. They require a legislative, not a legal-technical response.[90]

Hence, it is primarily through the political process that conflicts between the investment law regime and non-investment obligations should be addressed.

This implies, in the first place, the drafting of 'better' IIAs: that is, agreements that will provide those called upon to construe their provisions with better guidance on how to address the interplay of investment protection standards with host states' other obligations, so as to ensure greater predictability and coherence in the interpretation of treaty terms. Recent treaty-making practice demonstrates that this can be done in several ways.[91] The most obvious solution is to insert specific provisions defining the relationship of the IIA with the rights and obligations that contracting parties may have under other agreements, either existing or prospective, and specifying how inconsistencies shall be resolved if they arise.[92] But addressing the interplay can also be done in less direct ways. In several IIAs of the latest generation, states have sought to clarify the scope of some of the most commonly invoked standards of treatment – such as expropriation, fair and equitable treatment and non-discrimination – by including interpretative language refining or reinterpreting the standards and thereby providing guidance to the interpreter on how to balance the competing objectives of investor protection and other concerns of the host state.[93] Such interpretative

---

[90] ILC, Report on Fragmentation, para. 484.

[91] For an overview of these developments, see particularly S. A. Spears, 'Making Way for the Public Interest in International Investment Agreements', in C. Brow and K. Miles (eds), *Evolution in Investment Treaty Law and Arbitration* (Cambridge University Press, 2011), pp. 271–97.

[92] See, e.g., Art. 32 of the 2007 Investment Agreement for the COMESA Common Investment Area.

[93] Interpretative language is sometimes included in annexes, as in the case of Annex B.13(1) of the 2004 Canadian Model FIPA, which clarifies the scope of indirect expropriation; Annexes A and B of the 2012 US Model BIT, which provide guidance on how to interpret the treaty's provisions on the minimum standard of treatment and expropriation; or Annex 2 of the 2009 ASEAN Comprehensive Investment Agreement, which clarifies the scope of the provisions on expropriation and compensation. Sometimes, interpretative guidance is directly provided in footnotes to the relevant provisions, as in the case of Arts 4(c) and 6 of the 2009 ASEAN Comprehensive Investment Agreement, which define the scope of protected investments and of the most-favoured-nation treatment clause, respectively. Eventually, interpretative guidance can also be added as an integral part of the provision concerned. Examples of this type of drafting are the detailed provisions on fair and equitable treatment (Art. 14), expropriation (Art. 20) or national treatment

language may not necessarily be included in the treaty, but can also be provided in a separate agreement adopted at the time of treaty's conclusion, in the sense of Article 31(2) of the VCLT. Alternatively (and sometimes in addition to this), general exceptions clauses have begun to be inserted into IIAs, providing contracting parties with the possibility of derogating – subject to several substantive or procedural requirements – from the obligations of the treaty in situations where compliance would prevent a party from adopting or enforcing measures necessary for the achievement of certain non-investment policy goals, such as the protection of human health or the natural environment.[94] Last, but not least, states have also sought to broaden the policy objectives of recent IIAs, by clarifying in the treaty preambles that investment protection must not be at the cost of other societal concerns or even by adding non-investment policy goals as self-standing treaty objectives, and thereby also providing guidance for interpreting treaty protections.[95] All in all, it is hoped that the new drafting will embolden investment tribunals to consider non-investment rules more often than they have done in the past and enable them to properly balance investors' rights against the regulatory concerns of the host states.

But as the large majority of current IIAs will remain in force for several years – while renegotiating the terms of existing IIAs is not particularly feasible, especially for countries like Germany, China or Switzerland with 100 and more agreements in force – states should also consider addressing the potential for normative conflicts by adopting interpretative statements to clarify the scope of substantive investment protection standards in their current IIAs. A known example of such practice is the Note of Interpretation adopted by the NAFTA Free Trade Commission in 2001, through which the NAFTA contracting parties clarified that the reference to the fair and equitable provision in Article 1105 of the NAFTA was

---

(Art. 17) of the 2007 Investment Agreement for the COMESA Common Investment Area. The latter's provision on national treatment even provides a test for assessing what 'like circumstances' are.

[94] See, e.g., Art. 10 of the 2004 Canadian Model FIPA, Art. 17 of the 2009 ASEAN Comprehensive Investment Agreement, or Art. 16 of the 2002 Japan–Korea BIT.

[95] See, e.g., the preamble of the 2004 Dutch Model BIT, which stipulates that the treaty objectives 'can be achieved without compromising health, safety and environmental measures of general application', or the preamble of the 2012 US Model BIT, which expresses the desire to achieve the treaty objectives 'in a manner consistent with the protection of health, safety, and the environment, and the promotion of internationally recognized labor rights'.

equivalent to the international minimum standards of aliens under customary international law, rejecting thereby the proposition made a few months earlier by the tribunal in *Pope & Talbot* that the fair and equitable treatment provision was an autonomous treaty standard that was 'additive' to the minimum standard of treatment.[96] While this has attracted criticism that the Note of Interpretation amounted to a treaty amendment that was not in the power of the Free Trade Commission to make, it is beyond doubt that the contracting parties to an IIA, as the masters of the treaty, retain the right to authoritatively interpret its provisions, even in the absence of formal clauses explicitly providing for such possibility.[97] Provided that they clearly establish a common understanding of the contracting parties, such interpretative statements will have to be 'read into the treaty' for the purpose of its interpretation, as Article 31(3)(a) of the VCLT clearly directs the interpreter to take into account 'any subsequent agreement between the parties regarding the interpretation of the treaty or the application of its provisions'. The danger, on the other hand, is that interpretative statements, in their effect, eventually result in treaty amendments proper. And, admittedly, the difference between an authoritative interpretation in the sense of Article 31(3)(a) of the VCLT and a treaty amendment in the sense of Article 39 of the VCLT may often be rather thin.[98] But while there is nothing that prohibits contracting parties making amendments to their IIAs, it is certain that modifications radically altering the level of protections will not be met with approval by investors who, albeit beneficiaries, are not parties to IIAs. These may legitimately expect that the level of protection available to their investments will not be subject to abrupt changes as a result of treaty amendments. On the other hand, there is also nothing that should warrant investors' expectation that the broadly formulated investment protection standards currently present in many IIAs should always be interpreted in their favour. States are perfectly justified in clarifying what the originally intended scope of these protection standards was through authoritative interpretations.

---

[96] *Pope & Talbot*, para. 110.

[97] Already the Permanent Court of International Justice confirmed the 'established principle that the right of giving an authoritative interpretation of a legal rule belongs solely to the person or body who has power to modify or suppress it'. *Delimitation of the Polish–Czechoslovakian Frontier (Question of Jaworzina) PCIJ Reports*, Series B, No. 8, p. 37.

[98] A. Aust, *Modern Treaty Law and Practice*, 2nd edn (Cambridge University Press, 2007), p. 239.

Authoritative interpretations – and also treaty amendments, for that matter – are not subject to any prescribed forms and certainly need not be effected through the conclusion of a supplementary treaty. This follows from Articles 31(3)(a) and 39 of the VCLT, which both use the word 'agreement' and not 'treaty'. Indeed, investment tribunals have already accepted that a subsequent agreement within the meaning of Article 31(3)(a) of the VCLT need not be concluded with the same formal requirements as a treaty.[99] The adoption of interpretative statements could easily be implemented in the context of existing IIAs, since the large majority of them provide the possibility of holding consultations on matters concerning the interpretation or application of the treaty at the request of either party. These 'consultation clauses' not only provide a mechanism to avoid or prevent potential disputes from arising between the contracting parties, but could thus be used as a setting for clarifying the meaning of specific treaty provisions. One instance of such an interpretative exercise has already occurred in the context of a dispute between the Czech Republic and CME. Following dissatisfaction with the application of the Netherlands–Czech Republic BIT by the tribunal in its Partial Award in that case, the Czech Republic requested that the Netherlands should hold consultations, the outcome of which was a common understanding between the parties regarding three issues of treaty interpretation that arose out of the Partial Award. The understanding was recorded in Agreed Minutes, which were formally signed and exchanged between the two governments and subsequently also taken into account by the tribunal in the Final Award.[100] At the same time, the case also demonstrates the potential for abuse of such consultative processes, as states that find themselves as respondents in a dispute with the foreign investor may seek to influence the outcome of litigation through the adoption of interpretative instruments. Yet both authoritative interpretations and treaty amendments require common agreement of all contracting parties, which means that the non-disputing state (i.e., the state of the investor's nationality) may always resist any attempts to unduly influence the dispute settlement process. In fact, there is essentially nothing wrong with the possibility that states effect clarifications of their obligations under IIAs even after a dispute has arisen. Some

---

[99] *Methanex* v. *United States*, UNCITRAL, Final Award, 3 August 2005, para. 20. See also *Philippe Gruslin* v. *Malaysia*, ICSID Case No. ARB/99/3, Award, 27 November 2000, para. 23.4.

[100] See *CME Czech Republic BV* v. *Czech Republic*, Final Award, 14 March 2003, paras 87–93, 437 and 504.

IIAs even expressly provide for the possibility of arbitral tribunals request-ing that the contracting parties adopt an interpretation on a specific point at issue,[101] or at least permit the intervention of non-disputing parties.[102] In the end, however, a greater involvement in the interpretative process may not always be in the interests of all states. Many capital-exporting states have not yet been exposed to litigation 'at the wrong end of the stick' and, without having themselves experienced the role of the respondent party in investment treaty arbitration, they may therefore have little incentive to implement any changes that could potentially result in a dilution of the protections contained in their IIAs.

V Conclusion

As this chapter has sought to demonstrate, there is more than one avenue available for investment tribunals to consider non-investment obligations in deciding investor–state disputes. The general latitude that investment tribunals enjoy with regard to the scope of legal rules that they are entitled to apply, as well as the rules on treaty interpretation that enable them to take account of the broader normative environment in the interpretative process, provide them with a sufficient degree of flexibility to properly consider obligations arising under instruments other than the investment treaty, without necessarily exceeding their jurisdictional limits. Of course, in a world that is 'irreducibly pluralistic', as we have been importantly reminded by the ILC, law cannot resolve in an abstract way the normative conflicts that may arise between different regimes.[103] The investment law regime, like any other subfield of international law, has its own priorities and preferences, which possibly do not coincide with those of the human rights regimes, environmental protection regimes or the European legal order. Invest-ment lawyers, like any other epistemic community, prioritise their own concerns and interests over those of others.[104] And these, as has often

---

[101] Japan–Mexico FTA (2004), Art. 89 or US–Uruguay BIT (2005), Art. 31.
[102] See, e.g., NAFTA, Art. 1128.   [103] ILC, Report on Fragmentation, para. 488.
[104] See generally on this problem M. Hirsch, 'The Interaction between International Invest-ment Law and Human Rights Treaties: A Sociological Perspective', in T. Broude and Y. Shany (eds), *Multi-sourced Equivalent Norms in International Law* (Oxford: Hart, 2011), pp. 115–42, who suggests that the reluctance to accord significant weight to non-investment obligations in international treaty arbitration can be attributed to the 'socio-cultural distance' between investment lawyers and practitioners in other international legal settings and the deep-rooted tensions between the relevant communities.

shown, may not necessarily coincide with those of other societal groups. This is why the regulation of the interaction between investment law and other subfields of international law requires primarily a policy response. Investment arbitral tribunals should not be entrusted with deciding which societal concerns have priority; their task is primarily in finding the precise balance between the acts that may reasonably be found to constitute interference with investors' rights, and acts that fall within the state's legitimate right to regulate.

21

Fragmentation, consolidation and the future relationship between international investment law and general international law

RALPH ALEXANDER LORZ

The structure of this book has proven to perfectly fit the peculiarities of the topic. The symmetry of the parts is already apparent at first glance: starting from the perspective of individual rights (humanitarian law and human rights), then turning to the issue of (sustainable) development, and eventually concluding by looking at the new actors that have come into play, that is, the regimes of the European Union (EU) and the World Trade Organization (WTO), which have the potential to compete with international investment law.

This kind of parallel structure might have an aesthetic value as such. However, a symmetry that just shows itself in the external appearance of an academic discourse would be a hollow form. Thus, the goal of any attempt to draw some general conclusions from this volume as a whole must be to identify a common thread, if there is any. And, fortunately enough, in our case this thread is clearly discernible.

I Fragmentation

Using one of the most widespread commonplaces in today's debates on public international law, it may be called *fragmentation* and includes, of course, its (undesirable) consequences and possible tendencies that may be able to counter it.[1] But why has fragmentation become the red thread of this book as well, apart from the fact that it has developed into one of the regular buzzwords in modern public international law?

Looking into history, it becomes obvious that public international law has always been a fragmented order. Different branches of this field have

---

[1] See, e.g., 'Fragmentation of International Law: Difficulties Arising from the Diversification and Expansion of International Law', Report of the Study Group of the International Law Commission, finalised by Martti Koskenniemi, UN Doc. A/CN.4/L.682, 13 April 2006.

existed since ancient times, each shaped by its own actors, who developed their own rules in and for their own era. Regardless of whether we consider diplomatic relations, treaty law, sovereignty and the attribution of territory, protection and rights of the individual or, perhaps most recently, sustainable development and environmental law: there was always a specific concern to be addressed, which was then taken up by international players especially interested in it, and so the norms to be developed were – at least in the first place – tailor-made to take care of these concerns and interests only.

There is probably no other way to achieve some kind of fundamental progress and re-orientation in public international law, since it is common knowledge that public international law is not a coherently designed legal order, but rather arises spontaneously from the concurring behaviour of the international law subjects and is typically developed through the conclusion of treaties.[2] And especially if a multilateral treaty is to be concluded, demanding that the negotiating treaty partners take into account all possible repercussions of their treaty project and its interactions with other existing legal instruments would be a safe way to destroy all prospects of success. It is only now that – because of the permanent intensification of these interactions and the much more comprehensive character of public international law compared with earlier times[3] – there is a deeper focus on the inherent fragmentation of this legal order and an increasing view of the latter as a problem. Multi-sourced Norms, be they equivalent or competing, have therefore moved to centre stage.

The challenge to overcome the problems of fragmentation and to strike a balance between the competing demands is a twofold one. First, in terms of the persons involved, it calls for bringing together the various legal communities that are still largely separate. And, of course, in terms of law, the overlapping rules must be identified and then, if possible, revisited and reviewed in order to eliminate potential incompatibilities. To be sure, this is much more easily said than done. In particular, when various multilateral treaties start to interact, the hurdle of negotiating some kind of compatibility regime without sacrificing the achievements embodied in those treaties seems to be almost insurmountable. The fact that different treaties usually also have different contracting partners that

---

[2] On the significance of treaties for the development of international law, see, e.g., Bruno Simma, 'From Bilateralism to Community Interest in International Law' 241 (1994-VI) *Recueil des Cours* 217, at pp. 322 *et seq.*

[3] Cf. Mehrdad Payandeh, Internationales Gemeinschaftsrecht (Heidelberg: Springer, 2010), *passim*.

can barely be brought together is just the most obvious obstacle in its way. Even within an identical group of contracting states, the different focuses of the parties involved – one might be more occupied with environmental concerns, a second with social rights and a third with securing economic advantages – will most likely make it very difficult to find a common ground of compatibility. Moreover, if specific institutions for the settlement of disputes are employed, which is another tendency clearly discoverable in the recent developments of treaty law,[4] each dispute will entail its own agenda, and the emphasis the respective institution puts on certain aspects of it will be shaped by the peculiar institutional interest[5] that flows from the subject matter of the treaty.[6]

Customary international law proves a bit more accessible for the performance of such attempts at facilitating compatibility. The inter-action between international investment law and the law of armed conflict – although the latter is now also largely codified – serves as a good example for what legal interpretation can achieve. The interaction itself has so far received little attention in academic comments and legal practice. However, it is conceivable that international humanitarian law might, for instance, shape the extent of the full protection and security standard that is part of the core of international investment agreements.[7] In particular, whereas under normal circumstances this standard boils down to a far-reaching guarantee of physical integrity, it might be reduced to a mere due diligence obligation when the state obliged to guarantee this protection finds itself in a state of war.

Another possibility for combining the two approaches mentioned is to include cross-references in the treaties themselves, which can then point to different legal orders and even regulate the question of priority. Article XI of the US–Argentina Bilateral Investment Treaty (BIT)[8] is an

---

[4] On the proliferation of international dispute settlement bodies, see, e.g., Yuval Shany, 'No Longer a Weak Department of Power? Reflections on the Emergence of a New International Judiciary', *European Journal of International Law* 20 (2009): 73.

[5] On the structural bias of international legal institutions in general, see Martti Koskenniemi, *From Apology to Utopia: The Structure of International Legal Argument* (Cambridge University Press, 2005), pp. 562–617.

[6] On conflicting jurisdictions of national and international courts in general, see Heiko Sauer, *Jurisdiktionskonflikte in Mehrebenensystemen* (Heidelberg: Springer, 2008).

[7] Cf., e.g., Freya Baetens, 'When International Rules Interact: International Investment Law and the Law of Armed Conflict', *Investment Treaty News*, 7 April 2011.

[8] Treaty between the United States of America and the Argentine Republic concerning the reciprocal encouragement and protection of investment, signed 14 November 1991, entered into force 20 October 1994, available at: www.unctad.org/sections/dite/iia/docs/bits/argentina_us.pdf, accessed 18 July 2012.

example of this kind. The provision explicitly allows the parties to the treaty to fulfil their obligations 'with respect to the maintenance or restoration of international peace or security', which essentially means that if the United Nations Security Council imposes binding obligations on the UN member states for this purpose, the BIT shall not be used to question the legality of the corresponding measures. Of course, this solution to the problem of potential incompatibility opens up other gates: for instance, questioning whether the demands from the Security Council could not be fulfilled otherwise than by domestic measures negatively affecting (certain) investments. And it cannot solve the fundamental problem of possible limits to the Security Council's powers.[9] If the Security Council placed a person on one of its infamous 'terror lists' and then called on the member states to seize his or her property without further (judicial) review, does this comprehensively exonerate a member state from all claims that might otherwise be brought against it on the basis of other treaties? The Court of Justice of the European Union has already ruled that the EU is obliged to respect its own order of fundamental rights, even when implementing a Security Council resolution, and has invalidated the corresponding legal instrument – a regulation enacted by the Council – because it blindly followed the requirements set by the UN.[10] It is easily conceivable that arbitral tribunals in the future might also ignore the compulsory character of Security Council resolutions under Article 25 of the UN Charter when it comes to determining possible damages inflicted upon an investor by the implementing act of a UN member state.

II Reconciliation

Notwithstanding all these problems, perhaps the best news to be taken from this book is that reconciliation is generally possible. That is to some extent already true in personal terms: we increasingly see people from the various branches of law who are capable of wearing different hats. And

---

[9] For an overview of the legal debate, see, e.g., Jochen Frowein and Nico Krisch, 'Introduction to Chapter VII', in Bruno Simma et al. (eds), *The Charter of the United Nations: A Commentary*, 2nd edn (Oxford University Press, 2002), pp. 701, 710.

[10] ECJ, Joined Cases C-402 and C-415/05 P, *Kadi v. Council of the European Union* and *Al Barakaat Int'l Found. v. Council of the European Union* [2008] ECR 299; cf. Mehrdad Payandeh and Heiko Sauer, 'European Union: UN Sanctions and EU Fundamental Rights', *International Journal of Constitutional Law* 7 (2009): 306.

as a matter of substantive law, many of these branches in public international law have common roots and traits. Taking human rights and international investment law as an example, one can determine that they share history, ancestry and heuristics,[11] so the journey from being a human rights lawyer to becoming an international investment lawyer (or vice versa) is not as far as it might at first seem.

Moreover, once this path of mutual exchange is taken, a lot of cross-fertilisation effects can be expected and mobilised. The treatment of the 'terror lists' mentioned above might serve as a useful indication. When the Court of Justice of the European Union decided to stand up against the Security Council on this issue, it did so technically through a challenge using the pertinent EU regulation. But in fact it was prompted by human rights considerations – and therefore essentially by public international law – to defend basic individual guarantees against the presumptuousness of the Security Council and its Sanctions Committee.

European Union law holds even more interesting illustrations in that respect. The Court of Justice has developed a very sophisticated case law to reconcile human rights – recognised as general principles of the EU's law under Article 6-III of the TEU and now enshrined in the new Charter of Fundamental Rights of the Union – and the fundamental freedoms of the common market. On the one hand, human rights might serve as possible restrictions to these freedoms; that happened, for example, in the *Schmidberger* case, where the Court of Justice endorsed the decision of the Austrian authorities to allow a demonstration on the most important highway running through the Alps, despite the fact that this created a considerable – albeit temporary – obstacle to the free movement of goods guaranteed by Articles 34 and 35 of the Treaty on the Functioning of the European Union (TFEU).[12] But what is even more interesting in terms of cross-fertilisation is the *Carpenter* case, where the Court of Justice prevented the wife of an EU citizen from being deported, reasoning that the disturbance to family life necessarily following from that would hamper the Union citizen in his rendering of services abroad and thereby infringe the fundamental freedom to provide services under Article 56 of the TFEU.[13]

---

[11] See, e.g., Pierre-Marie Dupuy, Ernst-Ulrich Petersmann and Francesco Francioni (eds) *Human Rights in International Investment Law and Arbitration* (Oxford University Press, 2009).

[12] ECJ, Case C-112/00, *Schmidberger* [2003] ECR I-5650.

[13] ECJ, Case C-60/00, *Carpenter* [2002] ECR I-6279.

Here the Court of Justice created a mutual reinforcement of these two different branches of EU law: it employed human rights in order to expand the realm of fundamental freedoms and, at the same time, used a fundamental freedom for the purpose of strengthening a human right. In effect, both human rights and fundamental freedoms turned into a kind of double-edged sword. This construction might serve as a model for the future relationship of international investment law and human rights law as well – and perhaps also for the interaction of international investment law with other fields of public international law, such as the provisions regarding climate change. A look at the issues of sustainable development confirms this perception from another angle and adds another promising field of work.[14] In general, development law is far less developed than investment law – there is not even a comprehensive normative concept of development, let alone a concept for its interaction with international investment law. But even though international development – and/or environmental – and economic lawyers often speak different languages, it is unavoidable that one needs to strike a balance here as well, for foreign direct investment is indispensable for sustainable development, but must, of course, be sustainable itself.

1 The 'judicial' way

In order to achieve the desired reconciliation, two ways are generally possible and do not mutually exclude each other. One is the pragmatic choice to leave consolidation of the different legal regimes to the judicial process, which in this case means leaving it to the arbitral process to find reasonable and acceptable solutions for incompatibilities under the individual circumstances of any given case. This is not at all impossible, as an analysis of the already existing case law reveals. The open standards usually employed in international investment agreements – such as fair and equitable treatment,[15] legitimate expectations[16] or full protection

---

[14] Cf. on the notion of sustainable development in international law in general, Ulrich Beyerlin, 'Sustainable Development', in Rüdiger Wolfrum (ed.), *Max Planck Encyclopedia of Public International Law* (Oxford University Press, 2009).

[15] On the standard of fair and equitable treatment, see, e.g., Jeswald Salacuse, *The Law of Investment Treaties* (Oxford University Press, 2010), pp. 218–44; Katia Yannaca-Small, 'Fair and Equitable Treatment Standard: Recent Developments', in August Reinisch (ed.), *Standards of Investment Protection* (Oxford University Press, 2008), pp. 111–30.

[16] Several arbitral tribunals have drawn upon the notion of legitimate expectations to define fair and equitable treatment; see, e.g., *Saluka Investments BV (the Netherlands)* v. *The*

and security[17] – leave sufficient room for interpretation in that respect. Moreover, especially with regard to (sustainable) development, one can refer back to the famous formula in one of the most widespread definitions of investment: namely, that it has to contribute to the host state's development in order to be protected.[18] However, relying on this method requires a lot of trust in the system, which right now seems rather to be taking a slight turn towards erosion of that trust. One of the reasons for this is the perceived inconsistency of the case law, and, indeed, investor-state arbitration is not the prime example that comes to mind if one thinks of coherence in jurisprudence. This development is probably again inevitable, given the independence and individuality of the arbitral tribunals in question and the lack of a doctrine of precedence and an institution of appeal.

2 The 'legislative' way

It therefore seems advisable to choose another way for parallel progress, which is to try to eliminate incompatibilities already at the stage of the treaty-making process. The classical instrument for this is the insertion of correspondence clauses into future international investment agreements, which can clarify their relationship to other international agreements and obligations. This instrument has already proven its feasibility in many different contexts. In particular, one sees references to environmental and labour standards, for example, in NAFTA,[19] the US Model

---

Czech Republic, UNCITRAL, Partial Award, 17 March 2006, paras 301–2; Técnicas Medioambientales Tecmed SA v. United Mexican States, ICSID Case No. ARB (AF)/00/2, Award, 29 May 2003, para. 154; for further examples, cf. Salacuse, The Law of Investment Treaties, pp. 231–37; Yannaca-Small, 'Fair and Equitable Treatment Standard', pp. 124–6. See also Ioana Tudor, The Fair and Equitable Treatment Standard in the International Law of Foreign Investment (Oxford University Press, 2008), pp. 163 et seq.; and the most recent publication by Roland Kläger, 'Fair and Equitable Treatment' in International Investment Law (Cambridge University Press, 2011).

[17] Regarding full protection and security, cf. again Salacuse, The Law of Investment Treaties, pp. 207–17; Giuditta Cordero Moss, 'Full Protection and Security', in August Reinisch (ed.), Standards of Investment Protection (Oxford University Press, 2008), pp. 131–50.

[18] This is part of the so-called 'Salini test', see Salini Costruttori SpA and Italstrade SpA v. Morocco, ICSID Case No. ARB/00/4, Decision on Jurisdiction, 23 July 2001, para. 52. For further information on judicial practice concerning an investment's contribution to the host state's development, cf. Christoph Schreuer, Loretta Malintoppi, August Reinisch and Anthony Sinclair, The ICSID Convention (Cambridge University Press, 2009), pp. 131–4.

[19] NAFTA, Art. 1106, paras 2, 6, Art. 1114.

BIT,[20] the International Institute for Sustainable Development draft[21] and the Canadian Foreign Investment Promotion and Protection Agreements,[22] to home state responsibilities, for example, in the OECD Guidelines[23] and other mechanisms of corporate social responsibility and the fight against corruption. Vice versa, there are specific chapters on investment within treaties dealing with sustainable development.[24] In addition, a nuanced definition of investment might be used at the outset, following the already mentioned case law in that regard.

But the usefulness of such clauses is not limited to these issues. In principle, the same is true for clauses that aim at reconciling international investment law and human rights obligations. And even in the long neglected field of international humanitarian law, examples of such corresponding provisions in the form of 'war clauses' already exist.[25] It is to be noted, though, that the work to be done here is far from easy. If one really wants to secure the compatibility of all these obligations when concluding a treaty, it will require much more extensive negotiations and skilful legal drafting than was required for traditional BITs. The politically beloved idea of just decorating a state visit and emphasising future economic cooperation by pulling a model treaty from the drawer and signing it on the occasion would then have to disappear.

III New players

Looking to the future, however, the inconveniences resulting from that might be offset, and the fragmentation problem as a whole reduced, by the new powerful players who are just about to enter the arena: the EU and the WTO.

---

[20] US Model BIT (2004), Arts 12, 13, available at: www.state.gov/documents/organization/117601.pdf, accessed 18 July 2012.

[21] IISD, Model International Agreement on Investment for Sustainable Development, 2005, Arts 14, 16, 18, 20, 21, available at: www.iisd.org/pdf/2005/investment_model_int_agreement.pdf, accessed 18 July 2012.

[22] Canada's Foreign Investment Promotion and Protection Agreement Model, 2004, Art. 11, available at: www.international.gc.ca/trade-agreements-accords-commerciaux/assets/pdfs/2004-FIPA-model-en.pdf, accessed 18 July 2012.

[23] OECD Guidelines for Multinational Enterprises, available at: www.oecd.org/dataoecd/56/36/1922428.pdf, accessed 18 July 2012.

[24] For an overview, see Marie-Claire Cordonier Segger and Duncan French, 'Governing Investment in Sustainable Development: Investment Mechanisms in Sustainable Development: Treaties and Voluntary Instruments', in Marie-Claire Cordonier Segger, Markus Gehring and Andrew Newcombe (eds), *Sustainable Development in World Investment Law* (Alphen aan den Rijn: Kluwer Law, 2011), pp. 645–80.

[25] See, e.g., Art. IV(3) of the United States–Argentina BIT.

1   The European Union

With regard to the European Union, Article 207 of the TFEU has newly endowed it with the exclusive competence to conclude future agreements on foreign direct investment, which would then be valid for all twenty-seven – or in the future even more – member states. This might, by and large, in the long run unify one-third of the world's existing BITs and thereby bring about an enormous simplification of the whole environment in international investment law.[26] To be sure, though, this is going to be a very long run. Even the transition from the old bilateral system to a new Union treaty regime will take an enormous amount of time and effort. The European Commission has taken the first step towards that goal by submitting a draft regulation on transitional arrangements for BITs between member states and third countries.[27] Moreover, it has issued a communication 'towards a comprehensive European international investment policy'.[28] But the political differences underneath will persist: the strong capital-exporting countries within the Union will continue to defend their bilateral achievements, whereas the Commission and the other member states will press for a level playing field. The critical comments on the Commission's proposals made by the Council at its Foreign Affairs meeting in Luxembourg on 25 October 2010 were only the first signal in this respect.[29] It was on 21 June 2012 when the EC European Commission unveiled a proposal for the future of investment arbitrations allowing member states to continue being respondents in some cases.[30]

---

[26] For an overview, see Ralph Alexander Lorz, 'Good News and Bad News for European Investors', *Global Arbitration Review* 6(3) (2011): 23.

[27] European Commission, 'Proposal for a Regulation of the European Parliament and of the Council establishing transitional arrangements for bilateral investment agreements between Member States and third countries', COM(2010)344 final, 7 July 2010.

[28] European Commission, 'Communication, Towards a comprehensive European international investment policy', COM(2010)343 final, 7 July 2010.

[29] Council of the European Union, 'Conclusions on a Comprehensive European International Investment Policy', 3041st Foreign Affairs Council meeting, Luxembourg, 25 October 2010.

[30] See, 'European Commission Unveils Proposal for Who Should Bear Brunt of Future Investment Arbitrations; Member States Could Continue to be Respondents in Some Cases', *ITA Reporter*, available at: www.iareporter.com/articles/20120621, accessed 18 July 2012; European Commission, 'Proposal for a Regulation of the European Parliament and of the Council establishing a framework for managing financial responsibility linked to investor–state dispute settlement tribunals established by international agreements to which the European Union is party', 2012/0163 (COD), COM(2012)335 final.

The different positions are prone to clash with regard to the possible abolition of intra-EU BITs, as well as to the replacement of extra-EU BITs through a new European Model BIT. As far as intra-EU BITs are at stake, the Court of Justice of the EU will further complicate the picture, since it is the final institution to rule on their compatibility with mandatory EU law. Concerning the development of an EU Model BIT, as of now, the interests of the EU member states themselves seem too far apart to allow for a coherent EU investment strategy. But the political organs of the Union – which also pursue their own institutional agendas – will continue to push for such a strategy. It is common knowledge in public international law that the processes of normative development are destined for a long run anyway. It remains to be seen whether in this case the result of the process turns out to be a dream or a nightmare. Currently the announcements, communiqués and resolutions of the various actors involved are just too disparate to work out exactly what the future behaviour of the Union will be.

The two most recent developments within the European Parliament – and thus within one institution only, which is noteworthy in itself – serve as very interesting illustrations to that end. On the one hand, the European Parliament (EP), on 6 April 2011, adopted a resolution that criticised the Council for its statement that, 'the new European legal framework should not negatively affect investor protection and guarantees enjoyed under the existing agreements', and instead called upon the Commission to 'better address the right to protect the public capacity to regulate and meet the EU's obligation to exercise policy coherence for development', which embodies a clear inclination towards a weaker investment protection in future EU investment treaties.[31] On the other hand, just one month later the very same Parliament adopted another resolution in this area that aims at restraining the Commission's possibilities to review BITs of member states and the reasons it may invoke in order to withdraw authorisation from them, which means that the EP is trying to protect the *status quo* of EU investment protection and to secure the member states' already existing agreements.[32] This discrepancy is a remarkable outcome of the current political process. It seems to defy all

---

[31] European Parliament, Resolution, Future European International Investment Policy, 2010/2203(INI), 6 April 2011.

[32] European Parliament, Position of the European Parliament, adopted at First Reading, with a view to the adoption of Regulation (EU) No. …/2011 of the European Parliament and of the Council establishing transitional arrangements for bilateral investment agreements between Member States and third countries, COD(2010)0197, 10 May 2011.

attempts at developing a unified and consistent strategy for the EU investment policy of the future and instead demonstrates how volatile the political majorities within the pivotal organs are.

It therefore remains an open question as to which direction the Union as a whole will take. If the dream scenario comes true, a new, well-designed European Model BIT will replace the lion's share of existing BITs in which European states are involved, thereby considerably streamlining the international investment regime as a whole and serving as a potential model for other regions of the world. In the nightmare version, all the existing BITs mentioned here will also vanish, but will either not be replaced at all or will be replaced by some kind of badly drafted instrument, which, among other things, leaves open the questions of interaction with other fields of public international law. It is at least for the experts involved in that process to make sure that the final result will be more dream than nightmare.

2   The World Trade Organization

Concerning the WTO, and international trade law in general, the admission must be made that, unlike the EU, where the competence was transferred only at the end of 2009, this is not a brand new story. By contrast, a relationship between international investment and trade law – resembling siblings or even twins – has existed from the very beginning. However, today it appears stronger and merits more attention than ever before. This is, of course, mainly due to the fact that the WTO and the new institutional perspective its inception introduced in 1994 offer a much better prospect for any kind of harmonisation in the realm of international economic law, as the general unification of substantive standards in international trade law amply illustrates. This gives rise to the hope that greater coherence and a generally better integration of the two complementary approaches, which international trade and investment law embody, can be achieved. Perhaps – again in the very long run – even a consolidation of these two legal regimes into one might be conceivable, especially since they often arrive at the same legal consequences anyway.

IV   Final thesis

One focal point where all the strands discussed in the various parts meet is fairly obvious: there is a lot of work ahead for all the lawyers who are active in international investment law as well as in the other fields of public international law under observation. Of course, one can decide to simply let matters run their course – experience shows that the arbitral tribunals concerned with pertinent cases and all the other actors in the field will always find pragmatic ways to handle upcoming problems and to settle the disputes arising from them. But as far as a systematic way is sought to take care of all the interactions between these diverse branches of law and of the balancing issues they entail, a new generation of BITs and legal instruments in the other fields of public international law will be needed – and that means a lot of drafting, reasoning and negotiating work for academics and practitioners alike.

INDEX

Abi-Saab, Professor Georges 245–6
Abs, Herman J. 268
African Charter on Human and
 Peoples' Rights 110
Agreement on Sanitary and
 Phytosanitary (SPS) Measures
 294–5, 300
 'non-arbitrariness' requirement
 under Articles 2.3 and 5.5 SPS
 319
Agreement on Subsidies and
 Countervailing Measures
 (SCM) 300
Agreement on Technical Barriers to
 Trade 294–5
Agreement on Trade-related
 Intellectual Property Rights
 (TRIPS) 294–5
Agreement on Trade-related
 Investment Measures (TRIMs)
 275, 300
aggression, crime of 63–4
aiding and abetting
 additional subjective requirement of
 Article 25(3)(c) Rome Statute
 76–7
 assisting commission of group crime,
 Article 25(3)(d) Rome Statute
 78–81
 concept of 74–6
Alianza Bolivariana para los
 Pueblos de Nuestra América
 (ALBA) movement 143,
 162–3
American Convention on Human
 Rights 110, 132–3, 163
 access 152–5

exhaustion of local remedies
 152–3
 legal persons 153–5
 benefits and risks 157–60
 Inter-American Commission on
 Human Rights 151, 158
 access 152–5
 exhaustion of local remedies
 152–3
 legal persons 153–5
 Inter-American Court of Human
 Rights 121, 137–8, 151, 158
 legal persons 154–5
 right to property 155–9
 right to property 151
 scope of protection 155–7
 supervisory organs 151
amicus curiae briefs 436–9
Annan, UN Secretary General Kofi 330
applicability of IIAs and sustainable
 development criterion xxxv,
 240–56
 contribution to 'development'/
 establishment of an 'investment'
 243–8, 488
 ICSID arbitrations double-barrel
 test 243–7
 ex ante rule-making carving out
 particular subject matter 242
 explaining 'resistance': obstacles to
 acceptance of 'sustainable
 development' 250–2
 investments not contributing to host
 state's national economy 241
 'measures not precluded' and
 'essential security interests'
 clauses 248–50

3m